CHRYSLER

COLT/CHALLENGER/CONQUEST/VISTA
1971-89 REPAIR MANUAL

CHILTON'S

Senior Vice President	Ronald A. Hoxter
Publisher & Editor-In-Chief	Kerry A. Freeman, S.A.E.
Executive Editors	Dean F. Morgantini, S.A.E., W. Calvin Settle, Jr., S.A.E.
Managing Editor	Nick D'Andrea
Senior Editors	Jacques Gordon, Michael L. Grady, Ben Greisler, S.A.E., Debra McCall, Kevin M. G. Maher, Richard J. Rivele, S.A.E., Richard T. Smith, Jim Taylor, Ron Webb
Project Managers	Martin J. Gunther, Will Kessler, A.S.E., Richard Schwartz
Production Manager	Andrea Steiger
Product Systems Manager	Robert Maxey
Director of Manufacturing	Mike D'Imperio
Editor	Dawn M. Hoch

CHILTON BOOK COMPANY

ONE OF THE **DIVERSIFIED PUBLISHING COMPANIES,**
A PART OF **CAPITAL CITIES/ABC, INC.**

Manufactured in USA
© 1997 Chilton Book Company
Chilton Way, Radnor, PA 19089
ISBN 0-8019-9062-9
Library of Congress Catalog Card No. 97-65889
1234567890 6543210987

Contents

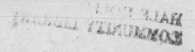

Contents

7 DRIVE TRAIN

8 SUSPENSION AND STEERING

9 BRAKES

10 BODY

GLOSSARY

MASTER INDEX

SAFETY NOTICE

Proper service and repair procedures are vital to the safe, reliable operation of all motor vehicles, as well as the personal safety of those performing repairs. This manual outlines procedures for servicing and repairing vehicles using safe, effective methods. The procedures contain many NOTES, CAUTIONS and WARNINGS which should be followed along with standard procedures to eliminate the possibility of personal injury or improper service which could damage the vehicle or compromise its safety.

It is important to note that the repair procedures and techniques, tools and parts for servicing motor vehicles, as well as the skill and experience of the individual performing the work vary widely. It is not possible to anticipate all of the conceivable ways or conditions under which vehicles may be serviced, or to provide cautions as to all of the possible hazards that may result. Standard and accepted safety precautions and equipment should be used when handling toxic or flammable fluids, and safety goggles or other protection should be used during cutting, grinding, chiseling, prying, or any other process that can cause material removal or projectiles.

Some procedures require the use of tools specially designed for a specific purpose. Before substituting another tool or procedure, you must be completely satisfied that neither your personal safety, nor the performance of the vehicle will be endangered.

Although information in this manual is based on industry sources and is complete as possible at the time of publication, the possibility exists that some car manufacturers made later changes which could not be included here. While striving for total accuracy, Chilton Book Company cannot assume responsibility for any errors, changes or omissions that may occur in the compilation of this data.

PART NUMBERS

Part numbers listed in this reference are not recommendation by Chilton for any product by brand name. They are references that can be used with interchange manuals and aftermarket supplier catalogs to locate each brand supplier's discrete part number.

SPECIAL TOOLS

Special tools are recommended by the vehicle manufacturer to perform their specific job. Use has been kept to a minimum, but where absolutely necessary, they are referred to in the text by the part number of the tool manufacturer. These tools can be purchased, under the appropriate part number, from your local dealer or regional distributor, or an equivalent tool can be purchased locally from a tool supplier or parts outlet. Before substituting any tool for the one recommended, read the SAFETY NOTICE at the top of this page.

ACKNOWLEDGMENTS

The Chilton Book Company expresses appreciation to Chrysler Corporation for their generous assistance.

1

GENERAL INFORMATION AND MAINTENANCE

HOW TO USE THIS BOOK

Chilton's Total Car Care manual is intended to help you learn more about the inner workings of your vehicle while saving you money on its upkeep and operation.

The beginning of the book will likely be referred to the most, since that is where you will find information for maintenance and tune-up. The other sections deal with the more complex systems of your vehicle. Operating systems from engine through brakes are covered to the extent that the average do-it-yourselfer becomes mechanically involved. This book will not explain such things as rebuilding a differential for the simple reason that the expertise required and the investment in special tools make this task uneconomical. It will, however, give you detailed instructions to help you change your own brake pads and shoes, replace spark plugs, and perform many more jobs that can save you money, give you personal satisfaction and help you avoid expensive problems.

A secondary purpose of this book is a reference for owners who want to understand their vehicle and/or their mechanics better. In this case, no tools at all are required.

Where to Begin

Before removing any bolts, read through the entire procedure. This will give you the overall view of what tools and supplies will be required. There is nothing more frustrating than having to walk to the bus stop on Monday morning because you were short one bolt on Sunday afternoon. So read ahead and plan ahead. Each operation should be approached logically and all procedures thoroughly understood before attempting any work.

All sections contain adjustments, maintenance, removal and installation procedures, and in some cases, repair or overhaul procedures. When repair is not considered practical, we tell you how to remove the part and then how to install the new or rebuilt replacement. In this way, you at least save the labor costs. Backyard repair of some components is just not practical.

Avoiding Trouble

Many procedures in this book require you to "label and disconnect . . ." a group of lines, hoses or wires. Don't be lulled into thinking you can remember where everything goes—you won't. If you hook up vacuum or fuel lines incorrectly, the vehicle will run poorly, if at all. If you hook up electrical wiring incorrectly, you may instantly learn a very expensive lesson.

You don't need to know the official or engineering name for each hose or line. A piece of masking tape on the hose and a piece on its fitting will allow you to assign your own label such as the letter A or a short name. As long as you remember your own code, the lines can be reconnected by matching similar letters or names. Do remember that tape will dissolve in gasoline or other fluids; if a component is to be washed or cleaned, use another method of identification. A permanent felt-tipped marker can be very handy for marking metal parts. Remove any tape or paper labels after assembly.

Maintenance or Repair?

It's necessary to mention the difference between maintenance and repair. Maintenance includes routine inspections, adjustments, and replacement of parts which show signs of normal wear. Maintenance compensates for wear or deterioration. Repair implies that something has broken or is not working. A need for repair is often caused by lack of maintenance. Example: draining and refilling the automatic transmission fluid is maintenance recommended by the manufacturer at specific mileage intervals. Failure to do this can ruin the transmission/transaxle, requiring very expensive repairs. While no maintenance program can prevent items from breaking or wearing out, a general rule can be stated: MAINTENANCE IS CHEAPER THAN REPAIR.

Two basic mechanic's rules should be mentioned here. First, whenever the left side of the vehicle or engine is referred to, it is meant to specify the driver's side. Conversely, the right side of the vehicle means the passenger's side. Second, most screws and bolts are removed by turning counterclockwise, and tightened by turning clockwise.

Safety is always the most important rule. Constantly be aware of the dangers involved in working on an automobile and take the proper precautions. See the information in this section regarding SERVICING YOUR VEHICLE SAFELY and the SAFETY NOTICE on the acknowledgment page.

Avoiding the Most Common Mistakes

Pay attention to the instructions provided. There are 3 common mistakes in mechanical work:

1. **Incorrect order of assembly, disassembly or adjustment.** When taking something apart or putting it together, performing steps in the wrong order usually just costs you extra time; however, it CAN break something. Read the entire procedure before beginning disassembly. Perform everything in the order in which the instructions say you should, even if you can't immediately see a reason for it. When you're taking apart something that is very intricate, you might want to draw a picture of how it looks when assembled at one point in order to make sure you get everything back in its proper position. We will supply exploded views whenever possible. When making adjustments, perform them in the proper order; often, one adjustment affects another, and you cannot expect even satisfactory results unless each adjustment is made only when it cannot be changed by any other.

2. **Overtorquing (or undertorquing).** While it is more common for overtorquing to cause damage, undertorquing may allow a fastener to vibrate loose causing serious damage. Especially when dealing with aluminum parts, pay attention to torque specifications and utilize a torque wrench in assembly. If a torque figure is not available, remember that if you are using the right tool to perform the job, you will probably not have to strain yourself to get a fastener tight enough. The pitch of most threads is so slight that the tension you put on the wrench will be multiplied many times in actual force on what you are tightening. A good example of how critical torque is can be seen in the case of spark plug in-

stallation, especially where you are putting the plug into an aluminum cylinder head. Too little torque can fail to crush the gasket, causing leakage of combustion gases and consequent overheating of the plug and engine parts. Too much torque can damage the threads or distort the plug, changing the spark gap.

There are many commercial products available for ensuring that fasteners won't come loose, even if they are not torqued just right (a very common brand is Loctite®). If you're worried about getting something together tight enough to hold, but loose enough to avoid mechanical damage during assembly, one of these products might offer substantial insurance. Before choosing a threadlocking compound, read the label on the package and make sure the product is compatible with the materials, fluids, etc. involved.

3. **Crossthreading.** This occurs when a part such as a bolt is screwed into a nut or casting at the wrong angle and forced. Crossthreading is more likely to occur if access is difficult. It helps to clean and lubricate fasteners, then to start threading with the part to be installed positioned straight in. Then, start the bolt, spark plug, etc. with your fingers. If you encounter resistance, unscrew the part and start over again at a different angle until it can be inserted and turned several times without much effort. Keep in mind that many parts, especially spark plugs, have tapered threads, so that gentle turning will automatically bring the part you're threading to the proper angle, but only if you don't force it or resist a change in angle. Don't put a wrench on the part until it's been tightened a couple of turns by hand. If you suddenly encounter resistance, and the part has not seated fully, don't force it. Pull it back out to make sure it's clean and threading properly.

Always take your time and be patient; once you have some experience, working on your vehicle may well become an enjoyable hobby.

TOOLS AND EQUIPMENT

Naturally, without the proper tools and equipment it is impossible to properly service your vehicle. It would also be virtually impossible to catalog every tool that you would need to perform all of the operations in this book. Of course, It would be unwise for the amateur to rush out and buy an expensive set of tools on the theory that he/she may need one or more of them at some time.

The best approach is to proceed slowly, gathering a good quality set of those tools that are used most frequently. Don't be misled by the low cost of bargain tools. It is far better to spend a little more for better quality. Forged wrenches, 6 or 12-point sockets and fine tooth ratchets are by far preferable to their less expensive counterparts. As any good mechanic can tell you, there are few worse experiences than trying to work on a vehicle with bad tools. Your monetary savings will be far outweighed by frustration and mangled knuckles.

Begin accumulating those tools that are used most frequently: those associated with routine maintenance and tune-up. In addition to the normal assortment of screwdrivers and pliers, you should have the following tools:

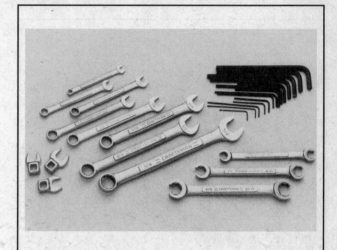

In addition to ratchets, a good set of wrenches and hex keys will be necessary

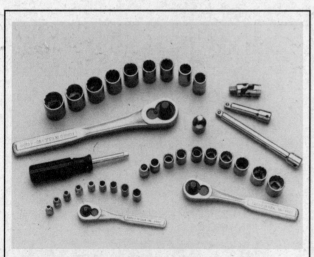

All but the most basic procedures will require an assortment of ratchets and sockets

A hydraulic floor jack and a set of jackstands are essential for lifting and supporting the vehicle

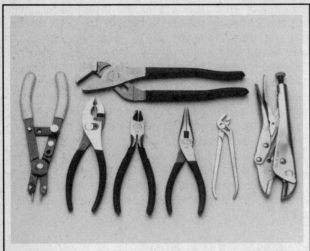

An assortment of pliers, grippers and cutters will be handy for old rusted parts and stripped bolt heads

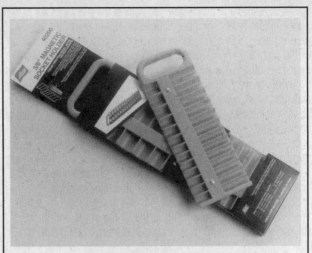

Tools from specialty manufacturers such as Lisle® are designed to make your job easier . . .

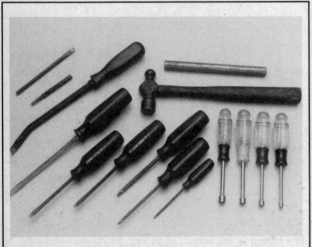

Various drivers, chisels and prybars are great tools to have in your toolbox

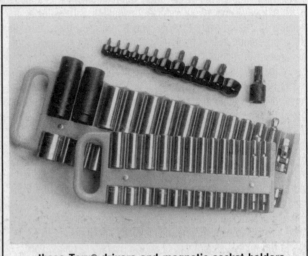

. . . these Torx® drivers and magnetic socket holders are just 2 examples of their handy products

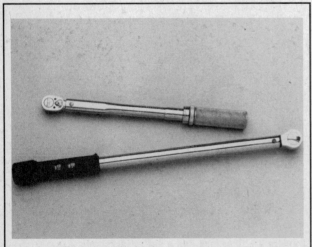

Many repairs will require the use of a torque wrench to assure the components are properly fastened

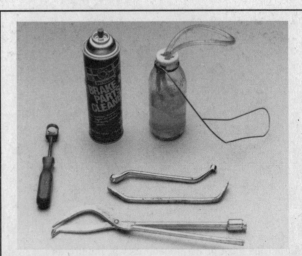

Although not always necessary, using specialized brake tools will save time

A few inexpensive lubrication tools will make maintenance easier

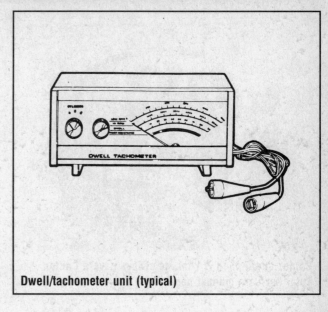

Dwell/tachometer unit (typical)

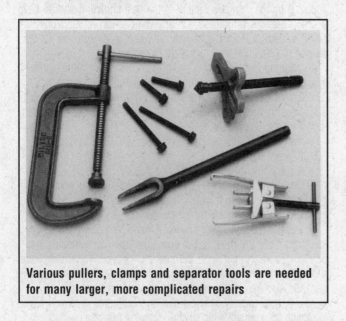

Various pullers, clamps and separator tools are needed for many larger, more complicated repairs

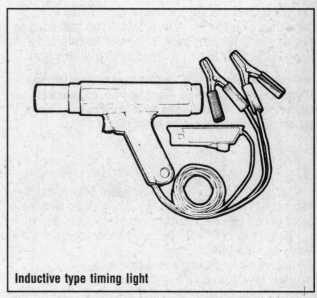

Inductive type timing light

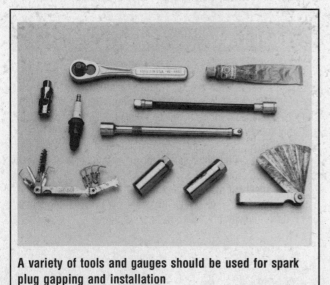

A variety of tools and gauges should be used for spark plug gapping and installation

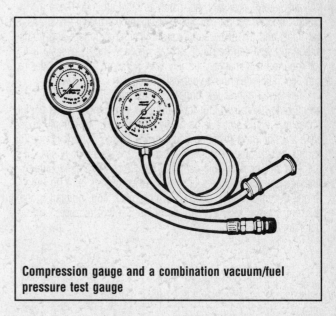

Compression gauge and a combination vacuum/fuel pressure test gauge

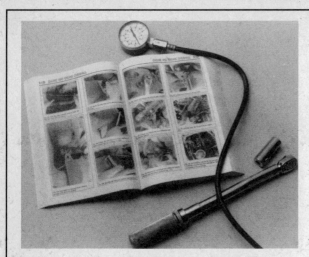

Proper information is vital, so always have a Chilton Total Car Care manual handy

• Wrenches/sockets and combination open end/box end wrenches in sizes from ⅛–¾ in. or 3mm–19mm (depending on whether your vehicle uses standard or metric fasteners) and a 13⁄16 in. or ⅝ in. spark plug socket (depending on plug type).

➡**If possible, buy various length socket drive extensions. Universal-joint and wobble extensions can be extremely useful, but be careful when using them, as they can change the amount of torque applied to the socket.**

• Jackstands for support.
• Oil filter wrench.
• Spout or funnel for pouring fluids.
• Grease gun for chassis lubrication (unless your vehicle is not equipped with any grease fittings—for details, please refer to information on Fluids and Lubricants found later in this section).
• Hydrometer for checking the battery (unless equipped with a sealed, maintenance-free battery).
• A container for draining oil and other fluids.
• Rags for wiping up the inevitable mess.

In addition to the above items there are several others that are not absolutely necessary, but handy to have around. These include Oil Dry® (or an equivalent oil absorbent gravel—such as cat litter) and the usual supply of lubricants, antifreeze and fluids, although these can be purchased as needed. This is a basic list for routine maintenance, but only your personal needs and desire can accurately determine your list of tools.

After performing a few projects on the vehicle, you'll be amazed at the other tools and non-tools on your workbench. Some useful household items are: a large turkey baster or siphon, empty coffee cans and ice trays (to store parts), ball of twine, electrical tape for wiring, small rolls of colored tape for tagging lines or hoses, markers and pens, a note pad, golf tees (for plugging vacuum lines), metal coat hangers or a roll of mechanics's wire (to hold things out of the way), dental pick or similar long, pointed probe, a strong magnet, and a small mirror (to see into recesses and under manifolds).

A more advanced set of tools, suitable for tune-up work, can be drawn up easily. While the tools are slightly more sophisticated, they need not be outrageously expensive. There are several inexpensive tach/dwell meters on the market that are every bit as good for the average mechanic as a professional model. Just be sure that it goes to a least 1200–1500 rpm on the tach scale and that it works on 4, 6 and 8-cylinder engines. (If you own one or more vehicles with a diesel engine, a special tachometer is required since diesels don't use spark plug ignition systems). The key to these purchases is to make them with an eye towards adaptability and wide range. A basic list of tune-up tools could include:

• Tach/dwell meter.
• Spark plug wrench and gapping tool.
• Feeler gauges for valve or point adjustment. (Even if your vehicle does not use points or require valve adjustments, a feeler gauge is helpful for many repair/overhaul procedures).

A tachometer/dwell meter will ensure accurate tune-up work on vehicles without electronic ignition. The choice of a timing light should be made carefully. A light which works on the DC current supplied by the vehicle's battery is the best choice; it should have a xenon tube for brightness. On any vehicle with an electronic ignition system, a timing light with an inductive pickup that clamps around the No. 1 spark plug cable is preferred.

In addition to these basic tools, there are several other tools and gauges you may find useful. These include:

• Compression gauge. The screw-in type is slower to use, but eliminates the possibility of a faulty reading due to escaping pressure.
• Manifold vacuum gauge.
• 12V test light.
• A combination volt/ohmmeter
• Induction Ammeter. This is used for determining whether or not there is current in a wire. These are handy for use if a wire is broken somewhere in a wiring harness.

As a final note, you will probably find a torque wrench necessary for all but the most basic work. The beam type models are perfectly adequate, although the newer click types (breakaway) are easier to use. The click type torque wrenches tend to be more expensive. Also keep in mind that all types of torque wrenches should be periodically checked and/or recalibrated. You will have to decide for yourself which better fits your purpose.

Special Tools

Normally, the use of special factory tools is avoided for repair procedures, since these are not readily available for the do-it-yourself mechanic. When it is possible to perform the job with more commonly available tools, it will be pointed out, but occasionally, a special tool was designed to perform a specific function and should be used. Before substituting another tool, you should be convinced that neither your safety nor the performance of the vehicle will be compromised.

Special tools can usually be purchased from an automotive parts store or from your dealer. In some cases special tools may be available directly from the tool manufacturer.

SERVICING YOUR VEHICLE SAFELY

It is virtually impossible to anticipate all of the hazards involved with automotive maintenance and service, but care and common sense will prevent most accidents.

The rules of safety for mechanics range from "don't smoke around gasoline," to "use the proper tool(s) for the job." The trick to avoiding injuries is to develop safe work habits and to take every possible precaution.

Do's

• Do keep a fire extinguisher and first aid kit handy.
• Do wear safety glasses or goggles when cutting, drilling, grinding or prying, even if you have 20–20 vision. If you wear glasses for the sake of vision, wear safety goggles over your regular glasses.
• Do shield your eyes whenever you work around the battery. Batteries contain sulfuric acid. In case of contact with the eyes or

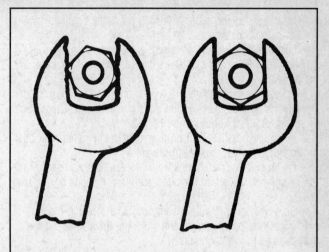

Using the correct size wrench will help prevent the possibility of rounding off a nut

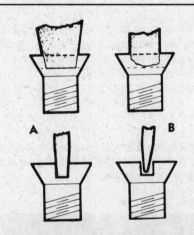

Screwdrivers should be kept in good condition to prevent injury or damage which could result if the blade slips from the screw

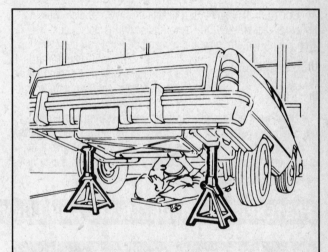

NEVER work under a vehicle unless it is supported using safety stands (jackstands)

skin, flush the area with water or a mixture of water and baking soda, then seek immediate medical attention.
• Do use safety stands (jackstands) for any undervehicle service. Jacks are for raising vehicles; jackstands are for making sure the vehicle stays raised until you want it to come down. Whenever the vehicle is raised, block the wheels remaining on the ground and set the parking brake.
• Do use adequate ventilation when working with any chemicals or hazardous materials. Like carbon monoxide, the asbestos dust resulting from some brake lining wear can be hazardous in sufficient quantities.
• Do disconnect the negative battery cable when working on the electrical system. The secondary ignition system contains EXTREMELY HIGH VOLTAGE. In some cases it can even exceed 50,000 volts.
• Do follow manufacturer's directions whenever working with potentially hazardous materials. Most chemicals and fluids are poisonous if taken internally.

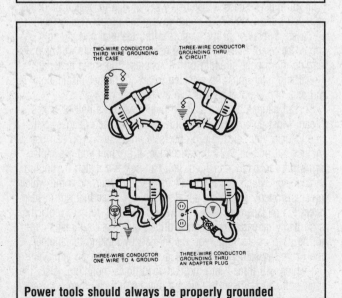

Power tools should always be properly grounded

• Do properly maintain your tools. Loose hammerheads, mushroomed punches and chisels, frayed or poorly grounded electrical cords, excessively worn screwdrivers, spread wrenches (open end), cracked sockets, slipping ratchets, or faulty droplight sockets can cause accidents.

• Likewise, keep your tools clean; a greasy wrench can slip off a bolt head, ruining the bolt and often harming your knuckles in the process.

• Do use the proper size and type of tool for the job at hand. Do select a wrench or socket that fits the nut or bolt. The wrench or socket should sit straight, not cocked.

• Do, when possible, pull on a wrench handle rather than push on it, and adjust your stance to prevent a fall.

• Do be sure that adjustable wrenches are tightly closed on the nut or bolt and pulled so that the force is on the side of the fixed jaw.

• Do strike squarely with a hammer; avoid glancing blows.

• Do set the parking brake and block the drive wheels if the work requires a running engine.

Don'ts

• Don't run the engine in a garage or anywhere else without proper ventilation—EVER! Carbon monoxide is poisonous; it takes a long time to leave the human body and you can build up a deadly supply of it in your system by simply breathing in a little every day. You may not realize you are slowly poisoning yourself. Always use power vents, windows, fans and/or open the garage door.

• Don't work around moving parts while wearing loose clothing. Short sleeves are much safer than long, loose sleeves. Hard-toed shoes with neoprene soles protect your toes and give a better grip on slippery surfaces. Jewelry such as watches, fancy belt buckles, beads or body adornment of any kind is not safe working around a vehicle. Long hair should be tied back under a hat or cap.

• Don't use pockets for toolboxes. A fall or bump can drive a screwdriver deep into your body. Even a rag hanging from your back pocket can wrap around a spinning shaft or fan.

• Don't smoke when working around gasoline, cleaning solvent or other flammable material.

• Don't smoke when working around the battery. When the battery is being charged, it gives off explosive hydrogen gas.

• Don't use gasoline to wash your hands; there are excellent soaps available. Gasoline contains dangerous additives which can enter the body through a cut or through your pores. Gasoline also removes all the natural oils from the skin so that bone dry hands will suck up oil and grease.

• Don't service the air conditioning system unless you are equipped with the necessary tools and training. When liquid or compressed gas refrigerant is released to atmospheric pressure it will absorb heat from whatever it contacts. This will chill or freeze anything it touches. Although refrigerant is normally non-toxic, R-12 becomes a deadly poisonous gas in the presence of an open flame. One good whiff of the vapors from burning refrigerant can be fatal.

• Don't use screwdrivers for anything other than driving screws! A screwdriver used as an prying tool can snap when you least expect it, causing injuries. At the very least, you'll ruin a good screwdriver.

• Don't use a bumper or emergency jack (that little ratchet, scissors, or pantograph jack supplied with the vehicle) for anything other than changing a flat! These jacks are only intended for emergency use out on the road; they are NOT designed as a maintenance tool. If you are serious about maintaining your vehicle yourself, invest in a hydraulic floor jack of at least a 1½ ton capacity, and at least two sturdy jackstands.

FASTENERS, MEASUREMENTS AND CONVERSIONS

Bolts, Nuts and Other Threaded Retainers

Although there are a great variety of fasteners found in the modern car or truck, the most commonly used retainer is the threaded fastener (nuts, bolts, screws, studs, etc). Most threaded retainers may be reused, provided that they are not damaged in use or during the repair. Some retainers (such as stretch bolts or torque prevailing nuts) are designed to deform when tightened or in use and should not be reinstalled.

Whenever possible, we will note any special retainers which should be replaced during a procedure. But you should always inspect the condition of a retainer when it is removed and replace any that show signs of damage. Check all threads for rust or corrosion which can increase the torque necessary to achieve the desired clamp load for which that fastener was originally selected. Additionally, be sure that the driver surface of the fastener has not been compromised by rounding or other damage. In some cases a driver surface may become only partially rounded, allowing the driver to catch in only one direction. In many of these occurrences, a fastener may be installed and tightened, but the driver would not be able to grip and loosen the fastener again. (This could lead to frustration down the line should that component ever need to be disassembled again).

If you must replace a fastener, whether due to design or damage, you must ALWAYS be sure to use the proper replacement. In all cases, a retainer of the same design, material and strength should be used. Markings on the heads of most bolts will help determine the proper strength of the fastener. The same material, thread and pitch must be selected to assure proper installation and safe operation of the vehicle afterwards.

Thread gauges are available to help measure a bolt or stud's thread. Most automotive and hardware stores keep gauges available to help you select the proper size. In a pinch, you can use another nut or bolt for a thread gauge. If the bolt you are replacing is not too badly damaged, you can select a match by finding another bolt which will thread in its place. If you find a nut which threads properly onto the damaged bolt, then use that nut to help select the replacement bolt. If however, the bolt you are replacing is so badly damaged (broken or drilled out) that its threads cannot be used as a gauge, you might start by looking for another bolt (from the same assembly or a similar location on your vehicle) which will thread into the damaged bolt's mounting. If so, the other bolt can be used to select a nut; the nut can then be used to select the replacement bolt.

Here are a few of the most common screw/bolt driver styles

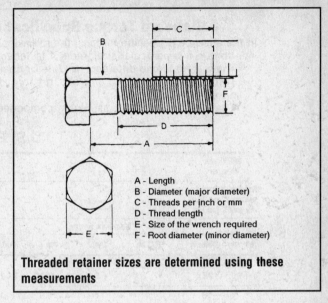

A - Length
B - Diameter (major diameter)
C - Threads per inch or mm
D - Thread length
E - Size of the wrench required
F - Root diameter (minor diameter)

Threaded retainer sizes are determined using these measurements

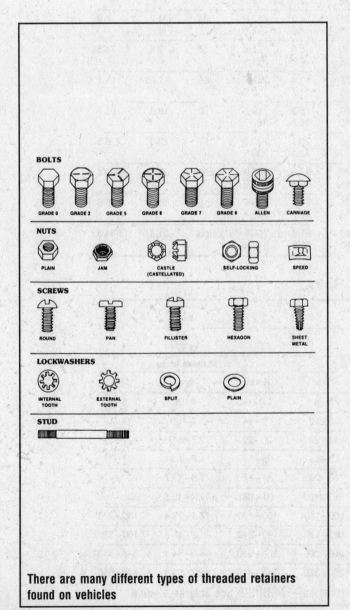

There are many different types of threaded retainers found on vehicles

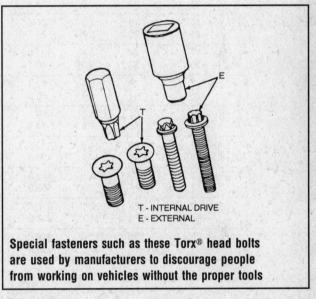

T - INTERNAL DRIVE
E - EXTERNAL

Special fasteners such as these Torx® head bolts are used by manufacturers to discourage people from working on vehicles without the proper tools

In all cases, be absolutely sure you have selected the proper replacement. Don't be shy, you can always ask the store clerk for help.

❄❄ WARNING

Be aware that when you find a bolt with damaged threads, you may also find the nut or drilled hole it was threaded into has also been damaged. If this is the case, you may have to drill and tap the hole, replace the nut or otherwise repair the threads. NEVER try to force a replacement bolt to fit into the damaged threads.

Torque

Torque is defined as the measurement of resistance to turning or rotating. It tends to twist a body about an axis of rotation. A common example of this would be tightening a threaded retainer such as a nut, bolt or screw. Measuring torque is one of the most

Standard Torque Specifications and Fastener Markings

In the absence of specific torques, the following chart can be used as a guide to the maximum safe torque of a particular size/grade of fastener.
- There is no torque difference for fine or coarse threads.
- Torque values are based on clean, dry threads. Reduce the value by 10% if threads are oiled prior to assembly.
- The torque required for aluminum components or fasteners is considerably less.

U.S. Bolts

SAE Grade Number	1 or 2			5			6 or 7		
Number of lines always 2 less than the grade number.									
Bolt Size (Inches)—(Thread)	Maximum Torque			Maximum Torque			Maximum Torque		
	Ft./Lbs.	Kgm	Nm	Ft./Lbs.	Kgm	Nm	Ft./Lbs.	Kgm	Nm
¼ — 20	5	0.7	6.8	8	1.1	10.8	10	1.4	13.5
— 28	6	0.8	8.1	10	1.4	13.6			
⁵⁄₁₆ — 18	11	1.5	14.9	17	2.3	23.0	19	2.6	25.8
— 24	13	1.8	17.6	19	2.6	25.7			
⅜ — 16	18	2.5	24.4	31	4.3	42.0	34	4.7	46.0
— 24	20	2.75	27.1	35	4.8	47.5			
⁷⁄₁₆ — 14	28	3.8	37.0	49	6.8	66.4	55	7.6	74.5
— 20	30	4.2	40.7	55	7.6	74.5			
½ — 13	39	5.4	52.8	75	10.4	101.7	85	11.75	115.2
— 20	41	5.7	55.6	85	11.7	115.2			
⁹⁄₁₆ — 12	51	7.0	69.2	110	15.2	149.1	120	16.6	162.7
— 18	55	7.6	74.5	120	16.6	162.7			
⅝ — 11	83	11.5	112.5	150	20.7	203.3	167	23.0	226.5
— 18	95	13.1	128.8	170	23.5	230.5			
¾ — 10	105	14.5	142.3	270	37.3	366.0	280	38.7	379.6
— 16	115	15.9	155.9	295	40.8	400.0			
⅞ — 9	160	22.1	216.9	395	54.6	535.5	440	60.9	596.5
— 14	175	24.2	237.2	435	60.1	589.7			
1 — 8	236	32.5	318.6	590	81.6	799.9	660	91.3	894.8
— 14	250	34.6	338.9	660	91.3	849.8			

Metric Bolts

Relative Strength Marking	4.6, 4.8			8.8		
Bolt Markings						
Bolt Size Thread Size x Pitch (mm)	Maximum Torque			Maximum Torque		
	Ft./Lbs.	Kgm	Nm	Ft./Lbs.	Kgm	Nm
6 x 1.0	2–3	.2–.4	3–4	3–6	4–.8	5–8
8 x 1.25	6–8	.8–1	8–12	9–14	1.2–1.9	13–19
10 x 1.25	12–17	1.5–2.3	16–23	20–29	2.7–4.0	27–39
12 x 1.25	21–32	2.9–4.4	29–43	35–53	4.8–7.3	47–72
14 x 1.5	35–52	4.8–7.1	48–70	57–85	7.8–11.7	77–110
16 x 1.5	51–77	7.0–10.6	67–100	90–120	12.4–16.5	130–160
18 x 1.5	74–110	10.2–15.1	100–150	130–170	17.9–23.4	180–230
20 x 1.5	110–140	15.1–19.3	150–190	190–240	26.2–46.9	160–320
22 x 1.5	150–190	22.0–26.2	200–260	250–320	34.5–44.1	340–430
24 x 1.5	190–240	26.2–46.9	260–320	310–410	42.7–56.5	420–550

Standard and metric bolt torque specifications based on bolt strengths—WARNING: use only as a guide

common ways to help assure that a threaded retainer has been properly fastened.

When tightening a threaded fastener, torque is applied in three distinct areas, the head, the bearing surface and the clamp load. About 50 percent of the measured torque is used in overcoming bearing friction. This is the friction between the bearing surface of the bolt head, screw head or nut face and the base material or washer (the surface on which the fastener is rotating). Approximately 40 percent of the applied torque is used in overcoming thread friction. This leaves only about 10 percent of the applied torque to develop a useful clamp load (the force which holds a joint together). This means that friction can account for as much as 90 percent of the applied torque on a fastener.

TORQUE WRENCHES

In most applications, a torque wrench can be used to assure proper installation of a fastener. Torque wrenches come in various designs and most automotive supply stores will carry a variety to suit your needs. A torque wrench should be used any time we supply a specific torque value for a fastener. A torque wrench can also be used if you are following the general guidelines in the accompanying charts. Keep in mind that because there is no worldwide standardization of fasteners, the charts are a general guideline and should be used with caution. Again, the general rule of "if you are using the right tool for the job, you should not have to strain to tighten a fastener" applies here.

Beam Type

The beam type torque wrench is one of the most popular types. It consists of a pointer attached to the head that runs the length of the flexible beam (shaft) to a scale located near the handle. As the wrench is pulled, the beam bends and the pointer indicates the torque using the scale.

Click (Breakaway) Type

Another popular design of torque wrench is the click type. To use the click type wrench you pre-adjust it to a torque setting. Once the torque is reached, the wrench has a reflex signalling fea-

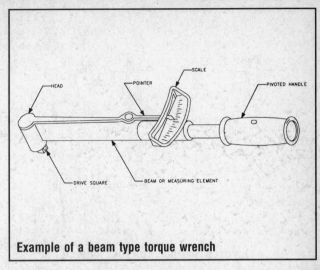

Example of a beam type torque wrench

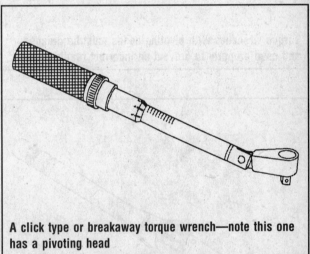

A click type or breakaway torque wrench—note this one has a pivoting head

ture that causes a momentary breakaway of the torque wrench body, sending an impulse to the operator's hand.

Pivot Head Type

Some torque wrenches (usually of the click type) may be equipped with a pivot head which can allow it to be used in areas of limited access. BUT, it must be used properly. To hold a pivot head wrench, grasp the handle lightly, and as you pull on the handle, it should be floated on the pivot point. If the handle comes in contact with the yoke extension during the process of pulling, there is a very good chance the torque readings will be inaccurate because this could alter the wrench loading point. The design of the handle is usually such as to make it inconvenient to deliberately misuse the wrench.

➡️**It should be mentioned that the use of any U-joint, wobble or extension will have an effect on the torque readings, no matter what type of wrench you are using. For the most accurate readings, install the socket directly on the wrench driver. If necessary, straight extensions (which hold a socket directly under the wrench driver) will have the least effect on the torque reading. Avoid any extension that alters the length of the wrench from the handle to the head/driving point (such as a crow's foot). U-joint or Wobble extensions can greatly affect the readings; avoid their use at all times.**

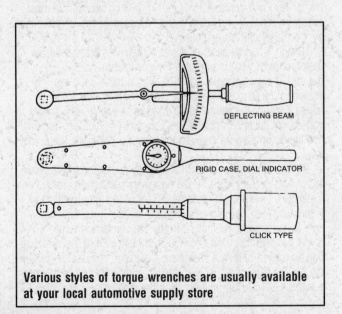

DEFLECTING BEAM

RIGID CASE, DIAL INDICATOR

CLICK TYPE

Various styles of torque wrenches are usually available at your local automotive supply store

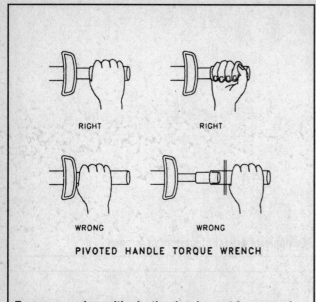

Torque wrenches with pivoting heads must be grasped and used properly to prevent an incorrect reading

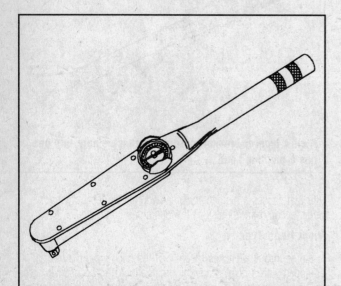

The rigid case (direct reading) torque wrench uses a dial indicator to show torque

Rigid Case (Direct Reading)

A rigid case or direct reading torque wrench is equipped with a dial indicator to show torque values. One advantage of these wrenches is that they can be held at any position on the wrench without affecting accuracy. These wrenches are often preferred because they tend to be compact, easy to read and have a great degree of accuracy.

TORQUE ANGLE METERS

Because the frictional characteristics of each fastener or threaded hole will vary, clamp loads which are based strictly on

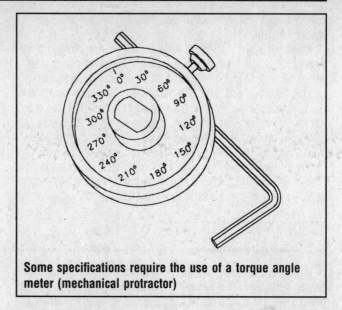

Some specifications require the use of a torque angle meter (mechanical protractor)

torque will vary as well. In most applications, this variance is not significant enough to cause worry. But, in certain applications, a manufacturer's engineers may determine that more precise clamp loads are necessary (such is the case with many aluminum cylinder heads). In these cases, a torque angle method of installation would be specified. When installing fasteners which are torque angle tightened, a predetermined seating torque and standard torque wrench are usually used first to remove any compliance from the joint. The fastener is then tightened the specified additional portion of a turn measured in degrees. A torque angle gauge (mechanical protractor) is used for these applications.

Standard and Metric Measurements

Throughout this manual, specifications are given to help you determine the condition of various components on your vehicle, or to assist you in their installation. Some of the most common measurements include length (in. or cm/mm), torque (ft. lbs., inch lbs. or Nm) and pressure (psi, in. Hg, kPa or mm Hg). In most cases, we strive to provide the proper measurement as determined by the manufacturer's engineers.

Though, in some cases, that value may not be conveniently measured with what is available in your toolbox. Luckily, many of the measuring devices which are available today will have two scales so the Standard or Metric measurements may easily be taken. If any of the various measuring tools which are available to you do not contain the same scale as listed in the specifications, use the accompanying conversion factors to determine the proper value.

The conversion factor chart is used by taking the given specification and multiplying it by the necessary conversion factor. For instance, looking at the first line, if you have a measurement in inches such as "free-play should be 2 in." but your ruler reads only in millimeters, multiply 2 in. by the conversion factor of 25.4 to get the metric equivalent of 50.8mm. Likewise, if the specification was given only in a Metric measurement, for example in Newton Meters (Nm), then look at the center column first. If the measurement is 100 Nm, multiply it by the conversion factor of 0.738 to get 73.8 ft. lbs.

CONVERSION FACTORS

LENGTH–DISTANCE

Inches (in.)	x 25.4	= Millimeters (mm)	x .0394	= Inches
Feet (ft.)	x .305	= Meters (m)	x 3.281	= Feet
Miles	x 1.609	= Kilometers (km)	x .0621	= Miles

VOLUME

Cubic Inches (in3)	x 16.387	= Cubic Centimeters	x .061	= in3
IMP Pints (IMP pt.)	x .568	= Liters (L)	x 1.76	= IMP pt.
IMP Quarts (IMP qt.)	x 1.137	= Liters (L)	x .88	= IMP qt.
IMP Gallons (IMP gal.)	x 4.546	= Liters (L)	x .22	= IMP gal.
IMP Quarts (IMP qt.)	x 1.201	= US Quarts (US qt.)	x .833	= IMP qt.
IMP Gallons (IMP gal.)	x 1.201	= US Gallons (US gal.)	x .833	= IMP gal.
Fl. Ounces	x 29.573	= Milliliters	x .034	= Ounces
US Pints (US pt.)	x .473	= Liters (L)	x 2.113	= Pints
US Quarts (US qt.)	x .946	= Liters (L)	x 1.057	= Quarts
US Gallons (US gal.)	x 3.785	= Liters (L)	x .264	= Gallons

MASS–WEIGHT

Ounces (oz.)	x 28.35	= Grams (g)	x .035	= Ounces
Pounds (lb.)	x .454	= Kilograms (kg)	x 2.205	= Pounds

PRESSURE

Pounds Per Sq. In. (psi)	x 6.895	= Kilopascals (kPa)	x .145	= psi
Inches of Mercury (Hg)	x .4912	= psi	x 2.036	= Hg
Inches of Mercury (Hg)	x 3.377	= Kilopascals (kPa)	x .2961	= Hg
Inches of Water (H_2O)	x .07355	= Inches of Mercury	x 13.783	= H_2O
Inches of Water (H_2O)	x .03613	= psi	x 27.684	= H_2O
Inches of Water (H_2O)	x .248	= Kilopascals (kPa)	x 4.026	= H_2O

TORQUE

Pounds–Force Inches (in·lb)	x .113	= Newton Meters (N·m)	x 8.85	= in–lb
Pounds–Force Feet (ft–lb)	x 1.356	= Newton Meters (N·m)	x .738	= ft–lb

VELOCITY

Miles Per Hour (MPH)	x 1.609	= Kilometers Per Hour (KPH)	x .621	= MPH

POWER

Horsepower (Hp)	x .745	= Kilowatts	x 1.34	= Horsepower

FUEL CONSUMPTION*

Miles Per Gallon IMP (MPG)	x .354	= Kilometers Per Liter (Km/L)
Kilometers Per Liter (Km/L)	x 2.352	= IMP MPG
Miles Per Gallon US (MPG)	x .425	= Kilometers Per Liter (Km/L)
Kilometers Per Liter (Km/L)	x 2.352	= US MPG

*It is common to covert from miles per gallon (mpg) to liters/100 kilometers (1/100 km), where mpg (IMP) x 1/100 km = 282 and mpg (US) x 1/100 km = 235.

TEMPERATURE

Degree Fahrenheit (°F)	= (°C x 1.8) + 32
Degree Celsius (°C)	= (°F – 32) x .56

Standard and metric conversion factors chart

SERIAL NUMBER IDENTIFICATION

Vehicle Identification

♦ **See Figures 1, 2 and 3**

The vehicle identification number plate is mounted on the instrument panel, adjacent to the lower corner of the windshield on the driver's side, and is visible through the windshield. The thirteen digit vehicle number is composed of a seven or eight digit identification number and a five or six digit serial number. The seventeen digit number, introduced in 1981, reflects the same information.

Engine Model

The engine model number is cast on the lower left side of the engine block or stamped near the engine serial number on the upper front side of the engine block.

Engine Serial Number

♦ **See Figure 4**

The engine serial number is stamped on a boss usually located on the right front top edge of the cylinder block.

Vehicle Body

♦ **See Figure 5**

The body number is located on the top center of the firewall in the engine compartment. The plate usually will also include, model, engine, transmission/transaxle and body paint color codes and identification.

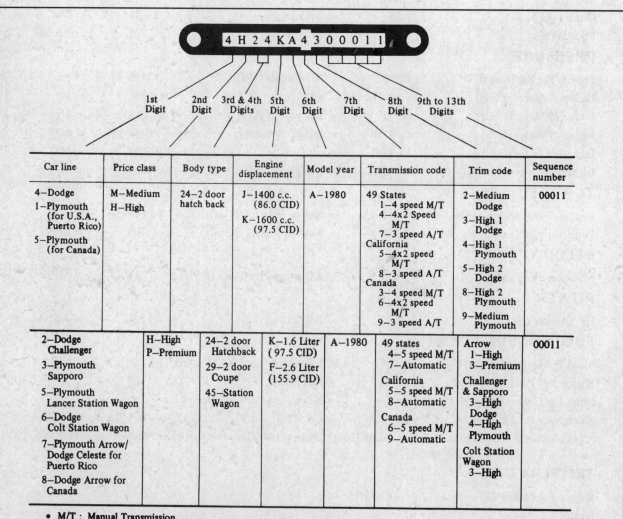

Car line	Price class	Body type	Engine displacement	Model year	Transmission code	Trim code	Sequence number
4—Dodge 1—Plymouth (for U.S.A., Puerto Rico) 5—Plymouth (for Canada)	M—Medium H—High	24—2 door hatch back	J—1400 c.c. (86.0 CID) K—1600 c.c. (97.5 CID)	A—1980	49 States 1—4 speed M/T 4—4x2 Speed M/T 7—3 speed A/T California 5—4x2 speed M/T 8—3 speed A/T Canada 3—4 speed M/T 6—4x2 speed M/T 9—3 speed A/T	2—Medium Dodge 3—High 1 Dodge 4—High 1 Plymouth 5—High 2 Dodge 8—High 2 Plymouth 9—Medium Plymouth	00011
2—Dodge Challenger 3—Plymouth Sapporo 5—Plymouth Lancer Station Wagon 6—Dodge Colt Station Wagon 7—Plymouth Arrow/ Dodge Celeste for Puerto Rico 8—Dodge Arrow for Canada	H—High P—Premium	24—2 door Hatchback 29—2 door Coupe 45—Station Wagon	K—1.6 Liter (97.5 CID) F—2.6 Liter (155.9 CID)	A—1980	49 states 4—5 speed M/T 7—Automatic California 5—5 speed M/T 8—Automatic Canada 6—5 speed M/T 9—Automatic	Arrow 1—High 3—Premium Challenger & Sapporo 3—High Dodge 4—High Plymouth Colt Station Wagon 3—High	00011

★ M/T : Manual Transmission

Fig. 1 Vehicle identification on models from 1971–80

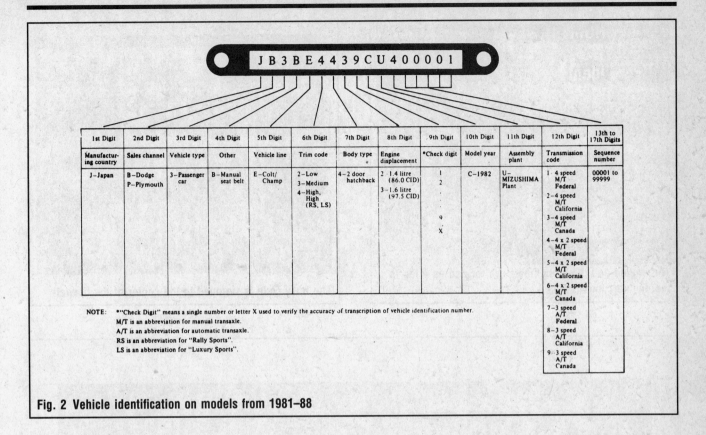

J B 3 B E 4 4 3 9 C U 4 0 0 0 0 1

1st Digit	2nd Digit	3rd Digit	4th Digit	5th Digit	6th Digit	7th Digit	8th Digit	9th Digit	10th Digit	11th Digit	12th Digit	13th to 17th Digits
Manufacturing country	Sales channel	Vehicle type	Other	Vehicle line	Trim code	Body type	Engine displacement	*Check digit	Model year	Assembly plant	Transmission code	Sequence number
J–Japan	B–Dodge P–Plymouth	3–Passenger car	B–Manual seat belt	E–Colt/Champ	2–Low 3–Medium 4–High, High (RS, LS)	4–2 door hatchback	2 - 1.4 litre (86.0 CID) 3–1.6 litre (97.5 CID)	1 2 . . 9 X	C–1982	U–MIZUSHIMA Plant	1 - 4 speed M/T Federal 2–4 speed M/T California 3–4 speed M/T Canada 4–4 x 2 speed M/T Federal 5–4 x 2 speed M/T California 6–4 x 2 speed M/T Canada 7–3 speed A/T Federal 8–3 speed A/T California 9–3 speed A/T Canada	00001 to 99999

NOTE: *"Check Digit" means a single number or letter X used to verify the accuracy of transcription of vehicle identification number.

M/T is an abbreviation for manual transaxle.

A/T is an abbreviation for automatic transaxle.

RS is an abbreviation for "Rally Sports".

LS is an abbreviation for "Luxury Sports".

Fig. 2 Vehicle identification on models from 1981–88

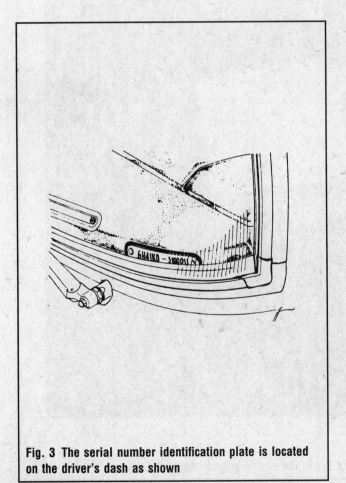

Fig. 3 The serial number identification plate is located on the driver's dash as shown

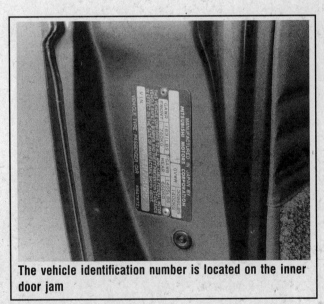

The vehicle identification number is located on the inner door jam

Transmission/Transaxle

The transmission (rear wheel drive models) serial number is stamped on the left side of the transmission case or on the clutch housing. The manual transaxle (front wheel drive models) serial number is stamped on housing of the transaxle case. On automatic transaxle models, the number is on a plate attached to the side of the transmission, or stamped on the boss of the oil pan flange.

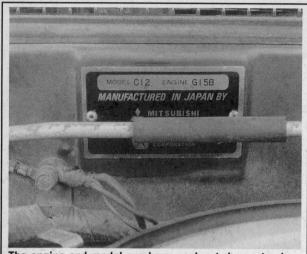

The engine and model numbers are located on a tag in the engine compartment

The body code is stamped in the center of the firewall

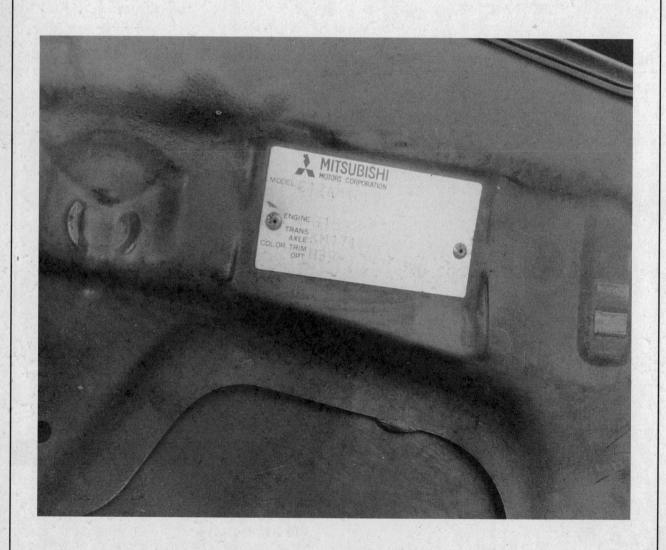

Transmission/transaxle identification numbers are located on a tag in the engine compartment

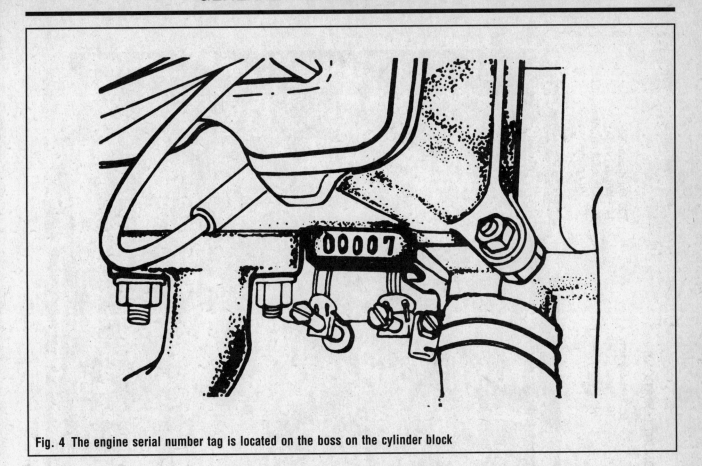

Fig. 4 The engine serial number tag is located on the boss on the cylinder block

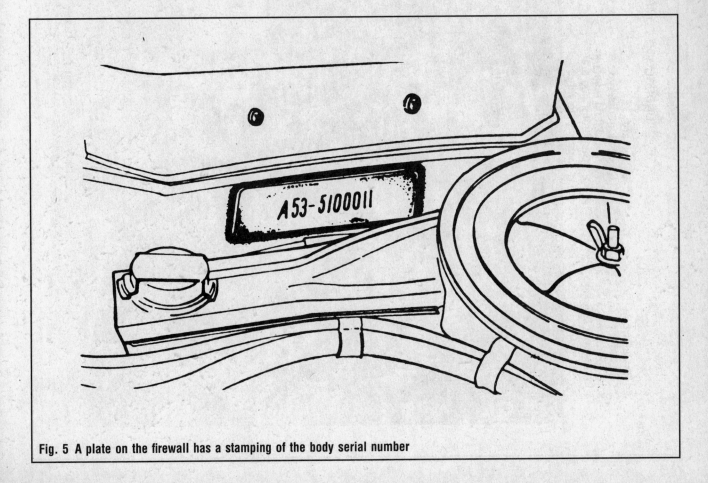

Fig. 5 A plate on the firewall has a stamping of the body serial number

UNDERHOOD COMPONENT LOCATIONS

1. Radiator cap
2. Radiator
3. Upper hose
4. Air intake snorkle
5. Battery
6. Coolant reservoir
7. Brake fluid reservoir
8. Distributor cap and spark plug wires
9. Battery tray
10. Heat shield
11. Air cleaner
12. Fuse block
13. Oil dipstick
14. Wiper blade
15. Chassis serial number
16. VIN plate

ROUTINE MAINTENANCE

Routine maintenance and driver's preventive maintenance are the most important steps that can be taken to extend the life of your car and avoid many expensive repairs.

Driver's preventive maintenance consists of taking only a minute every day (or so) to check the various fluid levels, hoses, belts, tire pressures and general visual condition of the engine and car body.

Routine maintenance calls for periodical service or replacement of parts and systems according to a schedule.

Air Cleaner

▶ **See Figures 6, 7, 8 and 9**

The air cleaner contains a dry filter element that keeps most dirt and dust from entering the engine via the carburetor or injection throttle body. Never run the engine (other than for adjusting) without a filter element. The dirt and dust entering the engine can cause expensive damage to the pistons, bearings, etc.

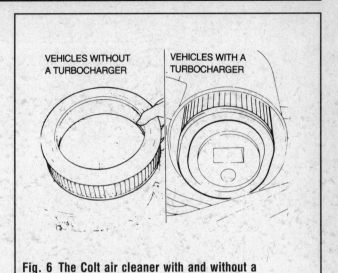

Fig. 6 The Colt air cleaner with and without a turbocharged engine

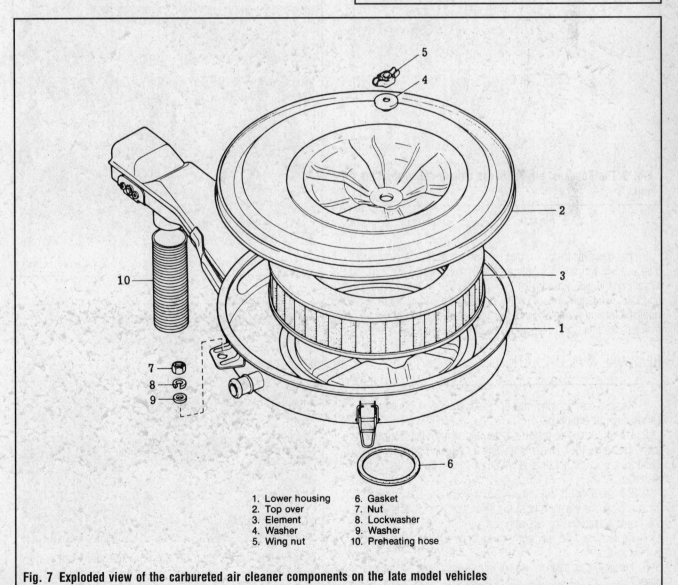

1. Lower housing
2. Top over
3. Element
4. Washer
5. Wing nut
6. Gasket
7. Nut
8. Lockwasher
9. Washer
10. Preheating hose

Fig. 7 Exploded view of the carbureted air cleaner components on the late model vehicles

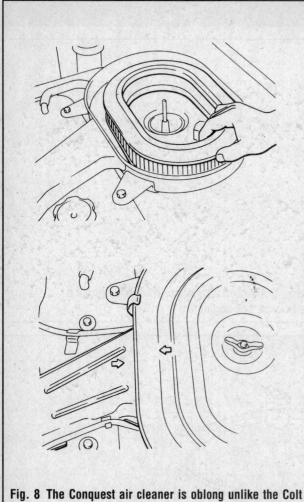

Fig. 8 The Conquest air cleaner is oblong unlike the Colt unit

Release the clamps . . .

. . . and remove the wing nut from the air cleaner cover

Proper maintenance of the cleaner element is vital. A clogged filter element will fail to supply sufficient fresh air to induction system and engine, causing an over-rich fuel/air mixture. Such a condition will result in poor engine performance and economy. Periodical cleaning or replacing of the filter element (refer to the maintenance chart) will help your car last longer and run better.

REMOVAL & INSTALLATION

1. Remove the top wing nuts or loosen the side mounted spring clips (if equipped).
2. Lift off the top of the air cleaner and remove the filter element. On some 1981 and later models a charcoal filter, is also located in the air cleaner, this is for vapor control and is not to be disturbed.
3. If the element is not too clogged by dirt, use compressed air and clean the element. Hold the air nozzle at least 50mm from the inside screen (or the element).
4. Replace the filter element if mileage or extreme dirt clogging is indicated.
5. Install the air cleaner element into position and secure the cover.

Remove the cover, then lift the filter out and inspect its condition

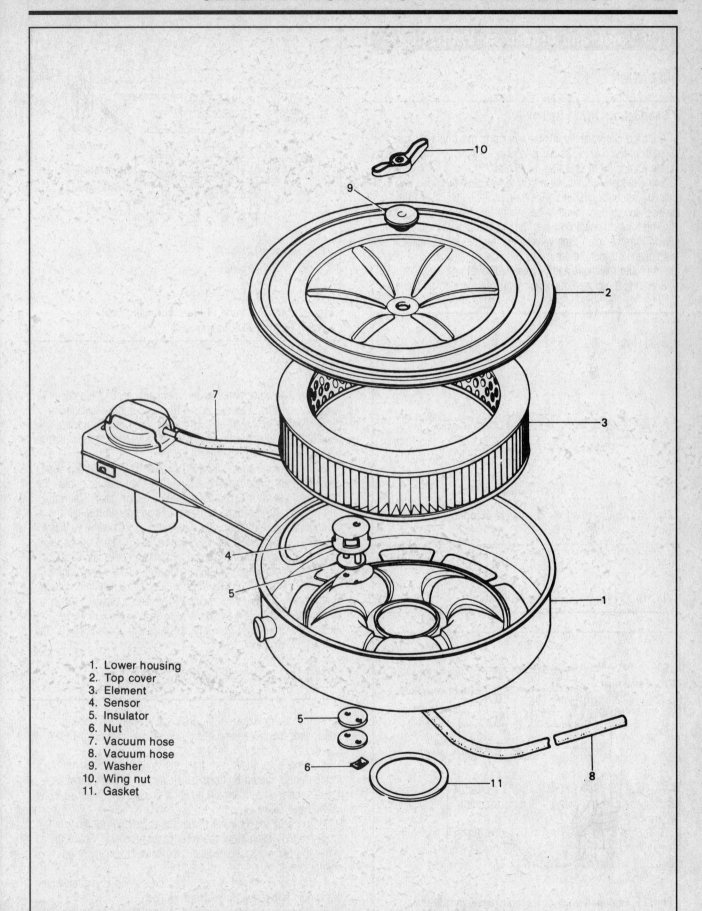

1. Lower housing
2. Top cover
3. Element
4. Sensor
5. Insulator
6. Nut
7. Vacuum hose
8. Vacuum hose
9. Washer
10. Wing nut
11. Gasket

Fig. 9 Exploded view of the carbureted air cleaner components on early model vehicles

PCV Valve and Crankcase Vent Filter

OPERATION

▶ **See Figures 10, 11 and 12**

A closed crankcase ventilation system is used on your car. The purpose of the closed system is to prevent blow-by gases, created by the engine, from escaping into the air.

Some models do not use a PCV valve, blow-by gases are passed through a hose from the front of the valve cover to the air cleaner, and through another hose from the rear of the valve cover into the intake manifold. At part throttle, the blow-by gases are drawn from the rear of the valve cover into the intake manifold. At wide opened throttle, the blow-by gases are drawn through both the front and rear hose and returned to the engine.

Servicing the closed crankcase ventilation system on models

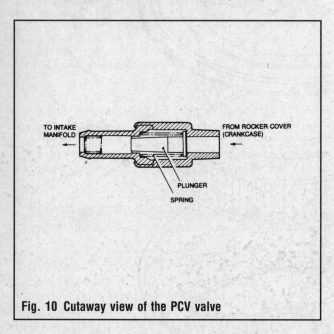

Fig. 10 Cutaway view of the PCV valve

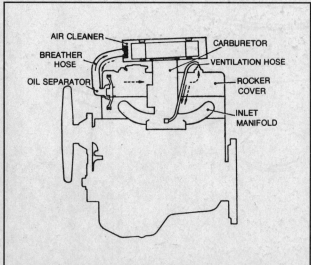

Fig. 11 Exploded view of the crankcase ventilation system without a PCV valve

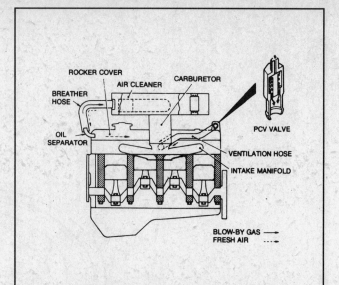

Fig. 12 Cutaway view of the crankcase ventilation system using a PCV valve

without a PCV valve amounts to a periodic check of the hoses (cracked or hard hoses should be replaced) and the cleaning of the wire mesh in the air cleaner and the fixed orifice on the intake manifold. The wire mesh (resembles steel wool) acts as a filter for the crankcase ventilation system.

On models equipped with a PCV valve, the PCV system supplies fresh air to the crankcase through the air cleaner. Inside the crankcase, the fresh air mixes with the blow-by gases. The mixture of fresh air and blow-by gases is then passed through the PCV valve and into the intake manifold. The PCV valve (usually mounted on the end of the valve cover) is a metered orifice that reacts to intake manifold vacuum, and has an adequate capacity for all normal driving conditions. However, under heavy engine loads or high speed driving there is less intake manifold vacuum and the blow-by gases exceed the PCV valve's capacity. When this happens, the blow-by gases back up into the air cleaner through the front hose, mix with fresh air and are reburned in the engine.

REMOVAL & INSTALLATION

1. Test the operation of the PCV valve, apply the parking brake, start the engine and allow it to operate at a normal idle speed.
2. Remove the PCV valve from the valve cover mounting. A hissing noise should be heard as air passes through the valve and a strong vacuum should be felt if you place a finger over the opened end of the valve.
3. To check the PCV valve with the engine not running, remove the PCV valve from the valve cover mounting. Shake the valve, if a rattling sound is heard, the valve is usually in operating condition.
4. If a rattling sound is not heard, or, suction is not felt when the engine is running, the valve is clogged.
5. Clean the valve and hose in solvent, check for air flow or rattle. Replace the valve and/or hose if necessary.

Separate the hose from the PCV valve

Unscrew the PCV valve from the valve cover

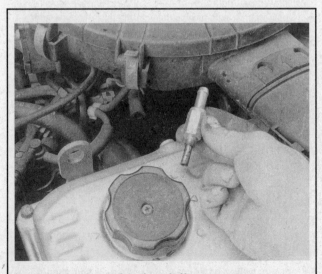

Inspect the valve and replace it if necessary

Fuel Filter

REMOVAL & INSTALLATION

Carbureted Engines

The fuel filter should be replaced, or at least checked for clogging every 12,000 miles. The fuel filter is of the in-line type and is located on the left side inner fender panel or low center of the firewall, on mechanical fuel pump equipped cars. On models equipped with electric fuel pumps, the fuel filter is located in the trunk, on sedan models, or in the left rear wheelhouse, on station wagons. Removal of the air cleaner assembly or battery and battery tray may be necessary, depending on year and model.

Fuel Injected Models

On models equipped with fuel injection, relieve fuel system pressure before replacing the filter. An electric fuel pump is used on these models and the filter is in the engine compartment. A connector, for checking the fuel function, is located under the battery tray. With the engine running, disconnect the harness, when the engine stops no pressure will remain in the system.

To remove the filter, loosen the hose clamps at both ends of the filter or unscrew the fittings and remove the fuel lines from the filter ends. Unclip the filter from the mounting bracket. Install a new filter. Start the engine and check for leaks. If a clogged filter is suspected, remove the filter and blow compressed air through the inlet and outlet fittings, reinstall the filter. Replace the old filter if needed.

Evaporative Emission Canister

Fuel vapors from the gas tank and carburetor (created by changes in temperature) are absorbed by a charcoal filled canister. When the engine is operating, the stored vapors are sucked out of the canister and fed back to, and burned in the combustion chambers. Some canisters are sealed, others contain a filter that must be cleaned. For proper service information refer to the following paragraph that covers the year of your car.

REMOVAL & INSTALLATION

1971–72 Models
▶ See Figure 13

Every 12,000 miles replace the air cleaner and filter in the canister. The air cleaner is located directly behind the side cover. Remove the retaining bolt and cover. Discard the old filter, insert the replacement, and tighten the nut. The canister itself must be completely replaced every 50,000 miles, as the activated charcoal gradually loses its effectiveness. Replacement is as follows:

1. Loosen and remove the two purge valve retaining bolts. Leave the hoses attached to the valve.
2. Loosen the purge valve-to-canister hose clamp at the canister and pull off the hose.
3. Loosen the expansion tank-to-canister hose clamp at the canister and remove the hose.
4. Remove the two canister bracket bolts and the canister.

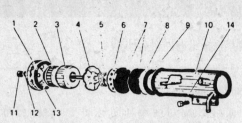

1. Gasket
2. Filter element
3. Spacer
4. Plate
5. Spring
6. Plate
7. Strainer
8. Paper filter
9. Gasket
10. Housing
11. Nut
12. Washer
13. Cover
14. Bolt

Fig. 13 Exploded view of the early evaporation emission canister components

5. Install the new canister, connect the hoses and tighten the mounting bracket.

➡**Inspect the hoses, replace any that are cracked, soft or collapsed.**

1973–89 Models
◆ **See Figure 14**

The canister or canisters should be replaced at specified intervals, as shown on the maintenance chart. Make sure all hoses are clamped and not dry rotted or broken. The canister filter, if equipped, should be inspected, cleaned or replaced at least every two years. Any clogging of the filter will inhibit air flow through the canister. Two different types of valves were used in the canister lines—refer to the emissions chapter for a detailed description of their function and necessary servicing. To replace the canister:

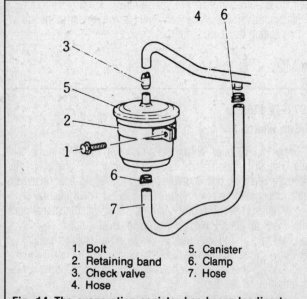

1. Bolt
2. Retaining band
3. Check valve
4. Hose
5. Canister
6. Clamp
7. Hose

Fig. 14 The evaporation canister has hoses leading to and from the unit

1. Remove the two connecting hoses from the canister.
2. Loosen and remove the canister retaining band bolt.
3. Remove the canister.
4. Check the hoses, replace any that are cracked, soft or collapsed. Install the new canister and connect the hoses.

Battery

GENERAL MAINTENANCE

All batteries, regardless of type, should be carefully secured by a battery hold-down device. If this is not done, the battery terminals or casing may crack from stress applied to the battery during vehicle operation. A battery which is not secured may allow acid to leak out, making it discharge faster; such leaking corrosive acid can also eat away components under the hood. A battery that is not sealed must be checked periodically for electrolyte level. You cannot add water to a sealed maintenance-free battery (though not all maintenance-free batteries are sealed), but a sealed battery must also be checked for proper electrolyte level as indicated by the color of the built-in hydrometer "eye."

Keep the top of the battery clean, as a film of dirt can help completely discharge a battery that is not used for long periods. A solution of baking soda and water may be used for cleaning, but be careful to flush this off with clear water. DO NOT let any of the solution into the filler holes. Baking soda neutralizes battery acid and will de-activate a battery cell.

✳✳ CAUTION

Always use caution when working on or near the battery. Never allow a tool to bridge the gap between the negative and positive battery terminals. Also, be careful not to allow a tool to provide a ground between the positive cable/terminal and any metal component on the vehicle. Either of these conditions will cause a short circuit leading to sparks and possible personal injury.

Batteries in vehicles which are not operated on a regular basis can fall victim to parasitic loads (small current drains which are constantly drawing current from the battery). Normal parasitic loads may drain a battery on a vehicle that is in storage and not used for 6–8 weeks. Vehicles that have additional accessories such as a cellular phone, an alarm system or other devices that increase parasitic load may discharge a battery sooner. If the vehicle is to be stored for 6–8 weeks in a secure area and the alarm system, if present, is not necessary, the negative battery cable should be disconnected at the onset of storage to protect the battery charge.

Remember that constantly discharging and recharging will shorten battery life. Take care not to allow a battery to be needlessly discharged.

BATTERY FLUID

✳✳ CAUTION

Battery electrolyte contains sulfuric acid. If you should splash any on your skin or in your eyes, flush the affected

area with plenty of clear water. If it lands in your eyes, get medical help immediately.

The fluid (sulfuric acid solution) contained in the battery cells will tell you many things about the condition of the battery. Because the cell plates must be kept submerged below the fluid level in order to operate, maintaining the fluid level is extremely important. And, because the specific gravity of the acid is an indication of electrical charge, testing the fluid can be an aid in determining if the battery must be replaced. A battery in a vehicle with a properly operating charging system should require little maintenance, but careful, periodic inspection should reveal problems before they leave you stranded.

Fluid Level

Check the battery electrolyte level at least once a month, or more often in hot weather or during periods of extended vehicle operation. On non-sealed batteries, the level can be checked either through the case on translucent batteries or by removing the cell caps on opaque-cased types. The electrolyte level in each cell

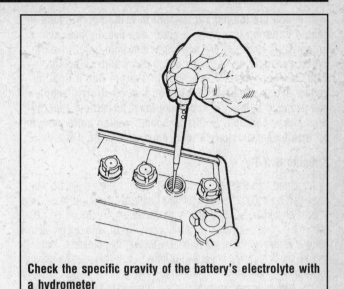

Check the specific gravity of the battery's electrolyte with a hydrometer

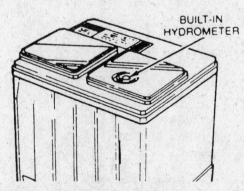

On non-maintenance free batteries, the level can be checked through the case on translucent batteries; the cell caps must be removed on other models

should be kept filled to the split ring inside each cell, or the line marked on the outside of the case.

If the level is low, add only distilled water through the opening until the level is correct. Each cell is separate from the others, so each must be checked and filled individually. Distilled water should be used, because the chemicals and minerals found in most drinking water are harmful to the battery and could significantly shorten its life.

If water is added in freezing weather, the vehicle should be driven several miles to allow the water to mix with the electrolyte. Otherwise, the battery could freeze.

Although some maintenance-free batteries have removable cell caps for access to the electrolyte, the electrolyte condition and level on all sealed maintenance-free batteries must be checked using the built-in hydrometer "eye." The exact type of eye varies between battery manufacturers, but most apply a sticker to the battery itself explaining the possible readings. When in doubt, refer to the battery manufacturer's instructions to interpret battery condition using the built-in hydrometer.

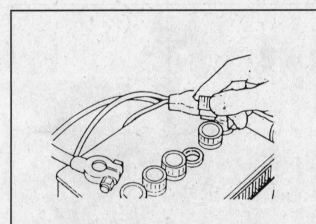

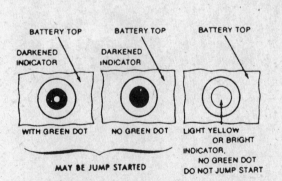

Location of indicator on sealed battery

Check the appearance of the charge indicator on top of the battery before attempting a jump start; if it's not green or dark, do not jump start the car

A typical sealed (maintenance-free) battery with a built-in hydrometer—NOTE that the hydrometer eye may vary between battery manufacturers; always refer to the battery's label

➡Although the readings from built-in hydrometers found in sealed batteries may vary, a green eye usually indicates a properly charged battery with sufficient fluid level. A dark eye is normally an indicator of a battery with sufficient fluid, but one which may be low in charge. And a light or yellow eye is usually an indication that electrolyte supply has dropped below the necessary level for battery (and hydrometer) operation. In this last case, sealed batteries with an insufficient electrolyte level must usually be discarded.

Specific Gravity

As stated earlier, the specific gravity of a battery's electrolyte level can be used as an indication of battery charge. At least once a year, check the specific gravity of the battery. It should be between 1.20 and 1.26 on the gravity scale. Most auto supply stores carry a variety of inexpensive battery testing hydrometers. These can be used on any non-sealed battery to test the specific gravity in each cell.

The battery testing hydrometer has a squeeze bulb at one end and a nozzle at the other. Battery electrolyte is sucked into the hydrometer until the float is lifted from its seat. The specific gravity is then read by noting the position of the float. If gravity is low in one or more cells, the battery should be slowly charged and checked again to see if the gravity has come up. Generally, if after charging, the specific gravity between any two cells varies more than 50 points (0.50), the battery should be replaced as it can no longer produce sufficient voltage to guarantee proper operation.

On sealed batteries, the built-in hydrometer is the only way of checking specific gravity. Again, check with your battery's manufacturer for proper interpretation of its built-in hydrometer readings.

CABLES

Once a year (or as necessary), the battery terminals and the cable clamps should be cleaned. Loosen the clamps and remove the cables, negative cable first. On batteries with posts on top, the use of a puller specially made for this purpose is recommended. These are inexpensive and available in most auto parts stores. Side terminal battery cables are secured with a small bolt.

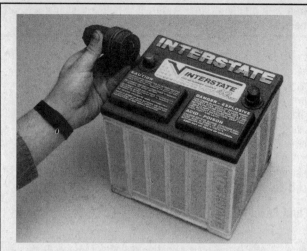

The underside of this special battery tool has a wire brush to clean post terminals

Place the tool over the terminals and twist to clean the post

Maintenance is performed with household items and with special tools like this post cleaner

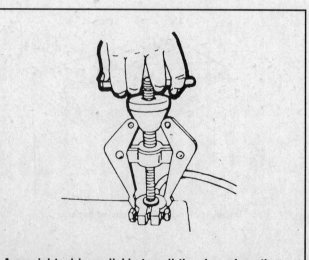

A special tool is available to pull the clamp from the post

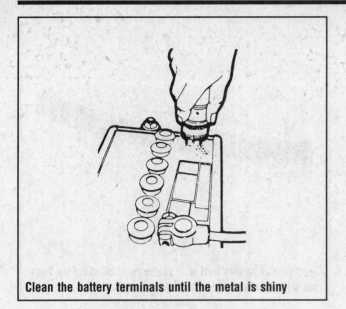

Clean the battery terminals until the metal is shiny

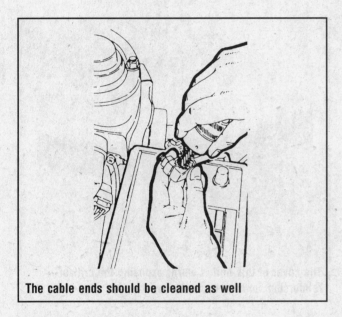

The cable ends should be cleaned as well

Clean the cable clamps and the battery terminal with a wire brush, until all corrosion, grease, etc., is removed and the metal is shiny. It is especially important to clean the inside of the clamp (an old knife is useful here) thoroughly, since a small deposit of foreign material or oxidation there will prevent a sound electrical connection and inhibit either starting or charging. Special tools are available for cleaning these parts, one type for conventional top post batteries and another type for side terminal batteries.

Before installing the cables, loosen the battery hold-down clamp or strap, remove the battery and check the battery tray. Clear it of any debris, and check it for soundness (the battery tray can be cleaned with a baking soda and water solution). Rust should be wire brushed away, and the metal given a couple coats of anti-rust paint. Install the battery and tighten the hold-down clamp or strap securely. Do not overtighten, as this can crack the battery case.

After the clamps and terminals are clean, reinstall the cables, negative cable last; DO NOT hammer the clamps onto post batter-

ies. Tighten the clamps securely, but do not distort them. Give the clamps and terminals a thin external coating of grease after installation, to retard corrosion.

Check the cables at the same time that the terminals are cleaned. If the cable insulation is cracked or broken, or if the ends are frayed, the cable should be replaced with a new cable of the same length and gauge.

CHARGING

✳✳ CAUTION

The chemical reaction which takes place in all batteries generates explosive hydrogen gas. A spark can cause the battery to explode and splash acid. To avoid serious personal injury, be sure there is proper ventilation and take appropriate fire safety precautions when connecting, disconnecting, or charging a battery and when using jumper cables.

A battery should be charged at a slow rate to keep the plates inside from getting too hot. However, if some maintenance-free batteries are allowed to discharge until they are almost "dead," they may have to be charged at a high rate to bring them back to "life." Always follow the charger manufacturer's instructions on charging the battery.

REPLACEMENT

When it becomes necessary to replace the battery, select one with a rating equal to or greater than the battery originally installed. Deterioration and just plain aging of the battery cables, starter motor, and associated wires makes the battery's job harder in successive years. The slow increase in electrical resistance over time makes it prudent to install a new battery with a greater capacity than the old.

Belts

INSPECTION

Inspect the belts for signs of glazing or cracking. A glazed belt will be perfectly smooth from slippage, while a good belt will have a slight texture of fabric visible. Cracks will usually start at the inner edge of the belt and run outward. All worn or damaged drive belts should be replaced immediately. It is best to replace all drive belts at one time, as a preventive maintenance measure, during this service operation.

ADJUSTING

Belts are normally adjusted by loosening the bolts of the accessory being driven and moving that accessory on its pivot points until the proper tension is applied to the belt. The accessory is held in this position while the bolts are tightened. To determine proper belt tension, you can purchase a belt tension guage or simply use the deflection method. To determine deflection, press inward on the belt at the mid-point of its longest straight run. The belt should deflect (move inward) ⅜-½ in. (10-30mm). A general rule for alternator belt tension is that the pulley should not be capable of being turned with hand pressure.

REMOVAL & INSTALLATION

To remove a V-style drive belt, simply loosen the accessory being driven and move it on its pivot point to free the belt. Then, remove the belt.

It is important to note that on engines with many driven accessories, several or all of the belts may have to be removed to get at the one to be replaced.

Deep cracks in this belt will cause flex, building up heat that will eventually lead to belt failure

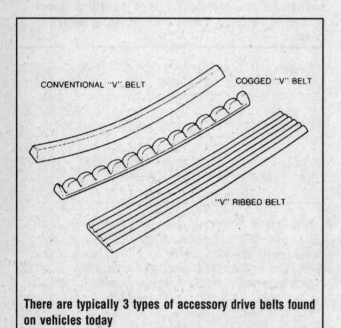

There are typically 3 types of accessory drive belts found on vehicles today

The cover of this belt is worn, exposing the critical reinforcing cords to excessive wear

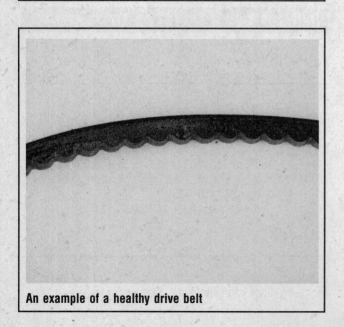

An example of a healthy drive belt

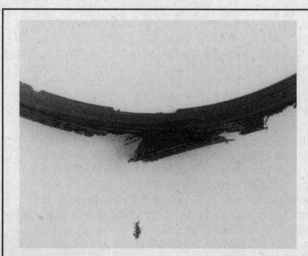

Installing too wide a belt can result in serious belt wear and/or breakage

Timing Belts

INSPECTION

Inspect both sides of the timing belt. Replace the belt with a new one if any of the following conditions exist:
- Hardening of black rubber back side is glossary without resilience and leaves no indent when press with a fingernail.
- Cracks on ruibber backing.
- Cracks or peeling of the canvas.
- Cracks on rib root.
- Cracks on belt sides.
- Missing teeth.
- Abnormal wear of belt sidea. The sides are normal if they are sharp as if cut by a knife.

If none of these conditions exist, the belt does not need replacment, unless it is at it's replacment interval.

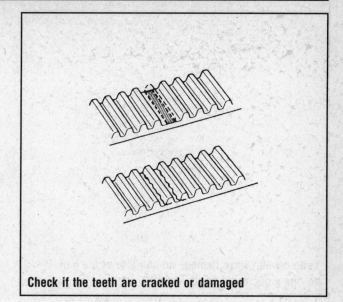

Check if the teeth are cracked or damaged

Do not bend, twist or turn the timing belt inside out. Never allow oil, water or steam to contact the belt

Inspect the timing belt for cracks, fraying, glazing or damage of any kind

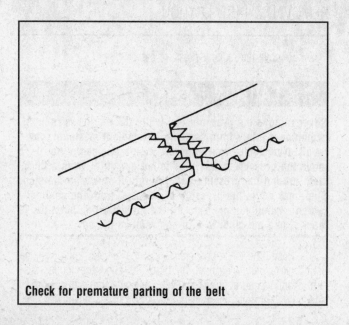

Check for premature parting of the belt

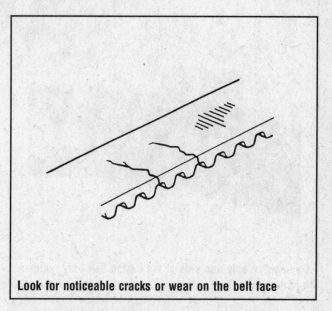

Look for noticeable cracks or wear on the belt face

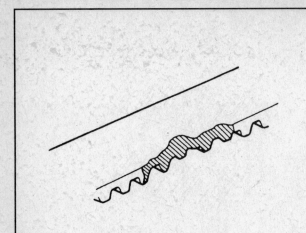

You may only have damage on one side of the belt; if so, the guide could be the culprit

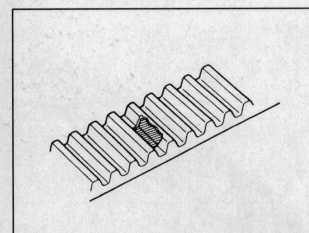

Foreign materials can get in between the teeth and cause damage

Damage on only one side of the timing belt may indicate a faulty guide

ALWAYS replace the timing belt at the interval specified by the manufacturer

Hoses

INSPECTION

Upper and lower radiator hoses along with the heater hoses should be checked for deterioration, leaks and loose hose clamps at least every 15,000 miles (24,000 km). It is also wise to check the hoses periodically in early spring and at the beginning of the fall or winter when you are performing other maintenance. A quick visual inspection could discover a weakened hose which might have left you stranded if it had remained unrepaired.

Whenever you are checking the hoses, make sure the engine and cooling system are cold. Visually inspect for cracking, rotting or collapsed hoses, and replace as necessary. Run your hand along the length of the hose. If a weak or swollen spot is noted when squeezing the hose wall, the hose should be replaced.

REMOVAL & INSTALLATION

1. Remove the radiator pressure cap.

✵✵ CAUTION

Never remove the pressure cap while the engine is running, or personal injury from scalding hot coolant or steam may result. If possible, wait until the engine has cooled to remove the pressure cap. If this is not possible, wrap a thick cloth around the pressure cap and turn it slowly to the stop. Step back while the pressure is released from the cooling system. When you are sure all the pressure has been released, use the cloth to turn and remove the cap.

2. Position a clean container under the radiator and/or engine draincock or plug, then open the drain and allow the cooling system to drain to an appropriate level. For some upper hoses, only a little coolant must be drained. To remove hoses positioned

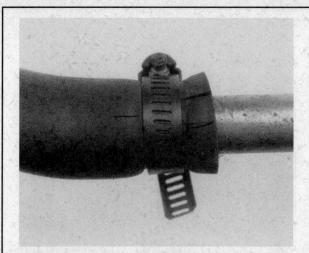

The cracks developing along this hose are a result of age-related hardening

A hose clamp that is too tight can cause older hoses to separate and tear on either side of the clamp

A soft spongy hose (identifiable by the swollen section) will eventually burst and should be replaced

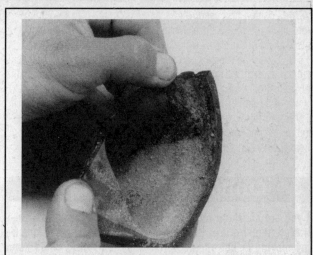

Hoses are likely to deteriorate from the inside if the cooling system is not periodically flushed

lower on the engine, such as a lower radiator hose, the entire cooling system must be emptied.

✳✳ CAUTION

When draining coolant, keep in mind that cats and dogs are attracted by ethylene glycol antifreeze, and are quite likely to drink any that is left in an uncovered container or in puddles on the ground. This will prove fatal in sufficient quantity. Always drain coolant into a sealable container. Coolant may be reused unless it is contaminated or several years old.

3. Loosen the hose clamps at each end of the hose requiring replacement. Clamps are usually either of the spring tension type (which require pliers to squeeze the tabs and loosen) or of the screw tension type (which require screw or hex drivers to loosen). Pull the clamps back on the hose away from the connection.

4. Twist, pull and slide the hose off the fitting, taking care not to damage the neck of the component from which the hose is being removed.

➡**If the hose is stuck at the connection, do not try to insert a screwdriver or other sharp tool under the hose end in an effort to free it, as the connection and/or hose may become damaged. Heater connections especially may be easily damaged by such a procedure. If the hose is to be replaced, use a single-edged razor blade to make a slice along the portion of the hose which is stuck on the connection, perpendicular to the end of the hose. Do not cut deep so as to prevent damaging the connection. The hose can then be peeled from the connection and discarded.**

5. Clean both hose mounting connections. Inspect the condition of the hose clamps and replace them, if necessary.

To install:

6. Dip the ends of the new hose into clean engine coolant to ease installation.

7. Slide the clamps over the replacement hose, then slide the hose ends over the connections into position.

8. Position and secure the clamps at least ¼ in. (6.35mm) from the ends of the hose. Make sure they are located beyond the raised bead of the connector.

9. Close the radiator or engine drains and properly refill the cooling system with the clean drained engine coolant or a suitable mixture of ethylene glycol coolant and water.

10. If available, install a pressure tester and check for leaks. If a pressure tester is not available, run the engine until normal operating temperature is reached (allowing the system to naturally pressurize), then check for leaks.

✳✳ CAUTION

If you are checking for leaks with the system at normal operating temperature, BE EXTREMELY CAREFUL not to touch any moving or hot engine parts. Once temperature has been reached, shut the engine OFF, and check for leaks around the hose fittings and connections which were removed earlier.

CV-Boots

INSPECTION

The CV (Constant Velocity) boots should be checked for damage each time the oil is changed and any other time the vehicle is raised for service. These boots keep water, grime, dirt and other damaging matter from entering the CV-joints. Any of these could cause early CV-joint failure which can be expensive to repair. Heavy grease thrown around the inside of the front wheel(s) and on the brake caliper/drum can be an indication of a torn boot. Thoroughly check the boots for missing clamps and tears. If the boot is damaged, it should be replaced immediately.

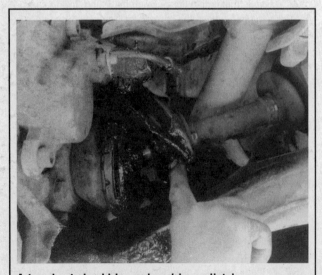

A torn boot should be replaced immediately

CV-boots must be inspected periodically for damage

Air Conditioning

➡ **Be sure to consult the laws in your area before servicing the air conditioning system. In most areas, it is illegal to perform repairs involving refrigerant unless the work is done by a certified technician. Also, it is quite likely that you will not be able to purchase refrigerant without proof of certification.**

SAFETY PRECAUTIONS

There are two major hazards associated with air conditioning systems and they both relate to the refrigerant gas. First, the refrigerant gas (R-12) is an extremely cold substance. When exposed to air, it will instantly freeze any surface it comes in contact with, including your eyes. The other hazard relates to fire. Although normally non-toxic, the R-12 gas becomes highly poisonous in the presence of an open flame. One good whiff of the vapor formed by burning R-12 can be fatal. Keep all forms of fire (including cigarettes) well clear of the air conditioning system.

Because of the inherent dangers involved with working on air conditioning systems and R-12 refrigerant, these safety precautions must be strictly followed.

• Avoid contact with a charged refrigeration system, even when working on another part of the air conditioning system or vehicle. If a heavy tool comes into contact with a section of tubing or a heat exchanger, it can easily cause the relatively soft material to rupture.

• When it is necessary to apply force to a fitting which contains refrigerant, as when checking that all system couplings are securely tightened, use a wrench on both parts of the fitting involved, if possible. This will avoid putting torque on refrigerant tubing. (It is also advisable to use tube or line wrenches when tightening these flare nut fittings.)

➡ **R-12 refrigerant is a chlorofluorocarbon which, when released into the atmosphere, can contribute to the depletion**

of the ozone layer in the upper atmosphere. Ozone filters out harmful radiation from the sun.

• Do not attempt to discharge the system without the proper tools. Precise control is possible only when using the service gauges and a proper A/C refrigerant recovery station. Wear protective gloves when connecting or disconnecting service gauge hoses.

• Discharge the system only in a well ventilated area, as high concentrations of the gas which might accidentally escape can exclude oxygen and act as an anesthetic. When leak testing or soldering, this is particularly important, as toxic gas is formed when R-12 contacts any flame.

• Never start a system without first verifying that both service valves are properly installed, and that all fittings throughout the system are snugly connected.

• Avoid applying heat to any refrigerant line or storage vessel. Charging may be aided by using water heated to less than 125°F (50°C) to warm the refrigerant container. Never allow a refrigerant storage container to sit out in the sun, or near any other source of heat, such as a radiator or heater.

• Always wear goggles to protect your eyes when working on a system. If refrigerant contacts the eyes, it is advisable in all cases to consult a physician immediately.

• Frostbite from liquid refrigerant should be treated by first gradually warming the area with cool water, and then gently applying petroleum jelly. A physician should be consulted.

• Always keep refrigerant drum fittings capped when not in use. If the container is equipped with a safety cap to protect the valve, make sure the cap is in place when the can is not being used. Avoid sudden shock to the drum, which might occur from dropping it, or from banging a heavy tool against it. Never carry a drum in the passenger compartment of a vehicle.

• Always completely discharge the system into a suitable recovery unit before painting the vehicle (if the paint is to be baked on), or before welding anywhere near refrigerant lines.

• When servicing the system, minimize the time that any refrigerant line or fitting is open to the air in order to prevent moisture or dirt from entering the system. Contaminants such as moisture or dirt can damage internal system components. Always replace O-rings on lines or fittings which are disconnected. Prior to installation coat, but do not soak, replacement O-rings with suitable compressor oil.

GENERAL SERVICING PROCEDURES

➡**It is recommended, and possibly required by law, that a qualified technician perform the following services.**

The most important aspect of air conditioning service is the maintenance of a pure and adequate charge of refrigerant in the system. A refrigeration system cannot function properly if a significant percentage of the charge is lost. Leaks are common because the severe vibration encountered underhood in an automobile can easily cause a sufficient cracking or loosening of the air conditioning fittings; allowing, the extreme operating pressures of the system to force refrigerant out.

The problem can be understood by considering what happens to the system as it is operated with a continuous leak. Because the expansion valve regulates the flow of refrigerant to the evaporator, the level of refrigerant there is fairly constant. The receiver/drier stores any excess refrigerant, and so a loss will first appear there as a reduction in the level of liquid. As this level nears the bottom of the vessel, some refrigerant vapor bubbles will begin to appear in the stream of liquid supplied to the expansion valve. This vapor decreases the capacity of the expansion valve very little as the valve opens to compensate for its presence. As the quantity of liquid in the condenser decreases, the operating pressure will drop there and throughout the high side of the system. As the R-12 continues to be expelled, the pressure available to force the liquid through the expansion valve will continue to decrease, and, eventually, the valve's orifice will prove to be too much of a restriction for adequate flow even with the needle fully withdrawn.

At this point, low side pressure will start to drop, and a severe reduction in cooling capacity, marked by freeze-up of the evaporator coil, will result. Eventually, the operating pressure of the evaporator will be lower than the pressure of the atmosphere surrounding it, and air will be drawn into the system wherever there are leaks in the low side.

Because all atmospheric air contains at least some moisture, water will enter the system and mix with the R-12 and the oil. Trace amounts of moisture will cause sludging of the oil, and corrosion of the system. Saturation and clogging of the filter/drier, and freezing of the expansion valve orifice will eventually result. As air fills the system to a greater and greater extent, it will interfere more and more with the normal flows of refrigerant and heat.

From this description, it should be obvious that much of the repairman's focus in on detecting leaks, repairing them, and then restoring the purity and quantity of the refrigerant charge. A list of general rules should be followed in addition to all safety precautions:

• Keep all tools as clean and dry as possible.

• Thoroughly purge the service gauges/hoses of air and moisture before connecting them to the system. Keep them capped when not in use.

• Thoroughly clean any refrigerant fitting before disconnecting it, in order to minimize the entrance of dirt into the system.

• Plan any operation that requires opening the system beforehand, in order to minimize the length of time it will be exposed to open air. Cap or seal the open ends to minimize the entrance of foreign material.

• When adding oil, pour it through an extremely clean and dry tube or funnel. Keep the oil capped whenever possible. Do not use oil that has not been kept tightly sealed.

• Use only R-12 refrigerant. Purchase refrigerant intended for use only in automatic air conditioning systems.

• Completely evacuate any system that has been opened for service, or that has leaked sufficiently to draw in moisture and air. This requires evacuating air and moisture with a good vacuum pump for at least one hour. If a system has been open for a considerable length of time it may be advisable to evacuate the system for up to 12 hours (overnight).

• Use a wrench on both halves of a fitting that is to be disconnected, so as to avoid placing torque on any of the refrigerant lines.

• When overhauling a compressor, pour some of the oil into a clean glass and inspect it. If there is evidence of dirt, metal particles, or both, flush all refrigerant components with clean refrigerant before evacuating and recharging the system. In addition, if metal particles are present, the compressor should be replaced.

• Schrader valves may leak only when under full operating pressure. Therefore, if leakage is suspected but cannot be located, operate the system with a full charge of refrigerant and look for leaks from all Schrader valves. Replace any faulty valves.

Additional Preventive Maintenance

USING THE SYSTEM

The easiest and most important preventive maintenance for your A/C system is to be sure that it is used on a regular basis. Running the system for five minutes each month (no matter what the season) will help assure that the seals and all internal components remain lubricated.

ANTIFREEZE

In order to prevent heater core freeze-up during A/C operation, it is necessary to maintain a proper antifreeze protection. Use a hand-held antifreeze tester (hydrometer) to periodically check the condition of the antifreeze in your engine's cooling system.

➡**Antifreeze should not be used longer than the manufacturer specifies.**

RADIATOR CAP

For efficient operation of an air conditioned vehicle's cooling system, the radiator cap should have a holding pressure which meets manufacturer's specifications. A cap which fails to hold these pressures should be replaced.

CONDENSER

Any obstruction of or damage to the condenser configuration will restrict the air flow which is essential to its efficient operation. It is therefore a good rule to keep this unit clean and in proper physical shape.

➡**Bug screens which are mounted in front of the condenser, (unless they are original equipment), are regarded as obstructions.**

CONDENSATION DRAIN TUBE

This single molded drain tube expels the condensation, which accumulates on the bottom of the evaporator housing, into the engine compartment. If this tube is obstructed, the air conditioning performance can be restricted and condensation buildup can spill over onto the vehicle's floor.

SYSTEM INSPECTION

➡**R-12 refrigerant is a chlorofluorocarbon which, when released into the atmosphere, can contribute to the depletion of the ozone layer in the upper atmosphere. Ozone filters out harmful radiation from the sun.**

The easiest and often most important check for the air conditioning system consists of a visual inspection of the system components. Visually inspect the air conditioning system for refrigerant leaks, damaged compressor clutch, compressor drive belt tension and condition, plugged evaporator drain tube, blocked condenser fins, disconnected or broken wires, blown fuses, corroded connections and poor insulation.

An antifreeze tester can be used to determine the freezing and boiling levels of the coolant

A refrigerant leak will usually appear as an oily residue at the leakage point in the system. The oily residue soon picks up dust or dirt particles from the surrounding air and appears greasy. Through time, this will build up and appear to be a heavy dirt impregnated grease. Most leaks are caused by damaged or missing O-ring seals at the component connections, damaged charging valve cores or missing service gauge port caps.

For a thorough visual and operational inspection, check the following:

1. Check the surface of the radiator and condenser for dirt, leaves or other material which might block air flow.

2. Check for kinks in hoses and lines. Check the system for leaks.

3. Make sure the drive belt is under the proper tension. When the air conditioning is operating, make sure the drive belt is free of noise or slippage.

4. Make sure the blower motor operates at all appropriate positions, then check for distribution of the air from all outlets with the blower on **HIGH**.

➡**Keep in mind that under conditions of high humidity, air discharged from the A/C vents may not feel as cold as expected, even if the system is working properly. This is because the vaporized moisture in humid air retains heat more effectively than does dry air, making the humid air more difficult to cool.**

Make sure the air passage selection lever is operating correctly. Start the engine and warm it to normal operating temperature, then make sure the hot/cold selection lever is operating correctly.

DISCHARGING, EVACUATING AND CHARGING

Discharging, evacuating and charging the air conditioning system must be performed by a properly trained and certified mechanic in a facility equipped with refrigerant recovery/recycling equipment that meets SAE standards for the type of system to be serviced.

If you don't have access to the necessary equipment, we recommend that you take your vehicle to a reputable service station to have the work done. If you still wish to perform repairs on the vehicle, have them discharge the system, then take your vehicle home and perform the necessary work. When you are finished, return the vehicle to the station for evacuation and charging. Just be sure to cap ALL A/C system fittings immediately after opening them and keep them protected until the system is recharged.

Windshield Wipers

ELEMENT (REFILL) CARE AND REPLACEMENT

For maximum effectiveness and longest element life, the windshield and wiper blades should be kept clean. Dirt, tree sap, road tar and so on will cause streaking, smearing and blade deterioration if left on the glass. It is advisable to wash the windshield carefully with a commercial glass cleaner at least once a month. Wipe off the rubber blades with the wet rag afterwards. Do not attempt to move wipers across the windshield by hand; damage to the motor and drive mechanism will result.

To inspect and/or replace the wiper blade elements, place the wiper switch in the **LOW** speed position and the ignition switch in the **ACC** position. When the wiper blades are approximately vertical on the windshield, turn the ignition switch to **OFF.**

Examine the wiper blade elements. If they are found to be cracked, broken or torn, they should be replaced immediately. Replacement intervals will vary with usage, although ozone deterioration usually limits element life to about one year. If the wiper pattern is smeared or streaked, or if the blade chatters across the glass, the elements should be replaced. It is easiest and most sensible to replace the elements in pairs.

If your vehicle is equipped with aftermarket blades, there are several different types of refills and your vehicle might have any kind. Aftermarket blades and arms rarely use the exact same type blade or refill as the original equipment. Here are some typical aftermarket blades; not all may be available for your vehicle:

The Anco® type uses a release button that is pushed down to allow the refill to slide out of the yoke jaws. The new refill slides back into the frame and locks in place.

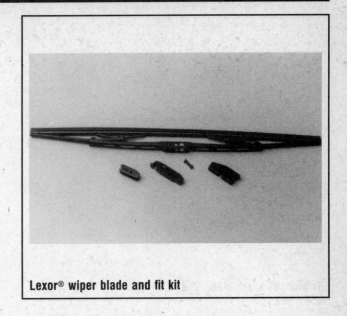

Lexor® wiper blade and fit kit

Pylon® wiper blade and adaptor

Bosch® wiper blade and fit kit

Trico® wiper blade and fit kit

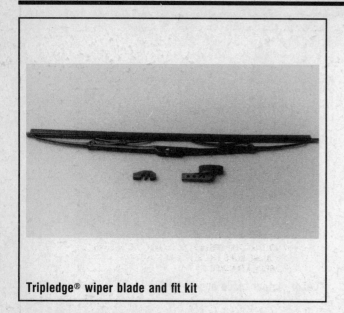

Tripledge® wiper blade and fit kit

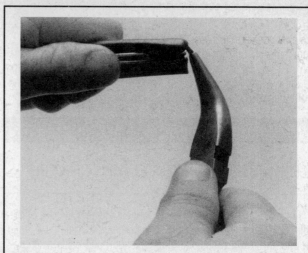

On Trico® wiper blades, the tab at the end of the blade must be turned up . . .

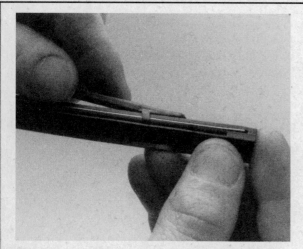

To remove and install a Lexor® wiper blade refill, slip out the old insert and slide in a new one

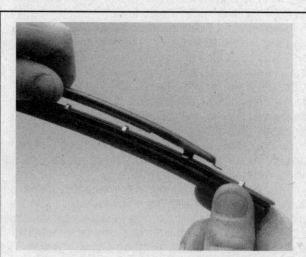

. . . then the insert can be removed. After installing the replacement insert, bend the tab back

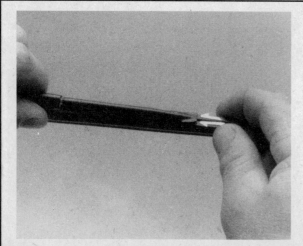

On Pylon® inserts, the clip at the end has to be removed prior to sliding the insert off

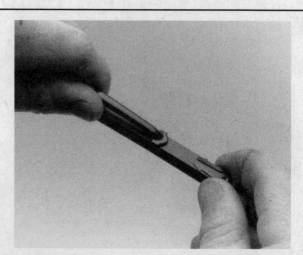

The Tripledge® wiper blade insert is removed and installed using a securing clip

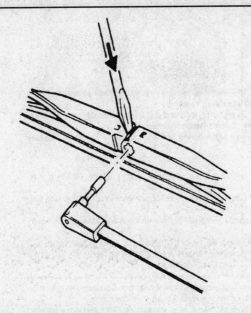

BLADE REPLACEMENT

1. CYCLE ARM AND BLADE ASSEMBLY TO UP POSITION-ON THE WINDSHIELD WHERE REMOVAL OF BLADE ASSEMBLY CAN BE PERFORMED WITHOUT DIFFICULTY. TURN IGNITION KEY OFF AT DESIRED POSITION.

2. TO REMOVE BLADE ASSEMBLY, INSERT SCREWDRIVER IN SLOT, PUSH DOWN ON SPRING LOCK AND PULL BLADE ASSEMBLY FROM PIN (VIEW A)

3. TO INSTALL, PUSH THE BLADE ASSEMBLY ON THE PIN SO THAT THE SPRING LOCK ENGAGES THE PIN (VIEW A). BE SURE THE BLADE ASSEMBLY IS SECURELY ATTACHED TO PIN

VIEW A

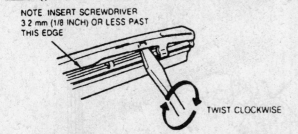

NOTE INSERT SCREWDRIVER 3 2 mm (1/8 INCH) OR LESS PAST THIS EDGE

TWIST CLOCKWISE

ELEMENT REPLACEMENT

1. INSERT SCREWDRIVER BETWEEN THE EDGE OF THE SUPER STRUCTURE AND THE BLADE BACKING DRIP (VIEW B) TWIST SCREWDRIVER SLOWLY UNTIL ELEMENT CLEARS ONE SIDE OF THE SUPER STRUCTURE CLAW

2. SLIDE THE ELEMENT INTO THE SUPER STRUCTURE CLAWS

VIEW B

4. INSERT ELEMENT INTO ONE SIDE OF THE END CLAWS (VIEW D) AND WITH A ROCKING MOTION PUSH ELEMENT UPWARD UNTIL IT SNAPS IN (VIEW E)

VIEW D

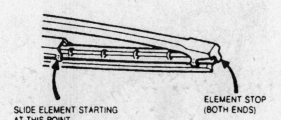

SLIDE ELEMENT STARTING AT THIS POINT

ELEMENT STOP (BOTH ENDS)

3. SLIDE THE ELEMENT INTO THE SUPER STRUCTURE CLAWS, STARTING WITH SECOND SET FROM EITHER END (VIEW C) AND CONTINUE TO SLIDE THE BLADE ELEMENT INTO ALL THE SUPER STRUCTURE CLAWS TO THE ELEMENT STOP (VIEW C)

VIEW C

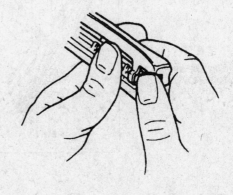

VIEW E

Trico® wiper blade insert (element) replacement

BLADE REPLACEMENT

1. Cycle arm and blade assembly to a position on the windshield where removal of blade assembly can be performed without difficulty. Turn ignition key off at desired position.
2. To remove blade assembly from wiper arm, pull up on spring lock and pull blade assembly from pin (View A). Be sure spring lock is not pulled excessively or it will become distorted.
3. To install, push the blade assembly onto the pin so that the spring lock engages the pin (View A). Be sure the blade assembly is securely attached to pin.

ELEMENT REPLACEMENT

1. In the plastic backing strip which is part of the rubber blade assembly, there is an 11.11mm (7/16 inch) long notch located approximately one inch from either end. Locate either notch.
2. Place the frame of the wiper blade assembly on a firm surface with either notched end of the backing strip visible.
3. Grasp the frame portion of the wiper blade assembly and push down until the blade assembly is tightly bowed.
4. With the blade assembly in the bowed position, grasp the tip of the backing strip firmly, pulling up and twisting C.C.W. at the same time. The backing strip will then snap out of the retaining tab on the end of the frame.
5. Lift the wiper blade assembly from the surface and slide the backing strip down the frame until the notch lines up with the next retaining tab, twist slightly, and the backing strip will snap out. Continue this operation with the remaining tabs until the blade element is completely detached from the frame.
6. To install blade element, reverse the above procedure, making sure all six (6) tabs are locked to the backing strip before installing blade to wiper arm.

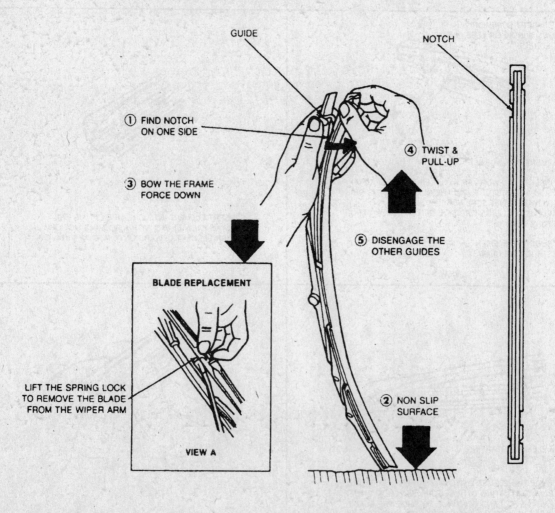

Tridon® wiper blade insert (element) replacement

Some Trico® refills are removed by locating where the metal backing strip or the refill is wider. Insert a small screwdriver blade between the frame and metal backing strip. Press down to release the refill from the retaining tab.

Other types of Trico® refills have two metal tabs which are unlocked by squeezing them together. The rubber filler can then be withdrawn from the frame jaws. A new refill is installed by inserting the refill into the front frame jaws and sliding it rearward to engage the remaining frame jaws. There are usually four jaws; be certain when installing that the refill is engaged in all of them. At the end of its travel, the tabs will lock into place on the front jaws of the wiper blade frame.

Another type of refill is made from polycarbonate. The refill has a simple locking device at one end which flexes downward out of the groove into which the jaws of the holder fit, allowing easy release. By sliding the new refill through all the jaws and pushing through the slight resistance when it reaches the end of its travel, the refill will lock into position.

To replace the Tridon® refill, it is necessary to remove the wiper blade. This refill has a plastic backing strip with a notch about 1 in. (25mm) from the end. Hold the blade (frame) on a hard surface so that the frame is tightly bowed. Grip the tip of the backing strip and pull up while twisting counterclockwise. The backing strip will snap out of the retaining tab. Do this for the remaining tabs until the refill is free of the blade. The length of these refills is molded into the end and they should be replaced with identical types.

Regardless of the type of refill used, be sure to follow the part manufacturer's instructions closely. Make sure that all of the frame jaws are engaged as the refill is pushed into place and locked. If the metal blade holder and frame are allowed to touch the glass during wiper operation, the glass will be scratched.

Tires and Wheels

Common sense and good driving habits will afford maximum tire life. Fast starts, sudden stops and hard cornering are hard on tires and will shorten their useful life span. Make sure that you don't overload the vehicle or run with incorrect pressure in the tires. Both of these practices will increase tread wear.

➡For optimum tire life, keep the tires properly inflated, rotate them often and have the wheel alignment checked periodically.

Inspect your tires frequently. Be especially careful to watch for bubbles in the tread or sidewall, deep cuts or underinflation. Replace any tires with bubbles in the sidewall. If cuts are so deep that they penetrate to the cords, discard the tire. Any cut in the sidewall of a radial tire renders it unsafe. Also look for uneven tread wear patterns that may indicate the front end is out of alignment or that the tires are out of balance.

TIRE ROTATION

Tires must be rotated periodically to equalize wear patterns that vary with a tire's position on the vehicle. Tires will also wear in an uneven way as the front steering/suspension system wears to the point where the alignment should be reset.

Rotating the tires will ensure maximum life for the tires as a

Unidirectional tires are identifiable by sidewall arrows and/or the word "rotation"

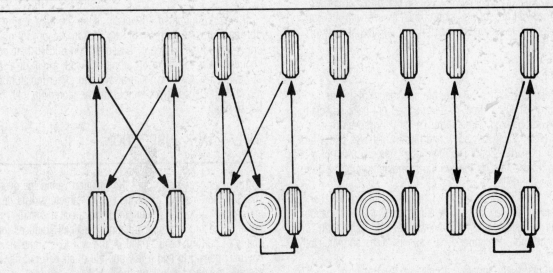

Common tire rotation patterns for 4 and 5-wheel rotations

set, so you will not have to discard a tire early due to wear on only part of the tread. Regular rotation is required to equalize wear.

When rotating "unidirectional tires," make sure that they always roll in the same direction. This means that a tire used on the left side of the vehicle must not be switched to the right side and vice-versa. Such tires should only be rotated front-to-rear or rear-to-front, while always remaining on the same side of the vehicle. These tires are marked on the sidewall as to the direction of rotation; observe the marks when reinstalling the tire(s).

Some styled or "mag" wheels may have different offsets front to rear. In these cases, the rear wheels must not be used up front and vice-versa. Furthermore, if these wheels are equipped with unidirectional tires, they cannot be rotated unless the tire is re-mounted for the proper direction of rotation.

➡The compact or space-saver spare is strictly for emergency use. It must never be included in the tire rotation or placed on the vehicle for everyday use.

TIRE DESIGN

For maximum satisfaction, tires should be used in sets of four. Mixing of different types (radial, bias-belted, fiberglass belted) must be avoided. In most cases, the vehicle manufacturer has designated a type of tire on which the vehicle will perform best. Your first choice when replacing tires should be to use the same type of tire that the manufacturer recommends.

When radial tires are used, tire sizes and wheel diameters should be selected to maintain ground clearance and tire load capacity equivalent to the original specified tire. Radial tires should always be used in sets of four.

✳✳ CAUTION

Radial tires should never be used on only the front axle.

When selecting tires, pay attention to the original size as marked on the tire. Most tires are described using an industry size code sometimes referred to as P-Metric. This allows the exact identification of the tire specifications, regardless of the manufacturer. If selecting a different tire size or brand, remember to check the installed tire for any sign of interference with the body or suspension while the vehicle is stopping, turning sharply or heavily loaded.

Snow Tires

Good radial tires can produce a big advantage in slippery weather, but in snow, a street radial tire does not have sufficient tread to provide traction and control. The small grooves of a street tire quickly pack with snow and the tire behaves like a billiard ball on a marble floor. The more open, chunky tread of a snow tire will self-clean as the tire turns, providing much better grip on snowy surfaces.

To satisfy municipalities requiring snow tires during weather emergencies, most snow tires carry either an M + S designation after the tire size stamped on the sidewall, or the designation "all-season." In general, no change in tire size is necessary when buying snow tires.

Most manufacturers strongly recommend the use of 4 snow tires on their vehicles for reasons of stability. If snow tires are fit-

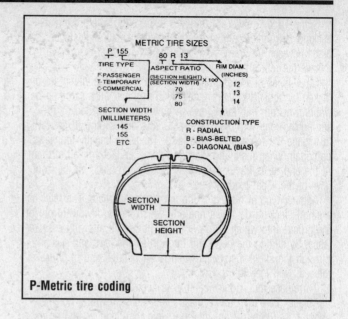

P-Metric tire coding

ted only to the drive wheels, the opposite end of the vehicle may become very unstable when braking or turning on slippery surfaces. This instability can lead to unpleasant endings if the driver can't counteract the slide in time.

Note that snow tires, whether 2 or 4, will affect vehicle handling in all non-snow situations. The stiffer, heavier snow tires will noticeably change the turning and braking characteristics of the vehicle. Once the snow tires are installed, you must re-learn the behavior of the vehicle and drive accordingly.

➡Consider buying extra wheels on which to mount the snow tires. Once done, the "snow wheels" can be installed and removed as needed. This eliminates the potential damage to tires or wheels from seasonal removal and installation. Even if your vehicle has styled wheels, see if inexpensive steel wheels are available. Although the look of the vehicle will change, the expensive wheels will be protected from salt, curb hits and pothole damage.

TIRE STORAGE

If they are mounted on wheels, store the tires at proper inflation pressure. All tires should be kept in a cool, dry place. If they are stored in the garage or basement, do not let them stand on a concrete floor; set them on strips of wood, a mat or a large stack of newspaper. Keeping them away from direct moisture is of paramount importance. Tires should not be stored upright, but in a flat position.

INFLATION & INSPECTION

The importance of proper tire inflation cannot be overemphasized. A tire employs air as part of its structure. It is designed around the supporting strength of the air at a specified pressure. For this reason, improper inflation drastically reduces the tires's ability to perform as intended. A tire will lose some air in day-to-day use; having to add a few pounds of air periodically is not necessarily a sign of a leaking tire.

Two items should be a permanent fixture in every glove compartment: an accurate tire pressure gauge and a tread depth gauge. Check the tire pressure (including the spare) regularly with a pocket type gauge. Too often, the gauge on the end of the air hose at your corner garage is not accurate because it suffers too much abuse. Always check tire pressure when the tires are cold, as pressure increases with temperature. If you must move the vehicle to check the tire inflation, do not drive more than a mile before checking. A cold tire is generally one that has not been driven for more than three hours.

A plate or sticker is normally provided somewhere in the vehicle (door post, hood, tailgate or trunk lid) which shows the proper pressure for the tires. Never counteract excessive pressure build-up by bleeding off air pressure (letting some air out). This will cause the tire to run hotter and wear quicker.

✷✷ CAUTION

Never exceed the maximum tire pressure embossed on the tire! This is the pressure to be used when the tire is at maximum loading, but it is rarely the correct pressure for everyday driving. Consult the owner's manual or the tire pressure sticker for the correct tire pressure.

Once you've maintained the correct tire pressures for several weeks, you'll be familiar with the vehicle's braking and handling personality. Slight adjustments in tire pressures can fine-tune these characteristics, but never change the cold pressure specification by more than 2 psi. A slightly softer tire pressure will give a softer ride but also yield lower fuel mileage. A slightly harder tire will give crisper dry road handling but can cause skidding on wet surfaces. Unless you're fully attuned to the vehicle, stick to the recommended inflation pressures.

All tires made since 1968 have built-in tread wear indicator bars that show up as ½ in. (13mm) wide smooth bands across the tire when 1/16 in. (1.5mm) of tread remains. The appearance of tread wear indicators means that the tires should be replaced. In fact, many states have laws prohibiting the use of tires with less than this amount of tread.

You can check your own tread depth with an inexpensive gauge or by using a Lincoln head penny. Slip the Lincoln penny (with Lincoln's head upside-down) into several tread grooves. If

Tires with deep cuts, or cuts which show bulging should be replaced immediately

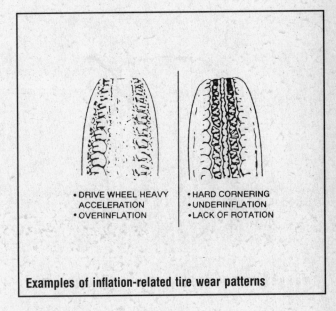

- DRIVE WHEEL HEAVY ACCELERATION
- OVERINFLATION

- HARD CORNERING
- UNDERINFLATION
- LACK OF ROTATION

Examples of inflation-related tire wear patterns

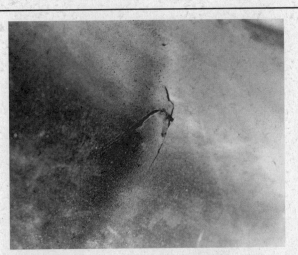

Tires should be checked frequently for any sign of puncture or damage

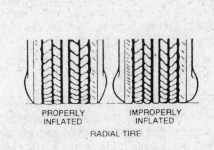

PROPERLY INFLATED   IMPROPERLY INFLATED

RADIAL TIRE

Radial tires have a characteristic sidewall bulge; don't try to measure pressure by looking at the tire. Use a quality air pressure gauge

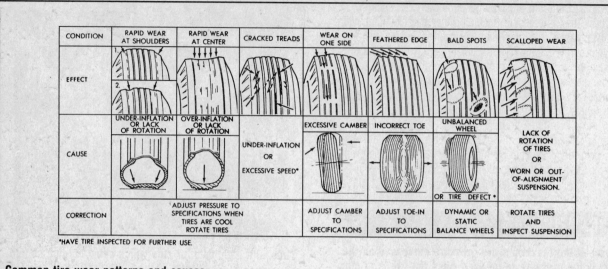

CONDITION	RAPID WEAR AT SHOULDERS	RAPID WEAR AT CENTER	CRACKED TREADS	WEAR ON ONE SIDE	FEATHERED EDGE	BALD SPOTS	SCALLOPED WEAR
EFFECT							
CAUSE	UNDER-INFLATION OR LACK OF ROTATION	OVER-INFLATION OR LACK OF ROTATION	UNDER-INFLATION OR EXCESSIVE SPEED*	EXCESSIVE CAMBER	INCORRECT TOE	UNBALANCED WHEEL OR TIRE DEFECT*	LACK OF ROTATION OF TIRES OR WORN OR OUT-OF-ALIGNMENT SUSPENSION.
CORRECTION	ADJUST PRESSURE TO SPECIFICATIONS WHEN TIRES ARE COOL ROTATE TIRES			ADJUST CAMBER TO SPECIFICATIONS	ADJUST TOE-IN TO SPECIFICATIONS	DYNAMIC OR STATIC BALANCE WHEELS	ROTATE TIRES AND INSPECT SUSPENSION

*HAVE TIRE INSPECTED FOR FURTHER USE.

Common tire wear patterns and causes

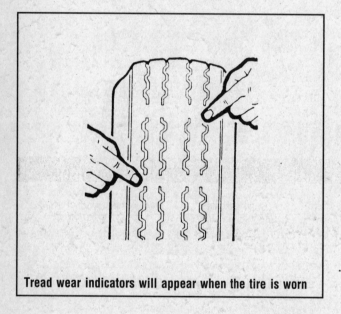

Tread wear indicators will appear when the tire is worn

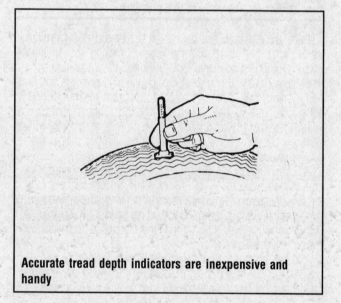

Accurate tread depth indicators are inexpensive and handy

you can see the top of Lincoln's head in 2 adjacent grooves, the tire has less than 1/16 in. (1.5mm) tread left and should be replaced. You can measure snow tires in the same manner by using the "tails" side of the Lincoln penny. If you can see the top of the Lincoln memorial, it's time to replace the snow tire(s).

CARE OF SPECIAL WHEELS

If you have invested money in magnesium, aluminum alloy or sport wheels, special precautions should be taken to make sure your investment is not wasted and that your special wheels look good for the life of the vehicle.

Special wheels are easily damaged and/or scratched. Occasionally check the rims for cracking, impact damage or air leaks. If any of these are found, replace the wheel. But in order to prevent this type of damage and the costly replacement of a special wheel, observe the following precautions:

• Use extra care not to damage the wheels during removal, in-

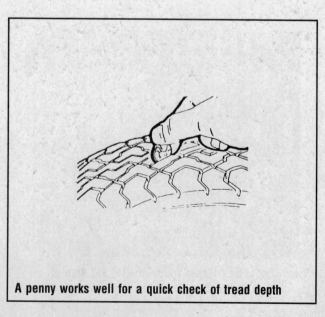

A penny works well for a quick check of tread depth

Tire inflation specifications can be found on the door jamb

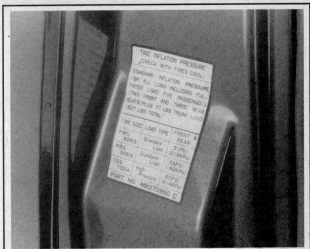

Be sure to inflate the tire according to its size and load type

stallation, balancing, etc. After removal of the wheels from the vehicle, place them on a mat or other protective surface. If they are to be stored for any length of time, support them on strips of wood. Never store tires and wheels upright; the tread may develop flat spots.

• When driving, watch for hazards; it doesn't take much to crack a wheel.

• When washing, use a mild soap or non-abrasive dish detergent (keeping in mind that detergent tends to remove wax). Avoid

cleansers with abrasives or the use of hard brushes. There are many cleaners and polishes for special wheels.

• If possible, remove the wheels during the winter. Salt and sand used for snow removal can severely damage the finish of a wheel.

• Make certain the recommended lug nut torque is never exceeded or the wheel may crack. Never use snow chains on special wheels; severe scratching will occur.

FLUIDS AND LUBRICANTS

Fuel and Oil Recommendations

◆ **See Figure 15**

Early 1970s vehicles will operate on regular, low lead gasoline of 91 octane; later models and all models equipped with a catalytic converter MUST use unleaded gasoline. Regular unleaded

gasoline is usually satisfactory, although using a higher octane may enhance vehicle performance.

Oil must be selected with regard to the anticipated temperatures during the period before the next oil change. Using the chart, select the oil viscosity for the lowest expected temperature and you will be assured of easy cold starting and sufficient engine protection. The oil you pour into your engine should have the designation SF marked on the top of its container.

Oil Viscosity Selection Chart

	Anticipated Temperature Range	SAE Viscosity
Multi-grade	Above 32°F	10W—40
		10W—50
		20W—40
		20W—50
		10W—30
	May be used as low as −10°F	10W—30
		10W—40
	Consistently below 10°F	5W—20
		5W—30
Single-grade	Above 32°F	30
	Temperature between +32°F and −10°F	10W

Fig. 15 Oil viscosity chart

Engine

OIL LEVEL CHECK

◆ **See Figure 16**

Checking the engine oil level at every full tank fuel stop is probably a good habit to have. Check the engine oil as follows:

1. Park the car on a level surface.

2. The engine may be either hot or cold when checking oil level. However, if it is hot, wait for a few minutes after the engine has been shut off to allow the oil to drain back into the crankcase. If the engine is cold, do not start it before checking the oil level.

3. Open the hood and locate the dipstick. Pull the dipstick from its tube, wipe it clean, and reinsert it.

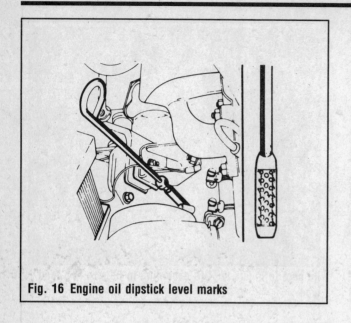

Fig. 16 Engine oil dipstick level marks

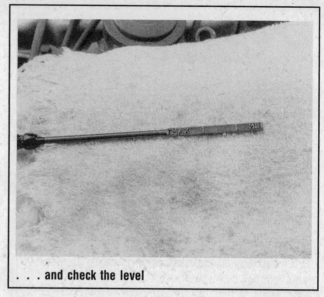

. . . and check the level

Locate the oil dipstick . . .

Remove the engine oil filler cap

. . . then remove the dipstick . . .

Using a funnel, fill the crankcase with clean fresh oil

4. Pull the dipstick again and, holding it horizontally, read the oil level. The oil should be between the top and add mark. If the oil is below the add mark, add oil of the proper viscosity through the capped opening of the valve cover.

➡ **The dipstick may have a reading of 3.5 max. on it. That figure is the oil pan capacity in liters.**

5. Insert the dipstick, and check the level again after adding any oil. Be careful not to overfill the crankcase. Approximately one quart of oil will raise the level from the low mark to the high mark. Excess oil will generally be consumed at an accelerated rate even if no damage to the engine seals occurs.

OIL AND FILTER CHANGE

Oil changes should be performed at intervals as described in your owners manual. However, it is a good idea to change the oil and oil filter at least twice a year, and to change the filter each time the oil is changed. If your car is being used under dusty conditions, change the oil and filter sooner. The same thing goes for cars being driven in stop and go city traffic, where acid and sludge buildup is a problem. The oil should also be changed more frequently in cars which are constantly driven at high speeds on expressways. The relatively high engine speeds associated with turnpike driving mean higher operating temperatures and a greater instance of oil foaming.

Always drain the oil after the engine has been run long enough to bring it to the normal operating temperature. Hot oil will flow easier and more contaminants will be removed with the oil than if it were drained cold. A large capacity drain pan, which can be purchased at any automotive supply store, will be more than paid back by savings from do-it-yourself oil changes. Another necessity is containers for the used oil. You will find that plastic bleach containers make excellent storage bottles.

Oil Change

1. Run the engine until it reaches the normal operating temperature. Raise and safely support the front of the car.

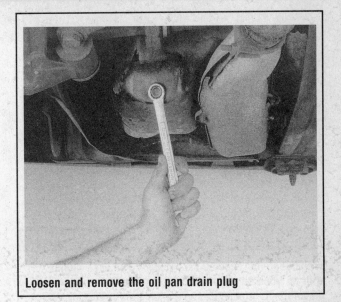
Loosen and remove the oil pan drain plug

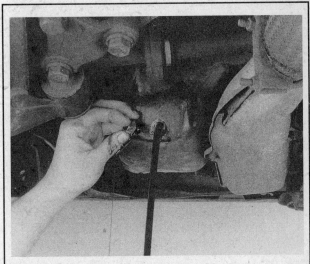
Have a drain pan in place to catch all the old engine oil

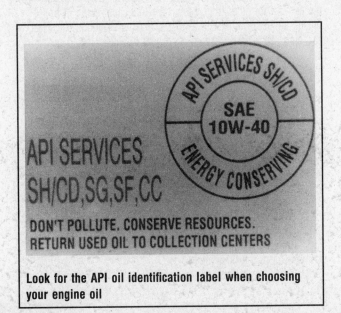
Look for the API oil identification label when choosing your engine oil

Using an oil filter wrench, loosen and remove the filter

2. Slide a drain pan under the oil pan drain plug.

3. Loosen the drain plug with a socket or box wrench, and then remove it by hand. Push in on the plug as you turn it out, so that no oil escapes until the plug is completely removed.

4. Allow the oil to drain into the pan.

5. Clean and install the drain plug, making sure that the gasket is still on the plug.

6. Refill the engine with oil. Start the engine and check for leaks.

Oil Filter Change

The car manufacturer recommends changing the oil filter at every other oil change, but it is more beneficial to replace the filter every time the oil is changed.

✳✳ CAUTION

Prolonged and repeated skin contact with used engine oil, with no effort to remove the oil, may be harmful. Follow these simple precautions when handling used motor oil. Avoid prolonged skin contact with used motor oil. Remove oil from skin by washing thoroughly with soap and water or waterless hand cleaner. Do not use gasoline, thinners or solvents. Avoid prolonged skin contact with oil-soaked clothing.

1. Drain the oil as already described.

2. Remove the lower splash shield, if necessary for clearance.

3. Slide a drain pan under the oil filter. Slowly turn the filter off with an oil filter wrench.

➡**Due to clearance problems on front wheel drive models, removing the alternator and replacing the filter from the top may be easier.**

To install:

4. Clean the oil filter adapter on the engine with a clean rag.

5. Oil the rubber seal on the replacement filter and install it. Tighten it until the seal is flush and then give it an additional ½ to ¾ turn.

Before installing a new oil filter, lightly coat the rubber gasket with clean oil

➡**On the 1979 and later front wheel drive Colt with 1597cc engines, the oil filter mounting flange distorts as the temperature changes. As a result, leakage past the oil filter gasket may occur between the time the engine is started from cold and the time it reaches operating temperature. In most cases, the leakage stops when the engine is hot. The factory-supplied filter and replacement MoPar filters have a thick, wide gasket which compensates for this occurrence. Most aftermarket filters do not have such a gasket. The best idea on these cars is to coat the oil filter gasket and mounting flange mating surfaces with gasket sealer, such as Permatex No.2, or its equivalent, not engine oil, prior to installation. Before applying the sealer, make certain that the mating surfaces are clean and free of oil. Screw the filter on in the normal manner.**

6. Install the splash pan. Fill the engine with the proper amount of oil. Start the engine and check for leaks.

Manual Transmission/Transaxle

FLUID RECOMMENDATIONS

A hypoid gear oil with an API classification of GL-4 or higher is required.

LEVEL CHECK

1. With the car parked on a level surface, or raised and supported safely and level, remove the filler plug from the left side of the transmission case; right front on front wheel drive models. The filler plug has a square head.

2. If lubricant begins to trickle out the hole, there is enough. Otherwise, carefully insert a finger (watch out for sharp threads) and check to see if the oil is up to the edge of the hole.

3. If not, add lubricant through the hole to raise the level to the edge of the filler hole. Most gear lubricants come in a plastic squeeze bottle with a nozzle, making additions easy. You can also use a squeeze bulb. Add gear oil GL4, Hypoid gear oil.

4. Replace the plug and check for leaks.

DRAIN AND REFILL

1. Jack up the front of the car and support it safely on stands.

2. Slide a drain pan under the transmission/transaxle.

3. Remove the filler plug and then the drain plug.

4. When the oil has been completely drained, install the drain plug.

5. Using the suction gun, refill the transmission/transaxle up to the level of the filler plug.

6. Install and tighten the filler plug.

Automatic Transmission/Transaxle

FLUID RECOMMENDATIONS

Automatic transmission/transaxle fluid type Dexron®II is required.

LEVEL CHECK

▶ **See Figures 17 and 18**

Check the level of the automatic transmission fluid every 2,000 miles.

✳✳ CAUTION

The electric cooling fan, on front wheel drive models, may switch at any time the engine is running. Keep hands away.

The dipstick has a high and low mark which are accurate for level indications only when the transmission is hot (normal operating temperature). The transmission is considered hot after 15 miles of highway driving.

1. Park the car on a level surface with the engine idling. Apply the parking brake.
2. Shift the transmission through all ranges and return the lever to the PARK position.
3. Remove the dipstick wipe it clean, then reinsert it firmly. Be certain that it has been pushed fully home. Remove the dipstick and check the fluid level while holding the dipstick horizontally. The level should be at or near the high mark.
4. If the fluid level is below the low mark, add Dexron®II type

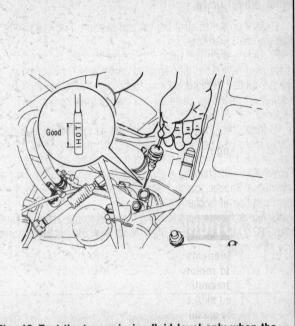

Fig. 18 Test the transmission fluid level only when the vehicle is HOT

automatic transmission fluid through the dipstick tube. This is more easily accomplished with the aid of a funnel and hose. Check the level often between additions, being careful not to overfill the transmission. Overfilling will cause slippage, seal damage, and overheating. Approximately one pint of fluid will raise the level from low to high.

➡**The fluid on the dipstick should be a bright red color. If it is discolored (brown or black), or smells burnt, serious transmission troubles, probably due to overheating, should be suspected. The transmission should be inspected to locate the cause of the burnt fluid.**

DRAIN AND REFILL

Rear Wheel Drive

The oil pan must be removed, since no drain plug is provided. Purchase a sufficient quantity of Dexron®II automatic transmission fluid and a pan gasket before starting this project.

1. Jack up the front of the car and support it safely on stands.
2. Slide a drain pan under the transmission. Loosen the rear oil pan bolts first, to allow most of the fluid to drain off without making a mess on your garage floor.
3. Remove the remaining bolts and drop the pan.
4. Discard the old gasket, clean the pan, and reinstall the pan with the new gasket.

➡**Tightening torque for the pan bolts is 8 to 13 ft. lbs. Tighten the bolts in a crisscross pattern. Don't overdo it, as the transmission case is aluminum.**

5. Refill the transmission through the dipstick tube. Check the level as previously described.

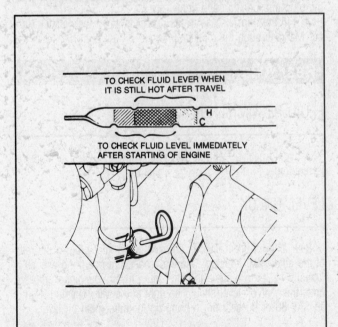

Fig. 17 Borg-Warner automatic transmission fluid dipstick with level indicators shown

Front Wheel Drive

1. Jack up the front of the car and support it on jackstands. Remove the lower cover.

2. Slide a drain pan under the differential and remove the drain plug. When the differential is completely drained, move the pan under the transmission. Remove the plug (on models equipped), or the transaxle oil pan (see the proceeding RWD section).

3. Install the drain plug(s). Clean all gasket mounting surfaces. Install the oil pan and new gasket. Tighten the mounting bolts to 8 ft. lbs. Fill the transmission with the required amount of Dexron®II fluid. Start the engine and allow to idle for at least two minutes. With the parking brake applied, move the selector to each position ending in PARK.

4. Add sufficient fluid to bring the level to the lower dipstick mark. Check the fluid level after the transmission is up to normal operating temperature.

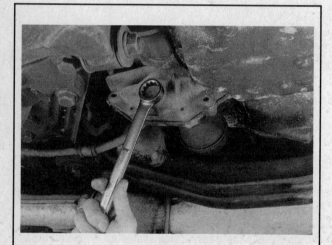

To drain the automatic transaxle loosen the drain plug on the differential housing . . .

. . . and allow the fluid to drain into a pan

PAN AND FILTER SERVICE

Drain the transmission/transaxle. With the oil pan removed, inspect the filter. If mileage servicing, or a clogged condition exists, remove the filter. Install a new filter and tighten the mounting bolts to 35 in. lbs. Install the oil pan and fill the transmission/transaxle with the proper amount of fluid.

Transfer Case

FLUID RECOMMENDATIONS

A hypoid gear oil with an API classification of GL-4 or higher is required.

LEVEL CHECK

A dipstick is provided for transfer case fluid level checks. Be sure the vehicle is parked on level ground. Remove the dipstick and wipe it clean. Insert the dipstick and remove it from the tube. If the level is between the upper and lower marks it is correct. Add fluid through the dipstick tube as required.

DRAIN AND REFILL

1. Place a suitable drain pan under the transfer case.
2. Remove the drain plug from the bottom of the transfer case.
3. Drain the gear oil. Wipe the drain plug threads clean. Screw the plug into position and tighten it.
4. Fill the transfer case to the proper level on the dipstick (upper Mark) through the dipstick tube.

Rear Axle

FLUID RECOMMENDATIONS

A hypoid gear oil with an API classification of GL-4 or higher is required.

LEVEL CHECK

Rear axle lubricant level is checked at the filler plug in the rear of the differential housing. Use the proper size open end wrench (usually ¹⁵/₁₆″) to remove the filler plug. Insert your finger into the hole; the gear oil level should be right at the plug opening. Use an SAE 80 or 90 gear oil to bring up the differential oil level.

DRAIN AND REFILL

Place a drain pan under the rear axle housing and remove the lower drain plug. When the fluid has stopped draining, clean the threads on the drain plug and screw it into the housing. Tighten the drain plug and fill the housing to the proper level through the filler plug hole.

Cooling System

▶ **See Figure 19**

At least once every 2 years, the engine cooling system should be inspected, flushed, and refilled with fresh coolant. If the coolant is left in the system too long, it loses its ability to prevent rust and corrosion. If the coolant has too much water, it won't protect against freezing.

The pressure cap should be looked at for signs of age or deterioration. Fan belt and other drive belts should be inspected and adjusted to the proper tension. (See checking belt tension).

Hose clamps should be tightened, and soft or cracked hoses replaced. Damp spots, or accumulations of rust or dye near hoses, water pump or other areas, indicate possible leakage, which must be corrected before filling the system with fresh coolant.

While you are checking the coolant level, check the radiator cap for a worn or cracked gasket. If the cap doesn't seal properly, fluid will be lost and the engine will overheat. Worn caps should be replaced with a new one.

Periodically clean any debris—leaves, paper, insects, etc.— from the radiator fins. Pick the large pieces off by hand. The smaller pieces can be washed away with water pressure from a hose.

Carefully straighten any bent radiator fins with a pair of needle nose pliers. Be careful—the fins are very soft. Don't wiggle the fins back and forth too much. Straighten them once and try not to move them again.

FLUID RECOMMENDATIONS

Coolant used (depending on winter temperatures) is usually a 50-50 mixture of ethylene glycol and water for year round use. Use a good quality antifreeze with water pump lubricants, rust inhibitors and other corrosion inhibitors along with acid neutralizers.

LEVEL CHECKS

On models without an expansion tank, if the engine is hot, allow it to cool for several minutes to reduce the pressure in the system. Using a rag, turn the radiator cap ¼ turn to the stop and allow all pressure to escape. Then, remove the cap. On models equipped with an expansion tank, check the level visually in the

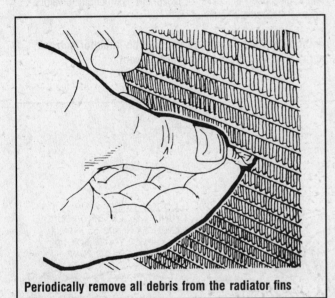

Periodically remove all debris from the radiator fins

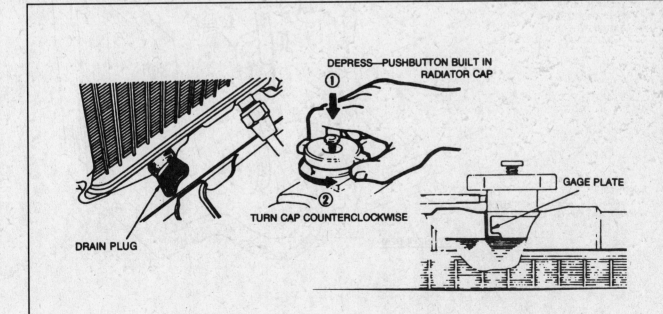

DEPRESS—PUSHBUTTON BUILT IN RADIATOR CAP

①

② TURN CAP COUNTERCLOCKWISE

DRAIN PLUG

GAGE PLATE

Fig. 19 Cooling system maintenance item locations

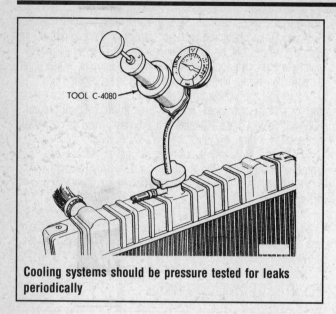

TOOL C-4080

Cooling systems should be pressure tested for leaks periodically

tank. It should be above the low mark. Never fill the tank over the upper mark.

Fill the radiator until the level is within 25mm of the radiator cap. It is best to add a 50/50 mix of antifreeze and water to avoid diluting the coolant in the system. Use permanent type antifreeze only.

DRAIN AND REFILL

Completely draining and refilling the cooling system every two years at least will remove accumulated rust, scale and other deposits.

1. Drain the existing antifreeze and coolant. Open the radiator and engine drain petcocks, or disconnect the bottom radiator hose, at the radiator outlet.

➡️**On older models, before opening the radiator petcock, spray it with some penetrating lubricant.**

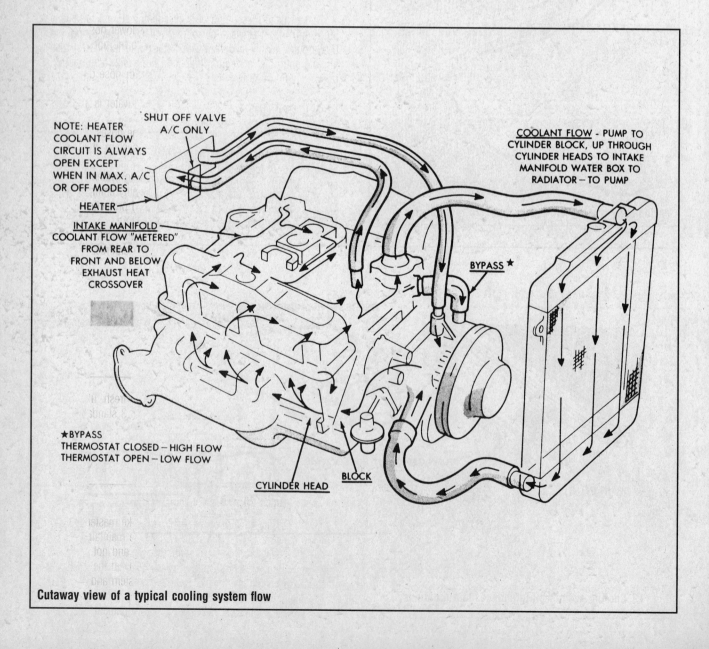

NOTE: HEATER COOLANT FLOW CIRCUIT IS ALWAYS OPEN EXCEPT WHEN IN MAX. A/C OR OFF MODES

SHUT OFF VALVE A/C ONLY

COOLANT FLOW - PUMP TO CYLINDER BLOCK, UP THROUGH CYLINDER HEADS TO INTAKE MANIFOLD WATER BOX TO RADIATOR – TO PUMP

HEATER

INTAKE MANIFOLD COOLANT FLOW "METERED" FROM REAR TO FRONT AND BELOW EXHAUST HEAT CROSSOVER

BYPASS ★

★BYPASS
THERMOSTAT CLOSED – HIGH FLOW
THERMOSTAT OPEN – LOW FLOW

CYLINDER HEAD   BLOCK

Cutaway view of a typical cooling system flow

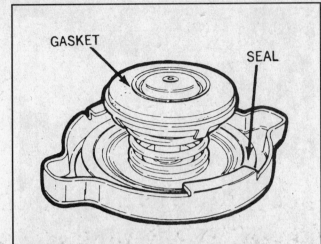

Be sure the rubber gasket on the radiator cap has a tight seal

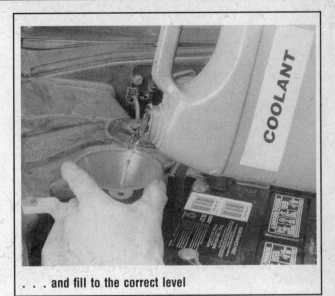

. . . and fill to the correct level

Carefully loosen the radiator petcock with a pair of pliers

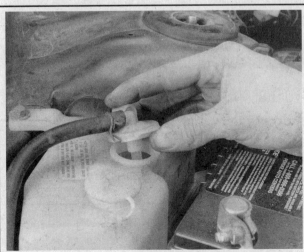

Once the radiator is full, remove the coolant reservoir tank lid . . .

2. Close the petcock or re-connect the lower hose and fill the system with water. Move the dash control to the hot position.

3. Add a can of quality radiator flush.

4. Idle the engine until the upper radiator hose gets hot.

5. Drain the system again.

6. Repeat this process until the drained water is clear and free of scale.

7. Close all petcocks and connect all the hoses.

8. If equipped with a coolant recovery system, flush the reservoir with water and leave empty.

9. Determine the capacity of your cooling system (see capacities specifications). Add a 50/50 mix of quality antifreeze (ethylene glycol) and water to provide the desired protection.

10. Run the engine to operating temperature.

11. Stop the engine and check the coolant level.

12. Check the level of protection with an antifreeze tester, replace the cap and check for leaks.

Brake Master Cylinder

FLUID RECOMMENDATIONS

When making additions of fluid, use only fresh, uncontaminated brake fluid meeting or exceeding DOT 3 standards.

LEVEL CHECK

▶ **See Figures 20 and 21**

Check the levels of brake fluid in the brake master cylinder reservoir(s) every 2 weeks. The fluid should be maintained to a level not below the bottom line on the reservoirs and not above the top line. Any sudden decrease in the level in any of the reservoirs indicates a probable leak in that particular system and should be checked out immediately.

Be careful not to spill any brake fluid on painted surfaces, be-

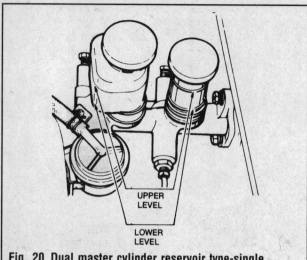

Fig. 20 Dual master cylinder reservoir type-single similar

If necessary, top off the master cylinder with the correct type of brake fluid

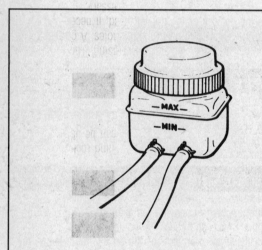

Fig. 21 This remotely mounted brake fluid reservoir is common on most vehicles

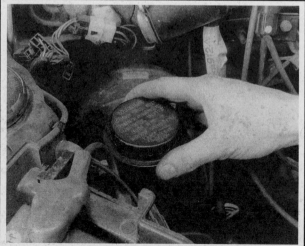

Remove the brake master cylinder cap and check the fluid level

cause it eats paint. Do not allow the fluid container or master cylinder reservoirs to remain open any longer than necessary; brake fluid absorbs moisture from the air, reducing its effectiveness and causing brake and clutch line corrosion.

Steering Gear

FLUID RECOMMENDATIONS

Add SAE 90 gear oil if the steering box needs filling.

LEVEL CHECK

Except Rack and Pinion and Power Steering: Remove the lower right bolt on the steering box cover and make sure that the oil level is approximately 18mm from the bolt hole. You can use a phillips screwdriver inserted through the hole to gauge the oil level.

Power Steering Pump

FLUID RECOMMENDATIONS

Dexron®II automatic transmission fluid should be used.

LEVEL CHECK

Depending on the model, the power steering pump reservoir will be equipped with a cap mounted dipstick or a see through case. The level should be between the high and low marks provided. Add fluid as required, but no higher than the upper full mark.

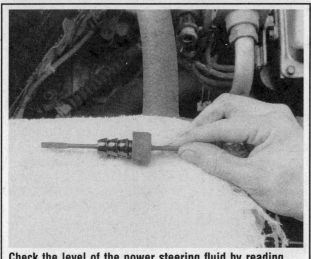

Check the level of the power steering fluid by reading the dipstick

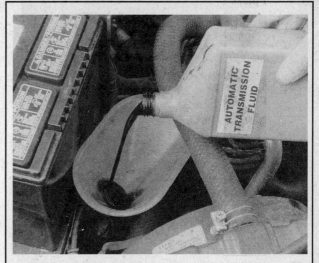

If necessary, top off the system with clean fresh fluid

OUTSIDE VEHICLE MAINTENANCE

Lock Cylinders

Apply graphite lubricant sparingly through the key slot. Insert the key and operate the lock several times to be sure that the lubricant is worked into the lock cylinder.

Door Hinges and Hinge Checks

Spray a silicone lubricant on the hinge pivot points to eliminate any binding conditions. Open and close the door several times to be sure that the lubricant is evenly and thoroughly distributed.

Liftgate

Spray a silicone lubricant on all of the pivot and friction surfaces to eliminate any squeaks or binds. Work the tailgate to distribute the lubricant.

Body Drain Holes

Be sure that the drain holes in the doors and rocker panels are cleared of obstruction. A small screwdriver can be used to clear them of any debris.

Chassis Greasing

Your car requires no regular chassis greasing. The lower ball joints are provided with plugged, threaded holes. A grease nipple can be installed and the ball joints lubricated, if necessary. No other lubrication points are provided or necessary.

Wheel Bearings

Refer to Chapter 7 for procedures on Front Wheel Drive vehicles, and Chapter 9 for Rear Wheel Drive models.

TRAILER TOWING

General Recommendations

Your vehicle was primarily designed to carry passengers and cargo. It is important to remember that towing a trailer will place additional loads on your vehicles engine, drivetrain, steering, braking and other systems. However, if you decide to tow a trailer, using the prior equipment is a must.

Local laws may require specific equipment such as trailer brakes or fender mounted mirrors. Check your local laws.

Trailer Weight

The weight of the trailer is the most important factor. A good weight-to-horsepower ratio is about 35:1, 35 lbs. of Gross Combined Weight (GCW) for every horsepower your engine develops. Multiply the engine's rated horsepower by 35 and subtract the weight of the vehicle passengers and luggage. The number remaining is the approximate ideal maximum weight you should tow, although a numerically higher axle ratio can help compensate for heavier weight.

Hitch (Tongue) Weight

Calculate the hitch weight in order to select a proper hitch. The weight of the hitch is usually 9–11% of the trailer gross weight and should be measured with the trailer loaded. Hitches fall into various categories: those that mount on the frame and rear bumper, the bolt-on type, or the weld-on distribution type used for larger trailers. Axle mounted or clamp-on bumper hitches should never be used.

Check the gross weight rating of your trailer. Tongue weight is usually figured as 10% of gross trailer weight. Therefore, a trailer with a maximum gross weight of 2000 lbs. will have a maximum tongue weight of 200 lbs. Class I trailers fall into this category. Class II trailers are those with a gross weight rating of 2000–3000 lbs., while Class III trailers fall into the 3500–6000 lbs. category. Class IV trailers are those over 6000 lbs. and are for use with fifth wheel trucks, only.

When you've determined the hitch that you'll need, follow the manufacturer's installation instructions, exactly, especially when it comes to fastener torques. The hitch will subjected to a lot of stress and good hitches come with hardened bolts. Never substitute an inferior bolt for a hardened bolt.

Cooling

ENGINE

Overflow Tank

One of the most common, if not THE most common, problems associated with trailer towing is engine overheating. If you have a cooling system without an expansion tank, you'll definitely need to get an aftermarket expansion tank kit, preferably one with at least a 2 quart capacity. These kits are easily installed on the radiator's overflow hose, and come with a pressure cap designed for expansion tanks.

Flex Fan

Another helpful accessory for vehicles using a belt-driven radiator fan is a flex fan. These fans are large diameter units designed to provide more airflow at low speeds, by using fan blades that have deeply cupped surfaces. The blades then flex, or flatten out, at high speed, when less cooling air is needed. These fans are far lighter in weight than stock fans, requiring less horsepower to drive them. Also, they are far quieter than stock fans. If you do decide to replace your stock fan with a flex fan, note that if your vehicle has a fan clutch, a spacer will be needed between the flex fan and water pump hub.

Oil Cooler

Aftermarket engine oil coolers are helpful for prolonging engine oil life and reducing overall engine temperatures. Both of these factors increase engine life. While not absolutely necessary in towing Class I and some Class II trailers, they are recommended for heavier Class II and all Class III towing. Engine oil cooler systems usually consist of an adapter, screwed on in place of the oil filter, a remote filter mounting and a multi-tube, finned heat exchanger, which is mounted in front of the radiator or air conditioning condenser.

TRANSMISSION

An automatic transmission is usually recommended for trailer towing. Modern automatics have proven reliable and, of course, easy to operate, in trailer towing. The increased load of a trailer, however, causes an increase in the temperature of the automatic

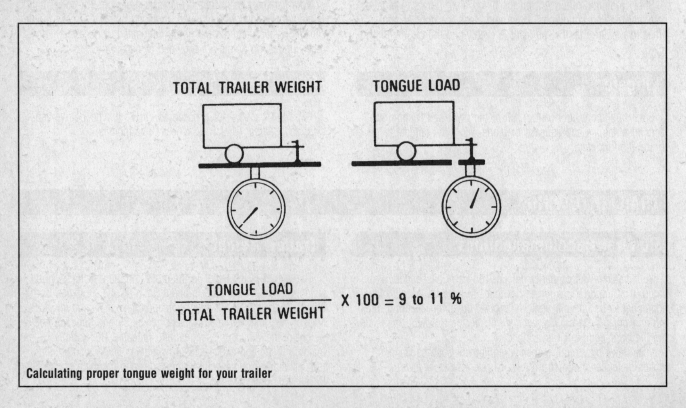

$$\frac{\text{TONGUE LOAD}}{\text{TOTAL TRAILER WEIGHT}} \times 100 = 9 \text{ to } 11\ \%$$

Calculating proper tongue weight for your trailer

transmission fluid. Heat is the worst enemy of an automatic transmission. As the temperature of the fluid increases, the life of the fluid decreases.

It is essential, therefore, that you install an automatic transmission cooler. The cooler, which consists of a multi-tube, finned heat exchanger, is usually installed in front of the radiator or air conditioning compressor, and hooked in-line with the transmission cooler tank inlet line. Follow the cooler manufacturer's installation instructions.

Select a cooler of at least adequate capacity, based upon the combined gross weights of the vehicle and trailer.

Cooler manufacturers recommend that you use an aftermarket cooler in addition to, and not instead of, the present cooling tank in your radiator. If you do want to use it in place of the radiator cooling tank, get a cooler at least two sizes larger than normally necessary.

➡A transmission cooler can, sometimes, cause slow or harsh shifting in the transmission during cold weather, until the fluid has a chance to come up to normal operating temperature. Some coolers can be purchased with or retrofitted with a temperature bypass valve which will allow fluid flow through the cooler only when the fluid has reached above a certain operating temperature.

Handling A Trailer

Towing a trailer with ease and safety requires a certain amount of experience. It's a good idea to learn the feel of a trailer by practicing turning, stopping and backing in an open area such as an empty parking lot.

JUMP STARTING A DEAD BATTERY

Whenever a vehicle is jump started, precautions must be followed in order to prevent the possibility of personal injury. Remember that batteries contain a small amount of explosive hydrogen gas which is a by-product of battery charging. Sparks should always be avoided when working around batteries, especially when attaching jumper cables. To minimize the possibility of accidental sparks, follow the procedure carefully.

✳✳ CAUTION

NEVER hook the batteries up in a series circuit or the entire electrical system will go up in smoke, including the starter!

Vehicles equipped with a diesel engine may utilize two 12 volt batteries. If so, the batteries are connected in a parallel circuit (positive terminal to positive terminal, negative terminal to negative terminal). Hooking the batteries up in parallel circuit increases battery cranking power without increasing total battery voltage output. Output remains at 12 volts. On the other hand, hooking two 12 volt batteries up in a series circuit (positive terminal to negative terminal, positive terminal to negative terminal) increases total battery output to 24 volts (12 volts plus 12 volts).

Jump Starting Precautions

• Be sure that both batteries are of the same voltage. Vehicles covered by this manual and most vehicles on the road today utilize a 12 volt charging system.
• Be sure that both batteries are of the same polarity (have the same terminal, in most cases NEGATIVE grounded).
• Be sure that the vehicles are not touching or a short could occur.
• On serviceable batteries, be sure the vent cap holes are not obstructed.
• Do not smoke or allow sparks anywhere near the batteries.
• In cold weather, make sure the battery electrolyte is not frozen. This can occur more readily in a battery that has been in a state of discharge.
• Do not allow electrolyte to contact your skin or clothing.

Jump Starting Procedure

1. Make sure that the voltages of the 2 batteries are the same. Most batteries and charging systems are of the 12 volt variety.
2. Pull the jumping vehicle (with the good battery) into a position so the jumper cables can reach the dead battery and that vehicle's engine. Make sure that the vehicles do NOT touch.
3. Place the transmissions/transaxles of both vehicles in **Neutral** (MT) or **P** (AT), as applicable, then firmly set their parking brakes.

➡If necessary for safety reasons, the hazard lights on both vehicles may be operated throughout the entire procedure without significantly increasing the difficulty of jumping the dead battery.

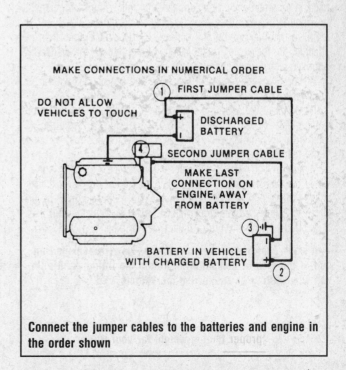

MAKE CONNECTIONS IN NUMERICAL ORDER

DO NOT ALLOW VEHICLES TO TOUCH

FIRST JUMPER CABLE

DISCHARGED BATTERY

SECOND JUMPER CABLE

MAKE LAST CONNECTION ON ENGINE, AWAY FROM BATTERY

BATTERY IN VEHICLE WITH CHARGED BATTERY

Connect the jumper cables to the batteries and engine in the order shown

4. Turn all lights and accessories OFF on both vehicles. Make sure the ignition switches on both vehicles are turned to the **OFF** position.

5. Cover the battery cell caps with a rag, but do not cover the terminals.

6. Make sure the terminals on both batteries are clean and free of corrosion or proper electrical connection will be impeded. If necessary, clean the battery terminals before proceeding.

7. Identify the positive (+) and negative (−) terminals on both batteries.

8. Connect the first jumper cable to the positive (+) terminal of the dead battery, then connect the other end of that cable to the positive (+) terminal of the booster (good) battery.

9. Connect one end of the other jumper cable to the negative (−) terminal on the booster battery and the final cable clamp to an engine bolt head, alternator bracket or other solid, metallic point on the engine with the dead battery. Try to pick a ground on the engine that is positioned away from the battery in order to minimize the possibility of the 2 clamps touching should one loosen during the procedure. DO NOT connect this clamp to the negative (−) terminal of the bad battery.

✳✳ CAUTION

Be very careful to keep the jumper cables away from moving parts (cooling fan, belts, etc.) on both engines.

10. Check to make sure that the cables are routed away from any moving parts, then start the donor vehicle's engine. Run the engine at moderate speed for several minutes to allow the dead battery a chance to receive some initial charge.

11. With the donor vehicle's engine still running slightly above idle, try to start the vehicle with the dead battery. Crank the engine for no more than 10 seconds at a time and let the starter cool for at least 20 seconds between tries. If the vehicle does not start in 3 tries, it is likely that something else is also wrong or that the battery needs additional time to charge.

12. Once the vehicle is started, allow it to run at idle for a few seconds to make sure that it is operating properly.

13. Turn ON the headlights, heater blower and, if equipped, the rear defroster of both vehicles in order to reduce the severity of voltage spikes and subsequent risk of damage to the vehicles' electrical systems when the cables are disconnected. This step is especially important to any vehicle equipped with computer control modules.

14. Carefully disconnect the cables in the reverse order of connection. Start with the negative cable that is attached to the engine ground, then the negative cable on the donor battery. Disconnect the positive cable from the donor battery and finally, disconnect the positive cable from the formerly dead battery. Be careful when disconnecting the cables from the positive terminals not to allow the alligator clips to touch any metal on either vehicle or a short and sparks will occur.

JACKING

▶ **See Figure 22 and 23**

Your vehicle was supplied with a jack for emergency road repairs. This jack is fine for changing a flat tire or other short term procedures not requiring you to go beneath the vehicle. If it is used in an emergency situation, carefully follow the instructions provided either with the jack or in your owner's manual. Do not attempt to use the jack on any portions of the vehicle other than specified by the vehicle manufacturer. Always block the diagonally opposite wheel when using a jack.

A more convenient way of jacking is the use of a garage or floor jack.

Never place the jack under the radiator, engine or transmission components. Severe and expensive damage will result when the jack is raised. Additionally, never jack under the floorpan or bodywork; the metal will deform.

Whenever you plan to work under the vehicle, you must support it on jackstands or ramps. Never use cinder blocks or stacks of wood to support the vehicle, even if you're only going to be under it for a few minutes. Never crawl under the vehicle when it is supported only by the tire-changing jack or other floor jack.

➡**Always position a block of wood or small rubber pad on top of the jack or jackstand to protect the lifting point's finish when lifting or supporting the vehicle.**

Small hydraulic, screw, or scissors jacks are satisfactory for raising the vehicle. Drive-on trestles or ramps are also a handy and safe way to both raise and support the vehicle. Be careful though, some ramps may be too steep to drive your vehicle onto without scraping the front bottom panels. Never support the vehicle on any suspension member (unless specifically instructed to do so by a repair manual) or by an underbody panel.

Jacking Precautions

The following safety points cannot be overemphasized:

• Always block the opposite wheel or wheels to keep the vehicle from rolling off the jack.

• When raising the front of the vehicle, firmly apply the parking brake.

• When the drive wheels are to remain on the ground, leave the vehicle in gear to help prevent it from rolling.

• Always use jackstands to support the vehicle when you are working underneath. Place the stands beneath the vehicle's jacking brackets. Before climbing underneath, rock the vehicle a bit to make sure it is firmly supported.

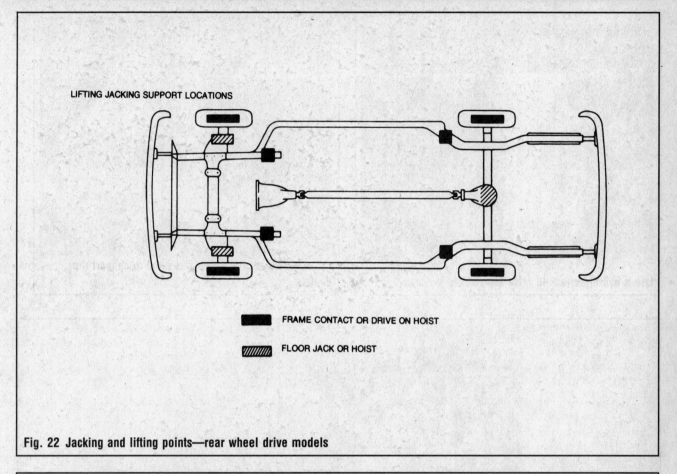

LIFTING JACKING SUPPORT LOCATIONS

▬ FRAME CONTACT OR DRIVE ON HOIST

▨ FLOOR JACK OR HOIST

Fig. 22 Jacking and lifting points—rear wheel drive models

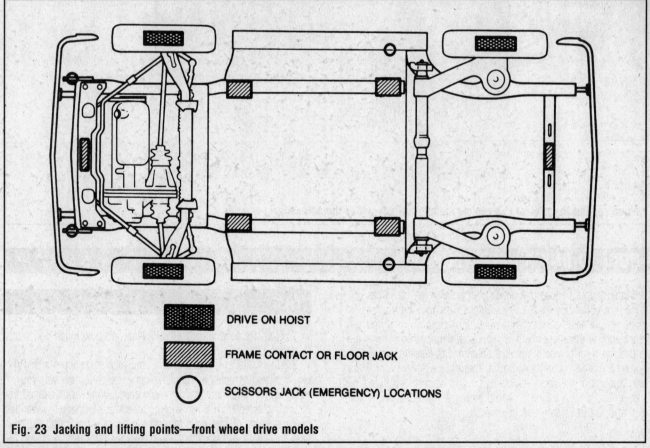

▨ DRIVE ON HOIST

▨ FRAME CONTACT OR FLOOR JACK

○ SCISSORS JACK (EMERGENCY) LOCATIONS

Fig. 23 Jacking and lifting points—front wheel drive models

Use a hydraulic jack to raise the vehicle . . .

. . . and be sure to use a jackstand to support the vehicle

When raising the rear of the vehicle, place the jack under the control arm

HOW TO BUY A USED VEHICLE

Many people believe that a two or three year old used car or truck is a better buy than a new vehicle. This may be true as most new vehicles suffer the heaviest depreciation in the first two years and, at three years old, a vehicle is usually not old enough to present a lot of costly repair problems. But keep in mind, when buying a non-warranted automobile, there are no guarantees. Whatever the age of the used vehicle you might want to purchase, this section and a little patience should increase your chances of selecting one that is safe and dependable.

Tips

1. First decide what model you want, and how much you want to spend.
2. Check the used car lots and your local newspaper ads. Privately owned vehicles are usually less expensive, however, you may not get a warranty that, in many cases, comes with a used vehicle purchased from a lot. Of course, some aftermarket warranties may not be worth the extra money, so this is a point you will have to debate and consider based on your priorities.

3. Never shop at night. The glare of the lights make it easy to miss faults on the body caused by accident or rust repair.

4. Try to get the name and phone number of the previous owner. Contact him/her and ask about the vehicle. If the owner of a lot refuses this information, look for a vehicle somewhere else.

A private seller can tell you about the vehicle and maintenance. But remember, there's no law requiring honesty from private citizens selling used vehicles. There is a law that forbids tampering with or turning back the odometer mileage. This includes both the private citizen and the lot owner. The law also requires that the seller or anyone transferring ownership of the vehicle must provide the buyer with a signed statement indicating the mileage on the odometer at the time of transfer.

5. You may wish to contact the National Highway Traffic Safety Administration (NHTSA) to find out if the vehicle has ever been included in a manufacturer's recall. Write down the year, model and serial number before you buy the vehicle, then contact NHTSA (there should be a 1-800 number that your phone company's information line can supply). If the vehicle was listed for a recall, make sure the needed repairs were made.

6. Refer to the Used Vehicle Checklist in this section and check all the items on the vehicle you are considering. Some items are more important than others. Only you know how much money you can afford for repairs, and depending on the price of the vehicle, may consider performing any needed work yourself. Beware, however, of trouble in areas that will affect operation, safety or emission. Problems in the Used Vehicle Checklist break down as follows:

• Numbers 1–8: Two or more problems in these areas indicate a lack of maintenance. You should beware.

• Numbers 9–13: Problems here tend to indicate a lack of proper care, however, these can usually be corrected with a tune-up or relatively simple parts replacement.

• Numbers 14–17: Problems in the engine or transmission can be very expensive. Unless you are looking for a project, walk away from any vehicle with problems in 2 or more of these areas.

7. If you are satisfied with the apparent condition of the vehicle, take it to an independent diagnostic center or mechanic for a complete check. If you have a state inspection program, have it inspected immediately before purchase, or specify on the bill of sale that the sale is conditional on passing state inspection.

8. Road test the vehicle—refer to the Road Test Checklist in this section. If your original evaluation and the road test agree—the rest is up to you.

USED VEHICLE CHECKLIST

➡ **The numbers on the illustrations refer to the numbers on this checklist.**

1. Mileage: Average mileage is about 12,000–15,000 miles per year. More than average mileage may indicate hard usage or could indicate many highway miles (which could be less detrimental than half as many tough around town miles).

2. Paint: Check around the tailpipe, molding and windows for overspray indicating that the vehicle has been repainted.

3. Rust: Check fenders, doors, rocker panels, window moldings, wheelwells, floorboards, under floormats, and in the trunk for signs of rust. Any rust at all will be a problem. There is no way to permanently stop the spread of rust, except to replace the part or panel.

➡ **If rust repair is suspected, try using a magnet to check for body filler. A magnet should stick to the sheet metal parts of the body, but will not adhere to areas with large amounts of filler.**

4. Body appearance: Check the moldings, bumpers, grille, vinyl roof, glass, doors, trunk lid and body panels for general overall condition. Check for misalignment, loose hold-down clips, ripples, scratches in glass, welding in the trunk, severe misalignment of body panels or ripples, any of which may indicate crash work.

5. Leaks: Get down and look under the vehicle. There are no normal leaks, other than water from the air conditioner evaporator.

6. Tires: Check the tire air pressure. One old trick is to pump the tire pressure up to make the vehicle roll easier. Check the tread wear, then open the trunk and check the spare too. Uneven wear is a clue that the front end may need an alignment.

7. Shock absorbers: Check the shock absorbers by forcing downward sharply on each corner of the vehicle. Good shocks will not allow the vehicle to bounce more than once after you let go.

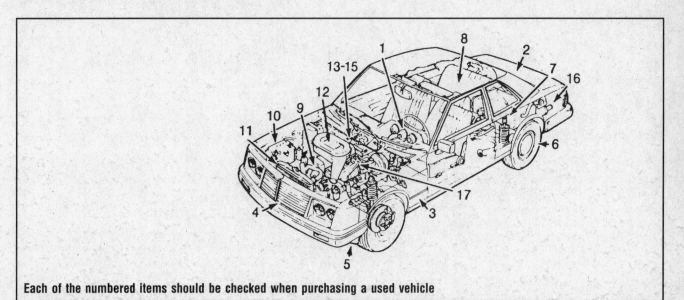

Each of the numbered items should be checked when purchasing a used vehicle

8. Interior: Check the entire interior. You're looking for an interior condition that agrees with the overall condition of the vehicle. Reasonable wear is expected, but be suspicious of new seat covers on sagging seats, new pedal pads, and worn armrests. These indicate an attempt to cover up hard use. Pull back the carpets and look for evidence of water leaks or flooding. Look for missing hardware, door handles, control knobs, etc. Check lights and signal operations. Make sure all accessories (air conditioner, heater, radio, etc.) work. Check windshield wiper operation.

9. Belts and Hoses: Open the hood, then check all belts and hoses for wear, cracks or weak spots.

10. Battery: Low electrolyte level, corroded terminals and/or cracked case indicate a lack of maintenance.

11. Radiator: Look for corrosion or rust in the coolant indicating a lack of maintenance.

12. Air filter: A severely dirty air filter would indicate a lack of maintenance.

13. Ignition wires: Check the ignition wires for cracks, burned spots, or wear. Worn wires will have to be replaced.

14. Oil level: If the oil level is low, chances are the engine uses oil or leaks. Beware of water in the oil (there is probably a cracked block or bad head gasket), excessively thick oil (which is often used to quiet a noisy engine), or thin, dirty oil with a distinct gasoline smell (this may indicate internal engine problems).

15. Automatic Transmission: Pull the transmission dipstick out when the engine is running. The level should read FULL, and the fluid should be clear or bright red. Dark brown or black fluid that has distinct burnt odor, indicates a transmission in need of repair or overhaul.

16. Exhaust: Check the color of the exhaust smoke. Blue smoke indicates, among other problems, worn rings. Black smoke can indicate burnt valves or carburetor problems. Check the exhaust system for leaks; it can be expensive to replace.

17. Spark Plugs: Remove one or all of the spark plugs (the most accessible will do, though all are preferable). An engine in good condition will show plugs with a light tan or gray deposit on the firing tip.

ROAD TEST CHECKLIST

1. Engine Performance: The vehicle should be peppy whether cold or warm, with adequate power and good pickup. It should respond smoothly through the gears.

2. Brakes: They should provide quick, firm stops with no noise, pulling or brake fade.

3. Steering: Sure control with no binding harshness, or looseness and no shimmy in the wheel should be expected. Noise or vibration from the steering wheel when turning the vehicle means trouble.

4. Clutch (Manual Transmission/Transaxle): Clutch action should give quick, smooth response with easy shifting. The clutch pedal should have free-play before it disengages the clutch. Start the engine, set the parking brake, put the transmission in first gear and slowly release the clutch pedal. The engine should begin to stall when the pedal is 1/2–3/4 of the way up.

5. Automatic Transmission/Transaxle: The transmission should shift rapidly and smoothly, with no noise, hesitation, or slipping.

6. Differential: No noise or thumps should be present. Differentials have no normal leaks.

7. Driveshaft/Universal Joints: Vibration and noise could mean driveshaft problems. Clicking at low speed or coast conditions means worn U-joints.

8. Suspension: Try hitting bumps at different speeds. A vehicle that bounces excessively has weak shock absorbers or struts. Clunks mean worn bushings or ball joints.

9. Frame/Body: Wet the tires and drive in a straight line. Tracks should show two straight lines, not four. Four tire tracks indicate a frame/body bent by collision damage. If the tires can't be wet for this purpose, have a friend drive along behind you and see if the vehicle appears to be traveling in a straight line.

Scheduled Maintenance

Emission Control System Maintenance	Service Intervals	Kilometers in Thousands Mileage in Thousands	24 15	48 30	72 45	80 50	96 60
Change Engine Oil Every 12 Months (Cars with a carburetor)	or		Every 12,000 Km (7,500 Miles)				
Replace Engine Oil Filter Every 12 Months (Cars with a carburetor)	or		X	X	X		X
Change Engine Oil Every 6 Months (Cars with a turbocharger)	or		Every 4,800 Km (3,000 Miles)				
Replace Engine Oil Filter Every 12 Months (Cars with a turbocharger)	or		Every 9,600 Km (6,000 Miles)				
Check Valve Clearance; Adjust as Required	at		X	X	X		X
Check Engine Idle Speed*1; Adjust as Required (Cars with a carburetor)	at		X	X	X		X
Clean Carburetor Choke Mechanism and Linkage *2	at			X			X
Replace Fuel Filter Every 5 Years	or					X	
Check Fuel System (Tank, Line and Connections) for Leaks Every 5 Years	or					X	
Replace Vacuum Hoses, Secondary Air Hoses, Crankcase Ventilation Hoses and Water Hoses Every 5 Years	or						X
Replace Fuel Hoses, Vapor Hoses and Fuel Filler Cap Every 5 Years	or					X	
Replace Turbocharger Air Intake Hoses and Oil Hose Every 5 Years	or						X
Replace Air Cleaner Element	at			X			X
Clean Crankcase Emission Control System (PCV Valve) Every 5 Years	or						X
Check Evaporative Emission Control System (Except Canister) for Leaks and Clogging Every 5 Years	or						X
Replace Canister	at					X	
Replace Spark Plugs	at			X			X
Replace Ignition Cables Every 5 Years	or						X
Replace Oxygen Sensor	at					X	

NOTE
*1: Recommended maintenance service item for California, and required maintenance service item except for California.
*2: Recommended maintenance service item except for California, and required maintenance service item for California.

Scheduled Maintenance

General Maintenance	Service Intervals		Kilometers in Thousands / Mileage in Thousands	24 / 15	48 / 30	72 / 45	80 / 50	96 / 60
Timing Belt	Replace	at						X
Drive Belt (for Water Pump and Alternator)	Replace	at			X			X
Manual Transaxle	Check Oil Level	at			X			X
Automatic Transaxle	Change Fluid	at			X			X
Cooling System	Check and Service as Required Every 12 Months	or		X	X	X		X
	Replace Engine Coolant Every 2 Years	or			X			X
Front Disc Brake Pads	Inspect for Wear Every 12 Months	or		X	X	X		X
Rear Drum Brake Linings and Rear Wheel Cylinders	Inspect for Wear and Leaks Every 2 Years	or			X			X
Brake Hoses	Check for Deterioration or Leaks Every 12 Months	or		X	X	X		X
Brake Fluid	Replace Every 4 Years	or						X
Ball Joint and Steering Linkage Seals, Steering and Drive Shaft Boots	Inspect for Grease Leaks and Damage Every 2 Years	or			X			X
Rear Wheel Bearings	Lubricate Grease Every 2 Years	or			X			X
Exhaust System (Connection Portion of Muffler, Pipings and Converter Heat Shield)	Check and Service as Required Every 12 Months	or		X	X	X		X

Severe Usage Maintenance

Maintenance Item	Service to be Performed		Mileage Intervals Kilometers in Thousands (Miles in Thousands) 24 (15)	48 (30)	72 (45)	96 (60)	Severe Usage Conditions A	B	C	D	E	F	G
Engine Oil	Change Every 3 Months	or	Every 4,800 Km (3,000 Miles)				X	X	X	X			X
Engine Oil Filter	Replace Every 6 Months	or	Every 9,600 Km (6,000 Miles)				X	X	X	X			X
Air Cleaner Element	Replace		More Frequently				X				X		
Crankcase Emission-Control System	Check and Clean as Required		More Frequently				X						
Spark Plugs	Replace	at	X (15)	X (30)	X (45)	X (60)	X		X				
Front Disc Brake Pads	Inspect for Wear		More Frequently				X					X	
Rear Drum Brake Linings and Rear Wheel Cylinders	Inspect for Wear and Leaks		More Frequently				X					X	

Severe usage conditions
A—Driving in dusty conditions
B—Police, taxi, or commercial type operation
C—Extensive idling
D—Short-trip operation at freezing temperatures (engine not thoroughly warmed up)
E—Driving in sandy areas
F—Driving in salty areas
G—More than 50% operation in heavy city traffic during hot weather above 32°C (90°F)

CAPACITIES-Rear Wheel Drive

Year	Model	Engine Displacement Liters (cc)	Engine Oil with Filter (qts.)	Transmission (pts.)			Drive Axle (pts.)	Gas Tank (gal.)	Cooling (qts.)	
				4-Spd	5-Spd	Auto.			W/AC	W/O AC
1971-73	All	1597	4.2	1.8		5.6	2	13.0 ①		7.2
1974-76	All	1597	4.2	1.8	2.4	6.8 ②	2.4	13.0 ①	6.4	6.4
		1994	5	1.8	2.4	6.8	2.4	13.0 ①	8	8
1977	All	1597	4.2	1.8	2.4	6.8	1.2	- ③	7.7	7.7
		1994	4.5	-	2.1	6.8	1.2	- ③	9.5	9.5
1978	All	1597	4.2	1.8	2.1	6.8	1.2	15.8	7.7	7.7
		1994	4.5	-	2.4	6.8	1.2	15.8	9.5	9.5
		2555	4.5	-	2.4	6.8	1.2	15.8	9.7	9.7
1979-83	All	1597	4.2	-	2.1	7.2	1.2	- ⑤	7.7	7.7
		1994	4.5	-	2.4	7.2	1.2	- ⑤	9.5	9.5
		2555	4.5	-	2.4	7.2	1.4 ④	⑤ ⑥	9.5	9.5
1984-89	Conquest	2555	5	-	2.4	7.4	2.7	19.8	9.7	9.7

1 Station wagon: 11 gallons
2 Borg-Warner: 5.6 quarts
3 Coupe, sedan and hatchback: 13.2 gallons hardtop: 13.5 gallons
4 1981-83: 2.7
5 Colt coupe, sedan 13.2 gallons Challenger: 15.8 gallons
   Station wagon: 14.0 (1979), 13.2 (1980) gallons
6 1981-83: 15.8 gallons

CAPACITIES-Front Wheel Drive

Year	Model	Engine Displacement Liters (cc)	Engine Oil with Filter (qts.)	Transmission (pts.)				Gas Tank (gal.)	Cooling (qts.)	
				4-Spd	5-Spd	Twin Stick	Auto.②		W/AC	W/O AC
1979-84	All	1410	3.7	4.4	-	4.4	-	10.6	-	4.7
		1597	4.2	4.4	4.4	-	12	10.6 ①	4.7	4.7
1985-86	All	1468	3.2	4.4	4.4	-	-	11.9	-	5.3
	Turbo	1597	3.7	-	4.9	-	12.3	11.9	5.3	5.3
	All	1997	4.2	-	4.9	4.9	12.3	13.2	7.4	7.4
	4WD Vista	1997	4.2	-	4.4	-	-	14.5	7.4	7.4
1987-89	All	1468	3.2	3.6	3.8	-	12.2	11.9	5.3	5.3
	Turbo	1597	3.7	-	3.8	-	12.2	11.9	5.3	5.3
	All	1997	4	-	5.3	-	12.3	13.2	7.4	7.4
	4WD Vista	1997	4	-	4.5	-	-	14.5	7.4	7.4

1 RS and LS models: 13.2
2 Includes torque converter drain and refill

ENGLISH TO METRIC CONVERSION: MASS (WEIGHT)

Current **mass** measurement is expressed in pounds and ounces (lbs. & ozs.). The metric unit of mass (or weight) is the kilogram (kg). Even although this table does not show conversion of masses (weights) larger than 15 lbs, it is easy to calculate larger units by following the data immediately below.

To convert ounces (oz.) to grams (g): multiply th number of ozs. by 28
To convert grams (g) to ounces (oz.): multiply the number of grams by .035

To convert pounds (lbs.) to kilograms (kg): multiply the number of lbs. by .45
To convert kilograms (kg) to pounds (lbs.): multiply the number of kilograms by 2.2

lbs	kg	lbs	kg	oz	kg	oz	kg
0.1	0.04	0.9	0.41	0.1	0.003	0.9	0.024
0.2	0.09	1	0.4	0.2	0.005	1	0.03
0.3	0.14	2	0.9	0.3	0.008	2	0.06
0.4	0.18	3	1.4	0.4	0.011	3	0.08
0.5	0.23	4	1.8	0.5	0.014	4	0.11
0.6	0.27	5	2.3	0.6	0.017	5	0.14
0.7	0.32	10	4.5	0.7	0.020	10	0.28
0.8	0.36	15	6.8	0.8	0.023	15	0.42

ENGLISH TO METRIC CONVERSION: TEMPERATURE

To convert Fahrenheit (°F) to Celsius (°C): take number of °F and subtract 32; multiply result by 5; divide result by 9
To convert Celsius (°C) to Fahrenheit (°F): take number of °C and multiply by 9; divide result by 5; add 32 to total

Fahrenheit (F)	Celsius (C)			Fahrenheit (F)	Celsius (C)			Fahrenheit (F)	Celsius (C)		
°F	°C	°C	°F	°F	°C	°C	°F	°F	°C	°C	°F
−40	−40	−38	−36.4	80	26.7	18	64.4	215	101.7	80	176
−35	−37.2	−36	−32.8	85	29.4	20	68	220	104.4	85	185
−30	−34.4	−34	−29.2	90	32.2	22	71.6	225	107.2	90	194
−25	−31.7	−32	−25.6	95	35.0	24	75.2	230	110.0	95	202
−20	−28.9	−30	−22	100	37.8	26	78.8	235	112.8	100	212
−15	−26.1	−28	−18.4	105	40.6	28	82.4	240	115.6	105	221
−10	−23.3	−26	−14.8	110	43.3	30	86	245	118.3	110	230
−5	−20.6	−24	−11.2	115	46.1	32	89.6	250	121.1	115	239
0	−17.8	−22	−7.6	120	48.9	34	93.2	255	123.9	120	248
1	−17.2	−20	−4	125	51.7	36	96.8	260	126.6	125	257
2	−16.7	−18	−0.4	130	54.4	38	100.4	265	129.4	130	266
3	−16.1	−16	3.2	135	57.2	40	104	270	132.2	135	275
4	−15.6	−14	6.8	140	60.0	42	107.6	275	135.0	140	284
5	−15.0	−12	10.4	145	62.8	44	112.2	280	137.8	145	293
10	−12.2	−10	14	150	65.6	46	114.8	285	140.6	150	302
15	−9.4	−8	17.6	155	68.3	48	118.4	290	143.3	155	311
20	−6.7	−6	21.2	160	71.1	50	122	295	146.1	160	320
25	−3.9	−4	24.8	165	73.9	52	125.6	300	148.9	165	329
30	−1.1	−2	28.4	170	76.7	54	129.2	305	151.7	170	338
35	1.7	0	32	175	79.4	56	132.8	310	154.4	175	347
40	4.4	2	35.6	180	82.2	58	136.4	315	157.2	180	356
45	7.2	4	39.2	185	85.0	60	140	320	160.0	185	365
50	10.0	6	42.8	190	87.8	62	143.6	325	162.8	190	374
55	12.8	8	46.4	195	90.6	64	147.2	330	165.6	195	383
60	15.6	10	50	200	93.3	66	150.8	335	168.3	200	392
65	18.3	12	53.6	205	96.1	68	154.4	340	171.1	205	401
70	21.1	14	57.2	210	98.9	70	158	345	173.9	210	410
75	23.9	16	60.8	212	100.0	75	167	350	176.7	215	414

ENGLISH TO METRIC CONVERSION: LENGTH

To convert inches (ins.) to millimeters (mm): multiply number of inches by 25.4

To convert millimeters (mm) to inches (ins.): multiply number of millimeters by .04

Inches	Decimals	Millimeters	Inches to millimeters inches	mm	Inches	Decimals	Millimeters	Inches to millimeters inches	mm
1/64	0.051625	0.3969	0.0001	0.00254	33/64	0.515625	13.0969	0.6	15.24
1/32	0.03125	0.7937	0.0002	0.00508	17/32	0.53125	13.4937	0.7	17.78
3/64	0.046875	1.1906	0.0003	0.00762	35/64	0.546875	13.8906	0.8	20.32
1/16	0.0625	1.5875	0.0004	0.01016	9/16	0.5625	14.2875	0.9	22.86
5/64	0.078125	1.9844	0.0005	0.01270	37/64	0.578125	14.6844	1	25.4
3/32	0.09375	2.3812	0.0006	0.01524	19/32	0.59375	15.0812	2	50.8
7/64	0.109375	2.7781	0.0007	0.01778	39/64	0.609375	15.4781	3	76.2
1/8	0.125	3.1750	0.0008	0.02032	5/8	0.625	15.8750	4	101.6
9/64	0.140625	3.5719	0.0009	0.02286	41/64	0.640625	16.2719	5	127.0
5/32	0.15625	3.9687	0.001	0.0254	21/32	0.65625	16.6687	6	152.4
11/64	0.171875	4.3656	0.002	0.0508	43/64	0.671875	17.0656	7	177.8
3/16	0.1875	4.7625	0.003	0.0762	11/16	0.6875	17.4625	8	203.2
13/64	0.203125	5.1594	0.004	0.1016	45/64	0.703125	17.8594	9	228.6
7/32	0.21875	5.5562	0.005	0.1270	23/32	0.71875	18.2562	10	254.0
15/64	0.234375	5.9531	0.006	0.1524	47/64	0.734375	18.6531	11	279.4
1/4	0.25	6.3500	0.007	0.1778	3/4	0.75	19.0500	12	304.8
17/64	0.265625	6.7469	0.008	0.2032	49/64	0.765625	19.4469	13	330.2
9/32	0.28125	7.1437	0.009	0.2286	25/32	0.78125	19.8437	14	355.6
19/64	0.296875	7.5406	0.01	0.254	51/64	0.796875	20.2406	15	381.0
5/16	0.3125	7.9375	0.02	0.508	13/16	0.8125	20.6375	16	406.4
21/64	0.328125	8.3344	0.03	0.762	53/64	0.828125	21.0344	17	431.8
11/32	0.34375	8.7312	0.04	1.016	27/32	0.84375	21.4312	18	457.2
23/64	0.359375	9.1281	0.05	1.270	55/64	0.859375	21.8281	19	482.6
3/8	0.375	9.5250	0.06	1.524	7/8	0.875	22.2250	20	508.0
25/64	0.390625	9.9219	0.07	1.778	57/64	0.890625	22.6219	21	533.4
13/32	0.40625	10.3187	0.08	2.032	29/32	0.90625	23.0187	22	558.8
27/64	0.421875	10.7156	0.09	2.286	59/64	0.921875	23.4156	23	584.2
7/16	0.4375	11.1125	0.1	2.54	15/16	0.9375	23.8125	24	609.6
29/64	0.453125	11.5094	0.2	5.08	61/64	0.953125	24.2094	25	635.0
15/32	0.46875	11.9062	0.3	7.62	31/32	0.96875	24.6062	26	660.4
31/64	0.484375	12.3031	0.4	10.16	63/64	0.984375	25.0031	27	690.6
1/2	0.5	12.7000	0.5	12.70					

ENGLISH TO METRIC CONVERSION: TORQUE

To convert foot-pounds (ft. lbs.) to Newton-meters: multiply the number of ft. lbs. by 1.3

To convert inch-pounds (in. lbs.) to Newton-meters: multiply the number of in. lbs. by .11

in lbs	N·m	in lbs	N·m	in lbs	N·m	in lbs	N·m	in lbs	N·m
0.1	0.01	1	0.11	10	1.13	19	2.15	28	3.16
0.2	0.02	2	0.23	11	1.24	20	2.26	29	3.28
0.3	0.03	3	0.34	12	1.36	21	2.37	30	3.39
0.4	0.04	4	0.45	13	1.47	22	2.49	31	3.50
0.5	0.06	5	0.56	14	1.58	23	2.60	32	3.62
0.6	0.07	6	0.68	15	1.70	24	2.71	33	3.73
0.7	0.08	7	0.78	16	1.81	25	2.82	34	3.84
0.8	0.09	8	0.90	17	1.92	26	2.94	35	3.95
0.9	0.10	9	1.02	18	2.03	27	3.05	36	4.0

ENGLISH TO METRIC CONVERSION: TORQUE

Torque is now expressed as either foot-pounds (ft./lbs.) or inch-pounds (in./lbs.). The metric measurement unit for torque is the Newton-meter (Nm). This unit—the Nm—will be used for all SI metric torque references, both the present ft./lbs. and in./lbs.

ft lbs	N-m	ft lbs	N-m	ft lbs	N-m	ft lbs	N-m
0.1	0.1	33	44.7	74	100.3	115	155.9
0.2	0.3	34	46.1	75	101.7	116	157.3
0.3	0.4	35	47.4	76	103.0	117	158.6
0.4	0.5	36	48.8	77	104.4	118	160.0
0.5	0.7	37	50.7	78	105.8	119	161.3
0.6	0.8	38	51.5	79	107.1	120	162.7
0.7	1.0	39	52.9	80	108.5	121	164.0
0.8	1.1	40	54.2	81	109.8	122	165.4
0.9	1.2	41	55.6	82	111.2	123	166.8
1	1.3	42	56.9	83	112.5	124	168.1
2	2.7	43	58.3	84	113.9	125	169.5
3	4.1	44	59.7	85	115.2	126	170.8
4	5.4	45	61.0	86	116.6	127	172.2
5	6.8	46	62.4	87	118.0	128	173.5
6	8.1	47	63.7	88	119.3	129	174.9
7	9.5	48	65.1	89	120.7	130	176.2
8	10.8	49	66.4	90	122.0	131	177.6
9	12.2	50	67.8	91	123.4	132	179.0
10	13.6	51	69.2	92	124.7	133	180.3
11	14.9	52	70.5	93	126.1	134	181.7
12	16.3	53	71.9	94	127.4	135	183.0
13	17.6	54	73.2	95	128.8	136	184.4
14	18.9	55	74.6	96	130.2	137	185.7
15	20.3	56	75.9	97	131.5	138	187.1
16	21.7	57	77.3	98	132.9	139	188.5
17	23.0	58	78.6	99	134.2	140	189.8
18	24.4	59	80.0	100	135.6	141	191.2
19	25.8	60	81.4	101	136.9	142	192.5
20	27.1	61	82.7	102	138.3	143	193.9
21	28.5	62	84.1	103	139.6	144	195.2
22	29.8	63	85.4	104	141.0	145	196.6
23	31.2	64	86.8	105	142.4	146	198.0
24	32.5	65	88.1	106	143.7	147	199.3
25	33.9	66	89.5	107	145.1	148	200.7
26	35.2	67	90.8	108	146.4	149	202.0
27	36.6	68	92.2	109	147.8	150	203.4
28	38.0	69	93.6	110	149.1	151	204.7
29	39.3	70	94.9	111	150.5	152	206.1
30	40.7	71	96.3	112	151.8	153	207.4
31	42.0	72	97.6	113	153.2	154	208.8
32	43.4	73	99.0	114	154.6	155	210.2

ENGLISH TO METRIC CONVERSION: FORCE

Force is presently measured in pounds (lbs.). This type of measurement is used to measure spring pressure, specifically how many pounds it takes to compress a spring. Our present force unit (the pound) will be replaced in SI metric measurements by the Newton (N). This term will eventually see use in specifications for electric motor brush spring pressures, valve spring pressures, etc.

To convert pounds (lbs.) to Newton (N): multiply the number of lbs. by 4.45

lbs	N	lbs	N	lbs	N	oz	N
0.01	0.04	21	93.4	59	262.4	1	0.3
0.02	0.09	22	97.9	60	266.9	2	0.6
0.03	0.13	23	102.3	61	271.3	3	0.8
0.04	0.18	24	106.8	62	275.8	4	1.1
0.05	0.22	25	111.2	63	280.2	5	1.4
0.06	0.27	26	115.6	64	284.6	6	1.7
0.07	0.31	27	120.1	65	289.1	7	2.0
0.08	0.36	28	124.6	66	293.6	8	2.2
0.09	0.40	29	129.0	67	298.0	9	2.5
0.1	0.4	30	133.4	68	302.5	10	2.8
0.2	0.9	31	137.9	69	306.9	11	3.1
0.3	1.3	32	142.3	70	311.4	12	3.3
0.4	1.8	33	146.8	71	315.8	13	3.6
0.5	2.2	34	151.2	72	320.3	14	3.9
0.6	2.7	35	155.7	73	324.7	15	4.2
0.7	3.1	36	160.1	74	329.2	16	4.4
0.8	3.6	37	164.6	75	333.6	17	4.7
0.9	4.0	38	169.0	76	338.1	18	5.0
1	4.4	39	173.5	77	342.5	19	5.3
2	8.9	40	177.9	78	347.0	20	5.6
3	13.4	41	182.4	79	351.4	21	5.8
4	17.8	42	186.8	80	355.9	22	6.1
5	22.2	43	191.3	81	360.3	23	6.4
6	26.7	44	195.7	82	364.8	24	6.7
7	31.1	45	200.2	83	369.2	25	7.0
8	35.6	46	204.6	84	373.6	26	7.2
9	40.0	47	209.1	85	378.1	27	7.5
10	44.5	48	213.5	86	382.6	28	7.8
11	48.9	49	218.0	87	387.0	29	8.1
12	53.4	50	224.4	88	391.4	30	8.3
13	57.8	51	226.9	89	395.9	31	8.6
14	62.3	52	231.3	90	400.3	32	8.9
15	66.7	53	235.8	91	404.8	33	9.2
16	71.2	54	240.2	92	409.2	34	9.4
17	75.6	55	244.6	93	413.7	35	9.7
18	80.1	56	249.1	94	418.1	36	10.0
19	84.5	57	253.6	95	422.6	37	10.3
20	89.0	58	258.0	96	427.0	38	10.6

ENGLISH TO METRIC CONVERSION: LIQUID CAPACITY

Liquid or fluid capacity is presently expressed as pints, quarts or gallons, or a combination of all of these. In the metric system the liter (l) will become the basic unit. Fractions of a liter would be expressed as deciliters, centiliters, or most frequently (and commonly) as milliliters.

To convert pints (pts.) to liters (l): multiply the number of pints by .47
To convert liters (l) to pints (pts.): multiply the number of liters by 2.1
To convert quarts (qts.) to liters (l): multiply the number of quarts by .95

To convert liters (l) to quarts (qts.): multiply the number of liters by 1.06
To convert gallons (gals.) to liters (l): multiply the number of gallons by 3.8
To convert liters (l) to gallons (gals.): multiply the number of liters by .26

gals	liters	qts	liters	pts	liters
0.1	0.38	0.1	0.10	0.1	0.05
0.2	0.76	0.2	0.19	0.2	0.10
0.3	1.1	0.3	0.28	0.3	0.14
0.4	1.5	0.4	0.38	0.4	0.19
0.5	1.9	0.5	0.47	0.5	0.24
0.6	2.3	0.6	0.57	0.6	0.28
0.7	2.6	0.7	0.66	0.7	0.33
0.8	3.0	0.8	0.76	0.8	0.38
0.9	3.4	0.9	0.85	0.9	0.43
1	3.8	1	1.0	1	0.5
2	7.6	2	1.9	2	1.0
3	11.4	3	2.8	3	1.4
4	15.1	4	3.8	4	1.9
5	18.9	5	4.7	5	2.4
6	22.7	6	5.7	6	2.8
7	26.5	7	6.6	7	3.3
8	30.3	8	7.6	8	3.8
9	34.1	9	8.5	9	4.3
10	37.8	10	9.5	10	4.7
11	41.6	11	10.4	11	5.2
12	45.4	12	11.4	12	5.7
13	49.2	13	12.3	13	6.2
14	53.0	14	13.2	14	6.6
15	56.8	15	14.2	15	7.1
16	60.6	16	15.1	16	7.6
17	64.3	17	16.1	17	8.0
18	68.1	18	17.0	18	8.5
19	71.9	19	18.0	19	9.0
20	75.7	20	18.9	20	9.5
21	79.5	21	19.9	21	9.9
22	83.2	22	20.8	22	10.4
23	87.0	23	21.8	23	10.9
24	90.8	24	22.7	24	11.4
25	94.6	25	23.6	25	11.8
26	98.4	26	24.6	26	12.3
27	102.2	27	25.5	27	12.8
28	106.0	28	26.5	28	13.2
29	110.0	29	27.4	29	13.7
30	113.5	30	28.4	30	14.2

ENGLISH TO METRIC CONVERSION: PRESSURE

The basic unit of pressure measurement used today is expressed as pounds per square inch (psi). The metric unit for psi will be the kilopascal (kPa). This will apply to either fluid pressure or air pressure, and will be frequently seen in tire pressure readings, oil pressure specifications, fuel pump pressure, etc.

To convert pounds per square inch (psi) to kilopascals (kPa): multiply the number of psi by 6.89

Psi	kPa	Psi	kPa	Psi	kPa	Psi	kPa
0.1	0.7	37	255.1	82	565.4	127	875.6
0.2	1.4	38	262.0	83	572.3	128	882.5
0.3	2.1	39	268.9	84	579.2	129	889.4
0.4	2.8	40	275.8	85	586.0	130	896.3
0.5	3.4	41	282.7	86	592.9	131	903.2
0.6	4.1	42	289.6	87	599.8	132	910.1
0.7	4.8	43	296.5	88	606.7	133	917.0
0.8	5.5	44	303.4	89	613.6	134	923.9
0.9	6.2	45	310.3	90	620.5	135	930.8
1	6.9	46	317.2	91	627.4	136	937.7
2	13.8	47	324.0	92	634.3	137	944.6
3	20.7	48	331.0	93	641.2	138	951.5
4	27.6	49	337.8	94	648.1	139	958.4
5	34.5	50	344.7	95	655.0	140	965.2
6	41.4	51	351.6	96	661.9	141	972.2
7	48.3	52	358.5	97	668.8	142	979.0
8	55.2	53	365.4	98	675.7	143	985.9
9	62.1	54	372.3	99	682.6	144	992.8
10	69.0	55	379.2	100	689.5	145	999.7
11	75.8	56	386.1	101	696.4	146	1006.6
12	82.7	57	393.0	102	703.3	147	1013.5
13	89.6	58	399.9	103	710.2	148	1020.4
14	96.5	59	406.8	104	717.0	149	1027.3
15	103.4	60	413.7	105	723.9	150	1034.2
16	110.3	61	420.6	106	730.8	151	1041.1
17	117.2	62	427.5	107	737.7	152	1048.0
18	124.1	63	434.4	108	744.6	153	1054.9
19	131.0	64	441.3	109	751.5	154	1061.8
20	137.9	65	448.2	110	758.4	155	1068.7
21	144.8	66	455.0	111	765.3	156	1075.6
22	151.7	67	461.9	112	772.2	157	1082.5
23	158.6	68	468.8	113	779.1	158	1089.4
24	165.5	69	475.7	114	786.0	159	1096.3
25	172.4	70	482.6	115	792.9	160	1103.2
26	179.3	71	489.5	116	799.8	161	1110.0
27	186.2	72	496.4	117	806.7	162	1116.9
28	193.0	73	503.3	118	813.6	163	1123.8
29	200.0	74	510.2	119	820.5	164	1130.7
30	206.8	75	517.1	120	827.4	165	1137.6
31	213.7	76	524.0	121	834.3	166	1144.5
32	220.6	77	530.9	122	841.2	167	1151.4
33	227.5	78	537.8	123	848.0	168	1158.3
34	234.4	79	544.7	124	854.9	169	1165.2
35	241.3	80	551.6	125	861.8	170	1172.1
36	248.2	81	558.5	126	868.7	171	1179.0

ENGLISH TO METRIC CONVERSION: PRESSURE

The basic unit of pressure measurement used today is expressed as pounds per square inch (psi). The metric unit for psi will be the kilopascal (kPa). This will apply to either fluid pressure or air pressure, and will be frequently seen in tire pressure readings, oil pressure specifications, fuel pump pressure, etc.

To convert pounds per square inch (psi) to kilopascals (kPa): multiply the number of psi by 6.89

Psi	kPa	Psi	kPa	Psi	kPa	Psi	kPa
172	1185.9	216	1489.3	260	1792.6	304	2096.0
173	1192.8	217	1496.2	261	1799.5	305	2102.9
174	1199.7	218	1503.1	262	1806.4	306	2109.8
175	1206.6	219	1510.0	263	1813.3	307	2116.7
176	1213.5	220	1516.8	264	1820.2	308	2123.6
177	1220.4	221	1523.7	265	1827.1	309	2130.5
178	1227.3	222	1530.6	266	1834.0	310	2137.4
179	1234.2	223	1537.5	267	1840.9	311	2144.3
180	1241.0	224	1544.4	268	1847.8	312	2151.2
181	1247.9	225	1551.3	269	1854.7	313	2158.1
182	1254.8	226	1558.2	270	1861.6	314	2164.9
183	1261.7	227	1565.1	271	1868.5	315	2171.8
184	1268.6	228	1572.0	272	1875.4	316	2178.7
185	1275.5	229	1578.9	273	1882.3	317	2185.6
186	1282.4	230	1585.8	274	1889.2	318	2192.5
187	1289.3	231	1592.7	275	1896.1	319	2199.4
188	1296.2	232	1599.6	276	1903.0	320	2206.3
189	1303.1	233	1606.5	277	1909.8	321	2213.2
190	1310.0	234	1613.4	278	1916.7	322	2220.1
191	1316.9	235	1620.3	279	1923.6	323	2227.0
192	1323.8	236	1627.2	280	1930.5	324	2233.9
193	1330.7	237	1634.1	281	1937.4	325	2240.8
194	1337.6	238	1641.0	282	1944.3	326	2247.7
195	1344.5	239	1647.8	283	1951.2	327	2254.6
196	1351.4	240	1654.7	284	1958.1	328	2261.5
197	1358.3	241	1661.6	285	1965.0	329	2268.4
198	1365.2	242	1668.5	286	1971.9	330	2275.3
199	1372.0	243	1675.4	287	1978.8	331	2282.2
200	1378.9	244	1682.3	288	1985.7	332	2289.1
201	1385.8	245	1689.2	289	1992.6	333	2295.9
202	1392.7	246	1696.1	290	1999.5	334	2302.8
203	1399.6	247	1703.0	291	2006.4	335	2309.7
204	1406.5	248	1709.9	292	2013.3	336	2316.6
205	1413.4	249	1716.8	293	2020.2	337	2323.5
206	1420.3	250	1723.7	294	2027.1	338	2330.4
207	1427.2	251	1730.6	295	2034.0	339	2337.3
208	1434.1	252	1737.5	296	2040.8	240	2344.2
209	1441.0	253	1744.4	297	2047.7	341	2351.1
210	1447.9	254	1751.3	298	2054.6	342	2358.0
211	1454.8	255	1758.2	299	2061.5	343	2364.9
212	1461.7	256	1765.1	300	2068.4	344	2371.8
213	1468.7	257	1772.0	301	2075.3	345	2378.7
214	1475.5	258	1778.8	302	2082.2	346	2385.6
215	1482.4	259	1785.7	303	2089.1	347	2392.5

Troubleshooting Basic Air Conditioning Problems

Problem	Cause	Solution
There's little or no air coming from the vents (and you're sure it's on)	• The A/C fuse is blown • Broken or loose wires or connections • The on/off switch is defective	• Check and/or replace fuse • Check and/or repair connections • Replace switch
The air coming from the vents is not cool enough	• Windows and air vent wings open • The compressor belt is slipping • Heater is on • Condenser is clogged with debris • Refrigerant has escaped through a leak in the system • Receiver/drier is plugged	• Close windows and vent wings • Tighten or replace compressor belt • Shut heater off • Clean the condenser • Check system • Service system
The air has an odor	• Vacuum system is disrupted • Odor producing substances on the evaporator case • Condensation has collected in the bottom of the evaporator housing	• Have the system checked/repaired • Clean the evaporator case • Clean the evaporator housing drains
System is noisy or vibrating	• Compressor belt or mountings loose • Air in the system	• Tighten or replace belt; tighten mounting bolts • Have the system serviced

Sight glass condition
  Constant bubbles, foam or oil streaks
  Clear sight glass, but no cold air
  Clear sight glass, but air is cold
  Clouded with milky fluid
	
	• Undercharged system
	
	• No refrigerant at all
	• System is OK
	• Receiver drier is leaking dessicant
		
		• Charge the system
		
		• Check and charge the system
		
		• Have system checked

Large difference in temperature of lines	• System undercharged	• Charge and leak test the system
Compressor noise	• Broken valves • Overcharged • Incorrect oil level • Piston slap • Broken rings • Drive belt pulley bolts are loose	• Replace the valve plate • Discharge, evacuate and install the correct charge • Isolate the compressor and check the oil level. Correct as necessary. • Replace the compressor • Replace the compressor • Tighten with the correct torque specification
Excessive vibration	• Incorrect belt tension • Clutch loose • Overcharged • Pulley is misaligned	• Adjust the belt tension • Tighten the clutch • Discharge, evacuate and install the correct charge • Align the pulley
Condensation dripping in the passenger compartment	• Drain hose plugged or improperly positioned • Insulation removed or improperly installed	• Clean the drain hose and check for proper installation • Replace the insulation on the expansion valve and hoses
Frozen evaporator coil	• Faulty thermostat • Thermostat capillary tube improperly installed • Thermostat not adjusted properly	• Replace the thermostat • Install the capillary tube correctly • Adjust the thermostat
Low side low—high side low	• System refrigerant is low • Expansion valve is restricted	• Evacuate, leak test and charge the system • Replace the expansion valve
Low side high—high side low	• Internal leak in the compressor—worn	• Remove the compressor cylinder head and inspect the compressor. Replace the valve plate assembly if necessary. If the compressor pistons, rings or

Troubleshooting Basic Air Conditioning Problems (cont.)

Problem	Cause	Solution
Low side high—high side low (cont.)		cylinders are excessively worn or scored replace the compressor
	• Cylinder head gasket is leaking	• Install a replacement cylinder head gasket
	• Expansion valve is defective	• Replace the expansion valve
	• Drive belt slipping	• Adjust the belt tension
Low side high—high side high	• Condenser fins obstructed	• Clean the condenser fins
	• Air in the system	• Evacuate, leak test and charge the system
	• Expansion valve is defective	• Replace the expansion valve
	• Loose or worn fan belts	• Adjust or replace the belts as necessary
Low side low—high side high	• Expansion valve is defective	• Replace the expansion valve
	• Restriction in the refrigerant hose	• Check the hose for kinks—replace if necessary
	• Restriction in the receiver/drier	• Replace the receiver/drier
	• Restriction in the condenser	• Replace the condenser
Low side and high side normal (inadequate cooling)	• Air in the system	• Evacuate, leak test and charge the system
	• Moisture in the system	• Evacuate, leak test and charge the system

Troubleshooting Basic Wheel Problems

Problem	Cause	Solution
The car's front end vibrates at high speed	• The wheels are out of balance • Wheels are out of alignment	• Have wheels balanced • Have wheel alignment checked/adjusted
Car pulls to either side	• Wheels are out of alignment • Unequal tire pressure • Different size tires or wheels	• Have wheel alignment checked/adjusted • Check/adjust tire pressure • Change tires or wheels to same size
The car's wheel(s) wobbles	• Loose wheel lug nuts • Wheels out of balance • Damaged wheel • Wheels are out of alignment • Worn or damaged ball joint • Excessive play in the steering linkage (usually due to worn parts) • Defective shock absorber	• Tighten wheel lug nuts • Have tires balanced • Raise car and spin the wheel. If the wheel is bent, it should be replaced • Have wheel alignment checked/adjusted • Check ball joints • Check steering linkage • Check shock absorbers
Tires wear unevenly or prematurely	• Incorrect wheel size • Wheels are out of balance • Wheels are out of alignment	• Check if wheel and tire size are compatible • Have wheels balanced • Have wheel alignment checked/adjusted

Troubleshooting Basic Tire Problems

Problem	Cause	Solution
The car's front end vibrates at high speeds and the steering wheel shakes	• Wheels out of balance • Front end needs aligning	• Have wheels balanced • Have front end alignment checked
The car pulls to one side while cruising	• Unequal tire pressure (car will usually pull to the low side) • Mismatched tires • Front end needs aligning	• Check/adjust tire pressure • Be sure tires are of the same type and size • Have front end alignment checked
Abnormal, excessive or uneven tire wear See "How to Read Tire Wear"	• Infrequent tire rotation • Improper tire pressure • Sudden stops/starts or high speed on curves	• Rotate tires more frequently to equalize wear • Check/adjust pressure • Correct driving habits
Tire squeals	• Improper tire pressure • Front end needs aligning	• Check/adjust tire pressure • Have front end alignment checked

Tire Size Comparison Chart

"Letter" sizes			Inch Sizes	Metric-inch Sizes		
"60 Series"	"70 Series"	"78 Series"	1965–77	"60 Series"	"70 Series"	"80 Series"
			5.50-12, 5.60-12	165/60-12	165/70-12	155-12
		Y78-12	6.00-12			
		W78-13	5.20-13	165/60-13	145/70-13	135-13
		Y78-13	5.60-13	175/60-13	155/70-13	145-13
			6.15-13	185/60-13	165/70-13	155-13, P155/80-13
A60-13	A70-13	A78-13	6.40-13	195/60-13	175/70-13	165-13
B60-13	B70-13	B78-13	6.70-13	205/60-13	185/70-13	175-13
			6.90-13			
C60-13	C70-13	C78-13	7.00-13	215/60-13	195/70-13	185-13
D60-13	D70-13	D78-13	7.25-13			
E60-13	E70-13	E78-13	7.75-13			195-13
			5.20-14	165/60-14	145/70-14	135-14
			5.60-14	175/60-14	155/70-14	145-14
			5.90-14			
A60-14	A70-14	A78-14	6.15-14	185/60-14	165/70-14	155-14
	B70-14	B78-14	6.45-14	195/60-14	175/70-14	165-14
	C70-14	C78-14	6.95-14	205/60-14	185/70-14	175-14
D60-14	D70-14	D78-14				
E60-14	E70-14	E78-14	7.35-14	215/60-14	195/70-14	185-14
F60-14	F70-14	F78-14, F83-14	7.75-14	225/60-14	200/70-14	195-14
G60-14	G70-14	G77-14, G78-14	8.25-14	235/60-14	205/70-14	205-14
H60-14	H70-14	H78-14	8.55-14	245/60-14	215/70-14	215-14
J60-14	J70-14	J78-14	8.85-14	255/60-14	225/70-14	225-14
L60-14	L70-14		9.15-14	265/60-14	235/70-14	
	A70-15	A78-15	5.60-15	185/60-15	165/70-15	155-15
B60-15	B70-15	B78-15	6.35-15	195/60-15	175/70-15	165-15
C60-15	C70-15	C78-15	6.85-15	205/60-15	185/70-15	175-15
	D70-15	D78-15				
E60-15	E70-15	E78-15	7.35-15	215/60-15	195/70-15	185-15
F60-15	F70-15	F78-15	7.75-15	225/60-15	205/70-15	195-15
G60-15	G70-15	G78-15	8.15-15/8.25-15	235/60-15	215/70-15	205-15
H60-15	H70-15	H78-15	8.45-15/8.55-15	245/60-15	225/70-15	215-15
J60-15	J70-15	J78-15	8.85-15/8.90-15	255/60-15	235/70-15	225-15
	K70-15		9.00-15	265/60-15	245/70-15	230-15
L60-15	L70-15	L78-15, L84-15	9.15-15			235-15
	M70-15	M78-15				255-15
		N78-15				

Note: Every size tire is not listed and many size comparisons are approximate, based on load ratings. Wider tires than those supplied new with the vehicle, should always be checked for clearance.

2

ENGINE PERFORMANCE AND TUNE-UP

TUNE-UP PROCEDURES

In order to extract the full measure of performance and economy from your engine it is essential that it be properly tuned at regular intervals. A regular tune-up will keep your vehicle's engine running smoothly and will prevent the annoying minor breakdowns and poor performance associated with an untuned engine.

A complete tune-up should be performed every 12,000 miles or twelve months, whichever comes first. This interval should be halved if the vehicle is operated under severe conditions, such as trailer towing, prolonged idling, continual stop and start driving, or if starting or running problems are noticed. It is assumed that the routine maintenance described in Section 1 has been kept up, as this will have a decided effect on the results of a tune-up. All of the applicable steps of a tune-up should be followed in order, as the result is a cumulative one.

If the specifications on the tune-up sticker in the engine compartment disagree with the Tune-Up Specifications chart in this chapter, the figures on the sticker must be used. The sticker often reflects changes made during the production run.

Spark Plugs

A typical spark plug consists of a metal shell surrounding a ceramic insulator. A metal electrode extends downward through the center of the insulator and protrudes a small distance. Located at the end of the plug and attached to the side of the outer metal shell is the side electrode. The side electrode bends in at a 90° angle so that its tip is just past and parallel to the tip of the center electrode. The distance between these two electrodes (measured in thousandths of an inch or hundredths of a millimeter) is called the spark plug gap.

The spark plug does not produce a spark but instead provides a gap across which the current can arc. The coil produces anywhere from 20,000 to 50,000 volts (depending on the type and application) which travels through the wires to the spark plugs. The current passes along the center electrode and jumps the gap to the side electrode, and in doing so, ignites the air/fuel mixture in the combustion chamber.

SPARK PLUG HEAT RANGE

Spark plug heat range is the ability of the plug to dissipate heat. The longer the insulator (or the farther it extends into the en-

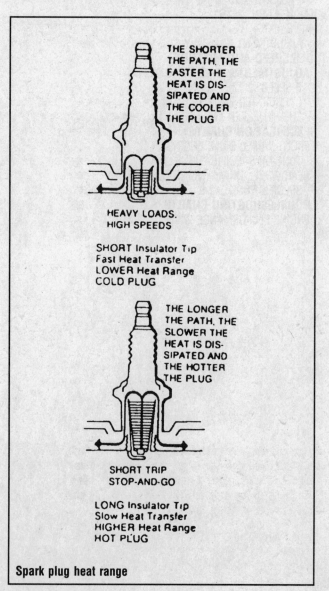

Cross-section of a spark plug

PORCELAIN INSULATOR

INSULATOR CRACKS OFTEN OCCUR HERE

SHELL

ADJUST FOR PROPER GAP

SIDE ELECTRODE (BEND TO ADJUST GAP)

CENTER ELECTRODE: FILE FLAT WHEN ADJUSTING GAP; DO NOT BEND

Spark plug heat range

THE SHORTER THE PATH, THE FASTER THE HEAT IS DISSIPATED AND THE COOLER THE PLUG

HEAVY LOADS, HIGH SPEEDS

SHORT Insulator Tip
Fast Heat Transfer
LOWER Heat Range
COLD PLUG

THE LONGER THE PATH, THE SLOWER THE HEAT IS DISSIPATED AND THE HOTTER THE PLUG

SHORT TRIP STOP-AND-GO

LONG Insulator Tip
Slow Heat Transfer
HIGHER Heat Range
HOT PLUG

gine), the hotter the plug will operate; the shorter the insulator (the closer the electrode is to the block's cooling passages) the cooler it will operate. A plug that absorbs little heat and remains too cool will quickly accumulate deposits of oil and carbon since it is not hot enough to burn them off. This leads to plug fouling and consequently to misfiring. A plug that absorbs too much heat will have no deposits but, due to the excessive heat, the electrodes will burn away quickly and might possibly lead to preignition or other ignition problems. Preignition takes place when plug tips get so hot that they glow sufficiently to ignite the air/fuel mixture before the actual spark occurs. This early ignition will usually cause a pinging during low speeds and heavy loads.

The general rule of thumb for choosing the correct heat range when picking a spark plug is: if most of your driving is long distance, high speed travel, use a colder plug; if most of your driving is stop and go, use a hotter plug. Original equipment plugs are generally a good compromise between the 2 styles and most people never have the need to change their plugs from the factory-recommended heat range.

REMOVAL & INSTALLATION

A set of spark plugs usually requires replacement after about 20,000–30,000 miles (32,000–48,000 km), depending on your style of driving. In normal operation plug gap increases about 0.001 in. (0.025mm) for every 2500 miles (4000 km). As the gap increases, the plug's voltage requirement also increases. It requires a greater voltage to jump the wider gap and about two to three times as much voltage to fire the plug at high speeds than at idle. The improved air/fuel ratio control of modern fuel injection combined with the higher voltage output of modern ignition systems will often allow an engine to run significantly longer on a set of standard spark plugs, but keep in mind that efficiency will drop as the gap widdens (along with fuel economy and power).

When you're removing spark plugs, work on one at a time. Don't start by removing the plug wires all at once, because, unless you number them, they may become mixed up. Take a minute before you begin and number the wires with tape.

1. Disconnect the negative battery cable, and if the vehicle has been run recently, allow the engine to thoroughly cool.

2. Carefully twist the spark plug wire boot to loosen it, then pull upward and remove the boot from the plug. Be sure to pull on the boot and not on the wire, otherwise the connector located inside the boot may become separated.

3. Using compressed air, blow any water or debris from the spark plug well to assure that no harmful contaminants are allowed to enter the combustion chamber when the spark plug is removed. If compressed air is not available, use a rag or a brush to clean the area.

➡**Remove the spark plugs when the engine is cold, if possible, to prevent damage to the threads. If removal of the plugs is difficult, apply a few drops of penetrating oil or silicone spray to the area around the base of the plug, and allow it a few minutes to work.**

4. Using a spark plug socket that is equipped with a rubber insert to properly hold the plug, turn the spark plug counterclockwise to loosen and remove the spark plug from the bore.

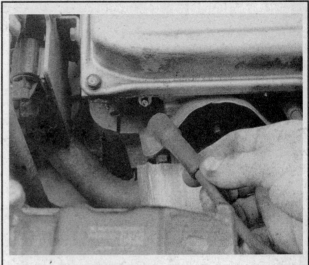

Pull the plug wire off by the boot

Loosen . . .

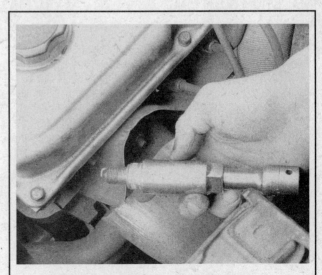

. . . then carefully remove and inspect the plug

✳✳ WARNING

Be sure not to use a flexible extension on the socket. Use of a flexible extension may allow a shear force to be applied to the plug. A shear force could break the plug off in the cylinder head, leading to costly and frustrating repairs.

To install:

5. Inspect the spark plug boot for tears or damage. If a damaged boot is found, the spark plug wire must be replaced.

6. Using a wire feeler gauge, check and adjust the spark plug gap. When using a gauge, the proper size should pass between the electrodes with a slight drag. The next larger size should not be able to pass while the next smaller size should pass freely.

7. Carefully thread the plug into the bore by hand. If resistance is felt before the plug is almost completely threaded, back the plug out and begin threading again. In small, hard to reach areas, an old spark plug wire and boot could be used as a threading tool. The boot will hold the plug while you twist the end of the wire and the wire is supple enough to twist before it would allow the plug to crossthread.

✳✳ WARNING

Do not use the spark plug socket to thread the plugs. Always carefully thread the plug by hand or using an old plug wire to prevent the possibility of crossthreading and damaging the cylinder head bore.

8. Carefully tighten the spark plug. If the plug you are installing is equipped with a crush washer, seat the plug, then tighten about 1/4 turn to crush the washer. If you are installing a tapered seat plug, tighten the plug to specifications provided by the vehicle or plug manufacturer.

9. Apply a small amount of silicone dielectric compound to the end of the spark plug lead or inside the spark plug boot to prevent sticking, then install the boot to the spark plug and push until it clicks into place. The click may be felt or heard, then gently pull back on the boot to assure proper contact.

INSPECTION & GAPPING

Check the plugs for deposits and wear. If they are not going to be replaced, clean the plugs thoroughly. Remember that any kind of deposit will decrease the efficiency of the plug. Plugs can be cleaned on a spark plug cleaning machine, which can sometimes be found in service stations, or you can do an acceptable job of cleaning with a stiff brush. If the plugs are cleaned, the electrodes must be filed flat. Use an ignition points file, not an emery board or the like, which will leave deposits. The electrodes must be filed perfectly flat with sharp edges; rounded edges reduce the spark plug voltage by as much as 50%.

Check spark plug gap before installation. The ground electrode (the L-shaped one connected to the body of the plug) must be parallel to the center electrode and the specified size wire gauge (please refer to the Tune-Up Specifications chart for details) must pass between the electrodes with a slight drag.

➡**NEVER adjust the gap on a used platinum type spark plug.**

Always check the gap on new plugs as they are not always set correctly at the factory. Do not use a flat feeler gauge when measuring the gap on a used plug, because the reading may be inaccurate. A round-wire type gapping tool is the best way to check the gap. The correct gauge should pass through the electrode gap with a slight drag. If you're in doubt, try one size smaller and one larger. The smaller gauge should go through easily, while the larger one shouldn't go through at all. Wire gapping tools usually have a bending tool attached. Use that to adjust the side electrode until the proper distance is obtained. Absolutely never attempt to bend the center electrode. Also, be careful not to bend the side electrode too far or too often as it may weaken and break off within the engine, requiring removal of the cylinder head to retrieve it.

A normally worn spark plug should have light tan or gray deposits on the firing tip

A carbon fouled plug, identified by soft, sooty, black deposits, may indicate an improperly tuned vehicle. Check the air cleaner, ignition components and engine control system

A physically damaged spark plug may be evidence of severe detonation in that cylinder. Watch that cylinder carefully between services, as a continued detonation will not only damage the plug, but could also damage the engine

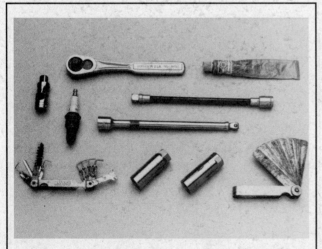

A variety of tools and gauges are needed for spark plug service

Checking the spark plug gap with a feeler gauge

An oil fouled spark plug indicates an engine with worn piston rings and/or bad valve seals allowing excessive oil to enter the chamber

This spark plug has been left in the engine too long, as evidenced by the extreme gap—Plugs with such an extreme gap can cause misfiring and stumbling accompanied by a noticeable lack of power

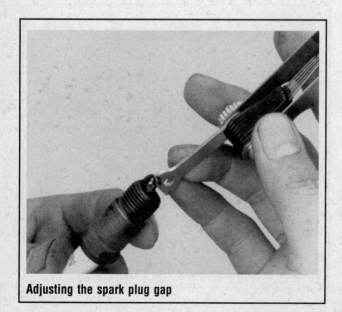

Adjusting the spark plug gap

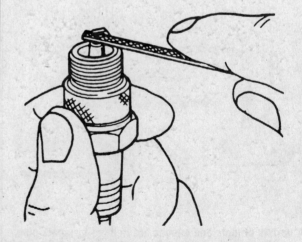

If the standard plug is in good condition, the electrode may be filed flat—CAUTION: do not file platinum plugs

Spark Plug Wires

INSPECTION

Visually inspect the spark plug cables for burns, cuts, or breaks in the insulation. Check the spark plug boots and the nipples on the distributor cap and coil. Replace any damaged wiring. If no physical damage is obvious, the wires can be checked with an ohmmeter for excessive resistance.

When installing a new set of spark plug cables, replace the cables one at a time so there will be no mixup. Start by replacing the longest cable first. Install the boot firmly over the spark plug. Route the wire exactly the same as the original. Insert the nipple firmly into the tower on the distributor cap. Repeat the process for each cable.

A bridged or almost bridged spark plug, identified by a build-up between the electrodes caused by excessive carbon or oil build-up on the plug

Checking individual plug wire resistance with a digital ohmmeter

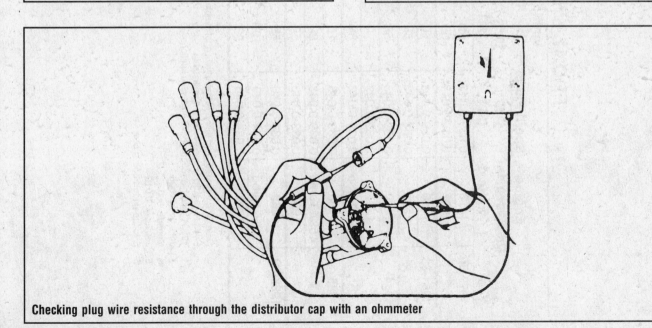

Checking plug wire resistance through the distributor cap with an ohmmeter

FRONT WHEEL DRIVE ENGINE TUNE-UP SPECIFICATIONS

Year	Engine Displacement Liters (cc)	Spark Plugs Gap (in.)	Ignition Timing (deg.) MT	Ignition Timing (deg.) AT	Distributor Dwell (deg.)	Distributor Gap (in.)	Idle Speed (rpm) MT	Idle Speed (rpm) AT	Valve Clearance In.	Valve Clearance Ex.
1979-80	1410	0.039-0.043	5B	-	49-55	0.018-0.021	850	-	0.006 ③	0.01
	1597	0.039-0.043	5B	5B	49-55	0.018-0.021	650	700	0.006 ③	0.01
1981-83	1410	0.039-0.043	5B	-	Electronic		650 ④	-	0.006 ③	0.01
	1597	0.039-0.043	5B	5B	Electronic		650 ④	700	0.006 ③	0.01
1984	1410	0.039-0.043	5B	-	Electronic		⑥	-	0.006 ⑤	0.01
	1597	0.039-0.043	-	5B	Electronic		-	700	0.006 ⑤	0.01
	1597 Turbo	0.039-0.043	8B	-	Electronic		⑥	-	0.006 ⑤	0.01
1985	1468	0.039-0.043	1B	1B	Electronic		⑥	⑥	0.006 ⑤	0.01
	1597 Turbo	0.039-0.043	8B	8B	Electronic		⑥	⑥	0.006 ⑤	0.01
	1997	0.039-0.043	5B	5B	Electronic		700	700	Hyd. ⑤	Hyd.
1986-89	1468	0.039-0.040	5B	5B	Electronic		⑥	⑥	0.006 ⑤	0.01
	1597 Turbo	0.039-0.040	10B	-	Electronic		⑥	⑥	0.006 ⑤	0.01
	1997	0.039-0.040	5B	5B	Electronic		⑥	⑥	Hyd. ⑤	Hyd.

Note: The information in this chart generally applicable to most vehicles. It is possible that specifications may have been changed on your particular car. If the figures found on the underhood

Hyd.: Hydraulic lash adjuster; not adjustable

1 1980 California models have electronic ignitions
3 Jet valve: 0.006
4 Canada: 850
5 Jet valve: 0.010
6 See the underhood sticker

REAR WHEEL DRIVE ENGINE TUNE-UP SPECIFICATIONS

Year	Engine Displacement Liters (cc)	Spark Plugs Gap (in.)	Ignition Timing (deg.) MT	AT	Distributor Dwell (deg.)	Gap (in.)	Idle Speed (rpm) MT	AT	Valve Clearance In.	Ex.
1971	1597	0.030	0	0	49-55	0.018-0.022	700-750	700-750	0.006	0.01
1972-73	1597	0.030	0	0	49-55	0.018-0.022	800-850	800-850	0.006	0.01
1974	1597	0.030	-	0	49-55	0.018-0.022	850	850	0.006	0.01
1974	1994	0.030	3B	3B	49-55	0.018-0.022	850	850	0.006	0.01
1975	1597	0.030	5A	5A	49-55	0.018-0.022	800-900	800-900	0.006	0.01
1975	1994	0.030	5A	5A	49-55	0.018-0.022	800-900	800-900	0.006	0.01
1976	1597	0.030	TDC	TDC	49-55	0.018-0.022	900-1000	800-900	0.006	0.01
1976	1994	0.030	3B	3B	49-55	0.018-0.022	900-1000	800-900	0.006	0.01
1977	1597	0.028-0.031	5B (1)	5B (1)	49-55	0.018-0.022	950 (2)	850 (2)	0.006	0.01
1977	1997	0.028-0.031	5B (1)	5B (1)	49-55	0.018-0.022	950 (2)	850 (2)	0.006	0.01
1978	1597	0.039-0.043 (3)	5B	5B	49-55	0.018-0.022	650 (2)	700 (2)	0.006 (6)	0.01
1978	1994	0.039-0.043 (3)	5B (3)	5B	49-55	0.018-0.022	650 (2)	700 (2)	0.006 (6)	0.01
1978	2555	0.039-0.043 (3)	7B (7)	7B	49-55	0.018-0.022	850 (2)	850 (2)	0.006 (6)	0.01
1979	1597	0.039-0.043 (3)	5B	5B	49-55	0.018-0.022	650 (8)	650 (8)	0.006 (6)	0.01
1979	1994	0.028-0.031	5B	5B	Electronic		850	850 (2)	0.006 (6)	0.01
1979	2555	0.039-0.043 (3)	7B	7B	Electronic		850	850	0.006 (6)	0.01
1980	1597	0.039-0.043 (3)	5B (11)	5B	49-55	0.018-0.022	750	750 (2)	0.006 (6)	0.01
1980	2555	0.039-0.043 (3)	7B	7B	Electronic		750	750 (2)	0.006 (6)	0.01
1981	1597	0.039-0.043 (3)	5B	5B	Electronic		650	700 (2)	0.006 (6)	0.01
1981	2555	0.039-0.043 (3)	7B	7B	Electronic		800	800 (2)	0.006 (6)	0.01
1982	1597	0.039-0.043 (3)	5B	5B	Electronic		700	750 (2)	0.006 (6)	0.01
1982	2555	0.039-0.043	7B	7B	Electronic		750	750 (2)	0.006 (6)	0.01
1983	2555	0.039-0.043	7B	7B	Electronic		750	800 (2)	0.006 (6)	0.01
1984-85	2555	0.039-0.043	10B	10B	Electronic		850	800	0.006 (6)	0.01
1986-89	2555	0.039-0.043	10B	10B	Electronic		850	850	(12)	(12)

Note: The information in this chart generally applicable to most vehicles. It is possible that specifications may have been changed on your particular car. If the figures found on the underhood sticker disagree, use the sticker information.

1 California-dual diaphragm: 5B High altitude-dual diaphragm: TDC
2 Canada: 850
3 Canada: 1597; 0.028-0.031 1994; 0.028-0.031 2555; 0.028-0.031
4 High altitude: 10B
5 California: 700 manual; 750 automatic Canada: 850

6 Jet valve (USA); 0.006
7 High altitude: 12B
8 California-1597 700 automatic
9 Canada only
10 California with electronic ignition Air gap:0.008-0.024

11 California: 7B
12 Hydraulic adjusters: jet valve 0.010 hot

REMOVAL & INSTALLATION

1. When removing spark plug wires, use great care.
2. Grasp and twist the insulator back and forth on the spark plug to free the insulator.

➡**Do not pull on the wire directly as it may become separated from the connector inside the insulator.**

To install:

3. Install each wire in or on the proper terminal of the distributor cap. Be sure the terminal connector inside the insulator is fully seated. The No. 1 terminal is identified on the cap.

4. Remove the brackets from the old spark plug wire set and install them on the new set in the same relative position. Install the wires in the brackets on the valve rocker arm covers. Connect the wires to the proper spark plugs. Install the coil high tension lead.

5. Wires must be positioned in the bracket in a special order to avoid cylinder cross-fire. Be sure to position the wire in the bracket in the order from front to rear.

FIRING ORDERS

♦ **See Figures 1, 2 and 3**

➡**To avoid confusion, remove and tag the spark plug wires one at a time, for replacement.**

If a distributor is not keyed for installation with only one orientation, it could have been removed previously and rewired. The resultant wiring would hold the corr firing order, but could change the relative placement of the plug towers in relation to the engine. For this reason it is imperative that you label all wires before disconnecting any of them. Also, before removal, compare the current wiring with the accompanying illustrations. If the current wiring does not match, make notes in your book to reflect how your engine is wired.

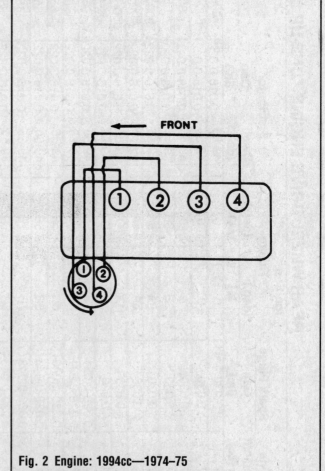

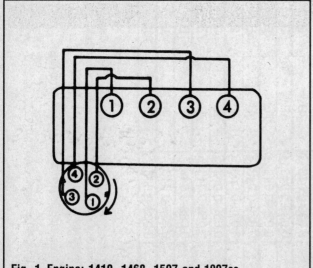

Fig. 1 Engine: 1410, 1468, 1597 and 1997cc
    Firing order: 1–3–4–2
    Distributor rotation: clockwise

Fig. 2 Engine: 1994cc—1974–75
    Firing order: 1–3–4–2
    Distributor rotation: counterclockwise

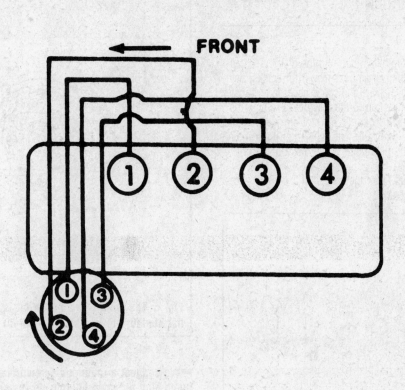

Fig 3 Engine: 1994 and 2555cc—1976 and later
Firing order: 1–3–4–2
Distributor rotation: clockwise

POINT TYPE IGNITION

Breaker Points and Condenser

The points function as a circuit breaker for the primary circuit of the ignition system. The ignition coil must boost the 12 volts of electrical pressure supplied by the battery to as much as 25,000 volts in order to fire the spark plugs. To do this, the coil depends on the points and condenser to make a clean break in the primary circuit.

The coil has both primary and secondary circuits. When the ignition is turned on, the battery supplies voltage through the coil and on to the points. The points are connected to ground, completing the primary circuit. As the current passes through the coil, a magnetic field is created in the iron center core of the coil. As the cam in the distributor turns, the points open and the primary circuit is interrupted. The magnetic field in the primary circuit of the coil collapses and cuts through the secondary circuit windings around the iron core. Because of the scientific phenomenon called electromagnetic induction, the battery voltage is at this point increased to a level sufficient to fire the spark plugs.

When the points open, the electrical charge in the primary circuit jumps the gap created between the two opened contacts of the points. If this charge were not transferred elsewhere, the metal contacts of the points would melt to change rapidly. If the gap is not maintained, the points will not break the primary circuit. If the primary circuit is not broken, the secondary circuit will not have enough voltage to fire the spark plugs.

The function of the condenser is to absorb excessive voltage from the points when they open and thus prevent the points from becoming pitted or burned.

There are two ways to check the breaker point gap. It can be done with a feeler gauge or a dwell meter. Either way you set the points, you are basically adjusting the amount of time that the points remain open. The time is measured in degrees of distributor rotation. When you measure the gap between the breaker points with a feeler gauge, you are setting the maximum amount the points will open when the rubbing block on the points is on the high point of the distributor cam. When you adjust the points with a dwell meter, you are adjusting the number of degrees that the points will remain closed before they start to open as a high point of the distributor cam approaches the rubbing block of the points.

When you replace a set of points, always replace the condenser at the same time.

When you change the point gap or dwell, you will also have changed the ignition timing. So, if the point gap or dwell is changed, the ignition timing must be adjusted also. Changing the ignition timing, however, does not affect the dwell of the breaker points.

REMOVAL & INSTALLATION

♦ **See Figures 4, 5 and 6**

1. Snap off the two spring clips that hold the distributor cap to the distributor. Remove the cap and examine it for cracks, deterioration, or carbon tracking. Replace the cap if necessary; transfer one wire at a time from the old cap to the new one. Examine the rotor for corrosion or wear and replace it if it's at all questionable.

2. Turn the engine with the crankshaft pulley until the rubbing block on the points is on the high point of the distributor cam. (Rotor removed).

3. Observe which screws retain the ground and primary wires. Remove the two retaining screws.

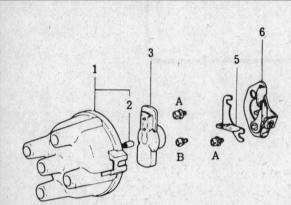

1. Distributor cap
2. Carbon button (1 and 2 are an assembly)
3. Rotor
5. Lubricator wick plate
6. Point set
A. Point and wick plate retaining screws
B. Eccentric adjusting screw (1971–74 models only)

Fig. 4 Exploded view of the tune-up related components on a breaker point ignition

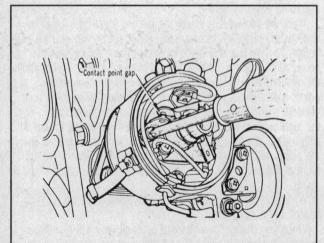

Fig. 5 The point gap adjustment is made with an eccentric screw—1971–74 models

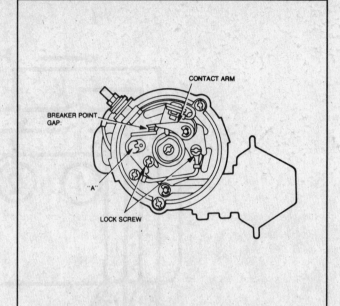

Fig. 6 The point gap adjustment is made by twisting a flat bladed tool in slot A—1975–80 models

➡We suggest a magnetic screwdriver, a screw start or some kind of screw holding device so you will not drop the retaining screws into the distributor or onto the ground.

To install:

4. Remove the distributor breaker points.

5. Install the new set of points; make sure that the pin on the bottom of the points engages the hole in the breaker plate.

6. Install the lubricator wick primary and ground wires and two retaining screws. Tighten the screws slightly snug.

7. Check to be sure that the rubbing block on the points is on the high part of the distributor cam.

8. On 1971–74 models, gap adjustment is made by turning the eccentric screw in or out as necessary to bring it within specs. On 1975 and later models, point adjustment is made by using a screwdriver in the slot provided and pivoting it to open or close the gap. Refer to the underhood decal or the Tune-Up specifications in this section for the correct point setting.

9. When the gap is correct, tighten the retaining screws.

10. Install the rotor and distributor cap.

11. The condenser is mounted on the outside of the distributor. Undo the mounting screw and the terminal screw or slide connector to replace the condenser.

DWELL ADJUSTMENT

1. Adjust the points with a feeler gauge as described.

2. Follow the directions that come with the dwell meter and connect it to your ignition circuit. One lead of the meter is connected to a ground and the other lead is to be connected to the distributor post on the coil. An adapter is usually provided for this purpose.

3. If the dwell meter has a zero set adjustment on it, make sure to zero the meter.

4. Start the engine and allow it to idle.

5. Observe the reading on the dwell meter. If the reading is within the specified range, turn OFF the engine and remove the dwell meter.

6. If the reading is above the specified range, the breaker point gap is too small. If the reading is below the specified range, the gap is too large. In either case, the engine must be stopped and the gap adjusted. After making the adjustment, start the engine and recheck the reading on the dwell meter. When the correct reading is obtained, disconnect the dwell meter.

7. Check and adjust the ignition timing.

ELECTRONIC IGNITION SYSTEM

Description and Operation

There are two major differences between the electronic ignition system and the point type system. First, the point and condenser are replaced by an induction type impulse sender. Second, an electronic ignition control unit has been added to amplify the electrical impulses between the distributor and the coil. The impulse sender is located inside the distributor where the points used to be. Instead of opening and closing an electrical circuit, the sender opens and closes a magnetic circuit. This induces impulses in a magnetic pick-up. The sender consists of a stator, pick-up, rotor signal (reluctor), and permanent magnet. The stator and reluctor each have the same number of teeth as there are cylinders. The permanent magnet creates a magnetic field which goes through the stator. The circuit is closed when the teeth are opposite each other. This means that the reluctor opens and closes the magnetic field while rotating. This generates current pulses in the magnetic pick-up. The electronic ignition control unit, located inside or outside of the distributor (depending on year, engine and model) usually consists of a power transmitter chip and ceramic board containing a monolithic IC (integrated circuit), several passive components and a thick film circuit. The electronic ignition control unit amplifies the impulses from the sender and controls the dwell angle.

IGNITION TIMING

Timing

Ignition timing is the measurement, in degrees of crankshaft rotation, of the point at which the spark plugs fire in each of the cylinders. It is measured in degrees before or after Top Dead Center (TDC) of the compression stroke. Ignition timing is controlled by turning the distributor body in the engine.

Ideally, the air/fuel mixture in the cylinder will be ignited by the spark plug just as the piston passes TDC of the compression stroke. If this happens, the piston will be beginning the power stroke just as the compressed and ignited air/fuel mixture starts to expand. The expansion of the air/fuel mixture then forces the piston down on the power stroke and turns the crankshaft.

Because it takes a fraction of a second for the spark plug to ignite the mixture in the cylinder, and the spark plug must fire a little before the piston reaches TDC. Otherwise, the mixture will not be completely ignited as the piston passes TDC and the full power of the explosion will not be used by the engine.

The timing measurement is given in degrees of crankshaft rotation before the piston reaches TDC (BTDC). If the setting for the ignition times is 5 degrees BTDC, each spark plug must fire 5 degrees before each piston reaches TDC. This only holds true, however, when the engine is at idle speed.

As the engine speed increases, the pistons go faster. The spark plugs have to ignite the fuel even sooner if it is to be completely ignited when the piston reaches TDC. To do this, the distributor has a means to advance the timing of the spark as the engine speed increases. This is accomplished by centrifugal weights within the distributor and, sometimes, a vacuum diaphragm mounted on the side of the distributor.

If the ignition is set too far advanced (BTDC), the ignition and expansion of the fuel in the cylinder will occur too soon and tend to force the piston down while it is still traveling up. This causes engine ping. If the ignition spark is set too far retarded after TDC (ATDC), the piston will have already passed TDC and started on its way down when the fuel is ignited. This will cause the piston to be forced down for only a portion of its travel. This will result in poor engine performance and lack of power.

The ignition timing is best checked with a timing light. This device is connected in series with the No. 1 spark plug or the coil wire, depending on type of timing light. The current that fires the spark plug also causes the timing light to flash.

Ignition timing should always be checked as a part of any tune-up. Timing is checked after the points have been adjusted or replaced.

INSPECTION AND ADJUSTMENT

1971–74 Models
▶ See Figure 7

1. Attach the timing light according to the instructions that came with the light.

2. Locate the timing tab on the front of the engine near the crankshaft pulley. Mark the **T** or appropriate line (check tune-up specifications), and the notch in the crankshaft pulley with chalk so they will be more visible.

3. Disconnect and plug the hose to the vacuum advance unit on the distributor.

4. Start the engine and allow it to reach operating temperature.

5. Shine the timing light at the crankshaft pulley marks. The marked line should align with pulley notch.

6. If the marks do not align, loosen the distributor mounting nut and rotate the distributor slowly in either direction to align the timing marks.

7. Tighten the mounting nut when the ignition timing is correct. Shut off engine and remove timing light.

8. The vacuum advance can be adjusted by means of a phillips screw located near the diaphragm. This adjustment is rarely needed. The checking procedure is performed in the same manner as outlined above, except that the vacuum line is left attached. Loosen the two retaining screws and turn the adjusting screw as necessary.

1975–78 Models
▶ See Figures 8 and 9

The distributor used from 1975 and later, is equipped with either a single or dual-diaphragm vacuum advance unit, depending upon the locale in which the car is sold, due to emission control regulations.

The retard section of the dual-diaphragm unit is located on the distributor side, with the advance section located on the opposite side of the advanced mechanism. The retard section is activated during the engine idle and deacceleration cycles.

At idle, the basic ignition timing is retarded to 5 degrees ATDC by the vacuum retard unit. Basic timing is checked with the rub-

ber plug removed from the advance/retard unit the vacuum lines are not removed and plugged as on the single unit diaphragm equipped distributor. To adjust the timing:

1. Attach the timing light and tachometer according to the instructions that came with the light or tachometer.

2. Locate the timing tab line on the front of the engine and the notch on the crankshaft pulley. Mark them with chalk.

3. Remove the rubber plug on dual diaphragm unit, or remove and plug the line on single units.

4. Start the engine and allow it to reach operating temperature, adjust idle speed if necessary.

5. Shine the timing light at the crankshaft pulley marks. The marked line should align with the pulley notch.

6. If the marks do not align, loosen the distributor mounting

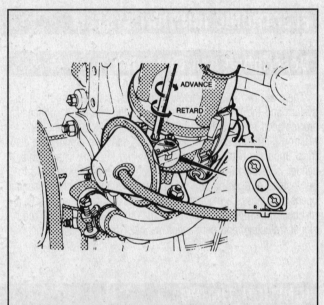

Fig. 8 Remove the rubber plug and fine tune the timing

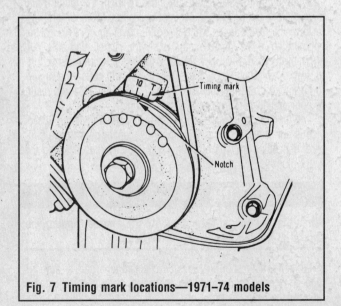

Fig. 7 Timing mark locations—1971-74 models

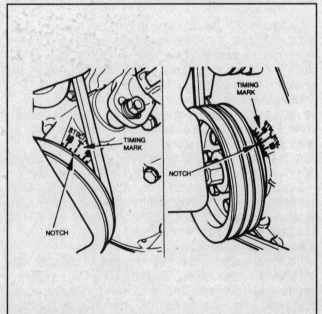

Fig. 9 Timing mark locations—1975 and later models shown

nut and rotate the distributor slowly in either direction to align the timing marks.

7. Tighten the mounting nut when the ignition timing is correct. Adjust idle speed.

8. Replace the rubber plug (dual diaphragm) and check the retarded timing. Adjustment is made by loosening the two diaphragm mounting screws and turning the phillips adjusting screw as necessary to bring timing into specs. Shut OFF engine and remove timing light.

1979 and Later Models

1. Attach the timing light and tachometer according to the instructions that came with the light or tachometer.

2. Locate the timing tab line on the front of the engine and the notch on the crankshaft pulley. Mark them with chalk.

3. Disconnect the vacuum advance hose and plug it, on models equipped. Start the engine and allow it to reach operating temperature. Adjust idle speed if necessary.

4. Shine the timing light at the crankshaft pulley marks. The marked line should align with the pulley notch.

5. If the marks do not align, loosen the distributor mounting nut and rotate the distributor slowly in either direction to align the timing marks.

6. Tighten the mounting nut when the ignition timing is correct, adjust idle speed. Shut OFF engine, remove timing light and tachometer.

➡**Some models are equipped with an ignition adjustment connector mounted on the fender well. After establishing the correct curb idle speed, on these models, stop the engine and disconnect the water-proof female connector from the adjustment connector. Connect a jumper wire to the ignition adjustment terminal and ground it. Start the engine and adjust the base timing as required. Stop the engine, remove the jumper and connect the water-proof connector. Start the engine and check the timing. The timing should have increased about five degrees.**

VALVE LASH

Valve adjustment determines how far the valves enter the cylinder and how long they stay open and closed.

If the valve clearance is too large, part of the lift of the camshaft will be used in removing the excessive clearance. Consequently, the valve will not be opening as far as it should. This condition has two effects: the valve train components will emit a tapping sound as they take up the excessive clearance and the engine will perform poorly because the valves don't open fully and allow the proper amount of gases to flow into and out of the engine.

If the valve clearance is too small, the intake valve and the exhaust valves will open too far and they will not fully seat on the cylinder head when they close. When a valve seats itself on the cylinder head, it does two things: it seals the combustion chamber so that none of the gases in the cylinder escape and it cools itself by transferring some of the heat it absorbs from the combustion in the cylinder to the cylinder head and to the engine's cooling system. If the valve clearance is too small, the engine will run poorly because of the gases escaping from the combustion chamber. The valves will also become overheated and will warp, since they cannot transfer heat unless they are touching the valve seat in the cylinder head.

➡**While all valve adjustments must be made as accurately as possible, it is better to have the valve adjustment slightly loose than slightly tight as a burned valve may result from overly tight adjustments.**

Valve

ADJUSTMENT

Models Without A Jet Valve
◆ See Figure 10

Valve clearance is adjusted with the engine stopped. When adjusting the valves cold, after the engine has been rebuilt or a valve job done on the cylinder head, proceed as follows:

1. Adjust the valves in the order as shown in hot adjustment—Step 8.

2. Turn the crankshaft pulley to bring the piston to top dead center (TDC) of the compression stroke of the cylinder being adjusted. Loosen the two rocker adjusting screw locknuts.

3. Using a 0.08mm feeler gauge for the intake and a 0.18mm gauge for the exhaust, turn the adjusting screw until the clearance is correct.

4. Tighten the locknuts to 7–9 ft. lbs.

The normal valve clearance adjustment, or final adjustment after the above initial cold adjustment, is performed as follows. To adjust the valves:

1. Run the engine until it reaches normal operating temperature and then turn it OFF.

2. Remove the air cleaner. Pull the large crankcase ventilation hose off the front of the air cleaner. Disconnect the two smaller hoses, one goes to the rear of the rocker arm cover and the other to the intake manifold.

Fig. 10 Adjusting the valve clearance on models without a jet valve

3. Loosen and remove the nuts and one bracket which attach the air cleaner to the rocker arm cover.

4. Lift the bottom housing of the air cleaner off of the carburetor and, with it, the hose coming up from the exhaust manifold heat stove.

5. Unsnap the spark plug wires from their clips on the rocker arm cover.

6. Loosen and remove the two rocker arm cover bolts. The rear bolt is a crankcase ventilation fitting, so you will have to use a deep socket or a box wrench.

7. Carefully lift the rocker arm cover off the cylinder head. Using a ⁵⁄₁₆″ allen socket (1597cc) or a regular socket (1994cc) and a torque wrench, make sure that the cylinder head bolts are all tightened to 58–62 ft. lbs. on 1597cc engines, 72–79 ft. lbs. on 1994cc engines.

8. Hot valve clearance is 0.15mm for the intake valves and 0.25mm for the exhaust.

9. Turn the crankshaft pulley to bring the piston to top dead center (TDC) of the compression stroke on the cylinder being adjusted. See step 8. Both valves will be closed at this point and the rocker arms will be resting on the heel of the camshaft lobe (the round side, not the egg-shaped side).

10. Loosen the two rocker arm adjusting screw locknuts.

11. Using the correct thickness feeler gauge, turn the adjusting screw until the gauge just snaps through the valve stem and the rocker arm.

12. Proceed to adjust the valves of each cylinder. Remember to bring each piston to TDC.

➡**The importance of correctly setting the valve clearance cannot be overemphasized. The clearance must be right or peak performance and efficiency will never be realized. Loose valve clearances will result in excessive wear and valve train chatter; tight valve clearance will result in burnt valve seats.**

13. Apply non-hardening sealer to the rocker arm cover gasket. Always use a new gasket.

14. Install the cover, hoses, spark plug wires and the air cleaner and remaining components. Tighten the rocker arm cover bolts to 4–5 ft. lbs.

15. Start the engine and check for leaks.

1978 and Later with Jet Valve

◗ **See Figures 11, 12 and 13**

➡**The 1985 and later Vista and late model Conquest engines have automatic lash adjusters incorporated in the rocker arms of the intake and exhaust valves. These valves are not adjustable. The Jet Valve is, however, adjustable in the same manner as other engines.**

A jet valve has been added to the combustion chamber (US models). Its adjuster is located on the intake valve rocker arm. The jet valve must be adjusted before the intake valve adjustment is done.

1. Start engine and allow it to reach normal operating temperature.

➡**Do not run engine with rocker arm cover removed, oil will be sprayed on to the hot exhaust manifold.**

2. Shut OFF engine and remove the rocker arm cover and all spark plugs.

3. Turn the crankshaft clockwise until the timing marks (TDC)

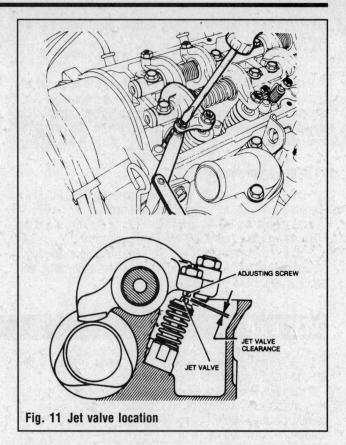

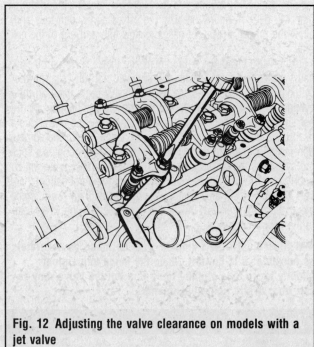

Fig. 11 Jet valve location

Fig. 12 Adjusting the valve clearance on models with a jet valve

are aligned. No. 1 piston should be at top dead center (TDC). When No. 1 piston is at TDC, the following valves can be adjusted: No. 1 intake, exhaust and jet valve. No. 2 intake and jet valve. No. 3 exhaust. Watch the valve operation on No. 1 cylinder while turning the crankshaft to close the exhaust valve and have the intake valve just begin to open. This places the No. 4 cylinder on TDC of its firing stroke and permits the adjustment of follow-

Exhaust Valve Closing	Adjust
No. 1 Cylinder	No. 4 Cylinder Valves
No. 2 Cylinder	No. 3 Cylinder Valves
No. 3 Cylinder	No. 2 Cylinder Valves
No. 4 Cylinder	No. 1 Cylinder Valves

Fig. 13 Exhaust valve closing chart

Tighten the screw until a slight drag is felt on the gauge

ing valves: No. 2 exhaust. No. 3 intake and jet valve. No. 4 intake, exhaust and jet valve.

➡On 1981 and later front wheel drive models with the K engine (1597cc) a crankshaft pulley access hole is located on the left side fender shield. Remove the covering plug and use a ratchet extension to turn the crankshaft when adjusting the valves.

4. Jet valves must be adjusted before the intake valve. To adjust the jet valves:

  a. Loosen the intake valve locknut and back off the adjustment screw two or more turns.

  b. Loosen the locknut on the jet valve adjusting screw. Turn the jet valve adjusting screw counter clockwise and insert a 0.15mm feeler gauge between the valve stem and the adjusting screw.

  c. Tighten the adjusting screw until it touches the feeler gauge.

➡The jet valve spring is weak, be careful not to force the jet valve in.

  d. After adjustment is made, hold the adjusting screw with a screwdriver and tighten the locknut.

5. Proceed to adjust the intake and the exhaust valves on the same cylinder as the jet valve you finished adjusting and move on to the next cylinder.

IDLE SPEED AND MIXTURE ADJUSTMENTS

Idle Speed

CARBURETED ENGINES

1971–72 Models

The Colt carburetor is equipped with five adjustment screws, but don't become immediately alarmed and confused. For tune-up purposes, we will only be using two of these screws: the curb idle screw and the throttle positioner screw. Other carburetor adjustments are outlined in Section 5. To set the idle speed:

1. Attach a dwell/tach to the engine. Start the engine and run it until the normal operating temperature is reached.

2. Observe the idle speed.

3. If your idle speed differs from those specified in the Tune-Up Specifications chart, turn the curb idle screw to correct it.

➡Make sure that you are turning the correct screw as shown in the illustration. Do not mistake the throttle positioner screw for the curb idle screw. Do not adjust the air/fuel mixture screw, readily identified by its plastic limiter cap. A CO meter is required to check any adjustment, so refer this service to your dealer or garage. If a CO meter is available, the specified CO values are 3.5%–5% for 1971, 3.5%+1% for 1972. To adjust the throttle positioner:

1. Bring the engine to operating temperature.

2. Attach a dwell/tachometer to the engine.

3. Disconnect and plug the hose which connects the air cleaner and the intake manifold at the manifold end.

4. Remove the air cleaner.

5. Disconnect the negative (green) solenoid lead from the terminal.

6. Accelerate the engine to 2,500 rpm a few times.

7. Maintain the engine speed and ground the green negative wire to the carburetor to switch the solenoid ON.

8. Release the throttle and check the engine rpm, which should be 1,350–1,450 rpm.

9. If the engine speed is incorrect, adjust the throttle positioner screw.

➡Some 1971 models are equipped with an adjusting nut rather than a screw, but the adjustment procedure is the same.

10. Install the solenoid wire and vacuum hose. Install the air cleaner.

1973–74 Models
▶ See Figures 14 and 15

This carburetor is similar to the one used on previous models except that the decel throttle positioner has been eliminated. On 1974 1600cc models equipped with a manual transmission and sold in California are additionally equipped with a decel dashpot.

Idle speed and mixture screws are in the same locations as 1971–72 models. Don't confuse them with the fast idle or dashpot screws.

1. Run the engine at idle speed until it reaches normal operating temperature.

2. Hook-up a tachometer and observe the idle speed.

3. If the idle speed differs from that given in the Tune-Up Specifications chart, turn the curb idle screw to correct it.

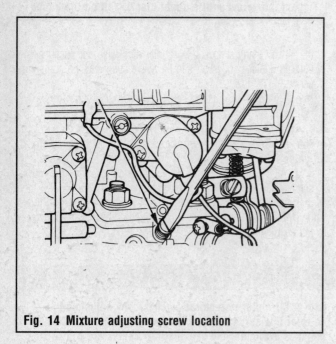
Fig. 14 Mixture adjusting screw location

➡ Air/fuel idle mixture should only be adjusted when a CO meter is available to obtain the CO level of 3–4.5%. To adjust the dashpot on models so equipped:

1. After adjusting the idle speed, push up on the lower end of the dashpot until it stops. Engine idle speed should increase to 1,500–2,000 rpm.

2. Quickly releasing the pushrod should cause the idle to drop to normal after a 1.5–3.5 second pause.

3. If the idle speed returns to normal too slowly, correct it with the adjustment screw.

1975–77 Models

1. Warm the engine to normal operating temperature.

2. Disconnect the air shut-off solenoid electrical plug. This is located under the air control valve which is on the left-side of the engine. This equipment is part of the air injection system.

3. Adjust the idle speed to 900 rpm on manual transmission cars or 800 rpm on automatic transmission cars. Do this with the carburetor idle speed adjusting screw on manual cars. Be careful that the screw doesn't contact the throttle arm. Use the throttle positioner screw on automatic cars.

4. Connect the air shut-off solenoid.

5. On manual cars, adjust engine speed to 1,000 rpm. On automatic cars, set the engine speed to 900 rpm.

6. On automatic cars only, remove the rubber plug from the vacuum unit on the distributor. Adjust the idle speed to 800 rpm, reinstall the rubber plug.

7. Race the engine to about 2,500 rpm a few times and observe that it returns to normal idle speed.

1978 and Later Models
▶ See Figure 16

1. Start and run the engine at idle until normal operating temperature is reached.

2. Check the chart in Chapter 4 or the underhood decal for the correct curb idle speed.

3. Connect a tachometer (follow the instructions that came with the meter) and adjust the idle speed screw until the correct rpm is reached.

4. Idle mixture adjustments should be made by an authorized

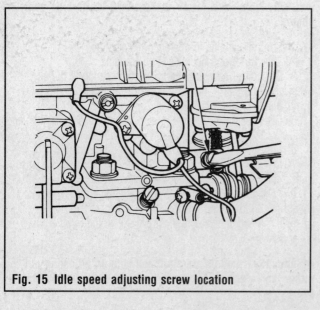
Fig. 15 Idle speed adjusting screw location

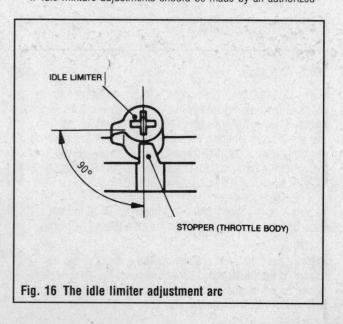
Fig. 16 The idle limiter adjustment arc

garage using a CO meter. However, a small amount of adjustment is possible (within the limits of the idle mixture screw limiter cap which must not be removed).

➡**Some late model carburetors have a tamper-proof, sealed idle mixture screw—these should not be unless the proper equipment is on hand to prevent incorrect adjustment.**

5. To adjust the idle mixture, first, adjust carb to correct curb idle speed. Next, watch the tachometer scale, listen to the engine and slowly turn the idle mixture screw clockwise. A drop in engine rpm or engine roughness will tell you when to stop. Then, slowly turn the mixture screw counterclockwise until once again you encounter rpm drop or engine roughness. A point in-between the clockwise or counterclockwise positions, that gives you the highest rpm or smoothest running engine, is the best setting.

6. Check and readjust the curb idle speed, if necessary.

7. Have your adjustment checked with a CO meter as soon as possible.

FUEL INJECTED ENGINES

◆ **See Figures 17, 18 and 19**

➡**This adjustment MUST be made any time the Idle Speed Control (ISC) servo, Throttle Position Sensor (TPS), mixing body or throttle body has been removed. A digital voltmeter is essential for this operation.**

1. Run the engine to normal operating temperature, then shut it OFF.

2. Disconnect the accelerator cable at the throttle lever on the mixing body.

3. Loosen the screws holding the TPS and turn it fully clockwise. Tighten the screws.

4. Turn the ignition switch to the ON position for at least 15 seconds, then turn it OFF. This will automatically set the ISC servo to the proper position.

5. Disconnect the ISC servo wiring connector.

6. Start the engine and check the idle speed with a tachometer. Idle speed should be 600 rpm. If not, adjust it with the adjusting screw as shown.

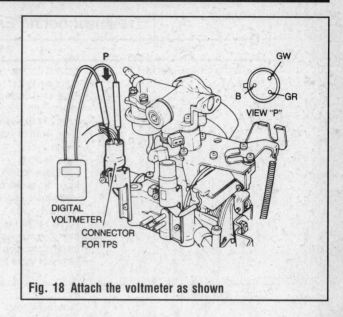

Fig. 18 Attach the voltmeter as shown

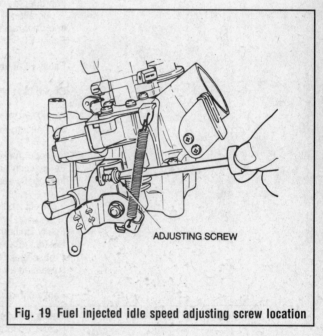

Fig. 19 Fuel injected idle speed adjusting screw location

7. Insert the digital voltmeter test probes in the TPS connector GW and B holes as shown.

8. Turn the ignition switch to the ON position. DO NOT START THE ENGINE!

9. Read the voltage. If indicated voltage is not 0.45–0.51v, loosen the TPS mounting screws and turn the sensor clockwise or counterclockwise until the indicated voltage is 0.48v. Tighten the screws and apply a thread-locking sealant.

10. Open the throttle valve fully and let it close. Recheck the indicated voltage. Adjust if necessary.

11. Remove the voltmeter and reconnect the wiring.

12. Start the engine. Recheck the idle speed. Adjust if necessary and stop the engine.

13. Turn the ignition switch to the ON position for at least 15 seconds, then turn it OFF.

14. Reconnect the cable, and adjust if necessary to remove any slack, using the adjusting nut at the throttle lever.

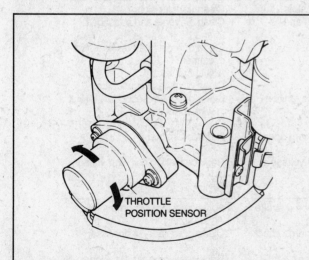

Fig. 17 The TPS can be adjusted after loosening the adjusting screws

Troubleshooting Engine Performance

Problem	Cause	Solution
Hard starting (engine cranks normally)	• Binding linkage, choke valve or choke piston	• Repair as necessary
	• Restricted choke vacuum diaphragm	• Clean passages
	• Improper fuel level	• Adjust float level
	• Dirty, worn or faulty needle valve and seat	• Repair as necessary
	• Float sticking	• Repair as necessary
	• Faulty fuel pump	• Replace fuel pump
	• Incorrect choke cover adjustment	• Adjust choke cover
	• Inadequate choke unloader adjustment	• Adjust choke unloader
	• Faulty ignition coil	• Test and replace as necessary
	• Improper spark plug gap	• Adjust gap
	• Incorrect ignition timing	• Adjust timing
	• Incorrect valve timing	• Check valve timing; repair as necessary
Rough idle or stalling	• Incorrect curb or fast idle speed	• Adjust curb or fast idle speed
	• Incorrect ignition timing	• Adjust timing to specification
	• Improper feedback system operation	• Refer to Chapter 4
	• Improper fast idle cam adjustment	• Adjust fast idle cam
	• Faulty EGR valve operation	• Test EGR system and replace as necessary
	• Faulty PCV valve air flow	• Test PCV valve and replace as necessary
	• Choke binding	• Locate and eliminate binding condition
	• Faulty TAC vacuum motor or valve	• Repair as necessary
	• Air leak into manifold vacuum	• Inspect manifold vacuum connections and repair as necessary
	• Improper fuel level	• Adjust fuel level
	• Faulty distributor rotor or cap	• Replace rotor or cap
	• Improperly seated valves	• Test cylinder compression, repair as necessary
	• Incorrect ignition wiring	• Inspect wiring and correct as necessary
	• Faulty ignition coil	• Test coil and replace as necessary
	• Restricted air vent or idle passages	• Clean passages
	• Restricted air cleaner	• Clean or replace air cleaner filler element
	• Faulty choke vacuum diaphragm	• Repair as necessary
Faulty low-speed operation	• Restricted idle transfer slots	• Clean transfer slots
	• Restricted idle air vents and passages	• Clean air vents and passages
	• Restricted air cleaner	• Clean or replace air cleaner filter element
	• Improper fuel level	• Adjust fuel level
	• Faulty spark plugs	• Clean or replace spark plugs
	• Dirty, corroded, or loose ignition secondary circuit wire connections	• Clean or tighten secondary circuit wire connections
	• Improper feedback system operation	• Refer to Chapter 4
	• Faulty ignition coil high voltage wire	• Replace ignition coil high voltage wire
	• Faulty distributor cap	• Replace cap
Faulty acceleration	• Improper accelerator pump stroke	• Adjust accelerator pump stroke
	• Incorrect ignition timing	• Adjust timing
	• Inoperative pump discharge check ball or needle	• Clean or replace as necessary
	• Worn or damaged pump diaphragm or piston	• Replace diaphragm or piston

Troubleshooting Engine Performance (cont.)

Problem	Cause	Solution
Faulty acceleration (cont.)	• Leaking carburetor main body cover gasket	• Replace gasket
	• Engine cold and choke set too lean	• Adjust choke cover
	• Improper metering rod adjustment (BBD Model carburetor)	• Adjust metering rod
	• Faulty spark plug(s)	• Clean or replace spark plug(s)
	• Improperly seated valves	• Test cylinder compression, repair as necessary
	• Faulty ignition coil	• Test coil and replace as necessary
	• Improper feedback system operation	• Refer to Chapter 4
Faulty high speed operation	• Incorrect ignition timing	• Adjust timing
	• Faulty distributor centrifugal advance mechanism	• Check centrifugal advance mechanism and repair as necessary
	• Faulty distributor vacuum advance mechanism	• Check vacuum advance mechanism and repair as necessary
	• Low fuel pump volume	• Replace fuel pump
	• Wrong spark plug air gap or wrong plug	• Adjust air gap or install correct plug
	• Faulty choke operation	• Adjust choke cover
	• Partially restricted exhaust manifold, exhaust pipe, catalytic converter, muffler, or tailpipe	• Eliminate restriction
	• Restricted vacuum passages	• Clean passages
	• Improper size or restricted main jet	• Clean or replace as necessary
	• Restricted air cleaner	• Clean or replace filter element as necessary
	• Faulty distributor rotor or cap	• Replace rotor or cap
	• Faulty ignition coil	• Test coil and replace as necessary
	• Improperly seated valve(s)	• Test cylinder compression, repair as necessary
	• Faulty valve spring(s)	• Inspect and test valve spring tension, replace as necessary
	• Incorrect valve timing	• Check valve timing and repair as necessary
	• Intake manifold restricted	• Remove restriction or replace manifold
	• Worn distributor shaft	• Replace shaft
	• Improper feedback system operation	• Refer to Chapter 4
Misfire at all speeds	• Faulty spark plug(s)	• Clean or replace spark plug(s)
	• Faulty spark plug wire(s)	• Replace as necessary
	• Faulty distributor cap or rotor	• Replace cap or rotor
	• Faulty ignition coil	• Test coil and replace as necessary
	• Primary ignition circuit shorted or open intermittently	• Troubleshoot primary circuit and repair as necessary
	• Improperly seated valve(s)	• Test cylinder compression, repair as necessary
	• Faulty hydraulic tappet(s)	• Clean or replace tappet(s)
	• Improper feedback system operation	• Refer to Chapter 4
	• Faulty valve spring(s)	• Inspect and test valve spring tension, repair as necessary
	• Worn camshaft lobes	• Replace camshaft
	• Air leak into manifold	• Check manifold vacuum and repair as necessary
	• Improper carburetor adjustment	• Adjust carburetor
	• Fuel pump volume or pressure low	• Replace fuel pump
	• Blown cylinder head gasket	• Replace gasket
	• Intake or exhaust manifold passage(s) restricted	• Pass chain through passage(s) and repair as necessary
	• Incorrect trigger wheel installed in distributor	• Install correct trigger wheel

Troubleshooting Engine Performance (cont.)

Problem	Cause	Solution
Power not up to normal	• Incorrect ignition timing	• Adjust timing
	• Faulty distributor rotor	• Replace rotor
	• Trigger wheel loose on shaft	• Reposition or replace trigger wheel
	• Incorrect spark plug gap	• Adjust gap
	• Faulty fuel pump	• Replace fuel pump
	• Incorrect valve timing	• Check valve timing and repair as necessary
	• Faulty ignition coil	• Test coil and replace as necessary
	• Faulty ignition wires	• Test wires and replace as necessary
	• Improperly seated valves	• Test cylinder compression and repair as necessary
	• Blown cylinder head gasket	• Replace gasket
	• Leaking piston rings	• Test compression and repair as necessary
	• Worn distributor shaft	• Replace shaft
	• Improper feedback system operation	• Refer to Chapter 4
Intake backfire	• Improper ignition timing	• Adjust timing
	• Faulty accelerator pump discharge	• Repair as necessary
	• Defective EGR CTO valve	• Replace EGR CTO valve
	• Defective TAC vacuum motor or valve	• Repair as necessary
	• Lean air/fuel mixture	• Check float level or manifold vacuum for air leak. Remove sediment from bowl
Exhaust backfire	• Air leak into manifold vacuum	• Check manifold vacuum and repair as necessary
	• Faulty air injection diverter valve	• Test diverter valve and replace as necessary
	• Exhaust leak	• Locate and eliminate leak
Ping or spark knock	• Incorrect ignition timing	• Adjust timing
	• Distributor centrifugal or vacuum advance malfunction	• Inspect advance mechanism and repair as necessary
	• Excessive combustion chamber deposits	• Remove with combustion chamber cleaner
	• Air leak into manifold vacuum	• Check manifold vacuum and repair as necessary
	• Excessively high compression	• Test compression and repair as necessary
	• Fuel octane rating excessively low	• Try alternate fuel source
	• Sharp edges in combustion chamber	• Grind smooth
	• EGR valve not functioning properly	• Test EGR system and replace as necessary
Surging (at cruising to top speeds)	• Low carburetor fuel level	• Adjust fuel level
	• Low fuel pump pressure or volume	• Replace fuel pump
	• Metering rod(s) not adjusted properly (BBD Model Carburetor)	• Adjust metering rod
	• Improper PCV valve air flow	• Test PCV valve and replace as necessary
	• Air leak into manifold vacuum	• Check manifold vacuum and repair as necessary
	• Incorrect spark advance	• Test and replace as necessary
	• Restricted main jet(s)	• Clean main jet(s)
	• Undersize main jet(s)	• Replace main jet(s)
	• Restricted air vents	• Clean air vents
	• Restricted fuel filter	• Replace fuel filter
	• Restricted air cleaner	• Clean or replace air cleaner filter element
	• EGR valve not functioning properly	• Test EGR system and replace as necessary
	• Improper feedback system operation	• Refer to Chapter 4

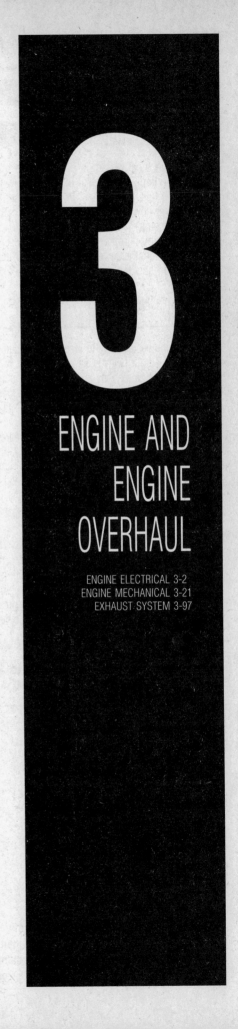

3

ENGINE AND ENGINE OVERHAUL

ENGINE ELECTRICAL

Understanding Electricity

For any electrical system to operate, there must be a complete circuit. This simply means that the power flow from the battery must make a full circle. When an electrical component is operating, power flows from the battery to the components, passes through the component (load) causing it to function, and returns to the battery through the ground path of the circuit. This ground may be either another wire or a metal part of the vehicle (depending upon how the component is designed).

BASIC CIRCUITS

Perhaps the easiest way to visualize a circuit is to think of connecting a light bulb (with two wires attached to it) to the battery. If one of the two wires was attached to the negative post (−) of the battery and the other wire to the positive post (+), the circuit would be complete and the light bulb would illuminate. Electricity could follow a path from the battery to the bulb and back to the battery. It's not hard to see that with longer wires on our light bulb, it could be mounted anywhere on the vehicle. Further, one wire could be fitted with a switch so that the light could be turned on and off. Various other items could be added to our primitive circuit to make the light flash, become brighter or dimmer under certain conditions, or advise the user that it's burned out.

Ground

Some automotive components are grounded through their mounting points. The electrical current runs through the chassis of the vehicle and returns to the battery through the ground (−) cable; if you look, you'll see that the battery ground cable connects between the battery and the body of the vehicle.

Load

Every complete circuit must include a "load" (something to use the electricity coming from the source). If you were to connect a

Damaged insulation can allow wires to break (causing an open circuit) or touch (causing a short circuit)

wire between the two terminals of the battery (DON'T do this, but take our word for it) without the light bulb, the battery would attempt to deliver its entire power supply from one pole to another almost instantly. This is a short circuit. The electricity is taking a short cut to get to ground and is not being used by any load in the circuit. This sudden and uncontrolled electrical flow can cause great damage to other components in the circuit and can develop a tremendous amount of heat. A short in an automotive wiring harness can develop sufficient heat to melt the insulation on all the surrounding wires and reduce a multiple wire cable to one sad lump of plastic and copper. Two common causes of shorts are broken insulation (thereby exposing the wire to contact with surrounding metal surfaces or other wires) or a failed switch (the pins inside the switch come out of place and touch each other).

Switches and Relays

Some electrical components which require a large amount of current to operate also have a relay in their circuit. Since these cir-

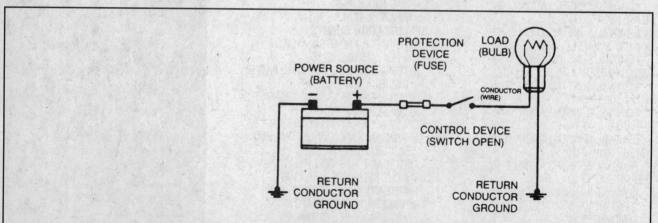

Here is an example of a simple automotive circuit. When the switch is closed, power from the positive battery terminal flows through the fuse, the switch and then the load (light bulb). The light illuminates and the circuit is completed through the return conductor and the vehicle ground. If the light did not work, the tests could be made with a voltmeter or test light at the battery, fuse, switch or bulb socket

cuits carry a large amount of current (amperage or amps), the thickness of the wire in the circuit (wire gauge) is also greater. If this large wire were connected from the load to the control switch on the dash, the switch would have to carry the high amperage load and the dash would be twice as large to accommodate wiring harnesses as thick as your wrist. To prevent these problems, a relay is used. The large wires in the circuit are connected from the battery to one side of the relay and from the opposite side of the relay to the load. The relay is normally open, preventing current from passing through the circuit. An additional, smaller wire is connected from the relay to the control switch for the circuit. When the control switch is turned on, it grounds the smaller wire to the relay and completes its circuit. The main switch inside the relay closes, sending power to the component without routing the main power through the inside of the vehicle. Some common circuits which may use relays are the horn, headlights, starter and rear window defogger systems.

Protective Devices

It is possible for larger surges of current to pass through the electrical system of your vehicle. If this surge of current were to reach the load in the circuit, it could burn it out or severely damage it. To prevent this, fuses, circuit breakers and/or fusible links are connected into the supply wires of the electrical system. These items are nothing more than a built-in weak spot in the system. It's much easier to go to a known location (the fusebox) to see why a circuit is inoperative than to dissect 15 feet of wiring under the dashboard, looking for what happened.

When an electrical current of excessive power passes through the fuse, the fuse blows (the conductor melts) and breaks the circuit, preventing the passage of current and protecting the components.

A circuit breaker is basically a self repairing fuse. It will open the circuit in the same fashion as a fuse, but when either the short is removed or the surge subsides, the circuit breaker resets itself and does not need replacement.

A fuse link (fusible link or main link) is a wire that acts as a fuse. One of these is normally connected between the starter relay and the main wiring harness under the hood. Since the starter is usually the highest electrical draw on the vehicle, an internal short during starting could direct about 130 amps into the wrong places. Consider the damage potential of introducing this current into a system whose wiring is rated at 15 amps and you'll understand the need for protection. Since this link is very early in the electrical path, it's the first place to look if nothing on the vehicle works, but the battery seems to be charged and is properly connected.

TROUBLESHOOTING

Electrical problems generally fall into one of three areas:
• The component that is not functioning is not receiving current.
• The component is receiving power but is not using it or is using it incorrectly (component failure).
• The component is improperly grounded.

The circuit can be can be checked with a test light and a jumper wire. The test light is a device that looks like a pointed screwdriver with a wire on one end and a bulb in its handle. A jumper wire is simply a piece of wire with alligator clips or spe-

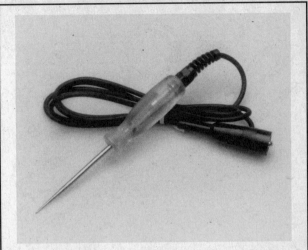

A 12 volt test light is useful when checking parts of a circuit for power

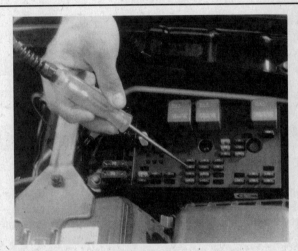

Here, someone is checking a circuit by making sure there is power to the component's fuse

cial terminals on each end. If a component is not working, you must follow a systematic plan to determine which of the three causes is the villain.

1. Turn ON the switch that controls the item not working.

➡Some items only work when the ignition switch is turned ON.

2. Disconnect the power supply wire from the component.
3. Attach the ground wire of a test light or a voltmeter to a good metal ground.
4. Touch the end probe of the test light (or the positive lead of the voltmeter) to the power wire; if there is current in the wire, the light in the test light will come on (or the voltmeter will indicate the amount of voltage). You have now established that current is getting to the component.
5. Turn the ignition or dash switch **OFF** and reconnect the wire to the component.

If there was no power, then the problem is between the battery and the component. This includes all the switches, fuses, relays and the battery itself. The next place to look is the fusebox; check

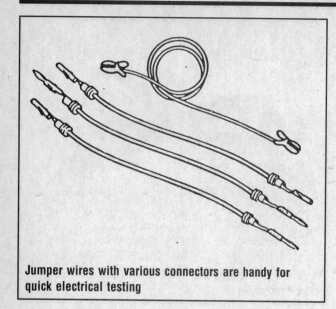

Jumper wires with various connectors are handy for quick electrical testing

carefully either by eye or by using the test light across the fuse clips. The easiest way to check is to simply replace the fuse. If the fuse is blown, and upon replacement, immediately blows again, there is a short between the fuse and the component. This is generally (not always) a sign of an internal short in the component. Disconnect the power wire at the component again and replace the fuse; if the fuse holds, the component is the problem.

✳✳ WARNING

DO NOT test a component by running a jumper wire from the battery UNLESS you are certain that it operates on 12 volts. Many electronic components are designed to operate with less voltage and connecting them to 12 volts could destroy them. Jumper wires are best used to bypass a portion of the circuit (such as a stretch of wire or a switch) that DOES NOT contain a resistor and is suspected to be bad.

If all the fuses are good and the component is not receiving power, find the switch for the circuit. Bypass the switch with the jumper wire. This is done by connecting one end of the jumper to the power wire coming into the switch and the other end to the wire leaving the switch. If the component comes to life, the switch has failed.

✳✳ WARNING

Never substitute the jumper for the component. The circuit needs the electrical load of the component. If you bypass it, you will cause a short circuit.

Checking the ground for any circuit can mean tracing wires to the body, cleaning connections or tightening mounting bolts for the component itself. If the jumper wire can be connected to the case of the component or the ground connector, you can ground the other end to a piece of clean, solid metal on the vehicle. Again, if the component starts working, you've found the problem.

A systematic search through the fuse, connectors, switches and the component itself will almost always yield an answer. Loose and/or corroded connectors, particularly in ground circuits, are becoming a larger problem in modern vehicles. The computers and on-board electronic (solid state) systems are highly sensitive to improper grounds and will change their function drastically if one occurs.

Remember that for any electrical circuit to work, ALL the connections must be clean and tight.

➡**For more information on Understanding and Troubleshooting Electrical Systems, please refer to Section 6 of this manual.**

Battery, Starting and Charging Systems

BASIC OPERATING PRINCIPLES

Battery

The battery is the first link in the chain of mechanisms which work together to provide cranking of the automobile engine. In most modern vehicles, the battery is a lead/acid electrochemical device consisting of six 2v subsections (cells) connected in series so the unit is capable of producing approximately 12v of electrical pressure. Each subsection consists of a series of positive and negative plates held a short distance apart in a solution of sulfuric acid and water.

The two types of plates are of dissimilar metals. This sets-up a chemical reaction, and it is this reaction which produces current flow from the battery when its positive and negative terminals are connected to an electrical accessory such as a lamp or motor. The continued transfer of electrons would eventually convert the sulfuric acid to water, and make the two plates identical in chemical composition. As electrical energy is removed from the battery, its voltage output tends to drop. Thus, measuring battery voltage and battery electrolyte composition are two ways of checking the ability of the unit to supply power. During engine cranking, electrical energy is removed from the battery. However, if the charging circuit is in good condition and the operating conditions are normal, the power removed from the battery will be replaced by the alternator which will force electrons back through the battery, reversing the normal flow, and restoring the battery to its original chemical state.

Starting System

The battery and starting motor are linked by very heavy electrical cables designed to minimize resistance to the flow of current. Generally, the major power supply cable that leaves the battery goes directly to the starter, while other electrical system needs are supplied by a smaller cable. During starter operation, power flows from the battery to the starter and is grounded through the vehicle's frame/body or engine and the battery's negative ground strap.

The starter is a specially designed, direct current electric motor capable of producing a great amount of power for its size. One thing that allows the motor to produce a great deal of power is its tremendous rotating speed. It drives the engine through a tiny pinion gear (attached to the starter's armature), which drives the very large flywheel ring gear at a greatly reduced speed. Another factor allowing it to produce so much power is that only intermittent operation is required of it. Thus, little allowance for air circulation is necessary, and the windings can be built into a very small space.

The starter solenoid is a magnetic device which employs the

small current supplied by the start circuit of the ignition switch. This magnetic action moves a plunger which mechanically engages the starter and closes the heavy switch connecting it to the battery. The starting switch circuit usually consists of the starting switch contained within the ignition switch, a neutral safety switch or clutch pedal switch, and the wiring necessary to connect these in series with the starter solenoid or relay.

The pinion, a small gear, is mounted to a one way drive clutch. This clutch is splined to the starter armature shaft. When the ignition switch is moved to the **START** position, the solenoid plunger slides the pinion toward the flywheel ring gear via a collar and spring. If the teeth on the pinion and flywheel match properly, the pinion will engage the flywheel immediately. If the gear teeth butt one another, the spring will be compressed and will force the gears to mesh as soon as the starter turns far enough to allow them to do so. As the solenoid plunger reaches the end of its travel, it closes the contacts that connect the battery and starter, then the engine is cranked.

As soon as the engine starts, the flywheel ring gear begins turning fast enough to drive the pinion at an extremely high rate of speed. At this point, the one-way clutch begins allowing the pinion to spin faster than the starter shaft so that the starter will not operate at excessive speed. When the ignition switch is released from the starter position, the solenoid is de-energized, and a spring pulls the gear out of mesh interrupting the current flow to the starter.

Some starters employ a separate relay, mounted away from the starter, to switch the motor and solenoid current on and off. The relay replaces the solenoid electrical switch, but does not eliminate the need for a solenoid mounted on the starter used to mechanically engage the starter drive gears. The relay is used to reduce the amount of current the starting switch must carry.

Charging System

The automobile charging system provides electrical power for operation of the vehicle's ignition system, starting system and all electrical accessories. The battery serves as an electrical surge or storage tank, storing (in chemical form) the energy originally produced by the engine driven generator. The system also provides a means of regulating output to protect the battery from being overcharged and to avoid excessive voltage to the accessories.

The storage battery is a chemical device incorporating parallel lead plates in a tank containing a sulfuric acid/water solution. Adjacent plates are slightly dissimilar, and the chemical reaction of the two dissimilar plates produces electrical energy when the battery is connected to a load such as the starter motor. The chemical reaction is reversible, so that when the generator is producing a voltage (electrical pressure) greater than that produced by the battery, electricity is forced into the battery, and the battery is returned to its fully charged state.

Newer automobiles use alternating current generators or alternators, because they are more efficient, can be rotated at higher speeds, and have fewer brush problems. In an alternator, the field usually rotates while all the current produced passes only through the stator winding. The brushes bear against continuous slip rings. This causes the current produced to periodically reverse the direction of its flow. Diodes (electrical one way valves) block the flow of current from traveling in the wrong direction. A series of diodes is wired together to permit the alternating flow of the stator to be rectified back to 12 volts DC for use by the vehicle's electrical system.

The voltage regulating function is performed by a regulator. The regulator is often built in to the alternator; this system is termed an integrated or internal regulator.

Ignition Coil

TESTING

▶ **See Figure 1**

The fastest way to check is by substituting a known good coil. If a coil is not on hand, proceed with one or more of the following tests.

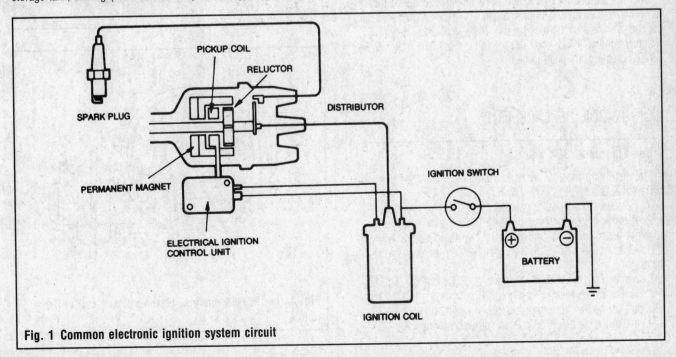

Fig. 1 Common electronic ignition system circuit

1. With the ignition switch on the ON position measure the voltage at the negative terminal of the ignition coil. If zero volts are shown, there is an open circuit in the coil.

2. Check the ignition coil resistance. If the engine will run allow it to reach normal operating temperature (the ignition coil should be hot). Shut OFF the engine and disconnect the high tension lead (coil wire) from the coil tower.

3. Measure primary resistance with an ohmmeter, connecting the coil minus and plus primary terminals. Resistance should be: $0.7–0.85\Omega$ through 1982; $1.04–1.3\Omega$ from 1983.

4. Measure the secondary resistance by connecting the ohmmeter between the contacts in the coil tower and the plus primary terminal. Resistance should be:
- 1971–82: $9–11k\Omega$
- 1983–85: $7.10–9.60k\Omega$
- 1986–89 1.5L engine: $11.6–15.8\Omega$
- 1986–89 1.6L engine: $9.4–12.6\Omega$
- Vista and Conquest: $10.8–13.2\Omega$.

5. Replace the coil if the voltage tests show zero volts or the resistances are not within specs.

TESTING THE EXTERNAL RESISTOR

1. With the ignition switch off: connect an ohmmeter between the terminals of the external resistor.

2. Obtain a reading from the ohmmeter. Resistance should be $1.22–1.49\Omega$.

3. If the reading on the ohmmeter is zero or not within specs, replace the resistor.

TESTING THE PICK-UP COIL

The pick-up coil may be tested while mounted in the distributor. Remove the cap and rotor and connect an ohmmeter between the two terminals of the pick-up coil. If the resistance is not within the limits, 1980—$1,050\Omega \pm 50\Omega$; 1981 and later—$920–1,120\Omega$, replace the pick-up coil.

PICK-UP COIL REPLACEMENT

▶ See Figures 2, 3, 4 and 5

The distributor must be removed from the engine. (See distributor removal procedure).

1. Remove the distributor cap and rotor.

2. Remove the center mounting bolt (screw) and remove the governor assembly. Take care not to mix up the governor springs (2), they must be installed in the same position. Remove the reluctor.

3. Remove the two mounting screws and take out the pick-up coil (79–80) or the pick-up coil and IC Igniter (from 1981). Carefully pull the Igniter from the pick-up coil (from 1981).

4. Install the new pick-up coil and other components.

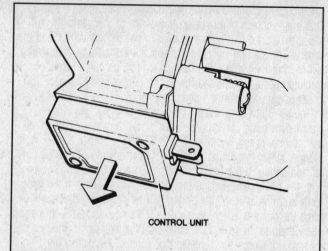
Fig. 2 Separate the control unit from the side of the distributor

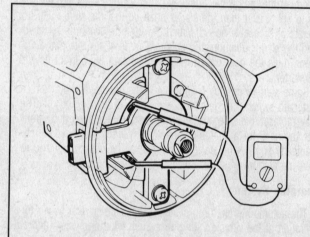
Fig. 3 Checking the pickup coil resistance—1979-80 models

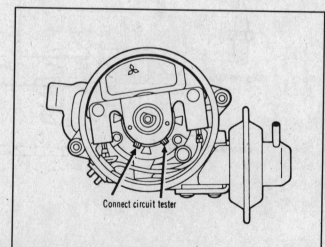
Connect circuit tester

Fig. 4 On 1981-89 models, test the pickup coil at these points

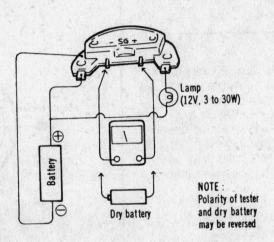

Fig. 5 On 1981-89 models, be sure to connect the igniter, battery and ohmmeter as shown

CONTROL UNIT TEST

The control unit is mounted on the side of the distributor (1979–80) and internally mounted (in the distributor on various models) from 1981.

1979–80 Models
▶ See Figure 6

With the control unit still mounted on the distributor: check for continuity between terminal C and the distributor housing. If the control unit is not mounted: check for continuity between terminal C and the metallic side of the unit. (See illustration). Alternately switch the leads of the meter: if there is continuity or an open circuit in both directions, the control unit is defective.

➡ **Only the transistors in the switching section of the control unit are checked by this test.**

Even if they test as good, the unit could still be defective.

1981 and Later Models

On various models equipped, connect the igniter unit, battery, lamp or ohmmeter as shown in the illustration. Apply signal voltage. If the lamp lights or ohms are read when voltage is applied, and goes out or reads no ohms when the voltage signal is removed, the igniter may be considered good.

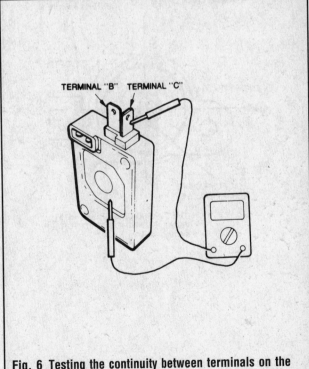

Fig. 6 Testing the continuity between terminals on the control unit with an ohmmeter

→Only the switching section of the control unit is checked with this test. Even if the unit tests as good, it could still be defective.

Distributor

REMOVAL & INSTALLATION

▶ **See Figures 7, 8, 9 and 10**

Although the distributor can be removed from the engine no matter which cylinder is about to fire, it is a good idea to have number one cylinder at TDC before distributor removal.

1. Disconnect the negative battery cable. Unsnap the two clips or unfasten (press down and turn clockwise) the two screws that hold on the distributor cap. Position the cap out of the way or remove the spark plug wires from the spark plugs (twist and pull on the boots), the coil wire from the coil and remove the cap and wires from the car.

2. Turn the engine clockwise (use a wrench on the crank pulley) until the rotor points to number one cylinder position and the

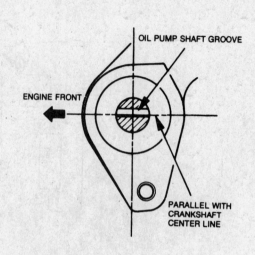

Fig. 8 Block mounted distributor oil pump gear alignment—1994cc engines

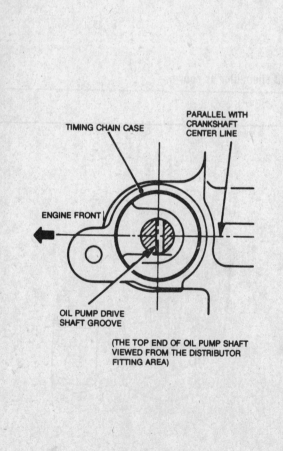

Fig. 7 Block mounted distributor oil pump gear alignment—1597cc engines

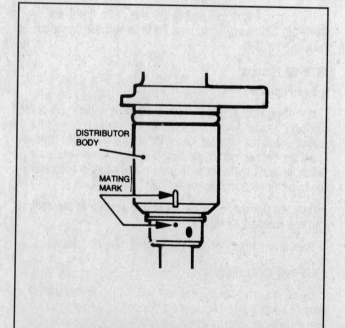

Fig. 9 Alignment of the factory markings—distributor housing and drive shaft spacer

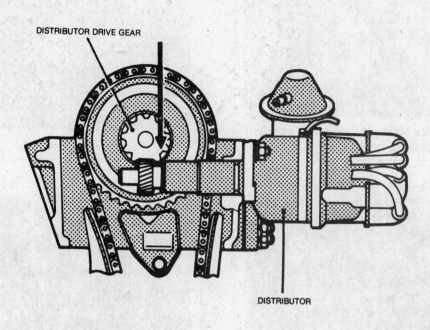

DISTRIBUTOR DRIVE GEAR

DISTRIBUTOR

Fig. 10 Common cylinder head mounted distributor cutaway view

Label the plug wires and remove the coil wire first

Mark the distributor location with a marker

Mark the exact position of the plug wires on the cap if the cap has no identification markings

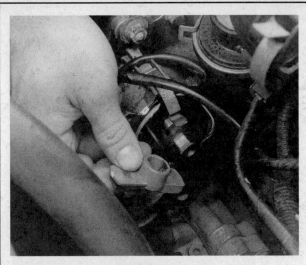

Remove the rotor and set aside

Unclamp and remove the distributor cap

Dont forget to label and disconnect the other distributor wiring

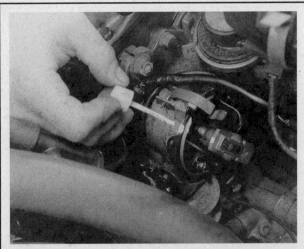

Place markings on the rotor and the distributor for installation purposes

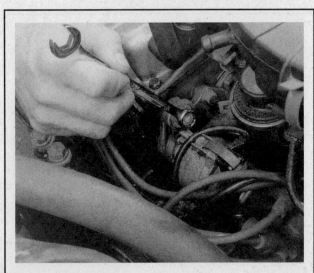

Loosen the distributor mounting bolt(s) . . .

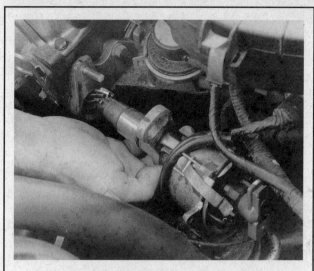

. . . **and carefully slide the unit out of the engine**

timing marks on the crankshaft pulley and the timing tab (refer to Section 2) are aligned at TDC.

3. Mark the distributor body to the exact place the rotor points. Matchmark both the distributor mounting flange and the engine block.

4. Disconnect the distributor primary wire or wiring harness. Remove the vacuum line (lines) from the advance unit. Loosen and remove the retaining nut from the mounting stud. Lift the distributor straight from the engine. The rotor may turn away slightly from your mark on the distributor body, make note of how far. When you reinstall the distributor this is the point to position the rotor.

To install:

5. If the engine has not been disturbed, i.e. the crankshaft was not turned, then install the distributor by placing the rotor in the same position it was in when the distributor was removed, carefully align the matchmarks and lower the distributor into the block or cylinder head. Always check the ignition timing whenever the distributor has been removed.

6. If the engine has been disturbed, i.e. rotated while the distributor was out, proceed as follows:

7. Turn the crankshaft so that the No. 1 piston is on the compression stroke and the timing marks are aligned.

8. Turn the distributor shaft so that the rotor points approximately 15° before the rotor position that you marked on the distributor. If you did not mark the distributor, line up the factory marks on the shaft and housing.

9. Insert the distributor into the engine. On block mounted distributors, if you meet resistance and slight wiggling of the rotor shaft does not help seat the distributor: the oil pump gear is probably out of alignment.

10. Do not force the distributor. Remove the distributor, and using a long screwdriver, turn the oil pump shaft so that it is vertical to the centerline of the crankshaft on 1597cc engines: parallel on 1994cc engines. (See illustrations).

11. When the distributor seats against the engine block or head, align the matchmarks and install the retaining nut. Do not tighten the retaining nut all the way, you still have to check the engine timing. Reinstall the rotor, cap, plug wires, coil lead, primary lead (or harness) and connect the vacuum hoses. Connect the negative battery cable. Start the engine, allow it to reach operating temperature and check the ignition timing (outlines in Section 2).

Alternator

GENERAL INFORMATION

The alternator charging system is a negative (−) ground system which consists of an alternator, a regulator, a charge indicator, a storage battery and wiring connecting the components, and fuse link wire.

The alternator is belt-driven from the engine. Energy is supplied from the alternator/regulator system to the rotating field through two brushes to two slip-rings. The slip-rings are mounted on the rotor shaft and are connected to the field coil. This energy supplied to the rotating field from the battery is called excitation current and is used to initially energize the field to begin the generation of electricity. Once the alternator starts to generate electricity, the excitation current comes from its own output rather than the battery.

The alternator produces power in the form of alternating current. The alternating current is rectified by 6 diodes into direct current. The direct current is used to charge the battery and power the rest of the electrical system.

When the ignition key is turned ON, current flows from the battery, through the charging system indicator light on the instrument panel, to the voltage regulator, and to the alternator. Since the alternator is not producing any current, the alternator warning light comes on. When the engine is started, the alternator begins to produce current and turns the alternator light off. As the alternator turns and produces current, the current is divided in two ways: part to the battery to charge the battery and power the electrical components of the vehicle, and part is returned to the alternator to enable it to increase its output. In this situation, the alternator is receiving current from the battery and from itself. A voltage regulator is wired into the current supply to the alternator to prevent it from receiving too much current which would cause it to put out too much current. Conversely, if the voltage regulator does not allow the alternator to receive enough current, the battery will not be fully charged and will eventually go dead.

The battery is connected to the alternator at all times, whether the ignition key is turned on or not. If the battery were shorted to ground, the alternator would also be shorted. This would damage the alternator. To prevent this, a fuse link is installed in the wiring between the battery and the alternator. If the battery is shorted, the fuse link is melted, protecting the alternator.

PRECAUTIONS

Your car is equipped with an alternator. Unlike the direct current (DC) generators used on many old cars, there are several precautions which must be strictly observed in order to avoid damaging the unit. They are:

1. Always observe proper polarity of the battery connections: be especially careful when jump starting the car. (See chapter one for jump starting procedures).

2. Never ground or short out the alternator or alternator regulator terminals.

3. Never operate the alternator with any of its or the battery's lead wires disconnected.

4. Always remove the battery or at least disconnect the ground cable while charging.

5. Always disconnect the battery ground cable while repairing or replacing an electrical component.

6. Never use a fast battery charger to jump start a dead battery.

7. Never attempt to polarize an alternator.

8. Never subject the alternator to excessive heat or dampness (for instance, steam cleaning the engine).

9. Never use arc welding equipment on the car with the alternator connected.

CHARGING SYSTEM TROUBLESHOOTING

There are many possible ways in which the charging system can malfunction. Often the source of a problem is difficult to diagnose, requiring special equipment and a good deal of experience. This is usually not the case, however, where the charging system fails completely and causes the dash board warning light to come on or the battery to become dead. To troubleshoot a complete system failure only two pieces of equipment are needed: a test light, to determine that current is reaching a certain point; and a current indicator (ammeter), to determine the direction of the current flow and its measurement in amps.

This test works under three assumptions:

1. The battery is known to be good and fully charged.

2. The alternator belt is in good condition and adjusted to the proper tension.

3. All connections in the system are clean and tight.

➡️**In order for the current indicator to give a valid reading, the car must be equipped with battery cables which are of the same gauge size and quality as original equipment battery cables.**

1. Turn off all electrical components on the car. Make sure the doors of the car are closed. If the car is equipped with a clock, disconnect the clock by removing the lead wire from the rear of the clock. Disconnect the positive battery cable from the battery and connect the ground wire on a test light to the disconnected positive battery cable. Touch the probe end of the test light to the positive battery post. The test light should not light. If the test light does light, there is a short or open circuit on the car.

2. Disconnect the voltage regulator wiring harness connector at the voltage regulator. Turn on the ignition key. Connect the wire on a test light to a good ground (engine bolt). Touch the probe end of a test light to the ignition wire connector into the voltage regulator wiring connector. This wire corresponds to the **I** terminal on the regulator. If the test light goes on, the charging system warning light circuit is complete. If the test light does not come on and the warning light on the instrument panel is on, either the resistor wire, which is parallel with the warning light, or the wiring to the voltage regulator, is defective. If the test light does not come on and the warning light is not on, either the bulb is defective or the power supply wire from the battery through the ignition

switch to the bulb has an open circuit. Connect the wiring harness to the regulator.

3. Examine the fuse link wire in the wiring harness from the starter relay to the alternator. If the insulation on the wire is cracked or split, the fuse link may be melted. Connect a test light to the fuse link by attaching the ground wire on the test light to an engine bolt and touching the probe end of the light to the bottom of the fuse link wire where it splices into the alternator output wire. If the bulb in the test light does not light, the fuse link is melted.

4. Start the engine and place a current indicator on the positive battery cable. Turn off all electrical accessories and make sure the doors are closed. If the charging system is working properly, the gauge will show a draw of less than 5 amps. If the system is not working properly, the gauge will show a draw of more than 5 amps. A charge moves the needle toward the battery, a draw moves the needle away from the battery. Turn the engine OFF.

5. Disconnect the wiring harness from the voltage regulator at the regulator connector. Connect a male spade terminal (solderless connector) to each end of a jumper wire. Insert one end of the wire into the wiring harness connector which corresponds to the **A** terminal on the regulator. Insert the other end of the wire into the wiring harness connector which corresponds to the **F** terminal on the regulator. Position the connector with the jumper wire installed so that it cannot contact any metal surface under the hood. Position a current indicator gauge on the positive battery cable. Have an assistant start the engine. Observe the reading on the current indicator. Have your assistant slowly raise the speed of the engine to about 2,000 rpm or until the current indicator needle stops moving, whichever comes first. Do not run the engine for more than a short period of time in this condition. If the wiring harness connector or jumper wire becomes excessively hot during this test, turn OFF the engine and check for a grounded wire in the regulator wiring harness. If the current indicator shows a charge of about three amps less than the output of the alternator, the alternator is working properly. If the previous tests showed a draw, the voltage regulator is defective. If the gauge does not show the proper charging rate, the alternator is defective.

REMOVAL & INSTALLATION

Rear Wheel Drive

♦ See Figure 11

1. Disconnect the negative battery cable. If the A/C compressor interferes with removal of the alternator, remove the compressor (with lines attached, if possible. If the lines must be disconnected, discharge the system safely before disconnecting). Tag (location) and remove the wires connected to the alternator.

2. Loosen and remove the top mounting nut and bolt. Loosen the bottom mounting nut and bolt. Push the alternator towards the engine and remove the drive belt.

3. Remove the bottom mounting nut and bolt: remove the alternator.

➡️**When removing the bottom mounting bolt do not loose any of the adjustment shims.**

To install:

4. Align the hole in the lower alternator leg with the hole in the mounting and insert the lower bolt. Remember to install any adjustment shims you removed. Install mounting nut but do not tighten at this time.

5. Install top mounting bolt and nut but do not tighten. Install drive belt and pull the alternator away from the engine to put pressure on the belt.

6. Adjust the drive belt to the proper tension and tighten top mounting bolt. Tighten lower mounting nut and bolt. (See Section 1 for proper belt adjustment).

Front Wheel Drive

1. Disconnect the negative battery cable.
2. Remove the condensor fan motor.
3. Remove the power steering oil pump from the bracket and position it out of the way with lines attached.
4. Remove the power steering pump bracket.
5. Disconnect the wiring harness from the alternator.
6. Loosen the lockbolt, the support bolt and the adjuster. Remove the drive belt.
7. Remove the mounting bolts and the alternator. If shims are provided for correct belt alignment, take note of their position for installation.

To install:

8. Place the alternator into position, with shims in their proper location.

9. Install the support bolt, adjuster and lockbolt. Do not tighten them until the drive belt is installed. After the drive belt is installed, tension the belt and tighten the mounting bolts.

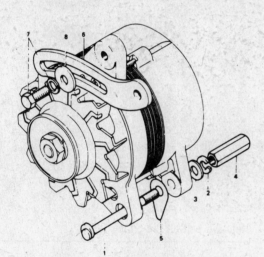

1. Bolt
2. Washer
3. Washer
4. Nut
5. Shim
6. Generator brace
7. Bolt
8. Washer

Fig. 11 Exploded view of the alternator mounting components

Label the plug wires and remove the coil wire first

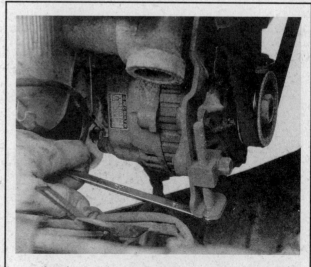

. . . then loosen the tension bolt

Pull the wire cap off the back of the alternator . . .

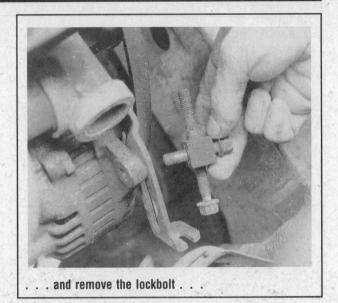

. . . and remove the lockbolt . . .

. . . then remove the wire nut, nut and washer

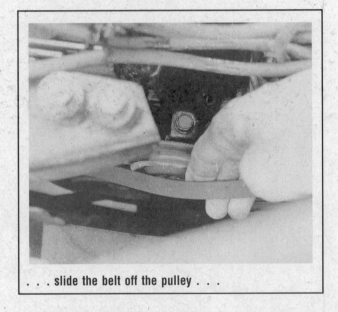

. . . slide the belt off the pulley . . .

If necessary, loosen the adjuster pulley . . .

. . . then remove the upper mounting bolt

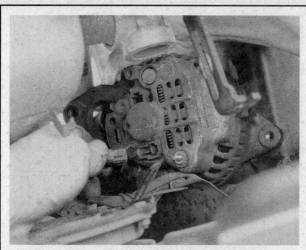

While holding the alternator with one hand, disconnect the plug in the back of the unit

Once all connections have been separated, remove the alternator out of the engine compartment

10. Install the power steering pump bracket and pump. Install the condenser fan and connect the battery cable.

Regulator

REMOVAL & INSTALLATION

1. Disconnect the ground cable from the battery.
2. Disconnect the electrical connector plug.
3. Loosen and remove the two mounting screws. Remove the regulator.

To install:

4. Clean the attaching area for proper grounding of the regulator.
5. Install the regulator. Do not overtighten the mounting screws or you will distort the case.
6. Connect the electrical plug and the battery cable.

➡A transistorized (electronic) voltage regulator was introduced in 1979. The regulator is either built into the alternator, or mounted on top.

VOLTAGE CHECK AND ADJUSTMENT

◗ **See Figures 12 and 13**

➡Check the voltage in a garage or other enclosed area if the outside temperature is lower than 68 F.

1. Connect a voltmeter by inserting clips into the (A) and (E) terminals of the regulator connector plug.

➡**Do not disconnect the plug.**

2. Disconnect one of the battery terminals while the engine is idling to unload the alternator.
3. Increase the alternator speed to approximately 4,000 rpm (engine speed of 2,000 rpm). The voltmeter should show a value of 14.3–15.8V at room temperature. If the reading is not within specifications, adjust the regulator as follows:
4. Carefully remove the two retaining screws and remove the regulator cover.
5. Adjust the constant voltage relay (located on the left) by bending the end of the coil side plate up or down as shown in the figure.
6. Bending the plate down reduces the voltage: bending it up increases the voltage.
7. The field (lamp) relay is adjusted in the same manner as the voltage relay.
8. After adjustment, recheck the voltage with the meter.
9. Install the cover, making sure that the seal is evenly compressed.

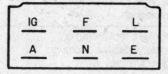

Fig. 12 Regulator connector plug test terminal locations

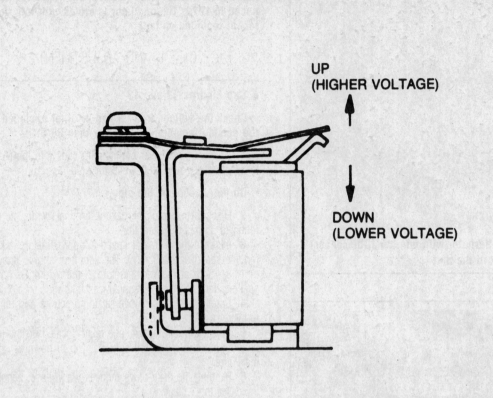

UP
(HIGHER VOLTAGE)

DOWN
(LOWER VOLTAGE)

Fig. 13 Adjusting the regulator on all models except built-in or alternator mounted

Troubleshooting Basic Charging System Problems

Problem	Cause	Solution
Noisy alternator	• Loose mountings • Loose drive pulley • Worn bearings • Brush noise • Internal circuits shorted (High pitched whine)	• Tighten mounting bolts • Tighten pulley • Replace alternator • Replace alternator • Replace alternator
Squeal when starting engine or accelerating	• Glazed or loose belt	• Replace or adjust belt
Indicator light remains on or ammeter indicates discharge (engine running)	• Broken fan belt • Broken or disconnected wires • Internal alternator problems • Defective voltage regulator	• Install belt • Repair or connect wiring • Replace alternator • Replace voltage regulator
Car light bulbs continually burn out— battery needs water continually	• Alternator/regulator overcharging	• Replace voltage regulator/alternator
Car lights flare on acceleration	• Battery low • Internal alternator/regulator problems	• Charge or replace battery • Replace alternator/regulator
Low voltage output (alternator light flickers continually or ammeter needle wanders)	• Loose or worn belt • Dirty or corroded connections • Internal alternator/regulator problems	• Replace or adjust belt • Clean or replace connections • Replace alternator or regulator

Battery

REMOVAL & INSTALLATION

1. Loosen the battery cable clamping nuts, negative (ground) cable first. Spread the battery cable terminals (or use a cable terminal puller. Remove the negative cable and then the positive cable.

2. Remove the battery hold-down frame nuts and the frame.

3. Put on work gloves or use a battery carrier and lift the battery from the engine compartment. Be careful not to tip the battery and spill acid on yourself or the car during removal. Automotive batteries contain a sulfuric acid electrolyte which is harmful to skin, clothing and paint finishes.

To install:

4. Carefully fit the battery into the engine compartment holder. Install the hold-down frame and tighten the retaining nuts.

5. Install the positive cable first, then the negative cable. Lightly coat the battery cables with petroleum jelly.

Alternator and Regulator Specifications

Year	Alternator Part No. or Manufacturer	Output (amps)	Part No. or Manufacturer	Field Relay Air Gap (in.)	Field Relay Point Gap (in.)	Regulator Air Gap (in.)	Regulator Point Gap (in.)	Volts @68°F
1971–72	AC2040K	40	RQ2220D	0.035–0.047	0.030–0.043	0.032–0.047	0.012–0.016	14.3–15.8
1973	AG2040K	40	RQB2220D	0.035–0.047	0.030–0.043	0.032–0.047	0.012–0.016	14.3–15.8
1974	AH2040K ①	40	RQB2220D	0.035–0.047	0.030–0.043	0.032–0.047	0.012–0.016	14.3–15.8
1975–76	AH2045K ①	45	RQB2220D	0.035–0.047	0.030–0.043	0.032–0.047	0.012–0.016	14.3–15.8

① K_1, with 1597 cc engine

Alternator, Regulator and Battery Specifications

Year	Engine	Rated Output	Rotation (Viewed from Pulley)	No Load Adjusted Voltage	Cover Temperature	Battery Capacity Ampere-Hour
1975	All	45A @ 12V	Clockwise	14.3 to 15.8V	68°F (20°C)	60
1976	All	45A @ 12V	Clockwise	14.2 to 15.3V	68°F (20°C)	60
1977	All	45A @ 12V	Clockwise	14.5 to 15.3V	68°F (20°C)	60
1978–89		45A @ 12V	Clockwise	14.5 to 15.3V	68°F (20°C)	36–52
		50A @ 12V	Clockwise	14.5 to 15.3V	68°F (20°C)	
		60A @ 12V	Clockwise	14.5 to 15.3V	68°F (20°C)	
		65A @ 12V	Clockwise	14.5 to 15.2V	68°F (20°C)	
		75A @ 12V	Clockwise	14.5 to 15.2V	68°F (20°C)	

① Coupe 1597 MT: 45 A.H.
  AT: 60 A.H.
Sedan all models: 60 A.H.
Hatchback 1597 MT, AT: 60 A.H.
  1994 MT: 45 A.H.
  AT: 60 A.H.
Station wagon 1597 MT, AT: 60 A.H.
  1994, 2600 ALL: 65 A.H.

② 1994 W/SS: off voltage: 4.0 to 5.8V
  on voltage: 0.5 to 3.5V

③ All models are equipped with sealed voltage regulators which cannot be adjusted if the readings vary from the specifications.

Starter

DIAGNOSIS

Starter Won't Crank The Engine

1. Dead battery.
2. Open starter circuit, such as:
   a. Broken or loose battery cables.
   b. Inoperative starter motor solenoid.
   c. Broken or loose wire from ignition switch to solenoid.
   d. Poor solenoid or starter ground.
   e. Bad ignition switch.
3. Defective starter internal circuit, such as:
   a. Dirty or burnt commutator.
   b. Stuck, worn or broken brushes.
   c. Open or shorted armature.
   d. Open or grounded fields.
4. Starter motor mechanical faults, such as:
   a. Jammed armature end bearings.
   b. Bad bearings, allowing armature to rub fields.
   c. Bent shaft.
   d. Broken starter housing.
   e. Bad starter drive mechanism.
   f. Bad starter drive or flywheel driven gear.
5. Engine hard or impossible to crank, such as:
   a. Hydrostatic lock, water in combustion chamber.
   b. Crankshaft seizing in bearings.
   c. Piston or ring seizing.
   d. Bent or broken connecting rod.
   e. Seizing of connecting rod bearings.
   f. Flywheel jammed or broken.

Starter Spins Freely, Won't Engage

1. Sticking or broken drive mechanism.
2. Damaged ring gear.

REMOVAL & INSTALLATION

1. Disconnect the battery ground (negative) cable from the battery.
2. Jack up and support (use a jackstand) the driver's side of the car.
3. Tag and remove the wires connected to the starter motor. Tagging the wires helps when reinstalling the starter motor.
4. Loosen and remove the two mounting bolts, make sure to support the weight of the starter motor.

To install:

5. Before installation of the motor, be sure to clean the mating surfaces of both the starter and the engine block.
6. Place the starter motor into position. Secure it with the mounting bolts. Connect the cables and wiring harness.

SOLENOID REPLACEMENT

1. Disconnect the negative battery cable.
2. Remove the starter motor.
3. Disconnect the field coil wire from the terminal connector on the solenoid.

4. Remove the mounting screws and the solenoid from the starter motor.

To install:

5. Place the solenoid over the spring and into position on the starter motor. Secure the solenoid with the mounting screws. Connect the field coil wire to the solenoid terminal.
6. Install the starter motor and connect the negative battery cable.

OVERHAUL

Direct Drive Starter

♦ See Figure 14

➡ **The starter must be removed to perform this procedure.**

1. Remove the wire connecting the starter solenoid to the starter.
2. Remove the two screws holding starter solenoid on the starter drive housing and remove the solenoid.
3. Remove the two long through bolts at the rear of the starter and separate the armature yoke from the armature.
4. Carefully remove the armature and the starter drive engagement lever from the front bracket, after making a mental note of the way they are positioned along with the attendant spring and spring retainer.
5. Loosen the two screws and remove the rear bracket.
6. Tap the stopper ring at the end of the drive gear engagement shaft in towards the drive gear to expose the snapring. Remove the snapring.
7. Pull the stopper, drive gear and overrunning clutch from the end of the shaft. For 1979 models with automatic transmission, remove the center bracket, spring and spring retainer. Inspect the pinion and spline teeth for wear or damage. If the engagement teeth are damaged, visually check the flywheel ring gear through the starter hole to insure that it is not damaged. It will be necessary to turn the engine over by hand to completely inspect the ring gear. Check the brushes for wear. Their service limit length is 11.5mm. Replace if necessary.
8. Assembly is performed in the following manner. For 1979 models with automatic transmissions, fit the spring retainer, spring and center bracket on the shaft.
9. Install the spring retainer and spring on the armature shaft.
10. Install the overrunning clutch assembly on the armature shaft.
11. Fit the stopper ring with its open side facing out on the shaft.
12. Install a new snapring and, using a gear puller, pull the stopper ring into place over the snapring.
13. Fit the small washer on the front end of the armature shaft.
14. Fit the engagement lever into the overrunning clutch and refit the armature into the front housing.
15. Fit the engagement lever spring and spring retainer into place and slide the armature yoke over the armature. Make sure you position the yoke with the spring retainer cutout space in line with the spring retainer.

➡ **Make sure the brushes are seated on the commutator.**

16. Replace the rear bracket and two retainer screws.
17. Install the two through bolts in the end of the yoke.
18. Refit the starter solenoid, making sure you fit the plunger

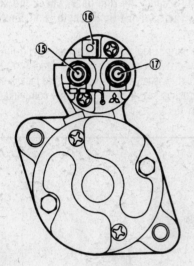
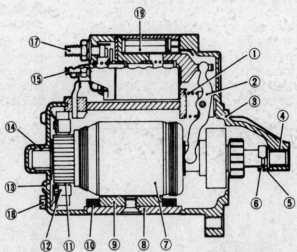

Sectional view

1. Spring	8. Yoke	14. Bearing
2. Lever	9. Pole	15. Terminal "M"
3. Front bracket	10. Field coil	16. Terminal "S"
4. Bearing	11. Brush	17. Terminal "B"
5. Ring	12. Brush holder	18. Through bolt
6. Stopper	13. Rear bracket	19. Magnetic switch
7. Armature		

Fig. 14 View of the direct drive starter motor

over the engagement lever. Install the screws and connect the wire running from the starter yoke to the starter solenoid.

Gear Reduction Type

▶ See Figure 15

➡**The starter must be removed to perform this procedure.**

1. Remove the wire connecting the starter solenoid to the starter.

2. Remove the two screws holding the solenoid and, pulling out, unhook it from the engagement lever.

3. Remove the two through bolts in the end of the starter and remove the two bracket screws. Pull off the rear bracket.

➡**Since the conical spring washer is contained in the rear bracket, be sure to take it out.**

4. Remove the yoke and brush holder assembly while pulling the brush upward.

5. Pull the armature assembly out of the mounting bracket.

6. On the side of the armature mounting bracket there is a small dust shield held on by two screws, remove the shield. Remove the snapring and washer located under the shield.

7. Remove the remaining bolts in the mounting bracket and separate the reduction case.

➡**Several washers will come out of the reduction case when you separate it. These adjust the armature end-play: do not lose them.**

8. Remove the reduction gear, lever and lever spring from the front bracket.

9. Use a brass drift or a deep socket to knock the stopper ring on the end of the shaft in toward the pinion. Remove the snapring. Remove the stopper, pinion and pinion shaft assembly.

10. Remove the ball bearings at both ends of the armature.

➡**The ball bearings are pressed into the front bracket and are not replaceable. Replace them together with the bracket. Inspect the pinion and spline teeth for wear or damage. If the pinion drive teeth are damaged, visually check the engine flywheel ring gear. Check the flywheel ring gear by looking through the starter motor mounting hole. It will be necessary to turn the engine over by hand to completely inspect the ring gear. Check the starter brushes for wear. Their service limit length is 11.5mm. Replace if necessary.**

11. Be sure to replace all the adjusting and thrust washers that you removed. When replacing the rear bracket, fit the conical spring pinion washer with its convex side facing out. Make sure that the brushes seat themselves on the commutator. Assemble the starter.

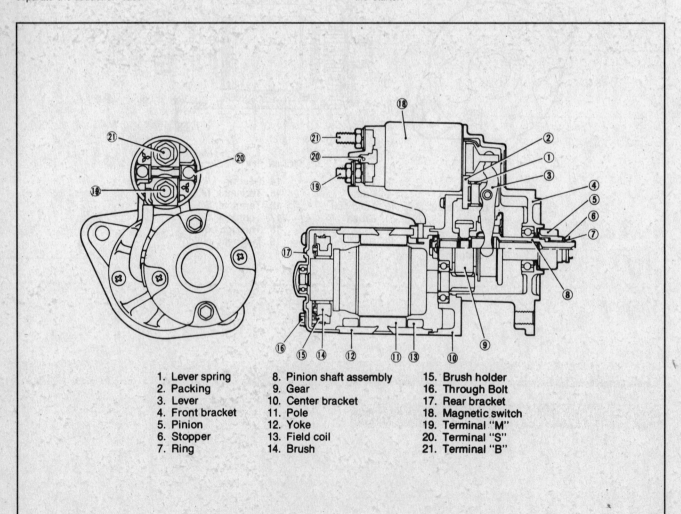

1. Lever spring	8. Pinion shaft assembly	15. Brush holder
2. Packing	9. Gear	16. Through Bolt
3. Lever	10. Center bracket	17. Rear bracket
4. Front bracket	11. Pole	18. Magnetic switch
5. Pinion	12. Yoke	19. Terminal "M"
6. Stopper	13. Field coil	20. Terminal "S"
7. Ring	14. Brush	21. Terminal "B"

Fig. 15 View of the gear reduction type starter motor

Troubleshooting Basic Starting System Problems

Problem	Cause	Solution
Starter motor rotates engine slowly	• Battery charge low or battery defective	• Charge or replace battery
	• Defective circuit between battery and starter motor	• Clean and tighten, or replace cables
	• Low load current	• Bench-test starter motor. Inspect for worn brushes and weak brush springs.
	• High load current	• Bench-test starter motor. Check engine for friction, drag or coolant in cylinders. Check ring gear-to-pinion gear clearance.
Starter motor will not rotate engine	• Battery charge low or battery defective	• Charge or replace battery
	• Faulty solenoid	• Check solenoid ground. Repair or replace as necessary.
	• Damage drive pinion gear or ring gear	• Replace damaged gear(s)
	• Starter motor engagement weak	• Bench-test starter motor
	• Starter motor rotates slowly with high load current	• Inspect drive yoke pull-down and point gap, check for worn end bushings, check ring gear clearance
	• Engine seized	• Repair engine
Starter motor drive will not engage (solenoid known to be good)	• Defective contact point assembly	• Repair or replace contact point assembly
	• Inadequate contact point assembly ground	• Repair connection at ground screw
	• Defective hold-in coil	• Replace field winding assembly
Starter motor drive will not disengage	• Starter motor loose on flywheel housing	• Tighten mounting bolts
	• Worn drive end busing	• Replace bushing
	• Damaged ring gear teeth	• Replace ring gear or driveplate
	• Drive yoke return spring broken or missing	• Replace spring
Starter motor drive disengages prematurely	• Weak drive assembly thrust spring	• Replace drive mechanism
	• Hold-in coil defective	• Replace field winding assembly
Low load current	• Worn brushes	• Replace brushes
	• Weak brush springs	• Replace springs

ENGINE MECHANICAL

Engine Overhaul Tips

Most engine overhaul procedures are fairly standard. In addition to specific parts replacement procedures and specifications for your individual engine, this section is also a guide to acceptable rebuilding procedures. Examples of standard rebuilding practice are given and should be used along with specific details concerning your particular engine.

Competent and accurate machine shop services will ensure maximum performance, reliability and engine life. In most instances it is more profitable for the do-it-yourself mechanic to remove, clean and inspect the component, buy the necessary parts and deliver these to a shop for actual machine work.

On the other hand, much of the rebuilding work (crankshaft, block, bearings, piston rods, and other components) is well within the scope of the do-it-yourself mechanic's tools and abilities. You will have to decide for yourself the depth of involvement you desire in an engine repair or rebuild.

TOOLS

The tools required for an engine overhaul or parts replacement will depend on the depth of your involvement. With a few exceptions, they will be the tools found in a mechanic's tool kit (see Section 1 of this manual). More in-depth work will require some or all of the following:
• A dial indicator (reading in thousandths) mounted on a universal base
• Micrometers and telescope gauges
• Jaw and screw-type pullers
• Scraper
• Valve spring compressor
• Ring groove cleaner
• Piston ring expander and compressor
• Ridge reamer
• Cylinder hone or glaze breaker
• Plastigage®
• Engine stand

The use of most of these tools is illustrated in this chapter. Many can be rented for a one-time use from a local parts jobber or tool supply house specializing in automotive work.

Occasionally, the use of special tools is called for. See the information on Special Tools and the Safety Notice in the front of this book before substituting another tool.

INSPECTION TECHNIQUES

Procedures and specifications are given in this chapter for inspecting, cleaning and assessing the wear limits of most major components. Other procedures such as Magnaflux® and Zyglo® can be used to locate material flaws and stress cracks. Magnaflux® is a magnetic process applicable only to ferrous materials. The Zyglo® process coats the material with a fluorescent dye penetrant and can be used on any material.

Checking for suspected surface cracks can be more readily made using spot check dye. The dye is sprayed onto the suspected area, wiped off and the area sprayed with a developer. Cracks will show up brightly.

OVERHAUL TIPS

Aluminum has become extremely popular for use in engines, due to its low weight. Observe the following precautions when handling aluminum parts:
• Never hot tank aluminum parts (the caustic hot tank solution will eat the aluminum.
• Remove all aluminum parts (identification tag, etc.) from engine parts prior to the tanking.
• Always coat threads lightly with engine oil or anti-seize compounds before installation, to prevent seizure.
• Never overtorque bolts or spark plugs especially in aluminum threads.

Stripped threads in any component can be repaired using any of several commercial repair kits (Heli-Coil®, Microdot®, Keenserts®, etc.).

When assembling the engine, any parts that will be exposed to frictional contact must be prelubed to provide lubrication at initial start-up. Any product specifically formulated for this purpose can be used, but engine oil is not recommended as a prelube in most cases.

When semi-permanent (locked, but removable) installation of bolts or nuts is desired, threads should be cleaned and coated with Loctite® or another similar, commercial non-hardening sealant.

REPAIRING DAMAGED THREADS

Several methods of repairing damaged threads are available. Heli-Coil® (shown here), Keenserts® and Microdot® are among the most widely used. All involve basically the same principle—drilling out stripped threads, tapping the hole and installing a pre-wound insert—making welding, plugging and oversize fasteners unnecessary.

Two types of thread repair inserts are usually supplied: a standard type for most inch coarse, inch fine, metric course and metric fine thread sizes and a spark lug type to fit most spark plug

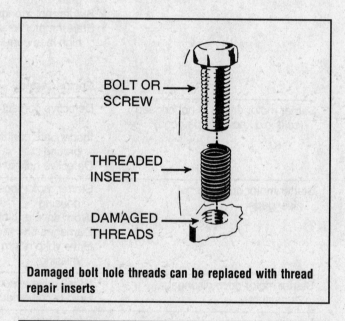

Damaged bolt hole threads can be replaced with thread repair inserts

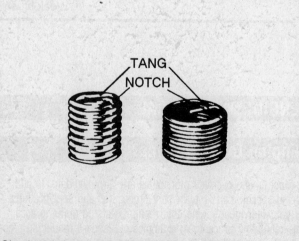

Standard thread repair insert (left), and spark plug thread insert

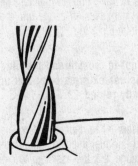

Drill out the damaged threads with the specified size bit. Be sure to drill completely through the hole or to the bottom of a blind hole

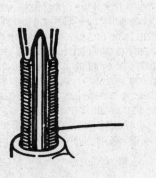

Using the kit, tap the hole in order to receive the thread insert. Keep the tap well oiled and back it out frequently to avoid clogging the threads

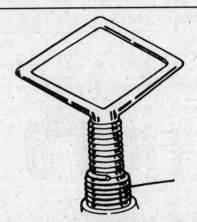

Screw the insert onto the installer tool until the tang engages the slot. Thread the insert into the hole until it is 1/4–1/2 turn below the top surface, then remove the tool and break off the tang using a punch

port sizes. Consult the individual tool manufacturer's catalog to determine exact applications. Typical thread repair kits will contain a selection of prewound threaded inserts, a tap (corresponding to the outside diameter threads of the insert) and an installation tool. Spark plug inserts usually differ because they require a tap equipped with pilot threads and a combined reamer/tap section. Most manufacturers also supply blister-packed thread repair inserts separately in addition to a master kit containing a variety of taps and inserts plus installation tools.

Before attempting to repair a threaded hole, remove any snapped, broken or damaged bolts or studs. Penetrating oil can be used to free frozen threads. The offending item can usually be removed with locking pliers or using a screw/stud extractor. After the hole is clear, the thread can be repaired, as shown in the series of accompanying illustrations and in the kit manufacturer's instructions.

Description

The engine is a compact, inline 4-cylinder powerplant. The engine block is a special cast iron alloy: the cylinder head and timing case cover are aluminum alloy. The engine is undersquare i.e., the stroke is larger than the bore. With this design, the surface area-to-volume ratio is smaller, which helps minimize hydrocarbons emissions. Five main bearings support the forged steel crankshaft. Forged connecting rods attach the aluminum pistons to the crankshaft. Full floating piston pins are used and are offset on the thrust side to minimize piston slap. Later model engines, in the United States, have the MCA-Jet system which allows better combustion (less emissions) and improved fuel economy through the use of a jet valve in each of the cylinders (see Section 4 for details).

The overhead camshaft is driven (depending on the year or engine) by the crank through a double-row, roller chain or a cogged rubber timing belt. The cam runs in five bearings (three on the 1410 and 1468cc engines) and operates directly on the rocker arms. Intake and exhaust rockers are mounted on separate shafts. Rockers act directly on the valves, which open and close in a hemispherical combustion chamber formed by a domed combustion chamber and a flat topped piston. The cylinder head is a cross-flow design. The carburetor feeds into the intake manifold on one side of the engine and the exhaust gases are exited through the exhaust manifold on the opposite side of the engine. This design permits much more efficient cylinder head porting (breathing).

A silent shaft engine is also offered. The silent shaft engine incorporates two chain or belt driven counterbalance shafts mounted in the cylinder block. The counterbalance shafts rotate at twice crankshaft speed and in opposite directions to balance out the usual vibration associated with a 4-cylinder engine.

Checking Engine Compression

A noticeable lack of engine power, excessive oil consumption and/or poor fuel mileage measured over an extended period are all indicators of internal engine wear. Worn piston rings, scored or worn cylinder bores, blown head gaskets, sticking or burnt valves and worn valve seats are all possible culprits here. A check of each cylinder's compression will help you locate the problems.

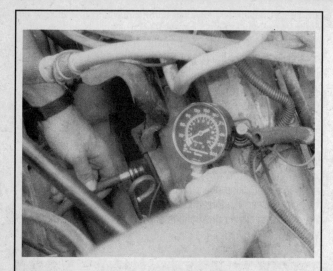

A screw-in type compression gauge is more accurate and easier to use without an assistant

As mentioned in the Tools and equipment portion of Section 1, a screw-in type compression gauge is more accurate than the type you simply hold against the spark plug hole, although it takes slightly longer to use. It's worth it to obtain a more accurate reading. Follow the procedures below.

1. Warm up the engine to normal operating temperature.
2. Remove all spark plugs.
3. Disconnect the high tension lead from the ignition coil.
4. On carbureted cars, fully open the throttle either by operating the carburetor throttle linkage by hand or by having an as-sistant floor the accelerator pedal. On fuel injected cars, disconnect the cold start valve and all injector connections.

5. Screw the compression gauge into the No. 1 spark plug hold until the fitting is snug.

→**Be careful not to crossthread the plug hold. On aluminum cylinder heads use extra care, as the threads in these heads are easily ruined.**

6. Ask an assistant to depress the accelerator pedal fully on both carbureted and fuel injected cars. Then, while you read the compression gauge, ask the assistant to crank the engine two or three times in short bursts using the ignition switch.
7. Read the compression gauge at the end of each series of cranks, and record the highest of these readings. Repeat this procedure for each of the engine's cylinders. Compare the highest reading of each cylinder.
8. A cylinder's compression pressure is usually acceptable if it is not less than 80% of maximum. The difference between each cylinder should be no more than 12–14 pounds.
9. If a cylinder is unusually low, pour a tablespoon of clean engine oil into the cylinder through the spark plug hold and repeat the compression test. If the compression comes up after adding the oil, it appears that that cylinder's piston rings or bore are damaged or worn. If the pressure remains low, the valves may not be seating properly (a valve job is needed), or the head gasket may be blown near that cylinder. If compression in any two adjacent cylinders is low, and if the addition of oil doesn't help the compression, there is leakage past the head gasket. Oil and coolant water in the combustion chamber can result from this problem. There may be evidence of water droplets on the engine dipstick when a head gasket has blown.

General Engine Specifications

Engine (cc)	Years	Fuel System Type	SAE net Horsepower @ rpm	SAE net Torque ft. lb. @ rpm	Bore x Stroke	Comp. Ratio	Oil Press. (psi.) @ 2000 rpm
1410	1979–84	2-bbl	70 @ 5200	78 @ 3000	2.91 x 3.23	8.8:1	50–64
1468	1985	2-bbl	77 @ 5300	84 @ 3000	2.97 x 3.23	9.4:1	50–64
1597	1971–73	2-bbl	100 @ 6300	101 @ 4000	3.03 x 3.39	8.5:1	28–57
	1974	2-bbl	83 @ 5600	83 @ 3600	3.03 x 3.39	8.5:1	28–57
	1975	2-bbl	79 @ 5300	86 @ 3000	3.03 x 3.39	8.5:1	57–71
	1976–78	2-bbl	83 @ 5500	89 @ 3500	3.03 x 3.39	8.5:1	57–71
	1979–84	2-bbl	77 @ 5200	78 @ 3000	3.03 x 3.39	8.5:1	57–71
1597 Turbo	1984–89	TBI	102 @ 5500	122 @ 3000	3.03 x 3.39	7.6:1	57–71
1994	1974–83	2-bbl	93 @ 5200	108 @ 3000	3.31 x 3.54	8.5:1	50–64
1997	1985–89	①	88 @ 5000	108 @ 3500	3.34 x 3.46	8.5:1	57–71
2555	1979–83	2-bbl	105 @ 5000	139 @ 2500	3.59 x 3.86	8.2:1	50–64
	1984–89	EFI/Turbo	145 @ 5000 ②	185 @ 2500	3.59 x 3.86	7.0:1	50–64

① 2 bbl or EFI
② Intercooled 170 @ 2500/220 @ 2500

Valve Specifications

Year & Engine	Seat Angle (deg)	Face Angle (deg)	Spring Test Pressure (lbs. @ in.)	Spring Installed Height (in.)	Stem to Guide Clearance (in.)		Stem Diameter (in.)	
					Intake	Exhaust	Intake	Exhaust
1979–84 1410cc	45	45	69 @ 1.417	1.417	.0012– .0024	.0020– .0035	.3147– .3153	.3147– .3153
1985–89 1468cc	45	45	69 @ 1.417	1.417	.0012– .0024	.0020– .0035	.3147– .3153	.3147– .3153
1971–89 1597cc	45	45	61 @ 1.470	1.470	.0012– .0024	.0020– .0035	.3147– .3153	.3147– .3153
1974–83 1994cc	45	45	61 @ 1.590	1.590	.0010– .0022	.0020– .0033	.3147– .3153	.3147– .3153
1985–89 1997cc	45	45	40 @ 1.591	1.591	.0012– .0024	.0020– .0035	.3147– .3153	.3147– .3153
1979–89 2555cc	45	45	61 @ 1.590	1.590	.0012– .0024	.0020– .0035	.3147– .3153	.3147– .3153
Jet Valve	45	45	5.5 @ .846	.846	—	—	——.1693——	

Camshaft Specifications

All measurements given in inches

Engine & Year	Journal Diameter					Bearing Clearance	Cam Height		End Play
	1	2	3	4	5		Int.	Exh.	
1410cc 1468cc	1.339	1.339	1.339	1.339	1.339	.0020– .0035	1.500	1.504	.002– .008
1597cc 1971–73	1.339	1.339	1.339	1.339	1.339	.0020– .0035	1.423	1.425	.002– .006
1597cc 1974–75	1.339	1.339	1.339	1.339	1.339	.0020– .0035	1.437	1.439	.002– .006
1597cc 1976–78	1.339	1.339	1.339	1.339	1.339	.0020– .0035	1.431	1.439	.002– .006
1597cc 1979–85	1.339	1.339	1.339	1.339	1.339	.0020– .0035	1.433	1.433	.002– .006
1994cc All	1.339	1.339	1.339	1.339	1.339	.0020– .0045	1.660	1.663	.004– .008
1997cc All	1.339	1.339	1.339	1.339	1.339	.0020– .0040	1.657	1.657	.004– .008
2555cc All	1.339	1.339	1.339	1.339	1.339	.0020– .0045	1.660 ①	1.663 ①	.004– .008

① 1984–89: 1.673

Crankshaft and Connecting Rod Specifications

All measurements given in inches

Engine & Year	Crankshaft				Connecting Rod		
	Main Bearing Journal Dia.	Main Bearing Oil Clearance	Shaft End Play	Thrust on No.	Journal Dia.	Oil Clearance	Side Clearance
1410cc 1468cc	1.8898	.0008–.0028	.002–.007	3	1.6535	.0004–.0024	.004–.010
1597cc 1971–76	2.2441	.0006–.0031	.002–.007	3	1.7717	.0004–.0028	.004–.010
1597cc 1977–89	2.2441	.0008–.0028	.002–.007	3	1.7717	.0004–.0028	.004–.010
1994cc All	2.5984	.0008–.0028	.002–.007	3	2.0866	.0008–.0028	.004–.010
1997cc 1985–89	2.2441	.0008–.0020	.002–.007	3	1.7717	.0008–.0020	.004–.010
2555cc 1979–83	2.5984	.0008–.0028	.002–.007	3	2.0866	.0008–.0028	.004–.010
2555cc 1984–89	2.3622	.0008–.0020	.002–.007	3	2.0866	.0008–.0024	.004–.010

Piston and Ring Specifications

All measurements given in inches

Engine & Year	Ring Gap			Ring Side Clearance			Piston to Bore Clearance
	#1 Compr.	#2 Compr.	Oil Control	#1 Compr.	#2 Compr.	Oil Control	
1410cc 1979–84	.0080–.0160	.0080–.0160	.0080–.0200	.0012–.0028	.0008–.0024	snug	.0008–.0016
1468cc 1985–89	.0080–.0160	.0080–.0160	.0080–.0200	.0012–.0028	.0008–.0024	snug	.0008–.0016
1597cc 1971–75	.0060–.0140	.0060–.0140	.0060–.0140	.0012–.0028	.0008–.0024	.0010–.0030	.0008–.0016
1597cc 1976–84	.0080–.0160	.0080–.0160	.0080–.0200	.0012–.0028	.0008–.0024	.0010–.0030	.0008–.0016
1597cc 1985–89	.0100–.0160	.0080–.0140	.0080–.0280	.0012–.0028	.0008–.0024	snug	.0008–.0016
1994cc 1974–75	.0118–.0197	.0098–.0177	.0098–.0177	.0012–.0028	.0008–.0024	.0008–.0026	.0008–.0016
1994cc 1976	.0098–.0157	.0098–.0177	.0098–.0177	.0024–.0039	.0008–.0024	.0008–.0024	.0008–.0016
1994cc 1977–83	.0098–.0177	.0098–.0177	.0078–.0354	.0024–.0039	.0008–.0024	.0008–.0024	.0008–.0016
1997cc 1985–89	.0098–.0127	.0079–.0138	.0080–.0276	.0012–.0028	.0008–.0024	snug	.0004–.0012
2555cc 1978–83	.0098–.0177	.0098–.0177	.0078–.0354	.0024–.0039	.0008–.0024	.0008–.0024	.0008–.0016
2555cc 1984–89	.0120–.0177	.0100–.0157	.0120–.0310	.0020–.0035	.0010–.0020	snug	.0012–.0020

Torque Specifications

All figures are given in ft. lb.

Engine & Year	Cyl. Head	Conn. Rod	Main Bearing	Crankshaft Damper	Flywheel	Manifold	
						Intake	Exhaust
1410cc 1979–84	50–54	23–25	37–39	37–43	94–101	11–14	11–14
1468cc 1985–89	50–54	23–25	37–39	47–54 ③	②	11–14	11–14
1597cc 1971–73	50–54	23–25	36–40	43–50	69–76	11–14	11–14
1597cc 1974–76	50–54	23–25	36–40	43–50	83–90	11–14	11–14
1597cc 1977–89	50–54	23–25	36–40	43–50	94–101 MT 84–90 AT	11–14	11–14
1994cc 1974–75	65–72	33–35	54–61	80–93	83–90	11–14	11–14
1994cc 1976–83	65–72	33–35	54–61	80–93	94–101 MT 84–90 AT	11–14	11–14
1997cc 1985–89	65–72	37–38	37–39	80–94	94–101 MT 84–90 AT ②	11–14	11–14
2555cc 1979–89	65–72 ①	33–35	54–61	80–93	94–101 MT 84–90 AT ②	11–14	11–14

① The head bolts marked #11 in the illustration showing torque sequence should be torque to 15 ft. lb. The bolts extend into the timing case cover.

② 1985–89. Both manual and automatic transmission torque is 94–101 ft. lb.

③ 1986–89: 55–72 ft. lbs.

Engine

REMOVAL & INSTALLATION

Rear Wheel Drive Models
◗ See Figures 16 and 17
➡ The factory recommends removing the engine and transmission as a unit.

1. Drain the cooling system. Open the radiator petcock and the engine drain plug.

✳✳ CAUTION

When draining engine coolant, keep in mind that cats and dogs are attracted to ethylene glycol antifreeze and could drink any that is left in an uncovered container or in puddles on the ground. This will prove fatal in sufficient quantity. Always drain coolant into a sealable container. Coolant should be reused unless it is contaminated or is several years old.

2. Disconnect and remove the battery.
3. Disconnect the coil, throttle positioner solenoid, fuel cut-off solenoid, alternator, starter, transmission switch, back-up light switch, and temperature and oil pressure gauge sending units.

✳✳ CAUTION

Please refer to Section 1 before discharging the compressor or disconnecting air conditioning lines. Damage to the air conditioning system or personal injury could result. Consult your local laws concerning refrigerant discharge and recycling. In many areas it may be illegal for anyone but a certified technician to service the A/C system. Always use an approved recovery station when discharging the air conditioning.

4. On cars with air conditioning, the refrigerant must be released from the system.
5. Remove all air cleaner hoses. Remove the wing nut (and snap clips) and the air cleaner top cover.
6. Remove the two retaining nuts and bracket and remove the air cleaner housing.
7. Disconnect the accelerator cable.
8. Remove and plug the heater hose.
9. Remove the exhaust manifold nuts and drop the pipe down and out of the way.
10. Disconnect and cap the fuel lines at the pump. On cars with fuel injection, see Section 5 for the procedure necessary to bleed the pressure from the system before disconnecting the lines.
11. Disconnect the vacuum hose from the canister purge valve located on the passenger side firewall. Remove the purge hose which runs from the valve to the intake manifold.

When removing nuts, bolts and other parts, place them in a tray or other container

12. Scribe a line around the hood hinges, then remove the hood. Place it away from the work area or it will invariably become scratched or dented.

13. Remove the grille, radiator cross panel, the radiator and condenser. Disconnect and plug the oil cooler lines on automatic transmission equipped cars.

14. Jack up the front of the car and support it on jackstands. Remove the splash shield.

15. Drain the engine oil and the transmission oil or fluid. Remove the driveshaft.

✳✳ CAUTION

The EPA warns that prolonged contact with used engine oil may cause a number of skin disorders, including cancer! You should make every effort to minimize you exposure to used engine oil. Protective gloves should be worn when changing the oil. Wash your hands and any other exposed skin areas as soon as possible after exposure to used engine oil. Soap and water, or waterless hand cleaner should be used.

16. Disconnect the speedometer cable and back-up switch wire. Remove the neutral switch wire on automatic cars.

17. On manual transmission cars: Disconnect the clutch cable from the clutch lever.

18. Remove the control rod and the cross shaft that are located under the transmission.

19. Unite and open the leather shift boot. Pull the rug back. Remove the four retaining bolts and remove the shift lever.

20. On automatic transmission cars: Disconnect the transmission control rod from the shift linkage.

21. On all transmission models: Attach the lifting device to the two engine brackets provided by the factory, one near the water neck at the front and the other on the passenger's side at the rear.

22. Raise the engine a slight amount and remove the retaining nuts on the side mounts and the rear crossmember mount.

23. Lift the engine out of the compartment by tilting it at approximately a 45° angle.

To install:

24. Check the condition of the engine mounts. There are three: left front, right front, and rear. If they are at all questionable, now is the time to replace them.

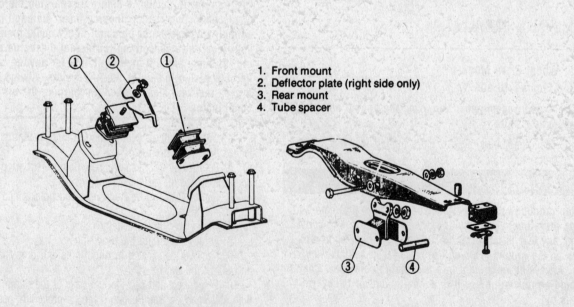

1. Front mount
2. Deflector plate (right side only)
3. Rear mount
4. Tube spacer

Fig. 16 Rear wheel drive engine mounting; most models similar

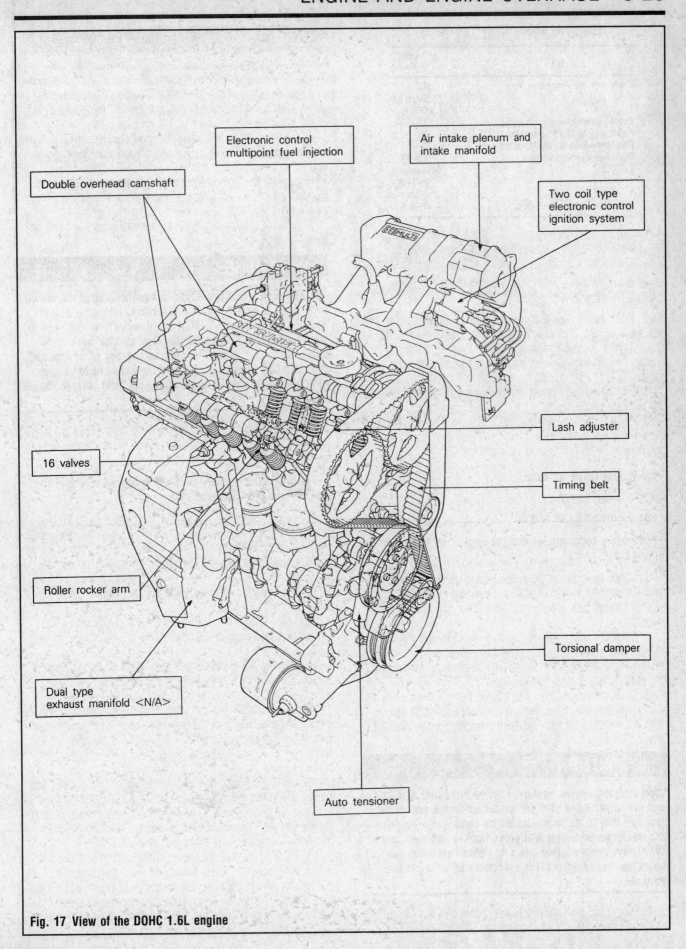

Fig. 17 View of the DOHC 1.6L engine

Engine Mounting Torques

Bolt	Torque (ft. lbs.)
Front mount-to-crossmember	15–17 (22–29 for 2000 cc)
Front mount-to-engine bracket nut	15–17
Front engine block-to-bracket bolt	29–36
Rear mount-to-support bracket	7–8.5
Rear mount-to-frame bolt	15–17 (Manual) 9–11.5 (Automatic)
Crossmember-to-body bolt	7–8.5

25. Installing the engine is basically a reverse of the removal procedure, noting the following:

26. Drape heavy rags over the rear of the cylinder head to prevent damaging the firewall when lowering the engine into place.

27. Tighten the two front mounts first, then the rear crossmember mount. All tightening torques are listed in the chart below.

28. Fill the cooling system, engine crankcase, and the transmission with the proper fluids.

29. Double check everything: fuel lines, coolant lines, electrical connections, and bolt torques. Then, and only then, start the engine and check for correct operation and leaks.

Front Wheel Drive Models

EXCEPT 4-WD VISTA

▸ See Figures 18, 19 and 20

➡The factory recommends that the engine and transaxle be removed as a unit.

1. Scribe the hood hinge outline on the underside of the hood. Remove the hood. Disconnect the battery cables (ground cable first) remove battery hold-down and battery. Remove the battery tray.

2. Remove the air cleaner assembly. Disconnect the purge control vacuum hose from the purge valve. Remove the purge control valve mounting bracket. Remove the windshield washer reservoir, radiator tank and carbon canister.

3. Drain the coolant from the radiator. Remove the radiator assembly with the electric cooling fan attached. Be sure to disconnect the fan wiring harness and the transmission cooler lines (if equipped).

✳✳ CAUTION

When draining engine coolant, keep in mind that cats and dogs are attracted to ethylene glycol antifreeze and could drink any that is left in an uncovered container or in puddles on the ground. This will prove fatal in sufficient quantity. Always drain coolant into a sealable container. Coolant should be reused unless it is contaminated or is several years old.

4. Disconnect the following cables, hoses and wires from the engine and transaxle: Clutch, Accelerator, Speedometer, Heater hose, Fuel lines, PCV vacuum line. High altitude compensator vacuum hose (Calif. Models), Bowl vent valve purge hose (U.S.A. Models), Inhibitor switch (Auto Trans), Control Cable (Auto Trans), Starter, Engine Ground Cable, Alternator, Water Temperature, Ignition Coil, Water Temperature Sensor, Back-up Light (Man. Trans), Oil Pressure Wires, and the ISC cable on fuel injected cars.

5. Remove the ignition coil. The next step will be to jack up the car. Before you do this, look around and make sure all wires and hoses are disconnected.

6. Jack up the front of the car after you block the rear wheels. Support the car on jackstands. Remove the splash shield (if equipped).

7. Drain the lubricant out of the transaxle, and drain the engine oil.

✳✳ CAUTION

The EPA warns that prolonged contact with used engine oil may cause a number of skin disorders, including cancer! You should make every effort to minimize you exposure to used engine oil. Protective gloves should be worn when changing the oil. Wash your hands and any other exposed skin areas as soon as possible after exposure to used engine oil. Soap and water, or waterless hand cleaner should be used.

8. Remove the right and left halfshafts from the transaxle and support them with wire. Plug the transaxle case holes so dirt cannot enter.

➡The driveshaft retainer circlip ring should be replaced whenever the shaft is removed.

9. Disconnect the assist rod and the control rod from the transaxle. If the car is equipped with a range selector, disconnect the selector cable.

10. Remove the mounting bolts/bolt from the front and rear roll control rods.

11. Disconnect the exhaust pipe from the engine and secure it with wire.

12. Loosen the engine and transaxle mounting bracket nuts. On turbocharged engines, disconnect the oil cooler tube.

13. Lower the car.

14. Attach a lifting device and shop crane or chain hoist to the engine. Remove the engine and transaxle mounting nuts and bolts.

15. Make sure the rear roll control rod is disconnected. Lift the engine and transaxle from the car. Make sure the transaxle does not hit the battery bracket when the engine and transaxle are lifted.

To install:

16. Lower the engine and transaxle carefully into position and loosely install the mounting bolts. Temporarily tighten the front and rear roll control rods mounting bolts. Lower the full weight of the engine and transaxle onto the mounts and tighten the nuts and bolts. Loosen and retighten the roll control rods.

17. Install the rest of the engine controls, lines and components. Make sure all cables, hoses and wires are connected. Fill the radiator with coolant, the transaxle with lubricant, and the engine with oil. Adjust the clutch cable and accelerator cable. Adjust the transaxle control rod. Take another check on everything you have done, start the engine and check for leaks.

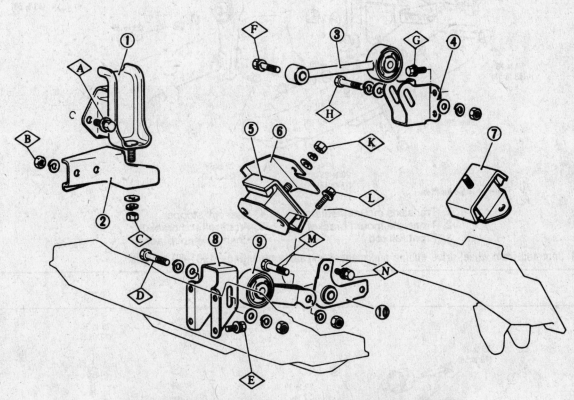

1. Transaxle mount insulator
2. Transaxle mount bracket
3. Roll rod, rear
4. Roll rod bracket
5. Engine mount front insulator
6. Heat protector
7. Engine mount rear insulator
8. Roll rod bracket
9. Roll rod, front
10. Roll rod bracket

Tightening torque   NM (ft-lb)
(A) 29 to 41 (22 to 30)
(B) 18 to 25 (13 to 18)
(C) 29 to 34 (22 to 25)
(D) 29 to 41 (22 to 30)
(E) 15 to 22 (11 to 16)
(F) 29 to 41 (22 to 30)
(G) 15 to 22 (11 to 16)
(H) 29 to 41 (22 to 30)
(K) 18 to 25 (13 to 18)
(L) 29 to 41 (22 to 30)
(M) 29 to 41 (22 to 30)
(N) 15 to 22 (11 to 16)

Fig. 18 Exploded view of the engine mounting and torque specifications—models through 1980

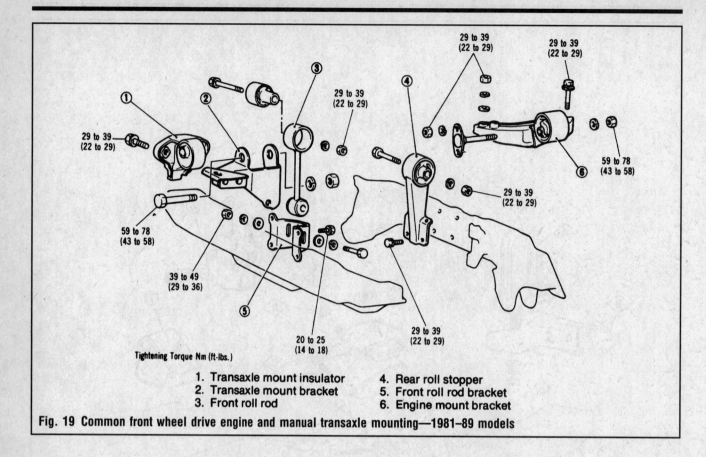

Tightening Torque Nm (ft-lbs.)

1. Transaxle mount insulator
2. Transaxle mount bracket
3. Front roll rod
4. Rear roll stopper
5. Front roll rod bracket
6. Engine mount bracket

Fig. 19 Common front wheel drive engine and manual transaxle mounting—1981–89 models

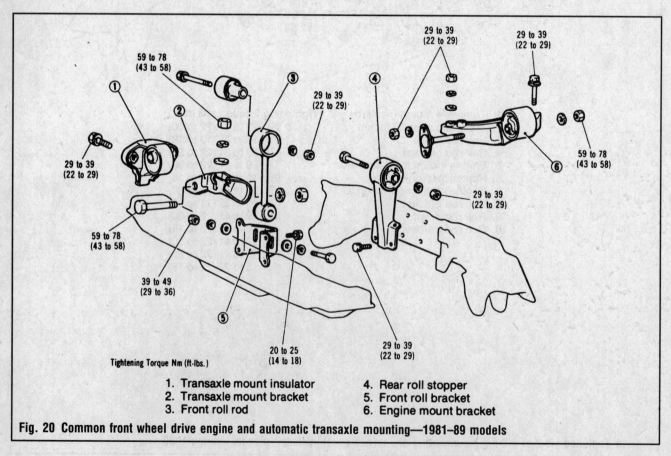

Tightening Torque Nm (ft-lbs.)

1. Transaxle mount insulator
2. Transaxle mount bracket
3. Front roll rod
4. Rear roll stopper
5. Front roll bracket
6. Engine mount bracket

Fig. 20 Common front wheel drive engine and automatic transaxle mounting—1981–89 models

4-WD VISTA

1. Scribe the hood hinge outlines on the underside of the hood. Remove the hood. Remove the battery, battery tray and bracket.
2. Disconnect the engine oil pressure switch and power steering pump connectors.
3. Disconnect the alternator harness.
4. Remove the air cleaner.
5. Remove the high tension cable from the distributor.
6. Disconnect the engine ground wire at the firewall.
7. Remove the windshield washer bottle.
8. Disconnect the brake booster vacuum hose.
9. Disconnect and tag all other vacuum lines connected to the engine.
10. Drain the coolant.

✳✳ CAUTION

When draining engine coolant, keep in mind that cats and dogs are attracted to ethylene glycol antifreeze and could drink any that is left in an uncovered container or in puddles on the ground. This will prove fatal in sufficient quantity. Always drain coolant into a sealable container. Coolant should be reused unless it is contaminated or is several years old.

11. Remove the coolant reservoir tank.
12. Remove the radiator.
13. Disconnect the heater hoses at the engine.
14. Disconnect the accelerator cable.
15. Disconnect the speed control cable.
16. Disconnect the speedometer cable at the transaxle.

✳✳ CAUTION

Please refer to Section 1 before discharging the compressor or disconnecting air conditioning lines. Damage to the air conditioning system or personal injury could result. Consult your local laws concerning refrigerant discharge and recycling. In many areas it may be illegal for anyone but a certified technician to service the A/C system. Always use an approved recovery station when discharging the air conditioning.

17. If the car is equipped with air conditioning, the system must be bled.
18. Disconnect the hoses at the air conditioning compressor and cap all openings immediately.
19. Disconnect the hoses at the power steering pump.
20. On fuel injected models, discharge the fuel system pressure. Disconnect the fuel return hose, then the fuel inlet hose, at the carburetor or fuel rail.
21. Disconnect the shift control cables at the transaxle.
22. Raise and support the car on jackstands.
23. Remove the lower cover and skid plate.
24. Drain the transaxle and transfer case.
25. Disconnect the oxygen sensor, and disconnect the exhaust pipe from the manifold.

26. Remove the driveshaft to the rear wheels.
27. Remove the clutch slave cylinder.
28. Disconnect the halfshafts at the transaxle.
29. Remove the transfer case extension stopper bracket.

➡ **The two top stopper bracket bolts are easier to get at from the engine compartment, using a T-type box wrench.**

30. Lower the vehicle to the ground.
31. Remove the nuts only, from the engine mount-to-body bracket.
32. Remove the range select control valves from the transaxle insulator bracket.
33. Remove the nut only, from the transaxle mounting insulator.
34. Remove the front roll insulator nut.
35. Remove the heat shield attaching bolt.
36. Remove the rear insulator-to-engine nut.
37. Remove the grille and valance panel.
38. Remove the A/C condenser.
39. Take up the weight of the engine with a shop crane attached to the lifting eyes.
40. Remove all the mounting bolts from which you previously removed the nuts.
41. Double check that you have disconnected all wiring, hoses and cables from the engine, transaxle and transfer case. Move the assembly forward slightly to a point at which it will clear the floorpan, and lift the whole assembly clear of the car.
42. Lower the engine and transaxle into position. Install the engine/transaxle mount attaching bolts and nuts loosely. Install the components in the reverse of removal. After the full weight of the engine/transaxle assembly lowered into position, tighten the mounting bolts and nuts. Observe the following torques:
- Transaxle stopper: 58 ft. lbs.
- Engine-to-body bracket bolts: 47 ft. lbs.
- Rear insulator: 29 ft. lbs.
- Transaxle mount nuts: 58 ft. lbs.
- Heat shield: 7 ft. lbs.
- Front roll bracket nuts: 36 ft. lbs.

Rocker Arm (Valve) Cover

REMOVAL & INSTALLATION

1. Remove air cleaner, air cleaner snorkel, mounting brackets and remove plug wires from mounting clip if necessary. Label vacuum hoses that are disconnected for reinstallation identification.
2. Disconnect breather hoses and remove cover mounting bolts. Remove valve cover.

To install:

3. Clean all mounting surfaces. Inspect the breather seal, camshaft end seal and valve cover end seals that are mounted on the cylinder head. Replace as necessary.
4. Install a new valve cover gasket into the mounting slot. Apply RTV sealant to the end seals and install the valve cover. Run engine until normal operating temperature is reached. Shut the engine OFF and check for oil leaks.

Remove the snorkel

. . . discard the old gasket

Loosen and remove the valve cover mounting bolts

Remove the valve cover and . . .

Rocker Arm and Shaft

To service the rocker arms or camshaft while the cylinder head is still mounted on the cylinder block and in the car:

1. Remove the breather hoses, purge hose and air cleaner. Disconnect the spark plug cables.

2. Turn the crankshaft until number 1 piston is on TDC (refer to Section 2).

3. Refer to the cylinder head removal portion in this section. Locate the engine size and year of your car as listed between Steps 7 and 11. Proceed with the steps pertaining to your car and remove the cam sprocket, timing chain/belt and rocker arm cover.

REMOVAL & INSTALLATION

Except 1985–89 1977cc and 2555cc Engines

▶ **See Figures 21, 22, 23 and 24**

If the cylinder head has been removed from the car or the preceding steps have been followed:

1. Matchmark the camshaft/rocker arm bearing caps to their cylinder head location (Except 1410cc and 1468cc engine).

2. Loosen the bearing cap bolts, or the rocker shaft bolts (1410cc and 1468cc engines) from the cylinder head but do not remove them from the caps or shafts. Lift the rocker assembly from the cylinder head as a unit.

3. The rocker arm assembly can be disassembled by the removal of the mounting bolts (and dowel pins on some models) from the bearing caps and or shafts.

➡**Keep the rocker arms and springs in the same order as disassembly. The left and right springs have different tension ratings and free length. Observe the location of the rocker arms as they are removed. Exhaust and intake, right and left are different. Do not get them mixed up.**

4. Observe the mating marks and reassemble the units, install the assembly in position on the cylinder head after all necessary service has been done.

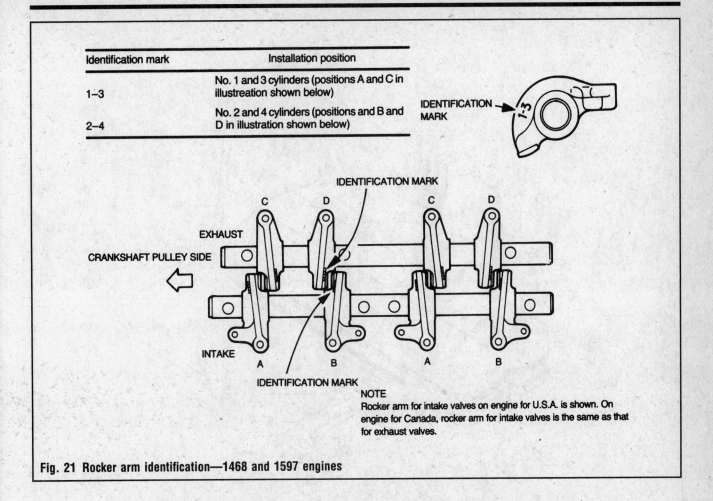

Identification mark	Installation position
1–3	No. 1 and 3 cylinders (positions A and C in illustreation shown below)
2–4	No. 2 and 4 cylinders (positions and B and D in illustration shown below)

NOTE
Rocker arm for intake valves on engine for U.S.A. is shown. On engine for Canada, rocker arm for intake valves is the same as that for exhaust valves.

Fig. 21 Rocker arm identification—1468 and 1597 engines

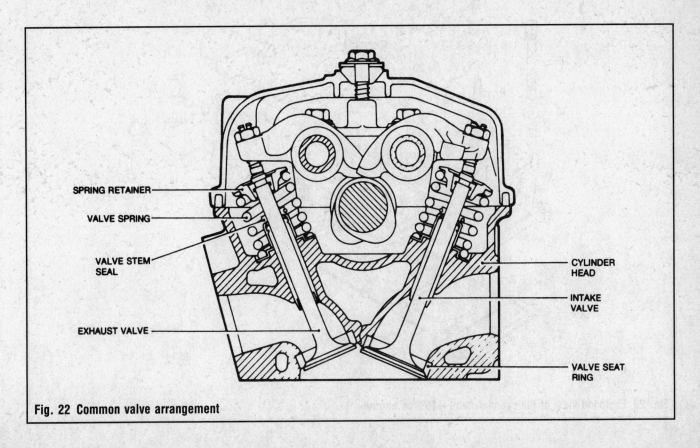

Fig. 22 Common valve arrangement

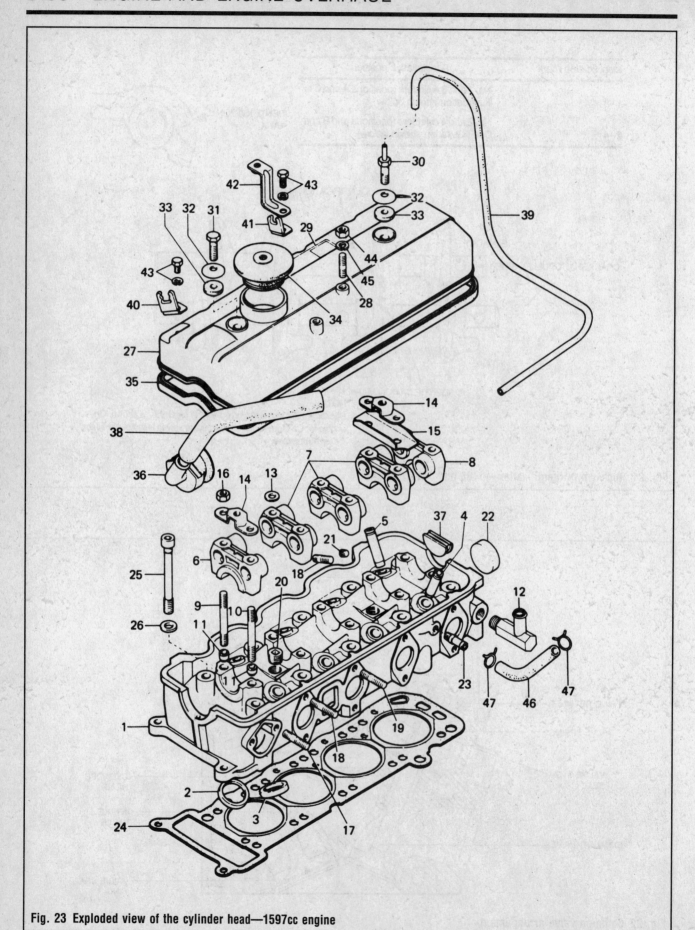

Fig. 23 Exploded view of the cylinder head—1597cc engine

1. Cylinder head
2. Intake valve seat
3. Exhaust valve seat
4. Intake valve guide
5. Exhaust valve guide
6. Front camshaft bearing cap
7. Center camshaft bearing caps
8. Rear camshaft bearing cap
9. Stud
10. Stud
11. Dowel bushing
12. Joint
13. Washer
14. Valve cover bracket
15. Baffle plate
16. Nut
17. Stud
18. Stud
19. Stud
20. Plug
21. Plug
22. Expansion plug
23. Hose fitting
24. Cylinder head gasket
25. Bolt
26. Washer
27. Valve cover
28. Stud
29. Label
30. Fitting/bolt
31. Bolt
32. Washer
33. Oil seal
34. Oil filler cap
35. Valve cover gasket
36. Breather
37. Seal
38. Breather hose
39. Hose
40. Spark plug wire bracket
41. Spark plug wire bracket
42. Air cleaner bracket
43. Bolt
44. Nut
45. Washer
46. Water hose
47. Clamp

Fig. 24 Cylinder head parts identification chart—1597cc engine

Loosen . . .

Lift the whole shaft assembly from the engine

. . . then remove the shaft mounting bolts

1997cc and 2555cc Engines

♦ See Figures 25 thru 33

➡A special tool, MD998443, is required to retain the automatic lash adjusters in this procedure.

1. Remove the rocker cover and gasket, and the timing belt cover.

2. Turn the crankshaft so that the #1 piston is at TDC compression. At this point, the timing mark on the camshaft sprocket and the timing mark on the head to the left of the sprocket will be aligned.

3. Remove the camshaft bearing cap bolts.

4. Install the automatic lash adjuster retainer tool, MD998443, to keep the adjuster from falling out of the rocker arms.

5. Lift off the bearing caps and rocker arm assemblies.

6. The rocker arms may now be removed from the shafts.

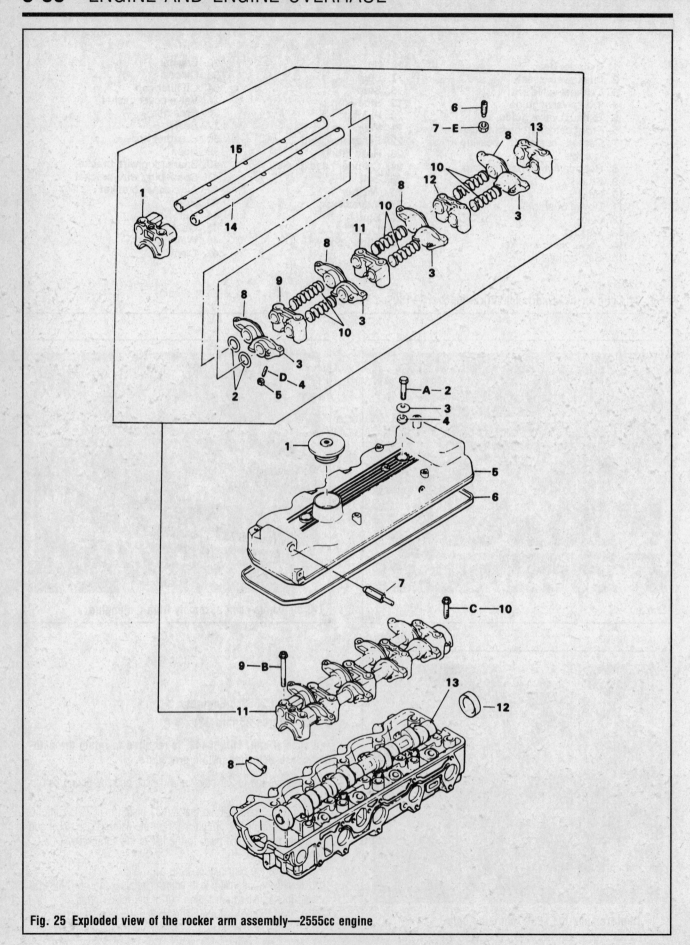

Fig. 25 Exploded view of the rocker arm assembly—2555cc engine

1. Oil filler cap
2. Bolt—8x40 (2)
3. Washer (2)
4. Oil seal (2)
5. Rocker cover
6. Rocker cover gasket
7. PCV valve
8. Semi-circular packing
9. Flange bolt (10)
10. Flange bolt—8x25 (2)
11. Rocker arm and shaft assembly
-1 Bearing cap, front
-2 Wave washer (2)
-3 Rocker arm "A" (4)
-4 Adjusting screw (4)
-5 Nut (4)
-6 Adjusting screw (8)
-7 Nut (8)
-8 Rocker arm "C" (4)

-9 Bearing cap, No. 2
-10 Rocker arm spring (6)
-11 Bearing cap, No. 3
-12 Bearing cap, No. 4
-13 Bearing cap, rear
-14 Rocker arm shaft, left
-15 Rocker arm shaft, right
12. Circular packing
13. Camshaft

	Nm	ft. lbs.
A	5–6.8	3.7–5.0
B	19–20	14–15
C	20–26	15–19
D	8–9.5	6–7
E	12–17	9–13

Fig. 26 Exploded view of the rocker arm assembly component list—2555cc engine

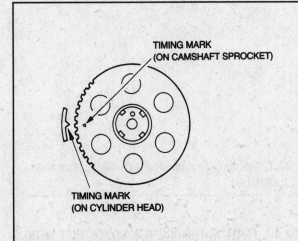

Fig. 27 Camshaft timing alignment mark for No. 1 TDC—1997 engine

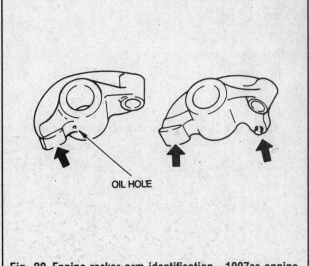

Fig. 29 Engine rocker arm identification—1997cc engine

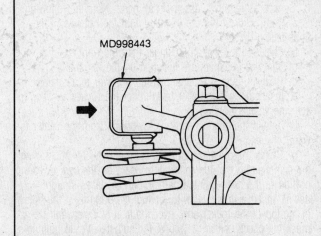

Fig. 28 The use of a lash adjuster holding tool may be necessary to perform this procedure

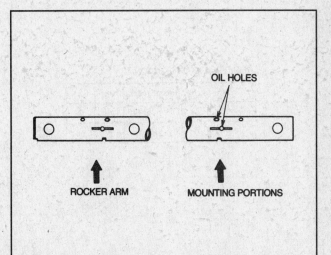

Fig. 30 Engine rocker arm shaft identification—1997cc engine

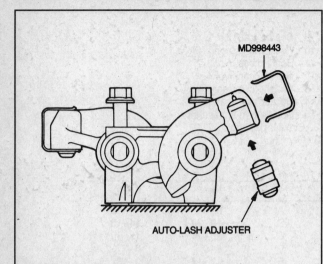

Fig. 31 Installing the automatic lash adjuster with special tool MD998443

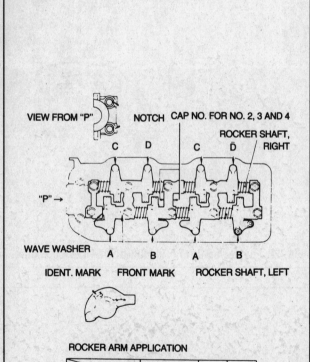

Fig. 32 Engine rocker arm shaft identification—1997cc engine

ROCKER ARM APPLICATION

	Ident. mark	In.	Ex.
No. 1 & 3 cyl.	1–3	A	C
No. 2 & 4 cyl.	2–4	B	D

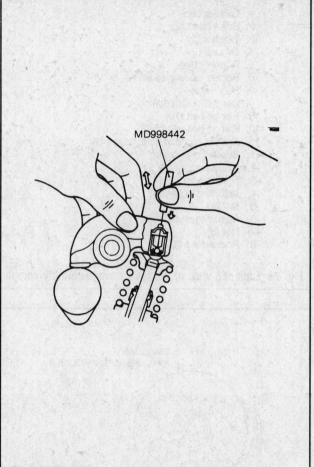

Fig. 33 Checking the automatic lash adjuster operation after installation

➡**KEEP ALL PARTS IN THE ORDER IN WHICH THEY WERE REMOVED. NONE OF THE PARTS ARE INTERCHANGEABLE.**

To install:

7. Check all parts for wear or damage. Replace any damaged or excessively worn part.

8. Service as required, assemble all parts. Note the following:

a. The rocker shafts are installed with the notches in the ends facing up.

b. The left rocker shaft is longer than the right.

c. The wave washers are installed on the left shaft.

d. Coat all parts with clean engine oil prior to assembly.

e. Insert the lash adjuster from under the rocker arm and install the special holding tool.

f. Tighten the bearing cap bolts, working from the center towards the ends, to 15 ft. lbs.

g. Check the operation of each lash adjuster by positioning the camshaft so that the rocker arm bears on the low, or round portion of the cam (pointed part of the cam faces straight down). Insert a thin steel wire, or tool MD998442 in the hole in the top of the rocker arm, over the lash adjuster, and depress the check ball at the top of the adjuster. While holding the check ball depressed, move the arm up and down. Looseness should be felt. Full plunger stroke should be 2.2mm. If not, remove, clean and bleed the lash adjuster.

Intake Manifold

REMOVAL & INSTALLATION

♦ **See Figures 34, 35 and 36**

The intake manifold is made from cast aluminum and should not be removed until the engine is cold.

1. Remove the air cleaner assembly.
2. Disconnect the fuel line (release fuel system pressure on fuel injected models before disconnecting any lines) and the EGR lines (models equipped with EGR) and tag and disconnect all vacuum hoses.
3. Disconnect the throttle positioner and fuel cut-off solenoid wires.

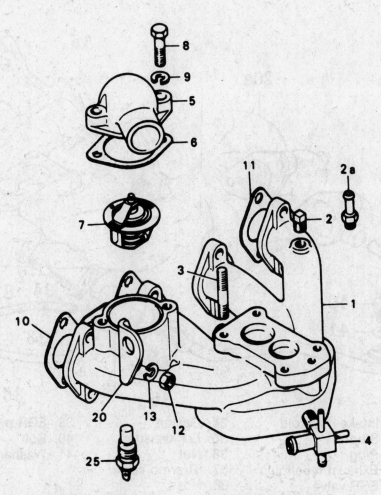

1. Intake manifold	9. Lock washer
2. Plug	10. Gasket
2A. Fitting	11. Gasket
3. Stud	12. Nut
4. Union fitting	13. Lock washer
5. Outlet neck	20. Engine lift bracket
6. Gasket	25. Temperature gauge
7. Thermostat	sending unit
8. Bolt	

Fig. 34 Exploded view of the intake manifold—1597cc engine

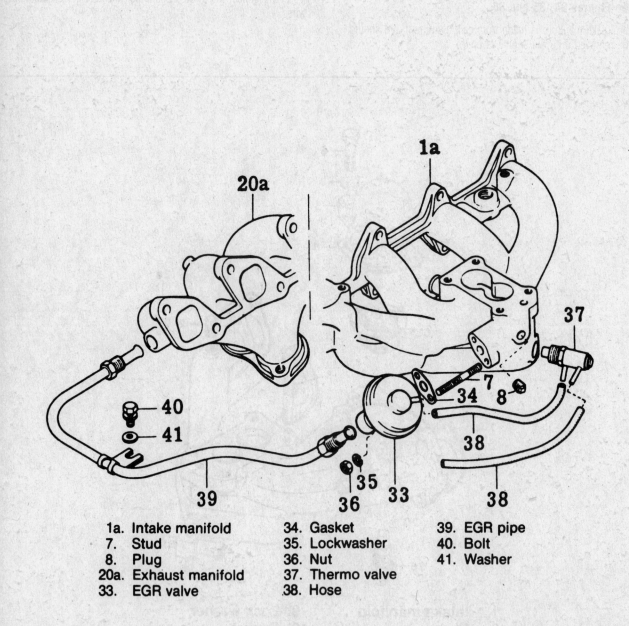

1a. Intake manifold	34. Gasket	39. EGR pipe
7. Stud	35. Lockwasher	40. Bolt
8. Plug	36. Nut	41. Washer
20a. Exhaust manifold	37. Thermo valve	
33. EGR valve	38. Hose	

Fig. 35 Exploded view of the intake and exhaust manifolds—1994cc engine

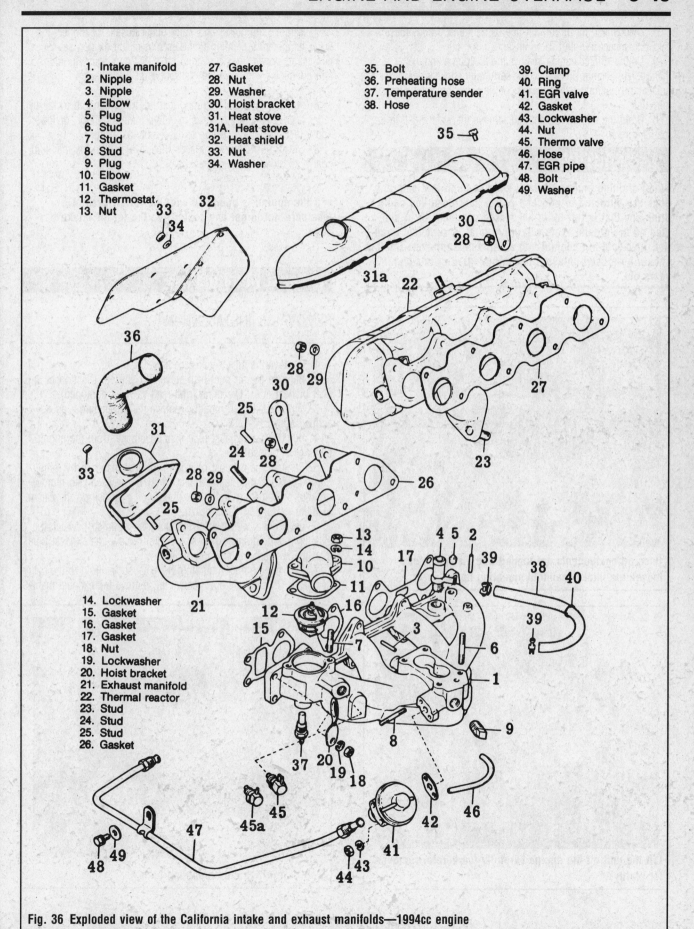

1. Intake manifold
2. Nipple
3. Nipple
4. Elbow
5. Plug
6. Stud
7. Stud
8. Stud
9. Plug
10. Elbow
11. Gasket
12. Thermostat
13. Nut
14. Lockwasher
15. Gasket
16. Gasket
17. Gasket
18. Nut
19. Lockwasher
20. Hoist bracket
21. Exhaust manifold
22. Thermal reactor
23. Stud
24. Stud
25. Stud
26. Gasket
27. Gasket
28. Nut
29. Washer
30. Hoist bracket
31. Heat stove
31A. Heat stove
32. Heat shield
33. Nut
34. Washer
35. Bolt
36. Preheating hose
37. Temperature sender
38. Hose
39. Clamp
40. Ring
41. EGR valve
42. Gasket
43. Lockwasher
44. Nut
45. Thermo valve
46. Hose
47. EGR pipe
48. Bolt
49. Washer

Fig. 36 Exploded view of the California intake and exhaust manifolds—1994cc engine

4. Disconnect the throttle linkage. On automatic transmission cars disconnect the shift cable linkage.

5. On the 1597cc engine, remove the fuel pump and the thermostat housing. Disconnect the carburetor choke water hose at the manifold. Also, disconnect the power brake booster vacuum line.

6. Drain the engine coolant and remove the water hose from the carburetor.

✷✷ CAUTION

When draining engine coolant, keep in mind that cats and dogs are attracted to ethylene glycol antifreeze and could drink any that is left in an uncovered container or in puddles on the ground. This will prove fatal in sufficient quantity. Always drain coolant into a sealable container. Coolant should be reused unless it is contaminated or is several years old.

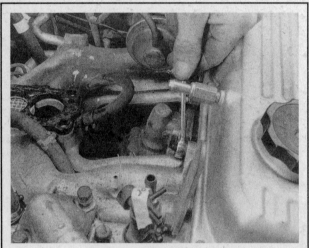

Once all components are tagged and disconnected, loosen the intake manifold mounting bolts

Lift the unit off the engine carefully (carburetor removed for clarity)

7. Remove the heater and water outlet hoses, disconnect the water temperature sending unit. Disconnect the oxygen sensor connector, power transistor connector, ISC connector, ignition coil connector, etc., and the distributor on fuel injected models.

8. Remove the mounting nuts that hold the manifold to the cylinder head. Remove the intake manifold and carburetor, or lower and upper sections with injector assembly as a unit.

9. Clean all mounting surfaces. Before installing the manifold, coat both sides with a gasket sealer.

➡ **If the engine is equipped with the jet air system, take care not to get any sealer into the jet air intake passage.**

Exhaust Manifold

REMOVAL & INSTALLATION

1. Remove the air cleaner assembly.

2. Remove the air duct-heat stove and shroud. Disconnect any EGR or heat lines. Disconnect the reed valve (if equipped).

3. On turbocharged models, remove the turbocharger as described above.

4. Remove the exhaust pipe support bracket from the engine block (if equipped).

5. Remove the exhaust pipe from exhaust manifold by removing the exhaust pipe flange nuts. It may be necessary to remove one nut or bolt from underneath the car. If you jack up the car, remember to support it on jackstands.

6. On models with a catalytic converter mounted between the exhaust manifold and exhaust pipe: first remove the exhaust pipe, then the secondary air supply pipe.

7. Remove the nuts mounting the exhaust manifold to the cylinder head. On cars without a converter, remove the exhaust mani-

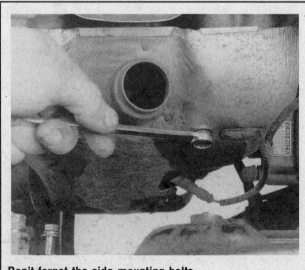

Don't forget the side mounting bolts

Loosen and remove the exhaust manifold mounting bolts

Remove any air injection and/or EGR system components in the way

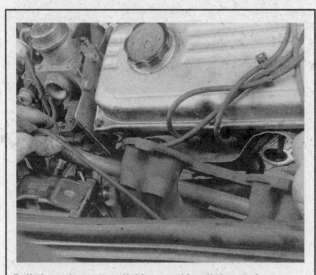
Pull the exhaust manifold assembly off the engine

fold. On cars with a converter, slide the manifold from the cylinder head so you have enough room to remove the converter mounting bolts. When the converter is disconnected, remove the exhaust manifold.

8. Install the exhaust manifold with new gaskets. New gaskets should be used, and on some engines, port liner gaskets are used.

Turbocharger

REMOVAL & INSTALLATION

▶ **See Figures 37 and 38**

Make sure that the engine and turbocharger are cold, preferably overnight cold, before removing the unit.

1. Remove the heat shield.
2. Remove the oxygen sensor from the catalytic converter.
3. Remove the converter-to-turbocharger nuts.
6. Remove the air intake pipe connecting bolt.
7. Remove the turbocharger mounting nuts and lift the unit off the engine.

To install:

8. Check the unit for any signs of cracks or damage. Make sure the turbine and compressor wheels turn freely. Apply air pressure through the nipple into the wastegate actuator and make sure that the wastegate actuator and linkage operate properly.

9. Place the turbocharger in position and secure. Torque all parts to the specification shown in the accompanying illustration. Before the oil pipe flare nut is installed at the top of the unit, pour clean engine oil into the turbocharger. Always use new gaskets.

Intercooler

REMOVAL & INSTALLATION

Conquest

1. Remove the air guide and header panels from around the intercooler.
2. Disconnect the air hoses at the intercooler.
3. Remove the intercooler bracket bolt and the bolt securing the intercooler to the bracket.
4. Lower the intercooler and remove it from under the car. Disconnect the air hose as the intercooler is lowered.

To install:

5. Check the fins for damage or bending. Check also for cracks or other damage.
6. Place the intercooler into position and secure it. Note that the air hoses have alignment marks for proper installation fit.

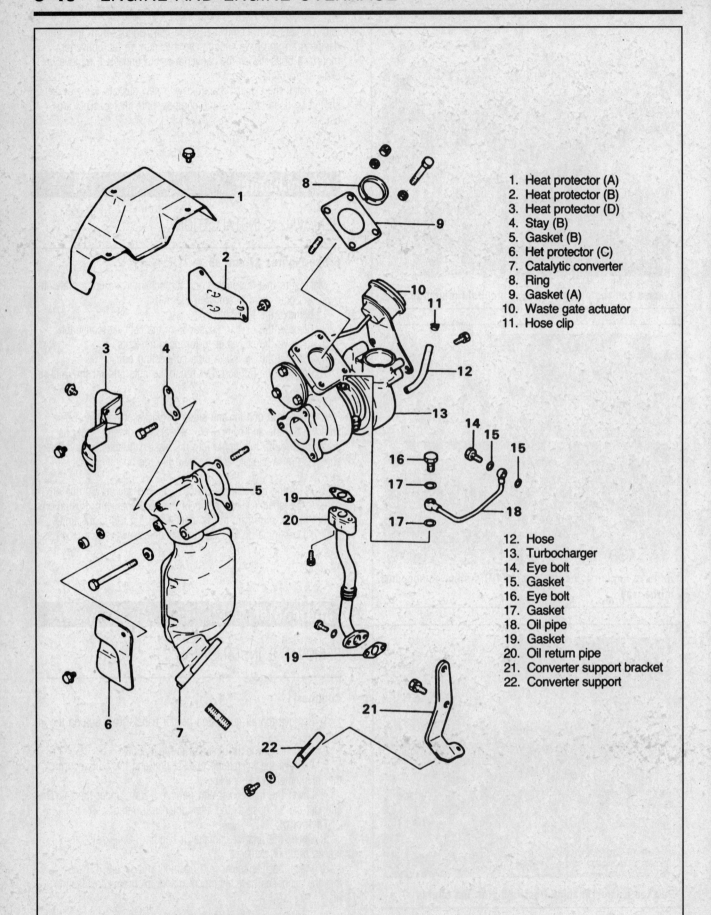

1. Heat protector (A)
2. Heat protector (B)
3. Heat protector (D)
4. Stay (B)
5. Gasket (B)
6. Het protector (C)
7. Catalytic converter
8. Ring
9. Gasket (A)
10. Waste gate actuator
11. Hose clip

12. Hose
13. Turbocharger
14. Eye bolt
15. Gasket
16. Eye bolt
17. Gasket
18. Oil pipe
19. Gasket
20. Oil return pipe
21. Converter support bracket
22. Converter support

Fig. 37 Exploded view of the Colt turbocharger

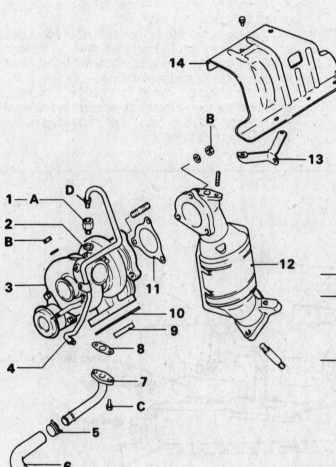

1. Oil pipe joint
2. Gasket
3. Turbocharger assembly
4. Oil pipe
5. Hose clamp(2)
6. Oil hose
7. Oil return pipe
8. Gasket
9. Ring
10. Gasket
11. Gasket
12. Catalytic converter
13. Heat protector stay
14. Heat protector

	Nm	ft. lbs.
A	22–26	16.5–19.5
B	49–68	37–50
C	8–9.5	6–7
D	16–23	13–17

Fig. 38 Exploded view of the Conquest turbocharger

Radiator

REMOVAL & INSTALLATION

◗ See Figure 39

✻✻ CAUTION

The electric cooling fan may operate when the engine is turned off, or at various times when the engine is running. Be careful when working around the fan. Disconnect the negative battery cable when servicing the cooling system components.

1. Disconnect the negative battery cable. Remove the splash panel from the bottom of the car. Drain the radiator by opening the petcock. Remove the shroud on models so equipped. On front wheel drive models disconnect the fan motor wiring harness.

✻✻ CAUTION

When draining engine coolant, keep in mind that cats and dogs are attracted to ethylene glycol antifreeze and could drink any that is left in an uncovered container or in puddles on the ground. This will prove fatal in sufficient quantity. Always drain coolant into a sealable container. Coolant should be reused unless it is contaminated or is several years old.

2. Disconnect the radiator hoses at the engine. On automatic transmission cars, disconnect and plug the transmission lines to the bottom of the radiator. On models that have an expansion tank be sure to disconnect the feed hose.

3. Remove the two retaining bolts from either side of the radiator. Lift out the radiator. On models with an electric cooling fan, the fan and motor may usually be left attached to the radiator and be removed with the radiator as one unit.

4. Install the radiator, connect the hoses, install the electric cooling fan, make sure the petcocks are closed and fill the system with the proper coolant mixture. Tighten the retaining bolts gradually in a criss-cross pattern.

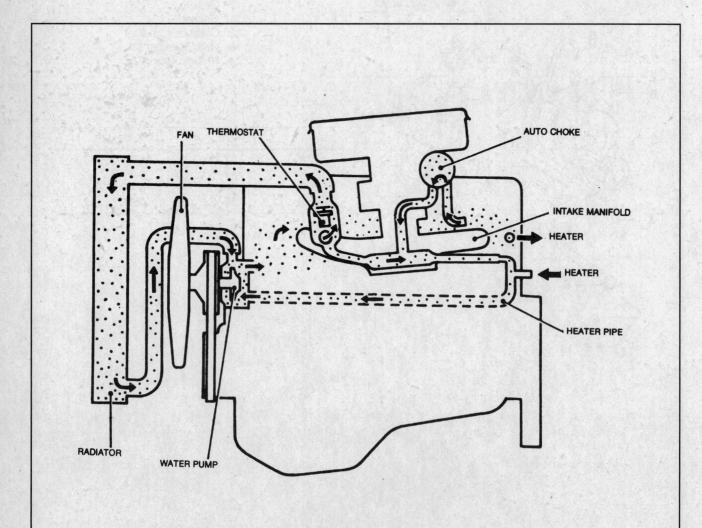

Fig. 39 Cutaway view of the cooling system on the 1597cc engine

After the coolant is drained, loosen the upper radiator hose

On the electric fan types, disconnect the wiring leading to the fan

Separate the hose from the upper radiator inlet

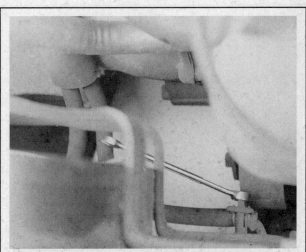

On automatic vehicles, disconnect the transmission cooler lines leading to the radiator

Disconnect the overflow hose

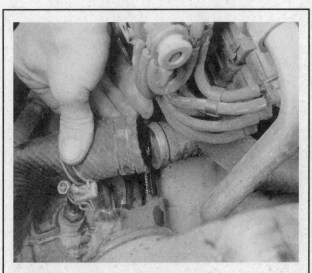

Remove the lower outlet radiator hose

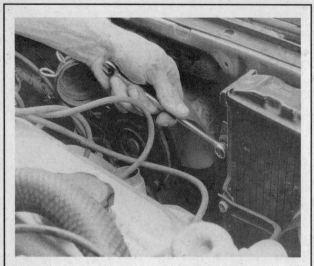

Unbolt the radiator from the mounting brackets

Lift the unit out of the engine compartment

On models with an electric fan, unbolt the housing

Lift the fan unit off the radiator as an assembly

Water Pump

REMOVAL & INSTALLATION

Rear Wheel Drive

▶ See Figure 40

1. Open the radiator petcock and the engine drain plug on the passenger's side. Drain the cooling system. Disconnect the battery ground (negative) cable.

✳✳ CAUTION

When draining engine coolant, keep in mind that cats and dogs are attracted to ethylene glycol antifreeze and could drink any that is left in an uncovered container or in puddles on the ground. This will prove fatal in sufficient quantity. Always drain coolant into a sealable container. Coolant should be reused unless it is contaminated or is several years old.

2. Remove all drive belts, pump mounted cooling fan/or drive pulley, and the alternator brace.
3. Unscrew the retaining nuts and bolts. Remove the water pump.
   To install:
4. Install a new gasket on the timing gear cover with sealer.
5. Apply sealer to the mating surface of the water pump. Install the pump. Tighten the nuts and bolts gradually in a criss-cross pattern to 11 ft. lbs. Don't overtighten the fasteners, the pump is aluminum.
6. Spin the pump to make sure that it doesn't interfere with the case.
7. Install the fan.
8. Install and tension the drive belts.
9. Refill the cooling system with a 50/50 mixture of antifreeze and water.

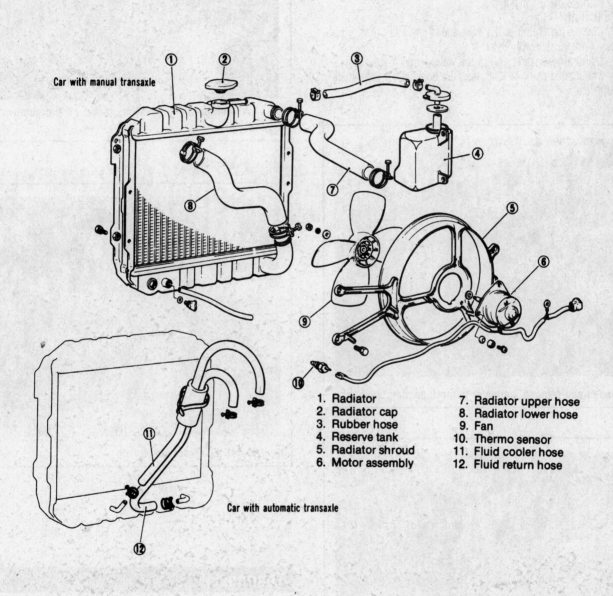

Car with manual transaxle

Car with automatic transaxle

1. Radiator
2. Radiator cap
3. Rubber hose
4. Reserve tank
5. Radiator shroud
6. Motor assembly
7. Radiator upper hose
8. Radiator lower hose
9. Fan
10. Thermo sensor
11. Fluid cooler hose
12. Fluid return hose

Fig. 40 Exploded view of the cooling system components—1597cc engine

Front Wheel Drive

1. Drain the cooling system.
2. Remove all drive belts and water pump pulley. It may be necessary to remove an engine mount, the power steering pump and alternator brace to gain necessary clearance, depending on model.
3. Remove the timing belt covers and timing belt tensioner, and timing belt as explained earlier in this section.
4. Remove the water pump bolts.
5. Remove the water pump.
To install:
6. Discard the O-ring in the front end of the water pipe. Install a new O-ring coated with water.
7. Using a new gasket, mount the water pump. Torque the bolts with a head mark 4–10 ft. lbs.: the bolts with a head mark 7–20 ft. lbs.

. . . and scrape the old mating gasket off the pump and engine

Loosen and remove the water pump mounting bolts

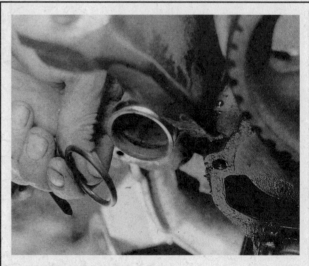

Dont forget to replace the O-ring

8. Assemble the remaining components, install the timing belt according to the previous instructions. Fill the system with a 50% mix of antifreeze.

Thermostat

REMOVAL & INSTALLATION

Rear Wheel Drive

The thermostat is located in the intake manifold under the upper radiator hose.
1. Drain the coolant below the level of the thermostat.

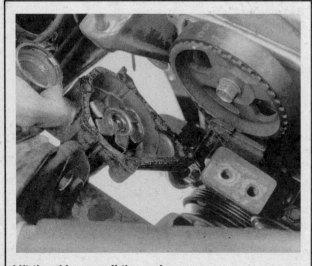

Lift the old pump off the engine . . .

✳✳ CAUTION

When draining engine coolant, keep in mind that cats and dogs are attracted to ethylene glycol antifreeze and could drink any that is left in an uncovered container or in puddles on the ground. This will prove fatal in sufficient quantity. Always drain coolant into a sealable container. Coolant should be reused unless it is contaminated or is several years old.

2. Remove the two retaining bolts and lift the thermostat housing off the intake manifold with the hose still attached.

➡If you are careful, it is not necessary to remove the upper radiator hose.

3. Lift the thermostat out of the manifold.

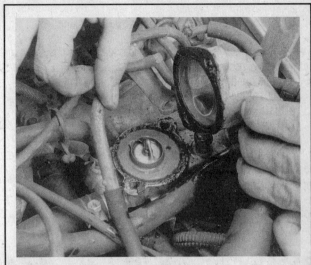

Lift the housing off the thermostat assembly . . .

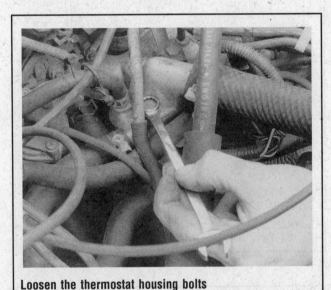

Loosen the thermostat housing bolts

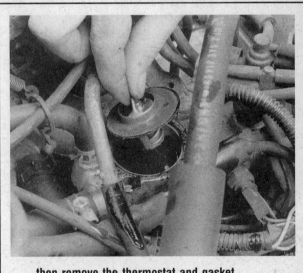

. . . then remove the thermostat and gasket

4. Install the thermostat. Use a new gasket and coat the mating surfaces with sealer.

Front Wheel Drive

1. Drain the cooling system to a point below the thermostat level.

✳✳ CAUTION

When draining the coolant, keep in mind that cats and dogs are attracted to the ethylene glycol antifreeze, and are quite likely to drink any that is left in an uncovered container or in puddles on the ground. This will prove fatal in sufficient quantity. Always drain the coolant into a sealable container. Coolant should be reused unless it is contaminated or several years old.

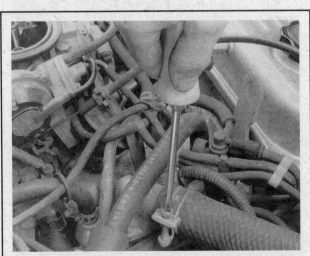

Remove the hose clamp and slide the hose off the end of the housing

2. Remove the air cleaner.

3. Disconnect the hose at the thermostat water pipe.

4. Remove the water pipe support bracket nut. The nut is also a manifold nut, and is very difficult to get to. A deep offset 12mm box wrench is necessary for removal and installation.

5. Unbolt and remove the thermostat housing and pipe.

6. Lift out the thermostat. Discard the gasket.

To install:

7. Clean the mating surfaces of the housing and manifold thoroughly.

8. Install the thermostat with the spring facing downward, and position a new gasket. The jiggle valve in the thermostat should be on the manifold side.

9. Install the housing and pipe assembly. Tighten the housing bolts to 10 ft. lbs.: the intake manifold nut to 14 ft. lbs.

10. Refill the system with a 50% antifreeze mix.

Cylinder Head

The timing chain/belt and the cam gear must be removed and secured together after the engine is turned to No. 1 cylinder at the TDC position. The exception being the 1410cc and 1468cc engines (see following paragraphs). The cylinder head bolts on the 1410cc, 1468cc, 1597cc and 1997cc engines require a $5/16$ inch Allen socket to remove. On 1994cc and 2555cc engines the cylinder head bolts are hex headed.

REMOVAL

▶ **See Figures 41 and 42**

Never remove the cylinder head unless the engine is absolutely cold, or the cylinder head will warp.

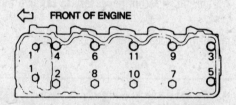

Fig. 42 Head bolt loosening sequence—2555cc engine

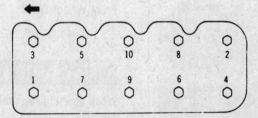

Fig. 41 Head bolt loosening sequence—1410, 1468, 1597 and 1997cc engines

Loosen the cylinder head bolts in the correct sequence

It is recommended to replace the cylinder head bolts with new ones

Lift the cylinder head off the block and set aside

Place clean rags in the open cylinders, then remove the old gasket and clean the mating surfaces

1. Turn the crankshaft to put No. 1 piston at top dead center with timing marks aligned.

2. Disconnect the negative cable from the battery. Remove the air cleaner assembly and the attached breather hoses. Drain the radiator coolant. Remove the upper radiator hose and disconnect the heater hoses.

✳✳ CAUTION

When draining the coolant, keep in mind that cats and dogs are attracted to the ethylene glycol antifreeze, and are quite likely to drink any that is left in an uncovered container or in puddles on the ground. This will prove fatal in sufficient quantity. Always drain the coolant into a sealable container. Coolant should be reused unless it is contaminated or several years old.

3. Remove the fuel line from the carburetor and fuel pump. On fuel injected engines, discharge the fuel pressure and disconnect the fuel lines. Disconnect the accelerator linkage, distributor vacuum lines, purge valve and water temperature gauge wire.

4. Remove the spark plug wires, spark plugs and the fuel pump. It is necessary to remove the distributor, mark the mounting flange location (see Section 2).

5. Remove the exhaust manifold.

6. Remove the intake manifold (see intake manifold removal).

➡**During the following procedures, do not turn the crankshaft from TDC.**

1410cc and 1468cc Engines

   a. Remove the timing belt cover. Be sure the knockout pin (cam sprocket) is at 12 o'clock and the cam sprocket mark and cylinder head pointer aligned at 3 o'clock.

   b. Loosen the timing belt tensioner mounting. Move the tensioner toward the water pump and secure it in that position. Remove the timing belt from the camshaft pulley.

➡The camshaft pulley need not be removed, and the timing belt may be left mounted on the crankshaft pulley.

c. Remove the rocker arm cover.

1971–76 1597cc Engine W/O Silent Shaft

a. Remove the rocker arm cover.

b. Position the crankshaft sprocket dowel pin between 1 and 2 o'clock, with the crank shaft pulley notch aligned with the timing mark T at the front of the timing chain case.

c. Matchmark the timing chain and the timing mark on the camshaft sprocket with white paint. Lock the chain to the sprocket with mechanics wire.

d. Remove the sprocket from the camshaft.

1597cc Engine With or Without Silent Shaft and 1997cc Engines

a. Align the timing mark on the upper under cover of the timing belt with that of the camshaft sprocket.

b. Matchmark the timing belt and the timing mark on the camshaft sprocket with a felt tip pen.

c. Remove the sprocket and insert a 50mm piece of timing belt or other material between the bottom of the camshaft sprocket and the sprocket holder on the timing belt lower front cover, to hold the sprocket and belt so that the valve timing will not be changed.

d. Remove the timing belt upper under cover and the rocker arm cover.

1973–75 1994cc Engine

a. Remove the rocker arm cover.

b. Position the camshaft sprocket dowel pin at the 12 o'clock position with the crankshaft pulley notch aligned with the TDC or T mark on the timing indicator scale.

c. Match the timing chain and the timing mark on the camshaft sprocket with white paint. Lock the chain to the sprocket with mechanics wire.

d. Remove the sprocket from the camshaft.

1976–83 1994cc and 2555cc Engines

a. Remove the rocker arm cover.

b. Position the camshaft sprocket dowel pin at the 12 o'clock position with the crankshaft pulley notch aligned with the timing mark T at the front of the timing chain case.

c. Match the timing chain with the timing mark on the camshaft sprocket.

d. Remove the camshaft sprocket bolt, distributor, gear and the sprocket from the camshaft.

All Engines

7. Loosen and remove the cylinder head bolts in two or three stages to avoid cylinder head warpage.

8. Remove the cylinder head from the engine block. Lift the head from the engine, locator pins in the engine block will prevent sliding.

INSTALLATION

◆ **See Figures 43 and 44**

1. Clean the cylinder head and block mating surfaces and install a new cylinder head gasket.

2. Position the cylinder head on the engine block, engage the dowel pins and install the cylinder head bolts.

3. Tighten the head bolts in three stages and then torque to specifications.

4. On 1977–85 1597 and 1997cc engines, install the timing belt upper under cover.

5. Locate the camshaft in the original position. Pull the camshaft sprocket, belt or chain up and install on the camshaft.

➡If you experience any difficulty while installing the timing chain, belt or sprocket: refer to the timing chain/belt installation section of this chapter.

6. If the dowel pin and the dowel pin hole do not line up between the sprocket and the spacer or camshaft, move the camshaft by bumping either of the two projections (provided at the rear of number two cylinder exhaust lobe of the camshaft) with a light hammer or other tool until the hole and pin align. Be certain that the crankshaft does not turn.

7. Install the camshaft sprocket bolt and distributor drive gear and tighten. (The gear is used on 1994cc and 2555cc engines from 1976).

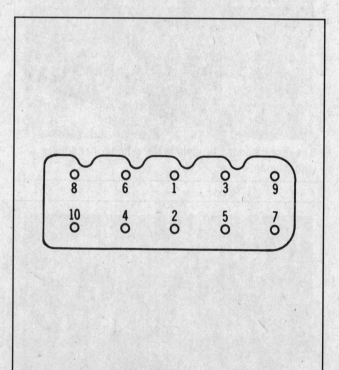

Fig. 43 Head bolt tightening sequence—1410, 1468, 1597 and 1997cc engines

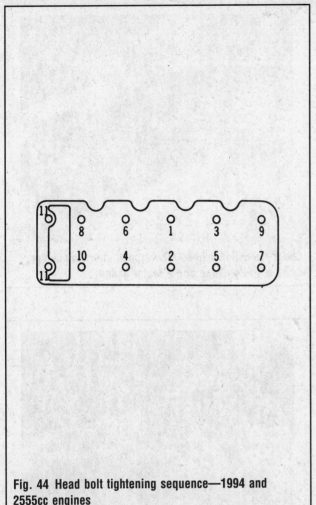

Fig. 44 Head bolt tightening sequence—1994 and 2555cc engines

8. Install the timing belt upper front cover and spark plug cable support or timing belt cover, depending on which model you are working on.

9. Apply sealant to the intake manifold gasket on both sides. Position the gasket and install the intake manifold. Tighten the nuts to specification. Be sure that no sealant enters the jet air passages on models that are equipped with jet valves.

10. Install the exhaust manifold gaskets and the exhaust manifold. Tighten the nuts to specifications.

11. Connect the exhaust pipe to the exhaust manifold assembly and tighten the nuts to specifications. Install the fuel pump and purge valve.

12. Install the water temperature gauge wire, heater hoses and the upper radiator hose. Connect the fuel lines, accelerator linkage and vacuum hoses. Install the distributor, spark plugs and spark plug wires, etc.

13. Fill the cooling system. Connect the negative battery cable.

14. Adjust the valve clearances to the cold engine specifications. (Refer to Section 2).

15. Install the gasket on the rocker arm cover and temporarily install the cover on the engine.

16. Start the engine and allow it to reach normal operating temperature. Stop the engine and remove the rocker arm cover.

17. Adjust the valves to hot engine specifications.

18. Reinstall the rocker arm cover and tighten securely.

19. Install the air cleaner, hoses purge valve hose and any other removed unit.

CLEANING AND INSPECTION

➡**With the cylinder head removed from the engine, the rocker arm assemblies and camshaft removed, the valves, valve springs and valve stem oil seals can not be serviced.**

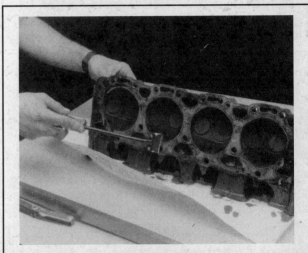

Use a gasket scraper to remove the bulk of the old head gasket from the mating surface

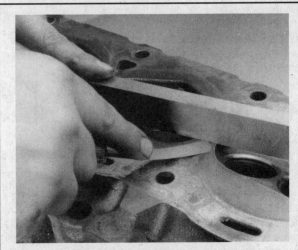

Check the cylinder head for flatness across the head surface

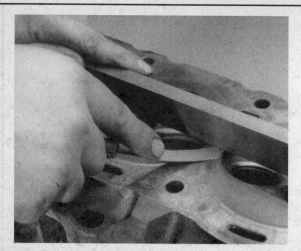

Checks should be made both straight across the cylinder head and at both diagonals

Check the cylinder head for warpage along the center using a straightedge and a feeler gauge

Since the machining of valve seats and valves, and the insertion of new valve guides or valve seats may tax the experience and equipment resources of the car owner, it is suggested that the cylinder head be taken to an automotive machine shop for rebuilding.

1. Remove the cylinder head from the car engine (see Cylinder Head Removal). Place the head on a workbench and remove any manifolds that are still connected. Remove all rocker arm assembly parts, if still installed and the camshaft (see Camshaft Removal).

2. Turn the cylinder head over so that the mounting surface is facing up and support evenly on wooden blocks.

3. Use a scraper and remove all of the gasket material and carbon stuck to the head mounting surface. Mount a wire carbon removal brush in an electric drill and clean away the carbon on the valve heads and head combustion chambers.

➡**When scraping or decarbonizing the cylinder head, take care not to damage or nick the gasket mounting surface or combustion chamber.**

4. Number the valve heads with a permanent felt-tipped marker for cylinder location.

RESURFACING

If the cylinder head is warped, resurfacing by an automotive machine shop, will be required. After cleaning the gasket surface, place a straightedge across the mounting surface of the head. Using feeler gauges, determine the clearance at the center and along the length between the head and straightedge. Measure clearance at the center and along the lengths of both diagonals. If warpage exceeds 0.08mm in a 152mm span, or 0.15mm over the total length the cylinder head must be resurfaced.

Be sure to check for warpage across the cylinder head at both diagonals

Jet Valves

REMOVAL & INSTALLATION

▶ **See Figure 45**

The jet valve can be removed from the cylinder head with the rocker arm either in place or removed. A special socket, tool No. MD998310, is helpful in removing the jet valve. Care must be taken not to twist the socket while removing the valve, it can be easily broken. When installing the valve, the torque is 14–16 ft. lbs.

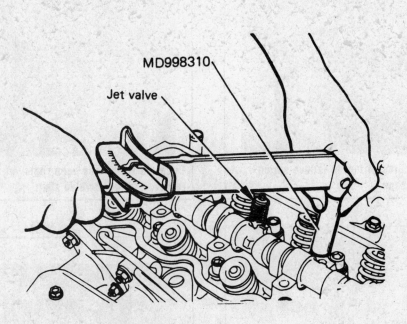

Fig. 45 Using a special tool for jet valve installation

Valves and Springs

REMOVAL & INSTALLATION

1. Block the head on its side, or install a pair of head-holding brackets made especially for valve removal.

2. Use a socket slightly larger than the valve stem and keepers, place the socket over the valve stem and gently hit the socket with a plastic hammer to break loose any varnish buildup.

3. Remove the valve keepers, retainer, spring shield (if equipped) and valve spring using a valve spring compressor (the locking C-clamp type is the easiest to use).

4. Do not mix removed parts. Place the parts from each valve in a separate container, numbered and identified for the valve and cylinder.

5. Remove and discard the valve stem oil seal, a new seal will be used at assembly time.

6. Remove the valve from the cylinder head and place, in order, through holes punched in a stiff piece of cardboard or stick in case the numbers marked on the valve head gets rubbed off.

To install:

7. Use an electric drill and rotary wire brush to clean the intake and exhaust valve ports, combustion chamber and valve seats. In some cases, the carbon build-up will have to be chipped away. Use a blunt pointed drift for carbon chipping, be careful around valve seat areas.

➡**When using a wire brush to clean carbon on the valve parts, valves, etc., be sure the deposits are actually removed, rather than burnished.**

8. Use a valve guide cleaning brush and safe solvent to clean the valve guides.

9. Clean the valves with a revolving wire brush. Heavy carbon deposits may be removed with blunt drift.

10. Wash and clean all valve springs, keepers, retaining caps,

Use a valve spring compressor tool to relieve spring tension from the valve caps

Once the spring has been removed, the O-ring may be removed from the valve stem

A small magnet will help in removal of the valve keepers

Be careful not to lose the valve keepers

A magnet may be helpful in removing the valve keepers

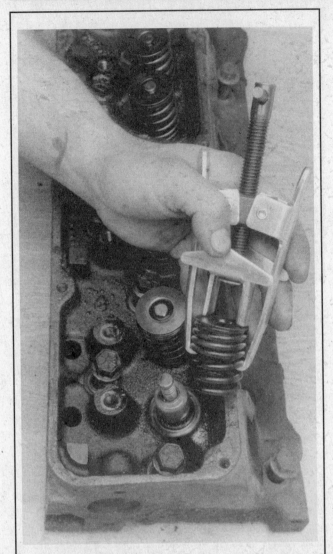

Remove the spring from the valve stem in order to access the seal

Remove the valve stem seal from the cylinder head

Invert the cylinder head and withdraw the valve from the cylinder head bore

A wire wheel may be used to clean the combustion chambers of carbon deposits

A dial gauge may be used to check valve stem-to-guide clearance

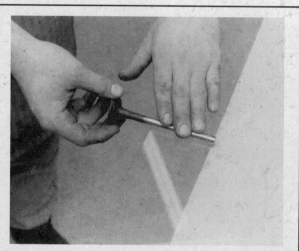

Valve stems may be rolled on a flat surface to check for bends

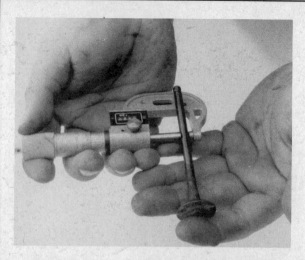

Use a micrometer to check the valve stem diameter

etc., in safe solvent. Remember to keep parts from each valve separate.

11. Check the cylinder head for cracks. Cracks usually start around the exhaust valve seat because it is the hottest part of the combustion chamber. If a crack is suspected but cannot be detected visually, have the area checked with a dye penetrant or other method by the machine shop.

12. After all cylinder head parts are reasonably clean check the valve stem-to-guide clearance. If a dial indicator is not on hand, a visual inspection can give you a fairly good idea if the guide, valve stem or both are worn.

13. Insert the valve into the guide until slightly away from the valve seat. Wiggle the valve sideways. A small amount of wobble is normal, excessive wobble means a worn guide and/or valve stem. If a dial indicator is on hand, mount the indicator so that gauge stem is 90° to the valve stem as close to the top of the valve guide as possible. Move the valve from the seat, and measure the valve guide-to-stem clearance by rocking the stem back and forth to actuate the dial indicator. Measure the valve stem using a micrometer and compare to specifications to determine whether stem or guide is causing excessive clearance.

14. The valve guide, if worn, must be repaired before the valve seats can be resurfaced. A new valve guide should be installed or, in some cases, knurled. Consult the automotive machine shop.

15. Valve faces and valve seats should be machined to specifications: the machine shop can handle the job for you. Only enough material to clean up any pits or grooves should be removed. The valve seat should not be too wide or too narrow. The valve face should contact the seat on their respective centers. The valve seat can be narrowed or widened as required.

16. After the valves and valve seats have been machined, they should be hand lapped. Use valve grinding compound and a small suction cupped valve stick. Place a small amount of compound on the valve face. Install the valve and rotate the valve face against the seat with the valve stick. Remove the valve and clean the compound from the valve face and seat. If the contact ring is too close to the outer edge of the valve face, narrow the seat: if too close to the inner edge widen the seat. If the edge of a valve head, after machining, is 1/32 inch or less replace the valve. The tip of the valve stem should also be dressed on the valve grinding machine, however do not remove too much material.

17. After all valve and valve seats have been machined, check the remaining valve train parts (springs, retainers, keepers, etc) for wear. Check the valve springs for straightness and tension.

18. Assemble the head using new valve stem guide seals. Lubricate the valve stems before installation. Check the valve spring installed height; shim or replace as necessary.

CHECKING VALVE SPRINGS

Place the valve spring on a flat surface next to a carpenters square. Measure the height of the spring, and rotate the spring against the edge of the square to measure distortion. If the spring height varies (by comparison) by more than 1.5mm or if the distortion exceeds 1.5mm, replace the spring.

Have the valve springs tested for spring pressure at the installed and compressed (installed height minus valve lift) height using a valve spring tester. Springs should be within one pound, plus or minus each other. Replace springs as necessary.

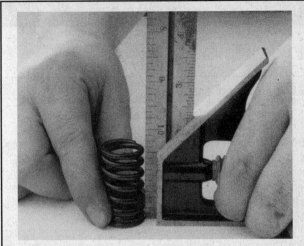

The valve spring should be straight up and down when placed like this

Use a caliper gauge to check the valve spring free-length

VALVE SPRING INSTALLED HEIGHT

After installing the valve spring, measure the distance between the spring mounting pad and the lower edge of the spring retainer. Compare the measurement to specifications. If the installed height is incorrect, add shim washers between the mounting pad and the base of the spring. Use only washers designed for spring shimming: available at parts houses.

VALVE STEM OIL SEALS

Positive valves seals are used. The seal fits over to top of the valve guide. Always install new valve stem seals when reassembling the cylinder head.

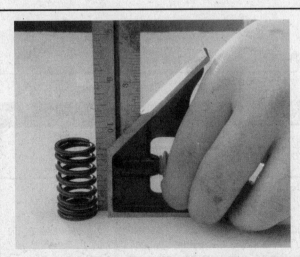

Check the valve spring for squareness on a flat service; a carpenter's square can be used

With the valve spring out of the way, the valve stem seals may now be replaced

Valve Seats

REMOVAL & INSTALLATION

▶ **See Figures 46 and 47**

The valve seat inserts are replaceable on all these engines.

1. With the valve removed, check the seat for wear, cracks, damage or uneven contact with the valve. If the damage or contact problem is slight, the valve may be refaced with a lapping compound and lapping tool. The compound is spread on the seat face and the valve inserted. The valve is then ground against the seat with the lapping tool, removing a small amount of metal and creating a polished surface.

2. If the damage or contact problem cannot be rectified by lapping, the insert can be cut with a special seat cutter which will remove the damaged material and cut the correct angle.

3. If the seat insert is cracked, too thin, or burnt, it must be replaced. An automotive machine shop can handle the job for you.

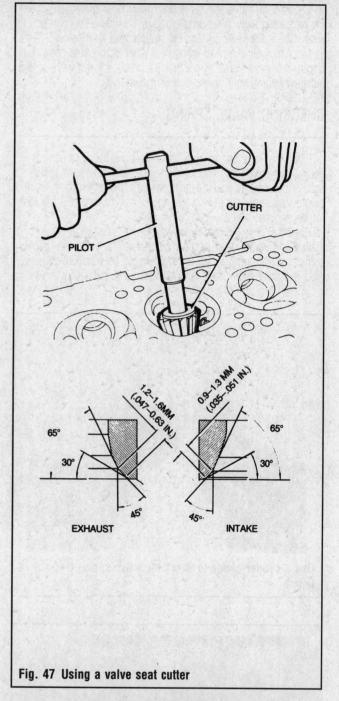

Fig. 47 Using a valve seat cutter

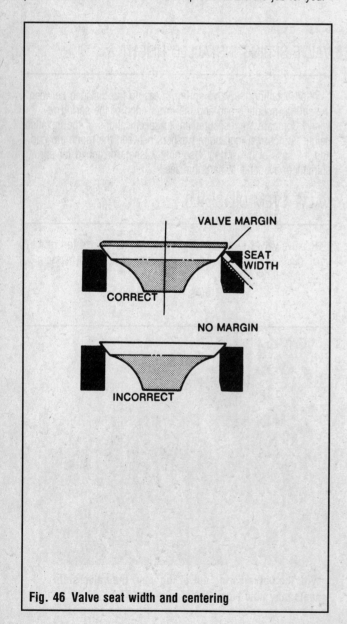

Fig. 46 Valve seat width and centering

Oil Pan

REMOVAL & INSTALLATION

▶ **See Figures 48 and 49**

The engine must be raised off its mounts to provide for the pan to clear the suspension crossmember. However, most of the front wheel drive models have enough clearance to provide for pan removal without raising the engine.

1. Jack up the front of the car and support it on stands.
2. Drain the oil.

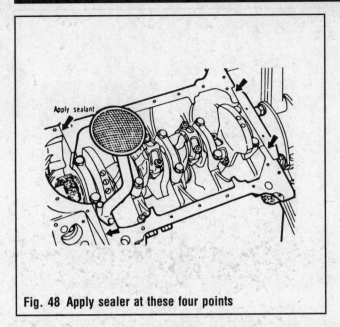

Fig. 48 Apply sealer at these four points

✳✳ CAUTION

The EPA warns that prolonged contact with used engine oil may cause a number of skin disorders, including cancer! You should make every effort to minimize you exposure to used engine oil. Protective gloves should be worn when changing the oil. Wash your hands and any other exposed skin areas as soon as possible after exposure to used engine oil. Soap and water, or waterless hand cleaner should be used.

3. Remove the underbody splash shield.

4. On rear wheel drive cars, remove the retaining nuts from the left and right engine mounts.

5. On rear wheel drive cars, place a jack under the bell housing. Use a board to evenly distribute the pressure and then raise the engine. Place blocks of wood between the mount and the frame to safely support the raised engine.

6. Remove the oil pan bolts, drop the pan, and slide it out from under the car.

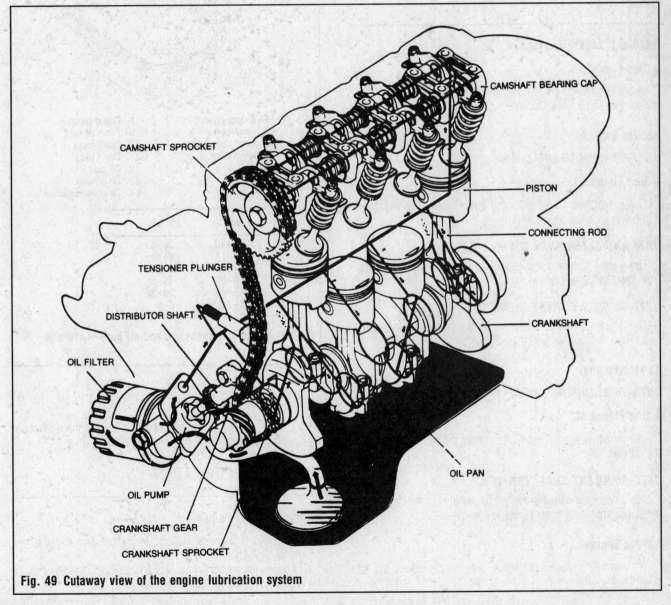

Fig. 49 Cutaway view of the engine lubrication system

To install:

7. Clean the mating surfaces of the oil pan and the engine block.

8. Apply sealer to the engine block at the block-to-chain case and block-to-rear oil seal case joint faces, on all but the 1410 & 1468cc. On the 1410 & 1468cc engines, apply a 4mm bead of RTV sealer along the groove in the oil pan.

9. Use a non-hardening sealer and secure a new gasket to the oil pan, on models that use a gasket.

10. Install the oil pan. Hand-tighten the retaining bolts.

11. Starting at one end of the pan, tighten the pan bolts to 48–72 in. lbs. in a criss-cross pattern.

12. Lower the engine and tighten the mount retaining nuts.

13. Install the oil pan drain plug.

14. Install the splash shield and lower the car.

15. Fill the crankcase with oil. Start the engine and check for leaks.

Oil Pump

LOCATIONS

1410 and 1468cc Engines

▶ **See Figure 50**

Use a gear driven oil pump mounted in the front case and driven directly by the crankshaft.

1597cc Engine

1971–77 WITH TIMING CHAIN

▶ **See Figure 51**

Use a rotor type oil pump located in the timing chaining case and driven by a crankshaft gear.

1978 AND LATER WITH TIMING BELT

Use a rotor type oil pump located on the lower left side of the front case and driven by the timing belt.

1977–80 SILENT SHAFT ENGINES

Use a gear type oil pump located on the front of the left counterbalance shaft and driven by the timing belt.

1994cc Engine

1974–75 STANDARD ENGINE

▶ **See Figure 52**

Use a rotor type oil pump located under the timing case, inside the oil pan.

1976–80 SILENT SHAFT ENGINE

Use a gear type oil pump located on the front of the right counterbalance shaft and driven by the timing chain.

1997cc Engine

The pump is located in the timing case, on the front of the left silent shaft.

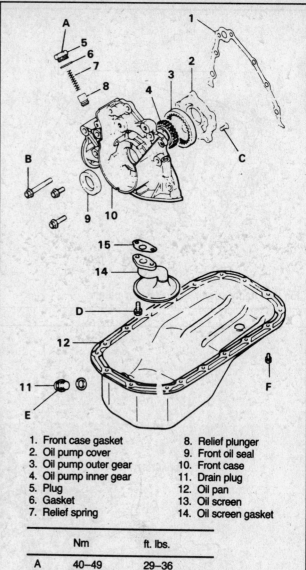

	Nm	ft. lbs.
A	40–49	29–36
B	12–14	9–10
C	8–9	6–7
D	18–24	13–18
E	35–44	26–32
F	6–7	5–6

1. Front case gasket
2. Oil pump cover
3. Oil pump outer gear
4. Oil pump inner gear
5. Plug
6. Gasket
7. Relief spring
8. Relief plunger
9. Front oil seal
10. Front case
11. Drain plug
12. Oil pan
13. Oil screen
14. Oil screen gasket

Fig. 50 Oil pump, front case and oil pan—1410 and 1468cc engines

2555cc Engine

Use a gear type oil pump located on the front of the right counterbalance shaft and driven by the timing chain.

REMOVAL & INSTALLATION

Oil Pan Located Pumps

1. Place No. 1 piston at TDC on the compression stroke (timing marks aligned).

2. Loosen the left and right engine mounts and raise and block the engine off of the mounting brackets.

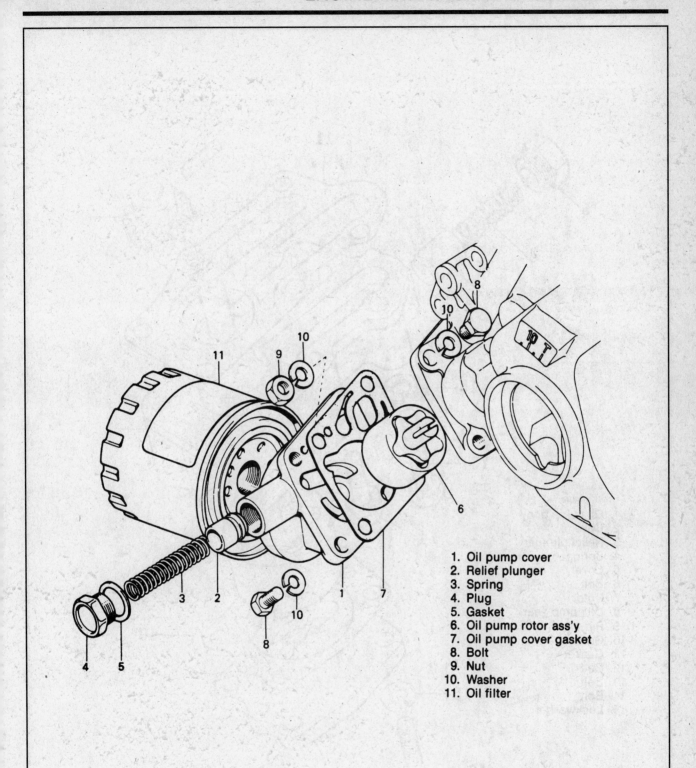

1. Oil pump cover
2. Relief plunger
3. Spring
4. Plug
5. Gasket
6. Oil pump rotor ass'y
7. Oil pump cover gasket
8. Bolt
9. Nut
10. Washer
11. Oil filter

Fig. 51 Exploded view of the oil pump components—1971–75 1597cc engine

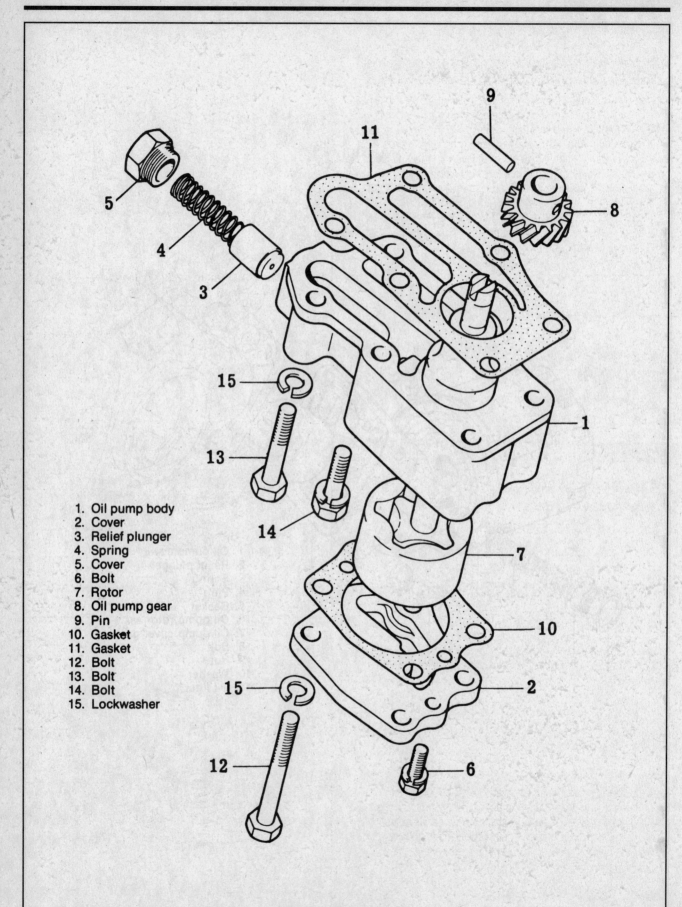

1. Oil pump body
2. Cover
3. Relief plunger
4. Spring
5. Cover
6. Bolt
7. Rotor
8. Oil pump gear
9. Pin
10. Gasket
11. Gasket
12. Bolt
13. Bolt
14. Bolt
15. Lockwasher

Fig. 52 Component breakdown of the oil pump—1971–75 1994cc engine

3. Remove the front splash shields, if necessary. Drain the oil, and remove the engine oil pan.

✳✳ CAUTION

The EPA warns that prolonged contact with used engine oil may cause a number of skin disorders, including cancer! You should make every effort to minimize your exposure to used engine oil. Protective gloves should be worn when changing the oil. Wash your hands and any other exposed skin areas as soon as possible after exposure to used engine oil. Soap and water, or waterless hand cleaner should be used.

4. Remove the screen and the oil pump from the engine block.
5. Be sure that No. 1 piston is still on TDC.
6. Remove the distributor cap and make sure that the rotor is pointing to the No. 1 position.

➡This should align the distributor pawl parallel with the crankshaft center line.

To install:

7. Align the mating marks of the distributor gear and body (if necessary). Insert the oil pump assembly with a new gasket into the engine block until the oil pump shaft gear is in mesh with the crankshaft gear and engaged with the distributor pawl.
8. Using a new gasket, install the oil pan, connect the engine mounts and install the splash shields.
9. Fill the engine with fresh oil, start the engine and check the ignition timing.

Timing Case Located Pumps

1410 AND 1468cc ENGINES

◆ **See Figures 53, 54, 55 and 56**

1. Remove the timing belt.
2. Remove the oil pan as previously described.
3. Remove the oil screen.
4. Unbolt and remove the front case assembly.
5. Remove the oil pump cover.
6. Remove the inner and outer gears from the front case.

➡The outer gear has no identifying marks to indicate direction of rotation. Clean the gear and mark it with an indelible marker.

7. Remove the plug, relief valve spring and relief valve from the case.

To install:

8. Check the front case for damage or cracks. Replace the front seal. Replace the oil screen O-ring. Clean all parts thoroughly with a safe solvent.
9. Check the pump gears for wear or damage. Clean the gears thoroughly and place them in position in the case to check the clearances. There is a crescent-shaped piece between the two gears. This piece is the reference point for two measurements. Use the following clearances for determining gear wear.
- Outer gear outer face-to-case: 0.10–0.20mm
- Outer gear teeth-to-crescent: 0.22–0.34mm
- Outer gear end-play: 0.04–0.10mm
- Inner gear teeth-to-crescent: 0.21–0.32mm
- Inner gear end-play: 0.04–0.10mm.

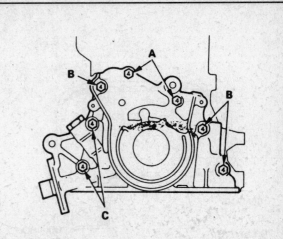

Fig. 53 Bolt identification on the timing cover—1410 and 1468 engines

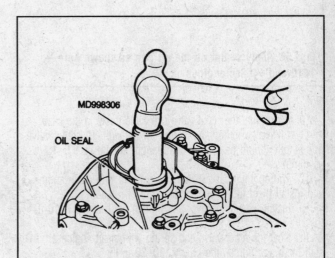

Fig. 54 Installing the front seal with a special tool—1410 and 1468cc engines

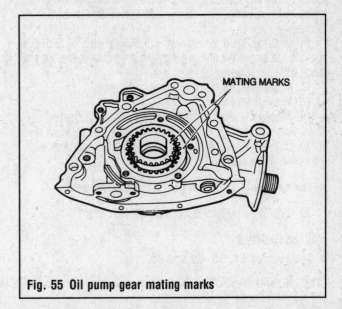

Fig. 55 Oil pump gear mating marks

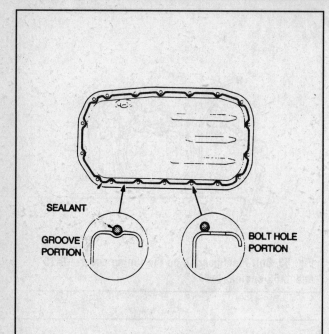

Fig. 56 Apply sealer on the oil pan as shown here— 1410 and 1468cc engines

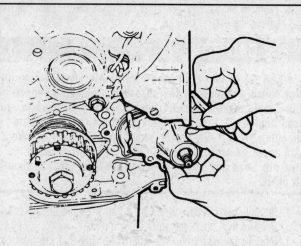

Fig. 57 Removing the oil pump cover from the 1597cc engine

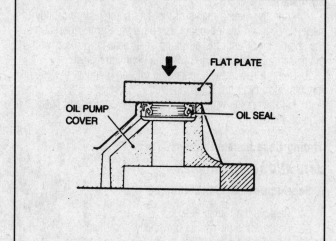

Fig. 58 Install the oil pump cover using a flat block on the 1597cc engine

10. Check that the relief valve can slide freely in the case.

11. Check the relief valve spring for damage. The relief valve free length should be 47mm. Load/length should be 9.5–13 lbs. at 40mm.

12. Thoroughly coat both oil pump gears with clean engine oil and install them in the correct direction of rotation.

13. Install the pump cover and tighten the bolts to 7–10 ft. lbs.

14. Coat the relief valve and spring with clean engine oil, install them and tighten the plug to 30–36 ft. lbs.

15. Position a new front case gasket, coated with sealer, on the engine and install the front case. Tighten the bolts to 10 ft. lbs. Note that the bolts have different shank lengths. Use the following guide and the accompanying illustration to determine which bolts go where. Bolts marked **A:** 20mm. **B:** 30mm. **C:** 60mm.

16. Coat the lips of a new seal with clean engine oil and slide it along the crankshaft until it touches the front case. Drive it into place with a seal drive.

17. Install the sprocket, timing belt and pulley.

18. Install the oil screen.

19. Thoroughly clean both the oil pan and engine mating surfaces. Apply a 4mm ide bead of RTV sealer in the groove of the oil pan mating surface. A 4mm is usually the first cut mark on the nozzle that comes with the tube of sealer.

➡ **You have only 15 minutes before the sealer sets.**

20. Tighten the oil pan bolts to 60–72 inch lbs.

1597cc ENGINES

▶ **See Figures 57, 58, 59 and 60**

1. Remove the timing belt.
2. Drain the oil.

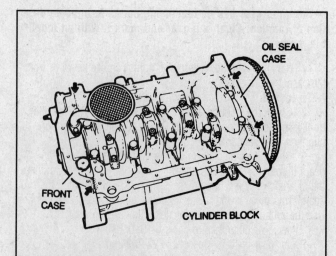

Fig. 59 Apply RTV sealer to the four points indicated by the arrows—1567cc engine

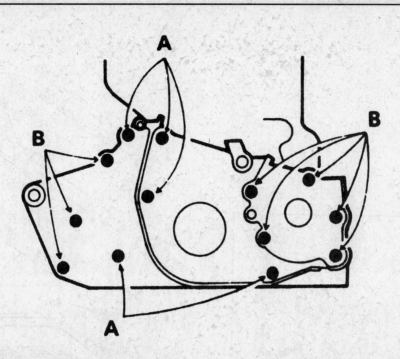

Fig. 60 Front case bolt identification—1597cc engine

❊❊ CAUTION

The EPA warns that prolonged contact with used engine oil may cause a number of skin disorders, including cancer! You should make every effort to minimize your exposure to used engine oil. Protective gloves should be worn when changing the oil. Wash your hands and any other exposed skin areas as soon as possible after exposure to used engine oil. Soap and water, or waterless hand cleaner should be used.

3. Remove the oil pan and screen.
4. Unbolt and remove the front case assembly.

➡If the front case assembly is difficult to remove from the block, there is a groove around the case into which a pry-bar may be inserted, to aid in removal. Pry slowly and evenly. Don't hammer!

5. Remove the oil pressure relief plug, spring and plunger.
6. Remove the nut and pull off the oil pump sprocket.
7. Remove the oil pump cover.
8. Remove the pump rotor.

To install:

9. Check the case for cracks and damage.
10. Check the oil screen for damage.
11. Replace the oil screen O-ring.
12. Thoroughly clean all parts in a safe solvent.
13. Place the rotor back in the case to check clearances:
• Side clearance: 0.06–0.12mm
• Tip clearance: 0.04–0.12mm
• Body clearance: 0.10–0.16mm
• Shaft-to-cover clearance: 0.02–0.05mm.
14. Check that the relief valve plunger slide smoothly in its bore.

15. Check the relief valve spring. The free length should be 47mm; the load/length should be 9.5 lb @ 40mm.
16. Install a new oil seal, coated with clean engine oil, into the oil pump cover. Drive it into place with a flat block.
17. Install a new cover gasket in the groove in the case.
18. Coat the rotor with clean engine oil and install it in the cover.
19. Install the cover and tighten the bolts.
20. Install the sprocket and tighten the nut to 28 ft. lbs.
21. Coat the oil relief valve plunger with clean engine oil and install it, along with the spring and plug.
22. Install a new case gasket, coated with sealer, on the block and install the case. Tighten the case bolts to 13 ft. lbs.

➡There are two different lengths of case bolts. In the accompanying illustration, the bolts labeled A are 35mm long: the ones marked B are 40mm long.

23. Install the screen. Tighten the bolts to 18 ft. lbs.
24. Install the oil pan as previously described.

1994, 1997, AND 2555cc ENGINES

▶ **See Figures 61 thru 66**

1. Remove the timing chain.
2. Remove the oil pump cover and gears.
3. Remove the relief valve plug, spring and plunger.
4. Thoroughly clean all parts in a safe solvent and check for wear and damage.
5. Clean all orifices and passages.
6. Place the gear back in the pump body and check clearances.
• Gear teeth-to-body: 0.10–0.15mm
• Driven gear end-play: 0.06–0.12mm
• Drive gear-to-bearing (front end): 0.020–0.045mm
• Drive gear-to-bearing (rear end): 0.043–0.066mm

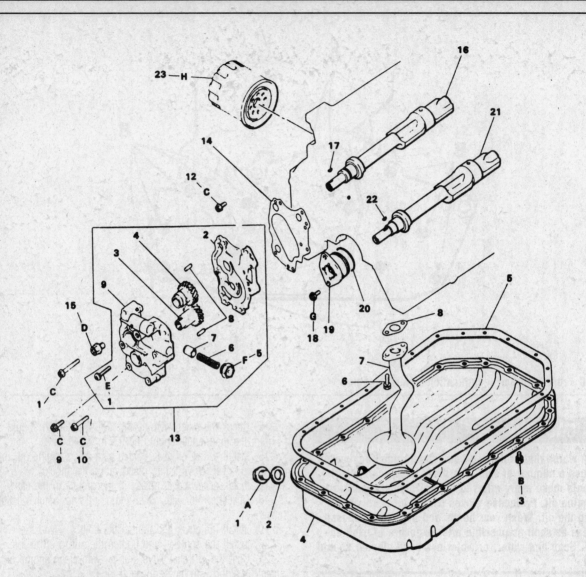

1. Oil drain plug
2. Oil drain plug gasket
3. Bolt (24)
4. Oil pan
5. Gasket
6. Bolt (2)
7. Oil screen
8. Oil screen gasket
9. Flange bolt—6x22
10. Flange bolt—6x38
11. Flange bolt—6x45
12. Flange bolt—6x16
13. Oil pump assembly
 -1 Screw
 -2 Oil pump cover
 -3 Oil pump drive gear
 -4 Oil pump driven gear
 -5 Plug
 -6 Relief spring
 -7 Relief valve
 -8 Pin (2)
 -9 Oil pump body

14. Oil pump gasket
15. Flange bolt
16. Silent shaft, right
17. Woodruff key
18. Flange bolt (2)
19. Thrust plate
20. O-ring
21. Silent shaft, left
22. Woodruff key
23. Oil filter

	Nm	ft. lbs.
A	59–78	44–57
B	6–7	4.5–5.5
C	10–11.5	7.5–8.5
D	59–68	44–50
E	8–9	6–7
F	30–44	22–32
G	10–11.5	7.5–8.5
H	11–12	8–9

Fig. 61 Exploded view of the engine oil system components—1994 and 2555cc engine

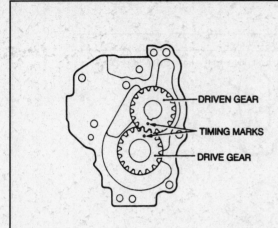

Fig. 62 the oil pump mating marks are dots in the gears—1994 and 2555cc engines

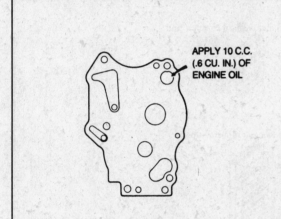

Fig. 63 To prime the pump, apply 10cc of clean engine oil into the delivery port—1994 and 2555cc engines

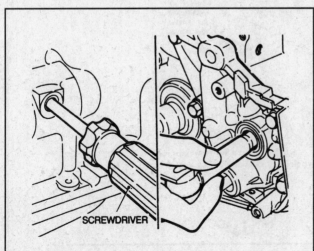

Fig. 64 On the 1997cc engine, insert an 8mm bar to hold the shaft into position

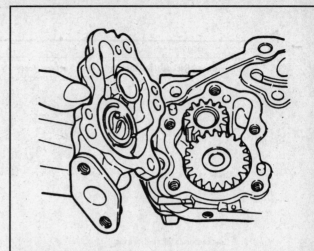

Fig. 65 Separating the oil pump cover on the 1997cc engine

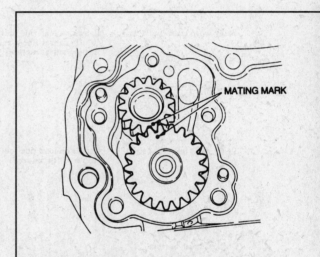

Fig. 66 The oil pump mating marks are dots in the gears—1997 engine

➡If gear replacement is necessary, the entire pump body must be replaced.

7. Check the relief valve spring for wear or damage. Free length should be 47mm; load/length should be 9.5 lb @ 40mm.

8. Assembly the pump components. Make sure that the gears are installed with the mating marks aligned.

Camshaft/Timing Chain/Belt

◆ See Figure 67

The correct installation and adjustment of the camshaft drive chain or belt is mandatory if the engine is to run properly. The camshaft controls the opening of the engine valves through coordination of the movement of the crankshaft and camshaft. When any given piston is on the intake stroke the corresponding intake valve must open to admit air/fuel mixture into the cylinder. When the same piston is on the compression and power strokes, both valves in that cylinder must be closed. When the piston is on the

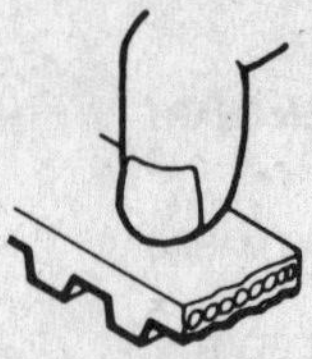

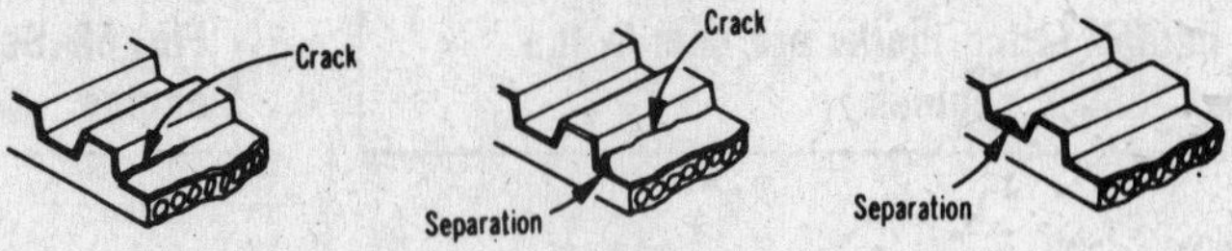

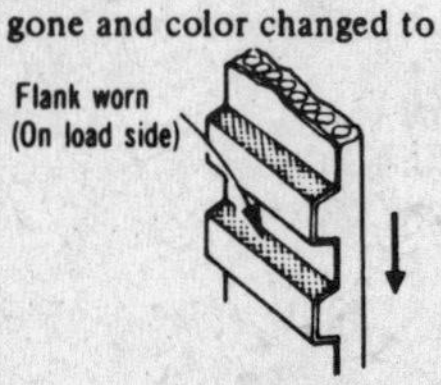

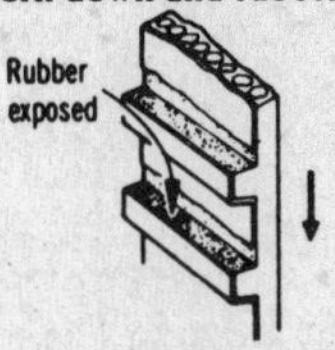

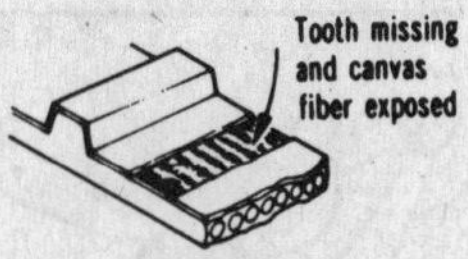

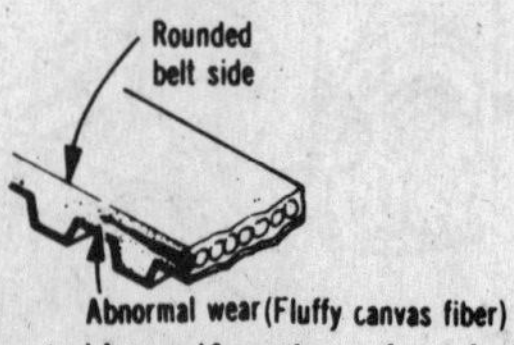

Description	Flaw conditions
1. Hardened back surface rubber	Back surface glossy. Non-elastic and so hard that even if a finger nail is forced into it, no mark is produced.
2. Cracked back surface rubber	
3. Cracked or exfoliated canvas	Crack Crack Crack Separation Separation
4. Badly worn teeth (initial stage)	Canvas on load side tooth flank worn (Fluffy canvas fibers, rubber gone and color changed to white, and unclear canvas texture) Flank worn (On load side)
5. Badly worn teeth (last stage)	Canvas on load side tooth flank worn down and rubber exposed (tooth width reduced) Rubber exposed
6. Cracked tooth bottom	Crack
7. Missing tooth	Tooth missing and canvas fiber exposed
8. Side of belt badly worn	Rounded belt side Abnormal wear (Fluffy canvas fiber) Note: Normal belt should have clear-cut sides as if cut by a sharp knife.
9. Side of belt cracked	

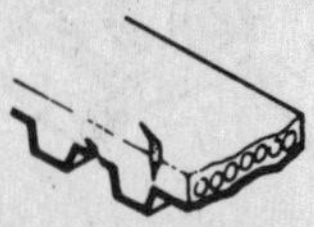

Fig. 67 Inspecting the timing belt wear

exhaust stroke, the exhaust valve for that cylinder must be open. If the opening and closing of the valves is not coordinated with the movements of the pistons, the engine will run poorly, if at all.

Timing Cover, Chain, Counterbalance Shafts, and Tensioner

REMOVAL & INSTALLATION

The following outlines are the recommended removal and installation procedures for the timing chain or belt. Some modifications to the procedures may be necessary due to added accessories, sheetmetal parts, or emission control units and connecting hoses.

➡The timing chain case is cast aluminum, so exercise caution when handling this part.

1971–77 1597cc Engine and 1974–75 1994cc Engine w/o Silent Shaft

♦ See Figures 68, 69, 70 and 71

1. Disconnect the negative battery cable. Drain the coolant. Disconnect and remove the radiator hoses. Remove the radiator.

✳✳ CAUTION

When draining the coolant, keep in mind that cats and dogs are attracted to ethylene glycol antifreeze, and are quite likely to drink any that is left in an uncovered container or in puddles on the ground. This will prove fatal in sufficient quantity. Always drain the coolant into a sealable container. Coolant should be reused unless it is contaminated or several years old.

2. Remove the alternator and accessory belts.
3. Rotate the crankshaft to bring No. 1 piston to TDC on the compression stroke, by aligning the notch on the crankshaft pulley with the T mark on the timing indicator scale.
4. Remove the crankshaft pulley and bolt.

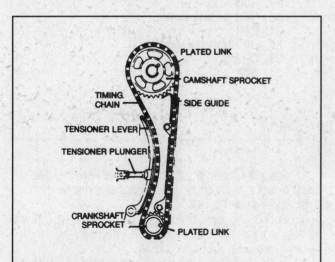

Fig. 68 Exploded view of the chain and tensioner—1597cc engine

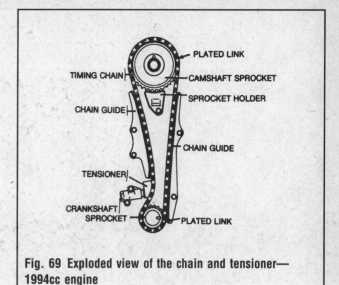

Fig. 69 Exploded view of the chain and tensioner—1994cc engine

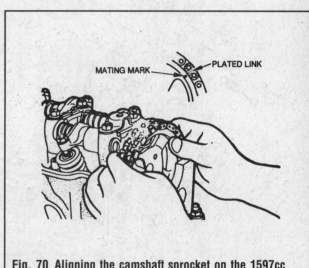

Fig. 70 Aligning the camshaft sprocket on the 1597cc engine

➡Do not move the crankshaft when removing the pulley. If the crankshaft is turned, return the shaft to the original position as in Step 3.

5. Remove the crankshaft pulley and bolt.
6. Remove the fan blades and the water pump assembly.
7. Remove the cylinder head assembly. (See cylinder head removal section).
8. Raise the car and support it safely on jackstands.
9. Drain the engine oil and remove the oil pan, oil pressure switch, oil filter, and oil pump.

➡Undercar splash pans may have to be removed to gain access to the oil pan.

10. Remove the chain tension holder, spring, and plunger, on the right side of the chain cover.
11. Remove the timing chain cover from the engine block.
12. Remove the oil slinger and crankshaft gear from the crankshaft. Do not loose the woodruff key from the crankshaft.

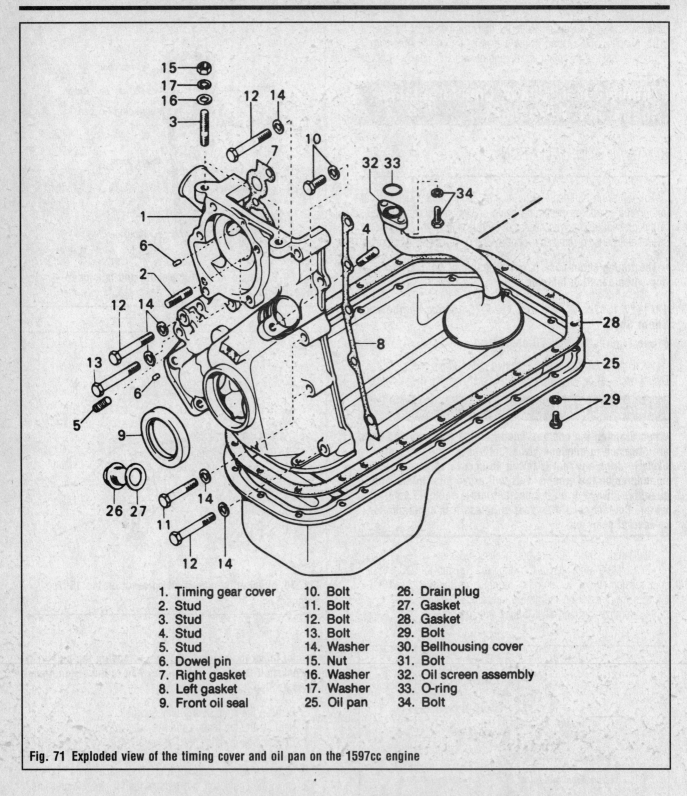

Fig. 71 Exploded view of the timing cover and oil pan on the 1597cc engine

1.	Timing gear cover	10. Bolt	26. Drain plug
2.	Stud	11. Bolt	27. Gasket
3.	Stud	12. Bolt	28. Gasket
4.	Stud	13. Bolt	29. Bolt
5.	Stud	14. Washer	30. Bellhousing cover
6.	Dowel pin	15. Nut	31. Bolt
7.	Right gasket	16. Washer	32. Oil screen assembly
8.	Left gasket	17. Washer	33. O-ring
9.	Front oil seal	25. Oil pan	34. Bolt

13. Remove the crankshaft and camshaft sprockets with the chain attached, from the engine block.

To install:

14. If needed, remove the chain tensioner lever and side guide.

15. If removed, install the chain tensioner lever and side guide, with the jet of the guide toward the chain and sprocket meshing point.

16. Be sure the No. 1 piston is at TDC. Using a new gasket, install the cylinder head assembly.

17. Rotate the camshaft until the dowel pin in between the 1 and 2 o'clock position on the 1597cc engines and at the 12 o'clock position on the 1994cc engines.

18. Position the crankshaft sprocket and the camshaft sprocket so that the punch marks on the sprockets align with the chrome or buff plated links of the timing chain.

19. Install the woodruff key on the crankshaft and while holding the timing chain and sprockets in position, install the sprockets onto the camshaft and the crankshaft.

20. If the dowel pin does not align with the hole in the camshaft sprocket, bump the camshaft on the projects provided to align the two. Install the camshaft sprocket bolt and tighten to 36 to 43 ft. lbs.

➡ **The chain must be fitted in the guide groove and against the tension lever.**

21. Install the woodruff key, crankshaft gear with the F mark toward the front on 1597cc engines, and with the C or A mark toward the front on the 1994cc engine. The oil slinger must be installed with its concave side facing the front of the engine.

22. Install a new gasket and seal on the front timing cover case and install the case on the engine block. Tighten the bolts to 11 to 13 ft. lbs.

23. Install the tensioner lever plunger and spring into the case and torque to 29–36 ft. lbs.

➡ **Because the timing chain is supported and stretched by the tensioner lever, it is important to align the marks on the sprockets and chain.**

24. Install the oil screen and oil pump.
25. Install the oil pan, oil filter, and the oil pressure gauge sender. Fill the oil pan.
26. Install any splash pans and lower the car to the floor.
27. Align the oil pump shaft in a vertical position on the 1597cc engine and in a horizontal position on the 1994cc engine. Align the distributor marks to fire No. 1 cylinder, and install distributor.
28. Install the crankshaft pulley and torque the bolt to 43–50 ft. lbs.
29. Install the water pump, fan blades, alternator and belt. Adjust the belt.
30. Install the radiator and radiator hoses, add coolant to the system, and connect the battery ground cable.
31. Refer to the Cylinder Head Installation Section and adjust the valves as for a cold engine. Temporarily install the rocker arm cover, start the engine, and warm it up.
32. Stop the engine and remove the rocker arm cover. Adjust the valves to the hot specifications.

1976–79 1994cc Engine and 2555cc Engine W/Silent Shaft

♦ **See Figures 72, 73 and 74**

1. Disconnect the battery ground (negative) cable. Drain the coolant. Disconnect and remove the radiator hoses. Remove the radiator.

✳✳ CAUTION

When draining the coolant, keep in mind that cats and dogs are attracted to ethylene glycol antifreeze, and are quite likely to drink any that is left in an uncovered container or in puddles on the ground. This will prove fatal in sufficient quantity. Always drain the coolant into a sealable container. Coolant should be reused unless it is contaminated or several years old.

2. Remove the alternator and accessory belts.
3. Rotate the crankshaft to bring No. 1 piston to TDC, on the compression stroke.
4. Mark and remove the distributor.

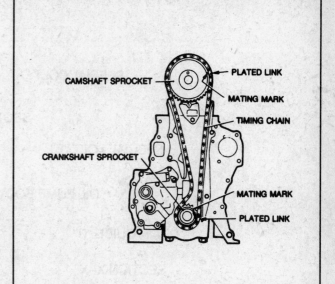

Fig. 72 Exploded view of the timing chain and gears on the engines with a silent shaft

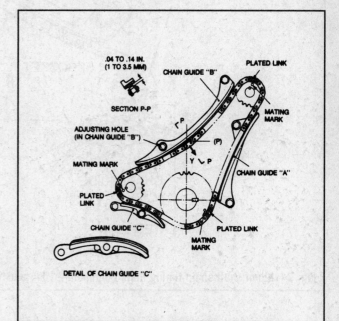

Fig. 73 Balance shaft and timing chain installation specifications

5. Remove the crankshaft pulley.
6. Remove the water pump assembly.
7. Remove the cylinder head. (See cylinder head removal section).

➡ **It may be possible to replace the timing chain without removing the cylinder head, however removing the head will make the job easier.**

8. Raise the front of the car and support it safely on jackstands.
9. Drain the engine oil and remove the oil pan and screen.

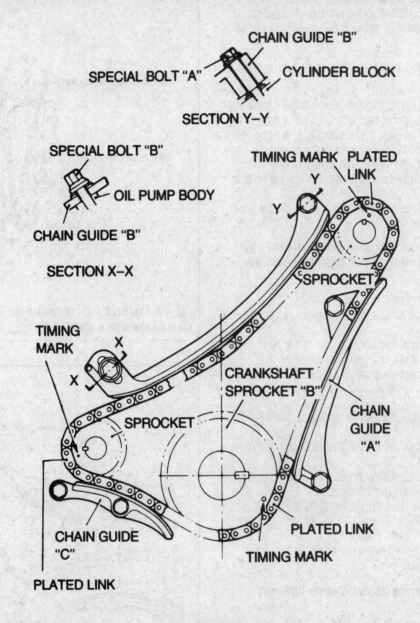

Fig. 74 Silent shaft chain timing mark alignment—1994 and 1997cc engines

✷✷ CAUTION

The EPA warns that prolonged contact with used engine oil may cause a number of skin disorders, including cancer! You should make every effort to minimize your exposure to used engine oil. Protective gloves should be worn when changing the oil. Wash your hands and any other exposed skin areas as soon as possible after exposure to used engine oil. Soap and water, or waterless hand cleaner should be used.

10. Remove the timing case cover.

11. Remove the chain guides, Side (A), Top (B), Bottom (C), from the B chain (outer). See illustration.

12. Remove the locking bolts from the B chain sprockets.

13. Remove the crankshaft sprocket, counterbalance shaft sprocket and the outer chain.

14. Remove the crankshaft and camshaft sprockets and the A (inner) chain.

15. Remove the camshaft sprocket holder and the chain guides, both left and right. Remove the tensioner spring and sleeve from the oil pump.

➡For further service to shafts and oil pump follow step 16 and 17.

16. Remove the oil pump by first removing the bolt locking the oil pump driven gear and the right counterbalance shaft, and then remove the oil pump mounting bolts. Remove the counterbalance shaft from the engine block.

➡**If the bolt locking the oil pump driven gear and the counterbalance shaft is hard to loosen, remove the oil pump and the shaft as a unit.**

17. Remove the left counterbalance shaft thrust washer and take the shaft from the engine block.

➡**If the tensioner rubber nose, or chain guide show wear, they should be replaced.**

To install:

18. Install the right counterbalance shaft into the engine block if removed.

19. Install the oil pump assembly if removed. Do not lose the woodruff key from the end of the counterbalance shaft. Torque the oil pump mounting bolts to 6–7 ft. lbs.

20. If they have been removed, tighten the counterbalance shaft and the oil pump driven gear mounting bolts.

➡**The counterbalance shaft and the oil pump can be installed as a unit, if necessary.**

21. Install the left counterbalance shaft into the engine block if removed.

22. Install a new O-ring on the thrust plate and install the unit into the engine block, using a pair of bolts without heads, as alignment guides.

➡**If the thrust plate is turned to align the bolts holes, the O-ring may be damaged.**

23. Remove the guide bolts and install the regular bolts into the thrust plate and tighten securely.

24. Rotate the crankshaft to bring No. 1 piston to TDC.

25. Using a new head gasket install the cylinder head.

26. Install the sprocket holder and the right and left chain guides.

27. Install the tensioner spring and sleeve on the oil pump body.

28. Install the camshaft and crankshaft sprockets on the timing chain, aligning the sprocket punch marks to the plate chain links.

29. While holding the sprocket and chain as a unit, install the crankshaft sprocket over the crankshaft and align it with the keyway.

30. Keeping the dowel pin hole on the camshaft in a vertical position, install the camshaft sprocket and chain on the camshaft.

➡**The sprocket timing mark and the plated chain link should be at the 2 to 3 o'clock position when correctly installed. The chain must be aligned in the right and left chain guides with the tensioner pushing against the chain. The tension for the inner chain is predetermined by spring tension.**

31. Install the crankshaft sprocket for the outer or **B** chain.

32. Install the two counterbalance shaft sprockets and align the punched mating marks with the plated linds of the chain.

33. Holding the two shaft sprockets and chain, install the outer chain in alignment with the mark on the crankshaft sprocket. Install the shaft sprockets on the counterbalance shaft and the oil pump driver gear. Install the lockbolts and recheck the alignment of the punch marks and the plated links.

34. Temporarily install the chain guides: Side (A), Top (B), and Bottom (C).

35. Tighten Side (A), chain guide securely.

36. Tighten Bottom (B) chain guide securely.

37. Adjust the position of the Top (B) chain guide, after shaking the right and left sprockets to collect any chain slack, so that when the chain is moved toward the center, the clearance between the chain guide and the chain links will be approximately 3.5mm. Tighten the Top (B) chain guide bolts.

38. Install the timing chain cover using a new gasket, being careful not to damage the front seal.

39. Install the oil screen and the oil pan, using a new gasket. Tighten the bolts to 54–66 inch lbs.

40. Install the crankshaft pulley, alternator and accessory belts, and the distributor.

41. Install the oil pressure switch, if removed, and install the negative battery cable.

42. Install the fan blades, radiator, fill the system with coolant and start the engine.

Timing Belt, Cover and Sprockets

REMOVAL & INSTALLATION

1597cc Engine W/O Silent Shaft 1597cc Engine W/Silent Shaft

◆ **See Figures 75, 76, 77, 78 and 79**

1. Disconnect the negative battery cable. On rear wheel drive cars, drain the coolant, disconnect the radiator hoses, remove the radiator.

✳✳ CAUTION

When draining the coolant, keep in mind that cats and dogs are attracted to the ethylene glycol antifreeze, and are quite likely to drink any that is left in an uncovered container or in puddles on the ground. This will prove fatal in sufficient quantity. Always drain the coolant into a sealable container. Coolant should be reused unless it is contaminated or several years old.

2. Remove the alternator and accessory belts. Remove the belt cover.

3. Rotate the crankshaft to bring No. 1 piston to TDC on the compression stroke. Align the notch on the crankshaft pulley with the T mark on the timing indicator scale and the timing mark on the upper under cover of the timing belt with the mark on the camshaft sprocket.

4. Remove the crankshaft pulley and bolt.

5. On rear wheel drive cars, remove the fan blades.

6. Remove the timing belt covers, upper front and lower front.

7. Remove the crankshaft sprocket bolt.

8. Loosen the tensioner mounting nut and bolt. Move the tensioner away from the belt and retighten the nut to keep the tensioner in the off position. Remove the tensioner.

➡**If the belt is all that needs servicing, proceed to the Installation section.**

9. Remove the camshaft sprocket, crankshaft sprocket, flange, and tensioner.

10. Silent shaft engines:

   a. Loosen the counterbalance shaft sprocket mounting bolt.

   b. Remove the belt tensioner and remove the timing belt.

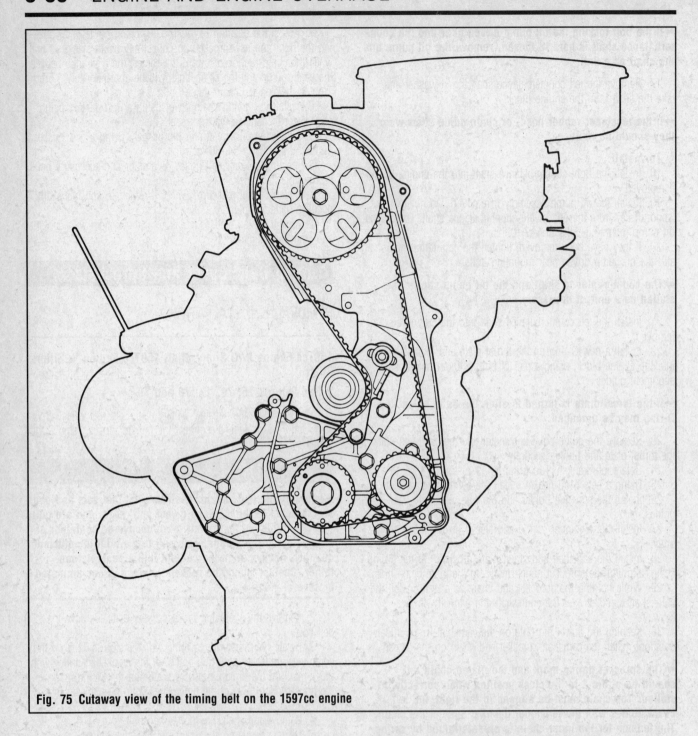

Fig. 75 Cutaway view of the timing belt on the 1597cc engine

c. Remove the crankshaft sprocket (inner) and counterbalance shaft sprocket.

d. Remove the upper and lower under timing belt covers.

11. The water pump or cylinder head may be removed at this point, depending upon the type of repairs needed.

12. Raise the front of the car and support it safely. Remove any interfering splash pans.

13. Drain the oil pan and remove the pan from the block.

✷✷ CAUTION

The EPA warns that prolonged contact with used engine oil may cause a number of skin disorders, including cancer!

You should make every effort to minimize your exposure to used engine oil. Protective gloves should be worn when changing the oil. Wash your hands and any other exposed skin areas as soon as possible after exposure to used engine oil. Soap and water, or waterless hand cleaner should be used.

14. Remove the oil pump sprocket and cover.

➡On the silent shaft engines, remove the plug at the bottom of the left side of the cylinder block and insert a screwdriver to keep the left counter balance shaft in position while removing the sprocket nut.

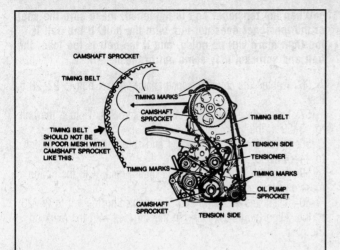

Fig. 76 Be sure the timing belt meshes correctly with the camshaft sprocket

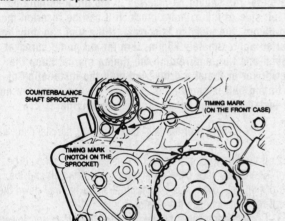

Fig. 77 Timing marks on timing belt silent shaft driven engines

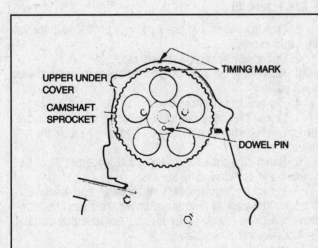

Fig. 78 Alignment marks on the crankshaft sprocket— 1597cc engine front view

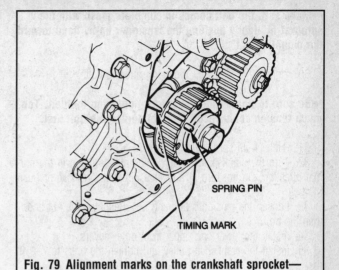

Fig. 79 Alignment marks on the crankshaft sprocket— 1597cc engine side view

15. Remove the front cover and oil pump as a unit, with the left counter shaft attached, if equipped.

16. Remove the oil pump gear and left counterbalance shaft.

➡️To aid in removal of the front cover, a driver groove is provided on the cover, above the oil pump housing. Avoid prying on the thinner parts of the housing flange or hammering on it to remove the case.

17. Remove the right counterbalance shaft from the engine block.

To install:

18. On the STANDARD ENGINE: Install a new front seal in the cover. Install a new gasket on the front of the cylinder block, and using a seal protector on the front of the crankshaft, install the front cover on the engine block.

19. Tighten the front case mounting bolts to 11–13 ft. lbs.

20. Install the oil screen, and using a new gasket, install the oil pan. Tighten bolts to 5–6 ft. lbs.

21. If the cylinder head and/or water pump had been removed reinstall them using new gaskets.

22. Install the upper and lower under covers.

23. Install the spacer, flange and crankshaft sprocket and tighten the bolt.

24. Align the timing mark on the crankshaft sprocket with the timing mark on the front case.

25. Align the camshaft sprocket timing mark with the upper under cover timing mark.

26. Install the tensioner spring and tensioner. Temporarily tighten the nut. Install the front end of the tensioner spring (bent at right angles) on the projection of the tensioner and the other end (straight) on the water pump body.

27. Loosen the nut and move the tensioner in the direction of the water pump. Lock it by tightening the nut.

28. Ensure that the sprocket timing marks are aligned, and install the timing belt. The belt should be installed on the crankshaft sprocket, the oil pump sprocket, and then the camshaft sprocket, in that order, while keeping the belt tight.

29. Loosen the tensioner mounting bolt and nut and allow the spring tension to move the tensioner against the belt.

➡️**Make sure the belt comes in complete mesh with the sprocket by lightly pushing the tensioner up by hand toward the mounting nut.**

30. Tighten the tensioner mounting nut and bolt.

➡️**Be sure to tighten the nut before tightening the bolt. Too much tension could result from tightening the bolt first.**

31. Recheck all sprocket alignments.
32. Turn the crankshaft through a complete rotation in the normal direction. Do not turn in a reverse direction or shake or push the belt.
33. Loosen the tensioner bolt and nut. Retighten the nut and then the bolt.
34. Install the lower and upper front outer covers.
35. Install the crankshaft pulley and tighten the bolts to 7–9 ft. lbs.
36. Install the alternator and belt and adjust. Install the distributor.
37. Install the radiator, fill the cooling system, and inspect for leaks.
38. On SILENT SHAFT ENGINES: Install a new front seal in the cover. Install the oil pump drive and driven gears in the front case, aligning the timing marks on the pump gears.
39. Install the left counterbalance shaft in the driven gear and temporarily tighten the bolt.
40. Install the right counterbalance shaft into the cylinder block.
41. Install an oil seal guide on the end of the crankshaft, and install a new gasket on the front of the engine block for the front cover.
42. Install a new front case packing. If equipped.
43. Insert the left counterbalance shaft into the engine block and at the same time, guide the front cover into place on the front of the engine block.
44. Insert a screwdriver at the bottom of the left side of the block and hold the left counterbalance shaft and tighten the bolt. Install the hole plug.
45. Install an O-ring on the oil pump cover and install it on the front cover.
46. Tighten the oil pump cover bolts and the front cover bolts to 11–13 ft. lbs.
47. Install the oil screen, and using a new gasket, install the oil pan.
48. Install the water pump and/or the cylinder head, if removed previously.
49. Install the upper and lower under covers.
50. Install the spacer on the end of the right counterbalance shaft, with the chambered edge toward the rear of the engine.
51. Install the counterbalance shaft sprocket and temporarily tighten the bolt.
52. Install the inner crankshaft sprocket and align the timing marks on the sprockets with those on the front case.
53. Install the inner tensioner (B) with the center of the pulley on the left side of the mounting bolt and with the pulley flange toward the front of the engine.
54. Lift the tensioner by hand, clockwise, to apply tension to the belt. Tighten the bolt to secure the tensioner.
55. Check that all alignment marks are in their proper places and the belt deflection is approximately ¼–½" on the tension side.

➡️**When the tensioner bolt is tightened, make sure the shaft of the tensioner does not turn with the bolt. If the belt is too tight there will be noise, and if the belt is too lose, the belt and sprocket may come out of mesh.**

56. Tighten the counterbalance shaft sprocket bolt to 22–29 ft. lbs.
57. Install the flange and crankshaft sprocket. Tighten the bolt to 43–50 ft. lbs.
58. Install the camshaft spacer and sprocket. Tighten the bolt to 44–57 ft. lbs.
59. Align the camshaft sprocket timing mark with the timing mark on the upper inner cover.
60. Install the oil pump sprocket, tightening the nut to 25–28 ft. lbs. Align the timing mark on the sprocket with the mark on the case.

➡️**To be assured that the phasing of the oil pump sprocket and the left counterbalance shaft is correct, a screwdriver or a metal rod should be inserted in the plugged hole on the left side of the cylinder block. If it can be inserted more than 60mm, the phasing is correct. If the tool can only be inserted approximately 25mm, turn the oil pump sprocket through one turn and realign the timing marks. Keep the screwdriver or metal rod inserted until the installation of the timing belt is completed. Remove the tool from the hole and install the plug, before starting the engine.**

61. Refer to Step 9 of the belt installation for the standard engine.
62. If the timing belt is correctly tensioned, there should be about 12mm clearance between the outside of the belt and the edge of the belt cover. This is measured about halfway down the side of the belt opposite the tensioner.
63. Complete the assembly by installing the upper and lower front covers.
64. Install the crankshaft pulley, alternator, and accessory belts, and adjust to specifications.
65. Install the radiator, fill the cooling system, and start the engine.

1410 and 1468cc Engines

◆ **See Figure 80**

1. Turn the engine until No. 1 piston is on TDC with the timing marks aligned.
2. Disconnect the negative battery cable.
3. Remove the fan drive belt, the fan blades, spacer and water pump pulley.
4. Remove the timing belt cover.
5. Loosen the timing belt tensioner mounting bolt and move the tensioner toward the water pump. Temporarily secure the tensioner.
6. Remove the crankshaft pulley and slide the belt off of the camshaft and crankshaft drive sprockets.
7. Inspect the drive sprockets for abnormal wear, cracks or damage and replace as necessary. Remove and inspect the tensioner. Check for smooth pulley rotation, excessive play or noise. Replace tensioner if necessary.

To install:

8. Reinstall the tensioner, if it was removed, and temporarily secure it close to the water pump.
9. Make sure that the timing mark on the camshaft sprocket

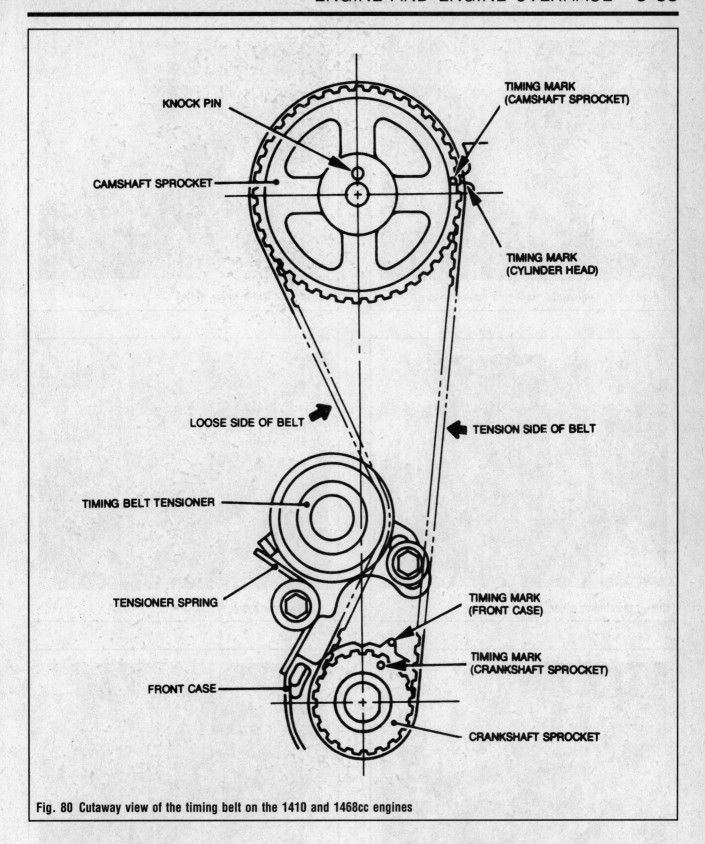

Fig. 80 Cutaway view of the timing belt on the 1410 and 1468cc engines

is aligned with the pointer on the cylinder head and that the crankshaft sprocket mark is aligned with the mark on the engine case.

10. Install the timing belt on the crankshaft sprocket.

11. Install the belt counterclockwise over the camshaft sprocket making sure there is no play on the tension side of the belt. Adjust the belt fore and aft so that it is centered on the sprockets.

12. Loosen the tensioner from its temporary position so that the spring pressure will allow it to contact the timing belt.

13. Rotate the crankshaft two complete turns in the normal rotation direction to remove any belt slack. Turn the crankshaft until the timing marks are lined up. If the timing has slipped, remove the belt and repeat the procedure.

If necessary, remove the right side engine mount

Loosen the water pump pulley . . .

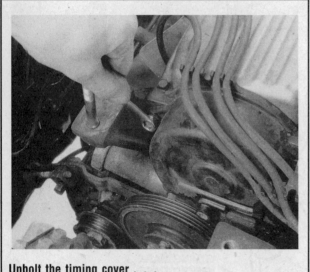

Unbolt the timing cover . . .

. . . and remove it

. . . and remove it

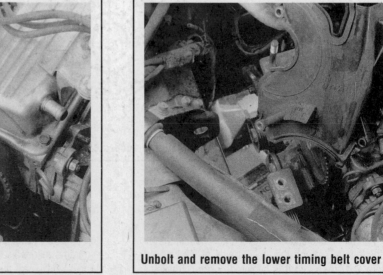

Unbolt and remove the lower timing belt cover

If necessary, remove the water pump

Loosen the upper . . .

Hold the crankshaft pulley bolt in place . . .

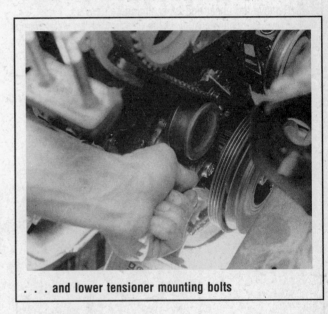

. . . and lower tensioner mounting bolts

. . . and remove the pulley mounting bolts

Slide the belt off the camshaft sprocket

14. Tighten the tensioner mounting bolts, slotted side (right) first then the spring side.

15. Once again rotate the engine two complete revolutions until the timing marks line up. Recheck the belt tension.

➡ **When the tension side of the timing bolt and the tensioner are pushed in horizontally with a moderate force (about 11 lbs.) and the cogged side of the belt covers about 6mm of the tensioner right side mounting bolt head, (across flats) the tension is correct.**

16. Install the timing belt cover, the water pump pulley, spacer, fan blades and drive belt.

17. Connect the negative battery cable.

1997cc Engine

▶ **See Figure 81**

➡ **An 8mm diameter metal bar is needed for this procedure.**

1. Remove the water pump drive belt and pulley.
2. Remove the crank adapter and crankshaft pulley.
3. Remove the upper and lower timing belt covers.
4. Move the tensioner fully in the direction of the water pump and temporarily secure it there.

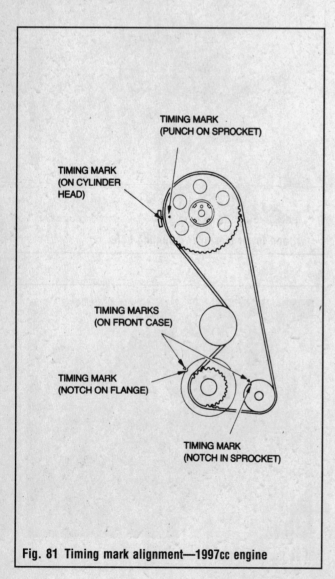

Fig. 81 Timing mark alignment—1997cc engine

5. If you are going to reuse the timing belt, make a paint mark on the belt to indicate the direction of rotation. Slip the belt from the sprockets.

➡ **Place the belt in an area where it will not be contacted by oil or other petroleum distillates.**

6. Remove the camshaft sprocket bolt and pull the sprocket from the camshaft.

7. Remove the crankshaft sprocket bolt and pull the crankshaft sprocket and flange from the crankshaft.

8. Remove the plug on the left side the block and insert an 8mm diameter metal bar in the opening to keep the silent shaft in position.

9. Remove the oil pump sprocket retaining nut and remove the oil pump sprocket.

10. Loosen the right silent shaft sprocket mounting bolt until it can be turned by hand.

11. Remove the silent shaft belt tensioner, and slip the silent shaft belt off its sprockets.

➡ **Do not attempt to turn the silent shaft sprocket or loosen its bolt while the belt is off.**

12. Remove the silent shaft belt sprocket from the crankshaft.

13. Check the belt for wear, damage or glossing. Replace it if any cracks, damage, brittleness or excessive wear are found.

To install:

14. Check the tensioners for a smooth rate of movement.

15. Replace any tensioner that shows grease leakage through the seal.

16. Install the silent shaft belt sprocket on the crankshaft, with the flat face toward the engine.

17. Apply light engine oil on the outer face of the spacer and install the spacer on the right silent shaft. The side with the rounded shoulder faces the engine.

18. Install the sprocket on the right silent shaft and install the bolt finger-tight.

19. Install the silent shaft belt and adjust the tension, by moving the tensioner into contact with the belt, tight enough to remove all slack. Tighten the tensioner bolt to 21 ft. lbs.

20. Tighten the silent shaft sprocket bolt to 28 ft. lbs.

21. Install the flange and crankshaft sprocket on the crankshaft. The flange conforms to the front of the silent shaft sprocket and the timing belt sprocket is installed with the flat face toward the engine.

➡ **The flange must be installed correctly or a broken belt will be the result.**

22. Install the washer and bolt in the crankshaft and tighten it to 94 ft. lbs.

23. Install the camshaft sprocket and bolt and tighten the bolt to 72 ft. lbs.

24. Install the timing belt tensioner, spacer and spring.

25. Align the timing mark on each sprocket with the corresponding mark on the front case.

26. Install the timing belt on the sprockets and move the tensioner against the belt with sufficient force to allow a deflection of 5–7mm along its longest straight run.

27. Tighten the tensioner bolt to 21 ft. lbs.

28. Install the upper and lower covers, the crankshaft pulley and the crank adapter. Tighten the bolts to 21 ft. lbs.

29. Remove the 8mm bar and install the plug.

Pistons and Connecting Rods

REMOVAL & INSTALLATION

◆ **See Figures 82 and 83**

➡**Although, in most cases, the pistons and connecting rods can be removed from the engine (after the cylinder head and oil pan are removed) while the engine is still in the car: it is far easier to work on the engine when removed from the car.**

If removing pistons with the engine still installed, disconnect the radiator hoses, automatic transmission cooler lines and radiator shroud. Unbolt front mounts before jacking up the engine and block the engine in position with wooden blocks between the mounts.

1. Remove the engine from the car. Remove cylinder head, oil pan and front cover.
2. Because the top piston ring does not travel to the very top of the cylinder bore, a ridge is built up between the end of the travel and the top of the cylinder. Pushing the piston and connecting rod assembly past the ridge is difficult and may cause damage to the piston. If new rings are installed the ridge has not been removed, ring breakage and piston damage can occur when the ridge is encountered at engine speed.
3. Turn the crankshaft to position the piston at the bottom of the cylinder bore. Cover the top of the piston with a rag. Install a ridge reamer in the bore and follow the manufacture's instructions to remove the ridge. Use caution, avoid cutting too deeply. Remove the rag and cutting from the top of the piston. Remove the ridge from all cylinders.
4. Check the edges of the connecting rod and bearing cap for numbers or matchmarks, if none are present mark the rod and cap numerically and in sequence from front to back of engine. The numbers or marks not only tell from which cylinder the piston came from but also helps ensure that the rod caps are installed in the correct matching position.
5. Turn the crankshaft until the connecting rod is at the bottom of travel. Remove the two attaching nuts and the bearing cap. Take two pieces of rubber tubing and cover the rod bolts to prevent crank or cylinder scoring. Use a wooden hammer handle to help push the piston and rod up and out of the cylinder. Reinstall the rod cap in proper position. Remove all pistons and connecting rods. Inspect cylinder walls and deglaze or hone as necessary.
6. Lubricate each piston, rod bearing and cylinder wall. Install a ring compressor over the piston, position the piston with mark toward front of engine and carefully install it into engine. Tap the piston into the bore with a wooden hammer handle or rubber hammer. Position connecting rod with bearing insert installed over the crank journal. Install the rod cap with bearing in proper position. Secure with rod nuts and torque to proper specifications. Install all of the remaining piston assemblies.

CLEANING AND INSPECTION

1. Use a piston ring expander and remove the rings from the piston.
2. Clean the ring grooves using an appropriate cleaning tool, exercise care to avoid cutting too deeply.

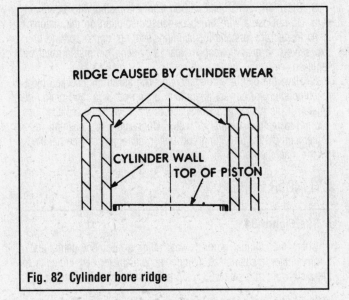

Fig. 82 Cylinder bore ridge

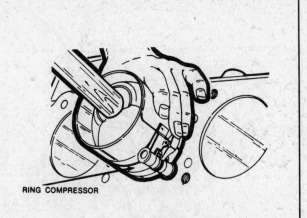

Fig. 83 Install a ring compressor around the piston, then install the assembly into the block as shown

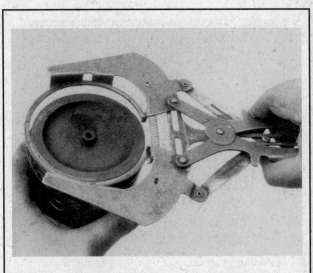

Use a ring expander tool to remove the piston rings

Clean the piston grooves using a ring groove cleaner

Measure the piston's outer diameter using a micrometer

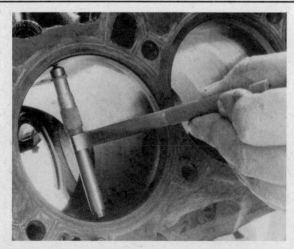

You can use a piece of an old ring to clean the piston grooves, BUT be careful, the ring is sharp

3. Clean all varnish and carbon from the piston with a safe solvent. Do not use a wire brush or caustic solution on the pistons.

4. Inspect the pistons for scuffing, scoring, cracks, pitting or excessive ring groove wear. If wear is evident, the piston must be replaced.

5. Have the piston and connecting rod assembly checked by a machine shop for correct alignment, piston pin wear and piston diameter. If the piston had Collapsed it will have to be replaced or knurled to restore original diameter. Connecting rod bushing replacement, piston pin fitting and piston changing can be handled by the machine shop.

CYLINDER BORE

▶ **See Figure 84**

Check the cylinder bore for wear using a telescope gauge and a micrometer, measure the cylinder bore diameter perpendicular to the piston pin at a point 63.5mm below the top of the engine

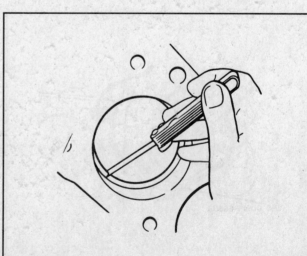

A telescoping gauge may be used to measure the cylinder bore diameter

Fig. 84 Using a gauge, check the piston ring and cap for wear

Removing cylinder glazing using a flexible hone

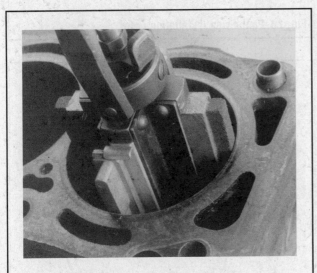

As with a ball hone, work the hone carefully up and down the bore to achieve the desired results

A solid hone can also be used to cross-hatch the cylinder bore

block. Measure the piston skirt perpendicular to the piston pin. The difference between the two measurements is the piston clearance. If the clearance is within specifications, finish honing or glaze breaking is all that is required. If clearance is excessive a slightly oversize piston may be required. If greatly oversize, the engine will have to be bored and 0.25mm or larger oversized pistons installed.

PISTON PINS

The pin connecting the piston and connecting rod is press fitted. If too much free-play develops take the piston assemblies to the machine shop and have oversize pins installed. Installing new rods or pistons requires the use of a press. Have the machine shop handle the job for you.

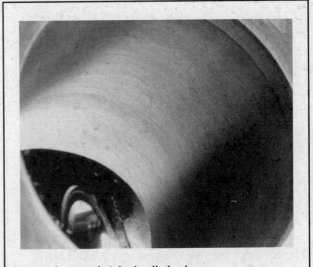

A properly cross-hatched cylinder bore

FITTING AND POSITIONING PISTON RINGS

♦ **See Figures 85, 86 and 87**

1. Take the new piston rings and care install, one at a time into the cylinder that they will be used in. Push the ring about 25mm below the top of the cylinder block using an inverted piston.

2. Use a feeler gauge and measure the distance between the ends of the ring, this is called measuring the ring end-gap. Compare the reading to the one called for in the specifications table. File the ends of the ring with a fine file to obtain necessary clearance.

➡**If inadequate ring end-gap is utilized, ring breakage will result.**

3. Inspect the ring grooves on the piston for excessive wear or taper. If necessary have the grooves recut for use with a standard ring and spacer. The machine shop can handle the job for you.

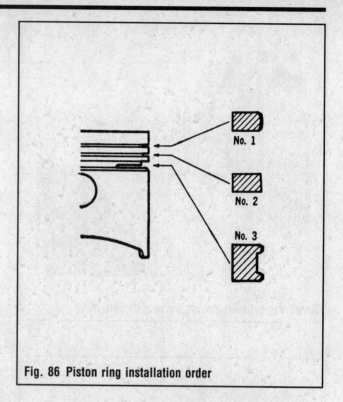

Fig. 86 Piston ring installation order

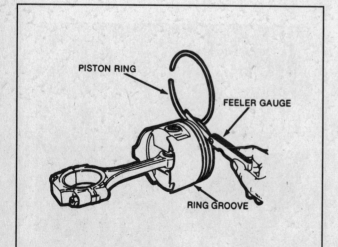

Most rings are marked to show which side should face upward

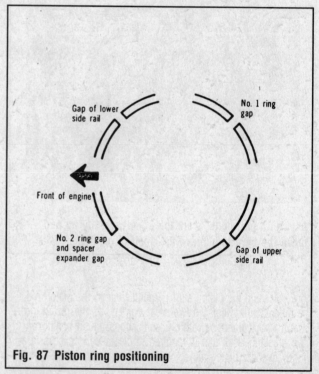

Fig. 87 Piston ring positioning

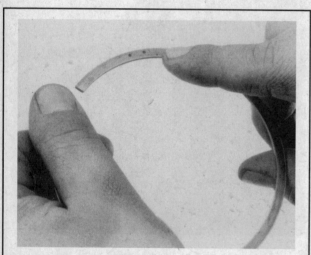

Fig. 85 Check the piston side clearance with a feeler gauge

4. Check the ring groove by rolling the new piston ring around the groove to check for burrs or carbon deposits. If any are found, remove with a fine file. Hold the ring in the groove and measure side clearance with a feeler gauge. If clearance is excessive, spacer(s) will have to be added.

➡**Always add spacers above the piston ring.**

5. Install the rings on the piston, lower ring first using a ring installing tool. Consult the instruction sheet that comes with the

rings to be sure they are installed with the correct side up. A mark on the ring usually faces upward.

6. When installing oil rings: install the center spreader (ring) in the groove. Hold the ends of the ring butted together (they must not overlap) and install the bottom rail (scraper) with the end about 25mm away from the butted end of the control ring. Install the top rail about 25mm away from the butted end of the control but on the opposite side from the lower rail.

7. Install the two compression rings (the rings usually have a stamped marked that faces up).

8. Consult the illustration with piston ring set instruction sheet for ring positioning, arrange the rings as shown, install a ring compressor and insert the piston and rod assembly into the engine.

ROD BEARING REPLACEMENT

1. Rod bearings can be installed when the pistons have been removed for servicing (rings etc) or, in most cases, while the engine is still in the car. Bearing replacement, however, is far easier with the engine out of the car and disassembled.

2. For in car service, remove the oil pan, spark plugs and front cover if necessary, Turn the engine until the connecting rod to be serviced is at the bottom of its travel. Remove the bearing cap, place two pieces of rubber hose over the rod cap bolts and push the piston and rod assembly up the cylinder bore until enough room is gained for bearing insert removal. Take care not to push the rod assembly up too far or the top ring will engage the cylinder ridge or come out of the cylinder and require head removal for reinstallation.

3. Clean the rod journal, the connecting rod end and the bearing cap after removing the old bearing inserts. Install the new inserts in the rod and bearing cap, lubricate them with oil. Position the rod over the crankshaft journal and install the rod cap. Make sure the cap and rod numbers match, torque the rod nuts to specifications.

4. Install the front cover, oil pan, etc.

Place rubber hose over the connecting rod studs to protect the crank and bores from damage

Rear Main Oil Seal

REMOVAL & INSTALLATION

◗ See Figures 88, 89 and 90

The rear main seal is located in a housing on the rear of the block. To replace the seal, it is necessary to remove the transmission and perform the work from underneath the car or remove the engine and perform the work on an engine stand or work bench.

➡ **On Front Wheel Drive models, the factory recommends that the engine be removed from the car.**

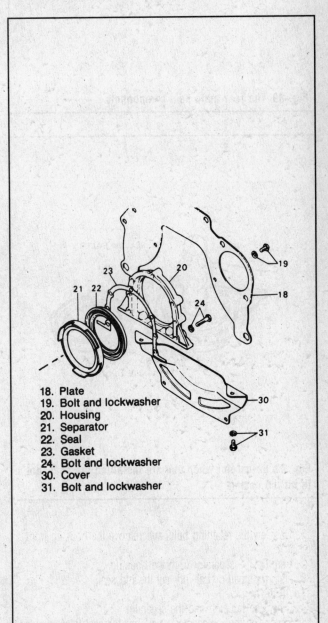

18. Plate
19. Bolt and lockwasher
20. Housing
21. Separator
22. Seal
23. Gasket
24. Bolt and lockwasher
30. Cover
31. Bolt and lockwasher

Fig. 88 Common rear main seal and components

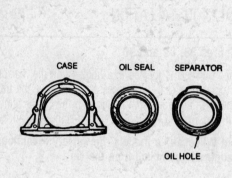

Fig. 89 The rear main seal components

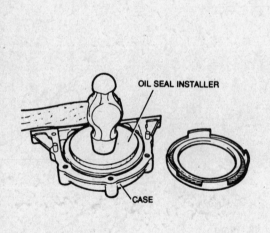

Fig. 90 Be careful when you are installing the seal, not to hit the casing

1. Unscrew the retaining bolts and remove the housing from the block.
2. Remove the separator from the housing.
3. Using a small prybar, pry out the old seal.

To install:

4. Clean the housing and the separator.
5. Lightly oil the replacement seal. Tap the seal into housing using a canister top or other circular piece of metal. The oil seal should be installed so that the seal plate fits into the inner contact surface of the seal case.
6. Install the separator into the housing so that the oil hole faces down.

7. Oil the lips of the seal and install the housing on the rear of the engine block.

Crankshaft and Main Bearings

REMOVAL & INSTALLATION

1. With the engine out of the car, remove the intake manifold, cylinder head, front cover, timing gears and/or chain, oil pan, oil pump and flywheel.
2. Remove the piston and rod assemblies. Remove the main bearing caps after marking them for position and direction.
3. Remove the crankshaft, bearing inserts and a rear main oil seal. Clean the engine block and cap bearing saddles. Clean the crankshaft and inspect for wear. Check the bearing journals with a micrometer for out-of-round condition and to determine what size rod and main bearing inserts to install.

A dial gauge may be used to check crankshaft end-play

Carefully pry the shaft back and forth while reading the dial gauge for play

A dial gauge may also be used to check crankshaft run-out

Turn the crankshaft slowly by hand while checking the gauge

Mounting a dial gauge to read crankshaft run-out

To install:

4. Install the main bearing upper inserts and rear main oil seal half into the engine block.

5. Lubricate the bearing inserts and the crankshaft journals. Slowly and carefully lower the crankshaft into position.

6. Install the bearing inserts and rear main seal into the bearing caps, install the caps working from the middle out. Torque cap bolts to specifications in stages, rotate the crankshaft after each torque stage.

7. Remove the bearing caps, one at a time and check the oil clearance with Plastigage. Reinstall if clearance is within specifications. Check the crankshaft end-play, if within specifications install connecting rod and piston assemblies with new rod bearing inserts. Check connecting rod bearing oil clearance and rod side play, if correct, assemble the rest of the engine.

BEARING OIL CLEARANCE

Remove the cap from the bearing to be checked. Using a clean, dry rag, thoroughly clean all of the oil from the crankshaft journal and bearing insert.

➡**Plastigage is soluble in oil: therefore, oil on the journal or bearing could result in erroneous readings.**

Place a piece of Plastigage along the width of the bearing insert, install the cap, and torque to specifications.

Remove the bearing cap, and determine the bearing clearance by comparing the squished width of Plastigage to the scale on the Plastigage envelope. Journal taper is determined by comparing the width of the Plastigage strip near its ends. Rotate the crankshaft 90° by hand, to determine journal eccentricity.

Apply a strip of gauging material to the bearing journal, then install and torque the cap

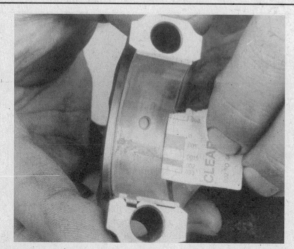

After the cap is removed again, use the scale supplied with the gauge material to check clearances

The notch on the the side of the bearing cap matches the groove on the bearing insert

➡️Do not rotate the crankshaft with the Plastigage installed. If bearing insert and journal appear intact, and are within tolerances, no further main bearing service is required. If bearing or journal appear defective, cause of failure should be determined before replacement.

CRANKSHAFT END-PLAY/CONNECTING ROD SIDE PLAY

Place a prybar between a main bearing cap and crankshaft casting taking care not to damage any journals. Pry backward and forward measure the distance between the thrust bearing (center main) and crankshaft with a feeler gauge. Compare reading with specifications. If too great a clearance is determined, a larger thrust bearing or crank machining may be required. Check with an automotive machine shop for their advice.

Connecting rod clearance between the rod and crankthrow casting can be checked with a feeler gauge. Pry the rod carefully to one side as far as possible and measure the distance on the other side of the rod.

CRANKSHAFT REPAIRS

If a journal is damaged on the crankshaft, repair is possible by having the crankshaft machined, after removal from engine to a standard undersize. Consult the machine shop for their advice.

COMPLETING THE REBUILDING PROCESS

▶ **See Figure 91**

Fill the oil pump with oil, to prevent cavitating (sucking air) on initial engine start up. Install the oil pump and the pickup tube on the engine. Coat the oil pan gasket as necessary, and install the gasket and the oil pan. Mount the flywheel and the crankshaft vibration damper or pulley on the crankshaft.

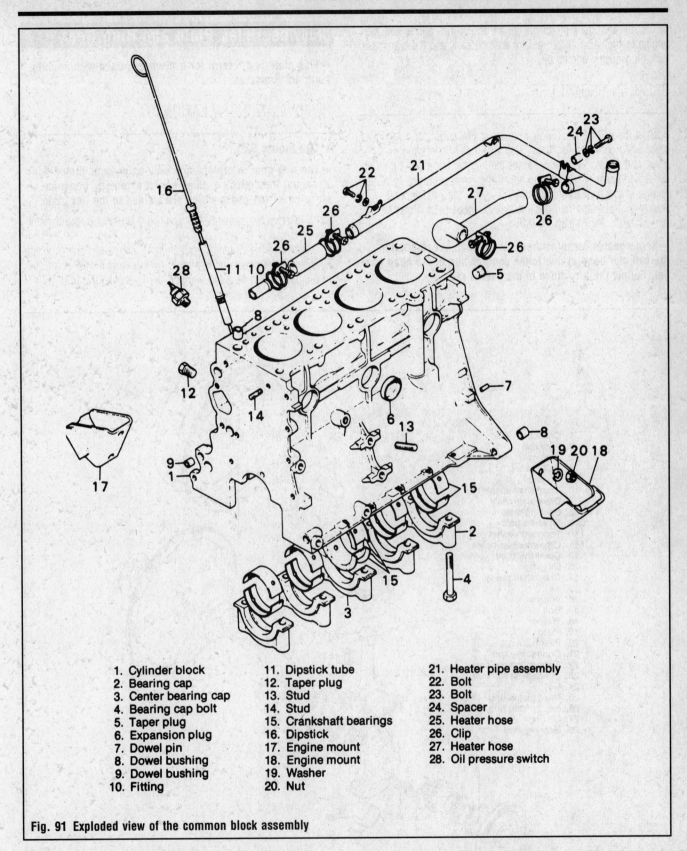

1. Cylinder block
2. Bearing cap
3. Center bearing cap
4. Bearing cap bolt
5. Taper plug
6. Expansion plug
7. Dowel pin
8. Dowel bushing
9. Dowel bushing
10. Fitting
11. Dipstick tube
12. Taper plug
13. Stud
14. Stud
15. Crankshaft bearings
16. Dipstick
17. Engine mount
18. Engine mount
19. Washer
20. Nut
21. Heater pipe assembly
22. Bolt
23. Bolt
24. Spacer
25. Heater hose
26. Clip
27. Heater hose
28. Oil pressure switch

Fig. 91 Exploded view of the common block assembly

➡**Always use new bolts when installing the flywheel. Inspect the clutch shaft pilot bushing in the crankshaft. If the bushing is excessively worn, remove it with an expanding puller and a slide hammer, and tap a new bushing into place.**

Position the engine, cylinder head side up. Lubricate the lifters, and install them into their bores. Install the cylinder head, and torque it as specified. Insert the pushrods (where applicable), and install the rocker shaft(s) (if so equipped) or position the rocker. Install the intake and exhaust manifolds, the carburetor(s), the distributor and spark plugs. Mount all accessories and install the engine in the car. Fill the radiator with coolant, and the crankcase with high quality engine oil.

BREAK-IN PROCEDURE

Start the engine, and allow it to run at low speed for a few minutes, while checking for leaks. Stop the engine, check the oil level, and fill as necessary. Restart the engine, and fill the cooling system to capacity. Check and adjust the ignition timing. Run the engine at low to medium speed (800–2,500 rpm) for approximately ½ hour, and retorque the cylinder head bolts. Road test the car, and check again for leaks.

➡**Some gasket manufacturers recommend not retorquing the cylinder head(s) due to the composition of the head gasket. Follow the directions in the gasket set.**

Flywheel/Flex Plate and Ring Gear

➡**Flex plate is the term for a flywheel mated with an automatic transmission.**

REMOVAL & INSTALLATION

◆ **See Figure 92**

➡**The ring gear is replaceable only on engines mated with a manual transmission. Engine with automatic transmissions have ring gears which are welded to the flex plate.**

1. Remove the transmission and, on 4-WD Vistas, the transfer case.
2. Remove the clutch, if equipped, or torque converter from the flywheel. The flywheel bolts should be loosened a little at a time in a cross pattern to avoid warping the flywheel. On trucks with

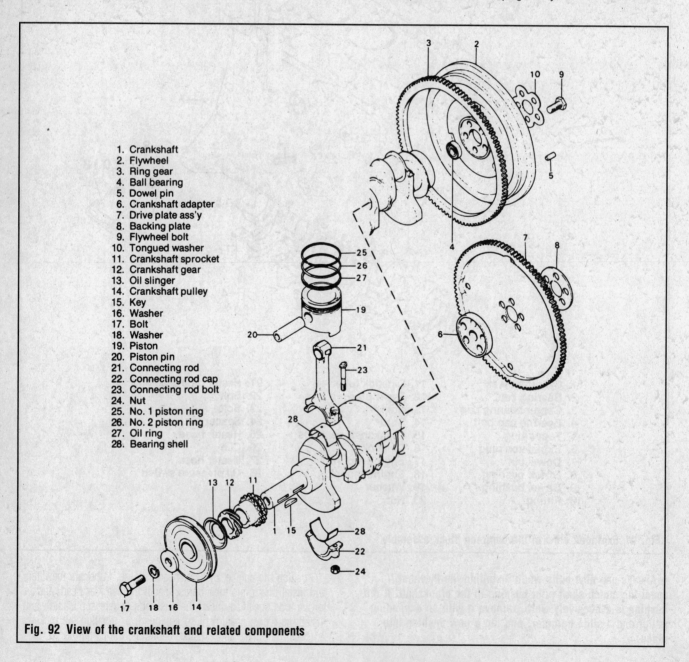

1. Crankshaft
2. Flywheel
3. Ring gear
4. Ball bearing
5. Dowel pin
6. Crankshaft adapter
7. Drive plate ass'y
8. Backing plate
9. Flywheel bolt
10. Tongued washer
11. Crankshaft sprocket
12. Crankshaft gear
13. Oil slinger
14. Crankshaft pulley
15. Key
16. Washer
17. Bolt
18. Washer
19. Piston
20. Piston pin
21. Connecting rod
22. Connecting rod cap
23. Connecting rod bolt
24. Nut
25. No. 1 piston ring
26. No. 2 piston ring
27. Oil ring
28. Bearing shell

Fig. 92 View of the crankshaft and related components

manual transmission, replace the pilot bearing in the end of the crankshaft if removing the flywheel.

3. The flywheel should be checked for cracks and glazing. It can be resurfaced by a machine shop.

4. If the ring gear is to be replaced, drill a hole in the gear between two teeth, being careful not to contact the flywheel surface. Using a cold chisel at this point, crack the ring gear and remove it.

5. Polish the inner surface of the new ring gear and heat it in an oven to about 600°F (315°C). Quickly place the ring gear on the flywheel and tap it into place, making sure that it is fully seated.

➡**Never heat the ring gear past 800°F (426°C), or the tempering will be destroyed.**

7. Installation is the reverse of removal. Tighten the bolts a little at a time in a cross pattern, to the torque figure shown in the Torque Specifications Chart.

EXHAUST SYSTEM

General Information

➡**Safety glasses should be worn at all times when working on or near the exhaust system. Older exhaust systems will almost always be covered with loose rust particles which will shower you when disturbed. These particles are more than a nuisance and could injure your eye.**

Whenever working on the exhaust system always keep the following in mind:
• Check the complete exhaust system for open seams, holes loose connections, or other deterioration which could permit exhaust fumes to seep into the passenger compartment.
• The exhaust system is usually supported by free-hanging rubber mountings which permit some movement of the exhaust system, but does not permit transfer of noise and vibration into the passenger compartment. Do not replace the rubber mounts with solid ones.
• Before removing any component of the exhaust system, ALWAYS squirt a liquid rust dissolving agent onto the fasteners for ease of removal. A lot of knuckle skin will be saved by following this rule. It may even be wise to spray the fasteners and allow them to sit overnight.

✳✳ CAUTION

Allow the exhaust system to cool sufficiently before spraying a solvent exhaust fasteners. Some solvents are highly flammable and could ignite when sprayed on hot exhaust components.

• Annoying rattles and noise vibrations in the exhaust system are usually caused by misalignment of the parts. When aligning the system, leave all bolts and nuts loose until all parts are properly aligned, then tighten, working from front to rear.
• When installing exhaust system parts, make sure there is enough clearance between the hot exhaust parts and pipes and hoses that would be adversely affected by excessive heat. Also make sure there is adequate clearance from the floor pan to avoid possible overheating of the floor.

Safety Precautions

For a number of reasons, exhaust system work can be the most dangerous type of work you can do on your car. Always observe the following precautions:
• Support the car extra securely. Not only will you often be working directly under it, but you'll frequently be using a lot of force, say, heavy hammer blows, to dislodge rusted parts. This can cause a car that's improperly supported to shift and possibly fall.
• Wear goggles. Exhaust system parts are always rusty. Metal chips can be dislodged, even when you're only turning rusted bolts. Attempting to pry pipes apart with a chisel makes the chips fly even more frequently.
• If you're using a cutting torch, keep it a great distance from either the fuel tank or lines. Stop what you're doing and feel the temperature of the fuel bearing pipes on the tank frequently. Even slight heat can expand and/or vaporize fuel, resulting in accumulated vapor, or even a liquid leak, near your torch.
• Watch where your hammer blows fall and make sure you hit squarely. You could easily tap a brake or fuel line when you hit an exhaust system part with a glancing blow. Inspect all lines and hoses in the area where you've been working.

✳✳ CAUTION

Be very careful when working on or near the catalytic converter. External temperatures can reach 1,500°F (816°C) and more, causing severe burns. Removal or installation should be performed only on a cold exhaust system.

Special Tools

A number of special exhaust system tools can be rented from auto supply houses or local stores that rent special equipment. A common one is a tail pipe expander, designed to enable you to join pipes of identical diameter.

It may also be quite helpful to use solvents designed to loosen rusted bolts or flanges. Soaking rusted parts the night before you do the job can speed the work of freeing rusted parts considerably. Remember that these solvents are often flammable. Apply only to parts after they are cool!

REPAIR

◆ **See Figures 93 thru 99**

Once or twice a year, check the muffler(s) and pipes for signs of corrosion and damage. Check the hangers and, or O-ring suspensions for wear, cracks or hardening. Check the heat shields (models equipped) for corrosion or damage. Replace components as necessary.

Early models are not equipped with catalytic converters. The system may be of a completely welded construction, or be partly

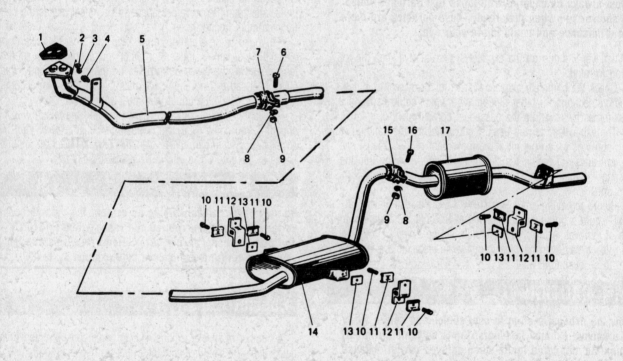

Fig. 93 Exploded view of an exhaust system without a catalytic converter—sedan and hardtop

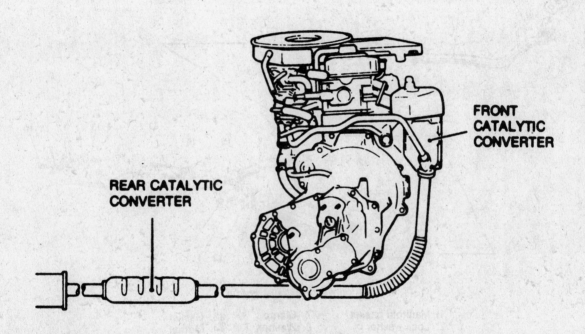

**FRONT
CATALYTIC
CONVERTER**

**REAR CATALYTIC
CONVERTER**

Fig. 94 Some front wheel drive models have two catalytic converters

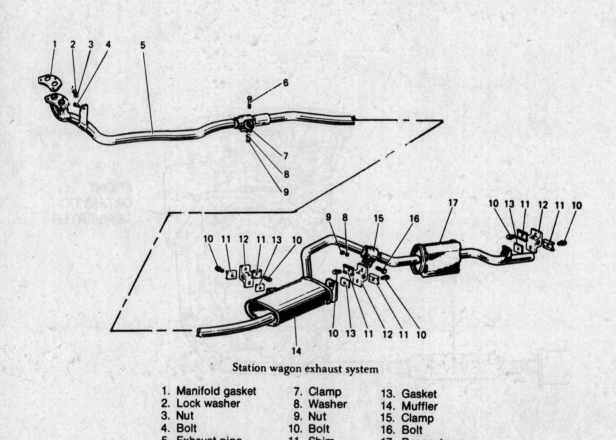

Station wagon exhaust system

1. Manifold gasket
2. Lock washer
3. Nut
4. Bolt
5. Exhaust pipe
6. Bolt
7. Clamp
8. Washer
9. Nut
10. Bolt
11. Shim
12. Hanger
13. Gasket
14. Muffler
15. Clamp
16. Bolt
17. Resonator

Fig. 95 Exploded view of an exhaust system without a catalytic converter—station wagon models

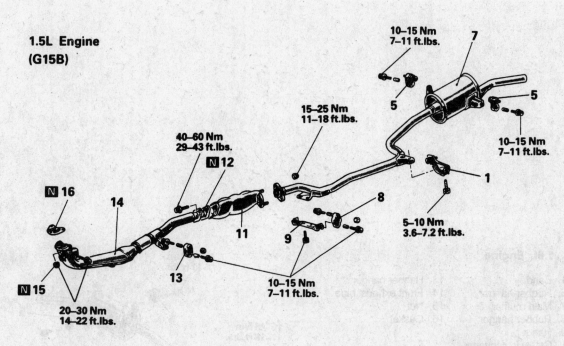

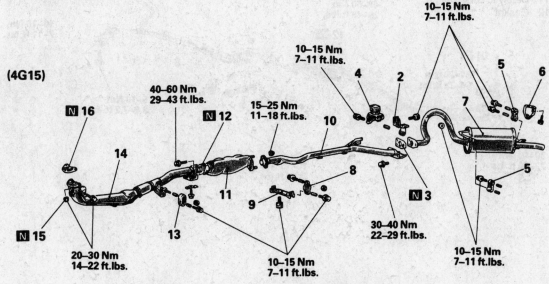

1. Band
2. Suspender
3. Gasket
4. Damper
5. Rubber hanger
6. Hanger bracket
7. Main muffler
8. Rubber hanger
9. Hanger
10. Center pipe assembly
11. Catalytic converter
12. Gasket
13. Rubber hanger
14. Front exhaust pipe
15. Nut
16. Gasket

Fig. 96 Exploded view of the Colt exhaust system—1.5L engine

1.6L Engine

1. Band
5. Rubber hanger
7. Main muffler
8. Rubber hanger
9. Hanger
11. Catalytic converter
12. Gasket
13. Rubber hanger
14. Front exhaust pipe
15. Nut
16. Gasket

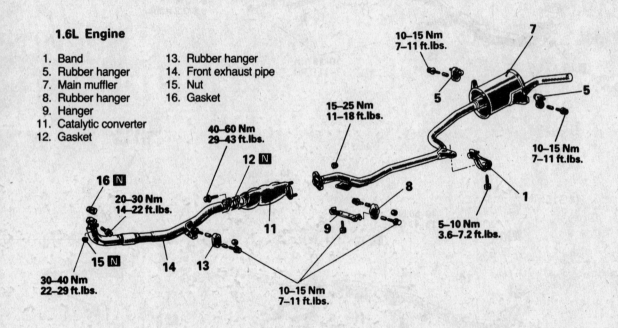

10–15 Nm
7–11 ft.lbs.

15–25 Nm
11–18 ft.lbs.

40–60 Nm
29–43 ft.lbs.

12 N

16 N

20–30 Nm
14–22 ft.lbs.

15 N

30–40 Nm
22–29 ft.lbs.

14

13

11

9

8

10–15 Nm
7–11 ft.lbs.

7

5

5

10–15 Nm
7–11 ft.lbs.

1

5–10 Nm
3.6–7.2 ft.lbs.

Fig. 97 Exploded view of the Colt exhaust system—1.6L engine

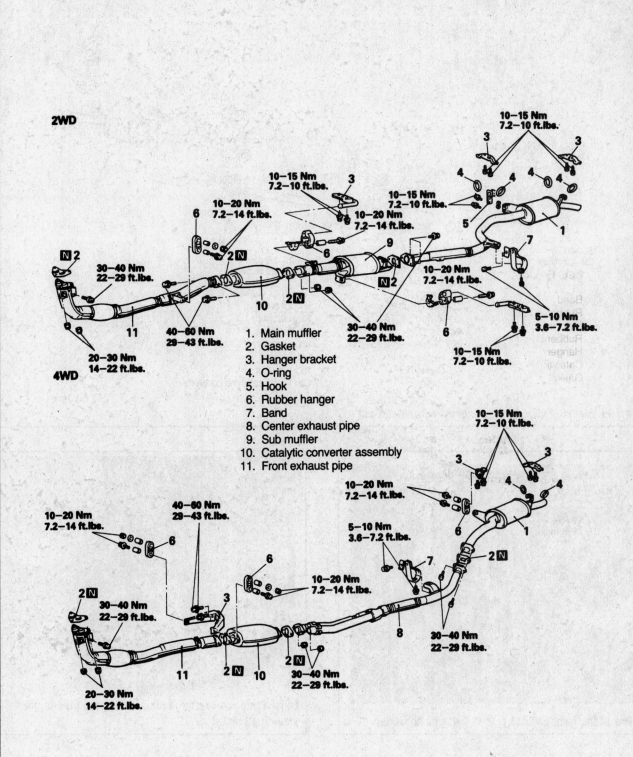

1. Main muffler
2. Gasket
3. Hanger bracket
4. O-ring
5. Hook
6. Rubber hanger
7. Band
8. Center exhaust pipe
9. Sub muffler
10. Catalytic converter assembly
11. Front exhaust pipe

Fig. 98 Exploded view of the Vista exhaust system

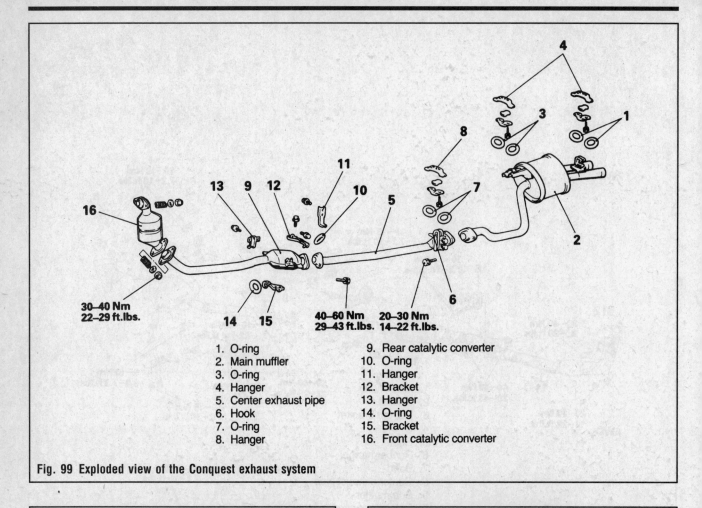

30–40 Nm
22–29 ft.lbs.

40–60 Nm
29–43 ft.lbs.

20–30 Nm
14–22 ft.lbs.

1. O-ring	9. Rear catalytic converter
2. Main muffler	10. O-ring
3. O-ring	11. Hanger
4. Hanger	12. Bracket
5. Center exhaust pipe	13. Hanger
6. Hook	14. O-ring
7. O-ring	15. Bracket
8. Hanger	16. Front catalytic converter

Fig. 99 Exploded view of the Conquest exhaust system

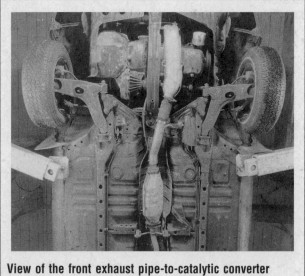

View of the front exhaust pipe-to-catalytic converter

Loosen and remove the bolts securing the pipe to the mounting bracket

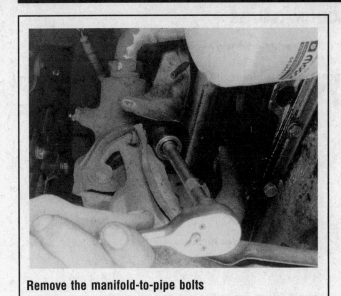

Remove the manifold-to-pipe bolts

Separate the pipe from the manifold and discard the old gasket

welded and clamped together. Replacement parts will determine how and what replacement procedures are required. That is, a welded system might be replaced with two or three clamp together pipes and mufflers.

Later models usually are equipped with a catalytic converter(s), which is attached to the exhaust manifold (usually front wheel drive models), or contained in the front exhaust pipe (rear wheel drive models). The exhaust system is usually bolted together. Replacement parts are usually the same as the original system, with the exception of some mufflers. The original system usually has the muffler and the inlet and tailpipe welded together. Some re-

placement companies supply the system in three pieces that are clamped together during installation. Splash shield removal will be required, in some cases, for removal and installation clearance.

Care should be taken when working on the exhaust system. Allow the muffler and pipes, an especially the converter to cool completely. Wear protective eye glasses or goggles to prevent rust or metal chips from falling in your eyes.

Use only the proper size sockets or wrenches when unbolting system components. Do not tighten completely until all components are attached, aligned, and suspended. Check the system for leaks after the installation is completed.

USING A VACUUM GAUGE

White needle = steady needle   *Dark needle = drifting needle*

The vacuum gauge is one of the most useful and easy-to-use diagnostic tools. It is inexpensive, easy to hook up, and provides valuable information about the condition of your engine.

Indication: Normal engine in good condition

Gauge reading: Steady, from 17–22 in./Hg.

Indication: Sticking valve or ignition miss

Gauge reading: Needle fluctuates from 15–20 in./Hg. at idle

Indication: Late ignition or valve timing, low compression, stuck throttle valve, leaking carburetor or manifold gasket.

Gauge reading: Low (15–20 in./Hg.) but steady

Indication: Improper carburetor adjustment, or minor intake leak at carburetor or manifold

NOTE: Bad fuel injector O-rings may also cause this reading.

Gauge reading: Drifting needle

Indication: Weak valve springs, worn valve stem guides, or leaky cylinder head gasket (vibrating excessively at all speeds).

NOTE: A plugged catalytic converter may also cause this reading.

Gauge reading: Needle fluctuates as engine speed increases

Indication: Burnt valve or improper valve clearance. The needle will drop when the defective valve operates.

Gauge reading: Steady needle, but drops regularly

Indication: Choked muffler or obstruction in system. Speed up the engine. Choked muffler will exhibit a slow drop of vacuum to zero.

Gauge reading: Gradual drop in reading at idle

Indication: Worn valve guides

Gauge reading: Needle vibrates excessively at idle, but steadies as engine speed increases

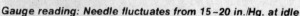

Troubleshooting Engine Mechanical Problems

Problem	Cause	Solution
External oil leaks	• Cylinder head cover RTV sealant broken or improperly seated	• Replace sealant; inspect cylinder head cover sealant flange and cylinder head sealant surface for distortion and cracks
	• Oil filler cap leaking or missing	• Replace cap
	• Oil filter gasket broken or improperly seated	• Replace oil filter
	• Oil pan side gasket broken, improperly seated or opening in RTV sealant	• Replace gasket or repair opening in sealant; inspect oil pan gasket flange for distortion
	• Oil pan front oil seal broken or improperly seated	• Replace seal; inspect timing case cover and oil pan seal flange for distortion
	• Oil pan rear oil seal broken or improperly seated	• Replace seal; inspect oil pan rear oil seal flange; inspect rear main bearing cap for cracks, plugged oil return channels, or distortion in seal groove
	• Timing case cover oil seal broken or improperly seated	• Replace seal
	• Excess oil pressure because of restricted PCV valve	• Replace PCV valve
	• Oil pan drain plug loose or has stripped threads	• Repair as necessary and tighten
	• Rear oil gallery plug loose	• Use appropriate sealant on gallery plug and tighten
	• Rear camshaft plug loose or improperly seated	• Seat camshaft plug or replace and seal, as necessary
Excessive oil consumption	• Oil level too high	• Drain oil to specified level
	• Oil with wrong viscosity being used	• Replace with specified oil
	• PCV valve stuck closed	• Replace PCV valve
	• Valve stem oil deflectors (or seals) are damaged, missing, or incorrect type	• Replace valve stem oil deflectors
	• Valve stems or valve guides worn	• Measure stem-to-guide clearance and repair as necessary
	• Poorly fitted or missing valve cover baffles	• Replace valve cover
	• Piston rings broken or missing	• Replace broken or missing rings
	• Scuffed piston	• Replace piston
	• Incorrect piston ring gap	• Measure ring gap, repair as necessary
	• Piston rings sticking or excessively loose in grooves	• Measure ring side clearance, repair as necessary
	• Compression rings installed upside down	• Repair as necessary
	• Cylinder walls worn, scored, or glazed	• Repair as necessary

Troubleshooting Engine Mechanical Problems

Problem	Cause	Solution
Excessive oil consumption (cont.)	• Piston ring gaps not properly staggered	• Repair as necessary
	• Excessive main or connecting rod bearing clearance	• Measure bearing clearance, repair as necessary
No oil pressure	• Low oil level	• Add oil to correct level
	• Oil pressure gauge, warning lamp or sending unit inaccurate	• Replace oil pressure gauge or warning lamp
	• Oil pump malfunction	• Replace oil pump
	• Oil pressure relief valve sticking	• Remove and inspect oil pressure relief valve assembly
	• Oil passages on pressure side of pump obstructed	• Inspect oil passages for obstruction
	• Oil pickup screen or tube obstructed	• Inspect oil pickup for obstruction
	• Loose oil inlet tube	• Tighten or seal inlet tube
Low oil pressure	• Low oil level	• Add oil to correct level
	• Inaccurate gauge, warning lamp or sending unit	• Replace oil pressure gauge or warning lamp
	• Oil excessively thin because of dilution, poor quality, or improper grade	• Drain and refill crankcase with recommended oil
	• Excessive oil temperature	• Correct cause of overheating engine
	• Oil pressure relief spring weak or sticking	• Remove and inspect oil pressure relief valve assembly
	• Oil inlet tube and screen assembly has restriction or air leak	• Remove and inspect oil inlet tube and screen assembly. (Fill inlet tube with lacquer thinner to locate leaks.)
	• Excessive oil pump clearance	• Measure clearances
	• Excessive main, rod, or camshaft bearing clearance	• Measure bearing clearances, repair as necessary
High oil pressure	• Improper oil viscosity	• Drain and refill crankcase with correct viscosity oil
	• Oil pressure gauge or sending unit inaccurate	• Replace oil pressure gauge
	• Oil pressure relief valve sticking closed	• Remove and inspect oil pressure relief valve assembly
Main bearing noise	• Insufficient oil supply	• Inspect for low oil level and low oil pressure
	• Main bearing clearance excessive	• Measure main bearing clearance, repair as necessary
	• Bearing insert missing	• Replace missing insert
	• Crankshaft end-play excessive	• Measure end-play, repair as necessary
	• Improperly tightened main bearing cap bolts	• Tighten bolts with specified torque
	• Loose flywheel or drive plate	• Tighten flywheel or drive plate attaching bolts
	• Loose or damaged vibration damper	• Repair as necessary

Troubleshooting Engine Mechanical Problems

Problem	Cause	Solution
Connecting rod bearing noise	• Insufficient oil supply	• Inspect for low oil level and low oil pressure
	• Carbon build-up on piston	• Remove carbon from piston crown
	• Bearing clearance excessive or bearing missing	• Measure clearance, repair as necessary
	• Crankshaft connecting rod journal out-of-round	• Measure journal dimensions, repair or replace as necessary
	• Misaligned connecting rod or cap	• Repair as necessary
	• Connecting rod bolts tightened improperly	• Tighten bolts with specified torque
Piston noise	• Piston-to-cylinder wall clearance excessive (scuffed piston)	• Measure clearance and examine piston
	• Cylinder walls excessively tapered or out-of-round	• Measure cylinder wall dimensions, rebore cylinder
	• Piston ring broken	• Replace all rings on piston
	• Loose or seized piston pin	• Measure piston-to-pin clearance, repair as necessary
	• Connecting rods misaligned	• Measure rod alignment, straighten or replace
	• Piston ring side clearance excessively loose or tight	• Measure ring side clearance, repair as necessary
	• Carbon build-up on piston is excessive	• Remove carbon from piston
Valve actuating component noise	• Insufficient oil supply	• Check for: (a) Low oil level (b) Low oil pressure (c) Wrong hydraulic tappets (d) Restricted oil gallery (e) Excessive tappet to bore clearance
	• Rocker arms or pivots worn	• Replace worn rocker arms or pivots
	• Foreign objects or chips in hydraulic tappets	• Clean tappets
	• Excessive tappet leak-down	• Replace valve tappet
	• Tappet face worn	• Replace tappet; inspect corresponding cam lobe for wear
	• Broken or cocked valve springs	• Properly seat cocked springs; replace broken springs
	• Stem-to-guide clearance excessive	• Measure stem-to-guide clearance, repair as required
	• Valve bent	• Replace valve
	• Loose rocker arms	• Check and repair as necessary
	• Valve seat runout excessive	• Regrind valve seat/valves
	• Missing valve lock	• Install valve lock
	• Excessive engine oil	• Correct oil level

Troubleshooting Engine Performance

Problem	Cause	Solution
Hard starting (engine cranks normally)	• Faulty engine control system component	• Repair or replace as necessary
	• Faulty fuel pump	• Replace fuel pump
	• Faulty fuel system component	• Repair or replace as necessary
	• Faulty ignition coil	• Test and replace as necessary
	• Improper spark plug gap	• Adjust gap
	• Incorrect ignition timing	• Adjust timing
	• Incorrect valve timing	• Check valve timing; repair as necessary
Rough idle or stalling	• Incorrect curb or fast idle speed	• Adjust curb or fast idle speed (If possible)
	• Incorrect ignition timing	• Adjust timing to specification
	• Improper feedback system operation	• Refer to Chapter 4
	• Faulty EGR valve operation	• Test EGR system and replace as necessary
	• Faulty PCV valve air flow	• Test PCV valve and replace as necessary
	• Faulty TAC vacuum motor or valve	• Repair as necessary
	• Air leak into manifold vacuum	• Inspect manifold vacuum connections and repair as necessary
	• Faulty distributor rotor or cap	• Replace rotor or cap (Distributor systems only)
	• Improperly seated valves	• Test cylinder compression, repair as necessary
	• Incorrect ignition wiring	• Inspect wiring and correct as necessary
	• Faulty ignition coil	• Test coil and replace as necessary
	• Restricted air vent or idle passages	• Clean passages
	• Restricted air cleaner	• Clean or replace air cleaner filter element
Faulty low-speed operation	• Restricted idle air vents and passages	• Clean air vents and passages
	• Restricted air cleaner	• Clean or replace air cleaner filter element
	• Faulty spark plugs	• Clean or replace spark plugs
	• Dirty, corroded, or loose ignition secondary circuit wire connections	• Clean or tighten secondary circuit wire connections
	• Improper feedback system operation	• Refer to Chapter 4
	• Faulty ignition coil high voltage wire	• Replace ignition coil high voltage wire (Distributor systems only)
	• Faulty distributor cap	• Replace cap (Distributor systems only)
Faulty acceleration	• Incorrect ignition timing	• Adjust timing
	• Faulty fuel system component	• Repair or replace as necessary
	• Faulty spark plug(s)	• Clean or replace spark plug(s)
	• Improperly seated valves	• Test cylinder compression, repair as necessary
	• Faulty ignition coil	• Test coil and replace as necessary

Troubleshooting Engine Performance

Problem	Cause	Solution
Faulty acceleration (cont.)	• Improper feedback system operation	• Refer to Chapter 4
Faulty high speed operation	• Incorrect ignition timing	• Adjust timing (if possible)
	• Faulty advance mechanism	• Check advance mechanism and repair as necessary (Distributor systems only)
	• Low fuel pump volume	• Replace fuel pump
	• Wrong spark plug air gap or wrong plug	• Adjust air gap or install correct plug
	• Partially restricted exhaust manifold, exhaust pipe, catalytic converter, muffler, or tailpipe	• Eliminate restriction
	• Restricted vacuum passages	• Clean passages
	• Restricted air cleaner	• Cleaner or replace filter element as necessary
	• Faulty distributor rotor or cap	• Replace rotor or cap (Distributor systems only)
	• Faulty ignition coil	• Test coil and replace as necessary
	• Improperly seated valve(s)	• Test cylinder compression, repair as necessary
	• Faulty valve spring(s)	• Inspect and test valve spring tension, replace as necessary
	• Incorrect valve timing	• Check valve timing and repair as necessary
	• Intake manifold restricted	• Remove restriction or replace manifold
	• Worn distributor shaft	• Replace shaft (Distributor systems only)
	• Improper feedback system operation	• Refer to Chapter 4
Misfire at all speeds	• Faulty spark plug(s)	• Clean or relace spark plug(s)
	• Faulty spark plug wire(s)	• Replace as necessary
	• Faulty distributor cap or rotor	• Replace cap or rotor (Distributor systems only)
	• Faulty ignition coil	• Test coil and replace as necessary
	• Primary ignition circuit shorted or open intermittently	• Troubleshoot primary circuit and repair as necessary
	• Improperly seated valve(s)	• Test cylinder compression, repair as necessary
	• Faulty hydraulic tappet(s)	• Clean or replace tappet(s)
	• Improper feedback system operation	• Refer to Chapter 4
	• Faulty valve spring(s)	• Inspect and test valve spring tension, repair as necessary
	• Worn camshaft lobes	• Replace camshaft
	• Air leak into manifold	• Check manifold vacuum and repair as necessary
	• Fuel pump volume or pressure low	• Replace fuel pump
	• Blown cylinder head gasket	• Replace gasket
	• Intake or exhaust manifold passage(s) restricted	• Pass chain through passage(s) and repair as necessary
Power not up to normal	• Incorrect ignition timing	• Adjust timing
	• Faulty distributor rotor	• Replace rotor (Distributor systems only)

Troubleshooting Engine Performance

Problem	Cause	Solution
Power not up to normal (cont.)	• Incorrect spark plug gap	• Adjust gap
	• Faulty fuel pump	• Replace fuel pump
	• Faulty fuel pump	• Replace fuel pump
	• Incorrect valve timing	• Check valve timing and repair as necessary
	• Faulty ignition coil	• Test coil and replace as necessary
	• Faulty ignition wires	• Test wires and replace as necessary
	• Improperly seated valves	• Test cylinder compression and repair as necessary
	• Blown cylinder head gasket	• Replace gasket
	• Leaking piston rings	• Test compression and repair as necessary
	• Improper feedback system operation	• Refer to Chapter 4
Intake backfire	• Improper ignition timing	• Adjust timing
	• Defective EGR component	• Repair as necessary
	• Defective TAC vacuum motor or valve	• Repair as necessary
Exhaust backfire	• Air leak into manifold vacuum	• Check manifold vacuum and repair as necessary
	• Faulty air injection diverter valve	• Test diverter valve and replace as necessary
	• Exhaust leak	• Locate and eliminate leak
Ping or spark knock	• Incorrect ignition timing	• Adjust timing
	• Distributor advance malfunction	• Inspect advance mechanism and repair as necessary (Distributor systems only)
	• Excessive combustion chamber deposits	• Remove with combustion chamber cleaner
	• Air leak into manifold vacuum	• Check manifold vacuum and repair as necessary
	• Excessively high compression	• Test compression and repair as necessary
	• Fuel octane rating excessively low	• Try alternate fuel source
	• Sharp edges in combustion chamber	• Grind smooth
	• EGR valve not functioning properly	• Test EGR system and replace as necessary
Surging (at cruising to top speeds)	• Low fuel pump pressure or volume	• Replace fuel pump
	• Improper PCV valve air flow	• Test PCV valve and replace as necessary
	• Air leak into manifold vacuum	• Check manifold vacuum and repair as necessary
	• Incorrect spark advance	• Test and replace as necessary
	• Restricted fuel filter	• Replace fuel filter
	• Restricted air cleaner	• Clean or replace air cleaner filter element
	• EGR valve not functioning properly	• Test EGR system and replace as necessary
	• Improper feedback system operation	• Refer to Chapter 4

Troubleshooting the Serpentine Drive Belt

Problem	Cause	Solution
Tension sheeting fabric failure (woven fabric on outside circumference of belt has cracked or separated from body of belt)	• Grooved or backside idler pulley diameters are less than minimum recommended • Tension sheeting contacting (rubbing) stationary object • Excessive heat causing woven fabric to age • Tension sheeting splice has fractured	• Replace pulley(s) not conforming to specification • Correct rubbing condition • Replace belt • Replace belt
Noise (objectional squeal, squeak, or rumble is heard or felt while drive belt is in operation)	• Belt slippage • Bearing noise • Belt misalignment • Belt-to-pulley mismatch • Driven component inducing vibration • System resonant frequency inducing vibration	• Adjust belt • Locate and repair • Align belt/pulley(s) • Install correct belt • Locate defective driven component and repair • Vary belt tension within specifications. Replace belt.
Rib chunking (one or more ribs has separated from belt body)	• Foreign objects imbedded in pulley grooves • Installation damage • Drive loads in excess of design specifications • Insufficient internal belt adhesion	• Remove foreign objects from pulley grooves • Replace belt • Adjust belt tension • Replace belt
Rib or belt wear (belt ribs contact bottom of pulley grooves)	• Pulley(s) misaligned • Mismatch of belt and pulley groove widths • Abrasive environment • Rusted pulley(s) • Sharp or jagged pulley groove tips • Rubber deteriorated	• Align pulley(s) • Replace belt • Replace belt • Clean rust from pulley(s) • Replace pulley • Replace belt
Longitudinal belt cracking (cracks between two ribs)	• Belt has mistracked from pulley groove • Pulley groove tip has worn away rubber-to-tensile member	• Replace belt • Replace belt
Belt slips	• Belt slipping because of insufficient tension • Belt or pulley subjected to substance (belt dressing, oil, ethylene glycol) that has reduced friction • Driven component bearing failure • Belt glazed and hardened from heat and excessive slippage	• Adjust tension • Replace belt and clean pulleys • Replace faulty component bearing • Replace belt
"Groove jumping" (belt does not maintain correct position on pulley, or turns over and/or runs off pulleys)	• Insufficient belt tension • Pulley(s) not within design tolerance • Foreign object(s) in grooves	• Adjust belt tension • Replace pulley(s) • Remove foreign objects from grooves

Troubleshooting the Serpentine Drive Belt

Problem	Cause	Solution
"Groove jumping" (belt does not maintain correct position on pulley, or turns over and/or runs off pulleys)	• Excessive belt speed • Pulley misalignment • Belt-to-pulley profile mismatched • Belt cordline is distorted	• Avoid excessive engine acceleration • Align pulley(s) • Install correct belt • Replace belt
Belt broken (Note: identify and correct problem before replacement belt is installed)	• Excessive tension • Tensile members damaged during belt installation • Belt turnover • Severe pulley misalignment • Bracket, pulley, or bearing failure	• Replace belt and adjust tension to specification • Replace belt • Replace belt • Align pulley(s) • Replace defective component and belt
Cord edge failure (tensile member exposed at edges of belt or separated from belt body)	• Excessive tension • Drive pulley misalignment • Belt contacting stationary object • Pulley irregularities • Improper pulley construction • Insufficient adhesion between tensile member and rubber matrix	• Adjust belt tension • Align pulley • Correct as necessary • Replace pulley • Replace pulley • Replace belt and adjust tension to specifications
Sporadic rib cracking (multiple cracks in belt ribs at random intervals)	• Ribbed pulley(s) diameter less than minimum specification • Backside bend flat pulley(s) diameter less than minimum • Excessive heat condition causing rubber to harden • Excessive belt thickness • Belt overcured • Excessive tension	• Replace pulley(s) • Replace pulley(s) • Correct heat condition as necessary • Replace belt • Replace belt • Adjust belt tension

Troubleshooting the Cooling System

Problem	Cause	Solution
High temperature gauge indication— overheating	• Coolant level low	• Replenish coolant
	• Improper fan operation	• Repair or replace as necessary
	• Radiator hose(s) collapsed	• Replace hose(s)
	• Radiator airflow blocked	• Remove restriction (bug screen, fog lamps, etc.)
	• Faulty pressure cap	• Replace pressure cap
	• Ignition timing incorrect	• Adjust ignition timing
	• Air trapped in cooling system	• Purge air
	• Heavy traffic driving	• Operate at fast idle in neutral intermittently to cool engine
		• Install proper component(s)
	• Incorrect cooling system component(s) installed	
	• Faulty thermostat	• Replace thermostat
	• Water pump shaft broken or impeller loose	• Replace water pump
	• Radiator tubes clogged	• Flush radiator
	• Cooling system clogged	• Flush system
	• Casting flash in cooling passages	• Repair or replace as necessary. Flash may be visible by removing cooling system components or removing core plugs.
	• Brakes dragging	• Repair brakes
	• Excessive engine friction	• Repair engine
	• Antifreeze concentration over 68%	• Lower antifreeze concentration percentage
	• Missing air seals	• Replace air seals
	• Faulty gauge or sending unit	• Repair or replace faulty component
	• Loss of coolant flow caused by leakage or foaming	• Repair or replace leaking component, replace coolant
	• Viscous fan drive failed	• Replace unit
Low temperature indication— undercooling	• Thermostat stuck open	• Replace thermostat
	• Faulty gauge or sending unit	• Repair or replace faulty component
Coolant loss—boilover	• Overfilled cooling system	• Reduce coolant level to proper specification
	• Quick shutdown after hard (hot) run	• Allow engine to run at fast idle prior to shutdown
	• Air in system resulting in occasional "burping" of coolant	• Purge system
	• Insufficient antifreeze allowing coolant boiling point to be too low	• Add antifreeze to raise boiling point
	• Antifreeze deteriorated because of age or contamination	• Replace coolant
	• Leaks due to loose hose clamps, loose nuts, bolts, drain plugs, faulty hoses, or defective radiator	• Pressure test system to locate source of leak(s) then repair as necessary

Troubleshooting the Cooling System (cont.)

Problem	Cause	Solution
Coolant loss—boilover	• Faulty head gasket • Cracked head, manifold, or block • Faulty radiator cap	• Replace head gasket • Replace as necessary • Replace cap
Coolant entry into crankcase or cylinder(s)	• Faulty head gasket • Crack in head, manifold or block	• Replace head gasket • Replace as necessary
Coolant recovery system inoperative	• Coolant level low • Leak in system • Pressure cap not tight or seal missing, or leaking • Pressure cap defective • Overflow tube clogged or leaking • Recovery bottle vent restricted	• Replenish coolant to FULL mark • Pressure test to isolate leak and repair as necessary • Repair as necessary • Replace cap • Repair as necessary • Remove restriction
Noise	• Fan contacting shroud • Loose water pump impeller • Glazed fan belt • Loose fan belt • Rough surface on drive pulley • Water pump bearing worn • Belt alignment	• Reposition shroud and inspect engine mounts (on electric fans inspect assembly) • Replace pump • Apply silicone or replace belt • Adjust fan belt tension • Replace pulley • Remove belt to isolate. Replace pump. • Check pulley alignment. Repair as necessary.
No coolant flow through heater core	• Restricted return inlet in water pump • Heater hose collapsed or restricted • Restricted heater core • Restricted outlet in thermostat housing • Intake manifold bypass hole in cylinder head restricted • Faulty heater control valve • Intake manifold coolant passage restricted	• Remove restriction • Remove restriction or replace hose • Remove restriction or replace core • Remove flash or restriction • Remove restriction • Replace valve • Remove restriction or replace intake manifold

NOTE: *Immediately after shutdown, the engine enters a condition known as heat soak. This is caused by the cooling system being inoperative while engine temperature is still high. If coolant temperature rises above boiling point, expansion and pressure may push some coolant out of the radiator overflow tube. If this does not occur frequently it is considered normal.*

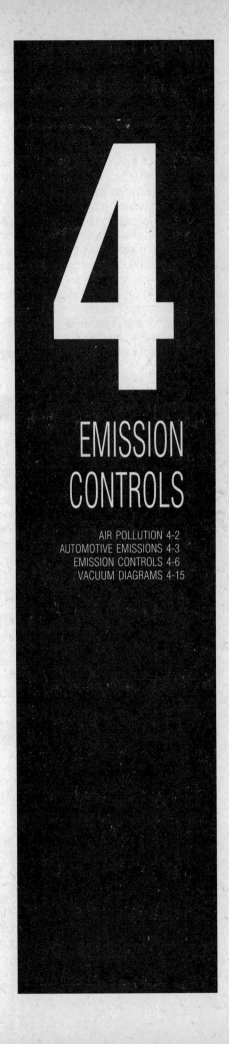

4

EMISSION CONTROLS

AIR POLLUTION

The earth's atmosphere, at or near sea level, consists approximately of 78 percent nitrogen, 21 percent oxygen and 1 percent other gases. If it were possible to remain in this state, 100 percent clean air would result. However, many varied sources allow other gases and particulates to mix with the clean air, causing our atmosphere to become unclean or polluted.

Some of these pollutants are visible while others are invisible, with each having the capability of causing distress to the eyes, ears, throat, skin and respiratory system. Should these pollutants become concentrated in a specific area and under certain conditions, death could result due to the displacement or chemical change of the oxygen content in the air. These pollutants can also cause great damage to the environment and to the many man made objects that are exposed to the elements.

To better understand the causes of air pollution, the pollutants can be categorized into 3 separate types, natural, industrial and automotive.

Natural Pollutants

Natural pollution has been present on earth since before man appeared and continues to be a factor when discussing air pollution, although it causes only a small percentage of the overall pollution problem. It is the direct result of decaying organic matter, wind born smoke and particulates from such natural events as plain and forest fires (ignited by heat or lightning), volcanic ash, sand and dust which can spread over a large area of the countryside.

Such a phenomenon of natural pollution has been seen in the form of volcanic eruptions, with the resulting plume of smoke, steam and volcanic ash blotting out the sun's rays as it spreads and rises higher into the atmosphere. As it travels into the atmosphere the upper air currents catch and carry the smoke and ash, while condensing the steam back into water vapor. As the water vapor, smoke and ash travel on their journey, the smoke dissipates into the atmosphere while the ash and moisture settle back to earth in a trail hundreds of miles long. In some cases, lives are lost and millions of dollars of property damage result.

Industrial Pollutants

Industrial pollution is caused primarily by industrial processes, the burning of coal, oil and natural gas, which in turn produce smoke and fumes. Because the burning fuels contain large amounts of sulfur, the principal ingredients of smoke and fumes are sulfur dioxide and particulate matter. This type of pollutant occurs most severely during still, damp and cool weather, such as at night. Even in its less severe form, this pollutant is not confined to just cities. Because of air movements, the pollutants move for miles over the surrounding countryside, leaving in its path a barren and unhealthy environment for all living things.

Working with Federal, State and Local mandated regulations and by carefully monitoring emissions, big business has greatly reduced the amount of pollutant introduced from its industrial sources, striving to obtain an acceptable level. Because of the mandated industrial emission clean up, many land areas and streams in and around the cities that were formerly barren of vegetation and life, have now begun to move back in the direction of nature's intended balance.

Automotive Pollutants

The third major source of air pollution is automotive emissions. The emissions from the internal combustion engines were not an appreciable problem years ago because of the small number of registered vehicles and the nation's small highway system. However, during the early 1950's, the trend of the American people was to move from the cities to the surrounding suburbs. This caused an immediate problem in transportation because the majority of suburbs were not afforded mass transit conveniences. This lack of transportation created an attractive market for the automobile manufacturers, which resulted in a dramatic increase in the number of vehicles produced and sold, along with a marked increase in highway construction between cities and the suburbs. Multi-vehicle families emerged with a growing emphasis placed on an individual vehicle per family member. As the increase in vehicle ownership and usage occurred, so did pollutant levels in and around the cities, as suburbanites drove daily to their businesses and employment, returning at the end of the day to their homes in the suburbs.

It was noted that a smoke and fog type haze was being formed and at times, remained in suspension over the cities, taking time to dissipate. At first this "smog," derived from the words "smoke" and "fog," was thought to result from industrial pollution but it was determined that automobile emissions shared the blame. It was discovered that when normal automobile emissions were exposed to sunlight for a period of time, complex chemical reactions would take place.

It is now known that smog is a photo chemical layer which develops when certain oxides of nitrogen (NOx) and unburned hydrocarbons (HC) from automobile emissions are exposed to sunlight. Pollution was more severe when smog would become stagnant over an area in which a warm layer of air settled over the top of the cooler air mass, trapping and holding the cooler mass at ground level. The trapped cooler air would keep the emissions from being dispersed and diluted through normal air flows. This type of air stagnation was given the name "Temperature Inversion."

TEMPERATURE INVERSION

In normal weather situations, surface air is warmed by heat radiating from the earth's surface and the sun's rays. This causes it to rise upward, into the atmosphere. Upon rising it will cool through a convection type heat exchange with the cooler upper air. As warm air rises, the surface pollutants are carried upward and dissipated into the atmosphere.

When a temperature inversion occurs, we find the higher air is no longer cooler, but is warmer than the surface air, causing the cooler surface air to become trapped. This warm air blanket can extend from above ground level to a few hundred or even a few thousand feet into the air. As the surface air is trapped, so are the pollutants, causing a severe smog condition. Should this stagnant air mass extend to a few thousand feet high, enough air movement with the inversion takes place to allow the smog layer to rise above ground level but the pollutants still cannot dissipate. This inversion can remain for days over an area, with the smog level only rising or lowering from ground level to a few hundred feet high. Meanwhile, the pollutant levels increase, causing eye irritation, respiratory problems, reduced visibility, plant damage and in some cases, even disease.

This inversion phenomenon was first noted in the Los Angeles, California area. The city lies in terrain resembling a basin and with certain weather conditions, a cold air mass is held in the basin while a warmer air mass covers it like a lid.

Because this type of condition was first documented as prevalent in the Los Angeles area, this type of trapped pollution was named Los Angeles Smog, although it occurs in other areas where a large concentration of automobiles are used and the air remains stagnant for any length of time.

HEAT TRANSFER

Consider the internal combustion engine as a machine in which raw materials must be placed so a finished product comes out. As in any machine operation, a certain amount of wasted material is formed. When we relate this to the internal combustion engine, we find that through the input of air and fuel, we obtain power during the combustion process to drive the vehicle. The by-product or waste of this power is, in part, heat and exhaust gases with which we must dispose.

AUTOMOTIVE EMISSIONS

Before emission controls were mandated on internal combustion engines, other sources of engine pollutants were discovered along with the exhaust emissions. It was determined that engine combustion exhaust produced approximately 60 percent of the total emission pollutants, fuel evaporation from the fuel tank and carburetor vents produced 20 percent, with the final 20 percent being produced through the crankcase as a by-product of the combustion process.

Exhaust Gases

The exhaust gases emitted into the atmosphere are a combination of burned and unburned fuel. To understand the exhaust emission and its composition, we must review some basic chemistry.

When the air/fuel mixture is introduced into the engine, we are mixing air, composed of nitrogen (78 percent), oxygen (21 percent) and other gases (1 percent) with the fuel, which is 100 percent hydrocarbons (HC), in a semi-controlled ratio. As the combustion process is accomplished, power is produced to move the vehicle while the heat of combustion is transferred to the cooling system. The exhaust gases are then composed of nitrogen, a diatomic gas (N_2), the same as was introduced in the engine, carbon dioxide (CO_2), the same gas that is used in beverage carbonation, and water vapor (H_2O). The nitrogen (N_2), for the most part, passes through the engine unchanged, while the oxygen (O_2) reacts (burns) with the hydrocarbons (HC) and produces the carbon dioxide (CO_2) and the water vapors (H_2O). If this chemical process would be the only process to take place, the exhaust emissions would be harmless. However, during the combustion pro-

The heat from the combustion process can rise to over 4000°F (2204°C). The dissipation of this heat is controlled by a ram air effect, the use of cooling fans to cause air flow and a liquid coolant solution surrounding the combustion area to transfer the heat of combustion through the cylinder walls and into the coolant. The coolant is then directed to a thin-finned, multi-tubed radiator, from which the excess heat is transferred to the atmosphere by 1 of the 3 heat transfer methods, conduction, convection or radiation.

The cooling of the combustion area is an important part in the control of exhaust emissions. To understand the behavior of the combustion and transfer of its heat, consider the air/fuel charge. It is ignited and the flame front burns progressively across the combustion chamber until the burning charge reaches the cylinder walls. Some of the fuel in contact with the walls is not hot enough to burn, thereby snuffing out or quenching the combustion process. This leaves unburned fuel in the combustion chamber. This unburned fuel is then forced out of the cylinder and into the exhaust system, along with the exhaust gases.

Many attempts have been made to minimize the amount of unburned fuel in the combustion chambers due to quenching, by increasing the coolant temperature and lessening the contact area of the coolant around the combustion area. However, design limitations within the combustion chambers prevent the complete burning of the air/fuel charge, so a certain amount of the unburned fuel is still expelled into the exhaust system, regardless of modifications to the engine.

cess, other compounds are formed which are considered dangerous. These pollutants are hydrocarbons (HC), carbon monoxide (CO), oxides of nitrogen (NOx) oxides of sulfur (SOx) and engine particulates.

HYDROCARBONS

Hydrocarbons (HC) are essentially fuel which was not burned during the combustion process or which has escaped into the atmosphere through fuel evaporation. The main sources of incomplete combustion are rich air/fuel mixtures, low engine temperatures and improper spark timing. The main sources of hydrocarbon emission through fuel evaporation on most vehicles used to be the vehicle's fuel tank and carburetor float bowl.

To reduce combustion hydrocarbon emission, engine modifications were made to minimize dead space and surface area in the combustion chamber. In addition, the air/fuel mixture was made more lean through the improved control which feedback carburetion and fuel injection offers and by the addition of external controls to aid in further combustion of the hydrocarbons outside the engine. Two such methods were the addition of air injection systems, to inject fresh air into the exhaust manifolds and the installation of catalytic converters, units that are able to burn traces of hydrocarbons without affecting the internal combustion process or fuel economy.

To control hydrocarbon emissions through fuel evaporation, modifications were made to the fuel tank to allow storage of the fuel vapors during periods of engine shut-down. Modifications were also made to the air intake system so that at specific times during engine operation, these vapors may be purged and burned by blending them with the air/fuel mixture.

CARBON MONOXIDE

Carbon monoxide is formed when not enough oxygen is present during the combustion process to convert carbon (C) to carbon dioxide (CO_2). An increase in the carbon monoxide (CO) emission is normally accompanied by an increase in the hydrocarbon (HC) emission because of the lack of oxygen to completely burn all of the fuel mixture.

Carbon monoxide (CO) also increases the rate at which the photo chemical smog is formed by speeding up the conversion of nitric oxide (NO) to nitrogen dioxide (NO_2). To accomplish this, carbon monoxide (CO) combines with oxygen (O_2) and nitric oxide (NO) to produce carbon dioxide (CO_2) and nitrogen dioxide (NO_2). ($CO + O_2 + NO \; CO_2 + NO_2$).

The dangers of carbon monoxide, which is an odorless and colorless toxic gas are many. When carbon monoxide is inhaled into the lungs and passed into the blood stream, oxygen is replaced by the carbon monoxide in the red blood cells, causing a reduction in the amount of oxygen supplied to the many parts of the body. This lack of oxygen causes headaches, lack of coordination, reduced mental alertness and, should the carbon monoxide concentration be high enough, death could result.

NITROGEN

Normally, nitrogen is an inert gas. When heated to approximately 2500°F (1371°C) through the combustion process, this gas becomes active and causes an increase in the nitric oxide (NO) emission.

Oxides of nitrogen (NOx) are composed of approximately 97–98 percent nitric oxide (NO). Nitric oxide is a colorless gas but when it is passed into the atmosphere, it combines with oxygen and forms nitrogen dioxide (NO_2). The nitrogen dioxide then combines with chemically active hydrocarbons (HC) and when in the presence of sunlight, causes the formation of photo-chemical smog.

Ozone

To further complicate matters, some of the nitrogen dioxide (NO_2) is broken apart by the sunlight to form nitric oxide and oxygen. (NO_2 + sunlight NO + O). This single atom of oxygen then combines with diatomic (meaning 2 atoms) oxygen (O_2) to form ozone (O_3). Ozone is one of the smells associated with smog. It has a pungent and offensive odor, irritates the eyes and lung tissues, affects the growth of plant life and causes rapid deterioration of rubber products. Ozone can be formed by sunlight as well as electrical discharge into the air.

The most common discharge area on the automobile engine is the secondary ignition electrical system, especially when inferior quality spark plug cables are used. As the surge of high voltage is routed through the secondary cable, the circuit builds up an electrical field around the wire, which acts upon the oxygen in the surrounding air to form the ozone. The faint glow along the cable with the engine running that may be visible on a dark night, is called the "corona discharge." It is the result of the electrical field passing from a high along the cable, to a low in the surrounding air, which forms the ozone gas. The combination of corona and ozone has been a major cause of cable deterioration. Recently, different and better quality insulating materials have lengthened the life of the electrical cables.

Although ozone at ground level can be harmful, ozone is beneficial to the earth's inhabitants. By having a concentrated ozone layer called the "ozonosphere," between 10 and 20 miles (16–32 km) up in the atmosphere, much of the ultra violet radiation from the sun's rays are absorbed and screened. If this ozone layer were not present, much of the earth's surface would be burned, dried and unfit for human life.

OXIDES OF SULFUR

Oxides of sulfur (SOx) were initially ignored in the exhaust system emissions, since the sulfur content of gasoline as a fuel is less than $1/10$ of 1 percent. Because of this small amount, it was felt that it contributed very little to the overall pollution problem. However, because of the difficulty in solving the sulfur emissions in industrial pollutions and the introduction of catalytic converter to the automobile exhaust systems, a change was mandated. The automobile exhaust system, when equipped with a catalytic converter, changes the sulfur dioxide (SO_2) into sulfur trioxide (SO_3).

When this combines with water vapors (H_2O), a sulfuric acid mist (H_2SO_4) is formed and is a very difficult pollutant to handle since it is extremely corrosive. This sulfuric acid mist that is formed, is the same mist that rises from the vents of an automobile battery when an active chemical reaction takes place within the battery cells.

When a large concentration of vehicles equipped with catalytic converters are operating in an area, this acid mist may rise and be distributed over a large ground area causing land, plant, crop, paint and building damage.

PARTICULATE MATTER

A certain amount of particulate matter is present in the burning of any fuel, with carbon constituting the largest percentage of the particulates. In gasoline, the remaining particulates are the burned remains of the various other compounds used in its manufacture. When a gasoline engine is in good internal condition, the particulate emissions are low but as the engine wears internally, the particulate emissions increase. By visually inspecting the tail pipe emissions, a determination can be made as to where an engine defect may exist. An engine with light gray or blue smoke emitting from the tail pipe normally indicates an increase in the oil consumption through burning due to internal engine wear. Black smoke would indicate a defective fuel delivery system, causing the engine to operate in a rich mode. Regardless of the color of the smoke, the internal part of the engine or the fuel delivery system should be repaired to prevent excess particulate emissions.

Diesel and turbine engines emit a darkened plume of smoke

from the exhaust system because of the type of fuel used. Emission control regulations are mandated for this type of emission and more stringent measures are being used to prevent excess emission of the particulate matter. Electronic components are being introduced to control the injection of the fuel at precisely the proper time of piston travel, to achieve the optimum in fuel ignition and fuel usage. Other particulate after-burning components are being tested to achieve a cleaner emission.

Good grades of engine lubricating oils should be used, which meet the manufacturers specification. Cut-rate oils can contribute to the particulate emission problem because of their low flash or ignition temperature point. Such oils burn prematurely during the combustion process causing emission of particulate matter.

The cooling system is an important factor in the reduction of particulate matter. The optimum combustion will occur, with the cooling system operating at a temperature specified by the manufacturer. The cooling system must be maintained in the same manner as the engine oiling system, as each system is required to perform properly in order for the engine to operate efficiently for a long time.

Crankcase Emissions

Crankcase emissions are made up of water, acids, unburned fuel, oil fumes and particulates. These emissions are classified as hydrocarbons (HC) and are formed by the small amount of unburned, compressed air/fuel mixture entering the crankcase from the combustion area (between the cylinder walls and piston rings) during the compression and power strokes. The head of the compression and combustion help to form the remaining crankcase emissions.

Since the first engines, crankcase emissions were allowed into the atmosphere through a road draft tube, mounted on the lower side of the engine block. Fresh air came in through an open oil filler cap or breather. The air passed through the crankcase mixing with blow-by gases. The motion of the vehicle and the air blowing past the open end of the road draft tube caused a low pressure area (vacuum) at the end of the tube. Crankcase emissions were simply drawn out of the road draft tube into the air.

To control the crankcase emission, the road draft tube was deleted. A hose and/or tubing was routed from the crankcase to the intake manifold so the blow-by emission could be burned with the air/fuel mixture. However, it was found that intake manifold vacuum, used to draw the crankcase emissions into the manifold, would vary in strength at the wrong time and not allow the proper emission flow. A regulating valve was needed to control the flow of air through the crankcase.

Testing, showed the removal of the blow-by gases from the crankcase as quickly as possible, was most important to the longevity of the engine. Should large accumulations of blow-by gases remain and condense, dilution of the engine oil would occur to form water, soots, resins, acids and lead salts, resulting in the formation of sludge and varnishes. This condensation of the blow-by gases occurs more frequently on vehicles used in numerous starting and stopping conditions, excessive idling and when the engine is not allowed to attain normal operating temperature through short runs.

Evaporative Emissions

Gasoline fuel is a major source of pollution, before and after it is burned in the automobile engine. From the time the fuel is refined, stored, pumped and transported, again stored until it is pumped into the fuel tank of the vehicle, the gasoline gives off unburned hydrocarbons (HC) into the atmosphere. Through the redesign of storage areas and venting systems, the pollution factor was diminished, but not eliminated, from the refinery standpoint. However, the automobile still remained the primary source of vaporized, unburned hydrocarbon (HC) emissions.

Fuel pumped from an underground storage tank is cool but when exposed to a warmer ambient temperature, will expand. Before controls were mandated, an owner might fill the fuel tank with fuel from an underground storage tank and park the vehicle for some time in warm area, such as a parking lot. As the fuel would warm, it would expand and should no provisions or area be provided for the expansion, the fuel would spill out of the filler neck and onto the ground, causing hydrocarbon (HC) pollution and creating a severe fire hazard. To correct this condition, the vehicle manufacturers added overflow plumbing and/or gasoline tanks with built in expansion areas or domes.

However, this did not control the fuel vapor emission from the fuel tank. It was determined that most of the fuel evaporation occurred when the vehicle was stationary and the engine not operating. Most vehicles carry 5–25 gallons (19–95 liters) of gasoline. Should a large concentration of vehicles be parked in one area, such as a large parking lot, excessive fuel vapor emissions would take place, increasing as the temperature increases.

To prevent the vapor emission from escaping into the atmosphere, the fuel systems were designed to trap the vapors while the vehicle is stationary, by sealing the system from the atmosphere. A storage system is used to collect and hold the fuel vapors from the carburetor (if equipped) and the fuel tank when the engine is not operating. When the engine is started, the storage system is then purged of the fuel vapors, which are drawn into the engine and burned with the air/fuel mixture.

EMISSION CONTROLS

Crankcase Ventilation System

OPERATION

▶ **See Figure 1**

A closed type crankcase ventilation system is used to prevent engine blow-by gases from escaping into the atmosphere.

A small fixed orifice, located in the intake manifold, is connected to the rear section of the rocker arm cover by a hose. Some later models have replaced the orifice with a PCV valve. The PCV valve is generally located in the hose from the rocker cover.

A larger hose is connected from the front of the rocker arm cover to the air cleaner assembly. Under light to medium carburetor throttle opening, the blow-by gases are drawn through the fixed orifice. Under heavy acceleration, both the fixed orifice and the large hose route the gases into the engine.

SERVICE

The only maintenance required is to regularly check the breather hose condition, clean the orifice in the intake manifold, and clean the steel wool filter, in the air cleaner. Replace the PCV valve (if equipped) when it becomes clogged.

To check for a clogged PCV valve; with the engine running, remove the valve from its mounting. A hissing sound should be heard and vacuum should be felt from the inlet (bottom) side of the valve. Turn off the engine, shake the valve. A clicking sound should come from the valve when it is shaken. If the valve fails either of these tests, replace it.

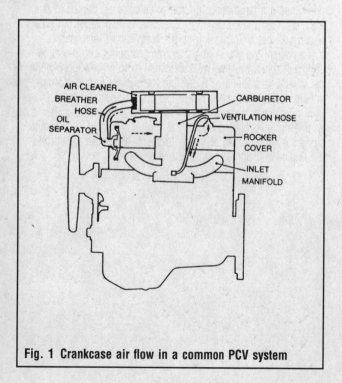

Fig. 1 Crankcase air flow in a common PCV system

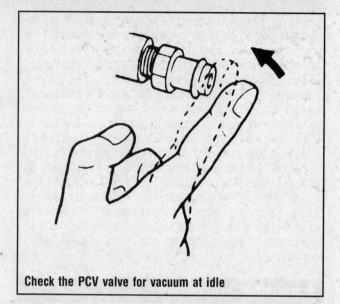

Check the PCV valve for vacuum at idle

REMOVAL & INSTALLATION

Remove the valve from its mounting. Disconnect the hose(s) from the valve. Install a new valve into the hose(s) and push the valve into the mounting.

Evaporative Emission Controls

OPERATION

▶ **See Figures 2 and 3**

This system is designed to prevent hydrocarbons from escaping into the atmosphere from the fuel tank, due to normal evaporation.

The parts of a typical system are: Separator tank: Located near the gasoline tank, used to accommodate expansion, and to allow maximum condensation of the fuel vapors. Canister: Located in the engine compartment to trap and retain gasoline vapors while the engine is not operating. When the engine is started, fresh air is drawn into the canister or canisters, removing the stored vapors, and is directed to the air cleaner. Vapor Check Valve: (1973–76) Used in the hose from the canister to the air cleaner to prevent vaporized fuel from entering the air cleaner during engine idling. Two-way Valve: (1977 and later) Because of different methods of tank venting and the use of a sealed gasoline tank cap, the two-way valve is used in the vapor lines. The valve relieves either pressure or vacuum in the tank. Purge Control Valve: (1977 and later) The purge control valve replaces the check valve used in previous years. During idle, the valve closes off the vapor passage to the air cleaner. Fuel Check Valve: (1976 and later) This valve is used to prevent fuel leakage in case of roll over. It is installed in the vapor line between the two-way valve and the canister on the coupe, sedan, and hatchback, and between the separator and the two-way valve on the station wagon. Bowl Vent Valve: (1980

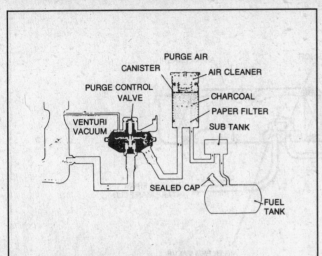

Fig. 2 Schematic of an early model evaporative emission system

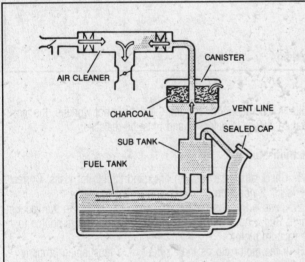

Fig. 3 Common late model evaporative emission system

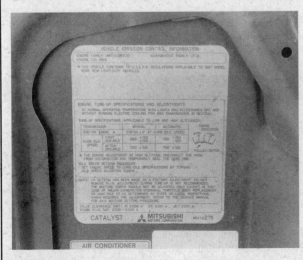

Vehicle emissions label located under the hood

and later) Controls carburetor bowl vapors between canister and carburetor. Carbon Element: (1980 and later) Element is located in the air cleaner to store vapors generated in the carburetor. Replace if clogged or dirty.

SERVICE

Be sure that all hoses are clamped and not dry-rotted or broken. Check the valves for cracks, signs of gasoline leakage, and proper operating condition.

The canister air filter should be inspected and changed at least every 24,000 miles.

REMOVAL & INSTALLATION

Charcoal Canister

1971–72 MODELS

1. Loosen and remove the two purge valve retaining bolts. Leave the hoses attached to the valve.

2. Loosen the purge valve-to-canister hose clamp at the canister and pull off the hose.

3. Loosen the expansion tank-to-canister hose clamp at the canister and remove the hose.

4. Remove the two canister bracket bolts and remove the canister.

5. Install the canister and connect the hoses.

1973 AND LATER

The canister or canisters used on these models is replaced periodically. No other maintenance is necessary except for an occasional check of connecting hose condition. To replace the canister:

1. Remove the two connecting hoses from the canister.
2. Loosen and remove the canister retaining band bolt.
3. Remove the canister.
4. Install the canister and connect the hoses. Replace any brittle hoses.

Thermostatically Controlled Air Cleaner

OPERATION

▶ **See Figure 4**

Carburetor equipped models are equipped with a thermostatically controlled air cleaner which maintains the intake air admitted to the carburetor between 95°F (35°C) and 105°F (41°C). To do this, the air cleaner snorkel has a movable door which allows intake air to be drawn from either a manifold heat stove (cold operation) or from under the hood (normal operation). The door is operated by a vacuum motor which is regulated by a bimetallic sensor located within the air cleaner. The sensor is connected by hoses to the intake manifold and the vacuum motor. At low temperatures, the sensor supplies manifold vacuum to the motor which then maintains the air door in a closed position. This allows only preheated air drawn from around the exhaust manifold to reach the carburetor. As the engine warms, the sensor allows less and less manifold vacuum to reach the motor. The vacuum motor be-

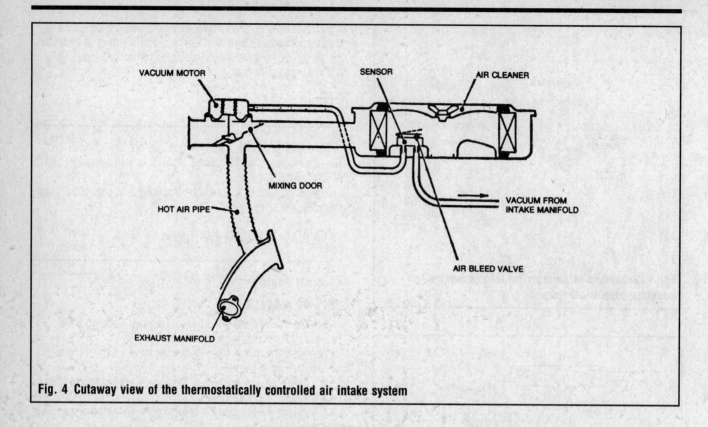

VACUUM MOTOR

SENSOR

AIR CLEANER

MIXING DOOR

HOT AIR PIPE

VACUUM FROM
INTAKE MANIFOLD

AIR BLEED VALVE

EXHAUST MANIFOLD

Fig. 4 Cutaway view of the thermostatically controlled air intake system

gins to open the door and permits cooler air to be drawn through the snorkel. When the engine reaches normal operating temperature, no vacuum reaches the motor and it closes off the exhaust manifold heat stove duct. A vacuum override provides cold air intake during periods of hard acceleration when exhaust manifold heated air is normally being supplied.

TESTING

Air Door

1. Either start with a cold engine or remove the air cleaner from the engine for at least half an hour. While cooling the air cleaner, leave the engine compartment hood open.

2. Tape a thermometer of known accuracy to the inside of the air cleaner so that it is near the temperature sensor unit. Install the air cleaner on the engine but do not fasten its wing nut.

3. Start the engine. With the engine cold and the outside temperature less than 90°F (32°C), the door should be in the **heat on** position (closed to outside air).

4. Operate the throttle lever rapidly to ½–¾ of its opening and release it. The air door should open to allow outside air to enter and then it should close again.

5. Allow the engine to warm up to normal operating temperature. Watch the door. When it opens to the outside air, remove the top from the air cleaner. The temperature should be over 90°F (32°C) and no more than 130°F (54°C); 115°F (46°C) is about normal. If the door does not work within these temperature ranges or fails to work at all, check for linkage or door binding.

6. If binding is not present and the air door is not working, proceed with the vacuum tests given below. If these indicate no

faults in the vacuum motor and the door is not working, the temperature sensor is defective and must be replaced.

Vacuum Motor

1. Check all of the vacuum lines and fittings for leaks, Correct any leaks. If none are found, proceed with the test.

2. Remove the hose which runs from the sensor to the vacuum motor. Run a hose directly from the manifold vacuum source to the vacuum motor.

3. If the motor closes the air door, it is functioning properly and the temperature sensor is defective.

4. If the motor does not close the door and no binding is present in its operation, the vacuum motor is defective and must be replaced.

➡**If an alternate vacuum source is applied to the motor, insert a vacuum gauge in the line by using a T-fitting. Apply at least 9 in.Hg of vacuum in order to operate the motor.**

Air Injection System (1975)

OPERATION

◆ **See Figure 5**

The air injection system pumps air to the exhaust gases in the exhaust manifold to further their combustion.

The system consists of a belt driven air pump, an air control valve, a check valve, air injection tubes, and electrical sensors to prevent exhaust manifold overheating.

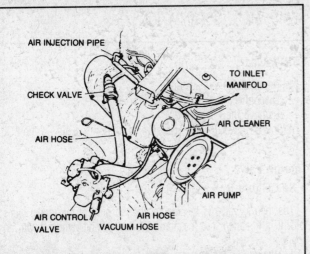

Fig. 5 Components of a common air injection system used by models in this manual

MAINTENANCE

Check the belt condition and the tension. Check the hose routing for kinks and the hoses for breaks and damage. Check for abnormal sounds from the pump or valves.

Clean the air pump air cleaner every 12,000 miles and replace it every 24,000 miles.

Secondary Air Supply System

DESCRIPTION

This system supplies air for the further combustion of unburned gases in the thermal reactor (California only) or exhaust manifold and consists of a reed valve, air hoses, and air passages built into the cylinder head.

The reed valve is operated by exhaust pulsations in the exhaust manifold. It draws fresh air through the air cleaner and supplies it to the exhaust ports.

MAINTENANCE

Check for damage to the air hoses and air pipes. Make sure the air passages are open in the head.

Pulse Air Feeder System (1981 and Later)

DESCRIPTION

The Pulse Air Feeder System supplies secondary air into the exhaust system between the front and rear catalytic converters to pro-

mote oxidation of exhaust emissions in the read converter. The system consists of a main reed valve, a subreed valve, air hoses and crankcase passages.

The main reed valve is actuated by pressure created by No. 3 piston. The subreed valve is actuated by exhaust pulsations. Fresh air is drawn through the air cleaner.

Exhaust Gas Recirculation System

OPERATION

▶ **See Figures 6 and 7**

The EGR system recirculates part of the exhaust gases into the combustion chambers. This dilutes the air/fuel mixture, reducing

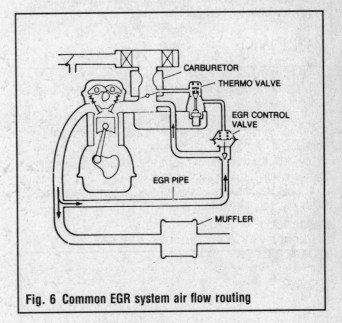

Fig. 6 Common EGR system air flow routing

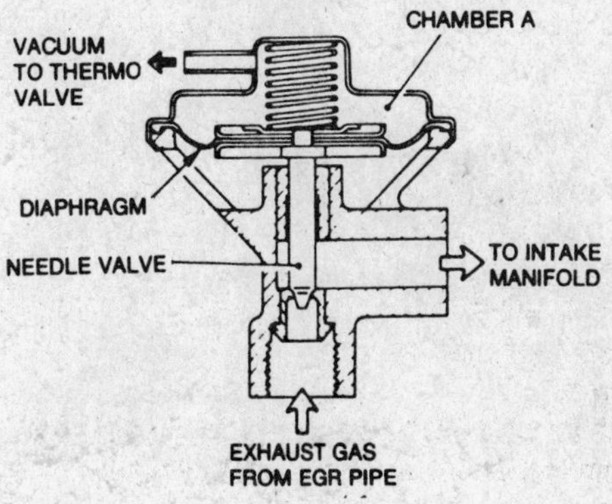

Fig. 7 Cutaway view of the EGR valve

formation of oxides of nitrogen in the exhaust gases by lowering the peak combustion temperatures.

The parts of a typical EGR system are:

• EGR valve—Operated by vacuum drawn from a point above the carburetor throttle plate. The vacuum controls the raising and lowering of the valve pintle to allow exhaust gases to pass from the exhaust system to the intake manifold.

• Thermo Valve—Used to stop EGR valve operation below approximately 131°F (55°C), in order improve cold driveability and starting.

• Dual EGR Valve—(1978 and Later) The EGR vacuum flow is suspended during idle and wide open throttle operation. The primary valve controls EGR flow when the throttle valve opening is relatively narrow, while the secondary control valve operates at wider openings.

• Sub-EGR Control Valve—Linked to the throttle valve to closely modulate the EGR gas flow.

MAINTENANCE

1. Check all vacuum hoses for cracks, breakage and correct installation.
2. Check EGR valve operation by applying vacuum to the EGR valve vacuum nipple with the engine idling. The idle should become rough.
3. Check the passages in the cylinder head and intake manifold for clogging. Clean as necessary.
4. Cold start the engine. The EGR port nipple should be open. When the coolant is warmed to over 131°F (55°C), the port should be closed.

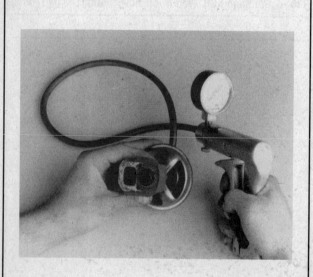

Some EGR valves may be tested using a vacuum pump by watching for diaphragm movement

REMOVAL & INSTALLATION

EGR Valve

1. Remove the vacuum hose.
2. Disconnect the exhaust line from the EGR valve.
3. Remove the EGR valve.
4. Install the EGR valve. Be sure to tighten the nut on the EGR line to 22–25 ft. lbs.

Thermo Valve

▶ **See Figure 8**

The thermo valve is located on the left side of the intake manifold. It is threaded into the manifold and can be removed with an openend wrench.

1. Disconnect the vacuum lines.
2. Using an open-end wrench, carefully turn the thermo valve out of the intake manifold.

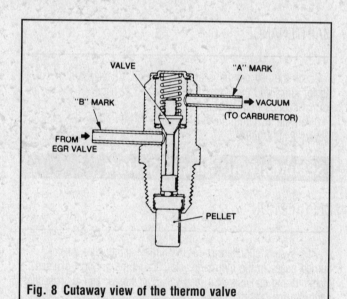

Fig. 8 Cutaway view of the thermo valve

A manifold vacuum gauge can be used to check a variety of vacuum-controlled components

3. Apply a good sealer to the valve threads before installation.

4. Connect the vacuum lines. The A nipple should be connected to the vacuum hose from the carburetor and the B nipple to the EGR valve.

Thermal Reactor

DESCRIPTION

This is used on 1975–77 California and High Altitude models. It is used to further the combustion of the exhaust gases. It consists of a shell and a core with heat insulation material between, mounted at the exhaust manifold.

MAINTENANCE

1. Listen for any abnormal sound from the reactor.
2. Check for cracks and damage.
3. Check the thermal reactor flange on the cylinder head for warpage.

➡**The thermal reactor must be replaced when defective. It cannot be disassembled.**

Maintenance Remainder Warning Light

DESCRIPTION

A light is located in or beside (depending on year and model) the speedometer assembly to alert the driver to the need for EGR system maintenance.

The device has a mileage sensor to light the visual signal at certain mileage intervals.

Upon completion of the required EGR system maintenance, the warning light can be turned off by resetting the switch. It is in the speedometer cable, on the left side junction of the cable behind the dash, or below it under the instrument panel. To reset the sensor, slide the switch.

Catalytic Converter

DESCRIPTION

The catalytic converter is used on 1978 and later models.

This unit or units (two used in 1981–83), replaces the thermal reactor. It is filled with catalyst to oxidize hydrocarbons and carbon monoxide in the exhaust gases. Two units are used on some late models.

MAINTENANCE

◆ **See Figure 9**

1. Check the core for cracks and damages.
2. If the idle carbon monoxide and hydrocarbon content ex-

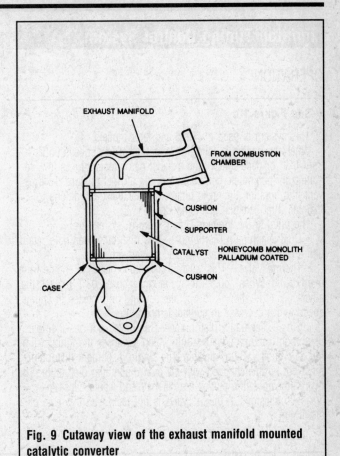

Fig. 9 Cutaway view of the exhaust manifold mounted catalytic converter

ceeds specifications and the ignition timing and idle mixture are correct, the converter must be replaced.

Jet Air System

DESCRIPTION

The jet air system is used on models from 1978 on.

A jet air passage is provided in the carburetor, intake manifold, and cylinder head to direct air to a jet valve, operated simultaneously with the intake valve.

On the intake stroke, jet air is forced into the combustion chamber because of the pressure difference between the ends of the air jet passage.

This jet of air produces a strong swirl in the combustion chamber scavenging the residual gases around the spark plug.

The jet air volume lessens with increased throttle opening. It is at a maximum at idle.

MAINTENANCE

Refer to Valve Lash Adjustment for adjusting jet valve clearance.

No maintenance is required, other than clearance adjustment during valve adjustment. The valve can be removed from the cylinder head for service or replacement.

Ignition Timing Control System

OPERATION

▶ **See Figure 10**

This system is used on 1975 and later models.

When the engine is idling or operating at low speeds under light load or deceleration, the exhaust gas temperature is low, resulting in incomplete combustion of the air/fuel mixture. To prevent this, ignition timing is retarded under these conditions to maintain high exhaust gas temperature.

The units in the Ignition Timing Control system are:

• Dual-Diaphragm Distributor—This distributor has both retard and advance mechanisms operated by vacuum.

• Thermo Valve—This valve is used to protect the engine from overheating. When coolant temperature reaches 203°F (95°C), the advance unit is allowed to operate, causing an increase in engine speed and a decrease in coolant temperature.

• Single diaphragm distributor—This distributor has a single diaphragm vacuum advance unit, which advances the ignition timing as engine vacuum dictates. The single diaphragm distributor must not be interchanged with the dual diaphragm distributor. The distributor operating curves are different and would cause increased emissions. A thermo valve is not used with this type of distributor.

MAINTENANCE

Distributor maintenance is at tune-up intervals.

Orifice Spark Advance Control

OPERATION

This is used on 1977 models only.

The OSAC valve is located in the vacuum line between the distributor and the carburetor. Its function is to delay vacuum advance during medium to high speed operation, when high vacuum would be present. It is used only with the single diaphragm distributor.

Deceleration Device

OPERATION

This is used on 1975, 1977 and later models.

Closing of the throttle valve on deceleration is delayed in order

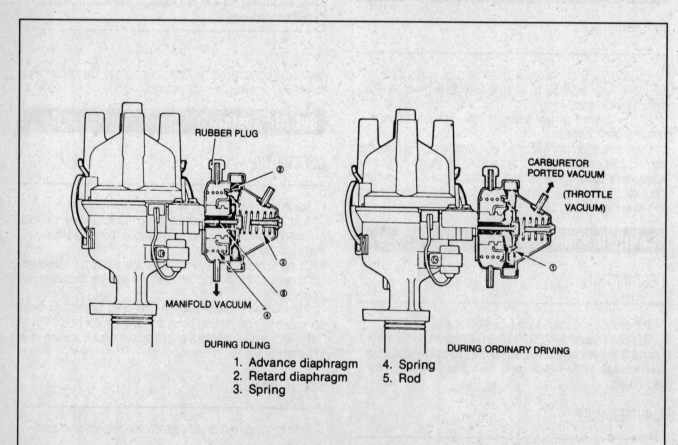

DURING IDLING
1. Advance diaphragm
2. Retard diaphragm
3. Spring

DURING ORDINARY DRIVING
4. Spring
5. Rod

Fig. 10 Dual diaphragm distributor operation

to burn the air/fuel mixture more thoroughly. A vacuum controlled dashpot, attached to the carburetor linkage is used.

A servo valve detects intake manifold vacuum and closes if vacuum exceeds a preset valve. Since the air in the dashpot diaphragm chamber cannot escape, the throttle linkage opening is temporarily retained. If the vacuum is below the preset value, the servo valve opens and the dashpot works normally.

MAINTENANCE

Inspect the hoses for breaks and damage, and the valve body for cracks.

ADJUSTMENT

1. Have the engine running, brakes locked, and a tachometer attached.
2. Push the dashpot rod, connected to the carburetor arm, upward and into the dashpot until it stops.
3. Note the rpm at the dashpot stop and adjust to the following specifications. Note the time required between suddenly releasing the dashpot rod and the return to normal curb idle.
4. The specifications are as follows:
- 1597cc engine, Calif. and H/Alt. Set speed: 1,800–2,000 rpm. Required time: 3–6 seconds
- 1994cc engine, Calif. Set speed: 1,400–1,600 rpm. Required time: 3–6 seconds.
- 1410cc and 1597cc engine, 49 states; 1994cc engine, 49 states. Set speed: 1,900–2,100 rpm. Required time: 3–6 seconds
- All engines, 1981 and later. Set speed: 1,900–2,100 rpm.

Mixture Control Valve

DESCRIPTION

This valve is used on 1977 and later models.

This control valve is used to supply additional air into the intake manifold to decrease manifold vacuum during deceleration, and is activated by the intake manifold vacuum level.

Manual Altitude Compensation System

DESCRIPTION

This system is used on 1977 and later models.

An off-on valve is used to increase the air supply to the carburetor to lean the mixture and decrease the EGR flow for high altitude operation.

MAINTENANCE

The required maintenance is to inspect any vacuum hoses and routing for kinks, breakage and cracks. The off-on valve should be on for high altitude and off for driving under 4,000 ft.

Feedback Carburetor (FBC) System

DESCRIPTION

The feedback carburetor system provides the capability to perform closed loop fuel control (adjusting fuel/air mixture to meet all driving conditions). It also provides the capability to control the secondary air system, the deceleration spark control system and the throttle opener system.

Input signals from a variety of sensors are fed to a microprocessor based electronic control unit (ECU). The ECU the generates output signals for all of the control functions.

The feedback carburetor is a two barrel, downdraft carburetor designed for closed loop system. When used in the closed loop system of mixture control, the carburetor includes special design features for optimum air/fuel mixtures during all ranges of engine operation. Fuel metering is accomplished through the use of three solenoid operated on/off valves (jet mixture, enrichment and deceleration solenoids), adding or reducing fuel to the engine.

The activation of the on/off valve is controlled by the length of the time current is supplied to the solenoid. The solenoid operates at a fixed frequency. By varying the amount of time the solenoid is energized during each cycle (defined as duty cycle), the air/fuel mixture delivered to the engine can be precisely controlled. The duty cycle to the solenoid is controlled by the ECU in response to the signals from the exhaust oxygen sensor, throttle position sensor, coolant sensor, engine speed and other sensors.

Incorporated in the feedback carburetor are eight basic systems of operation: fuel inlet, primary metering, secondary metering, accelerating pump, choke, jet mixture, enrichment and fuel cutoff.

OPERATION

Electronic Control Unit (ECU)

The electronic control unit is mounted in the passenger compartment and consists of a printed circuit board mounted in a protective metal box. It receives analog inputs from the sensors and converts them into digital signals. These signals and various discrete inputs are processed and used by the ECU in controlling fuel delivery, secondary air, deceleration spark and throttle opener managements.

Air/Fuel Control

The feedback carburetor air/fuel control ratio is controlled by the ECU. The ECU monitors the throttle position, engine speed, coolant temperature, intake air temperature, and exhaust oxygen concentration to calculate the fuel flow required to yield the desired air/fuel ratios for all operating conditions. Closed loop control is used to adjust the fuel flow to yield a near stoichiometeric air/fuel ratio (optimum of 15:1) when required. The fuel flow is modified to account for special operating conditions, such as hot starts, acceleration and deceleration.

Adaptive Memory Control

During closed loop operation, the ECU controls the duty cycle of the jet mixture control solenoid, based on the output voltage signal from the exhaust oxygen sensor. The mean values of the duty cycle are stored in a Random Access Memory (RAM) and the last values are stored, even when the ignition is turned OFF.

Secondary Air Control

A solenoid is used to control the air control valve signal vacuum. The solenoid is controlled by the ECU, based on the engine speed, idle position and coolant temperature. The valve sends air to the exhaust manifold.

Deceleration Spark Control

In order to decrease the hydrocarbon (HC) emissions during vehicle deceleration, ignition timing is advanced by the solenoid operated vacuum valve on the distributor. The valve changes the vacuum to intake manifold vacuum. The solenoid is controlled by the ECU, based on engine speed.

Exhaust Oxygen Sensor

The oxygen sensor is mounted in the exhaust manifold. The output signal from the sensor, which varies with the oxygen content of the exhaust gas stream, is provided to the ECU for use in controlling closed loop compensation of fuel delivery.

Coolant Temperature Sensor

The coolant temperature sensor is installed in the intake manifold. The sensor provides data to the ECU for use in controlling fuel delivery and secondary air management.

Engine Speed Sensor

The engine speed sensor signal comes from the ignition coil. Electric signals are sent to the ECU, where the time between pulses is used to calculate engine speed. Engine speed is used in controlling fuel delivery, secondary air management, deceleration spark and throttle opener management.

Throttle Position Sensor

The throttle position sensor is a carburetor mounted potentiometer. The TPS provides throttle angle information to the ECU to be used in controlling the fuel delivery and secondary air management.

Vacuum Sensor Switch

The switch is mounted on the floor board or the inside fender and is turned on when the throttle valve is in the closed (engine idling) position. Information from the switch is provided to the ECU for use in controlling fuel delivery and secondary air management.

Intake Air Temperature Sensor

The sensor is located in the air cleaner. The function of this sensor is to measure the air intake temperature. The temperature information is provided to the ECU for use in controlling fuel delivery.

Jet Mixture System

The jet mixture system supplies fuel to the engine through jet mixture passages and jet valves for optimum air/fuel mixtures. This system is calibrated by the jet mixture solenoid, which responses to an electrical impulse from the ECU. If the oxygen sensor detects a lean condition, the ECU energizes the solenoid at increasing duty cycles to enrich the mixture. If the oxygen sensor detects a rich condition, the solenoid receives a signal from the ECU to decrease the duty cycle to lean out the mixture. Thus, the solenoid is constantly responding to an electrical signal from the ECU to provide efficient control of the air/fuel mixture.

Enrichment System

The enrichment system consists of a metering jet and an enrichment solenoid operated on/off valve, which constantly provides additional fuel for the main metering system. The activation of the on/off valve is controlled by the length of time the current is supplied to the solenoid. When additional fuel is required, such as under heavy acceleration, heavy engine loads, cold start or warm up operation, the ECU energizes the solenoid at preset duty cycles.

Electronically Controlled Fuel Injection (ECI) System

OPERATION

The ECI system consists of an electric control unit (ECU), two fuel injectors, an air flow sensor and other components.

The amount of fuel metered by the two injectors is determined by an electrical signal supplied by the ECU. The ECU monitors various engine and vehicle parameters, needed to calculate fuel delivery time (the frequency and duration of injection) of the injectors.

The fuel delivery time is modified by the ECU according to such operating conditions as cranking, cold starting, altitude, acceleration, deceleration and so on. The fuel is drawn from the fuel tank and forced by the electric fuel pump to the pressure line through a fuel filter. At the end of the fuel line, a fuel pressure regulator controls the fuel pressure at a preset value. Excess fuel is returned to the fuel tank by a return line.

The fuel injectors are installed in a mixer assembly and inject fuel upstream of the throttle valve. When a solenoid coil on the injector is energized, a needle valve opens injecting fuel, for the length of time determined by the ECU to match the operating conditions at hand. Each injector features a swirl nozzle that atomizes the fuel at a higher combustion efficiency.

Multi-Point (MPI) Fuel Injection System

OPERATION

The MPI system functions to control the air/fuel mixture to the optimum ratio. The various engine operating conditions are determined at the ECU according to signals input from various sensors, as a result of this information, the fuel injectors (one for each cylinder) are controlled according to driving conditions.

The injectors inject fuel to each manifold port, in the sequential firing order of each cylinder. The air/fuel ratio control is determined by the injection time of each injector as controlled by the ECU. During the start (cranking) process, there are two fuel injections simultaneously for each of the four cylinders.

VACUUM DIAGRAMS

Following are vacuum diagrams for most of the engine and emissions package combinations covered by this manual. Because vacuum circuits will vary based on various engine and vehicle options, always refer first to the vehicle emission control information label, if present. Should the label be missing, or should vehicle be equipped with a different engine from the vehicle's original equipment, refer to the diagrams below for the same or similar configuration.

If you wish to obtain a replacement emissions label, most manufacturers make the labels available for purchase. The labels can usually be ordered from a local dealer.

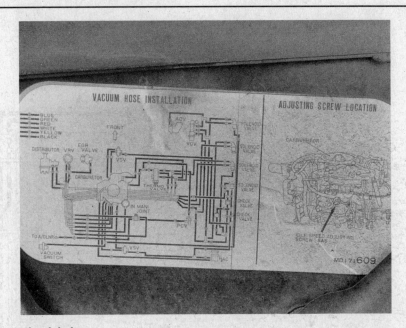

Common vacuum hose routing label

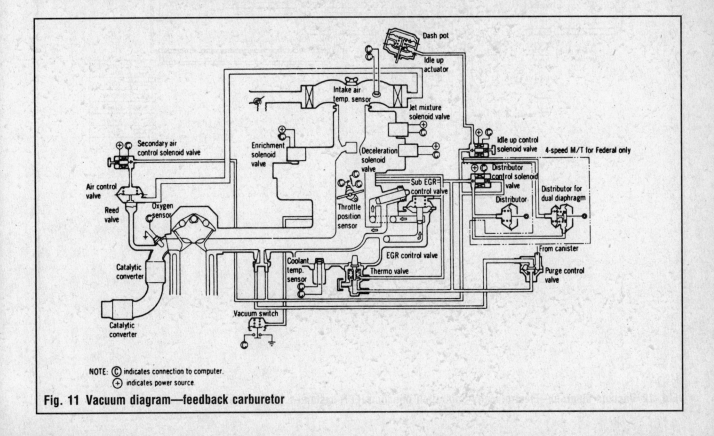

NOTE: Ⓒ indicates connection to computer.
⊕ indicates power source.

Fig. 11 Vacuum diagram—feedback carburetor

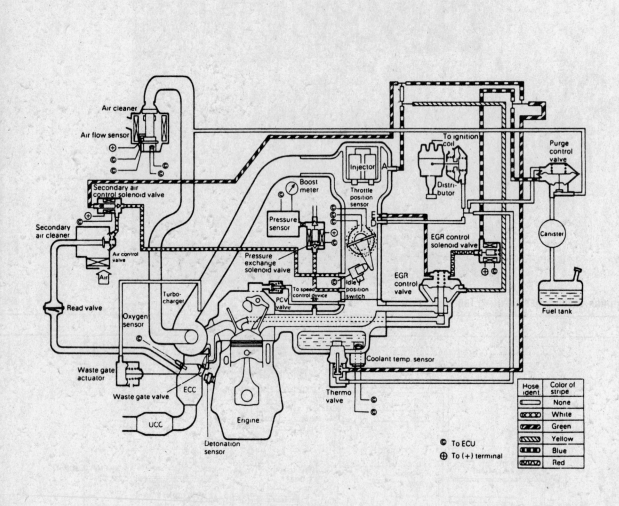

Fig. 12 Vacuum diagram—Electronically Controlled Injection (ECI) system—1.6L Turbo engine

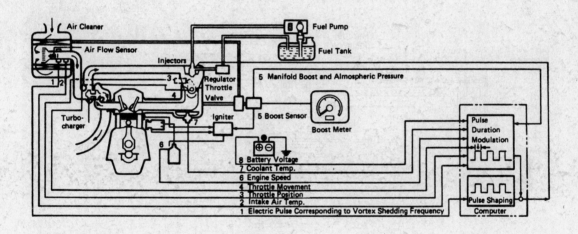

Fig. 13 Schematic of the Electronically Controlled Injection (ECI) system—2.6L engine

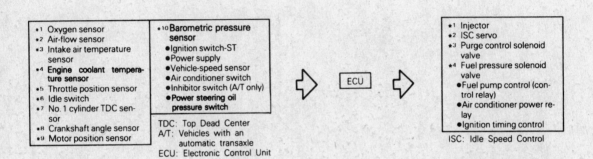

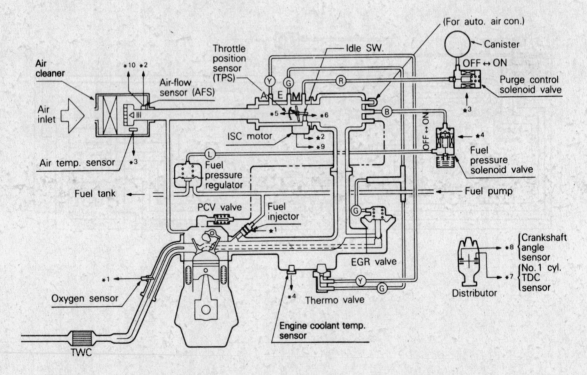

PCV: Positive Crankcase Ventilation
TWC: Three-Way Catalytic converter

Fig. 14 Vacuum diagram—Multiport Fuel Injection (MPI) system

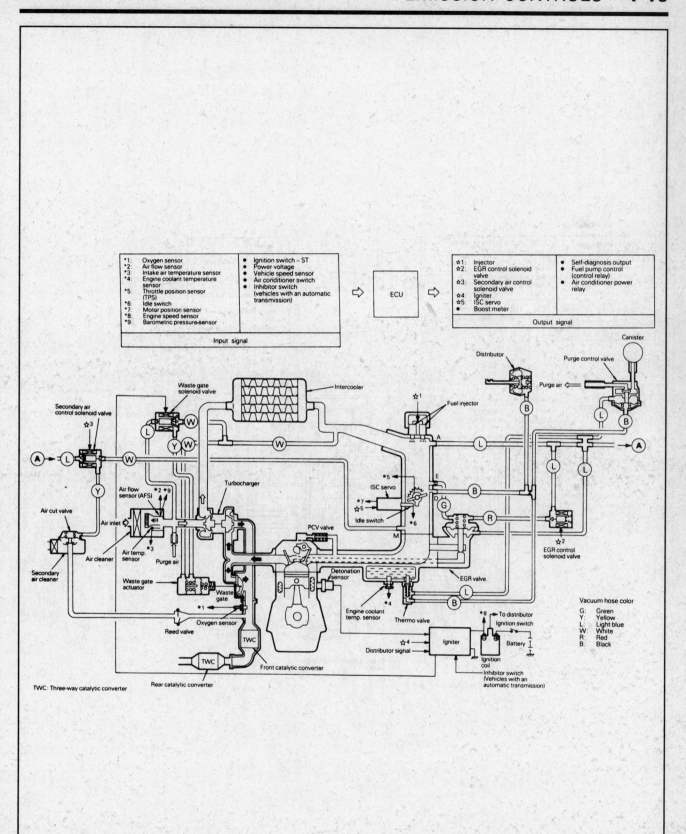

Fig. 15 Vacuum diagram—Conquest with Electronically Controlled Injection (ECI) system

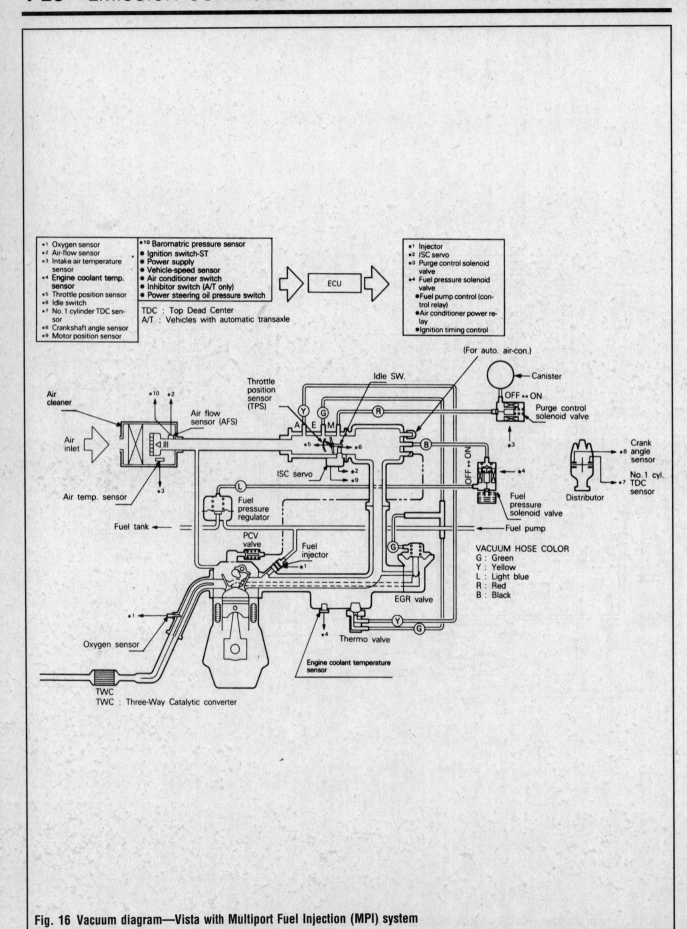

Fig. 16 Vacuum diagram—Vista with Multiport Fuel Injection (MPI) system

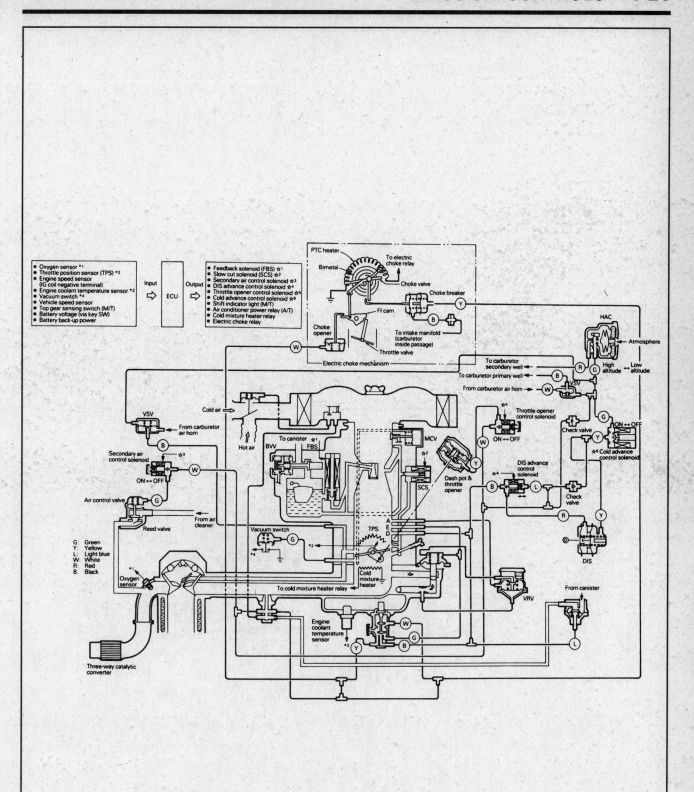

Fig. 17 Vacuum diagram—Colt with Feedback Carburetor (FBC) system

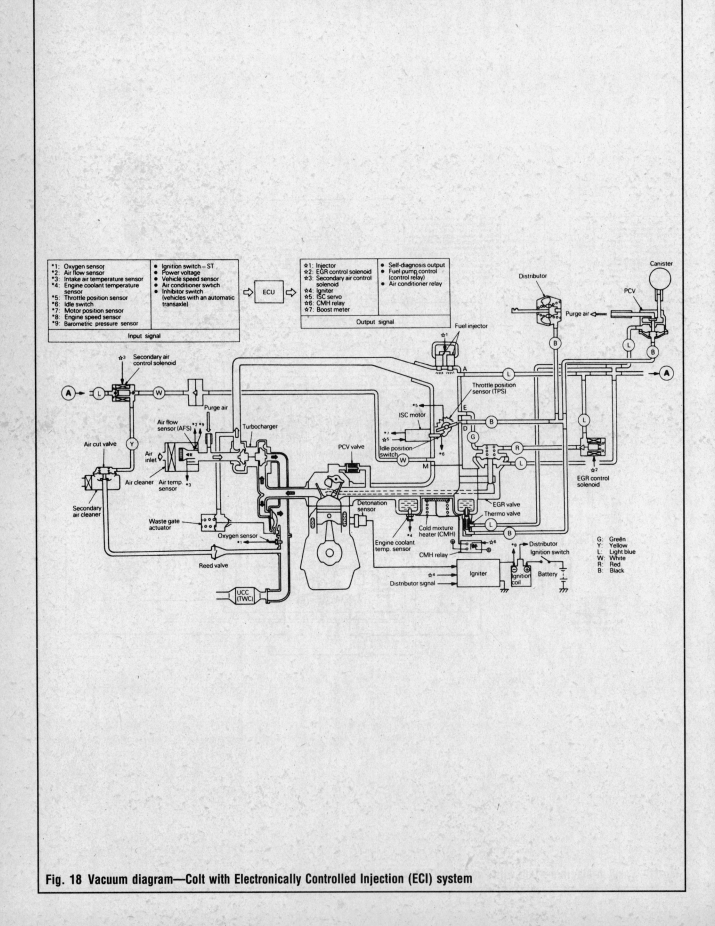

Fig. 18 Vacuum diagram—Colt with Electronically Controlled Injection (ECI) system

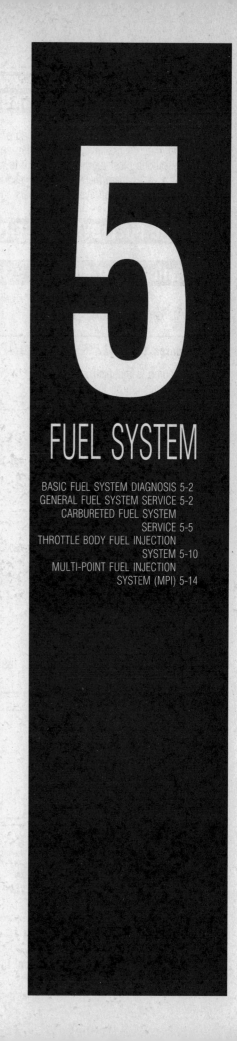

5

FUEL SYSTEM

BASIC FUEL SYSTEM DIAGNOSIS

When there is a problem starting or driving a vehicle, two of the most important checks involve the ignition and the fuel systems. The questions most mechanics attempt to answer first, "is there spark?" and "is there fuel?" will often lead to solving most basic problems. For ignition system diagnosis and testing, please refer to the information on engine electrical components and ignition systems found earlier in this manual. If the ignition system checks out (there is spark), then you must determine if the fuel system is operating properly (is there fuel?).

GENERAL FUEL SYSTEM SERVICE

Mechanical Fuel Pump

REMOVAL & INSTALLATION

♦ **See Figures 1 and 1a**

The fuel pump is mounted on the side of the engine and is driven by an eccentric on the camshaft.

➡**If the engine is set with No. 1 piston at top dead center, the eccentric pressure on the fuel pump arm will be reduced, thus making removal and installation easier.**

1. Remove the air cleaner, heat duct and, depending on model, any other component interfering with pump removal. Remove the plastic pump shield, if equipped. Disconnect the fuel lines (plug the line from the fuel tank).
2. Remove the two mounting bolts or nuts and remove the fuel pump. Remove the gasket and insulator.

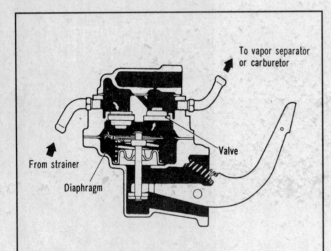

Fig. 1 Cross-section of the mechanical fuel pump—1.6L engine

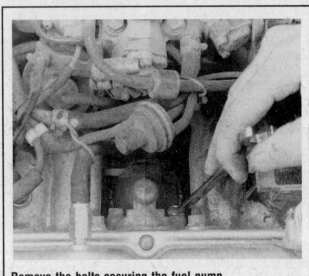

Remove the bolts securing the fuel pump

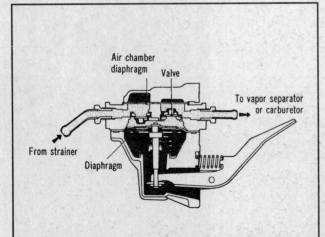

Fig. 1a Cross-section of the mechanical fuel pump—2.0L engine

Once separated, discard the old spacer and gasket and replace with new ones

3. Clean all pump mounting surfaces.

4. Apply a non-hardening sealer to all gasket surfaces. Place the fuel pump into position and secure it with the mounting bolts or nuts.

5. Connect the fuel lines. Install the plastic shield on models equipped, and all other components removed.

TESTING

Disconnect the fuel line from the carburetor and attach a pressure tester to the end of the line. Crank the engine. The tester should show psi as listed on Tune-Up charts.

Electric Fuel Pump

♦ **See Figures 2 and 3**

Some early models and all turbocharged or fuel injected cars are equipped with an electric fuel pump. On the early models the fuel pump is mounted in the trunk on sedans and hardtops and in the left rear wheel housing on station wagons. On the turbocharged Colt and fuel injected Vista, the fuel pump is in the gas tank. On the Conquest, it is on the frame rail, behind the left rear wheel, and on later models is located on the fuel tank.

REMOVAL & INSTALLATION

Except Turbocharged and/or Injected Engines

1. Disconnect the negative battery ground cable.

2. Open the trunk or, on station wagons, remove the left rear wheel housing trim.

3. Disconnect the fuel lines.

4. Make a note of the electrical connections and then detach them from the pump.

5. Remove the retaining screws and remove the pump.

6. Install the new pump. Connect the fuel lines and electrical connector. Be sure that you reconnect the wiring correctly. Connect the battery cable.

Fuel Injected Colt and Vista

♦ **See Figure 4**

✳✳ CAUTION

The electric fuel pump supplies fuel under high pressure. The system pressure must be relieved before servicing the fuel system. Working around gasoline is extremely dangerous unless precautions are taken! NEVER smoke! Make sure the electrical system is disconnected. Avoid prolonged contact of gasoline with the skin. Wear safety glasses. Avoid prolonged breathing of gasoline vapors.

1. Reduce pressure in the fuel lines as follows: Remove the rear seat cushion and carpet. Note the fuel pump wire running

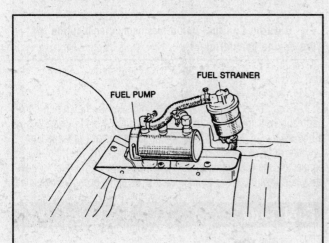

Fig. 2 Fuel pump mounting on sedan and hardtop models

Fig. 4 Unbolt the fuel pump from the gas tank. Arrows indicate the bolt locations

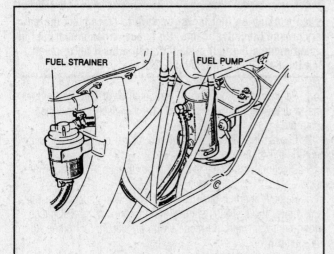

Fig. 3 Fuel pump mounting on station wagon models

along the floor. It has an inwire connector in it. Start the engine and uncouple the connector in the wire. Let the engine stop by itself. Turn the key to OFF. Disconnect the negative battery cable.

2. Remove the fuel tank as described at the end of this chapter.

3. Disconnect the hoses at the pump.

4. Unbolt and remove the pump.

5. Install the new pump. Use a new gasket. Connect the fuel lines, inline connector and battery cable.

Conquest

▶ **See Figure 5**

1. See Step 1 of the Colt procedure above, to reduce fuel line pressure.

2. On early Conquest models. Disconnect the negative battery cable. Raise and support the rear of the car on jackstands.

3. Remove the left rear wheel.

4. Loosen the fuel tank mounting strap nut and lower the tank slightly.

5. Remove the fuel pump support.

6. Disconnect the hoses from the pump and remove the pump.

7. Connect the fuel lines. Install the new pump. Connect the inline electrical connector and the battery cable.

➡ **On late Conquest models, the fuel pump is tank mounted. It is necessary to remove the fuel tank for fuel pump service. Refer to the Colt/Vista procedure.**

TROUBLESHOOTING

▶ **See Figure 6**

If the fuel pump doesn't work.

1. Check the fuse.

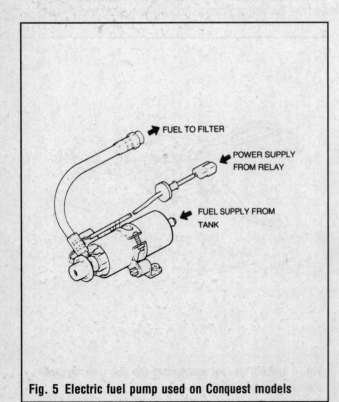

Fig. 5 Electric fuel pump used on Conquest models

FUEL TO FILTER

POWER SUPPLY FROM RELAY

FUEL SUPPLY FROM TANK

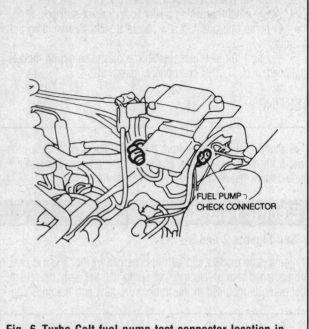

FUEL PUMP CHECK CONNECTOR

Fig. 6 Turbo Colt fuel pump test connector location in the engine compartment

2. Check all wiring connections.

3. Check the control relay which is located in the engine compartment, next to the ignition coil. If the engine starts when the ignition switch is turned to START but stops when it is turned to ON, the relay is defective. Jumper terminals 1 and 2 of the test connector, the fuel pump should operate. If the pump fails to operate when the jumper is connected, the pump is probably defective.

Fuel Tank

REMOVAL & INSTALLATION

✳✳ CAUTION

When working on fuel tanks, be sure to disconnect the battery ground (negative) cable. On turbocharged and/or fuel injected models the fuel system pressure must be relieved. See the Fuel Pump procedures, above.

1. Remove the drain plug (if equipped) or disconnect the fuel line to drain the fuel from the tank. On the Vista, remove the spare tire.

2. Loosen the fuel hose (main and return) clamps and disconnect the fuel lines.

3. Disconnect the filler hose and breather hose from the filler neck.

4. Remove the fuel tank mounting band while supporting the tank. Lower the fuel tank slightly and disconnect the fuel gauge wiring connector and, on models with an electric fuel pump, the fuel pump wiring.

5. Remove the fuel tank.

6. Place the fuel tank into position. Connect the wiring connectors. Secure the tank and connect the fuel lines.

CARBURETED FUEL SYSTEM SERVICE

Carburetor

ADJUSTMENTS

Throttle Linkage
1973–77 MODELS

Throttle linkage is adjusted at the clamp which joins the accelerator pedal rod to the carburetor rod. With the carburetor throttle valves closed (engine at normal operating temperature) the distance between the top of the clamp and the toe-board should be about 35mm. The distance between the end of the connecting rod to the toe-board should be a minimum or 10mm, and the clearance between the stopper bolt and the pedal lever should be 0–20mm.

1978–88 MODELS

On non-feedback carburetors: Adjust the stopper bolt at the firewall, to a distance of 10–20mm from the inside of the bolt holding bracket, to the contact point of the pedal lever, while holding the carburetor throttle plates closed. The yoke at the carburetor end of the accelerator rod is serrated to allow the yoke to be loosened and moved so that a minimal readjustment of the stopper adjusting bolt is needed to give the proper throttle release and opening. On feedback carburetor models: The cable free-play is adjusted by; turning the ignition switch to the On position for 15 seconds, without the engine running. Loosen the adjusting nut so that the throttle lever is free, turn the adjusting nut until the throttle lever just starts to move. Back the nut off one turn and lock the adjusting nut. Make sure the idle position switch touches the stopper.

Float and Fuel Level
▶ **See Figure 7**
1971–83 MODELS

A sight glass is fitted at the float chamber and the fuel level can be checked without disassembling the carburetor. Normal fuel level is within the level mark on the sight glass.

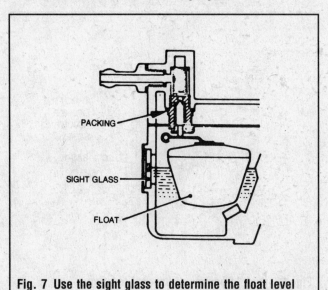

Fig. 7 Use the sight glass to determine the float level

The fuel level adjustment is corrected by increasing or decreasing the number of needle valve packings between the valve and top cover. The float level may be off 2.7mm above or below the level mark and the operation of the engine would not be affected.

1984–88 MODELS

This procedure is for non-feedback carburetors:
1. Invert the float chamber cover with a gasket mounted.
2. Position a universal float level gauge and measure the distance from the bottom of the float to the surface of the float chamber cover. The gap should be 20mm.
3. If the measurement is not within specifications, shims under the needle seat must be changed. Shim kits containing three different thickness shims are available.

Fast Idle Speed

1. On non-feedback carburetors: Start the engine and open the throttle valve about 45°. Manually close the choke valve and slowly return the throttle valve to the stop position.
2. With a tachometer connected, check that the fast idle speed is 2,000 rpm or lower. (Not less than 1,700 rpm). Adjust the speed as necessary with the fast idle speed screw. On earlier models, bend the cam operating link rod to alter the fast idle.
3. Cold start the engine and check the automatic choke and fast idle operation.
4. On feedback carburetors: Run the engine until normal operating temperature is reached. Shut off the engine.
5. Remove the air cleaner and attach a tachometer.
6. Disconnect the vacuum hose from the choke opener. Set the choke lever on the second highest detent of the fast idle cam.
7. Start the engine and check the fast idle speed on the tachometer. Models with an automatic transaxle should be 2,700 rpm. Models with a manual transaxle should be 2,800 rpm.
8. Adjust the fast idle speed with the fast idle adjustment screw.
9. Connect the vacuum hose to the choke opener. Check that the opener cancels the fast idle.

Secondary Throttle Blade

The secondary throttle blade stop screw is adjusted to keep the throttle blade from closing too tightly. This adjustment is only made with the carburetor off of the engine. The screw is set at the factory and doesn't normally need adjustment.

Automatic Choke
1971–79 MODELS

The choke case has five projections. Align the center projection with the punch mark of the bimetal case.

1980–88 MODELS
▶ **See Figures 8, 9 and 10**

On non-feedback carburetors: The choke is adjusted by turning the screw located on the choke spring bracket. The latest model years could have a tamper resistant cover on the screw. If choke adjustment is absolutely necessary the cover must be removed. A new cover should be installed on the screw after adjustment.
On feedback carburetors:
1. Remove the air cleaner and choke mechanism cover.

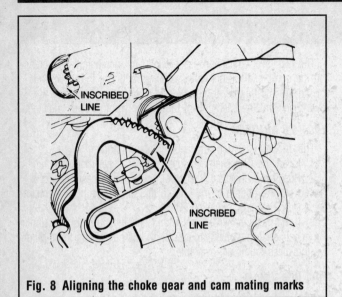

Fig. 8 Aligning the choke gear and cam mating marks

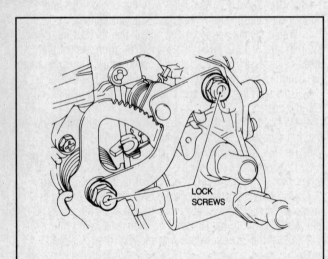

Fig. 9 The choke bracket lockscrews are located on the end of the cam—1985 feedback carburetor shown

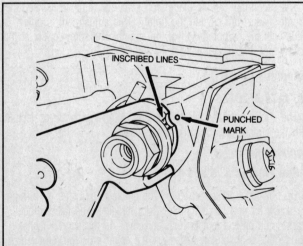

Fig. 10 Alignment of the mating marks on the arm and float chamber

➡Some models might have headless, tamperproof screws securing the choke mechanism cover. These have to be drilled out. In that case, it's easier to remove the carburetor.

2. Remove the bracket bridging the choke spring gear and choke actuating cam.

3. Slip the choke strangler spring from the choke lever. Align the scribed black line on the choke gear with the mark below the teeth on the actuating cam and reassemble all parts.

4. Temporarily tighten the lower bracket screw.

5. Move the arm at the upper screw to align the center line scribed in the notch on the arm with the punch mark on the float chamber.

6. Tighten the screws.

7. Install the cover with new screws.

Throttle Opener

1979–84 MODELS

◆ See Figure 11

The system is not available on California models. The throttle opener increases engine rpm if it drops below a specified amount. The system can be adjusted if necessary:

1. Attach a tachometer, check and adjust the curb idle if needed.

2. Turn off all accessories and disconnect the electric radiator fan.

3. Warm the engine to normal operating temperature.

4. Remove pressure on the throttle opener by lifting the unit with a finger. Do not push on the throttle opener lever or rod. Adjust the throttle opener screw to obtain 800 to 900 rpm.

FROM 1985 EXCEPT 4-WD VISTA

1. Check the vacuum hoses and electrical connectors.

2. Disconnect the vacuum hose at the throttle opener nipple.

3. Connect a vacuum pump to the throttle opener nipple.

4. Connect a tachometer to the engine.

5. Run the engine to normal operating temperature at idle.

6. Apply 300mmHg vacuum with the pump. The idle speed should increase. If not, replace the throttle opener dashpot.

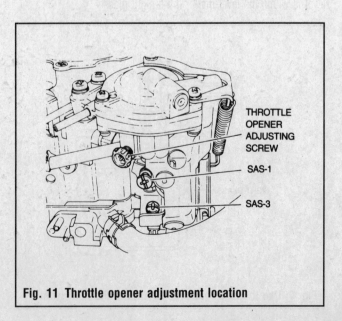

Fig. 11 Throttle opener adjustment location

4-WD VISTA

1. Turn all lights and accessories off.
2. Place the transaxle in neutral.
3. Disconnect the electric fan connector.
4. Apply the parking brake.
5. Make sure that the wheels are in the straight ahead position.
6. Connect a tachometer to the engine. Make sure that the curb idle has been adjusted to specification.
7. Turn on the heater or air conditioner and check the engine speed. The speed should increase to 700–800 rpm. If not, set it there by turning the throttle opener adjusting screw.
8. Turn the air conditioner or heater off and on several times to verify that the throttle opener responds.

Throttle Position Sensor

USA FROM 1985

▶ See Figure 12

1. Disconnect the TPS connector.
2. Check the resistance with an ohmmeter between terminals 2 and 3 (the bottom, adjacent terminals in the connector). With the throttle closed, resistance should be 1.2. Resistance should slowly increase to 4.9 at wide open throttle.

➡**Due to the complex nature of modern fuel systems, comprehensive diagnosis and testing procedures fall outside the confines of this manual.**

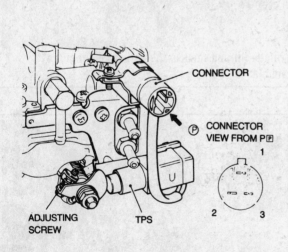

Fig. 12 Check the resistance between terminals 2 and 3 of the throttle position sensor with an ohmmeter

REMOVAL & INSTALLATION

1. Remove the air cleaner. Pull the large crankcase ventilation hose off the front of the air cleaner. Disconnect the two smaller hoses, one goes to the rear of the rocker arm cover and one to the intake manifold.
2. Loosen and remove the two nuts and one bracket which attach the air cleaner to the rocker arm cover.
3. Lift the bottom housing of the air cleaner off of the carburetor and, with it, the hose coming up from the exhaust manifold heat stove.
4. Disconnect the wiring to the throttle position solenoid and the fuel cutoff solenoid.
5. Disconnect the accelerator rod and, on cars equipped with automatic transmissions, the shift rod.
6. Remove the fuel line and vacuum lines.
7. Remove the plug on the passenger's side of the cylinder block and drain the coolant.

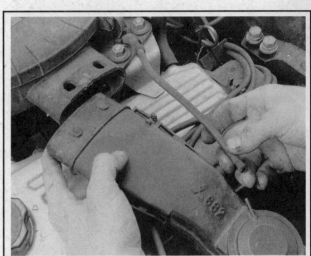

If applicable, remove the snorkel attached to the air cleaner

If present, remove the bolts securing the air cleaner. . .

. . . then lift the air cleaner assembly off the carburetor

. . . then remove the mounting bolts

Be sure to label the hoses before disconnecting them

Carefully lift and remove the carburetor from the manifold

Loosen . . .

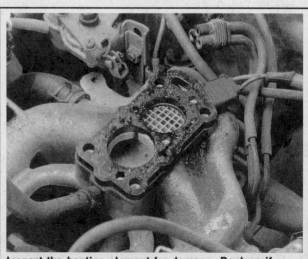

Inspect the heating element for damage. Replace if necessary

➡ **Not draining the cooling system will allow the antifreeze/ water mixture to leak down into the intake manifold and enter the combustion chambers where it can do all sorts of damage.**

8. Disconnect the water hose which runs between the carburetor and the cylinder head.

9. Unscrew the four retaining nuts and remove the carburetor.

10. Install the carburetor. Use a new mounting gasket and sealer.

OVERHAUL

♦ See Figure 13

Efficient carburetion depends greatly on careful cleaning and inspection during overhaul, since dirt, gum, water, or varnish in or on the carburetor parts are often responsible for poor performance.

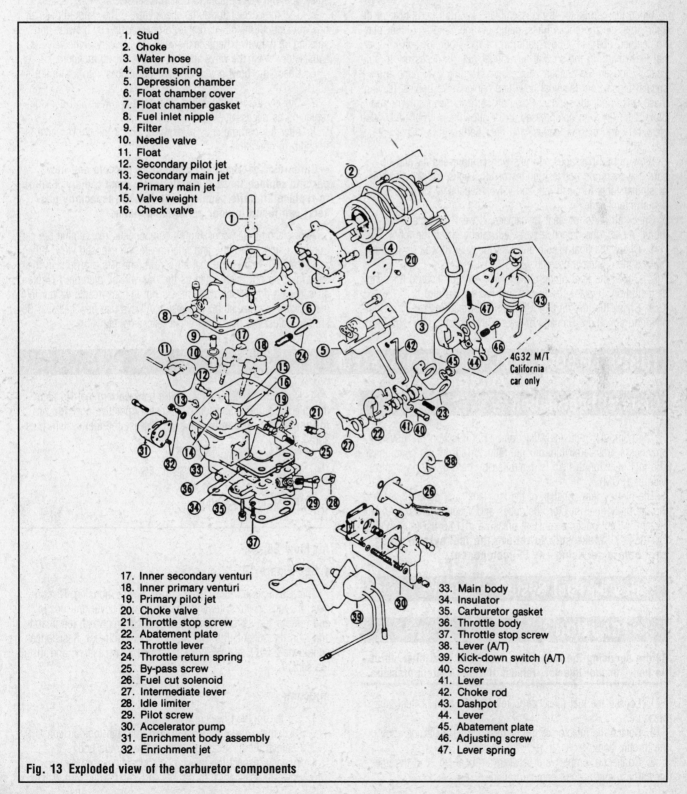

1. Stud
2. Choke
3. Water hose
4. Return spring
5. Depression chamber
6. Float chamber cover
7. Float chamber gasket
8. Fuel inlet nipple
9. Filter
10. Needle valve
11. Float
12. Secondary pilot jet
13. Secondary main jet
14. Primary main jet
15. Valve weight
16. Check valve

17. Inner secondary venturi
18. Inner primary venturi
19. Primary pilot jet
20. Choke valve
21. Throttle stop screw
22. Abatement plate
23. Throttle lever
24. Throttle return spring
25. By-pass screw
26. Fuel cut solenoid
27. Intermediate lever
28. Idle limiter
29. Pilot screw
30. Accelerator pump
31. Enrichment body assembly
32. Enrichment jet

33. Main body
34. Insulator
35. Carburetor gasket
36. Throttle body
37. Throttle stop screw
38. Lever (A/T)
39. Kick-down switch (A/T)
40. Screw
41. Lever
42. Choke rod
43. Dashpot
44. Lever
45. Abatement plate
46. Adjusting screw
47. Lever spring

4G32 M/T California car only

Fig. 13 Exploded view of the carburetor components

Overhaul your carburetor in a clean, dustfree area. Carefully disassemble the carburetor, referring often to the exploded views. Keep all similar and lookalike parts segregated during disassembly and cleaning to avoid accidental interchange during assembly. Make a note of all jet sizes.

➡**Specific procedures for rebuilding your carburetor and illustration exploded view sheets are provided with the rebuilding kit.**

When the carburetor is disassembled, wash all parts (except diaphragms, electric choke units, pump plunger, and any other plastic, leather, fiber, or rubber parts) in clean carburetor solvent. Do not leave parts in the solvent any longer than is necessary to sufficiently loosen the deposits. Excessive cleaning may remove the special finish from the float bowl and choke valve bodies, leaving these parts unfit for service. Rinse all parts in clean solvent and blow them dry with compressed air or allow them to air dry. Wipe clean all cork, plastic, leather, and fiber parts with a clean, lint-free cloth.

Blow out all passages and jets with compressed air and be sure that there are not restrictions or blockages. Never use wire or similar tools to clean jets and valves separately to avoid accidental interchange.

Check all parts for wear or damage. If wear or damage is found, replace the defective parts. Especially check the following:

1. Check the float needle and seat for wear. If wear is found; replace the complete assembly.

2. Check the float hinge pin for wear and the float(s) for dents or distortion. Replace the float if fuel has leaked into it.

3. Check the throttle and choke shaft bores for wear or an out-of-round condition. Damage or wear to the throttle arm, shaft, or shaft bore will often require replacement of the throttle body. These parts require a close tolerance of fit; wear may allow air leakage, which could affect starting and idling.

➡**Throttle shafts and bushings are not included in overhaul kits. They can be purchased separately.**

4. Inspect the idle mixture adjusting needles for burrs or grooves. Any such condition requires replacement of the needle, since you will not be able to obtain a satisfactory idle.

5. Test the accelerator pump check valves. They should pass air one way but not the other. Test for proper seating by blowing and sucking on the valve. Replace the valve if necessary. If the valve is satisfactory, wash the valve again to remove breath moisture.

6. Check the bowl cover for warped surfaces with a straight edge.

7. Closely inspect the valves and seats for wear and damage, replacing as necessary.

8. After the carburetor is assembled, check the choke valve for freedom of operation.

➡**Carburetor overhaul kits contain all gaskets and new parts to replace those that deteriorate most rapidly. Failure to replace all parts supplied with the kit (especially gaskets) can result in poor performance later.**

After cleaning and checking all components, reassemble the carburetor, using new parts and referring to the exposed view. When reassembling, make sure that all screws and jets are right in their seats, but do not overtighten as the tips will be distorted. Tighten all screws gradually, in rotation. Do not tighten needle valves into their seats; uneven jetting will result. Always use new gaskets. Be sure to adjust the float level when reassembling.

THROTTLE BODY FUEL INJECTION SYSTEM

General Information

The computer regulated, Electronic Fuel Injection (EFI) system provides a precise air/fuel mixture ratio for all driving conditions. The fuel injection system is controlled by the Powertrain Control Module (PCM).

The fuel system consists of the fuel tank, fuel pump, fuel filter, throttle body, fuel injector, fuel tubes and vacuum tubes. The fuel system is kept under a constant pressure of 14.5 psi (100 kPa) for 1984–89. **Make sure to relieve the fuel system pressure before servicing any EFI component.**

Relieving Fuel System Pressure

✳✳ CAUTION

Before servicing the fuel pump, fuel lines, fuel filter, throttle body, or fuel injector, release the fuel system pressure.

1. Loosen the fuel filler cap to release any built-up fuel tank pressure.

2. Detach the injector wiring harness connector at the edge of the throttle body.

3. Connect a jumper wire between terminal No. 1 of the injector harness and a good engine ground.

4. Connect a second jumper wire between terminal No. 2 of the injector harness and touch the battery positive post **for no longer than 5 seconds**—this will release the fuel system pressure.

5. Remove the jumper wires.

6. Continue with the fuel system service.

COMPONENT TESTING

Air Flow Sensor

◗ **See Figure 14**

The sensor is located inside the air cleaner housing. Disconnect the sensor wires, remove the air cleaner cover and unclip and remove the sensor. Check the resistance between terminal 1 and 4 in the sensor (the two adjacent top terminals). Resistance should be 2.5kΩ at 68°F (20°C). Service as necessary, and install the sensor.

Injectors

1. Set the ignition switch to OFF.
2. Disconnect the high tension lead from the ignition coil.
3. Remove the air intake pipe from the throttle body.
4. Visually inspect the injectors for cleanliness.
5. Have an assistant turn the key to START while you watch

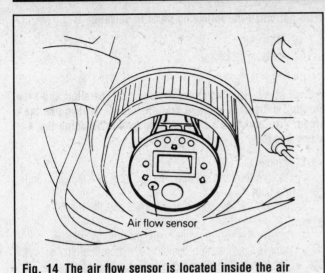

Fig. 14 The air flow sensor is located inside the air cleaner housing

the injectors. A good squirt from each injector should be observed.

6. Have your assistant turn the key to OFF. No leakage should occur.

7. Reconnect the coil wire. If the injectors do not perform properly, proceed to the injector coil test below.

Injector Coil

1. Turn the ignition switch to OFF.
2. Disconnect the wires from the injectors.
3. Check across the injector coil leads with an ohmmeter. Resistance should be 2.0–3.0Ω. If not, replace the injector.
4. Reconnect the wires.

Idle Switch

▶ See Figure 15

1. Turn the ignition switch OFF.
2. Disconnect the ISC servo.
3. Check for continuity between pole 2 (see accompanying il-

lustration) of the connector, and the throttle body. With the throttle body at idle, there should be continuity; with the throttle wide open, there should be no continuity. With the throttle open, the lever should break contact with the idle switch.

4. If the continuity test is defective, replace the ISC servo.
5. Reconnect the wiring.

ISC Servo

▶ See Figure 16

1. Without disconnecting the ISC servo, connect a voltmeter between terminal 3 in the illustration and the throttle body.

2. Turn the ignition switch from OFF to ON, and keep it at ON for at least 15 seconds. The voltmeter should indicate 11–13v, then momentarily drop to 1v or less, and return to 6–13v. This indicates normal operation.

3. Turn the switch OFF and remove the voltmeter.

ISC Servo Motor

1. With the ignition switch OFF, disconnect the ISC servo.
2. Check the motor coil with an ohmmeter for continuity between terminals 1 and 4. Resistance should be 7.0–10.0Ω. If not, replace the servo assembly.

3. Make sure there is no continuity between either terminal 1 or 4 and the throttle body.

4. If there is continuity, there is a short in the coil and the servo must be replaced.

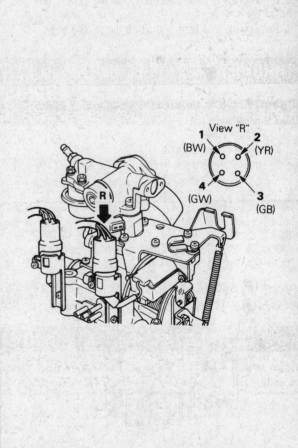

Fig. 16 Using an ohmmeter, test for continuity between the throttle body and terminal 3 of the ISC servo

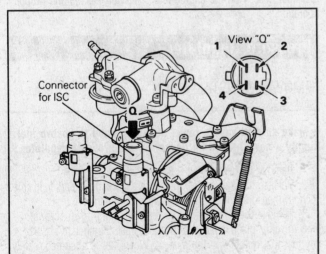

Fig. 15 Check for continuity between terminal 2 of the idle switch connector and the throttle body

Throttle Position Sensor
♦ See Figure 17

1. With the ignition switch OFF, disconnect the TPS connector.
2. Check resistance across terminals 1 and 3 (top and bottom left) of the connector. Resistance should be 4.0–6.0kΩ.
3. Using a circuit test, cross connect terminals 1 and 3 or 2 and 3. Operate the throttle valve slowly from idle to wide open. The resistance should change smoothly.
4. Remove the testers and connect the wires.

Throttle Body

REMOVAL

♦ See Figure 18

1. Reduce system pressure. Disconnect the battery ground cable.
2. Drain the coolant to a point below the intake manifold.
3. Remove the coolant hose at the throttle body.
4. Disconnect the air inlet pipe.
5. Disconnect the throttle cable.
6. Mark and disconnect all vacuum hoses at the throttle body.
7. Mark and disconnect all wiring at the throttle body.
8. Disconnect and cap the fuel inlet and return lines. When removing the inlet line, remove the two bolts and slowly pull the pipe, allowing the residual pressure to escape. Do not pull the line right off.
9. Remove the four bolts and lift off the throttle body.

DISASSEMBLY

➡Do not remove or disassemble the following parts:
 a. ISC servo.
 b. Throttle valve.
 c. Injector holder screens.
 d. Fuel return nipple.

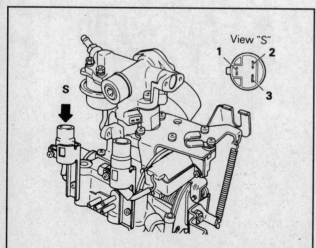

Fig. 17 Check the resistance across terminals 1 and 3 of the connector on the throttle position sensor

➡Do not clean the following parts in solvent:
 a. TPS sensor.
 b. Variable resistor.
 c. ISC servo.

➡Most screw-type fasteners are securely installed and may be more difficult to remove than they look. Always use the proper size and type screwdriver to avoid damaging the screw heads.

1. Remove the TPS.
2. Remove the hose between the fuel pressure regulator and the mixing body.
3. Remove the injector retainer screws and lift out the retainer.
4. Remove the fuel pressure regulator from the retainer.
5. Remove the pulsation damper cover from the retainer and take out the spring and diaphragm.
6. Pull the injector from the throttle body. Use your fingers; never grab the injectors with pliers!
7. Remove the injector gaskets from the throttle body.
8. Remove the throttle return spring and damper spring.
9. Remove the ISC servo mounting bracket screws and lift off the servo and bracket.
10. Unbolt and remove the upper half of the throttle body assembly.

ASSEMBLY

1. Clean all parts, noting the earlier cautions.
2. Assembly the components. Use new gaskets and seals. Never reuse a gasket or seal. When installing the injectors, use finger pressure only. Injector retainer screws are torques to 12–16 in. lb. Make all necessary adjustments described above.

INSTALLATION

Install the throttle body. Torque the top half mounting screws to 14 ft. lbs. Always use new gaskets. Use a new O-ring on the fuel inlet hose. Run the engine and check for leakage and proper operation.

Pressure Regulator

REMOVAL & INSTALLATION

➡Make sure to have a towel or rag on hand to absorb fuel. Supply a new O-ring and gasket for the pressure regulator.

1. Remove the air cleaner and air hoses.
2. Release the fuel system pressure as described earlier in this section, then disconnect the negative battery cable.
3. Remove the 3 fuel pressure regulator hold-down screws, then **quickly** place a rag over the fuel inlet chamber to absorb any fuel that remains in the system. When fuel is absorbed, safely dispose of the rag.
4. Pull the pressure regulator from the throttle body. Carefully remove the old O-ring and gasket.

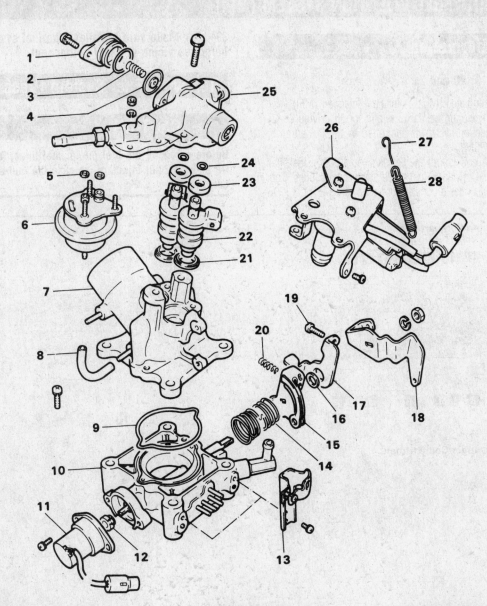

1. Pulsation damper cover
2. O-ring
3. Spring
4. Pulsation damper
5. O-ring (2)
6. Fuel pressure regulator
7. Mixing body
8. Hose
9. Seal ring
10. Throttle body assembly
11. Throttle position sensor
12. Joint
13. Connector bracket
14. Return spring
15. Throttle lever
16. Ring
17. Free lever
18. Kickdown lever
19. Adjusting screw
20. Spring
21. Seal ring (2)
22. Injector (2)
23. Collar (2)
24. O-ring (2)
25. Injector holder
26. ISC servo assembly
27. Damper spring
28. Return spring

Fig. 18 Exploded view of the throttle body unit

To install:

5. Carefully install a new O-ring and gasket onto the regulator.

6. Position the pressure regulator onto the throttle body. Press it into place squarely so as to properly seat the O-ring and gasket.

7. Install the 3 hold-down screws and tighten them to 40 inch lbs. (4.5 Nm).

8. Connect the negative battery cable.

9. Start the engine and check for fuel leaks with the air cleaner off, then install the air cleaner and hoses.

MULTI-POINT FUEL INJECTION SYSTEM (MPI)

General Information

▶ See Figures 19, 20 and 21

The computer regulated, Multi-Point Fuel Injection (MFI) system provides a precise air/fuel mixture ratio for all driving conditions. The fuel injection system is controlled by the Powertrain Control Module (PCM).

The fuel system consists of the fuel tank, fuel pump, fuel filter, throttle body, 4 fuel injectors, fuel tubes and vacuum tubes. The fuel system is kept under a constant pressure of 53–57 psi (366–

394 kPa). **Make sure to relieve the fuel system pressure before servicing any MFI component.**

Relieving Fuel System Pressure

✳✳ CAUTION

Before servicing the fuel pump, fuel lines, fuel filter, throttle body, or fuel injectors, release the fuel system pressure.

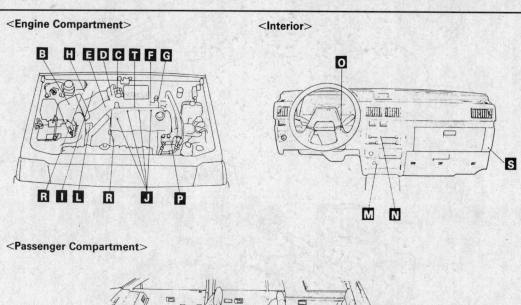

Name	Symbol	Name	Symbol
Air conditioner relay	A	Ignition timing adjustment terminal	H
Air conditioner switch	N	Inhibitor siwth (A/T models)	L
Air-flow sensor (incorporating intake air temperature sensor and barometric pressure sensor)	B	Injector	J
		ISC motor (idle switch, motor position sensor)	C
Crank angle sensor and No. 1 cylinder TDC sensor	G	MPI control relay	M
EGR control solenoid valve*	R	Oxygen sensor	K
EGR temperature sensor*	T	Power steering oil pressure switch	P
Engine control unit	Q	Purge control solenoid valve	I
Engine coolant temperature sensor	E	Self-diagnosis connector	S
Fuel pump checker terminal	H	Throttle position sensor	D
Ignition coil (power transistor)	F	Vehicle-speed sensor (reed switch)	O

NOTE
The "Name" column is arranged in alphabetical order.
*: <California>

Fig. 19 MPI component locations—1989 Colt Vista shown

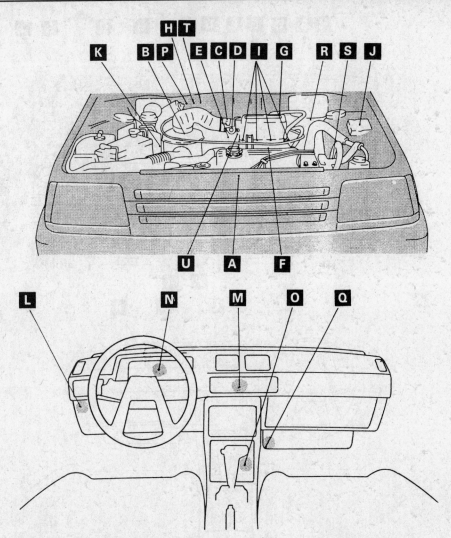

Name	Symbol	Name	Symbol
Air conditioner relay	J	Ignition coil (power transistor)	F
Air conditioner switch	M	Ignition timing adjustment terminal	P
Air flow sensor (incorporating intake air temperature sensor and barometric pressure sensor)	B	Inhibitor switch (A/T models)	K
Crank angle sensor	G	Injector	I
Diagnosis terminal	Q	MPI control relay	L
EGR control solenoid valve*	T	Oxygen sensor	A
EGR temperature sensor*	U	Power steering oil pressure switch	S
Engine control unit	O	Purge control solenoid valve	H
Engine coolant temperature sensor	E	Throttle position sensor	D
Fuel pump checker terminal	R	Vehicle speed sensor (reed switch)	N
Idle speed control servo (idle switch, motor position sensor)	C	–	–

NOTE
*: <California>

Fig. 20 MPI component locations—1989 Colt wagon, 1.5L engine shown

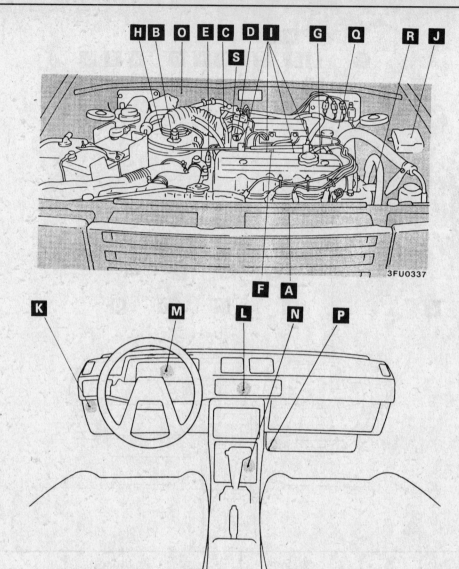

3FU0337

Name	Symbol	Name	Symbol
Air conditioner relay	J	Ignition coil (power transistor)	F
Air conditioner switch	L	Ignition timing adjustment terminal	O
Air flow sensor (incorporating intake air temperature sensor and barometric pressure sensor)	B	Injector	I
Crank angle sensor	G	MPI control relay	K
Diagnosis terminal	P	Oxygen sensor	A
EGR temperature sensor*	S	Power steering oil pressure switch	R
Engine control unit	N	Purge control solenoid valve	H
Engine coolant temperature sensor	E	Throttle position sensor	D
Fuel pump checker terminal	Q	Vehicle speed sensor (reed switch)	M
Idle speed control servo (idle switch, motor position sensor)	C	—	—

NOTE
*: <California>

Fig. 21 MPI component locations—1989 Colt wagon, 1.8L engine shown

1. Loosen the fuel filler cap to release any built-up fuel tank pressure.

2. Detach the injector wiring harness connector from the engine or main harness.

3. Connect a jumper wire between terminal No. 1 of the injector harness and a good engine ground.

4. Connect a second jumper wire between terminal No. 2 of the injector harness and touch the battery positive post **for no longer than 5 seconds**—this will release the fuel system pressure.

5. Remove the jumper wires.

6. Continue with the fuel system service.

Throttle Body and Injectors

REMOVAL & INSTALLATION

▶ **See Figures 22 thru 26**

1. Release the fuel system pressure. Disconnect the negative battery cable.

2. Drain the cooling system level to a point below the radiator and by-pass hose connections at the engine. Disconnect the hose from the engine.

3. Remove the air intake hose from the throttle body. Disconnect the electrical harness connectors. Remove the throttle body.

4. Remove the fuel pressure regulator.

5. Remove the fuel line to the injector delivery pipe.

6. Remove the mounting bolts and the fuel delivery pipe and fuel injectors as an assembly.

➡**When lifting the delivery pipe from the engine, take care not to drop the fuel injectors.**

7. Remove the injectors for the delivery tube by twisting them while pulling them out of the tube.

8. Measure the resistance between the injector terminals. Resistance should be 2–3Ω. Replace the injector if the proper resistance is not present.

9. Clean all gasket and O-ring mounting surfaces.

To install:

10. Install new O-ring insulators to the delivery tube mounting points on the intake manifold.

11. Install the fuel injectors into the delivery tube. Install a new grommet and O-ring on the injector. Apply a film of light oil to the O-rings.

12. Push the injector into the delivery while twisting it. After the injector is seated in the delivery tube, make sure that it will turn freely. If the injector binds, the O-ring may be jammed. Remove the injector and check the O-ring. Service as necessary and install the injector.

13. Position the fuel delivery rail over the intake manifold mounting points. Line up the injectors and secure the fuel pipe.

14. Apply a film of light oil on the fuel pressure (new) O-ring. Turn the locknut up till it reaches the top of the threads next to the regulator body. Screw the fuel pressure into the delivery pipe by hand. When the regulator bottoms, back it off until the nipple is parallel with the distributor cap towers. Tighten the locknut to secure the regulator.

15. Connect the fuel line. Install the throttle body with a new mounting gasket.

16. Connect the wire harnesses, water hoses and air inlet hose. Fill the cooling system and connect the battery cable.

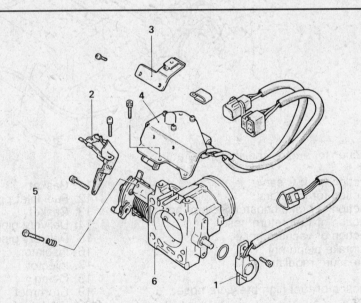

Disassembly steps

1. Throttle position sensor
2. Throttle bracket
3. Connector bracket
4. ISC servo assembly
5. Throttle valve set screw
6. Throttle body

Fig. 22 Disassembly of the throttle body on the MPI system—1989 Colt Vista shown

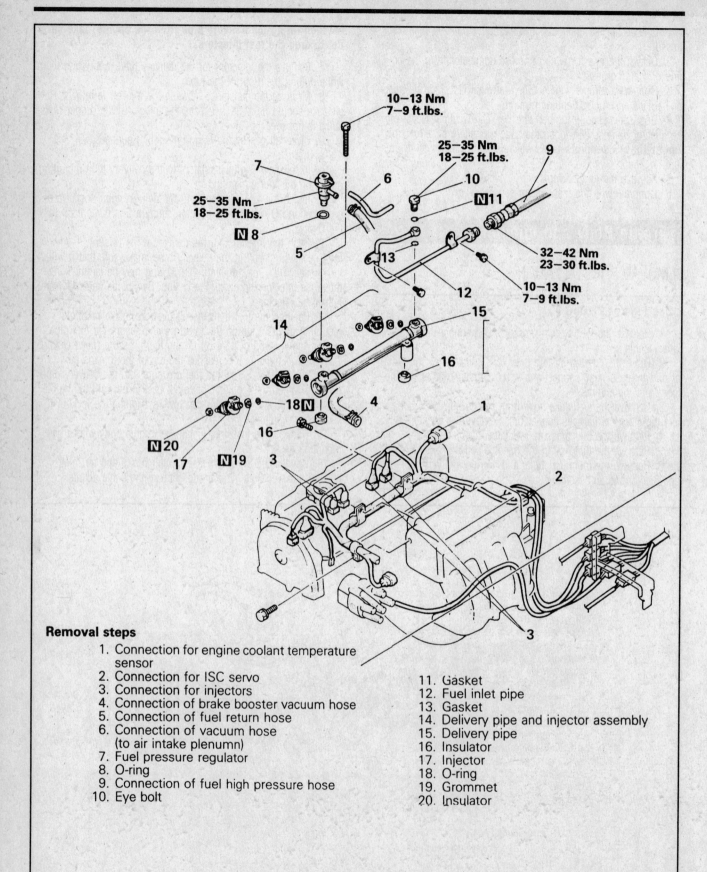

10—13 Nm
7—9 ft.lbs.

25—35 Nm
18—25 ft.lbs.

9

7

10

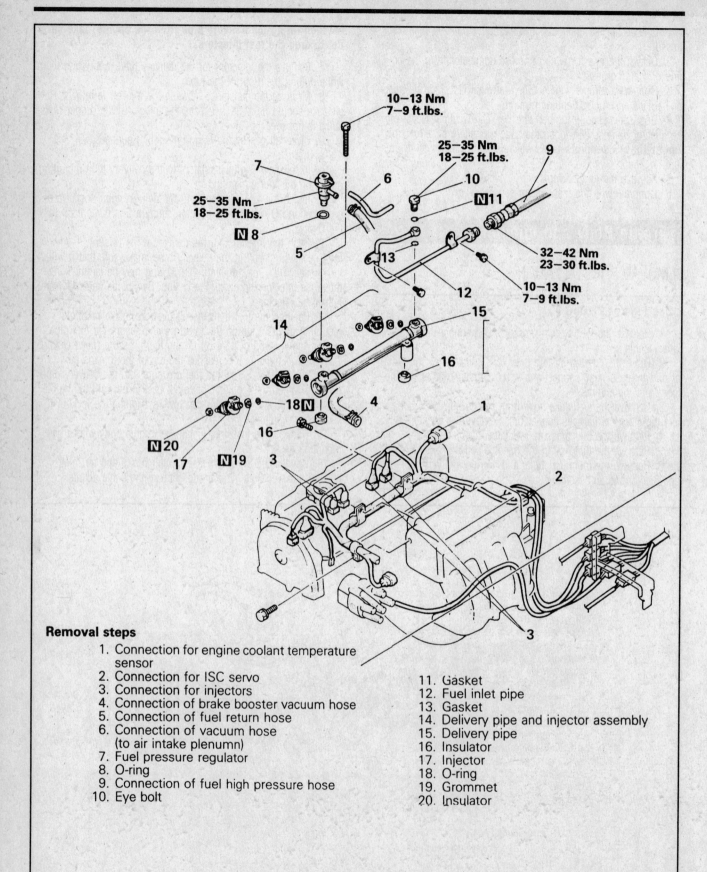11

6

25—35 Nm
18—25 ft.lbs.

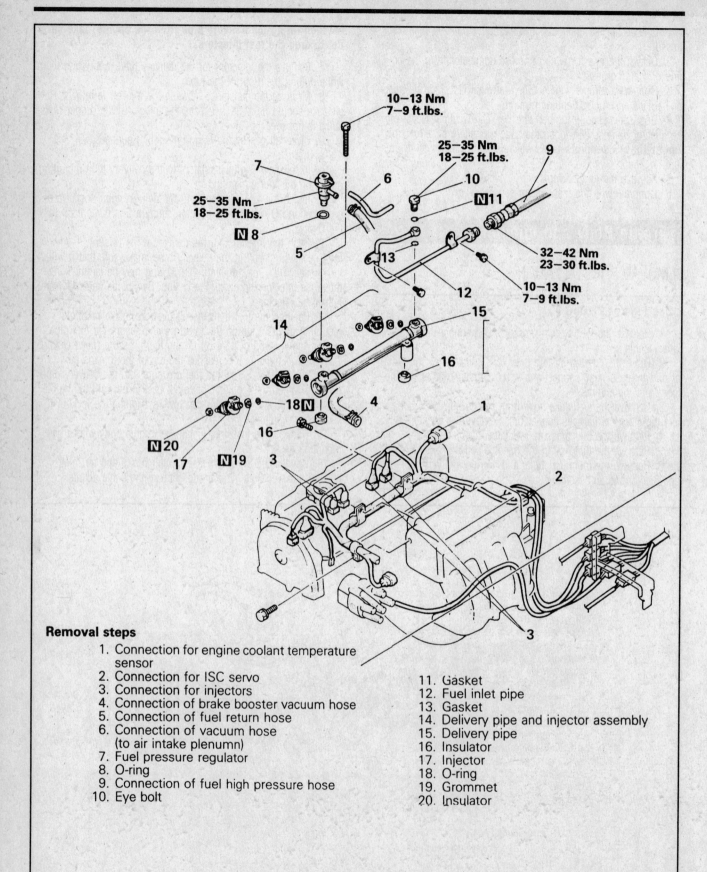8

5

13

32—42 Nm
23—30 ft.lbs.

12

10—13 Nm
7—9 ft.lbs.

14

15

16

18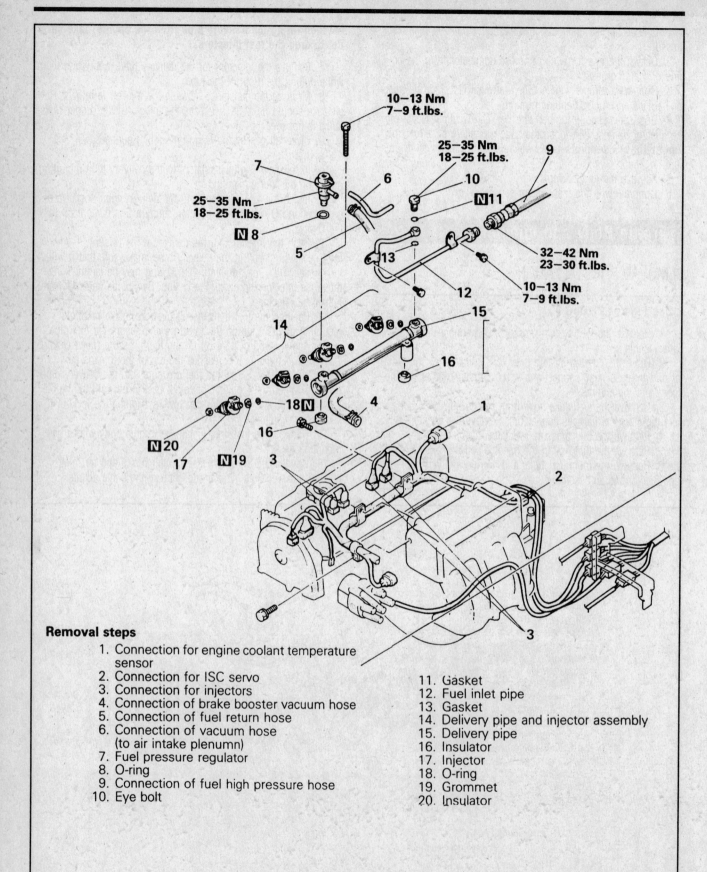

4

1

20

16

2

17

19

3

3

Removal steps

1. Connection for engine coolant temperature
   sensor
2. Connection for ISC servo
3. Connection for injectors
4. Connection of brake booster vacuum hose
5. Connection of fuel return hose
6. Connection of vacuum hose
   (to air intake plenumn)
7. Fuel pressure regulator
8. O-ring
9. Connection of fuel high pressure hose
10. Eye bolt

11. Gasket
12. Fuel inlet pipe
13. Gasket
14. Delivery pipe and injector assembly
15. Delivery pipe
16. Insulator
17. Injector
18. O-ring
19. Grommet
20. Insulator

Fig. 23 MPI injector removal and installation—1989 Colt Vista shown

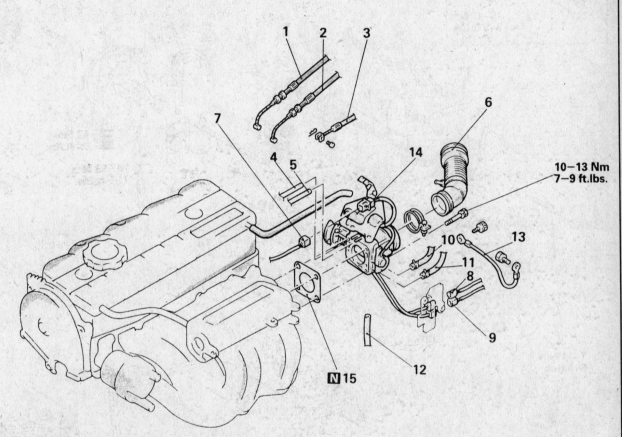

Removal steps

1. Connction of speed control cable (Vehicles with an auto-cruise control system)
2. Connection of accelerator cable
3. Throttle control cable (Vehicles with an automatic transaxle)
4. EGR vacuum hose connection
5. Purge control valve vacuum hose connection
6. Air intake hose connection
7. ISC motor connector
8. MPS connector
9. TPS connector
10. Water hose connection
11. Water by-pass hose connection
12. Vacuum hose connection
13. Ground cable
14. Throttle body
15. Gasket

Fig. 24 Throttle body removal and installation—1989 Colt Vista shown

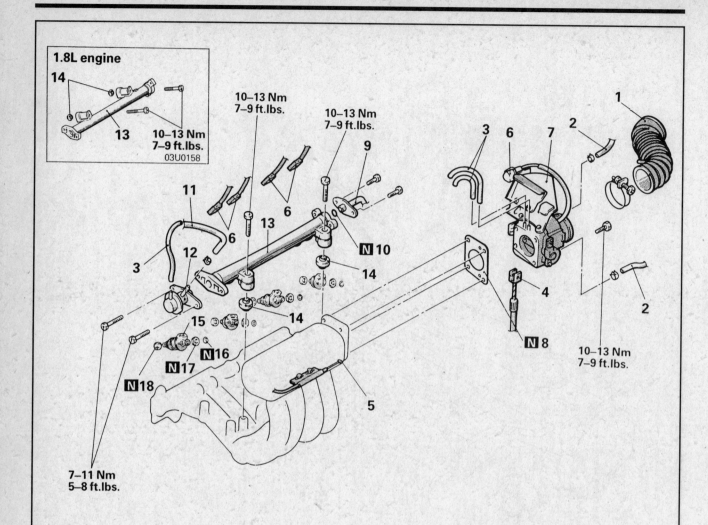

1.8L engine

14

13

10–13 Nm
7–9 ft.lbs.

03U0158

10–13 Nm
7–9 ft.lbs.

10–13 Nm
7–9 ft.lbs.

9

11

13

6

6

6

3

12

10

14

3

6

7

2

1

4

8

2

2

10–13 Nm
7–9 ft.lbs.

15

16

17

18

5

7–11 Nm
5–8 ft.lbs.

Removal steps

1. Connection for air intake hose
2. Connection for water hose
3. Connection for vacuum hose
4. Connection for throttle control cable
5. Connection for accelerator cable
6. Connection for control wiring harness
7. Throttle body
8. Gasket
9. Connection for fuel high pressure hose
10. O-ring
11. Connection for fuel return hose
12. Fuel pressure regulator
13. Delivery pipe
14. Insulator
15. Injector
16. O-ring
17. Grommet
18. Insulator

Fig. 25 MPI injector and throttle body removal—Colt wagon, 1.5 and 1.8L engines

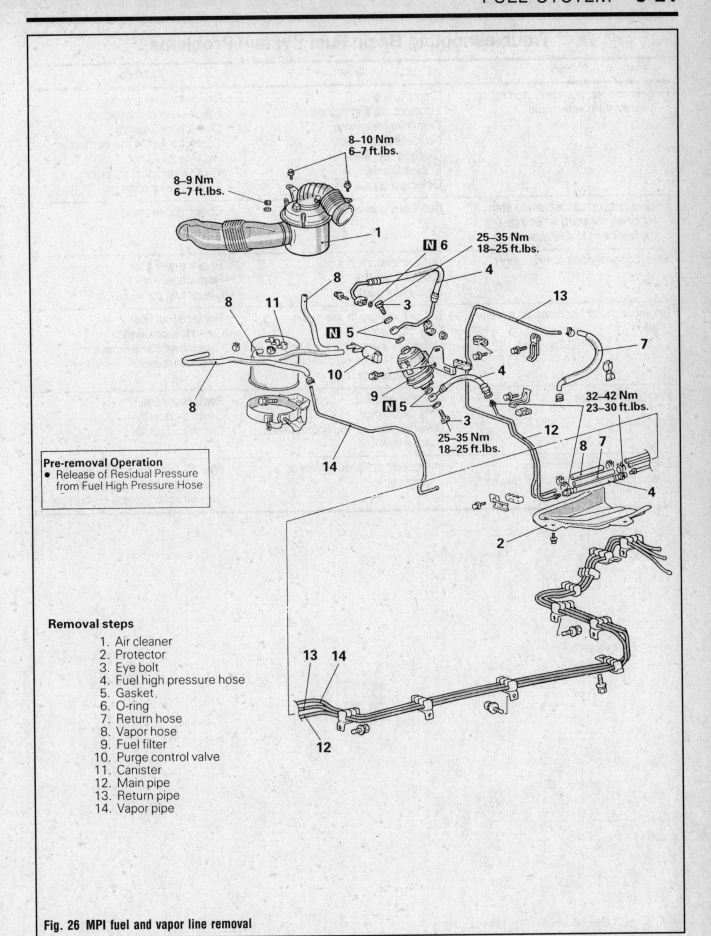

Fig. 26 **MPI fuel and vapor line removal**

8–10 Nm
6–7 ft.lbs.

8–9 Nm
6–7 ft.lbs.

25–35 Nm
18–25 ft.lbs.

32–42 Nm
23–30 ft.lbs.

25–35 Nm
18–25 ft.lbs.

Pre-removal Operation
- Release of Residual Pressure
  from Fuel High Pressure Hose

Removal steps

1. Air cleaner
2. Protector
3. Eye bolt
4. Fuel high pressure hose
5. Gasket
6. O-ring
7. Return hose
8. Vapor hose
9. Fuel filter
10. Purge control valve
11. Canister
12. Main pipe
13. Return pipe
14. Vapor pipe

Troubleshooting Basic Fuel System Problems

Problem	Cause	Solution
Engine cranks, but won't start (or is hard to start) when cold	• Empty fuel tank • Incorrect starting procedure • Defective fuel pump • No fuel in carburetor • Clogged fuel filter • Engine flooded • Defective choke	• Check for fuel in tank • Follow correct procedure • Check pump output • Check for fuel in the carburetor • Replace fuel filter • Wait 15 minutes; try again • Check choke plate
Engine cranks, but is hard to start (or does not start) when hot— (presence of fuel is assumed)	• Defective choke	• Check choke plate
Rough idle or engine runs rough	• Dirt or moisture in fuel • Clogged air filter • Faulty fuel pump	• Replace fuel filter • Replace air filter • Check fuel pump output
Engine stalls or hesitates on acceleration	• Dirt or moisture in the fuel • Dirty carburetor • Defective fuel pump • Incorrect float level, defective accelerator pump	• Replace fuel filter • Clean the carburetor • Check fuel pump output • Check carburetor
Poor gas mileage	• Clogged air filter • Dirty carburetor • Defective choke, faulty carburetor adjustment	• Replace air filter • Clean carburetor • Check carburetor
Engine is flooded (won't start accompanied by smell of raw fuel)	• Improperly adjusted choke or carburetor	• Wait 15 minutes and try again, without pumping gas pedal • If it won't start, check carburetor

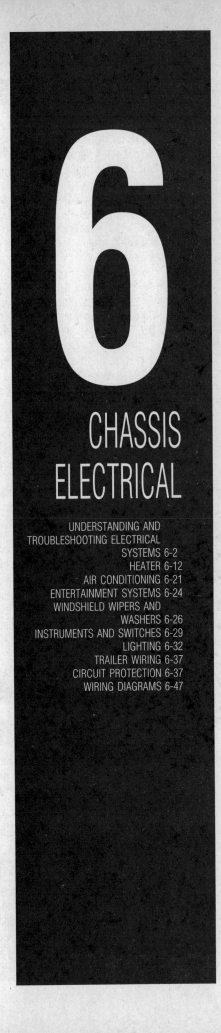

6

CHASSIS ELECTRICAL

UNDERSTANDING AND TROUBLESHOOTING ELECTRICAL SYSTEMS

Over the years import and domestic manufacturers have incorporated electronic control systems into their production lines. In fact, electronic control systems are so prevalent that all new cars and trucks built today are equipped with at least one on-board computer. These electronic components (with no moving parts) should theoretically last the life of the vehicle, provided that nothing external happens to damage the circuits or memory chips.

While it is true that electronic components should never wear out, in the real world malfunctions do occur. It is also true that any computer-based system is extremely sensitive to electrical voltages and cannot tolerate careless or haphazard testing/service procedures. An inexperienced individual can literally cause major damage looking for a minor problem by using the wrong kind of test equipment or connecting test leads/connectors with the ignition switch **ON**. When selecting test equipment, make sure the manufacturer's instructions state that the tester is compatible with whatever type of system is being serviced. Read all instructions carefully and double check all test points before installing probes or making any test connections.

The following section outlines basic diagnosis techniques for dealing with automotive electrical systems. Along with a general explanation of the various types of test equipment available to aid in servicing modern automotive systems, basic repair techniques for wiring harnesses and connectors are also given. Read the basic information before attempting any repairs or testing. This will provide the background of information necessary to avoid the most common and obvious mistakes that can cost both time and money. Although the replacement and testing procedures are simple in themselves, the systems are not, and unless one has a thorough understanding of all components and their function within a particular system, the logical test sequence these systems demand cannot be followed. Minor malfunctions can make a big difference, so it is important to know how each component affects the operation of the overall system in order to find the ultimate cause of a problem without replacing good components unnecessarily. It is not enough to use the correct test equipment; the test equipment must be used correctly.

Safety Precautions

✳✳ CAUTION

Whenever working on or around any electrical or electronic systems, always observe these general precautions to prevent the possibility of personal injury or damage to electronic components.

• Never install or remove battery cables with the key **ON** or the engine running. Jumper cables should be connected with the key **OFF** to avoid power surges that can damage electronic control units. Engines equipped with computer controlled systems should avoid both giving and getting jump starts due to the possibility of serious damage to components from arcing in the engine compartment if connections are made with the ignition **ON**.

• Always remove the battery cables before charging the battery. Never use a high output charger on an installed battery or attempt to use any type of "hot shot" (24 volt) starting aid.

• Exercise care when inserting test probes into connectors to insure good contact without damaging the connector or spreading the pins. Always probe connectors from the rear (wire) side, NOT the pin side, to avoid accidental shorting of terminals during test procedures.

• Never remove or attach wiring harness connectors with the ignition switch **ON**, especially to an electronic control unit.

• Do not drop any components during service procedures and never apply 12 volts directly to any component (like a solenoid or relay) unless instructed specifically to do so. Some component electrical windings are designed to safely handle only 4 or 5 volts and can be destroyed in seconds if 12 volts are applied directly to the connector.

• Remove the electronic control unit if the vehicle is to be placed in an environment where temperatures exceed approximately 176°F (80°C), such as a paint spray booth or when arc/gas welding near the control unit location.

Understanding Basic Electricity

Understanding the basic theory of electricity makes electrical troubleshooting much easier. Several gauges are used in electrical troubleshooting to see inside the circuit being tested. Without a basic understanding, it will be difficult to understand testing procedures.

THE WATER ANALOGY

Electricity is the flow of electrons—hypothetical particles thought to constitute the basic stuff of electricity. Many people have been taught electrical theory using an analogy with water. In a comparison with water flowing in a pipe, the electrons would be the water. As the flow of water can be measured, the flow of electricity can be measured. The unit of measurement is amperes, frequently abbreviated amps. An ammeter will measure the actual amount of current flowing in the circuit.

Just as the water pressure is measured in units such as pounds per square inch, electrical pressure is measured in volts. When a voltmeter's two probes are placed on two live portions of an electrical circuit with different electrical pressures, current will flow through the voltmeter and produce a reading which indicates the difference in electrical pressure between the two parts of the circuit.

While increasing the voltage in a circuit will increase the flow of current, the actual flow depends not only on voltage, but on the resistance of the circuit. The standard unit for measuring circuit resistance is an ohm, measured by an ohmmeter. The ohmmeter is somewhat similar to an ammeter, but incorporates its own source of power so that a standard voltage is always present.

CIRCUITS

An actual electric circuit consists of four basic parts. These are: the power source, such as a generator or battery; a hot wire, which conducts the electricity under a relatively high voltage to the component supplied by the circuit; the load, such as a lamp, motor, resistor or relay coil; and the ground wire, which carries the current back to the source under very low voltage. In such a circuit the bulk of the resistance exists between the point where the hot wire is connected to the load, and the point where the load is grounded. In an automobile, the vehicle's frame or body, which is made of steel, is used as a part of the ground circuit for many of the electrical devices.

Remember that, in electrical testing, the voltmeter is connected in parallel with the circuit being tested (without disconnecting any wires) and measures the difference in voltage between the locations of the two probes; that the ammeter is connected in series with the load (the circuit is separated at one point and the ammeter inserted so it becomes a part of the circuit); and the ohmmeter is self-powered, so that all the power in the circuit should be off and the portion of the circuit to be measured contacted at either end by one of the probes of the meter.

For any electrical system to operate, it must make a complete circuit. This simply means that the power flow from the battery must make a complete circle. When an electrical component is operating, power flows from the battery to the component, passes through the component causing it to perform it to function (such as lighting a light bulb) and then returns to the battery through the ground of the circuit. This ground is usually (but not always) the metal part of the vehicle on which the electrical component is mounted.

Perhaps the easiest way to visualize this is to think of connecting a light bulb with two wires attached to it to your vehicle's battery. The battery in your vehicle has two posts (negative and positive). If one of the two wires attached to the light bulb was attached to the negative post of the battery and the other wire was attached to the positive post of the battery, you would have a complete circuit. Current from the battery would flow out one post, through the wire attached to it and then to the light bulb, where it would pass through causing it to light. It would then leave the light bulb, travel through the other wire, and return to the other post of the battery.

AUTOMOTIVE CIRCUITS

The normal automotive circuit differs from this simple example in two ways. First, instead of having a return wire from the bulb to the battery, the light bulb return the current to the battery through the chassis of the vehicle. Since the negative battery cable is attached to the chassis and the chassis is made of electrically conductive metal, the chassis of the vehicle can serve as a ground wire to complete the circuit. Secondly, most automotive circuits contain switches to turn components on and off.

Some electrical components which require a large amount of current to operate also have a relay in their circuit. Since these circuits carry a large amount of current, the thickness of the wire in the circuit (gauge size) is also greater. If this large wire were connected from the component to the control switch on the instrument panel, and then back to the component, a voltage drop would occur in the circuit. To prevent this potential drop in voltage, an electromagnetic switch (relay) is used. The large wires in the circuit are connected from the vehicle battery to one side of the relay, and from the opposite side of the relay to the component. The relay is normally open, preventing current from passing through the circuit. An additional, smaller wire is connected from the relay to the control switch for the circuit. When the control switch is turned on, it grounds the smaller wire from the relay and completes the circuit.

SHORT CIRCUITS

If you were to disconnect the light bulb (from the previous example of a light-bulb being connected to the battery by two wires) from the wires and touch the two wires together (please take our word for this; don't try it), the result will be a shower of sparks. A similar thing happens (on a smaller scale) when the power supply wire to a component or the electrical component itself becomes grounded before the normal ground connection for the circuit. To prevent damage to the system, the fuse for the circuit blows to interrupt the circuit—protecting the components from damage. Because grounding a wire from a power source makes a complete circuit—less the required component to use the power—the phenomenon is called a short circuit. The most common causes of short circuits are: the rubber insulation on a wire breaking or rubbing through to expose the current carrying core of the wire to a metal part of the car, or a shorted switch.

Some electrical systems on the vehicle are protected by a circuit breaker which is, basically, a self-repairing fuse. When either of the described events takes place in a system which is protected by a circuit breaker, the circuit breaker opens the circuit the same way a fuse does. However, when either the short is removed from the circuit or the surge subsides, the circuit breaker resets itself and does not have to be replaced as a fuse does.

Troubleshooting

When diagnosing a specific problem, organized troubleshooting is a must. The complexity of a modern automobile demands that you approach any problem in a logical, organized manner. There are certain troubleshooting techniques that are standard:

1. Establish when the problem occurs. Does the problem appear only under certain conditions? Were there any noises, odors, or other unusual symptoms?

2. Isolate the problem area. To do this, make some simple tests and observations; then eliminate the systems that are working properly. Check for obvious problems such as broken wires, dirty connections or split/disconnected vacuum hoses. Always check the obvious before assuming something complicated is the cause.

3. Test for problems systematically to determine the cause once the problem area is isolated. Are all the components functioning properly? Is there power going to electrical switches and motors? Is there vacuum at vacuum switches and/or actuators? Is there a mechanical problem such as bent linkage or loose mounting screws? Performing careful, systematic checks will often turn up most causes on the first inspection without wasting time checking components that have little or no relationship to the problem.

4. Test all repairs after the work is done to make sure that the problem is fixed. Some causes can be traced to more than one component, so a careful verification of repair work is important in order to pick up additional malfunctions that may cause a problem to reappear or a different problem to arise. A blown fuse, for example, is a simple problem that may require more than another fuse to repair. If you don't look for a problem that caused a fuse to blow, a shorted wire (for example) may go undetected.

Experience has shown that most problems tend to be the result of a fairly simple and obvious cause, such as loose or corroded connectors or air leaks in the intake system. This makes careful inspection of components during testing essential to quick and accurate troubleshooting.

BASIC TROUBLESHOOTING THEORY

Electrical problems generally fall into one of three areas:
• The component that is not functioning is not receiving current.
• The component itself is not functioning.
• The component is not properly grounded.

Problems that fall into the first category are by far the most complicated. It is the current supply system to the component which contains all the switches, relay, fuses, etc.

The electrical system can be checked with a test light and a jumper wire. A test light is a device that looks like a pointed screwdriver with a wire attached to it. It has a light bulb in its handle. A jumper wire is a piece of insulated wire with an alligator clip attached to each end.

If a light bulb is not working, you must follow a systematic plan to determine which of the three causes is the villain.

1. Turn on the switch that controls the inoperable bulb.
2. Disconnect the power supply wire from the bulb.
3. Attach the ground wire to the test light to a good metal ground.
4. Touch the probe end of the test light to the end of the power supply wire that was disconnected from the bulb. If the bulb is receiving current, the test light will go on.

➡️**If the bulb is one which works only when the ignition key is turned on (turn signal), make sure the key is turned on.**

If the test light does not go on, then the problem is in the circuit between the battery and the bulb. As mentioned before, this includes all the switches, fuses, and relays in the system. Turn to a wiring diagram and find the bulb on the diagram. Follow the wire that runs back to the battery. The problem is an open circuit between the battery and the bulb. If the fuse is blown and, when replaced, immediately blows again, there is a short circuit in the system which must be located and repaired. If there is a switch in the system, bypass it with a jumper wire. This is done by connecting one end of the jumper wire to the power supply wire into the switch and the other end of the jumper wire to the wire coming out of the switch. If the test light illuminates with the jumper wire installed, the switch or whatever was bypassed is defective.

➡️**Never substitute the jumper wire for the bulb, as the bulb is the component required to use the power from the power source.**

5. If the bulb in the test light goes on, then the current is getting to the bulb that is not working in the car. This eliminates the first of the three possible causes. Connect the power supply wire and connect a jumper wire from the bulb to a good metal ground. Do this with the switch which controls the bulb works with jumper wire installed, then it has a bad ground. This is usually caused by the metal area on which the bulb mounts to the vehicle being coated with some type of foreign matter.

6. If neither test located the source of the trouble, then the light bulb itself is defective.

The above test procedure can be applied to any of the components of the chassis electrical system by substituting the component that is not working for the light bulb. Remember that for any electrical system to work, all connections must be clean and tight.

TEST EQUIPMENT

➡️**Pinpointing the exact cause of trouble in an electrical system can sometimes only be accomplished by the use of special test equipment. The following describes different types of commonly used test equipment and explains how to use them in diagnosis. In addition to the information covered below, the tool manufacturer's instructions booklet (provided with the tester) should be read and clearly understood before attempting any test procedures.**

Jumper Wires

Jumper wires are simple, yet extremely valuable, pieces of test equipment. They are basically test wires which are used to bypass sections of a circuit. The simplest type of jumper wire is a length of multi-strand wire with an alligator clip at each end. Jumper wires are usually fabricated from lengths of standard automotive wire and whatever type of connector (alligator clip, spade connector or pin connector) that is required for the particular vehicle being tested. The well equipped tool box will have several different styles of jumper wires in several different lengths. Some jumper wires are made with three or more terminals coming from a common splice for special purpose testing. In cramped, hard-to-reach areas it is advisable to have insulated boots over the jumper wire terminals in order to prevent accidental grounding, sparks, and possible fire, especially when testing fuel system components.

Jumper wires are used primarily to locate open electrical circuits, on either the ground (−) side of the circuit or on the hot (+) side. If an electrical component fails to operate, connect the jumper wire between the component and a good ground. If the component operates only with the jumper installed, the ground circuit is open. If the ground circuit is good, but the component does not operate, the circuit between the power feed and component may be open. By moving the jumper wire successively back from the lamp toward the power source, you can isolate the area of the circuit where the open is located. When the component stops functioning, or the power is cut off, the open is in the segment of wire between the jumper and the point previously tested. You can sometimes connect the jumper wire directly from the

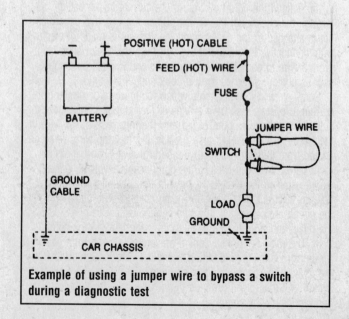

Example of using a jumper wire to bypass a switch during a diagnostic test

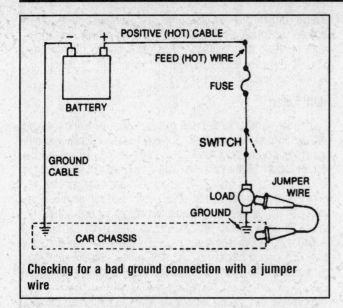

Checking for a bad ground connection with a jumper wire

Like the jumper wire, the 12 volt test light is used to isolate opens in circuits. But, whereas the jumper wire is used to bypass the open to operate the load, the 12 volt test light is used to locate the presence of voltage in a circuit. If the test light glows, you know that there is power up to that point; if the 12 volt test light does not glow when its probe is inserted into the wire or connector, you know that there is an open circuit (no power). Move the test light in successive steps back toward the power source until the light in the handle does glow. When it glows, the open is between the probe and point which was probed previously.

➡ **The test light does not detect that 12 volts (or any particular amount of voltage) is present; it only detects that some voltage is present. It is advisable before using the test light to touch its terminals across the battery posts to make sure the light is operating properly.**

Self-Powered Test Lights

The self-powered test light usually contains a 1.5 volt penlight battery. One type of self-powered test light is similar in design to the 12 volt unit. This type has both the battery and the light in the handle, along with a pick-type probe tip. The second type has the light toward the open tip, so that the light illuminates the contact point. The self-powered test light is a dual purpose piece of test equipment. It can be used to test for either open or short circuits when power is isolated from the circuit (continuity test). A powered test light should not be used on any computer controlled system or component unless specifically instructed to do so. Many engine sensors can be destroyed by even this small amount of voltage applied directly to the terminals.

Voltmeters

A voltmeter is used to measure voltage at any point in a circuit, or to measure the voltage drop across any part of a circuit. It can also be used to check continuity in a wire or circuit by indicating current flow from one end to the other. Analog voltmeters usually have various scales on the meter dial and a selector switch to allow the selection of different voltages. The voltmeter has a positive and a negative lead. To avoid damage to the meter, always connect the negative lead to the negative (−) side of the circuit (to ground or nearest the ground side of the circuit) and connect the positive lead to the positive (+) side of the circuit (to the power source or the nearest power source). Note that the negative voltmeter lead will always be black and that the positive voltmeter will always be some color other than black (usually red).

Depending on how the voltmeter is connected into the circuit, it has several uses. A voltmeter can be connected either in parallel or in series with a circuit and it has a very high resistance to current flow. When connected in parallel, only a small amount of current will flow through the voltmeter current path; the rest will flow through the normal circuit current path and the circuit will work normally. When the voltmeter is connected in series with a circuit, only a small amount of current can flow through the circuit. The circuit will not work properly, but the voltmeter reading will show if the circuit is complete or not.

Ohmmeters

The ohmmeter is designed to read resistance (which is measured in ohms or Ω) in a circuit or component. Although there are several different styles of ohmmeters, all analog meters will usually have a selector switch which permits the measurement of

battery to the hot terminal of the component, but first make sure the component uses 12 volts in operation. Some electrical components, such as fuel injectors, are designed to operate on about 4 volts and running 12 volts directly to the injector terminals can cause damage.

By inserting an in-line fuse holder between a set of test leads, a fused jumper wire can be used for bypassing open circuits. Use a 5 amp fuse to provide protection against voltage spikes. When in doubt, use a voltmeter to check the voltage input to the component and measure how much voltage is normally being applied.

✳✳ CAUTION

Never use jumpers made from wire that is of lighter gauge than that which is used in the circuit under test. If the jumper wire is of too small a gauge, it may overheat and possibly melt. Never use jumpers to bypass high resistance loads in a circuit. Bypassing resistances, in effect, creates a short circuit. This may, in turn, cause damage and fire. Jumper wires should only be used to bypass lengths of wire.

Unpowered Test Lights

The 12 volt test light is used to check circuits and components while electrical current is flowing through them. It is used for voltage and ground tests. Twelve volt test lights come in different styles but all have three main parts; a ground clip, a probe, and a light. The most commonly used 12 volt test lights have pick-type probes. To use a 12 volt test light, connect the ground clip to a good ground and probe wherever necessary with the pick. The pick should be sharp so that it can be probed into tight spaces.

✳✳ CAUTION

Do not use a test light to probe electronic ignition spark plug or coil wires. Never use a pick-type test light to probe wiring on computer controlled systems unless specifically instructed to do so. Any wire insulation that is pierced by the test light probe should be taped and sealed with silicone after testing.

different ranges of resistance (usually the selector switch allows the multiplication of the meter reading by 10, 100, 1000, and 10,000). A calibration knob allows the meter to be set at zero for accurate measurement. Since all ohmmeters are powered by an internal battery, the ohmmeter can be used as a self-powered test light. When the ohmmeter is connected, current from the ohmmeter flows through the circuit or component being tested. Since the ohmmeter's internal resistance and voltage are known values, the amount of current flow through the meter depends on the resistance of the circuit or component being tested.

The ohmmeter can be used to perform a continuity test for opens or shorts (either by observation of the meter needle or as a self-powered test light), and to read actual resistance in a circuit. It should be noted that the ohmmeter is used to check the resistance of a component or wire while there is no voltage applied to the circuit. Current flow from an outside voltage source (such as the vehicle battery) can damage the ohmmeter, so the circuit or component should be isolated from the vehicle electrical system before any testing is done. Since the ohmmeter uses its own voltage source, either lead can be connected to any test point.

➡**When checking diodes or other solid state components, the ohmmeter leads can only be connected one way in order to measure current flow in a single direction. Make sure the positive (+) and negative (−) terminal connections are as described in the test procedures to verify the one-way diode operation.**

In using the meter for making continuity checks, do not be concerned with the actual resistance readings. Zero resistance, or any ohm reading, indicates continuity in the circuit. Infinite resistance indicates an open in the circuit. A high resistance reading where there should be none indicates a problem in the circuit. Checks for short circuits are made in the same manner as checks for open circuits except that the circuit must be isolated from both power and normal ground. Infinite resistance indicates no continuity to ground, while zero resistance indicates a dead short to ground.

Ammeters

An ammeter measures the amount of current flowing through a circuit in units called amperes or amps. Amperes are units of electron flow which indicate how fast the electrons are flowing through the circuit. Since Ohms Law dictates that current flow in a circuit is equal to the circuit voltage divided by the total circuit resistance, increasing voltage also increases the current level (amps). Likewise, any decrease in resistance will increase the amount of amps in a circuit. At normal operating voltage, most circuits have a characteristic amount of amperes, called "current draw" which can be measured using an ammeter. By referring to a specified current draw rating, measuring the amperes, and comparing the two values, one can determine what is happening within the circuit to aid in diagnosis. An open circuit, for example, will not allow any current to flow so the ammeter reading will be zero. More current flows through a heavily loaded circuit or when the charging system is operating.

An ammeter is always connected in series with the circuit being tested. All of the current that normally flows through the circuit must also flow through the ammeter; if there is any other path for the current to follow, the ammeter reading will not be accurate. The ammeter itself has very little resistance to current flow and therefore will not affect the circuit, but it will measure current draw only when the circuit is closed and electricity is flowing. Ex-

cessive current draw can blow fuses and drain the battery, while a reduced current draw can cause motors to run slowly, lights to dim and other components to not operate properly. The ammeter can help diagnose these conditions by locating the cause of the high or low reading.

Multimeters

Different combinations of test meters can be built into a single unit designed for specific tests. Some of the more common combination test devices are known as Volt/Amp testers, Tach/Dwell meters, or Digital Multimeters. The Volt/Amp tester is used for charging system, starting system or battery tests and consists of a voltmeter, an ammeter and a variable resistance carbon pile. The voltmeter will usually have at least two ranges for use with 6, 12 and/or 24 volt systems. The ammeter also has more than one range for testing various levels of battery loads and starter current draw. The carbon pile can be adjusted to offer different amounts of resistance. The Volt/Amp tester has heavy leads to carry large amounts of current and many later models have an inductive ammeter pickup that clamps around the wire to simplify test connections. On some models, the ammeter also has a zero-center scale to allow testing of charging and starting systems without switching leads or polarity. A digital multimeter is a voltmeter, ammeter and ohmmeter combined in an instrument which gives a digital readout. These are often used when testing solid state circuits because of their high input impedance (usually 10 megohms or more).

The tach/dwell meter that combines a tachometer and a dwell (cam angle) meter is a specialized kind of voltmeter. The tachometer scale is marked to show engine speed in rpm and the dwell scale is marked to show degrees of distributor shaft rotation. In most electronic ignition systems, dwell is determined by the control unit, but the dwell meter can also be used to check the duty cycle (operation) of some electronic engine control systems. Some tach/dwell meters are powered by an internal battery, while others take their power from the vehicle battery in use. The battery powered testers usually require calibration (much like an ohmmeter) before testing.

TESTING

Open Circuits

To use the self-powered test light or a multimeter to check for open circuits, first isolate the circuit from the vehicle's 12 volt power source by disconnecting the battery or wiring harness connector. Connect the test light or ohmmeter ground clip to a good ground and probe sections of the circuit sequentially with the test light. (start from either end of the circuit). If the light is out/or there is infinite resistance, the open is between the probe and the circuit ground. If the light is on/or the meter shows continuity, the open is between the probe and end of the circuit toward the power source.

Short Circuits

By isolating the circuit both from power and from ground, and using a self-powered test light or multimeter, you can check for shorts to ground in the circuit. Isolate the circuit from power and ground. Connect the test light or ohmmeter ground clip to a good ground and probe any easy-to-reach test point in the circuit. If the light comes on or there is continuity, there is a short somewhere in the circuit. To isolate the short, probe a test point at either end of the isolated circuit (the light should be on/there should be continuity). Leave the test light probe engaged and open connectors, switches, remove parts, etc., sequentially, until the light goes out/continuity is broken. When the light goes out, the short is between the last circuit component opened and the previous circuit opened.

➡**The battery in the test light and does not provide much current. A weak battery may not provide enough power to illuminate the test light even when a complete circuit is made (especially if there are high resistances in the circuit). Always make sure that the test battery is strong. To check the battery, briefly touch the ground clip to the probe; if the light glows brightly the battery is strong enough for testing. Never use a self-powered test light to perform checks for opens or shorts when power is applied to the electrical system under test. The 12 volt vehicle power will quickly burn out the light bulb in the test light.**

Available Voltage Measurement

Set the voltmeter selector switch to the 20V position and connect the meter negative lead to the negative post of the battery. Connect the positive meter lead to the positive post of the battery and turn the ignition switch **ON** to provide a load. Read the voltage on the meter or digital display. A well charged battery should register over 12 volts. If the meter reads below 11.5 volts, the battery power may be insufficient to operate the electrical system properly. This test determines voltage available from the battery and should be the first step in any electrical trouble diagnosis procedure. Many electrical problems, especially on computer controlled systems, can be caused by a low state of charge in the battery. Excessive corrosion at the battery cable terminals can cause a poor contact that will prevent proper charging and full battery current flow.

Normal battery voltage is 12 volts when fully charged. When the battery is supplying current to one or more circuits it is said to be "under load." When everything is off the electrical system is under a "no-load" condition. A fully charged battery may show about 12.5 volts at no load; will drop to 12 volts under medium load; and will drop even lower under heavy load. If the battery is partially discharged the voltage decrease under heavy load may be excessive, even though the battery shows 12 volts or more at no load. When allowed to discharge further, the battery's available voltage under load will decrease more severely. For this reason, it is important that the battery be fully charged during all testing procedures to avoid errors in diagnosis and incorrect test results.

Voltage Drop

When current flows through a resistance, the voltage beyond the resistance is reduced (the larger the current, the greater the reduction in voltage). When no current is flowing, there is no voltage drop because there is no current flow. All points in the circuit which are connected to the power source are at the same voltage as the power source. The total voltage drop always equals the total source voltage. In a long circuit with many connectors, a series of small, unwanted voltage drops due to corrosion at the connectors can add up to a total loss of voltage which impairs the operation of the normal loads in the circuit. The maximum allowable voltage drop under load is critical, especially if there is more than one high resistance problem in a circuit because all voltage drops are cumulative. A small drop is normal due to the resistance of the conductors.

INDIRECT COMPUTATION OF VOLTAGE DROPS

1. Set the voltmeter selector switch to the 20 volt position.
2. Connect the meter negative lead to a good ground.
3. While operating the circuit, probe all loads in the circuit with the positive meter lead and observe the voltage readings. A drop should be noticed after the first load. But, there should be little or no voltage drop before the first load.

DIRECT MEASUREMENT OF VOLTAGE DROPS

1. Set the voltmeter switch to the 20 volt position.
2. Connect the voltmeter negative lead to the ground side of the load to be measured.
3. Connect the positive lead to the positive side of the resistance or load to be measured.
4. Read the voltage drop directly on the 20 volt scale.

Too high a voltage indicates too high a resistance. If, for example, a blower motor runs too slowly, you can determine if perhaps there is too high a resistance in the resistor pack. By taking voltage drop readings in all parts of the circuit, you can isolate the problem. Too low a voltage drop indicates too low a resistance. Take the blower motor for example again. If a blower motor runs too fast in the MED and/or LOW position, the problem might be isolated in the resistor pack by taking voltage drop readings in all parts of the circuit to locate a possibly shorted resistor.

HIGH RESISTANCE TESTING

1. Set the voltmeter selector switch to the 4 volt position.
2. Connect the voltmeter positive lead to the positive post of the battery.
3. Turn on the headlights and heater blower to provide a load.
4. Probe various points in the circuit with the negative voltmeter lead.
5. Read the voltage drop on the 4 volt scale. Some average maximum allowable voltage drops are:
- FUSE PANEL: 0.7 volts
- IGNITION SWITCH: 0.5 volts
- HEADLIGHT SWITCH: 0.7 volts
- IGNITION COIL (+): 0.5 volts
- ANY OTHER LOAD: 1.3 volts

➡**Voltage drops are all measured while a load is operating; without current flow, there will be no voltage drop.**

Resistance Measurement

The batteries in an ohmmeter will weaken with age and temperature, so the ohmmeter must be calibrated or "zeroed" before taking measurements. To zero the meter, place the selector switch in its lowest range and touch the two ohmmeter leads together. Turn the calibration knob until the meter needle is exactly on zero.

➡**All analog (needle) type ohmmeters must be zeroed before use, but some digital ohmmeter models are automatically calibrated when the switch is turned on. Self-calibrating digital ohmmeters do not have an adjusting knob, but its a good idea to check for a zero readout before use by touching the leads together. All computer controlled systems require the use of a digital ohmmeter with at least 10 megohms impedance for testing. Before any test procedures are attempted, make sure the ohmmeter used is compatible with the electrical system or damage to the on-board computer could result.**

To measure resistance, first isolate the circuit from the vehicle power source by disconnecting the battery cables or the harness connector. Make sure the key is **OFF** when disconnecting any components or the battery. Where necessary, also isolate at least one side of the circuit to be checked in order to avoid reading parallel resistances. Parallel circuit resistances will always give a lower reading than the actual resistance of either of the branches. When measuring the resistance of parallel circuits, the total resistance will always be lower than the smallest resistance in the circuit. Connect the meter leads to both sides of the circuit (wire or component) and read the actual measured ohms on the meter scale. Make sure the selector switch is set to the proper ohm scale for the circuit being tested to avoid misreading the ohmmeter test value.

✳✳ WARNING

Never use an ohmmeter with power applied to the circuit. Like the self-powered test light, the ohmmeter is designed to operate on its own power supply. The normal 12 volt automotive electrical system current could damage the meter!

Wiring Harnesses

The average automobile contains about ½ mile of wiring, with hundreds of individual connections. To protect the many wires from damage and to keep them from becoming a confusing tangle, they are organized into bundles, enclosed in plastic or taped together and called wiring harnesses. Different harnesses serve different parts of the vehicle. Individual wires are color coded to help trace them through a harness where sections are hidden from view.

Automotive wiring or circuit conductors can be in any one of three forms:

1. Single strand wire
2. Multi-strand wire
3. Printed circuitry

Single strand wire has a solid metal core and is usually used inside such components as alternators, motors, relays and other devices. Multi-strand wire has a core made of many small strands of wire twisted together into a single conductor. Most of the wiring in an automotive electrical system is made up of multi-strand wire, either as a single conductor or grouped together in a harness. All wiring is color coded on the insulator, either as a solid color or as a colored wire with an identification stripe. A printed circuit is a thin film of copper or other conductor that is printed on an insulator backing. Occasionally, a printed circuit is sandwiched between two sheets of plastic for more protection and flexibility. A complete printed circuit, consisting of conductors, insulating material and connectors for lamps or other components is called a printed circuit board. Printed circuitry is used in place of individual wires or harnesses in places where space is limited, such as behind instrument panels.

Since automotive electrical systems are very sensitive to changes in resistance, the selection of properly sized wires is critical when systems are repaired. A loose or corroded connection or a replacement wire that is too small for the circuit will add extra resistance and an additional voltage drop to the circuit. A ten per-cent voltage drop can result in slow or erratic motor operation, for example, even though the circuit is complete. The wire gauge number is an expression of the cross-section area of the conductor. The most common system for expressing wire size is the American Wire Gauge (AWG) system.

Gauge numbers are assigned to conductors of various cross-section areas. As gauge number increases, area decreases and the conductor becomes smaller. A 5 gauge conductor is smaller than a 1 gauge conductor and a 10 gauge is smaller than a 5 gauge. As the cross-section area of a conductor decreases, resistance increases and so does the gauge number. A conductor with a higher gauge number will carry less current than a conductor with a lower gauge number.

➡**Gauge wire size refers to the size of the conductor, not the size of the complete wire. It is possible to have two wires of the same gauge with different diameters because one may have thicker insulation than the other.**

12 volt automotive electrical systems generally use 10, 12, 14, 16 and 18 gauge wire. Main power distribution circuits and larger accessories usually use 10 and 12 gauge wire. Battery cables are usually 4 or 6 gauge, although 1 and 2 gauge wires are occasionally used. Wire length must also be considered when making repairs to a circuit. As conductor length increases, so does resistance. An 18 gauge wire, for example, can carry a 10 amp load for 10 feet without excessive voltage drop; however if a 15 foot wire is required for the same 10 amp load, it must be a 16 gauge wire.

An electrical schematic shows the electrical current paths when a circuit is operating properly. It is essential to understand how a circuit works before trying to figure out why it doesn't. Schematics break the entire electrical system down into individual circuits and show only one particular circuit. In a schematic, no attempt is made to represent wiring and components as they physically appear on the vehicle; switches and other components are shown as simply as possible. Face views of harness connectors show the cavity or terminal locations in all multi-pin connectors to help locate test points.

If you need to backprobe a connector while it is on the component, the order of the terminals must be mentally reversed. The wire color code can help in this situation, as well as a keyway, lock tab or other reference mark.

WIRING REPAIR

Soldering is a quick, efficient method of joining metals permanently. Everyone who has the occasion to make wiring repairs should know how to solder. Electrical connections that are soldered are far less likely to come apart and will conduct electricity much better than connections that are only "pig-tailed" together. The most popular (and preferred) method of soldering is with an electrical soldering gun. Soldering irons are available in many sizes and wattage ratings. Irons with higher wattage ratings deliver higher temperatures and recover lost heat faster. A small soldering iron rated for no more than 50 watts is recommended, especially on electrical systems where excess heat can damage the components being soldered.

There are three ingredients necessary for successful soldering;

proper flux, good solder and sufficient heat. A soldering flux is necessary to clean the metal of tarnish, prepare it for soldering and to enable the solder to spread into tiny crevices. When soldering, always use a rosin core solder which is non-corrosive and will not attract moisture once the job is finished. Other types of flux (acid core) will leave a residue that will attract moisture and cause the wires to corrode. Tin is a unique metal with a low melting point. In a molten state, it dissolves and alloys easily with many metals. Solder is made by mixing tin with lead. The most common proportions are 40/60, 50/50 and 60/40, with the percentage of tin listed first. Low priced solders usually contain less tin, making them very difficult for a beginner to use because more heat is required to melt the solder. A common solder is 40/60 which is well suited for all-around general use, but 60/40 melts easier and is preferred for electrical work.

Soldering Techniques

Successful soldering requires that the metals to be joined be heated to a temperature that will melt the solder, usually 360–460°F (182–238°C). Contrary to popular belief, the purpose of the soldering iron is not to melt the solder itself, but to heat the parts being soldered to a temperature high enough to melt the solder when it is touched to the work. Melting flux-cored solder on the soldering iron will usually destroy the effectiveness of the flux.

➡**Soldering tips are made of copper for good heat conductivity, but must be "tinned" regularly for quick transference of heat to the project and to prevent the solder from sticking to the iron. To "tin" the iron, simply heat it and touch the flux-cored solder to the tip; the solder will flow over the hot tip. Wipe the excess off with a clean rag, but be careful as the iron will be hot.**

After some use, the tip may become pitted. If so, simply dress the tip smooth with a smooth file and "tin" the tip again. Flux-cored solder will remove oxides but rust, bits of insulation and oil or grease must be removed with a wire brush or emery cloth. For maximum strength in soldered parts, the joint must start off clean and tight. Weak joints will result in gaps too wide for the solder to bridge.

If a separate soldering flux is used, it should be brushed or swabbed on only those areas that are to be soldered. Most solders contain a core of flux and separate fluxing is unnecessary. Hold the work to be soldered firmly. It is best to solder on a wooden board, because a metal vise will only rob the piece to be soldered of heat and make it difficult to melt the solder. Hold the soldering tip with the broadest face against the work to be soldered. Apply solder under the tip close to the work, using enough solder to give a heavy film between the iron and the piece being soldered, while moving slowly and making sure the solder melts properly. Keep the work level or the solder will run to the lowest part and favor the thicker parts, because these require more heat to melt the solder. If the soldering tip overheats (the solder coating on the face of the tip burns up), it should be retinned. Once the soldering is completed, let the soldered joint stand until cool. Tape and seal all soldered wire splices after the repair has cooled.

Wire Harness Connectors

Most connectors in the engine compartment or that are otherwise exposed to the elements are protected against moisture and dirt which could create oxidation and deposits on the terminals.

These special connectors are weather-proof. All repairs require the use of a special terminal and the tool required to service it. This tool is used to remove the pin and sleeve terminals. If removal is attempted with an ordinary pick, there is a good chance that the terminal will be bent or deformed. Unlike standard blade type terminals, these weather-proof terminals cannot be straightened once they are bent. Make certain that the connectors are properly seated and all of the sealing rings are in place when connecting leads. On some models, a hinge-type flap provides a backup or secondary locking feature for the terminals. Most secondary locks are used to improve connector reliability by retaining the terminals if the small terminal lock tangs are not positioned properly.

Molded-on connectors require complete replacement of the connection. This means splicing a new connector assembly into the harness. All splices should be soldered to insure proper contact. Use care when probing the connections or replacing terminals in them as it is possible to short between opposite terminals. If this happens to the wrong terminal pair, it is possible to damage certain components. Always use jumper wires between connectors for circuit checking and never probe through weatherproof seals.

Open circuits are often difficult to locate by sight because corrosion or terminal misalignment are hidden by the connectors. Merely wiggling a connector on a sensor or in the wiring harness may correct the open circuit condition. This should always be considered when an open circuit or a failed sensor is indicated. Intermittent problems may also be caused by oxidized or loose connections. When using a circuit tester for diagnosis, always probe connections from the wire side. Be careful not to damage sealed connectors with test probes.

All wiring harnesses should be replaced with identical parts, using the same gauge wire and connectors. When signal wires are spliced into a harness, use wire with high temperature insulation only. It is seldom necessary to replace a complete harness. If replacement is necessary, pay close attention to insure proper harness routing. Secure the harness with suitable plastic wire clamps to prevent vibrations from causing the harness to wear in spots or contact any hot components.

➡**Weatherproof connectors cannot be replaced with standard connectors. Instructions are provided with replacement connector and terminal packages. Some wire harnesses have mounting indicators (usually pieces of colored tape) to mark where the harness is to be secured.**

In making wiring repairs, its important that you always replace damaged wires with wiring of the same gauge as the wire being replaced. The heavier the wire, the smaller the gauge number. Wires are color-coded to aid in identification and whenever possible the same color coded wire should be used for replacement. A wire stripping and crimping tool is necessary to install solderless terminal connectors. Test all crimps by pulling on the wires; it should not be possible to pull the wires out of a good crimp.

Wires which are open, exposed or otherwise damaged are repaired by simple splicing. Where possible, if the wiring harness is accessible and the damaged place in the wire can be located, it is best to open the harness and check for all possible damage. In an inaccessible harness, the wire must be bypassed with a new insert, usually taped to the outside of the old harness.

When replacing fusible links, be sure to use fusible link wire, NOT ordinary automotive wire. Make sure the fusible segment is of the same gauge and construction as the one being replaced and double the stripped end when crimping the terminal connector for a good contact. The melted (open) fusible link segment of the wiring harness should be cut off as close to the harness as possible, then a new segment spliced in as described. In the case of a damaged fusible link that feeds two harness wires, the harness connections should be replaced with two fusible link wires so that each circuit will have its own separate protection.

➡ **Most of the problems caused in the wiring harness are due to bad ground connections. Always check all vehicle ground connections for corrosion or looseness before performing any power feed checks to eliminate the chance of a bad ground affecting the circuit.**

Hard-Shell Connectors

Unlike molded connectors, the terminal contacts in hard-shell connectors can be replaced. Weatherproof hard-shell connectors with the leads molded into the shell have non-replaceable terminal ends. Replacement usually involves the use of a special terminal removal tool that depresses the locking tangs (barbs) on the connector terminal and allows the connector to be removed from the rear of the shell. The connector shell should be replaced if it shows any evidence of burning, melting, cracks, or breaks. Replace individual terminals that are burnt, corroded, distorted or loose.

➡ **The insulation crimp must be tight to prevent the insulation from sliding back on the wire when the wire is pulled. The insulation must be visibly compressed under the crimp tabs, and the ends of the crimp should be turned in for a firm grip on the insulation.**

The wire crimp must be made with all wire strands inside the crimp. The terminal must be fully compressed on the wire strands with the ends of the crimp tabs turned in to make a firm grip on the wire. Check all connections with an ohmmeter to insure a good contact. There should be no measurable resistance between the wire and the terminal when connected.

Fusible Links

The fuse link is a short length of special, Hypalon (high temperature) insulated wire, integral with the engine compartment wiring harness and should not be confused with standard wire. It is several wire gauges smaller than the circuit which it protects. Under no circumstances should a fuse link replacement repair be made using a length of standard wire cut from bulk stock or from another wiring harness.

To repair any blown fuse link use the following procedure:
1. Determine which circuit is damaged, its location and the cause of the open fuse link. If the damaged fuse link is one of three fed by a common No. 10 or 12 gauge feed wire, determine the specific affected circuit.
2. Disconnect the negative battery cable.
3. Cut the damaged fuse link from the wiring harness and discard it. If the fuse link is one of three circuits fed by a single feed wire, cut it out of the harness at each splice end and discard it.
4. Identify and procure the proper fuse link with butt connectors for attaching the fuse link to the harness.

➡ **Heat shrink tubing must be slipped over the wire before crimping and soldering the connection.**

5. To repair any fuse link in a 3-link group with one feed:
   a. After cutting the open link out of the harness, cut each of the remaining undamaged fuse links close to the feed wire weld.
   b. Strip approximately ½ in. (13mm) of insulation from the detached ends of the two good fuse links. Insert two wire ends into one end of a butt connector, then carefully push one stripped end of the replacement fuse link into the same end of the butt connector and crimp all three firmly together.

➡ **Care must be taken when fitting the three fuse links into the butt connector as the internal diameter is a snug fit for three wires. Make sure to use a proper crimping tool. Pliers, side cutters, etc. will not apply the proper crimp to retain the wires and withstand a pull test.**

   c. After crimping the butt connector to the three fuse links, cut the weld portion from the feed wire and strip approximately ½ in. (13mm) of insulation from the cut end. Insert the stripped end into the open end of the butt connector and crimp very firmly.
   d. To attach the remaining end of the replacement fuse link, strip approximately ½ in. (13mm) of insulation from the wire end of the circuit from which the blown fuse link was removed, and firmly crimp a butt connector or equivalent to the stripped wire. Then, insert the end of the replacement link into the other end of the butt connector and crimp firmly.
   e. Using rosin core solder with a consistency of 60 percent tin and 40 percent lead, solder the connectors and the wires at the repairs then insulate with electrical tape or heat shrink tubing.
6. To replace any fuse link on a single circuit in a harness, cut out the damaged portion, strip approximately ½ in. (13mm) of insulation from the two wire ends and attach the appropriate replacement fuse link to the stripped wire ends with two proper size butt connectors. Solder the connectors and wires, then insulate.
7. To repair any fuse link which has an eyelet terminal on one end such as the charging circuit, cut off the open fuse link behind the weld, strip approximately ½ in. (13mm) of insulation from the cut end and attach the appropriate new eyelet fuse link to the cut stripped wire with an appropriate size butt connector. Solder the connectors and wires at the repair, then insulate.
8. Connect the negative battery cable to the battery and test the system for proper operation.

➡ **Do not mistake a resistor wire for a fuse link. The resistor wire is generally longer and has print stating, "Resistor-don't cut or splice."**

When attaching a single No. 16, 17, 18 or 20 gauge fuse link to a heavy gauge wire, always double the stripped wire end of the fuse link before inserting and crimping it into the butt connector for positive wire retention.

Add-On Electrical Equipment

The electrical system in your vehicle is designed to perform under reasonable operating conditions without interference between

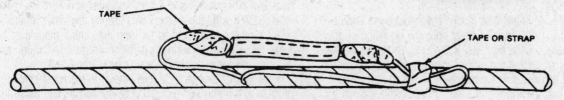

REMOVE EXISTING VINYL TUBE SHIELDING
REINSTALL OVER FUSE LINK BEFORE CRIMPING
FUSE LINK TO WIRE ENDS

TAPE

TAPE OR STRAP

TYPICAL REPAIR USING THE SPECIAL #17 GA. (9.00" LONG-YELLOW) FUSE LINK REQUIRED FOR THE AIR/COND.
CIRCUITS (2) #687E and #261A LOCATED IN THE ENGINE COMPARTMENT

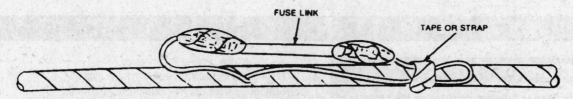

FUSE LINK

TAPE OR STRAP

TYPICAL REPAIR FOR ANY IN-LINE FUSE LINK USING THE SPECIFIED GAUGE FUSE LINK FOR THE SPECIFIC CIRCUIT

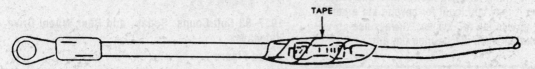

TAPE

TYPICAL REPAIR USING THE EYELET TERMINAL FUSE LINK OF THE SPECIFIED GAUGE FOR ATTACHMENT TO A CIRCUIT WIRE END

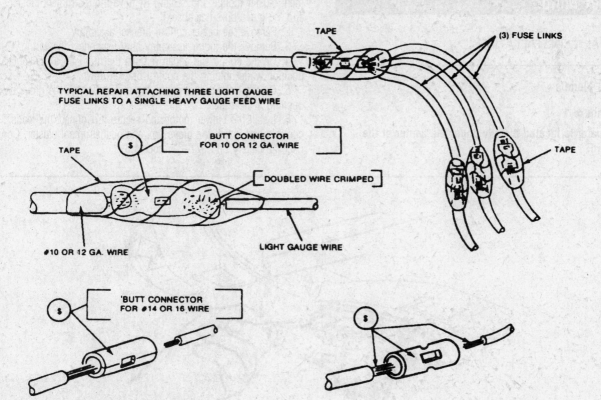

TAPE

(3) FUSE LINKS

TYPICAL REPAIR ATTACHING THREE LIGHT GAUGE
FUSE LINKS TO A SINGLE HEAVY GAUGE FEED WIRE

TAPE

BUTT CONNECTOR
FOR 10 OR 12 GA. WIRE

DOUBLED WIRE CRIMPED

#10 OR 12 GA. WIRE

LIGHT GAUGE WIRE

TAPE

BUTT CONNECTOR
FOR #14 OR 16 WIRE

FUSIBLE LINK REPAIR PROCEDURE

**General fusible link repair—never replace a fusible link with regular wire or a fusible link rated at a higher amperage
than the one being replaced**

components. Before any additional electrical equipment is installed, it is recommended that you consult your dealer or a reputable repair facility that is familiar with the vehicle and its systems.

If the vehicle is equipped with mobile radio equipment and/or mobile telephone, it may have an effect upon the operation of any on-board computer control modules. Radio Frequency Interference (RFI) from the communications system can be picked up by the vehicle's wiring harnesses and conducted into the control module, giving it the wrong messages at the wrong time. Although well shielded against RFI, the computer should be further protected by taking the following measures:

• Install the antenna as far as possible from the control module. For instance, if the module is located behind the center console area, then the antenna should be mounted at the rear of the vehicle.

• Keep the antenna wiring a minimum of eight inches away from any wiring running to control modules and from the module itself. NEVER wind the antenna wire around any other wiring.

• Mount the equipment as far from the control module as possible. Be very careful during installation not to drill through any wires or short a wire harness with a mounting screw.

• Insure that the electrical feed wire(s) to the equipment are properly and tightly connected. Loose connectors can cause interference.

• Make certain that the equipment is properly grounded to the vehicle. Poor grounding can damage expensive equipment.

HEATER

✳✳ CAUTION

Please refer to Section 1 before discharging the compressor or disconnecting air conditioning lines. Damage to the air conditioning system or personal injury could result. Consult your local laws concerning refrigerant discharge and recycling. In many areas it may be illegal for anyone but a certified technician to service the A/C system. Always use an approved recovery station when discharging the air conditioning.

Blower Motor

REMOVAL & INSTALLATION

1971–76 Models

▶ See Figure 1

➡The heater is located directly under the center of the dashboard.

1. Disconnect the negative battery cable.
2. Unplug the two electrical leads from the motor.
3. Remove the three retaining screws and remove the motor.
4. Install the motor and secure it with the mounting screws. Connect the wiring and battery cable.

1977–83 Colt Coupe, Sedan, and Rear Wheel Drive Hatchback

▶ See Figure 2

1. Disconnect the negative battery cable. Remove the instrument cluster (coupe and sedan). Remove the instrument cluster and the glove box (hatchback).
2. Remove the heater control bracket assembly.
3. Remove the motor assembly and disconnect the wiring.
4. On the coupe and sedan remove the motor in a horizontal position while holding the control bracket down.
5. On the Hatchback, remove the motor through the glove box opening, if necessary.
6. Install the blower motor and secure it. Connect the leads, controls and install the glove box and/or instrument cluster. Connect the battery on 1977–81 models.

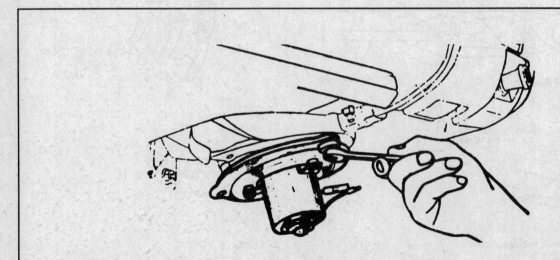

Fig. 1 The heater blower motor unbolts from the heater unit

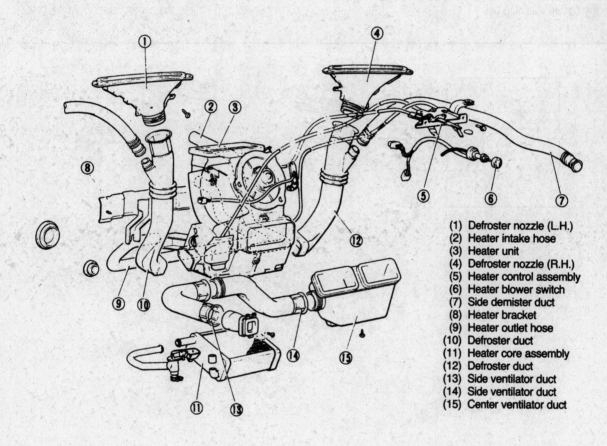

(1) Defroster nozzle (L.H.)
(2) Heater intake hose
(3) Heater unit
(4) Defroster nozzle (R.H.)
(5) Heater control assembly
(6) Heater blower switch
(7) Side demister duct
(8) Heater bracket
(9) Heater outlet hose
(10) Defroster duct
(11) Heater core assembly
(12) Defroster duct
(13) Side ventilator duct
(14) Side ventilator duct
(15) Center ventilator duct

Fig. 2 Exploded view of the heater unit—1979–82 Colt

Station Wagon

▶ **See Figure 3**

1. Disconnect the negative battery cable. Remove the instrument cluster and the meter cluster.

2. Disconnect the wiring to the motor.

3. Remove the motor assembly.

4. Install the blower motor and connect the wiring. Install the meter/instrument cluster and connect the battery cable.

1979–84 Front Wheel Drive Colt Models

1. Disconnect the battery ground cable. Remove the center console and parcel tray, if equipped.

2. Remove the center vent duct and defroster duct. Remove the instrument panel trim. Remove the two heater unit top bolts and loosen the bottom attaching bolt.

3. Disconnect the wiring to the motor.

4. Tilt the heater unit toward yourself, remove the three motor attaching bolts and remove the motor.

5. The blower fan may be removed from the shaft if necessary.

6. Install the fan to the motor shaft. Install the motor and connect the wiring. Install the heater mounting bolts, the ducts and the trim. Install the center console and parcel tray if removed. Connect the battery cable.

1985–89 Colt

▶ **See Figure 4**

1. Disconnect the negative battery cable. Remove the glove box and parcel tray.

2. Disconnect the changeover control wire and duct.

3. Remove the blower case.

4. Unbolt and remove the blower motor from the case.

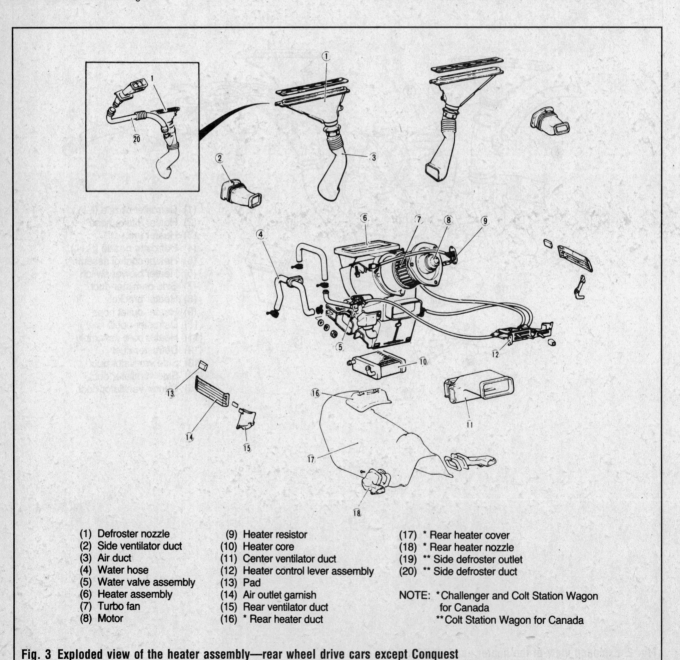

(1)	Defroster nozzle	(9)	Heater resistor	(17)	* Rear heater cover
(2)	Side ventilator duct	(10)	Heater core	(18)	* Rear heater nozzle
(3)	Air duct	(11)	Center ventilator duct	(19)	** Side defroster outlet
(4)	Water hose	(12)	Heater control lever assembly	(20)	** Side defroster duct
(5)	Water valve assembly	(13)	Pad		
(6)	Heater assembly	(14)	Air outlet garnish	NOTE:	* Challenger and Colt Station Wagon
(7)	Turbo fan	(15)	Rear ventilator duct		for Canada
(8)	Motor	(16)	* Rear heater duct		** Colt Station Wagon for Canada

Fig. 3 Exploded view of the heater assembly—rear wheel drive cars except Conquest

1. Water valve assembly
2. Heater core
3. Heater hose (B)
4. Heater hose (A)
5. Heater relay
6. Heater unit case
7. Duct
8. Blower case
9. Resistor
10. Fan
11. Blower motor
12. Heater control assembly
13. Blower switch

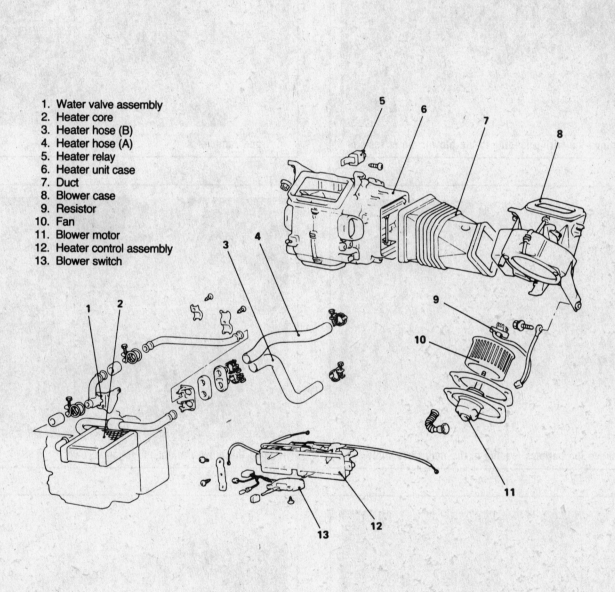

Fig. 4 Exploded view of the heater unit—1985 Colt

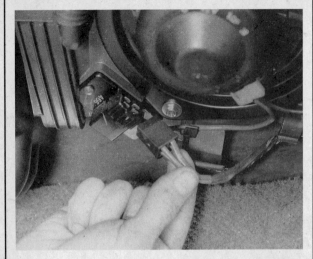

Remove the wiring leading to the blower motor resistor

. . . and remove

Remove the harness leading to the motor assembly

Remove the blower motor mounting screws . . .

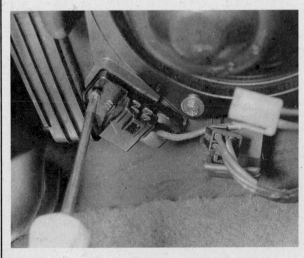

If necessary, unscrew the blower motor resistor . . .

. . . and separate the unit from the motor housing

5. The fan is removable from the motor shaft.

6. Install the fan to the blower motor shaft. Install the blower motor and case. Connect the control wire and duct. Install the glove box and parcel tray. Connect the battery cable.

Vista

1. Disconnect the negative battery cable. Remove the upper and lower glove boxes.

2. Disconnect the wiring and duct from the blower assembly.

3. Remove the blower motor mounting bolts and lift out the motor. If the entire blower case is to be removed, the instrument panel will have to be removed first.

4. Install the blower motor. Connect the wiring and duct. Install the glove boxes and connect the battery cable.

Conquest

▶ **See Figure 5**

1. Disconnect the negative battery cable. Remove the lower panel cover and the glove box.

2. Disconnect the air changeover cable from the blower.

3. Disconnect the duct from the blower.

4. Disconnect the blower wiring.

5. Unbolt and remove the blower motor.

6. Install the blower motor. Connect the wiring and the duct.

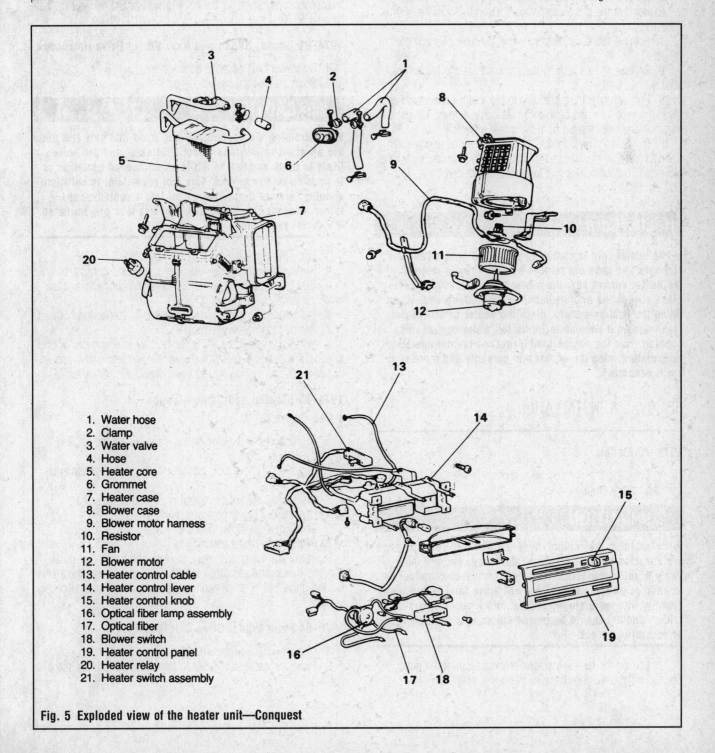

1. Water hose
2. Clamp
3. Water valve
4. Hose
5. Heater core
6. Grommet
7. Heater case
8. Blower case
9. Blower motor harness
10. Resistor
11. Fan
12. Blower motor
13. Heater control cable
14. Heater control lever
15. Heater control knob
16. Optical fiber lamp assembly
17. Optical fiber
18. Blower switch
19. Heater control panel
20. Heater relay
21. Heater switch assembly

Fig. 5 Exploded view of the heater unit—Conquest

Connect the changeover cable. Install the glove box and lower panel cover.

7. Connect the battery cable.

1981 and Later Challenger

1. Disconnect the negative battery cable. Remove the lower instrument pad cover assembly from under the glove box.

2. Remove the passenger side console cover.

3. Remove the glove box to center support attaching screw.

4. Loosen the stops at either side of the glove box so that the glove box swings free.

5. Disconnect the glove box light.

6. Remove the glove compartment assembly from the instrument pad.

7. Remove the ducts, heater fan switch connector and control cables.

8. Remove three attaching bolts and lift out the blower assembly.

9. Remove the wiring bracket and the motor connector. Remove the vent tube and three motor attaching screws. Lift out the motor and remove the fan from the motor assembly.

10. Install the blower motor. Connect the wiring and bracket. Connect the control cable, switch connector and ducts. Install the glove box, console cover and lower instrument pad cover. Connect the battery cable.

Heater Core

➡The heater core is contained within the heater case unit. The core and case are remove as a unit. Upon removal of the heater control box, the heater core is removable. Replace all gaskets and insulation in its proper place. When filling the cooling system, place the heater control to the maximum heat position to insure full water control valve opening. Run the engine until it reaches normal operating temperature, stop the engine and carefully add more coolant if necessary.

REMOVAL & INSTALLATION

1971–76 Models

1. Open the radiator petcock and drain the coolant. Disconnect the battery ground cable.

✳✳ CAUTION

When draining the coolant, keep in mind that cats and dogs are attracted to ethylene glycol antifreeze, and are quite likely to drink any that is left in an uncovered container or in puddles on the ground. This will prove fatal in sufficient quantity. Always drain the coolant into a sealable container. Coolant should be reused unless it is contaminated or several years old.

2. Loosen the retaining screws at the bottom of the radio which are tightened together with the center cover.

3. Press down on the top center padding and pull it out.

4. Remove the three heater control knobs.

5. Remove the retaining screws at the bottom of the console cover which are tightened together with the ashtray.

6. Slide the console and radio out toward yourself.

7. Disconnect the radio wiring and remove the console.

8. Remove the two heater control wires at the heater.

9. Remove the heater control assembly.

10. Disconnect the two water hoses. Disconnect the two ducts at the heater.

11. Remove the heater unit.

12. Install the heater and attach all hoses and controls. Install the console and radio. Fill the cooling system and connect the battery cable.

1974–81 Coupe, Sedan and Rear Wheel Drive Hatchback

1. Disconnect the negative battery cable.

2. Drain the cooling system.

✳✳ CAUTION

When draining the coolant, keep in mind that cats and dogs are attracted to ethylene glycol antifreeze, and are quite likely to drink any that is left in an uncovered container or in puddles on the ground. This will prove fatal in sufficient quantity. Always drain the coolant into a sealable container. Coolant should be reused unless it is contaminated or several years old.

3. Place the water valve in the OFF position.

4. Remove the under tray, defroster nozzle and console box.

5. Disconnect each heater control wire and connectors at the heater assembly.

6. Disconnect the water hoses, heater duct and wiring harness.

7. Remove the heater assembly.

8. Install the heater assembly Connect all hoses, ducts, wiring harness and controls. Install the console, defroster nozzle and under tray. Fill the cooling system and connect the battery cable.

1974–83 Hardtop and Station Wagon
▶ See Figure 6

1. Disconnect the negative battery cable. Drain the cooling system.

2. Remove the glove box, instrument cluster and console assembly.

3. Disconnect the heater control wires at the heater box.

4. Remove the heater control assembly.

5. Disconnect all heater hoses and air ducts.

6. Remove the heater assembly.

7. Install the heater assembly. Connect the hoses and ducts. Connect the control assembly. Install the console, instrument cluster and glove box. Fill the cooling system and connect the battery cable.

1979–84 Front Wheel Drive Colt Models

1. Disconnect the negative battery cable.

2. Place the water valve lever in the HOT position. Drain the coolant.

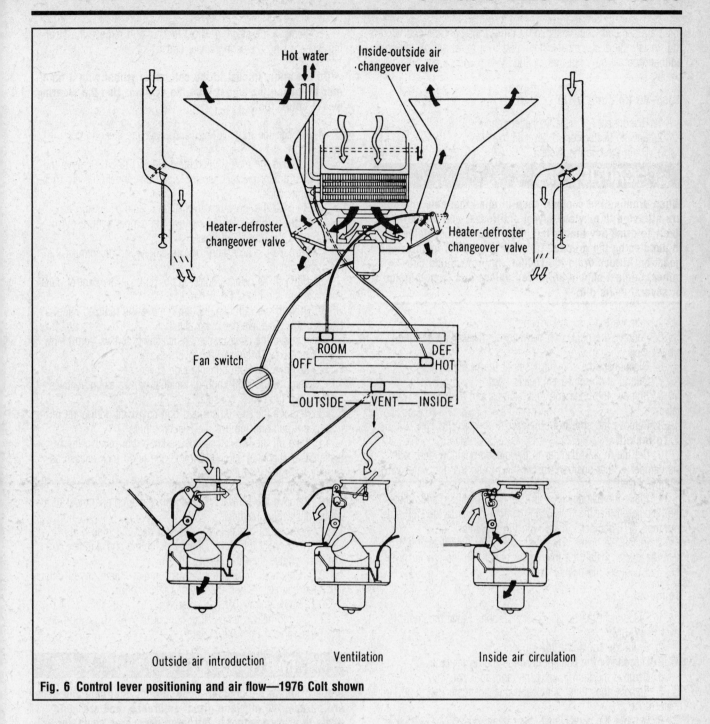

Fig. 6 Control lever positioning and air flow—1976 Colt shown

3. Remove the center console and parcel tray, if equipped.

4. Remove the center ventilation duct and the defroster duct. Disconnect the instrument trim panel and cluster hood.

5. Disconnect all control wires at the heater unit.

6. Disconnect the heater hose from the engine. Remove the clamps from the hoses. Disconnect the heater wiring harness.

7. Remove the two top mounting bolts and the one lower nut. Remove the heater assembly.

8. Install the heater assembly. Be sure the grommets through which the heater hoses pass when entering the passenger compart-

ment are secured when installing. Connect the controls and wiring. Install the ducts, cluster hood and trim panel. Install the console and parcel tray. Fill the cooling system and connect the battery cable.

1985–89 Colt and Vista

1. Disconnect the negative battery cable.
2. Set the heater control lever to WARM.
3. Drain the cooling system.

❄❄ CAUTION

When draining the coolant, keep in mind that cats and dogs are attracted to ethylene glycol antifreeze, and are quite likely to drink any that is left in an uncovered container or in puddles on the ground. This will prove fatal in sufficient quantity. Always drain the coolant into a sealable container. Coolant should be reused unless it is contaminated or several years old.

4. Remove the instrument panel.
5. Remove the duct from between the heater unit and the blower case.
6. Disconnect the coolant hoses at the heater case.
7. Unbolt and remove the heater case.
8. Remove the hose and pipe clamps and remove the water valve.
9. Remove the core from the case.

To install:

10. Set the mixing damper to the closed position, and, with the damper in that position, install the rod so that the water valve is fully closed.
11. Place the damper lever in the VENT position, and adjust the linkage so that the FOOT/DEF damper opens to the DEF side and the VENT damper is level with the separator.
12. Install the hoses. They are marked for flow direction. Connect the ducts. Install the instrument panel. Fill the cooling system and connect the battery cable.

Conquest

1. Disconnect the negative battery cable. Move the control lever to WARM.
2. Drain the coolant at the radiator.
3. Disconnect the coolant hoses at the heater unit.
4. Remove the instrument panel and floor console.
5. Remove the center ventilation duct, defroster duct and lap heater duct.
6. Remove the center instrument panel brace.
7. Remove the heater control assembly.
8. Remove the three screws and lift out the heater case.
9. Check the core for leaks, clogging and bent fins. Replace or repair as necessary.
10. Replace any cracked hoses or damaged insulation. Install the heater assembly. Install the control assembly, ducts, instrument panel and floor console. Connect the hose and fill the cooling system. Connect the battery cable.

1981 and Later Challenger

1. Disconnect the negative battery cable.
2. Remove the steering wheel horn pad attaching screws, from the back of the steering wheel. Remove the horn pad.

3. Remove the steering wheel locknut and remove the steering wheel using a steering wheel puller tool.

➡**Do not apply impact to the column or wheel with a hammer to loosen the wheel from the column. Use the steering wheel puller tool.**

4. Loosen the tilt lock lever and lower the steering column fully.
5. Remove the meter (instrument cluster) hood. Remove the meter (instrument cluster) assembly and disconnect the electrical cable connectors.
6. Remove the inner box from the console accessory box. Press on the spring catch, to remove the remote control mirror switch from the accessory box.
7. Remove the accessory box assembly and disconnect the electrical wiring.
8. Pull off the heater control knob, pull out the control panel and take out the illumination harness.
9. Pull off the radio knobs and remove the radio to panel attaching nuts. Remove the radio panel.
10. Remove the cover assembly attaching screws from below the glove box and remove the cover assembly.
11. Remove the both console side covers.
12. Remove the shift knob on manual transmission vehicles and remove the center console.
13. Remove the instrument pad bolt covers at both ends of the instrument pad and remove the attaching nuts.
14. Take off the hood lock release knob and remove the release cable attaching screws. Remove the hood lock release assembly from the instrument pad.
15. Remove the defroster garnish.
16. Remove the screws attaching the glove compartment to the center dash reinforcement.
17. Remove all remaining instrument pad attaching bolts.
18. Disconnect the clock, glove box, chime and dimmer control and remove the instrument pad.
19. Disconnect the defogger switch, radio, chime driver, defogger relay connectors and the antenna feeder end.
20. Remove the center reinforcement.
21. Set the heater temperature control to WARM position and drain the coolant from the radiator.

❄❄ CAUTION

When draining the coolant, keep in mind that cats and dogs are attracted to ethylene glycol antifreeze, and are quite likely to drink any that is left in an uncovered container or in puddles on the ground. This will prove fatal in sufficient quantity. Always drain the coolant into a sealable container. Coolant should be reused unless it is contaminated or several years old.

22. From the engine compartment, remove the heater hoses from the heater assembly.
23. From under the dash, remove the heater ducts from the heater assembly. To remove the rear seat heater duct, move the outlet control link to the VENT side, insert a finger into the outlet and remove the duct from inside heater.
24. Disconnect the power relay wiring, remove three attaching bolts and remove the heater assembly. Remove the heat core.

25. Install the heater core and heater assembly. Connect the control harness and controls. Connect all dusts, accessories, panels, and moldings. Install the steering wheel assembly. Connect the hoses and fill the cooling system. Connect the negative battery cable.

→Connect the heater hoses in a fully seated position on the inlet and outlet fittings of the heater core assembly, so they will not leak. Adjust the heater control cable by setting the control panel to COOL and heater unit lever on COOL and tighten the cable at that position.

AIR CONDITIONING

✵✵ CAUTION

Please refer to Section 1 before discharging the compressor or disconnecting air conditioning lines. Damage to the air conditioning system or personal injury could result. Consult your local laws concerning refrigerant discharge and recycling. In many areas it may be illegal for anyone but a certified technician to service the A/C system. Always use an approved recovery station when discharging the air conditioning.

Evaporator Core

REMOVAL & INSTALLATION

♦ See Figures 7, 8, 9, 10 and 10A

1. Discharge the A/C refrigerant system safely (see Section 1).
2. Disconnect the negative battery cable.
3. Remove the evaporator drain hose.

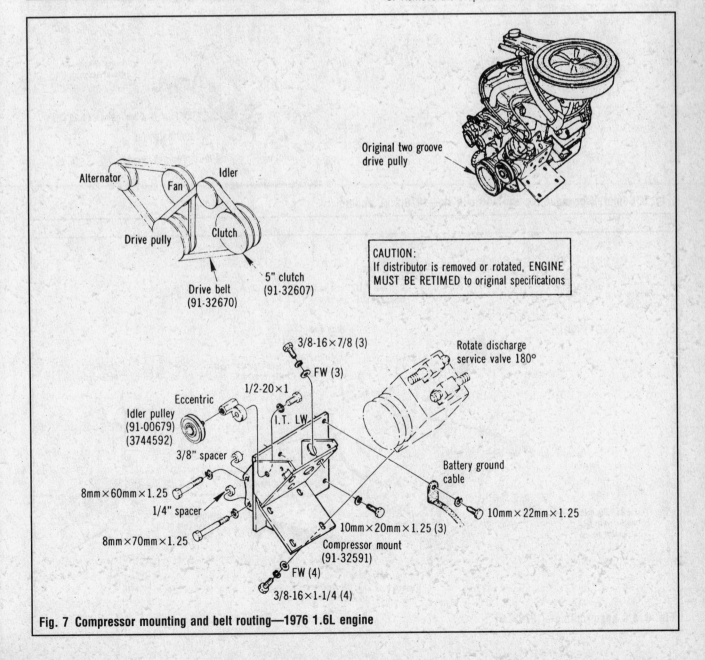

CAUTION:
If distributor is removed or rotated, ENGINE MUST BE RETIMED to original specifications

Fig. 7 Compressor mounting and belt routing—1976 1.6L engine

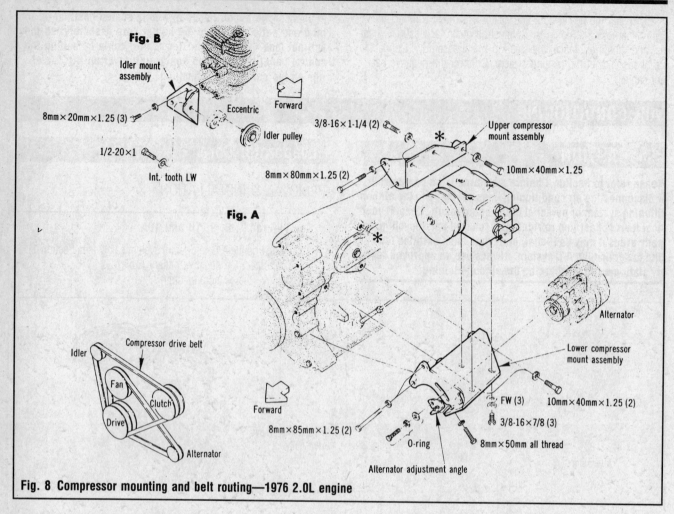

Fig. 8 Compressor mounting and belt routing—1976 2.0L engine

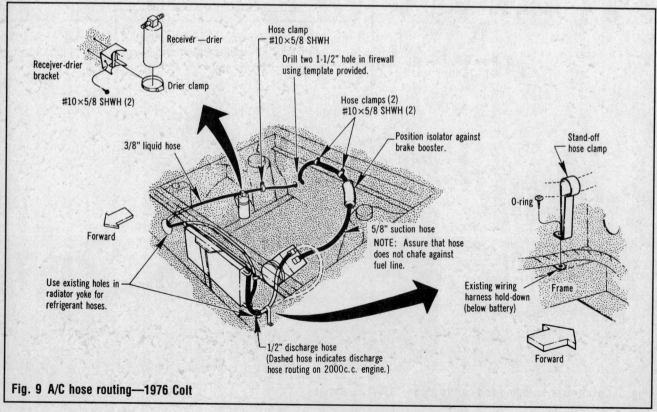

Fig. 9 A/C hose routing—1976 Colt

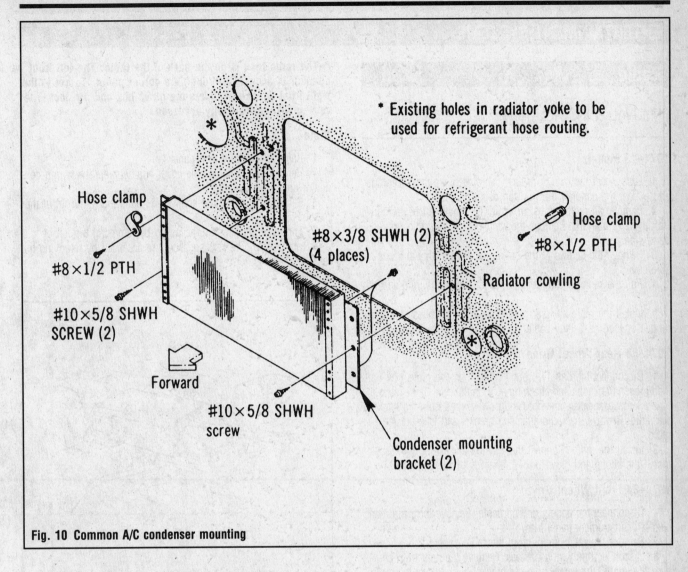

* Existing holes in radiator yoke to be used for refrigerant hose routing.

Hose clamp

#8×1/2 PTH

#10×5/8 SHWH SCREW (2)

Forward

#10×5/8 SHWH screw

#8×3/8 SHWH (2) (4 places)

Hose clamp
#8×1/2 PTH

Radiator cowling

Condenser mounting bracket (2)

Fig. 10 Common A/C condenser mounting

4. Disconnect the liquid and suction refrigerant lines from the evaporator (engine side). Remove the firewall insulator O-rings.

5. Remove the glove box and dash trim insert.

6. Remove the heater ducts and disconnect the duct joints from the heater case.

7. Disconnect the switch and main wire harness from the evaporator.

8. Remove the evaporator case mounting nuts and bolts, lower the case assembly and remove it from the vehicle.

9. Separate the case halves by removing the spring clips. Remove the expansion valve and other components to free the evaporator core from the case mounting.

To install:

10. Install the evaporator, connect components and the expansion valve.

11. Assemble the evaporator case and mount in under the dash.

12. Connect the wiring harness, duct connections to the heater and install the ducts.

13. Install the glove box and trim panel.

14. Install the firewall insulators. Connect the refrigerant lines using new O-rings lubricated with refrigerant oil.

15. Connect the evaporator drain hose. Connect the negative battery cable. Charge the A/C refrigerant system.

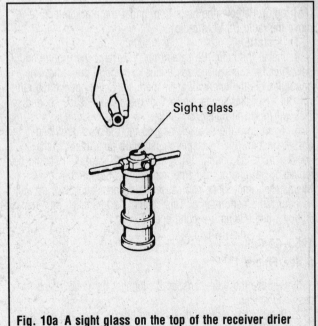

Sight glass

Fig. 10a A sight glass on the top of the receiver drier will allow you to see any air bubbles in the system

ENTERTAINMENT SYSTEMS

Radio

REMOVAL & INSTALLATION

1971–73 Models

1. Disconnect the battery ground cable. Remove the fastenings and extract the padding from on top of the radio.
2. Remove all radio knobs. In addition, remove all heater control levers and knobs. Remove the wing nut on the radio right-hand side.
3. Remove the screws at the bottom of the ash tray and console cover.
4. Pull the radio slightly forward. Disconnect all wiring and lift out.
5. Install the radio and secure it. Install the switches and padding. Connect the battery cable.

1974–83 Rear Wheel Drive

1. Disconnect the battery ground cable. Remove glove box then loosen the knobs and attaching nuts on the front of the radio.
2. Remove speaker, antenna, and power wires from the back of the radio. Remove the radio attaching bracket and take out the radio.
3. Install the radio. Connect the antenna and wiring harnesses. Install the knobs and glove box. Connect the battery cable.

1979–84 Front Wheel Drive

1. Disconnect the battery ground cable. Remove the instrument cluster or instrument panel trim.
2. Remove the radio knobs from the radio panel.
3. Disconnect the wiring harness. Remove the nuts from behind the knobs, the screw from the bracket and remove the radio (AM radio). Remove the bolts from under the brackets and remove the radio (AM/FM radio).
To install:
4. Install the radio. Be careful not to reverse the ground and power leads. This will cause serious damage to the radio. The power lead is the one with an inline fuse. Never operate the radio without a speaker connected or with the speaker leads shorted. This will result in transistor failure.
5. To remove the speaker, remove the radio as described above. Unscrew the four speaker retaining nuts. Remove the speaker from the bottom. When replacing a speaker, it should be replaced with one of the same impedance, measured in ohms. Mismatched impedance can cause rapid transistor failure as well as poor radio performance. This should also be taken into consideration when adding a second speaker.

1985–89 Colt
▶ **See Figure 11**

1. Remove the floor console. Disconnect the radio wiring harness and antenna.
2. Remove the radio and mounting bracket from the console.
3. Install the radio and mounting bracket to the console and install the console.

➡The radio fuse is on the back of the radio. The left front speaker is accessed through the corner panel. To get to the right front speaker, remove the glove box and air duct. The rear speakers are easily accessed.

Vista

1. Remove the radio trim panel.
2. Remove the console side cover and seperate the wiring connector and antenna cable.
3. Remove the mounting screws and slide the radio out of the panel.
4. The front speakers are accessed by removing the left or right trim panels. The rear speakers are accessed by removing the rear door trim panels.

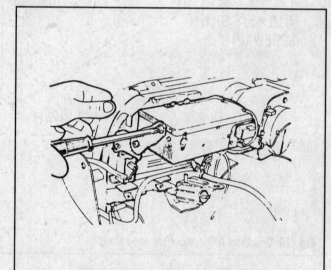

Fig. 11 Unscrew the radio from the mounting bracket, then separate the wiring from the back of the unit

To access the faceplate retaining nut, remove the front . . .

. . . and rear radio knobs

Remove the mounting nuts on either side of the radio knob locations

With a wrench, remove the nuts . . .

If equipped, pry off the metal rear mounting face plate

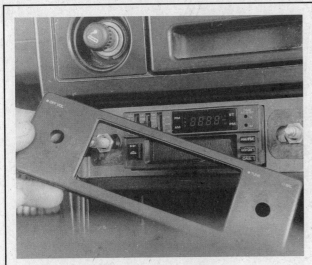

. . . and lift the faceplate off the radio

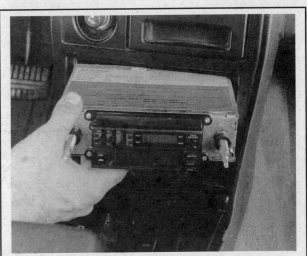

Slide the radio out of the dash, then separate the unit from the harness

5. Install the radio. Connect the wiring harnesses and antenna. Install the console cover and trim panel.

Conquest

1. Remove the front console box.
2. Remove the radio trim panel.
3. Remove the attaching screws and lift out the radio and mounting bracket.

4. To remove the front speaker, the instrument panel pad must first be removed.
5. The door speakers are accessed by removing the door trim panels.
6. The rear speakers are accessed by removing the rear trim panels.
7. Install the radio. Install the trim panel and front console box.

WINDSHIELD WIPERS AND WASHERS

Wiper Blade and Arm

REMOVAL & INSTALLATION

▸ See Figure 12

The windshield wiper arm and blade assembly is retained to the wiper linkage pivot by a locknut. The wiper arm will usually have a park position, that is, lift the arm away from the windshield to a point where the arm spring will hold it away from the windshield. Lift up the nut cover (where the arm meets the pivot linkage). Loosen the nut until the arm can be pulled off of the pivot. Put the arm on the pivot and tighten the nut. Close the nut cover and carefully lower the arm and blade to the windshield. The blade is retained to the arm by a clip or removal pin. Squeeze the clip, or twist the pin out of the retaining hole, depending on style.

Front Windshield Wiper Motor

➡ The wiper motor may be located on either the right or left side of the front deck, depending upon the year and model. A wiper removing hole is provided to gain access to the linkage for removal purposes.

REMOVAL & INSTALLATION

All Except Vista, Conquest, 1985–89 Colt
▸ See Figure 13

1. Remove the motor bracket and body retaining bolts.
2. Remove the wiper arm shaft nut on the driver's side of the car and pull the motor assembly out toward yourself.
3. Remove the bushing and disconnect the motor crank arm and linkage.

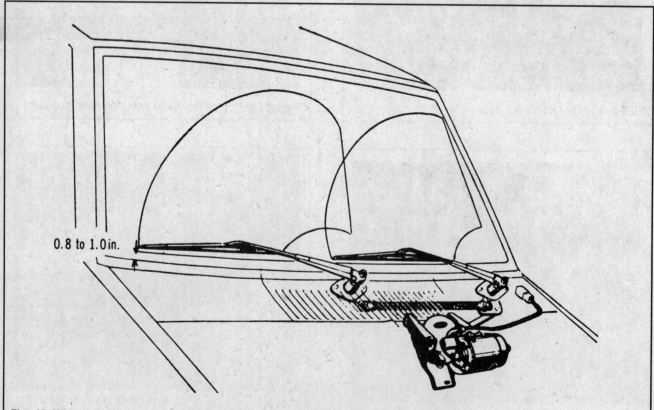

0.8 to 1.0 in.

Fig. 12 When installing the wiper blades, make sure the height of the blade-to-windshield is correct

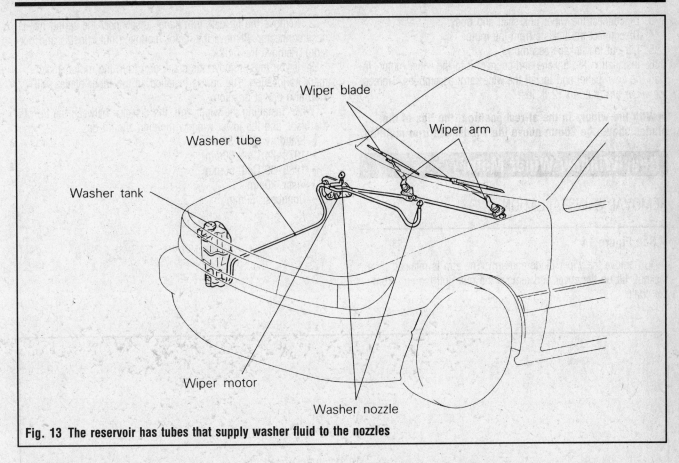

Fig. 13 The reservoir has tubes that supply washer fluid to the nozzles

4. Install the motor. Connect the drive link and install the body retaining

Vista, 1985–89 Colt

1. Remove the wiper arm assemblies.
2. Remove the front cowl trim plate.
3. Remove the pivot shaft mounting nuts and push the pivot shaft toward the inside.
4. Disconnect the linkage from the motor and lift out the linkage.
5. Unbolt and remove the motor.
6. Install the motor. Connect the linkage and mount the pivots. Install the cowl trim plate and wiper arm assemblies.

When installing the arms, the at-rest position of the blade tips-to-windshield molding should be:
- Vista Passenger's side: 30mm
  Driver's side: 25mm
- Colt Passenger's side: 20mm
  Driver's side: 15mm

Conquest

1. Remove the wiper arm and pivot shaft mounting nut, re-move the arms and push the shaft toward the inside.
2. Remove the cover from the wiper access hole on the right side of the front deck panel.
3. Loosen the wiper motor mounting bolts, pull the motor out slightly, disconnect the motor from the linkage, then remove the motor and linkage. If you are going to remove the motor's crank arm, mark its position first.
4. Install the motor. Connect the linkage. Mount the pivots and linkage. Install the cover and wiper arm assemblies. Install the wi-

per arm so that the blade tip-to-windshield molding distance, at rest, is 12mm.

Windshield Wiper Linkage

REMOVAL & INSTALLATION

➡On models not listed below, the linkage is removed with the wiper motor.

Rear Wheel Drive Cars Except Conquest

1. Remove the wiper arm.
2. Remove the wiper arm retaining nuts and push the shaft in toward the body.
3. Remove the wiper motor and bracket assembly.
4. Pull the wiper linkage out through the access hole. To dis-connect the wiper linkage, press the bushing out by hand while holding the crank arm and linkage parallel.
5. When installing the wiper arm shaft on the body, insert the shaft bracket positioning boss into the marching hole in the body.
6. Before installing the center shaft bracket, remove the canister and make sure that the shaft bracket boss is inserted in the hole.
7. Adjust the wiper blade position in the stopped position ap-proximately 12–19mm above the windshield molding or rubber seal then tighten the wiper arm nuts to 8–12 ft. lbs.

1979–84 Front Wheel Drive Colt

1. Remove the wiper arms.
2. Remove the cowl trim panel.

3. Disconnect the wiper link shaft and body.

4. Disconnect the linkage from the motor.

5. Lift out the linkage assembly.

6. Installation the linkage and connect it to the wiper motor. Install the cowl panel and install the wiper arm assemblies. Tighten the wiper arm nuts to 12 ft. lbs.

➡ **With the wipers in the at-rest position, the tips of the blades should be 20mm above the windshield trim molding.**

Rear Window Wiper Motor

REMOVAL & INSTALLATION

▶ **See Figure 14**

1. Remove the wiper blade and arm. The arm is retained by a locknut, lift up the cover and remove the nut: pull the arm from the shaft.

2. Remove the lift gate trim panel, disconnect the wiring harness connector. Remove the motor mounting nuts (inside and outside). Remove the motor.

3. If you must remove the crank arm from the motor, match mark its location. The arm is installed so the wiper blades will stop at a preset position.

When installing the wiper arm, the distance between the tip of the blade and the lower window molding should be:

- Station wagon: 5mm
- 1979–84 Colt: 80mm
- 1985–89 Colt: 60mm
- Vista: 20mm
- Conquest: 50mm

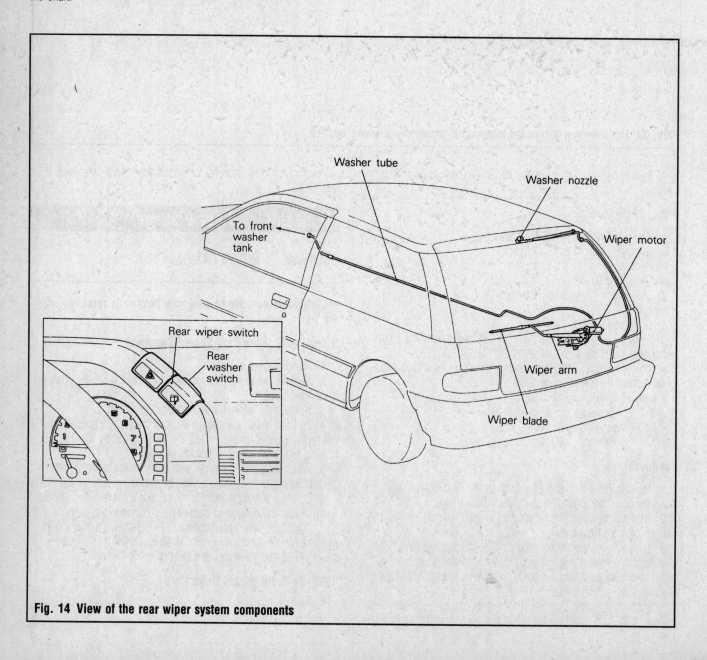

Fig. 14 View of the rear wiper system components

INSTRUMENTS AND SWITCHES

Instrument Cluster

REMOVAL & INSTALLATION

1971–73 Models

♦ **See Figure 15**

1. Disconnect the negative battery cable. Loosen the adjusting knob and drop the steering wheel to its lowest position.
2. Remove the two retaining screws at the bottom of the instrument cluster.
3. Lift and pull the instrument cluster out of the two clips at the top.
4. Disconnect the gauge wiring and the speedometer cable.
5. Remove the instrument cluster.
6. Install the cluster after connecting the wiring harnesses and speedometer cable. Connect the battery cable.

1974–78 Colt Except 1978 Station Wagon

♦ **See Figure 16**

➡**Disconnect the battery ground cable before cluster removal.**

1. Loosen screws at the upper and lower part of the instrument cluster. Loosen the screws holding the heater control knobs, ash tray, and cigarette lighter from their respective brackets, if necessary. Remove blind cover, if equipped on the right side of the glove box and remove the attaching screws on the right side of the cluster.

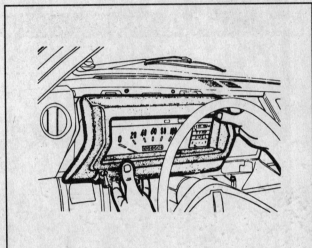

Fig. 15 Removing the instrument cluster on 1971–73 models

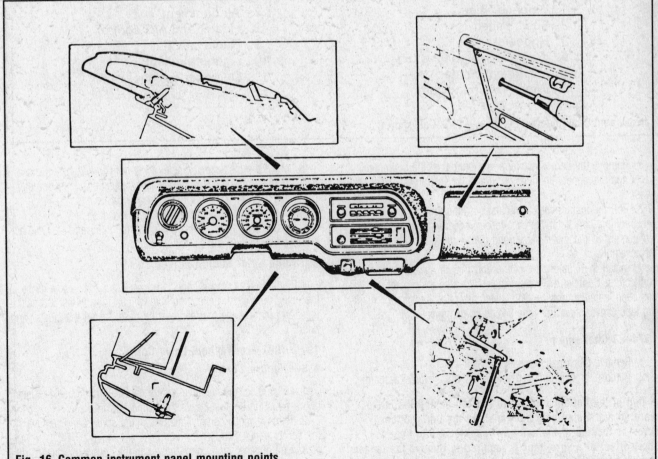

Fig. 16 Common instrument panel mounting points

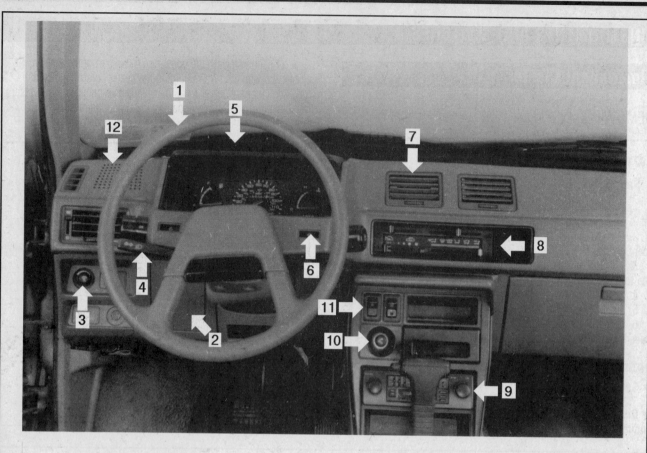

1. Steering wheel
2. Fuse panel
3. Rheostat
4. Wiper/Turn signal switch
5. Instrument cluster
6. Wiper switch indicator
7. Air duct vent
8. Heater and A/C control
9. Radio
10. Lighter element
11. Defogger switch
12. Speaker grille

Instrument panel component view—1987 Colt shown

2. Remove the harness cover at the bottom of the instrument panel and disconnect lighting switch and the instrument panel harness.

3. Pull the instrument panel cluster a little toward you, disconnect multiple connector, antenna feeder, speaker connector, heater fan connector and meter cables and then remove instrument cluster assembly.

4. Install the cluster after connecting the wiring and component connectors. Connect the battery cable. After the instrument cluster has been installed, draw out the meter cables as long as the marking tape can be seen from the engine compartment.

1974–83 Challenger

1. Remove the negative battery cable.
2. Remove three screws from the bottom of the cluster assembly.

➡**Two of the bottom screws are located behind the brake warning and fasten seat belt lens and the third bottom screw is located at the ash tray opening. A thin tipped screwdriver or a wire hook is required to remove the lenses to gain access to the screws.**

3. Move the instrument cluster away from the dash and disconnect the meter connections, heater fan connections, speedometer cable and any other connector or ground cables.

4. Remove the cluster assembly from the dash.

5. Install the cluster after connecting the components. Connect the negative battery cable.

1978 and Later Station Wagon

The instrument cluster hood is removed separately to expose the instrument cluster attaching screws, attaching wires and cables, and remove the cluster from the dash. Install the cluster and hood.

1979–1982 Front Wheel Drive Colt

▶ **See Figure 17**

1. Disconnect the negative battery cable. Remove the 4 cluster hood mounting screws. Leave the connectors in place.

2. Remove the 5 corner panel mounting screws and remove the corner panel.

3. Pull out the hood connector, push the connector claw to disengage the connector and remove the hood.

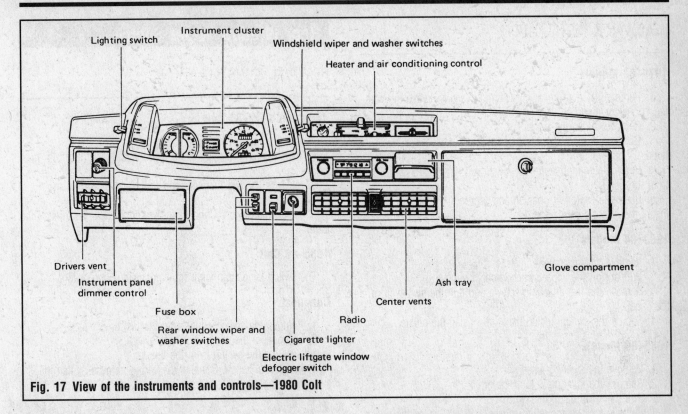

Fig. 17 View of the instruments and controls—1980 Colt

4. Remove the 4 cluster mounting screws and lift the cluster, disconnecting the speedometer cable and wiring connectors.

5. Install the cluster after connecting the wiring harness and speedometer cable. Install the cluster hood and corner panel. Connect the battery cable.

1983–84 Colt

1. Disconnect the negative battery cable. Remove the steering wheel.

2. Remove the heater control knobs.

3. Remove the cluster panel attaching screws.

4. Remove the light switch, wiper switch, clock and indicator connectors.

5. Remove the cluster panel.

6. Remove the combination meter attaching screws.

7. Pull the combination meter out slightly and disconnect the speedometer cable and electrical connectors. Lift out the combination meter.

8. Install the cluster after connecting the wiring harness and speedometer cable. Install the steering wheel and connect the battery cable.

1985–89 Colt

1. Disconnect the negative battery cable. Remove the steering wheel.

2. Remove the glove box.

3. Remove the instrument panel heater duct.

4. Remove the parcel tray.

5. Remove the steering column lower cover.

6. Disconnect the light switch and wiper switch connectors.

7. Remove the steering column upper cover.

8. Remove the instrument cluster hood screws and lift off the hood.

9. Remove the cluster mounting screws and pull the cluster

slightly forward. Disconnect the speedometer cable and electrical connectors and lift out the cluster.

10. Install the cluster after connecting the wiring harness and speedometer cable. Install the steering column cover, parcel tray heater duct and glove box. Install the steering wheel and connect the battery cable.

Conquest

➡️**The following procedure applies to both the conventional needle-type gauge cluster and to the liquid crystal display type. Because the LCD gauges are composed of very delicate components, they must not be subjected to severe shocks. Furthermore, the LCD gauges must not be disassembled.**

1. Disconnect the negative battery cable. Remove the cluster hood attaching screws.

2. Pull outward on both bottom side edges of the hood; and, while holding it in that position, pull it upward and off.

3. Disconnect the wiring to the hood switches.

4. Remove the cluster case attaching screws.

5. Pull both sides of the lower part of the cluster case up and toward you.

6. Disconnect the speedometer cable from the back of the case.

7. Disconnect all wiring at the back of the case and lift the case out.

8. Install the cluster after connecting the wiring harnesses and speedometer cable. Install the cluster hood. Connect the battery cable.

Windshield Wiper Switch

➡️**On most late models, the wiper switch is integral with the turn signal switch. For wiper switch service on those cars, follow the procedures under Turn Signal Switch, in Section 8.**

REMOVAL & INSTALLATION

1979–82 Models

1. Remove the instrument cluster hood screws. Leave the wiring connector alone.
2. Remove the corner panel.
3. Disconnect the cluster hood connector and remove the hood.
4. Remove the knob from the switch and remove the switch from the hood.
5. Place the switch in position and secure it. Install the knob. Install the hood, corner panel.

1983–84 Models

1. Remove the instrument cluster.
2. Pull out on the wiper switch knob to remove it.
3. Remove the two attaching screws and pull the switch from the panel.
4. Secure the switch, install the knob. Install the cluster.

1985–89 Models

1. Remove the steering wheel.
2. Remove the steering column cover.
3. Pull the knob off of the switch.
4. Remove the two mounting screws and pull the switch out.
5. Secure the switch. Install the knob and steering column cover. Install the steering wheel.

Rear Window Wiper Switch

REMOVAL & INSTALLATION

Vista and 1979–84 Colt

1. Pry the switch bezel from the panel.
2. Reach behind the panel and disconnect the wiring from the switch.
3. Depress the two retainers and pull the switch from the panel.
4. Install the switch. Connect the wiring harness and install the bezel.

1985–89 Colt

The switch is integral with the windshield wiper switch.

Conquest

1. Remove the switch panel from the instrument panel.
2. Disconnect the wiring from the switch.
3. Separate the switch from the bezel.
4. Install the switch. Connect the wiring harness. Install the switch panel.

LIGHTING

Headlights

REMOVAL & INSTALLATION

Rear Wheel Drive Cars Except Conquest

1. Remove the grille or grilles covering the headlights.
2. Unscrew the retaining screws and pull the bulb out from its mounting.

➡ **Do not unscrew the adjustment screws or a headlight adjustment will be required.**

3. Unplug the electrical connectors and remove the bulb.
4. Install the replacement bulb. Install the grille covers.

Conquest

1. Using the pop-up switch (not the headlight switch), raise the headlights.
2. Disconnect the negative battery cable.
3. Remove 3 outside and 2 inside screws from the headlight bezel. Pull the bezel up and forward to remove it.
4. Remove the 4 headlight trim ring mounting screws (don't mistakenly touch the headlight aiming screws), and remove the trim ring.

5. Pull the headlight out enough to disconnect the wiring plug. Remove the headlight.
6. Connect the wiring plug and install the headlight. Secure the trim ring retainer and bezel. Connect the battery cable. Check operation.

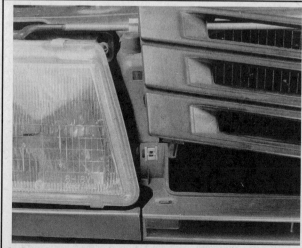

It may be necessary to remove the grille prior to headlamp removal

Unscrew the bulb retainer for the headlamp

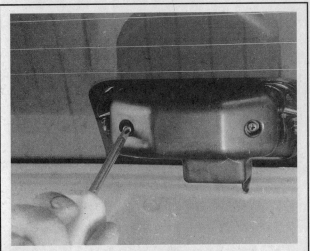

Lift the trunk lid and unscrew the third brake light housing

Using a clean rag (not your hands!) remove the headlamp bulb

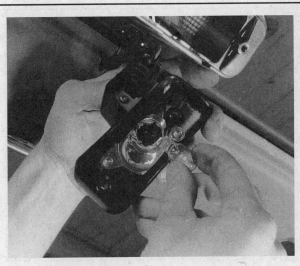

The light bulb should pull out of the socket with ease

Front Wheel Drive

1. Remove the front side marker lights (Vista). Grille lower garnish (Colt).
2. Remove the radiator grille (Early Colts).
3. Remove the headlight bezel.
4. Remove the headlight mounting screws. Don't disturb the headlight aiming screws.
5. Using needlenosed pliers, unhook the spring from the headlight support panel. Remove the plug connector and remove the bulb.

Third Brake Lamp Bulb

REMOVAL & INSTALLATION

1. Open the trunk lid assembly.
2. Unscrew the outer portion of the lamp assembly.

3. Separate the outer portion from the lamp assembly.
4. Pull the bulb from its mounting socket and inspect. Replace if necessary.

To install:

5. Install the bulb into the socket.
6. Place the outer portion of the lamp onto the brake light assembly and tighten the mounting screws.
7. Check the operation of the unit and close the trunk lid.

License Plate Bulb

REMOVAL & INSTALLATION

1. Remove the upper and lower mounting screws on the lamp lens.
2. Check the gasket on the lens for any deterioration.
3. Remove the bulb and replace if necessary.
4. Reverse the procedure to install.

Remove the lower mounting screw . . .

Remove the bulb and replace if necessary

. . . and the upper screw on the license plate lamp

Turn Signal/Side Marker Lamps

REMOVAL & INSTALLATION

1. Unscrew the side marker lens from the body of the vehicle.
2. Remove the lens and mounting screws.
3. Check the gasket for any deterioration.
4. Remove the bulb and replace if necessary.
To install:
5. Place the new bulb into position and check for operation.
6. Install the lens on the body of the vehicle and tighten the mounting screws.

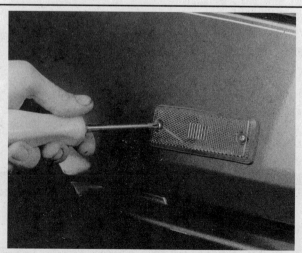

Once removed, inspect the gasket mating material for deterioration

The front side marker lamp lens is retained by two screws

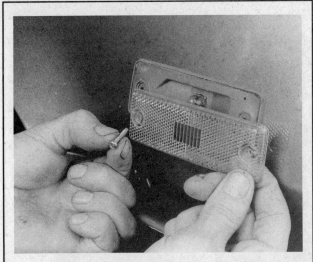

Once the lens is removed, you can access the bulb

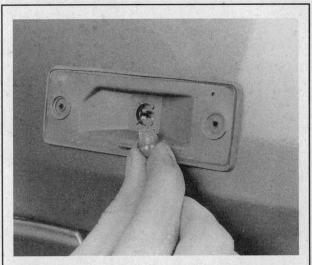

Remove the bulb and replace with a new one if needed

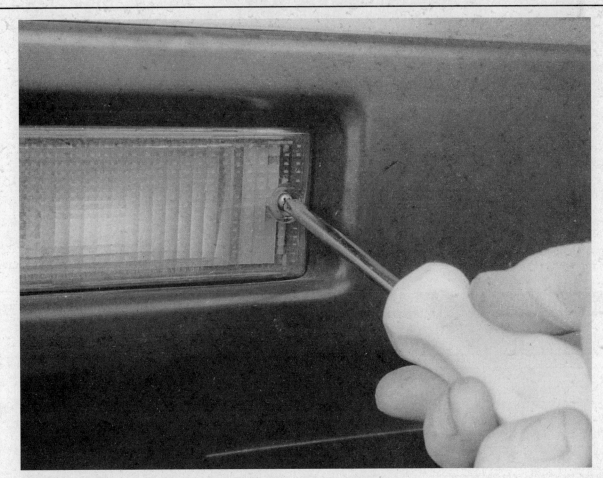

The front turn signal lens is removed in a similar manner to the side marker

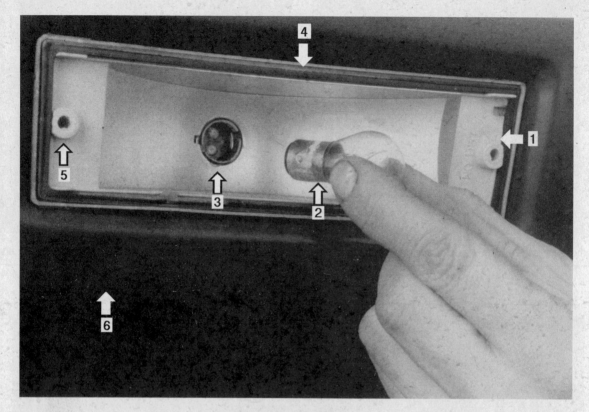

1. Bulb size indication
2. Bulb
3. Socket
4. Gasket
5. Screw location
6. Bumper

On some models the bulb type will be imprinted in the lamp body

Rear Tail Lamp

REMOVAL & INSTALLATION

1. On some models, there are no mounting screws on the tail lamp. Simply and carefully pry the lens off the body of the car. If there are mounting screws, remove them.

2. From the inside of some models, remove the trim panel to access the lamp bulbs. If not, remove the lamp bulbs from the exterior of the vehicle.

3. Under the interior trim panel, unclamp the bulb housing from the body of the car.

4. Then remove the bulbs from their sockets.

5. Reverse to install.

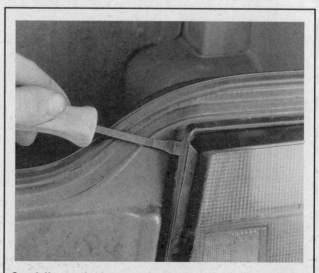

Carefully pry the lamp assembly from the vehicle body

Some rear tail lamp assemblies are sealed with butyl sealer

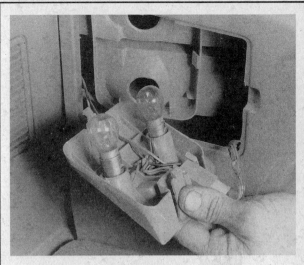

. . . and pull the unit straight out

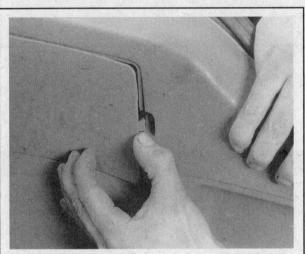

For bulb replacement, (on some models) there is an access trim panel inside the hatch area

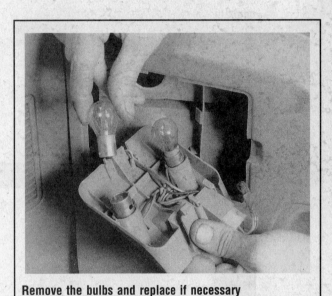

Remove the bulbs and replace if necessary

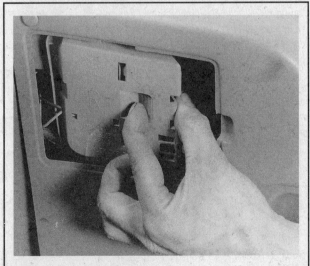

Unclamp the bulb housing . . .

Dome Light

REMOVAL & INSTALLATION

1. Unsnap the lens from the dome lamp body.
2. Remove the bulb.
3. Unscrew the housing assembly from the roof.
4. Separate the wiring harness from the body and lamp assembly.

To install:

5. Join the wiring harness connectors and place the lamp body into position.
6. Tighten the lamp body to the roof.
7. Insert a light bulb in place and snap the lens on the lamp body.

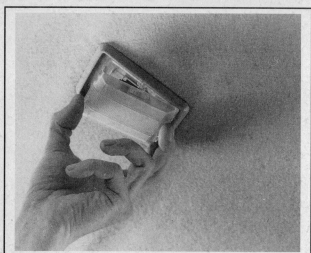

If you dome light bulb is blown, simply unsnap the lens from the housing . . .

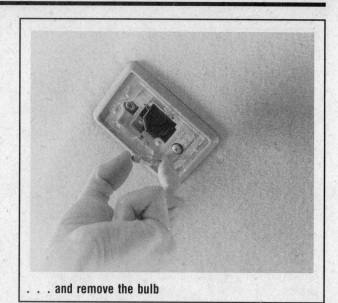

. . . and remove the bulb

Turn Signal and Hazard Flashers

The flashers are located under the left side of the instrument panel. If the turn signals operate in only one direction, a bulb is probably burned out. If they operate in neither direction, a bulb on each side may be burned out, or the flasher may be defective.

REMOVAL & INSTALLATION

1. Pull the flasher from its spring clip mounting.
2. Unplug and discard the flasher. Plug in the new flasher.
3. Replace the flasher in the spring clip and check operation.

TRAILER WIRING

Wiring the vehicle for towing is fairly easy. There are a number of good wiring kits available and these should be used, rather than trying to design your own.

All trailers will need brake lights and turn signals as well as tail lights and side marker lights. Most areas require extra marker lights for overwide trailers. Also, most areas have recently required back-up lights for trailers, and most trailer manufacturers have been building trailers with back-up lights for several years.

Additionally, some Class I, most Class II and just about all Class III trailers will have electric brakes. Add to this number an accessories wire, to operate trailer internal equipment or to charge the trailer's battery, and you can have as many as seven wires in the harness.

Determine the equipment on your trailer and buy the wiring kit necessary. The kit will contain all the wires needed, plus a plug adapter set which includes the female plug, mounted on the bumper or hitch, and the male plug, wired into, or plugged into the trailer harness.

When installing the kit, follow the manufacturer's instructions. The color coding of the wires is usually standard throughout the industry. One point to note: some domestic vehicles, and most imported vehicles, have separate turn signals. On most domestic vehicles, the brake lights and rear turn signals operate with the same bulb. For those vehicles with separate turn signals, you can purchase an isolation unit so that the brake lights won't blink whenever the turn signals are operated, or, you can go to your local electronics supply house and buy four diodes to wire in series with the brake and turn signal bulbs. Diodes will isolate the brake and turn signals. The choice is yours. The isolation units are simple and quick to install, but far more expensive than the diodes. The diodes, however, require more work to install properly, since they require the cutting of each bulb's wire and soldering in place of the diode.

One, final point, the best kits are those with a spring loaded cover on the vehicle mounted socket. This cover prevents dirt and moisture from corroding the terminals. Never let the vehicle socket hang loosely; always mount it securely to the bumper or hitch.

CIRCUIT PROTECTION

Fuses

▶ **See Figures 18, 19 and 20**

On rear wheel drive cars except Conquest the fuse block is located beneath the instrument panel above the headlight dimmer floor switch or on the driver's side front pillar post. On Conquest and front wheel drive cars, the fuse panel is located in the instrument panel, just to the left of the steering column.

Some components have inline fuses at or near the component. Check your owner's manual to determine the location of these fuses. Fuse holders are labeled as to their service and the correct

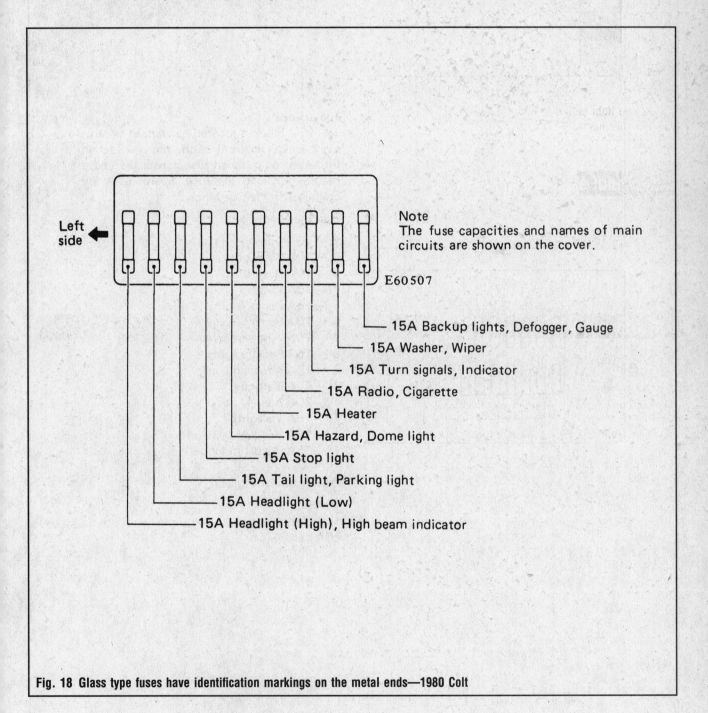

Note
The fuse capacities and names of main circuits are shown on the cover.

E60507

- 15A Backup lights, Defogger, Gauge
- 15A Washer, Wiper
- 15A Turn signals, Indicator
- 15A Radio, Cigarette
- 15A Heater
- 15A Hazard, Dome light
- 15A Stop light
- 15A Tail light, Parking light
- 15A Headlight (Low)
- 15A Headlight (High), High beam indicator

Left side

Fig. 18 Glass type fuses have identification markings on the metal ends—1980 Colt

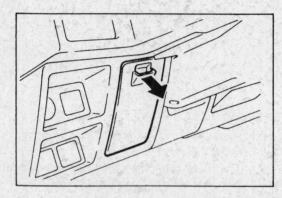

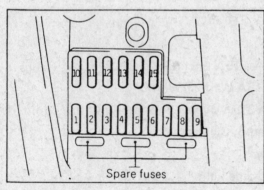

Spare fuses

Fuses

Fuse Block

The fuse block is located beneath the instrument cluster in front of the driver's seat. In the event of a blown fuse, locate the cause before replacing the fuse. Spare fuses are contained in the fuse block.

Fuse load capacity

1 — 10A Dome light
2 — 10A Stoplights
3 — 10A Hazard
4 — 15A Wiper
5 — 15A Radio
6 — 10A Horn
7 — 10A Turn signals
8 — 10A Backup lights
9 — 10A Air-conditioner
10 — 20A Defogger
11 — 20A Heater
12 — 10A Taillights
14 — 15A Headlight (lower)
15 — 15A Headlight (upper)

Identification of fuse

10A Red
15A Light blue
20A Yellow

Fig. 19 The newer models have plastic push-in type fuses. They are color coded and marked—1985 Colt

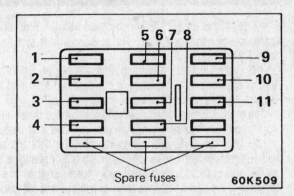

Spare fuses

60K509

Fuses

Fuse Block

The fuse block is located beneath the instrument cluster in front of the driver's seat. In the event of a blown fuse, locate the cause before replacing the fuse. Spare fuses are contained in the fuse block.

1— 10A Dome light
2— 10A Stoplights
3— 10A Hazard
4— 20A Defogger
5— 20A Heater
6— 10A Horn
7— 15A Wiper
8— 15A Radio
9— 10A Turn signals
10— 10A Backup lights
11— 10A Liftgate

Identification of fuse
10A Red
15A Light blue
20A Yellow

NOTE

The fuse capacities and names of main circuits are shown on the cover.
If a fuse blows frequently, take your car to an authorized dealer for inspection.

Fig. 20 Fuse block on the 1985 Vista, other Vistas similar

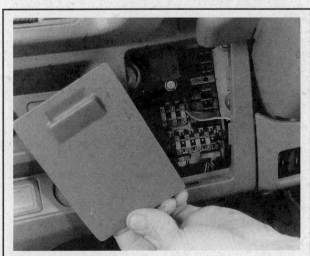

Remove the fuse box cover (usually under or in the dash)

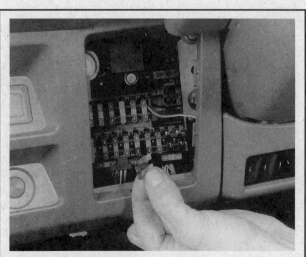

Pull the bad fuse with either your fingers or a special fuse puller

amperage. Always replace blown fuses with new ones of the correct amperage. Otherwise electrical overloads and possible wiring damage will result.

Fusible Links

▶ **See Figures 21 and 22**

Fusible links are sections of wire, with special insulation, designed to melt under electrical overload. Replacements are simply spliced into the wire. There may be as many as five of these in the engine compartment wiring harnesses.

Some fusible links are a cartrige type found in a relay box. Refer to your onwers manual.

REPLACEMENT

1. Disconnect the battery ground cable.
2. Disconnect the fusible link from the junction block or starter solenoid.
3. Cut the harness directly behind the connector to remove the damaged fusible link.
4. Strip the harness wire approximately 12mm.
5. Connect the new fusible link to the harness wire using a crimp on connector. Solder the connection using rosin core solder.
6. Tape all exposed wires with plastic electrical tape.
7. Connect the fusible link to the junction block or starter solenoid and reconnect the battery ground cable.

Seat Belt/Starter Interlock System

All 1974 and some 1975 are equipped with the Federally required starter interlock system. The purpose of this system is to force the wearing of seat belts.

The system includes a warning light and buzzer, weight sensors in the front seats, switches in the outboard front seal belt retractors, and an electronic control module.

The electronic control module requires that the driver and right front passenger first sit down, then pull out their seat belts. If this is not done, the starter will not operate, but the light and buzzer will. The sequence must be followed each time the engine is started unless the driver and passenger have remained seated and buckled. If the seat belts have been pulled out and left buckled, the engine will not start. The switches in the retractors must be cycled for each start. If the belts are released after the start, the light and buzzer will operate.

If the system should fail, preventing starting, the interlock bypass switch under the hood can be used. This switch permits one start without interference from the interlock system. This by-pass switch can also be used for servicing purposes.

TROUBLESHOOTING

If the starter will not crank or the warning buzzer will not shut off, perform the following checks:

Problem: Front seat occupant sits on a prebuckled seat belt.

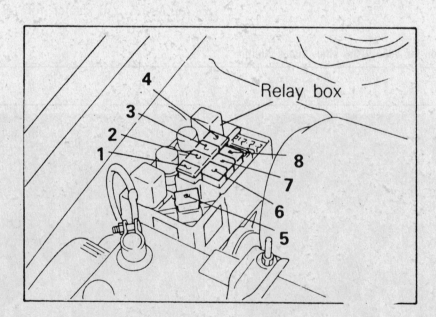

Fig. 21 A relay/fusible link box is located in the engine compartment on most models

FUSIBLE LINKS

For the fusible links, the cartridge type is employed; they are located in the relay box (within the engine compartment).

No.	Circuit	Housing color	Rated capacity (A)
1	MPI circuit	Blue	20
2	Headlight circuit	Green	40
3	Radiator fan motor circuit	Pink or *Green	30 or *40
4	Ignition circuit	Green	40
5	Alternator circuit, fusible link ⑥, ⑦, ⑧ circuit	Black	80
6	Multi-purpose fuse power supply	Green	40
7	Power window circuit	Pink	30
8	Defogger circuit	Pink	30

NOTE
The * symbol indicates applicability to DOHC models for the U.S.

Fig. 22 Capacity chart for the relay/fusible link chart—1989 Colt shown, others similar

Solution: Unbuckle the prebuckled belt, fully retract, extract, and then rebuckle the belt.

Problem: The front seat occupants are buckled, but the starter will not crank.

Solution: The unoccupied seat sensor switch stuck closed before the seat was occupied. Reset the unoccupied seat sensor switches by applying and then releasing 50 lbs. or more of weight to the seat directly over the seat sensor switches.

Problem: Starter will not crank with a heavy parcel on the front seat.

Solution: Buckle the seat belt around the parcel somewhere else in the car. Unbuckle the seat belt when the parcel is removed from the front seat.

Problem: Starter will not crank due to starter interlock system component failure.

Solution: An emergency starter interlock override switch is located under the hood on the fender apron. Depress the red push button on the switch and release it. This will allow one complete cycle of the ignition key from OFF to Start and back to OFF. Do not tape the button down as this will result in deactivation of the override feature.

DISABLING THE STARTER INTERLOCK SYSTEM

Cars built after October 29, 1974 are no longer required to have the interlock system. The system may be legally disabled on cars which have it, but the following procedure must be used:

1. Open the hood and locate the override switch and terminal connector attached to it.

2. Remove the brown and the blue/yellow wire. After cutting these wires, splice them together.

3. To remove the buzzer, remove the terminal connector from the buzzer and tape it to the wiring harness to prevent it from rattling. The buzzer now can be removed and discarded. Federal law requires that the warning light still be operable, so do not disconnect it.

Troubleshooting Basic Lighting Problems

Problem	Cause	Solution
Lights		
One or more lights don't work, but others do	• Defective bulb(s) • Blown fuse(s) • Dirty fuse clips or light sockets • Poor ground circuit	• Replace bulb(s) • Replace fuse(s) • Clean connections • Run ground wire from light socket housing to car frame
Lights burn out quickly	• Incorrect voltage regulator setting or defective regulator • Poor battery/alternator connections	• Replace voltage regulator • Check battery/alternator connections
Lights go dim	• Low/discharged battery • Alternator not charging • Corroded sockets or connections • Low voltage output	• Check battery • Check drive belt tension; repair or replace alternator • Clean bulb and socket contacts and connections • Replace voltage regulator
Lights flicker	• Loose connection • Poor ground • Circuit breaker operating (short circuit)	• Tighten all connections • Run ground wire from light housing to car frame • Check connections and look for bare wires
Lights "flare"—Some flare is normal on acceleration—if excessive, see "Lights Burn Out Quickly"	• High voltage setting	• Replace voltage regulator
Lights glare—approaching drivers are blinded	• Lights adjusted too high • Rear springs or shocks sagging • Rear tires soft	• Have headlights aimed • Check rear springs/shocks • Check/correct rear tire pressure
Turn Signals		
Turn signals don't work in either direction	• Blown fuse • Defective flasher • Loose connection	• Replace fuse • Replace flasher • Check/tighten all connections
Right (or left) turn signal only won't work	• Bulb burned out • Right (or left) indicator bulb burned out • Short circuit	• Replace bulb • Check/replace indicator bulb • Check/repair wiring
Flasher rate too slow or too fast	• Incorrect wattage bulb • Incorrect flasher	• Flasher bulb • Replace flasher (use a variable load flasher if you pull a trailer)
Indicator lights do not flash (burn steadily)	• Burned out bulb • Defective flasher	• Replace bulb • Replace flasher
Indicator lights do not light at all	• Burned out indicator bulb • Defective flasher	• Replace indicator bulb • Replace flasher

Troubleshooting Basic Turn Signal and Flasher Problems

Most problems in the turn signals or flasher system, can be reduced to defective flashers or bulbs, which are easily replaced. Occasionally, problems in the turn signals are traced to the switch in the steering column, which will require professional service.

F = Front   R = Rear   ● = Lights off   o ⇒ Lights on

Problem		Solution
Turn signals light, but do not flash		• Replace the flasher
No turn signals light on either side		• Check the fuse. Replace if defective. • Check the flasher by substitution • Check for open circuit, short circuit or poor ground
Both turn signals on one side don't work		• Check for bad bulbs • Check for bad ground in both housings
One turn signal light on one side doesn't work		• Check and/or replace bulb • Check for corrosion in socket. Clean contacts. • Check for poor ground at socket
Turn signal flashes too fast or too slow		• Check any bulb on the side flashing too fast. A heavy-duty bulb is probably installed in place of a regular bulb. • Check the bulb flashing too slow. A standard bulb was probably installed in place of a heavy-duty bulb. • Check for loose connections or corrosion at the bulb socket
Indicator lights don't work in either direction		• Check if the turn signals are working • Check the dash indicator lights • Check the flasher by substitution
One indicator light doesn't light		• On systems with 1 dash indicator: See if the lights work on the same side. Often the filaments have been reversed in systems combining stoplights with taillights and turn signals. Check the flasher by substitution • On systems with 2 indicators: Check the bulbs on the same side Check the indicator light bulb Check the flasher by substitution

Troubleshooting Basic Dash Gauge Problems

Problem	Cause	Solution
Coolant Temperature Gauge		
Gauge reads erratically or not at all	• Loose or dirty connections • Defective sending unit	• Clean/tighten connections • Bi-metal gauge: remove the wire from the sending unit. Ground the wire for an instant. If the gauge registers, replace the sending unit.
	• Defective gauge	• Magnetic gauge: disconnect the wire at the sending unit. With ignition ON gauge should register COLD. Ground the wire; gauge should register HOT.
Ammeter Gauge—Turn Headlights ON (do not start engine). Note reaction		
Ammeter shows charge Ammeter shows discharge Ammeter does not move	• Connections reversed on gauge • Ammeter is OK • Loose connections or faulty wiring • Defective gauge	• Reinstall connections • Nothing • Check/correct wiring • Replace gauge
Oil Pressure Gauge		
Gauge does not register or is inaccurate	• On mechanical gauge, Bourdon tube may be bent or kinked	• Check tube for kinks or bends preventing oil from reaching the gauge
	• Low oil pressure	• Remove sending unit. Idle the engine briefly. If no oil flows from sending unit hole, problem is in engine.
	• Defective gauge	• Remove the wire from the sending unit and ground it for an instant with the ignition ON. A good gauge will go to the top of the scale.
	• Defective wiring	• Check the wiring to the gauge. If it's OK and the gauge doesn't register when grounded, replace the gauge.
	• Defective sending unit	• If the wiring is OK and the gauge functions when grounded, replace the sending unit
All Gauges		
All gauges do not operate	• Blown fuse • Defective instrument regulator	• Replace fuse • Replace instrument voltage regulator
All gauges read low or erratically	• Defective or dirty instrument voltage regulator	• Clean contacts or replace
All gauges pegged	• Loss of ground between instrument voltage regulator and car • Defective instrument regulator	• Check ground • Replace regulator
Warning Lights		
Light(s) do not come on when ignition is ON, but engine is not started	• Defective bulb • Defective wire	• Replace bulb • Check wire from light to sending unit
	• Defective sending unit	• Disconnect the wire from the sending unit and ground it. Replace the sending unit if the light comes on with the ignition ON.
Light comes on with engine running	• Problem in individual system • Defective sending unit	• Check system • Check sending unit (see above)

Troubleshooting the Heater

Problem	Cause	Solution
Blower motor will not turn at any speed	• Blown fuse • Loose connection • Defective ground • Faulty switch • Faulty motor • Faulty resistor	• Replace fuse • Inspect and tighten • Clean and tighten • Replace switch • Replace motor • Replace resistor
Blower motor turns at one speed only	• Faulty switch • Faulty resistor	• Replace switch • Replace resistor
Blower motor turns but does not circulate air	• Intake blocked • Fan not secured to the motor shaft	• Clean intake • Tighten security
Heater will not heat	• Coolant does not reach proper temperature • Heater core blocked internally • Heater core air-bound • Blend-air door not in proper position	• Check and replace thermostat if necessary • Flush or replace core if necessary • Purge air from core • Adjust cable
Heater will not defrost	• Control cable adjustment incorrect • Defroster hose damaged	• Adjust control cable • Replace defroster hose

WIRING DIAGRAMS

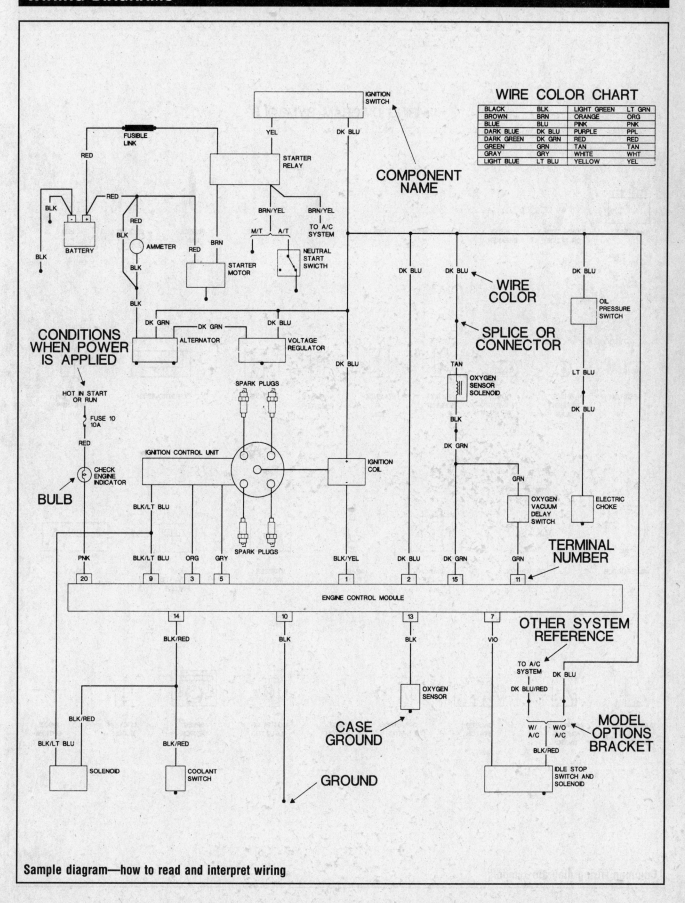

WIRE COLOR CHART

BLACK	BLK	LIGHT GREEN	LT GRN
BROWN	BRN	ORANGE	ORG
BLUE	BLU	PINK	PNK
DARK BLUE	DK BLU	PURPLE	PPL
DARK GREEN	DK GRN	RED	RED
GREEN	GRN	TAN	TAN
GRAY	GRY	WHITE	WHT
LIGHT BLUE	LT BLU	YELLOW	YEL

Sample diagram—how to read and interpret wiring

WIRING DIAGRAM SYMBOLS

BATTERY   CONNECTOR OR SPLICE   CIRCUIT BREAKER   CAPACITOR   COIL   DIODE   FUSE   FUSIBLE LINK   GROUND   LED

RESISTOR   SINGLE FILAMENT BULB   DUAL FILAMENT BULB   HEATING ELEMENT   SOLENOID OR COIL   VARIABLE RESISTOR   CRYSTAL   POTENTIOMETER   HORN OR SPEAKER

ALTERNATOR   DISTRIBUTOR ASSEMBLY   IGNITION COIL   SPARK PLUG   STEPPER MOTOR   HEAT ACTIVATED SWITCH   RELAY

NORMALLY OPEN SWITCH   NORMALLY CLOSED SWITCH   GANGED SWITCH   3-POSITION SWITCH   REED SWITCH   MOTOR OR ACTUATOR   SPEED SENSOR   JUNCTION BLOCK   MODEL OPTIONS BRACKET

Common wiring diagram symbols

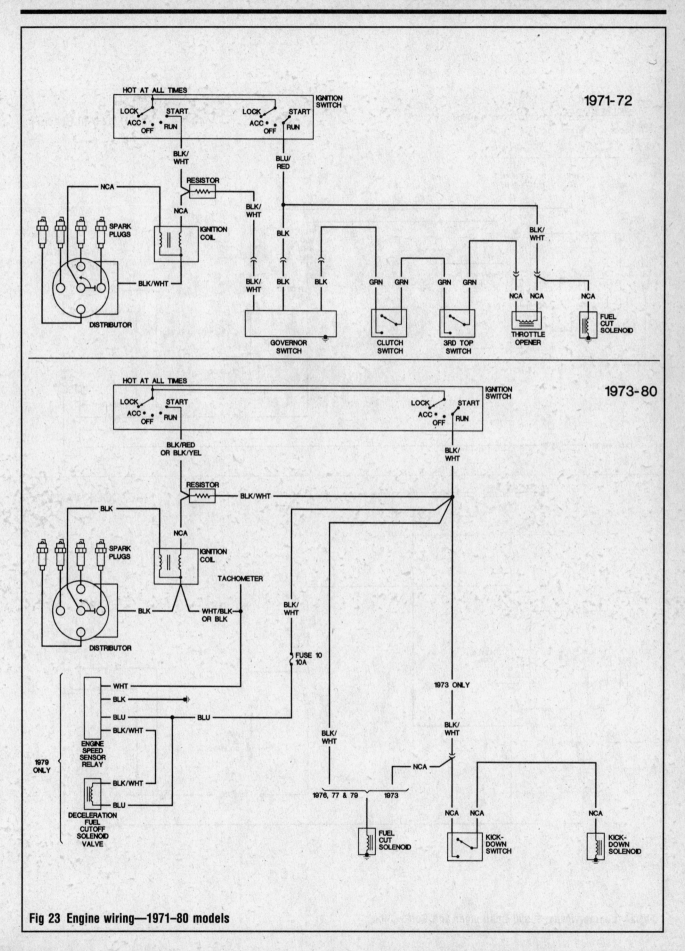

Fig 23 Engine wiring—1971–80 models

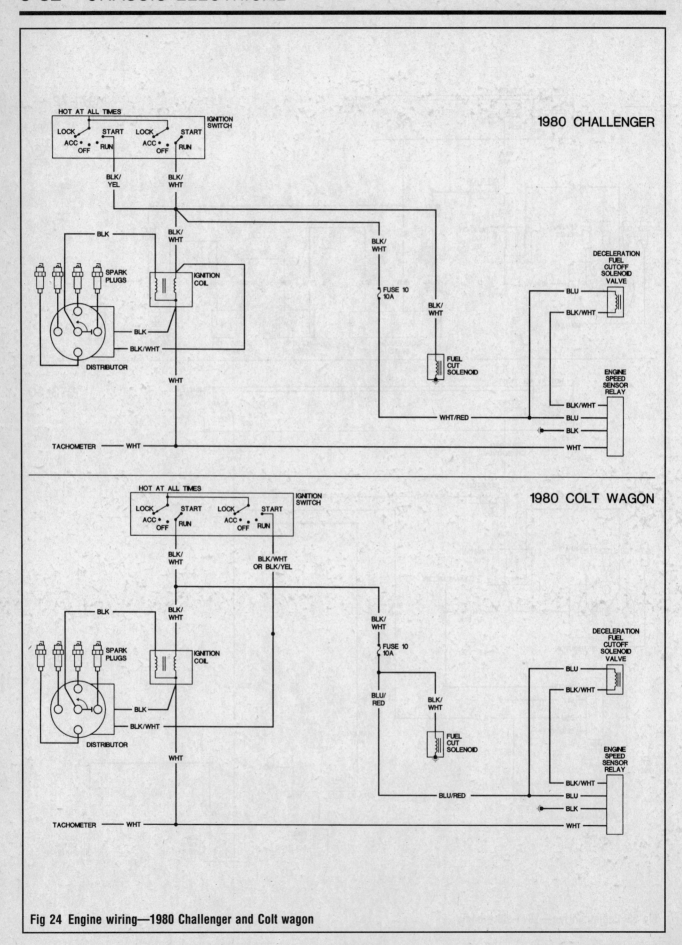

Fig 24 Engine wiring—1980 Challenger and Colt wagon

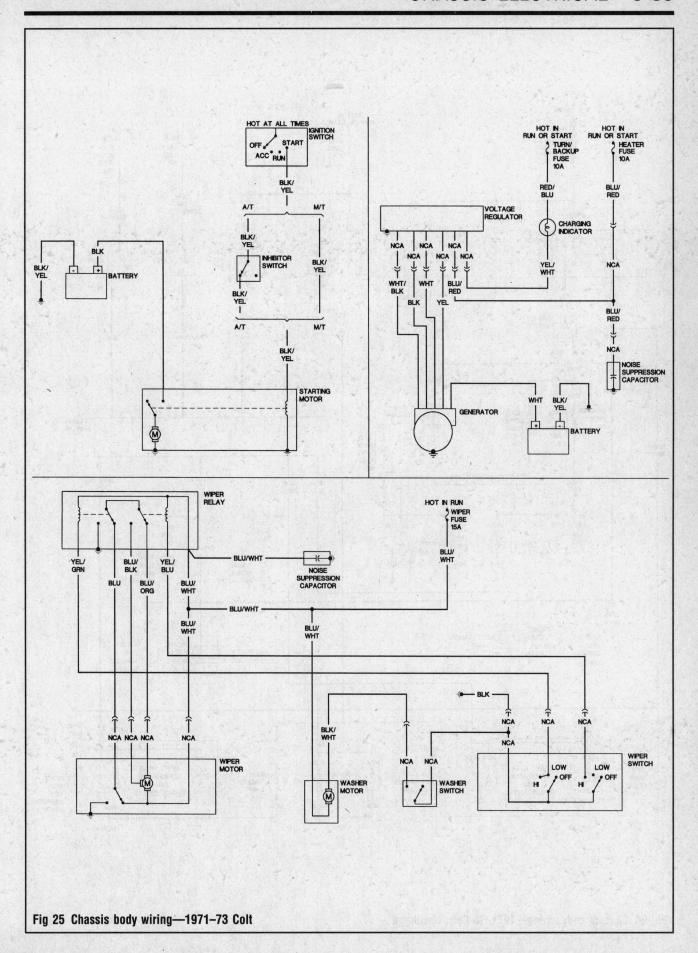

Fig 25 Chassis body wiring—1971–73 Colt

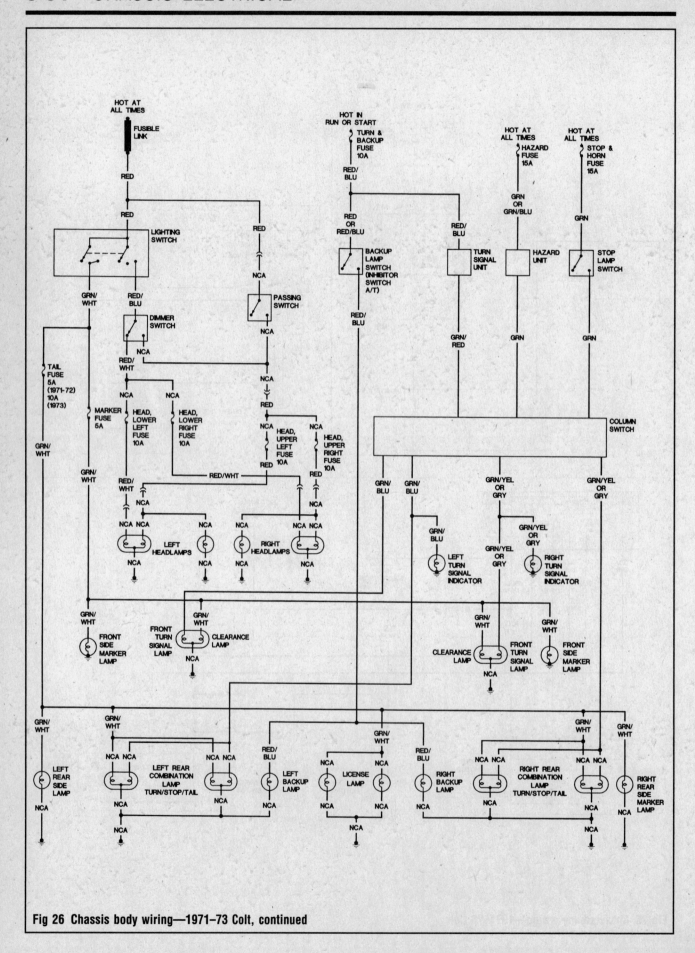

Fig 26 Chassis body wiring—1971-73 Colt, continued

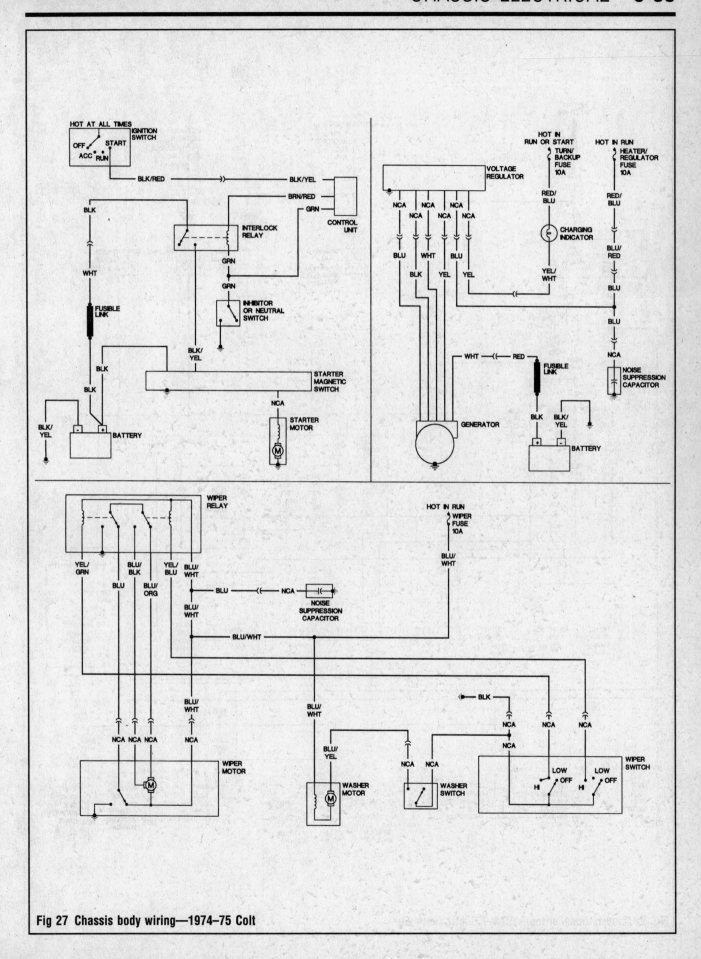

Fig 27 Chassis body wiring—1974-75 Colt

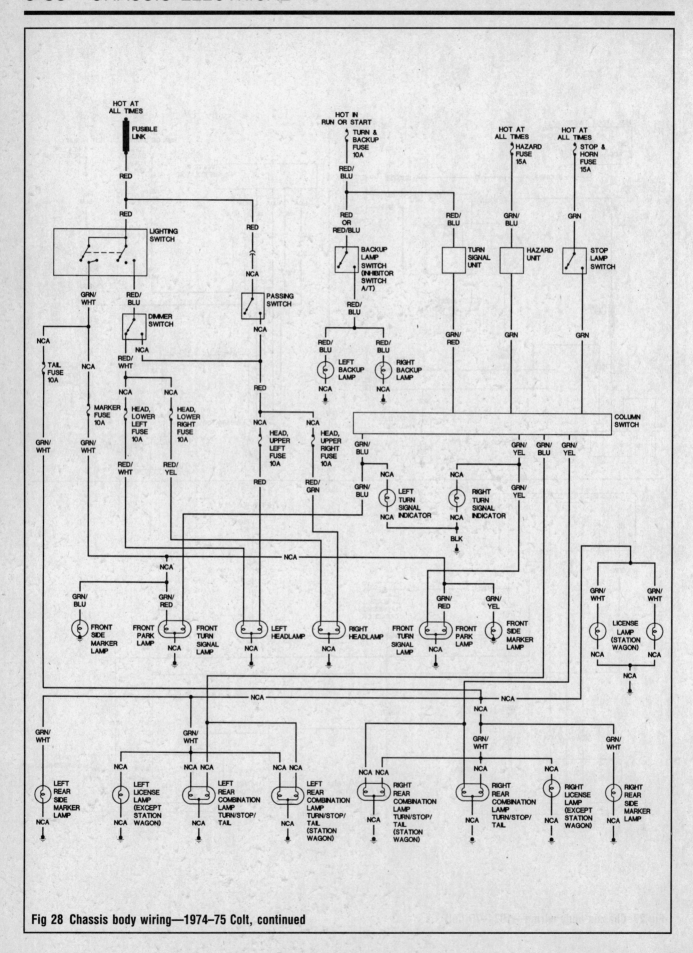

Fig 28 Chassis body wiring—1974-75 Colt, continued

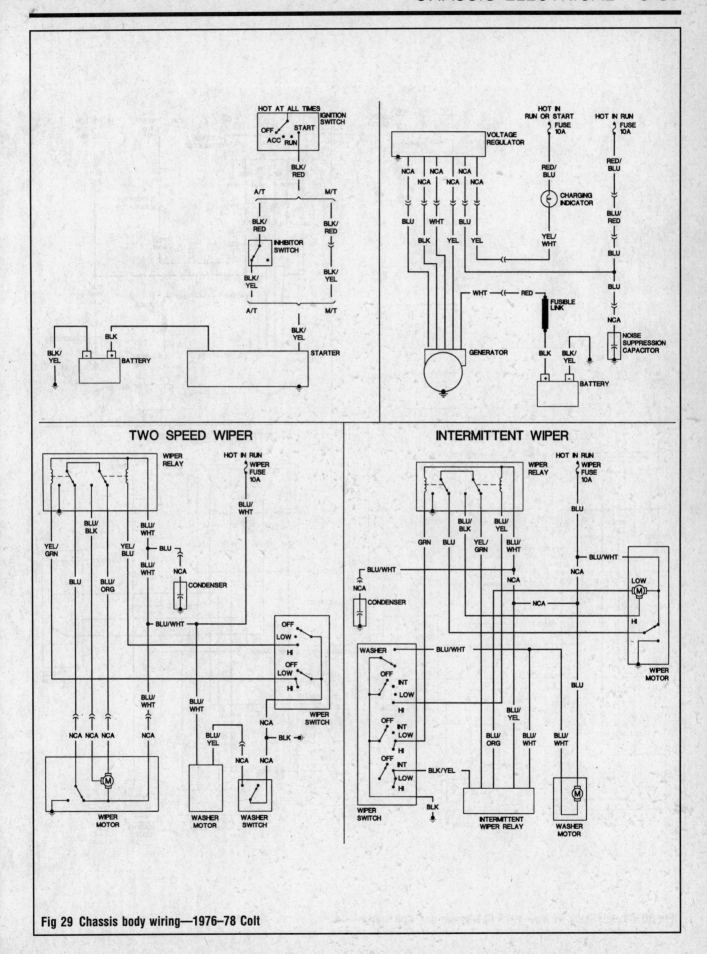

Fig 29 Chassis body wiring—1976–78 Colt

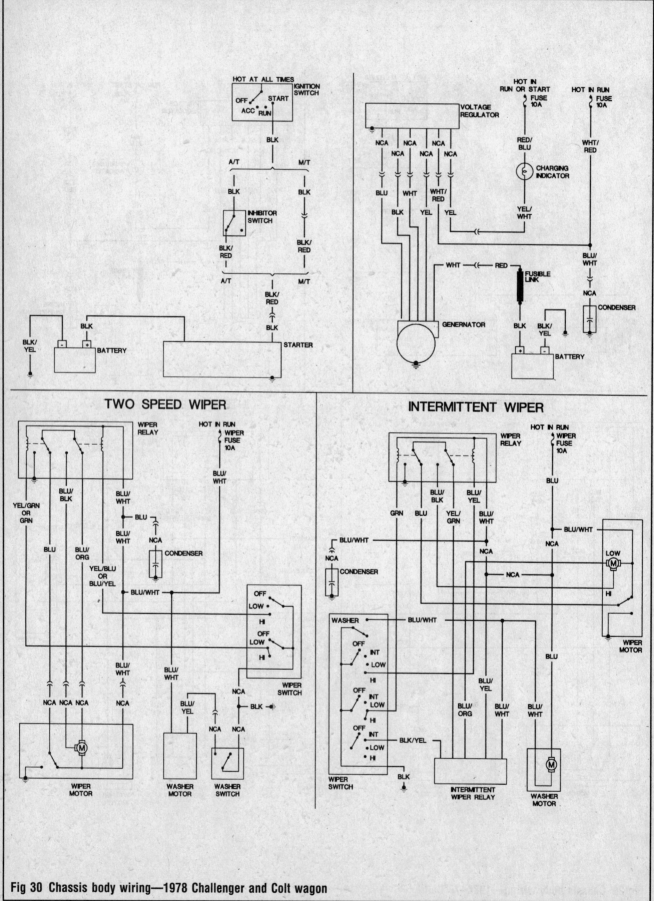

Fig 30 Chassis body wiring—1978 Challenger and Colt wagon

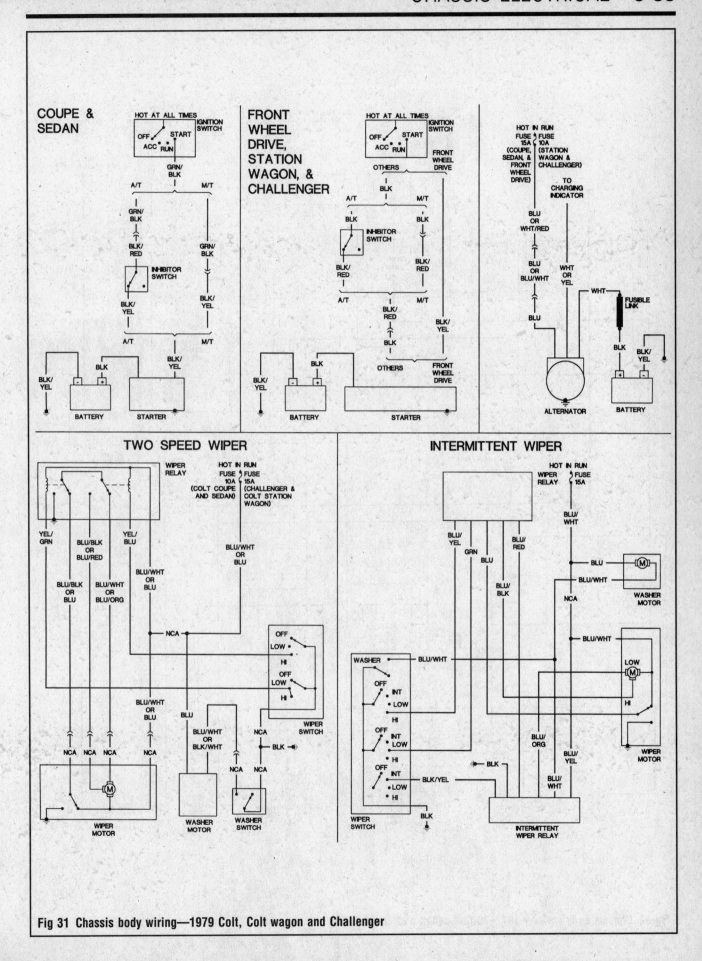

Fig 31 Chassis body wiring—1979 Colt, Colt wagon and Challenger

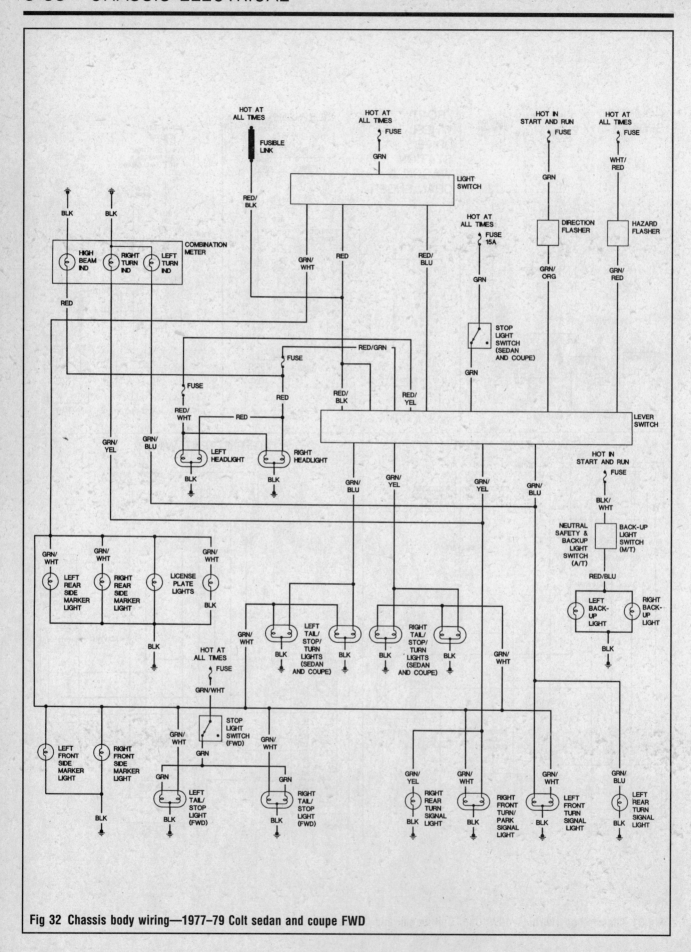

Fig 32 Chassis body wiring—1977–79 Colt sedan and coupe FWD

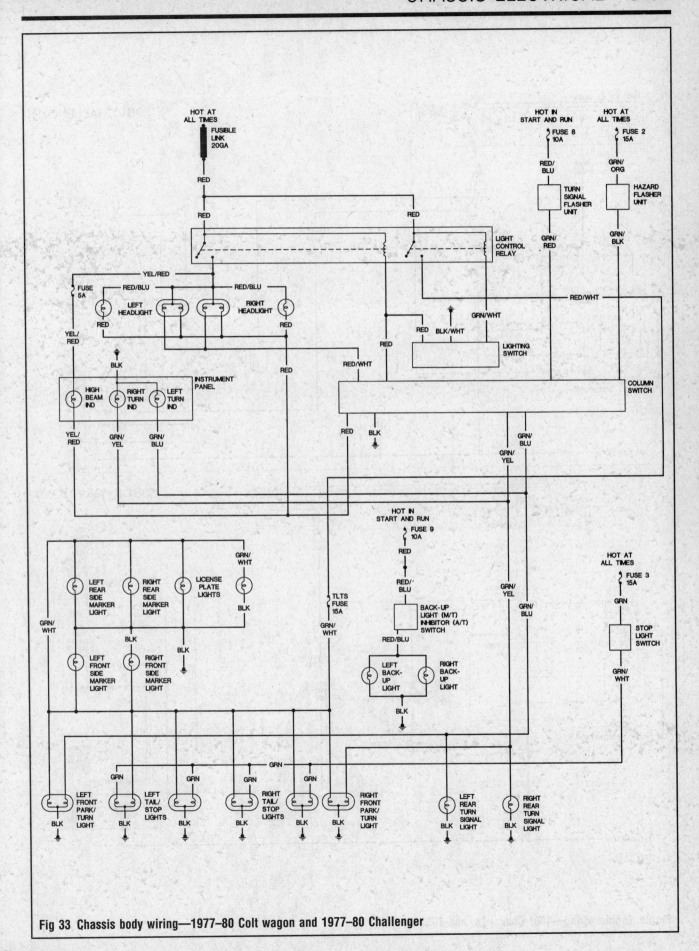

Fig 33 Chassis body wiring—1977-80 Colt wagon and 1977-80 Challenger

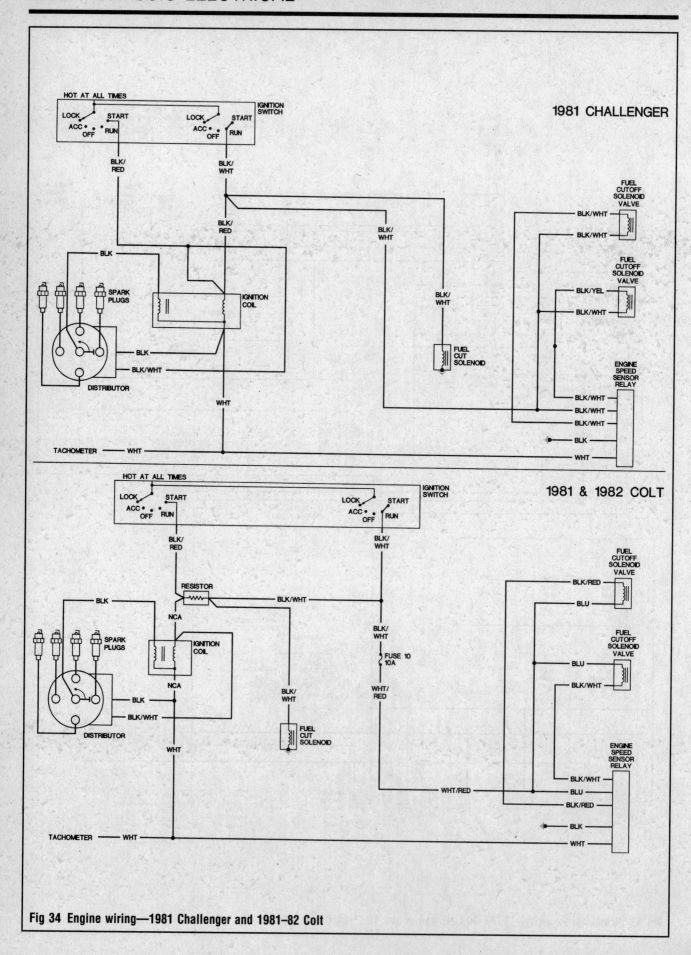

Fig 34 Engine wiring—1981 Challenger and 1981–82 Colt

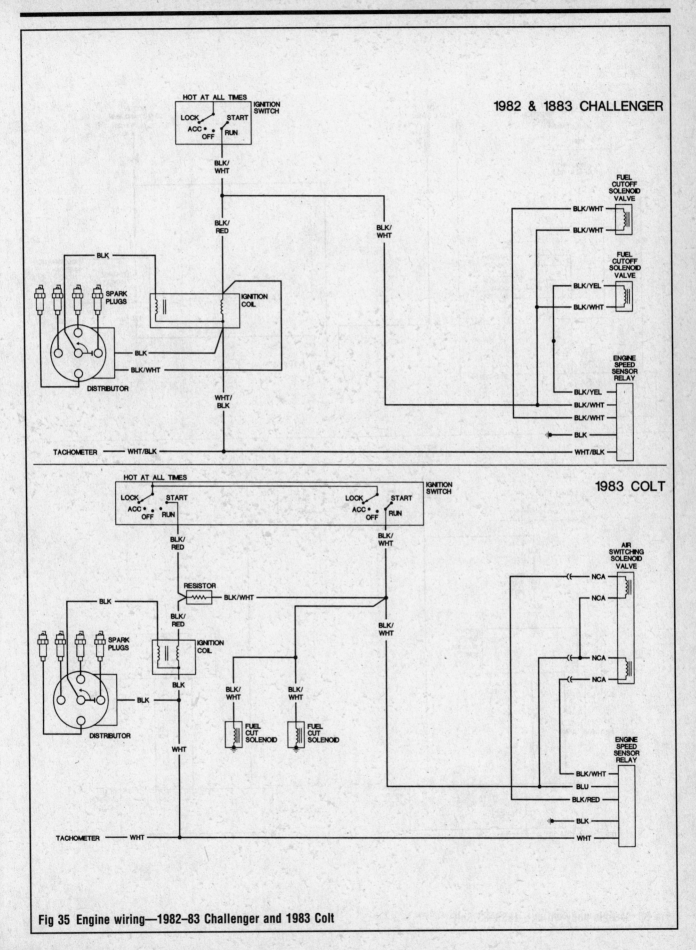

Fig 35 Engine wiring—1982-83 Challenger and 1983 Colt

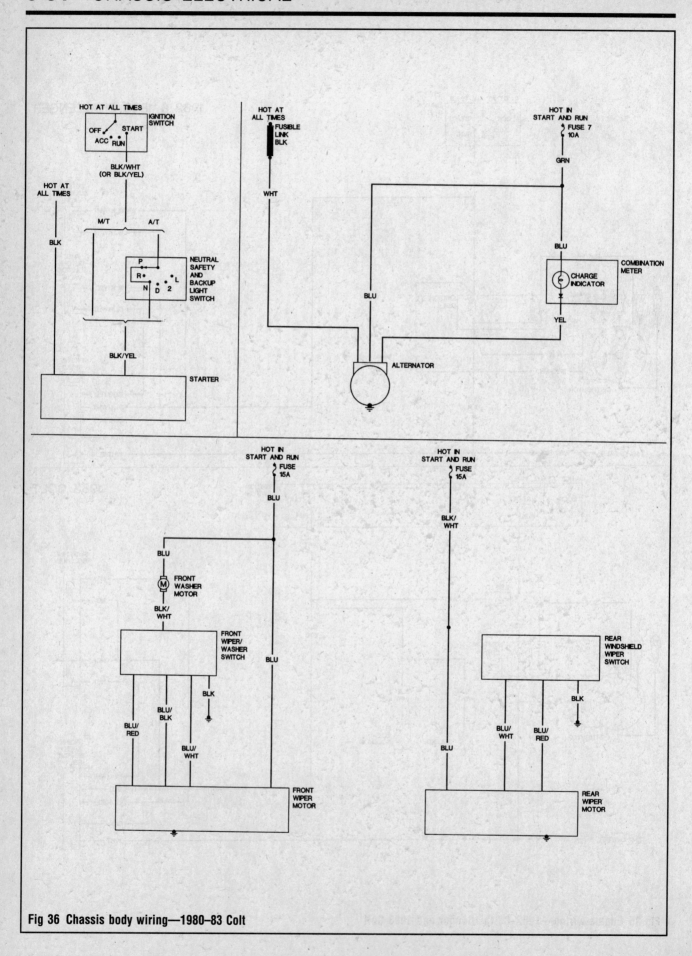

Fig 36 Chassis body wiring—1980-83 Colt

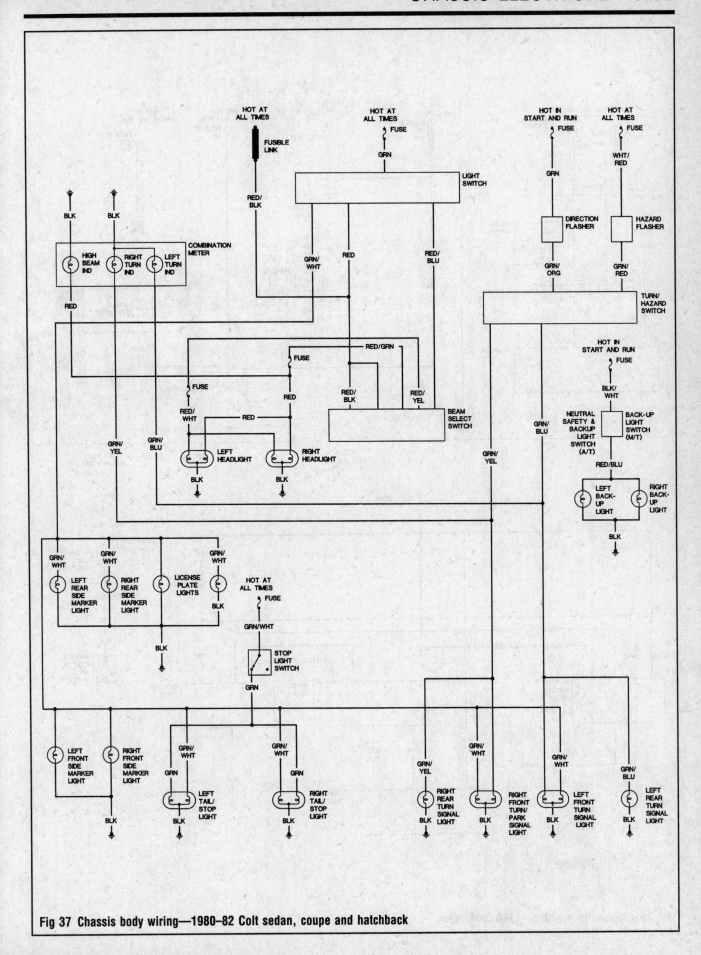

Fig 37 Chassis body wiring—1980–82 Colt sedan, coupe and hatchback

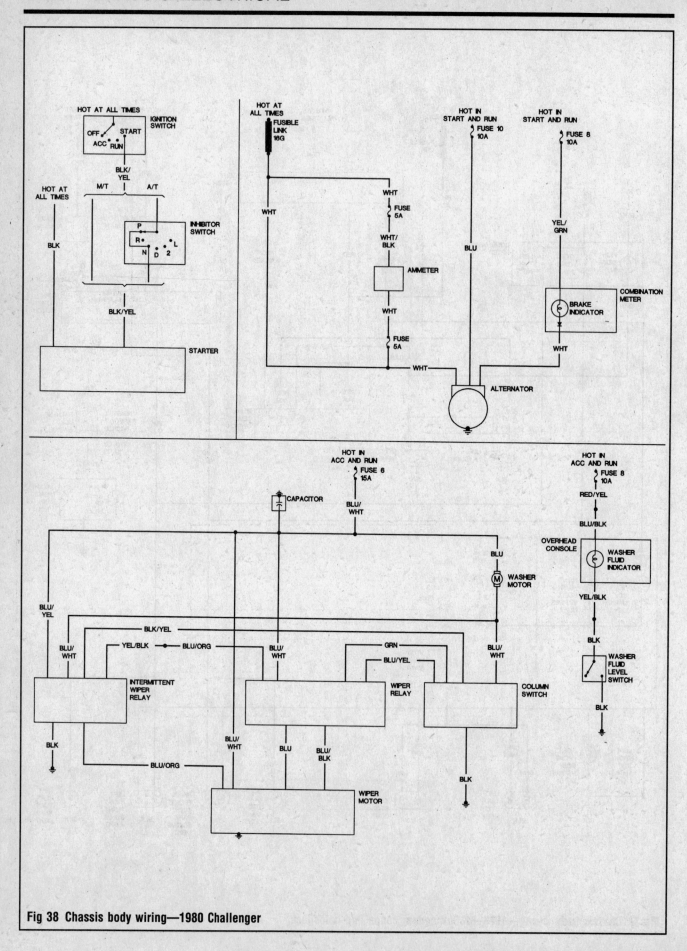

Fig 38 Chassis body wiring—1980 Challenger

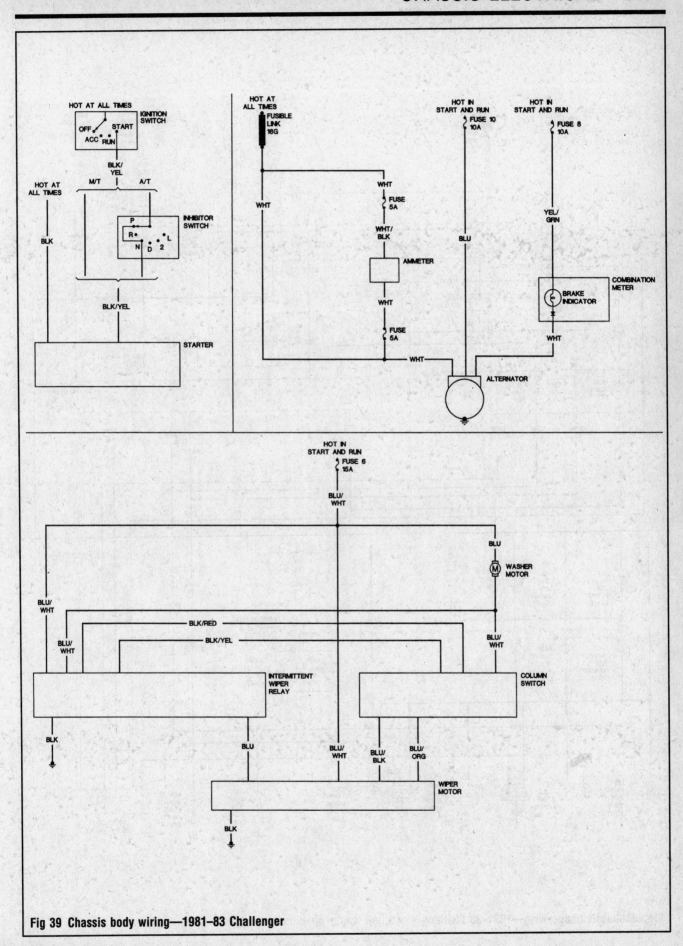

Fig 39 Chassis body wiring—1981-83 Challenger

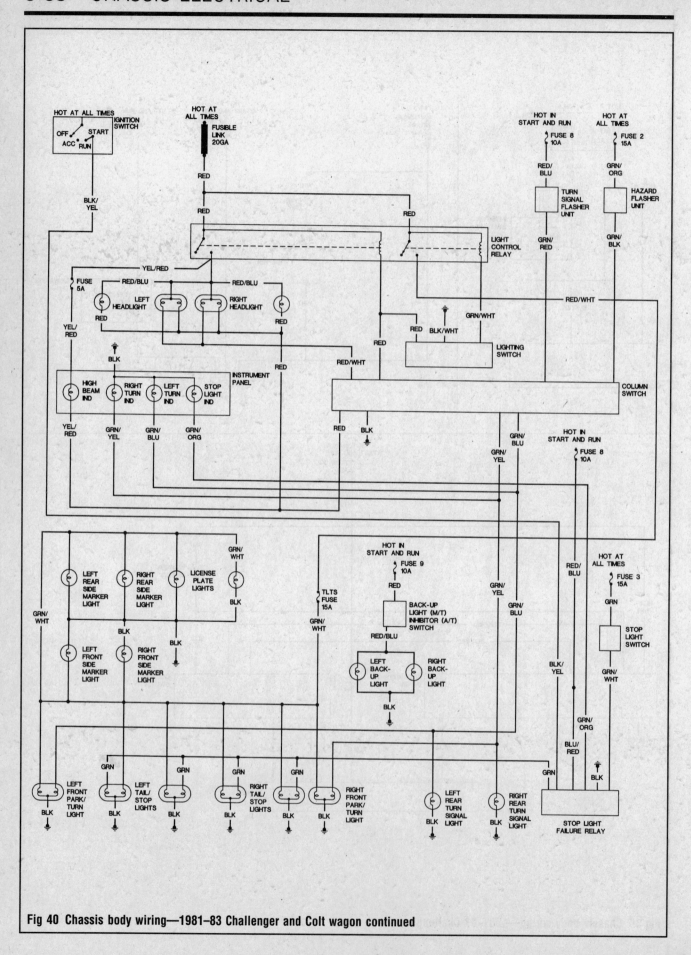

Fig 40 Chassis body wiring—1981-83 Challenger and Colt wagon continued

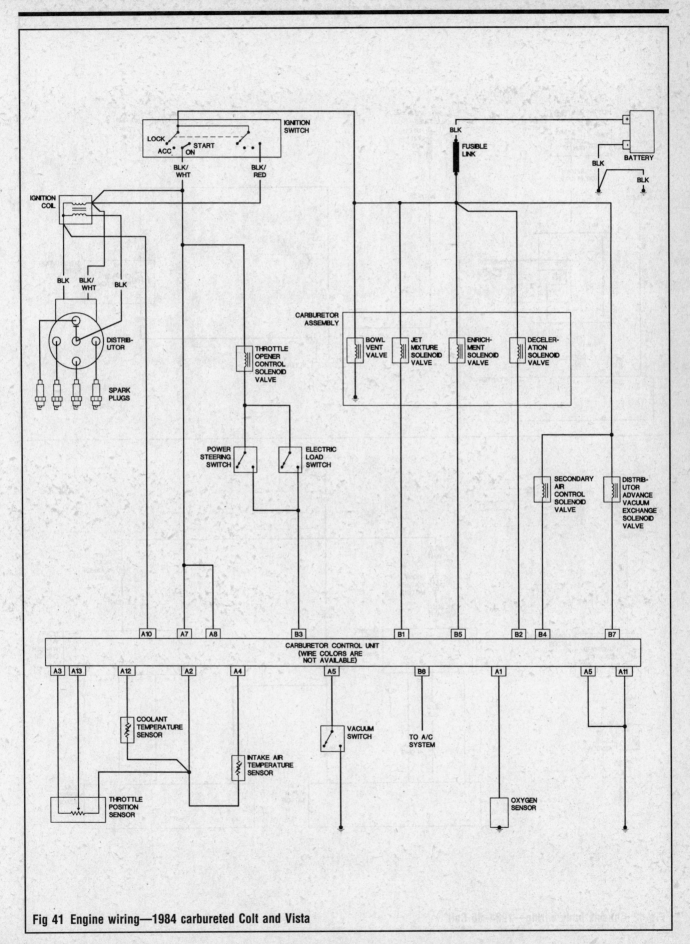

Fig 41 Engine wiring—1984 carbureted Colt and Vista

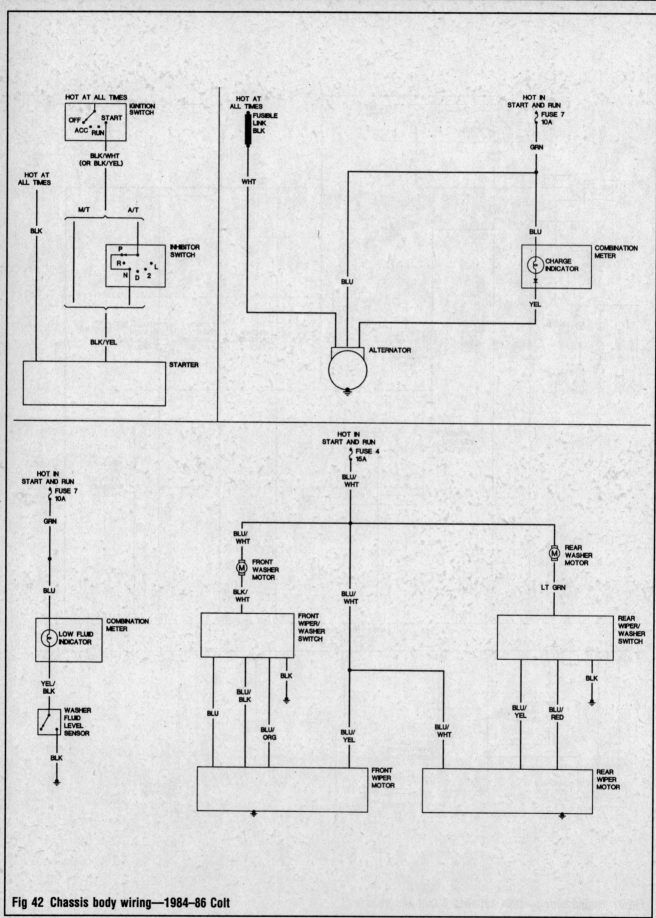

Fig 42 Chassis body wiring—1984–86 Colt

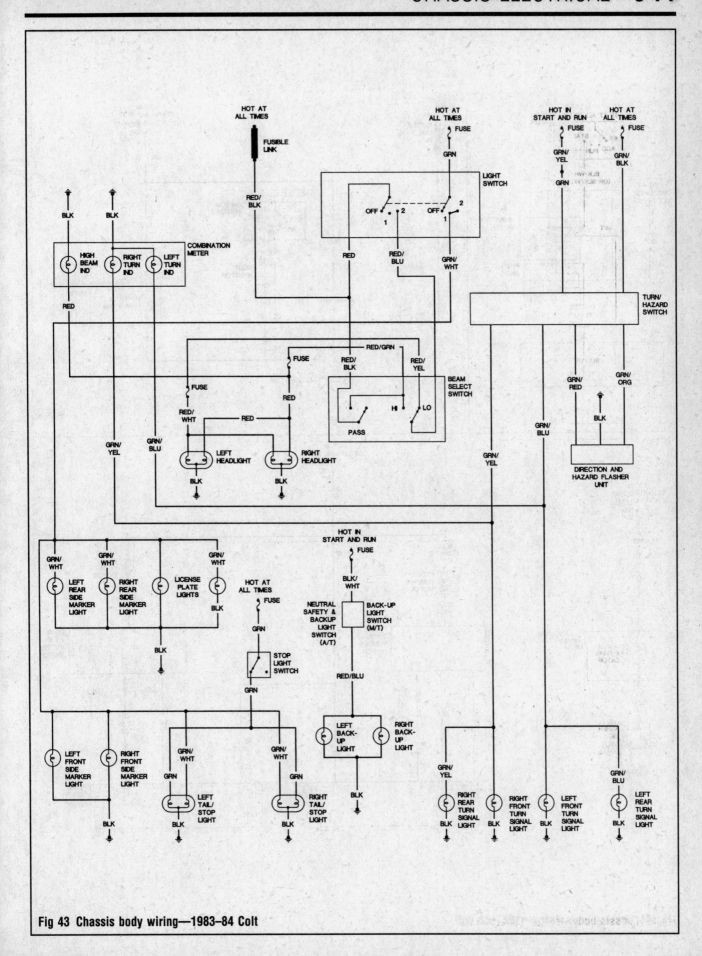

Fig 43 Chassis body wiring—1983–84 Colt

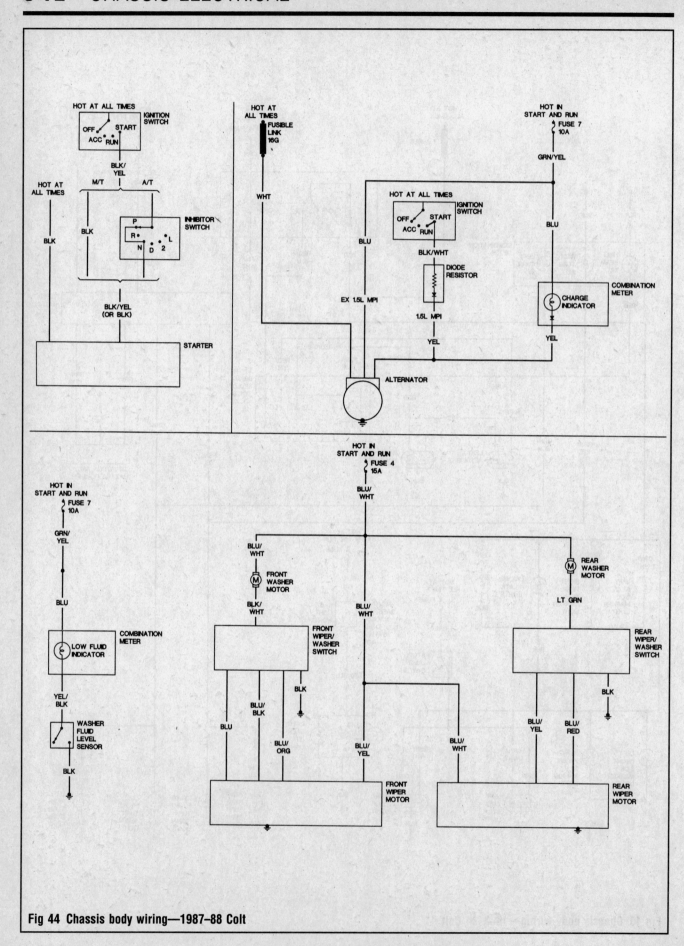

Fig 44 Chassis body wiring—1987-88 Colt

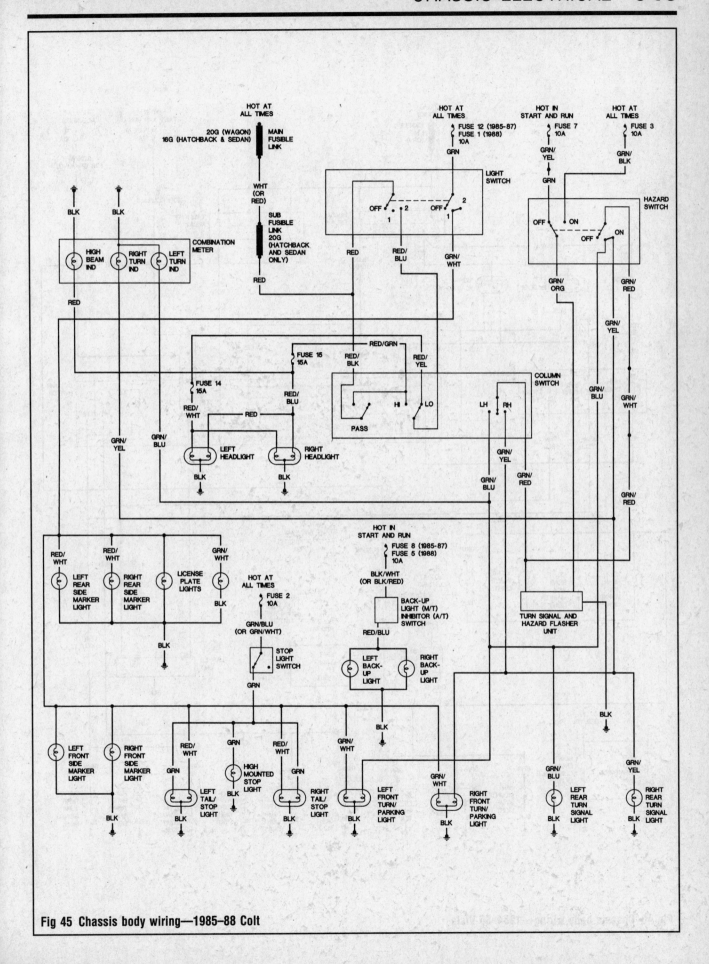

Fig 45 Chassis body wiring—1985-88 Colt

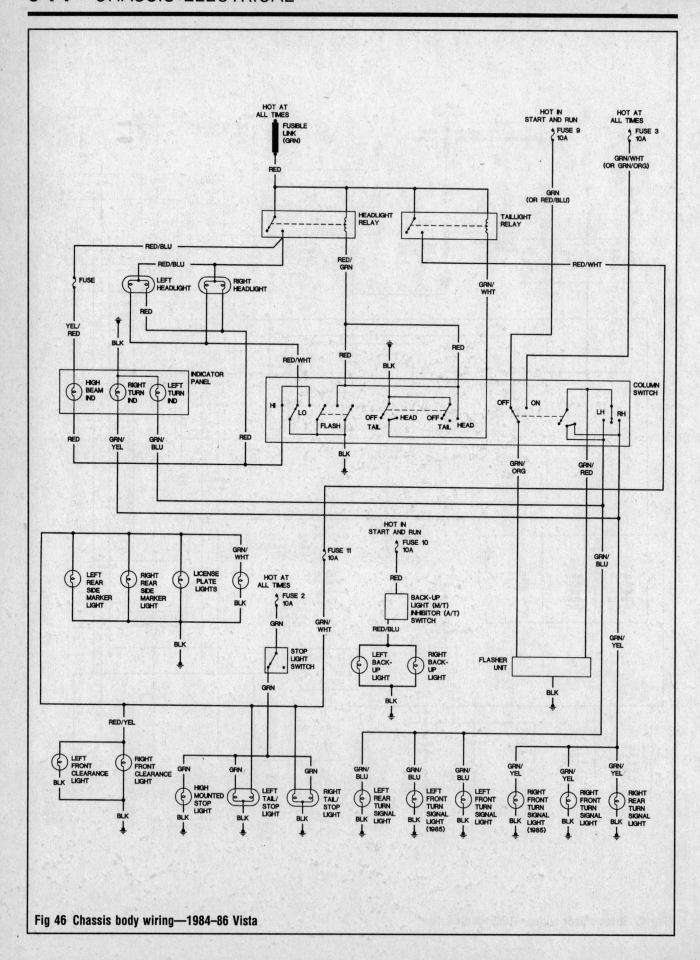

Fig 46 Chassis body wiring—1984-86 Vista

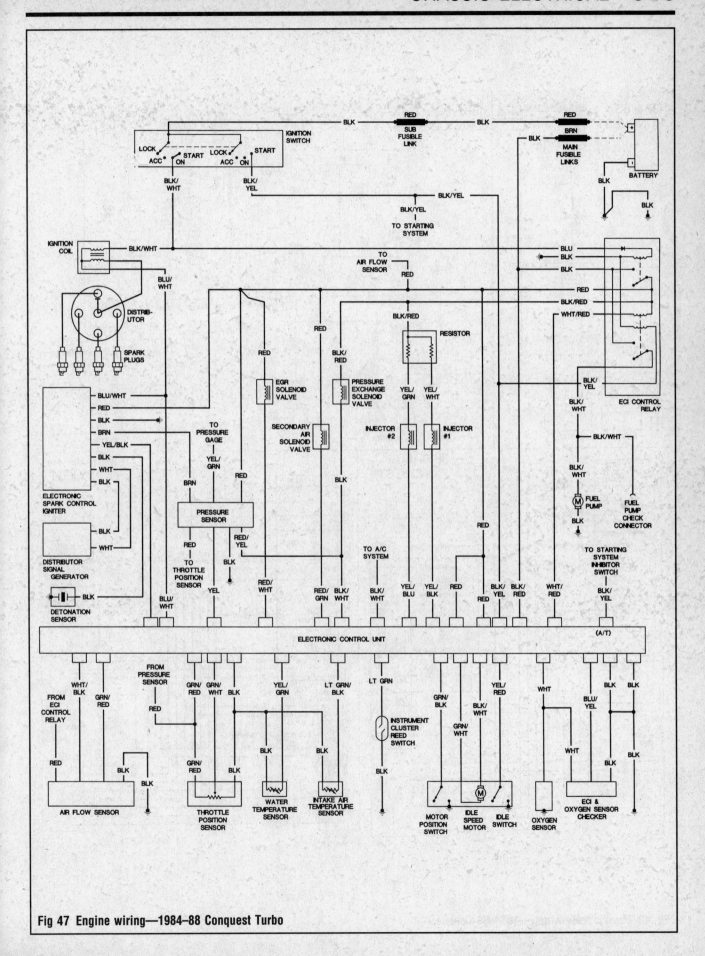

Fig 47 Engine wiring—1984-88 Conquest Turbo

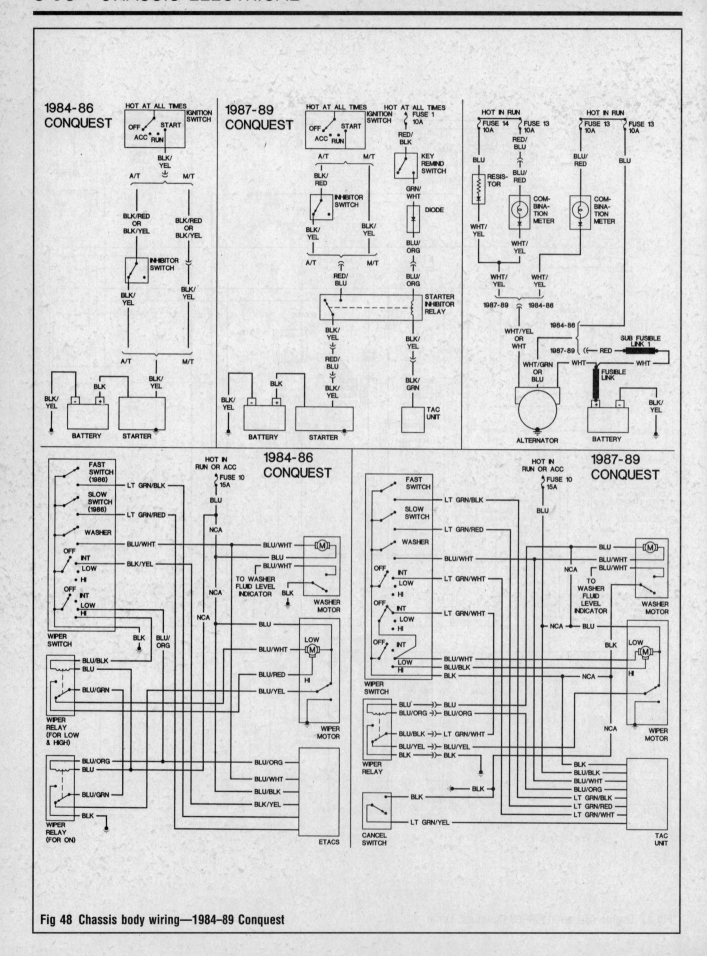

Fig 48 Chassis body wiring—1984-89 Conquest

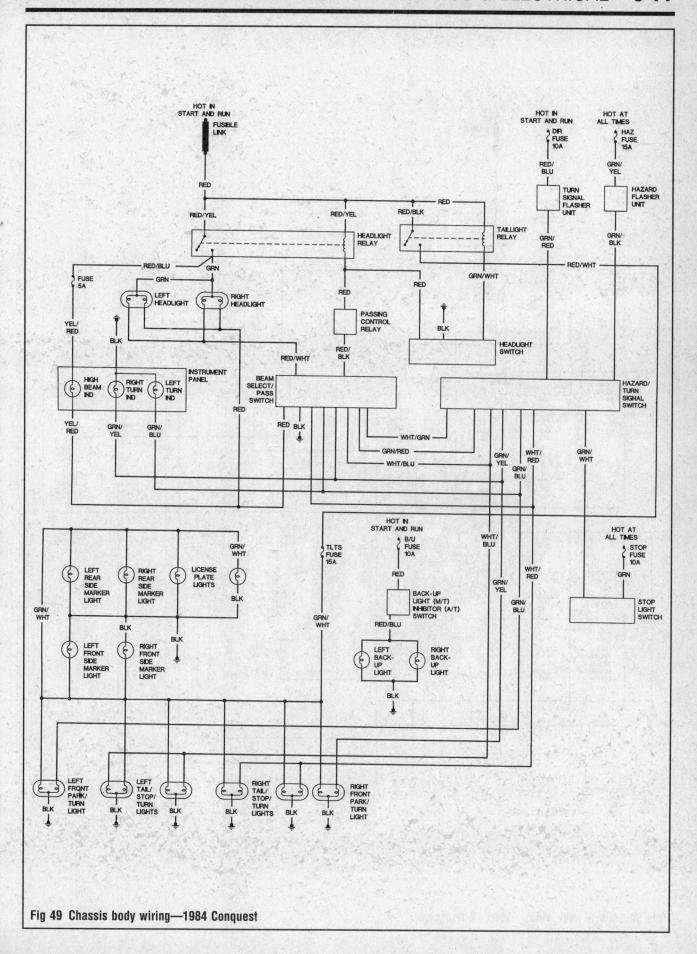

Fig 49 Chassis body wiring—1984 Conquest

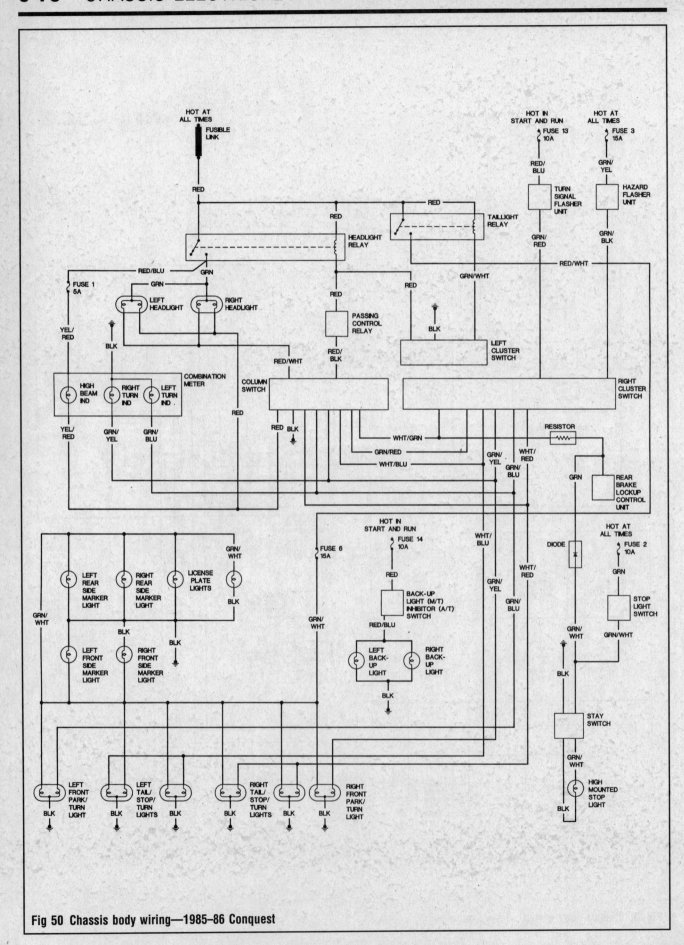

Fig 50 Chassis body wiring—1985-86 Conquest

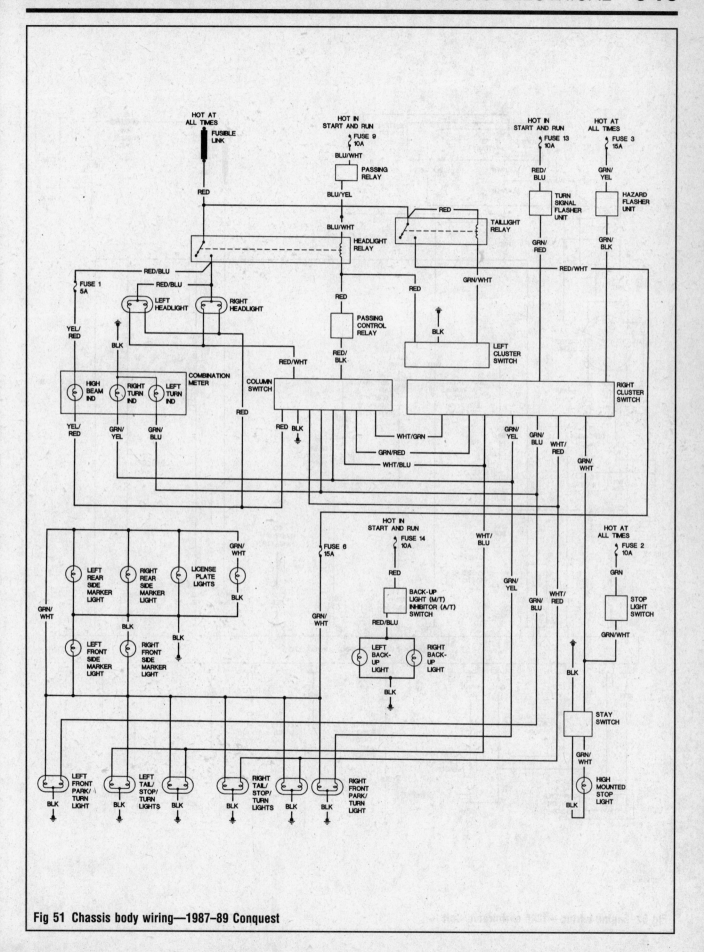

Fig 51 Chassis body wiring—1987–89 Conquest

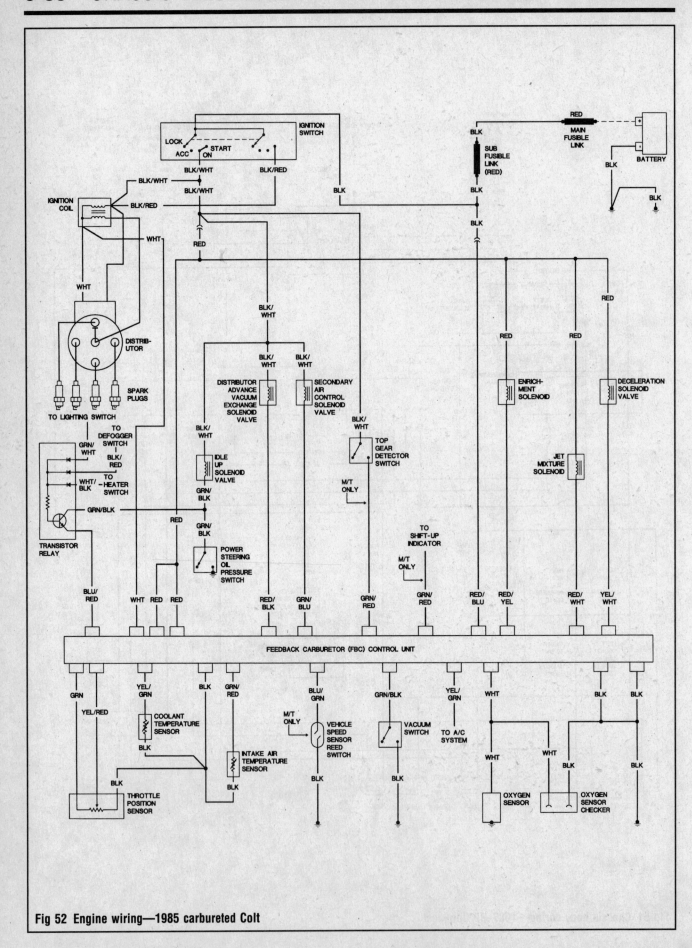

Fig 52 Engine wiring—1985 carbureted Colt

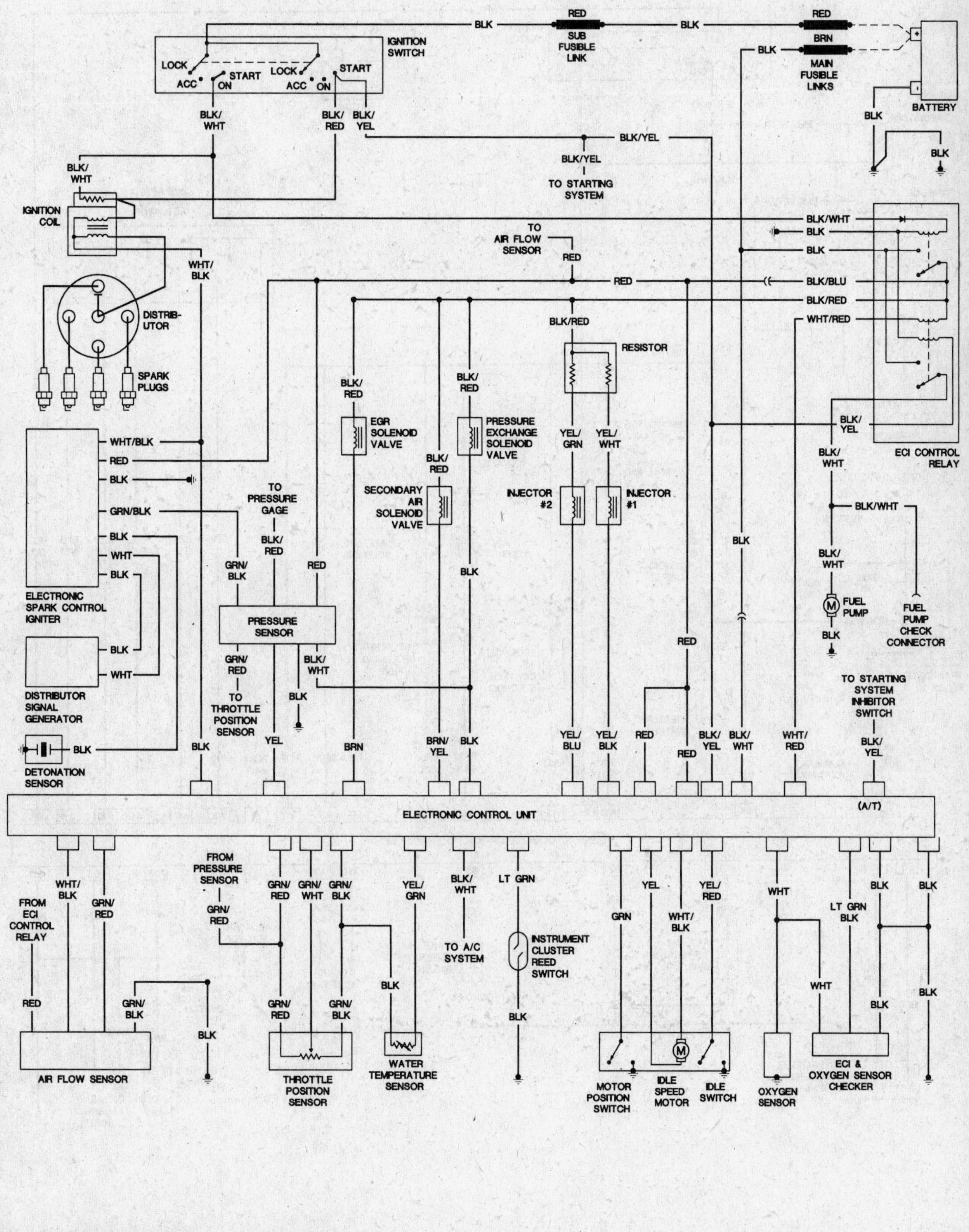

Fig 53 Engine wiring—1984–85 Colt Turbo

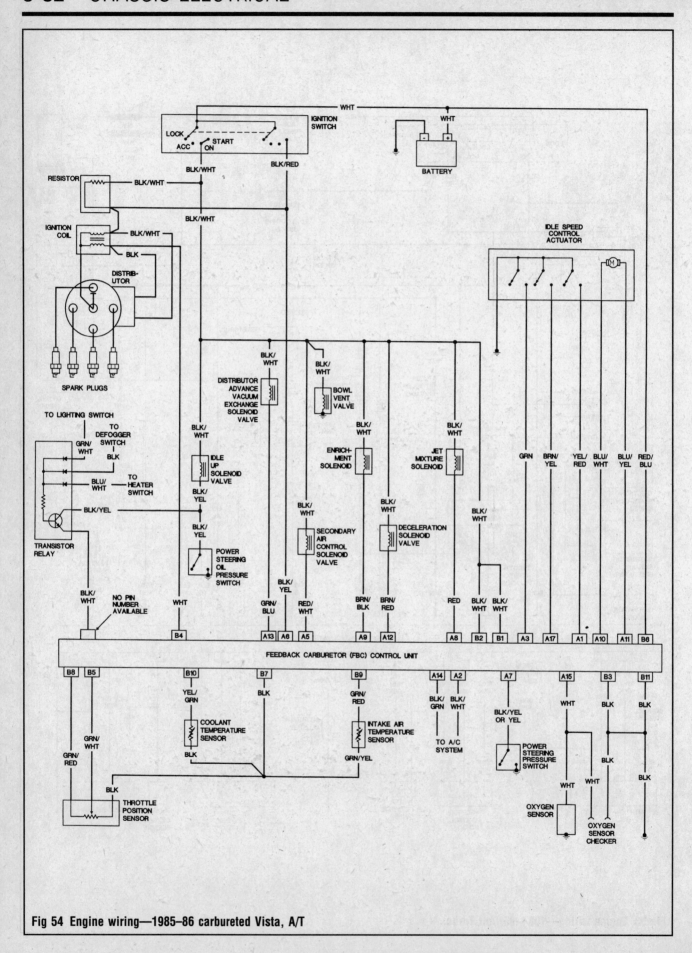

Fig 54 Engine wiring—1985–86 carbureted Vista, A/T

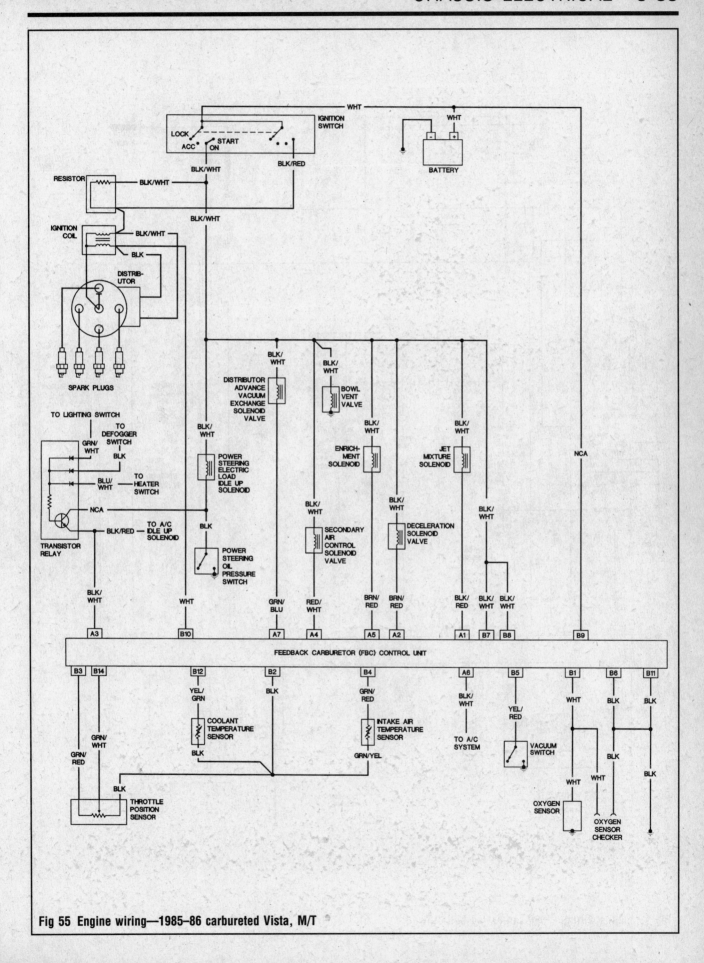

Fig 55 Engine wiring—1985–86 carbureted Vista, M/T

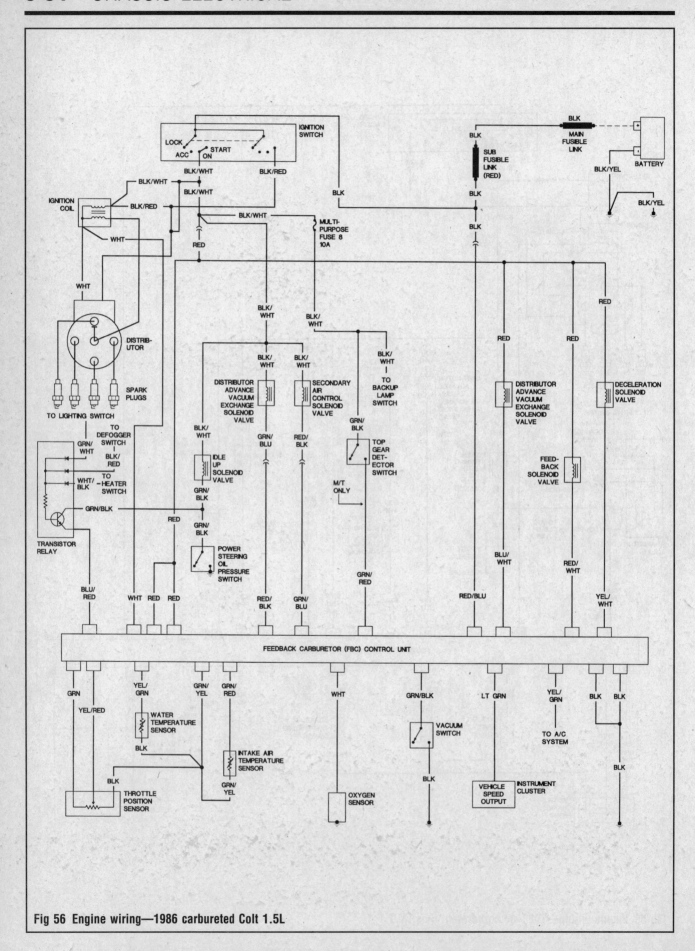

Fig 56 Engine wiring—1986 carbureted Colt 1.5L

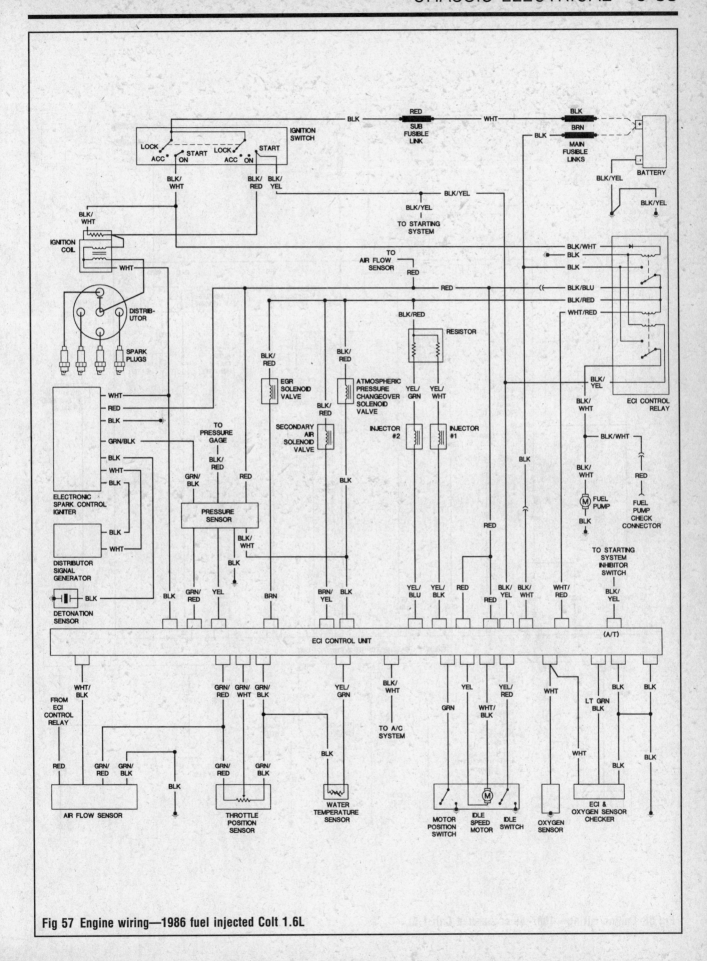

Fig 57 Engine wiring—1986 fuel injected Colt 1.6L

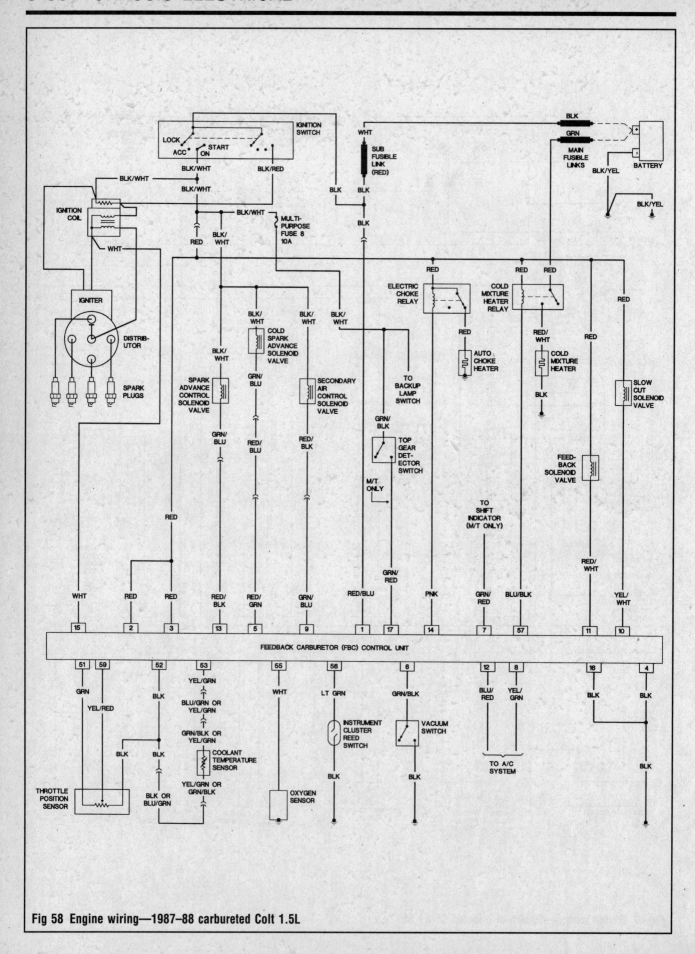

Fig 58 Engine wiring—1987–88 carbureted Colt 1.5L

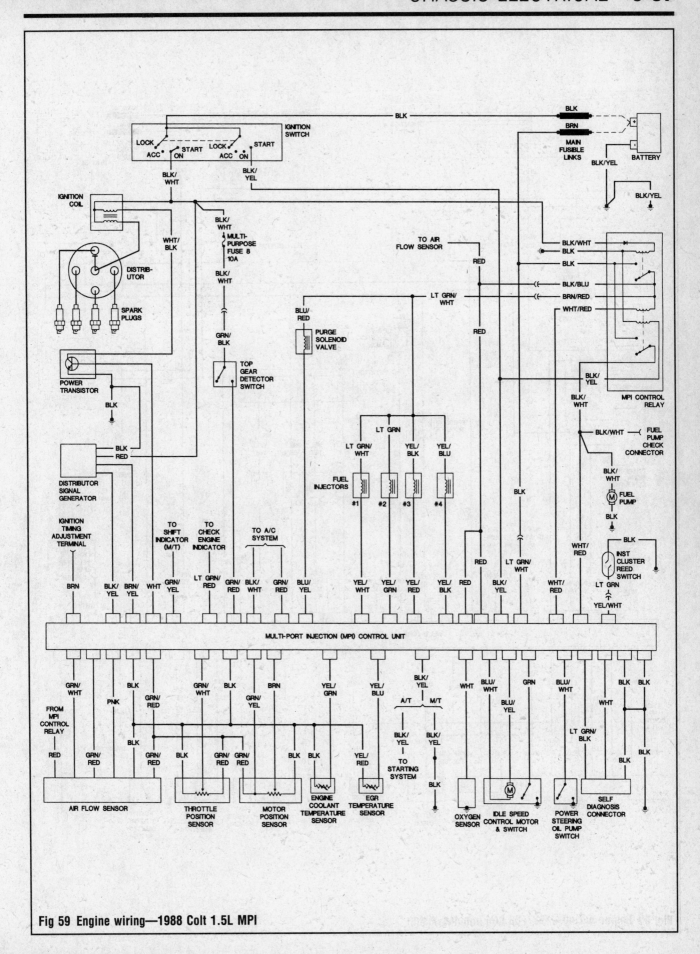

Fig 59 Engine wiring—1988 Colt 1.5L MPI

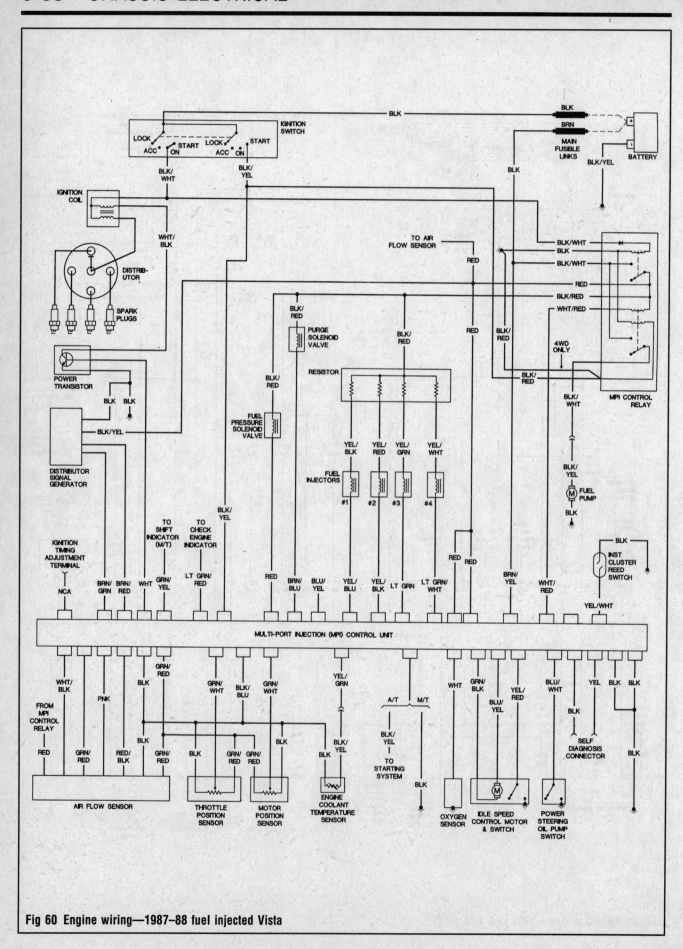

Fig 60 Engine wiring—1987–88 fuel injected Vista

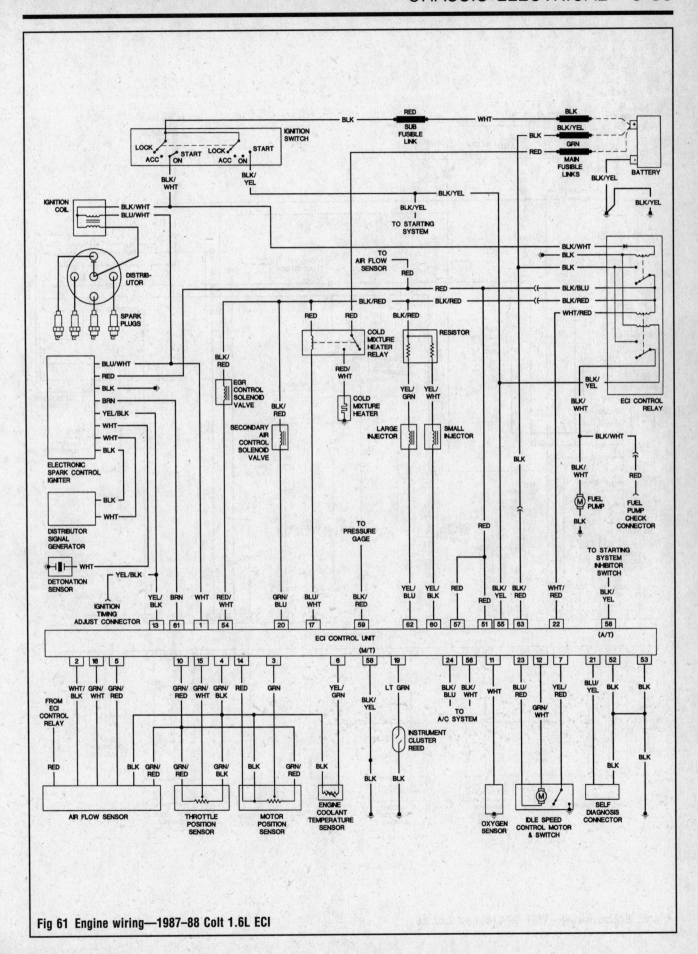

Fig 61 Engine wiring—1987–88 Colt 1.6L ECI

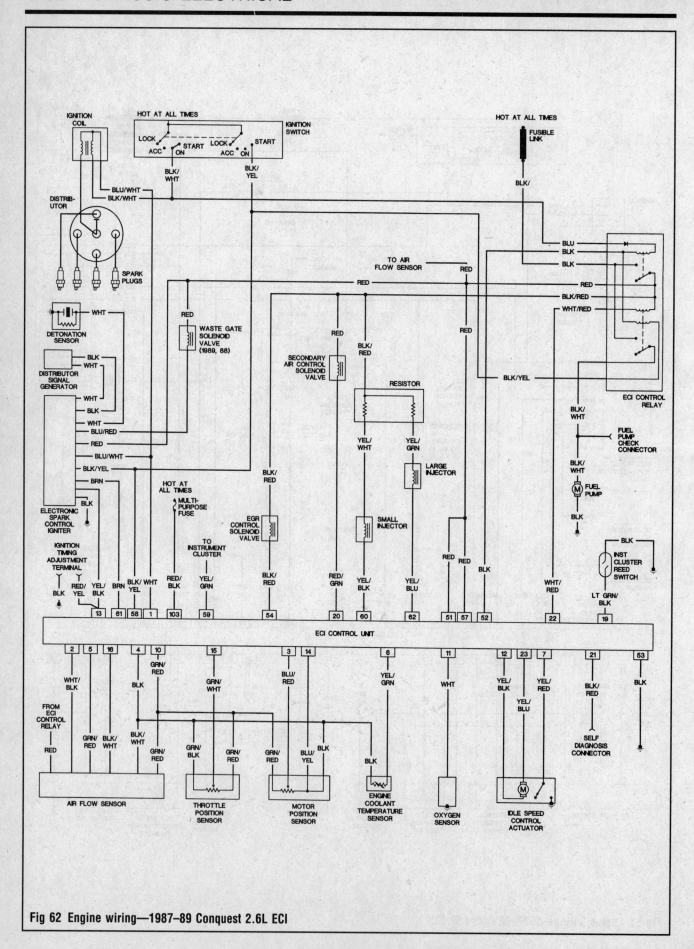

Fig 62 Engine wiring—1987-89 Conquest 2.6L ECI

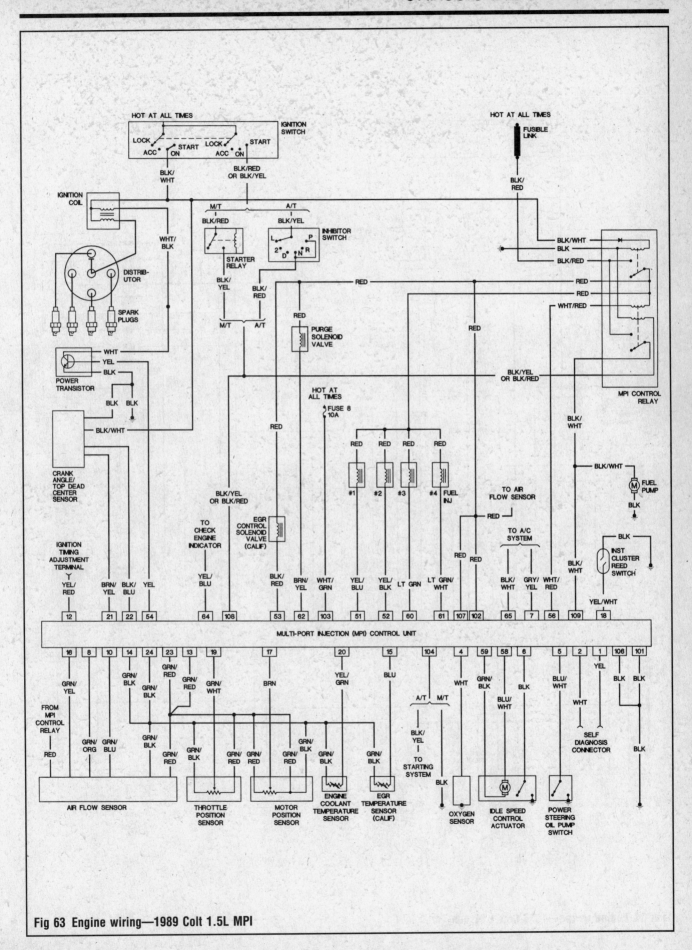

Fig 63 Engine wiring—1989 Colt 1.5L MPI

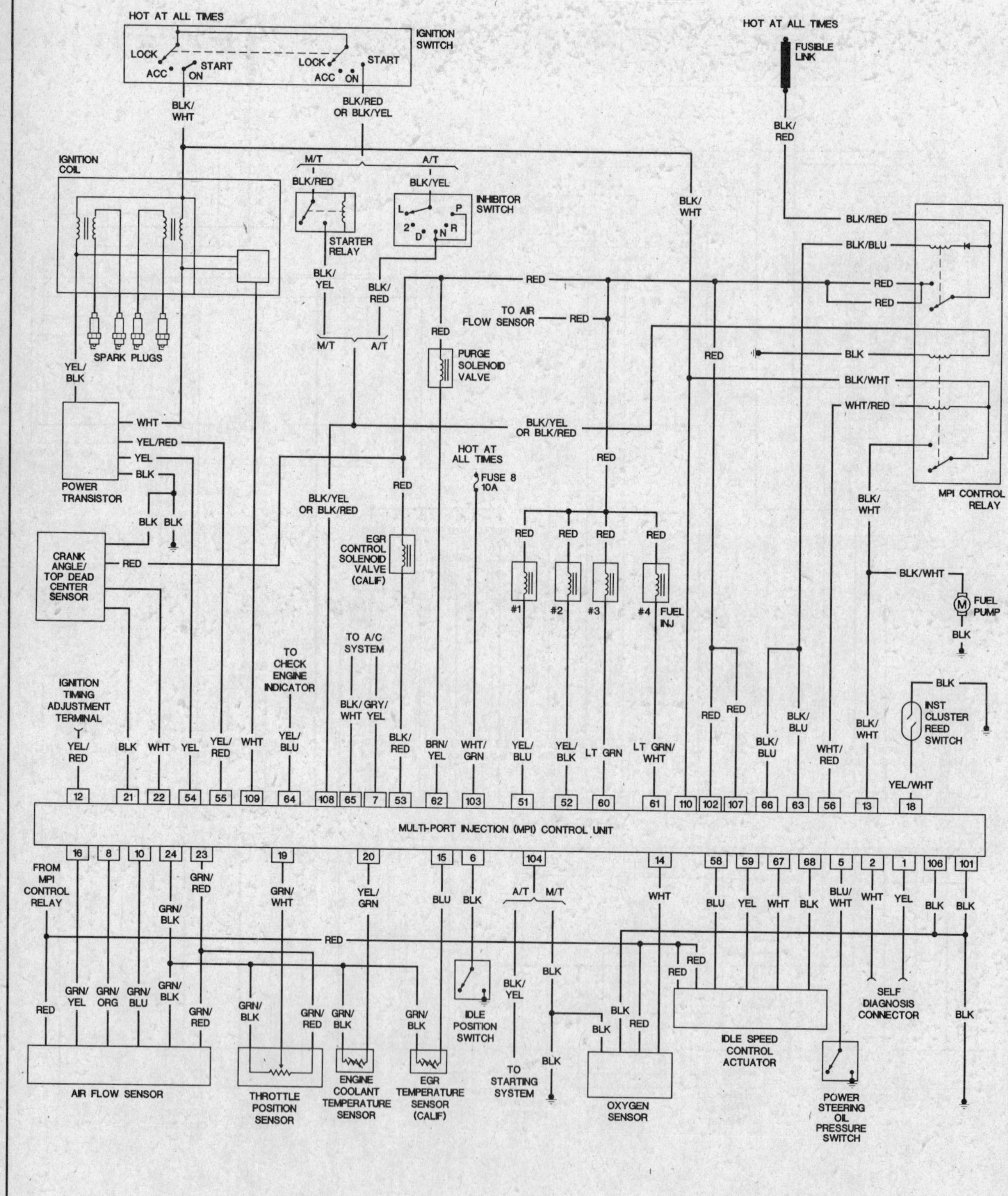

Fig 64 Engine wiring—1989 Colt 1.6L non-Turbo MPI

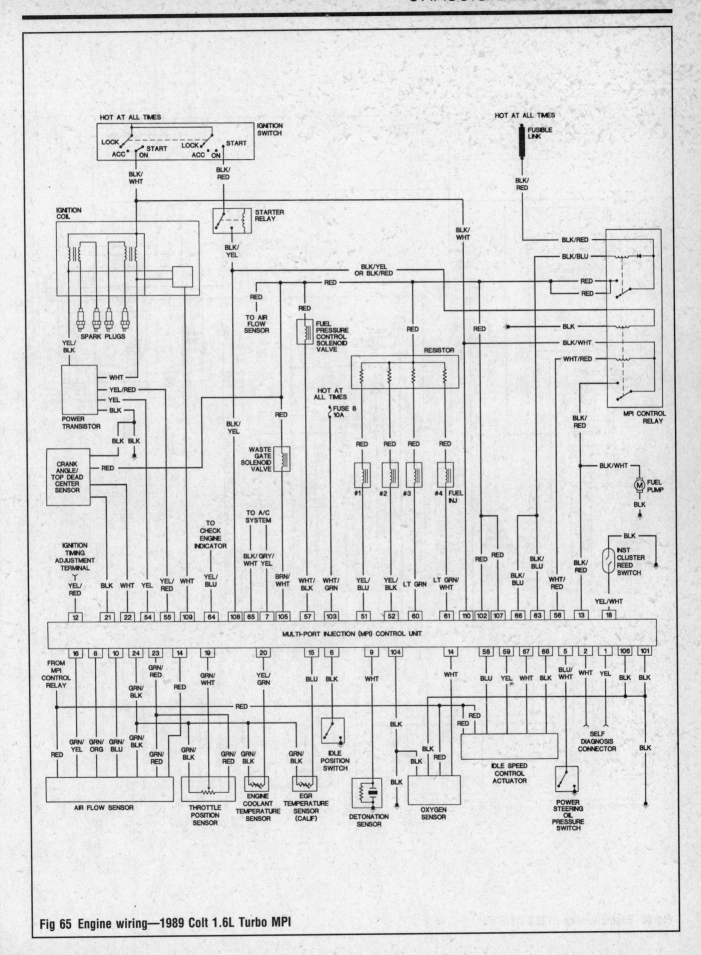

Fig 65 Engine wiring—1989 Colt 1.6L Turbo MPI

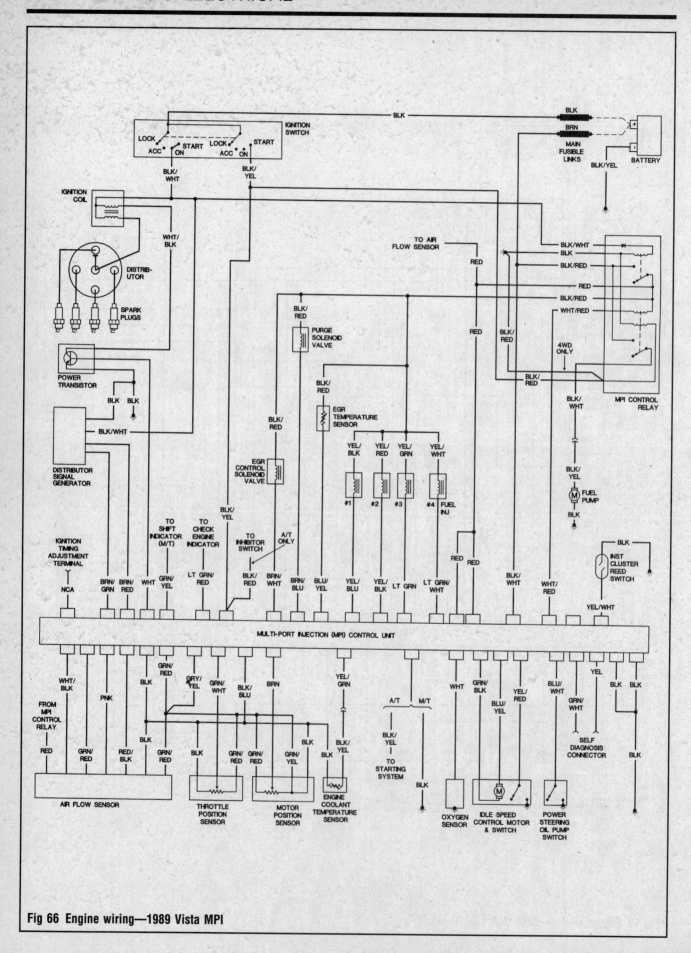

Fig 66 Engine wiring—1989 Vista MPI

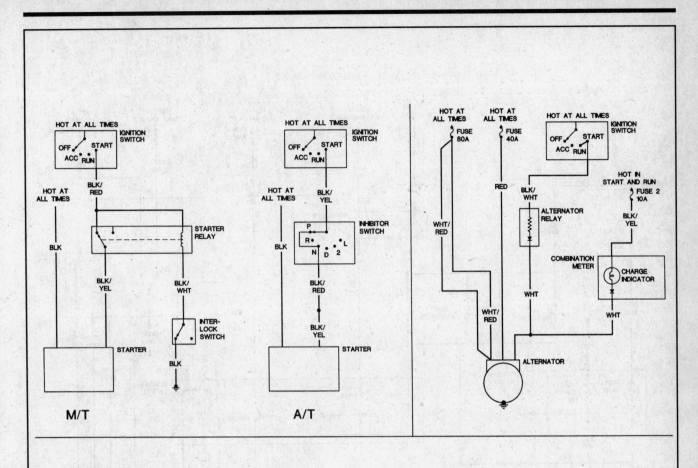

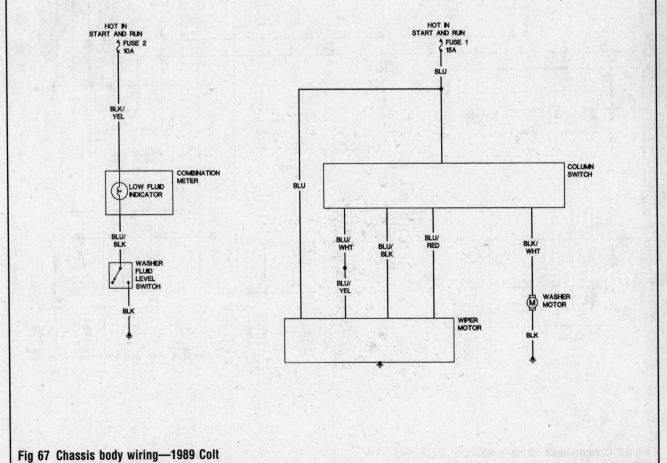

Fig 67 Chassis body wiring—1989 Colt

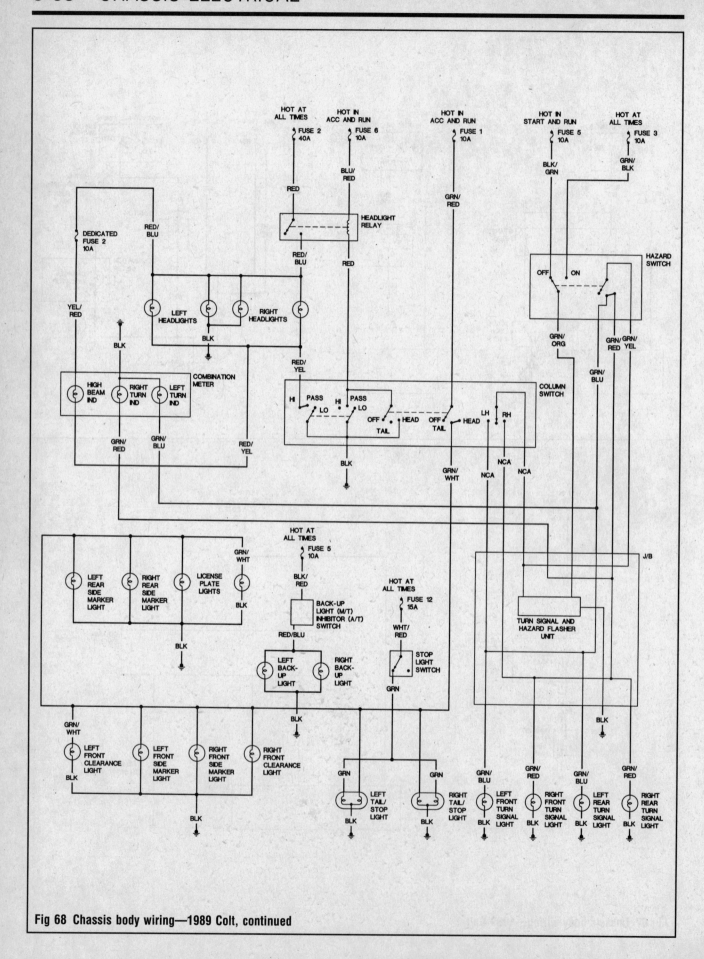

Fig 68 Chassis body wiring—1989 Colt, continued

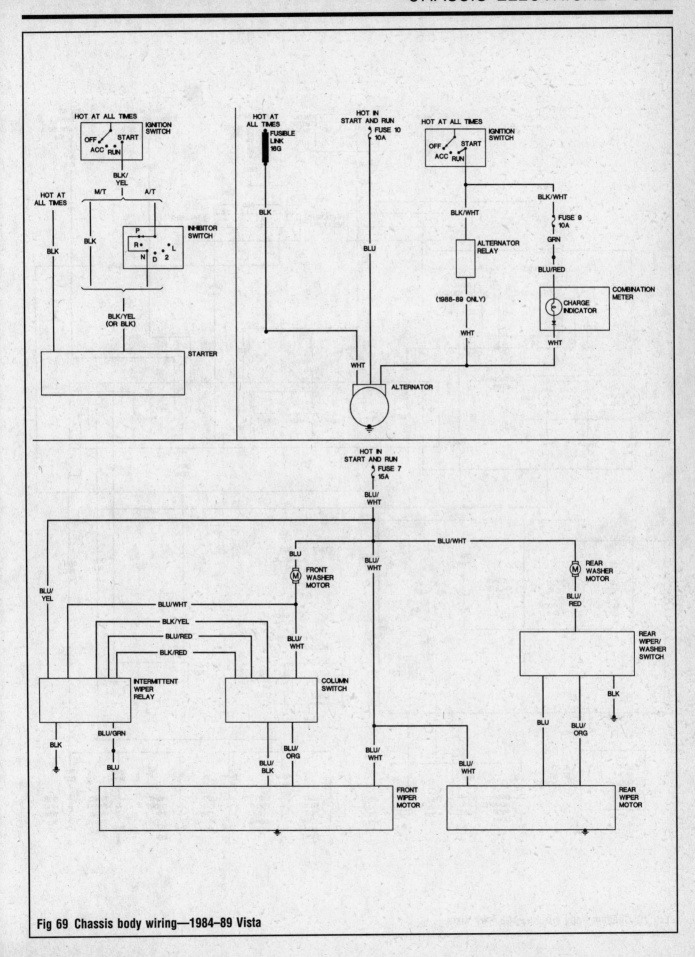

Fig 69 Chassis body wiring—1984–89 Vista

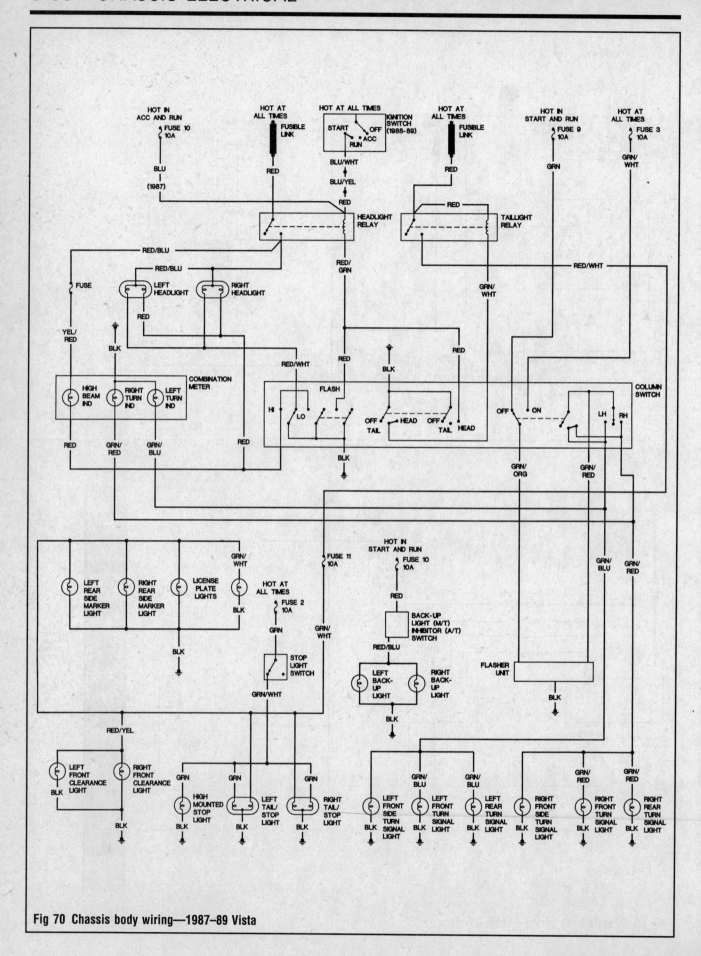

Fig 70 Chassis body wiring—1987-89 Vista

7

DRIVE TRAIN

MANUAL TRANSMISSION

Understanding the Manual Transmission

Because of the way an internal combustion engine breathes, it can produce torque (or twisting force) only within a narrow speed range. Most overhead valve pushrod engines must turn at about 2500 rpm to produce their peak torque. Often by 4500 rpm, they are producing so little torque that continued increases in engine speed produce no power increases.

The torque peak on overhead camshaft engines is, generally, much higher, but much narrower.

The manual transmission and clutch are employed to vary the relationship between engine RPM and the speed of the wheels so that adequate power can be produced under all circumstances. The clutch allows engine torque to be applied to the transmission input shaft gradually, due to mechanical slippage. The vehicle can, consequently, be started smoothly from a full stop.

The transmission changes the ratio between the rotating speeds of the engine and the wheels by the use of gears. 4-speed or 5-speed transmissions are most common. The lower gears allow full engine power to be applied to the rear wheels during acceleration at low speeds.

The clutch driveplate is a thin disc, the center of which is splined to the transmission input shaft. Both sides of the disc are covered with a layer of material which is similar to brake lining and which is capable of allowing slippage without roughness or excessive noise.

The clutch cover is bolted to the engine flywheel and incorporates a diaphragm spring which provides the pressure to engage the clutch. The cover also houses the pressure plate. When the clutch pedal is released, the driven disc is sandwiched between the pressure plate and the smooth surface of the flywheel, thus forcing the disc to turn at the same speed as the engine crankshaft.

The transmission contains a mainshaft which passes all the way through the transmission, from the clutch to the driveshaft. This shaft is separated at one point, so that front and rear portions can turn at different speeds.

Power is transmitted by a countershaft in the lower gears and reverse. The gears of the countershaft mesh with gears on the mainshaft, allowing power to be carried from one to the other. Countershaft gears are often integral with that shaft, while several of the mainshaft gears can either rotate independently of the shaft or be locked to it. Shifting from one gear to the next causes one of the gears to be freed from rotating with the shaft and locks another to it. Gears are locked and unlocked by internal dog clutches which slide between the center of the gear and the shaft. The forward gears usually employ synchronizers; friction members which smoothly bring gear and shaft to the same speed before the toothed dog clutches are engaged.

Transmission

REMOVAL & INSTALLATION

Rear Wheel Drive, Except Conquest

➡**The clutch housing and transmission are removed as a unit.**

1. Disconnect the battery cables, negative cable first.
2. Remove the battery cable from the starter and fasten it away from the transmission.
3. Remove the starter.
4. Remove the top two clutch housing bolts.
5. From inside the passenger compartment: Untie the leather or rubber shift boot and pull the rug back over the shift lever. If the car is equipped with a console it is necessary to remove same for access to the shift lever retaining plate etc.
6. Place the four speed transmission in second gear and the five speed transmission in first gear. Unscrew the four retaining bolts and remove the gearshift lever from the tailshaft housing.
7. From underneath the vehicle: Jack up the front of the car and support it on stands.
8. Drain the transmission oil.
9. Disconnect the transmission back-up light switch and the speedometer cable.
10. Remove the driveshaft.
11. Disconnect the exhaust pipe at the manifold and the engine side bracket. Drop the pipe down and out of the way.
12. Disconnect the clutch cable.
13. Position a jack under the transmission cover to support it when the crossmember is removed. Use a board between the cover and the jack.
14. Remove the two attaching bolts from the transmission-to-crossmember mount.
15. Unscrew the two bolts at each side of the crossmember and remove the crossmember.
16. Remove the remaining bolts from the clutch housing.
17. Pull the transmission rearward and lower it to the floor.

➡**When removing the transmission, pull it straight back so as not to damage the pilot bearing, clutch disc, or pressure plate.**

18. Lube the mainshaft splines with white lube. Raise the transmission on the floor jack until the mainshaft is level with the clutch disc, and at the same degree of engine slant.
19. Push the jack and transmission forward until the mainshaft enters the clutch disc. Wiggle the transmission to align the splines and push the transmission forward until it is in position

against the engine. When wiggling the transmission, do not knock it off of the jack.

20. Secure the transmission to the engine with the mounting bolts. Install the crossmember and lower the transmission. Secure the transmission to the crossmember. Install the driveshaft.

21. Connect the clutch cable, the exhaust pipe, speedometer cable and back-up light switch.

22. Install the gearshift lever and console. Install the upper bell housing bolts. Install the starter motor. Fill the transmission with lubricant. Adjust the clutch. Lower the vehicle and connect the battery cables.

23. When installing the gearshift assembly, position the lever in First gear so that the nylon bushing is vertical. Make sure that no dirt enters the transmission housing during the installation of the shifter.

Conquest

1. Remove the console, place the shift lever in Neutral and remove the gearshift lever. Raise and support the front and rear of the car on jackstands.

2. Remove the driveshaft.

3. Drain the transmission.

4. Disconnect the speedometer cable and switch at the transmission.

5. Remove the clutch slave cylinder.

6. Remove the lower bell housing cover.

7. Remove the starter.

8. Remove the two upper transmission mounting bolts.

9. Support the transmission with a floor jack.

10. Remove the remaining transmission mounting bolts.

11. Remove the engine support bracket, insulator assembly and ground strap.

12. Place the shift lever in the NEUTRAL position. Remove the trim plate and unbolt the shifter assembly, removing it and the stopper plate underneath it.

13. Cover the rear of the cylinder head with a heavy cloth to prevent damage from contact with the firewall.

14. Slowly lower the jack, pull it rearward to disengage the transmission from the clutch.

15. Raise the transmission on the jack until the mainshaft is level with the clutch disc. Push the transmission forward until the mainshaft enters the clutch. Raise or lower the jack as required and push the transmission into position against the engine. Secure it with the mounting bolts.

16. Install the mount and support bracket, then secure the transmission. Remove the jack. Install the starter and lower bell housing shield. Attach the speedometer cable and switch connector. Install the driveshaft and fill the transmission with lubricant. Install the clutch slave cylinder. Install the gearshift lever (in Neutral) and the console. Bleed the clutch if necessary.

17. Tighten the transmission mounting bolts to 35 ft. lbs.; the starter bolts to 20 ft. lbs. Lower the vehicle.

OVERHAUL

4-Speed KM110

◆ **See Figure 1**

1. Remove the clutch control lever shaft and arm.

2. Remove the speedometer driven gear.

3. Remove the backup light switch.

4. Remove the extension housing. It may be necessary to tap it with a soft mallet to break it loose.

5. Turn the transmission upside down (on its top) and remove the bottom cover.

6. Remove the snapring and take out the speedometer drive gear.

7. Tap off the main drive gear bearing retainer.

8. Remove the countershaft retainer.

9. Remove the countershaft from the rear of the case. Remove the forty needle bearings, both front and rear spacers and the front and rear thrust washers also.

10. Remove the reverse idler gear, needle bearings, spacer and front thrust washer from the idler gear shaft.

11. Remove the reverse idler gear shaft locking bolt and pull the idler gear shaft from the rear of the case.

12. Remove the three plugs on the right side of the case, then the poppet spring and balls.

13. Remove the reverse gear, reverse shift rail and fork.

14. Drive the shift rail and fork springs off with a ³⁄₁₆ in. punch.

15. Remove each shift rail and selector out of the rear of the case and then remove the shift fork.

16. Pull the mainshaft assembly rearward and off of the bearing retainer.

17. Remove the main drive gear synchronizer ring and pilot needle bearing.

18. Remove the snapring and pull the mainshaft rear bearing retainer off of the bearing.

19. Remove the locknut.

20. Hold the mainshaft with the forward end down and strike it against a wooden block to make the bearing fall off.

21. Remove the spacer, first gear needle bearing, spacer bushing, synchronizer ring, first-second speed synchronizer assembly, synchronizer ring, second speed gear and the needle bearing.

22. Remove the snapring from the front end of the mainshaft and then remove the third-fourth speed synchronizer assembly, synchronizer ring, third speed gear and the needle bearing.

23. Remove the main drive gear assembly from the front of the case.

24. Remove the snapring(s) and remove the bearing using an appropriate puller.

25. Remove the shifter and control shaft lock pin with a punch.

26. Remove the return spring and pull off the control shaft. Inspect all of the disassembled parts. Replace as necessary.

To assemble:

27. Press the main drive gear bearing into place and install a select fitted snapring to bring the end-play down to 0–0.05mm.

28. Assemble the synchronizers. Install the needle bearings and third speed gear onto the mainshaft from the front. Install the synchronizer ring and the third-fourth synchronizer assembly.

29. Install the first-second speed synchronizer.

30. Install a snapring to bring the the synchronizer end-play down to 0–0.08mm. Third gear end-play should be 0.025–0.200mm.

31. Install the needle bearing, second speed gear, synchronizer ring and first-second speed synchronizer assembly onto the mainshaft.

32. Force the synchronizer assembly forward and check the second speed gear end-play. Play should be 0.025–0.200mm.

33. Install the first gear spacer ring, needle bearing, synchronizer ring, first speed gear and spacer. Force these parts forward and check the end-play. Play should be 0.025–0.200mm.

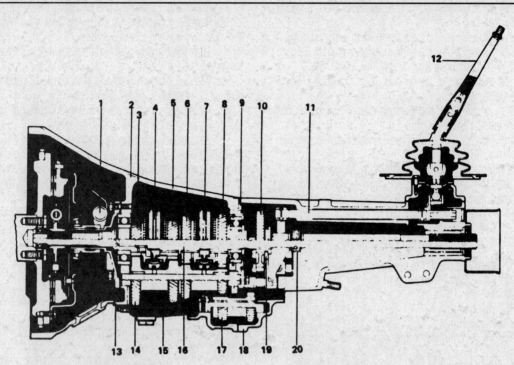

1. Clutch control shaft
2. Transmission case
3. Main drive gear
4. Synchronizer sleeve (for third-fourth speeds)
5. Third-speed gear
6. Second-speed gear
7. Synchronizer sleeve (for first-second speeds)
8. First-speed gear
9. Rear bearing retainer
10. Reverse gear
11. Control shaft
12. Transmission control lever assembly
13. Front gear bearing retainer
14. Counter gear
15. Under cover
16. Mainshaft
17. Reverse idler gear, front
18. Extension housing
19. Shift fork
20. Speedometer drive gear

Fig. 1 Cross-section of the KM110 4 speed transmission

34. Press on the mainshaft bearing. Tighten the locknut to 72. ft. lbs. and install the locking key.

35. Install the snapring on the rear bearing retainer and install the retainer. A snapring should be selected that will give an end-play of 0–0.15mm.

36. Temporarily install the counter gear, front and rear thrust washers and shaft. Measure the end-play of the counter gear. If the end-play is not between 0.05–0.20mm, correct it by selecting a suitable rear thrust washer of correct thickness. Make certain that the thrust washer tongue fits properly in the slot made into the transmission case.

37. Install the needle rollers and the bearing spacers in the front and rear bores of the counter gear. Apply grease to the rollers to prevent them from falling out of position. Install the spacers on the outside of the rollers.

38. Attach the front thrust washer and the rear thrust washer that have been selected to provide proper end-play. Hold them in place with grease. Install the counter gear into the case.

39. Secure the counter gear by tightening the stopper plate. Install the reverse idler shaft and gear. Install the shift forks and rails.

40. Fill the front bearing oil seal lip with grease. Apply sealant to the packing. Install the seal.

41. When installing the front bearing retainer, check the thickness of the packing. Thickness, top and bottom, should be

0.3mm. Adjust bearing clearance with the proper thickness shim.

42. Install the speedometer driven gear onto the mainshaft.

43. Apply sealant to the packing and lockbolts and install the extension housing to the transmission case.

44. Install the backup light switch and ball.

45. Install the speedometer driven gear and lockplate.

46. Install the bottom cover. Tighten the bolts in a criss-cross pattern to 6–7 ft. lbs.

47. Install the control lever assembly, with the shifter in the second speed position, and the nylon bushing in the vertical position.

5-Speed KM119

➡**Special tools are needed, the are: Rear Stopper Plate MD998244, Front Stopper Plate MD998243 and Mainshaft Support MD998241, or equivalent.**

1. Remove the inspection cover.
2. Remove the backup light switch and ball.
3. Loosen the extension housing bolts, but do not remove them.
4. Loosen the plunger plug and place the shift lever in reverse. Remove the bolts and pull off the extension housing.
5. Remove the snapring, speedometer drive gear and ball.

6. Remove the snapring, mainshaft rear bearing, and bearing front snapring.

7. Remove the reverse idler gear and related parts.

8. Loosen and remove the mainshaft intermediate locknut and countershaft gear rear end locknut.

9. Remove the three poppet spring covers, springs and balls from the right side of the case.

10. Use a punch and drive the split pin retainers from the first-second and third-fourth shift forks.

11. Pull the first-second shift rail toward the rear of the case. Remove the counter fifth gear and ball bearing with the rail.

12. Pull the third-fourth shift rail toward the rear of the case.

13. Remove the mainshaft nut.

14. Remove the fifth-reverse synchronizer assembly, the fifth gear and the fifth-reverse shift rail and fork.

15. Remove the two interlock plungers.

16. Remove the spacer and reverse counter gear.

17. Remove the rear retainer.

18. Remove the front bearing retainer and spacer.

19. At this point, the special tools MD998244 and MD998243, the front and rear stopper plates are needed.

20. Insert the rear stopper plate tool between the clutch gear and synchronizer ring of the third speed gear, and the front stopper plate tool between the clutch gear and the synchronizer ring of the maindrive gear.

21. Remove the mainshaft bearing snapring and bearing. Slide the mainshaft support tool in place over the mainshaft to support it.

22. Remove the main drive gear bearing snaprings. Remove the bearing using an appropriate puller.

23. Remove the front and rear stopper plate tools.

24. Remove the countershaft gear front bearing snapring. Remove the front bearing using a puller.

25. Remove the countershaft gear rear bearing snapring. Remove the bearing with a puller.

26. Remove the mainshaft support tool. Lower the mainshaft and take the first speed gear rear spacer out of the case.

27. Shift the third-fourth synchronizer sleeve to the third speed side to permit easy removal of the countershaft gear.

28. Remove the countershaft gear.

29. Remove the first-second and third-fourth shift forks.

30. Remove the main drive gear.

31. Remove the mainshaft assembly and disassemble it into its component parts.

To assemble:

32. Inspect all parts, replace as necessary. Assemble the mainshaft components onto the mainshaft.

33. Insert the mainshaft into the case.

34. Install the synchronizer ring and needle bearing on the main drive gear and insert it into the case from the front.

35. Install the first-second and third-fourth shift forks, the third-fourth synchronizer sleeve and the countershaft.

36. Install the countershaft gear.

37. Support the countershaft gear, install the snapring and press on the bearing.

38. Install the countershaft front bearing outer race into the case first, the the needle bearing.

39. Drive the bearing into place using a soft drift and hammer.

40. Support the mainshaft rear end.

41. Insert the front stopper plate tool between the maindrive gear and the synchronizer ring. Install the rear stopper plate tool between the third speed gear and the synchronizer ring.

42. Install the main drive gear bearing snapring and drive the bearing into position. Install the select fit snapring onto the main drive gear to maintain a clearance, between the bearing inner race and the snapring of 0.05mm.

43. Remove the mainshaft support tool and install the snapring on the mainshaft bearing. Drive the bearing into position and remove the front and rear stopper plates.

44. Apply grease to the front bearing oil seal lip and drive the seal into place in the front bearing retainer.

45. Check the clearance between the front bearing retainer and the maindrive gear. Select and install a spacer to provide a clearance of 0–0.1mm.

46. Install the front bearing retainer.

47. Install the rear retainer.

48. Install the counter reverse gear and spacer.

49. Install the two interlock plungers.

50. Assemble the fifth-reverse synchronizer.

51. Install the spacer on the mainshaft.

52. Install the synchronizer ring, fifth gear, needle bearing and sleeve to the synchronizer.

53. Install the synchronizer assembly and the fifth-reverse shift rod and fork on the mainshaft.

54. Install the mainshaft locknut.

55. Insert the third-fourth shift rail into the rear of the case and into the shift forks.

56. Insert the first-second shift rail in the same way.

57. Align the fifth countergear with the relieved portion of the shift rail and install both parts simultaneously. Install the bearing.

58. Align the spring pin holes of the shift forks and rails. Install the spring pins The pins must not project out of the forks and the split of the pin must be parallel with the rail.

59. Install the poppet balls and springs. Install the plugs until the heads are flush with the case surface. The springs must be installed with the tapered ends inside the balls. The first-second spring is longest.

60. Tighten the mainshaft locknut to 70–90 ft. lbs. and the countershaft locknut to 50–70 ft. lbs.

61. Insert the reverse idler shaft into the case.

62. Install the spacer bushing, gear, needle bearing and thrust washer. Tighten the nut to 20–40 ft. lbs. Align the split of the nut with the cotter pin hole and install a cotter pin.

63. Install the rear bearing on the mainshaft. Install a select fit snapring to provide the clearance of 0–0.2mm between the bearing inner race and the snapring.

64. Install the speedometer drive gear and snapring.

65. Assemble the extension housing components.

66. Install the extension housing to the case. When installing, tilt the shifter down and to the left and fit the lever in the grooves provided in the selector.

67. Install the neutral return plungers and ball, screw in the plugs until they are flush with the case.

68. Install the backup light switch and ball.

69. Install the bottom cover and tighten the bolts to 6–7 ft. lbs.

70. Install the control lever assembly.

5-Speed KM132

▶ **See Figures 2 thru 15**

1. Remove the cover plate.

2. Remove the backup light switch and ball.

3. Remove the extension housing attaching bolts. Back off the

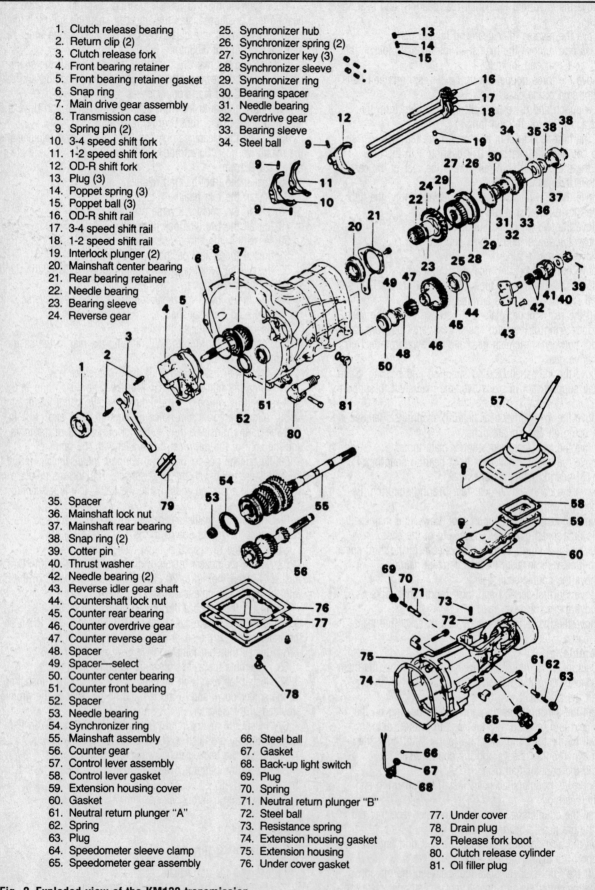

1. Clutch release bearing
2. Return clip (2)
3. Clutch release fork
4. Front bearing retainer
5. Front bearing retainer gasket
6. Snap ring
7. Main drive gear assembly
8. Transmission case
9. Spring pin (2)
10. 3-4 speed shift fork
11. 1-2 speed shift fork
12. OD-R shift fork
13. Plug (3)
14. Poppet spring (3)
15. Poppet ball (3)
16. OD-R shift rail
17. 3-4 speed shift rail
18. 1-2 speed shift rail
19. Interlock plunger (2)
20. Mainshaft center bearing
21. Rear bearing retainer
22. Needle bearing
23. Bearing sleeve
24. Reverse gear

25. Synchronizer hub
26. Synchronizer spring (2)
27. Synchronizer key (3)
28. Synchronizer sleeve
29. Synchronizer ring
30. Bearing spacer
31. Needle bearing
32. Overdrive gear
33. Bearing sleeve
34. Steel ball

35. Spacer
36. Mainshaft lock nut
37. Mainshaft rear bearing
38. Snap ring (2)
39. Cotter pin
40. Thrust washer
42. Needle bearing (2)
43. Reverse idler gear shaft
44. Countershaft lock nut
45. Counter rear bearing
46. Counter overdrive gear
47. Counter reverse gear
48. Spacer
49. Spacer—select
50. Counter center bearing
51. Counter front bearing
52. Spacer
53. Needle bearing
54. Synchronizer ring
55. Mainshaft assembly
56. Counter gear
57. Control lever assembly
58. Control lever gasket
59. Extension housing cover
60. Gasket
61. Neutral return plunger "A"
62. Spring
63. Plug
64. Speedometer sleeve clamp
65. Speedometer gear assembly

66. Steel ball
67. Gasket
68. Back-up light switch
69. Plug
70. Spring
71. Neutral return plunger "B"
72. Steel ball
73. Resistance spring
74. Extension housing gasket
75. Extension housing
76. Under cover gasket

77. Under cover
78. Drain plug
79. Release fork boot
80. Clutch release cylinder
81. Oil filler plug

Fig. 2 Exploded view of the KM132 transmission

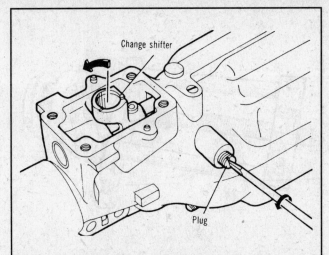

Fig. 3 Back off the neutral return plunger B, then turn the change shifter down to the left

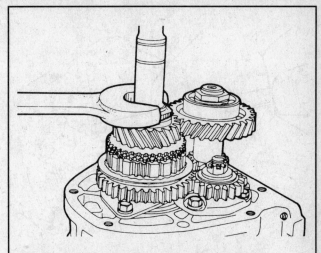

Fig. 6 Bend the lockwasher back, then loosen the locknuts on the main and countershaft rear ends

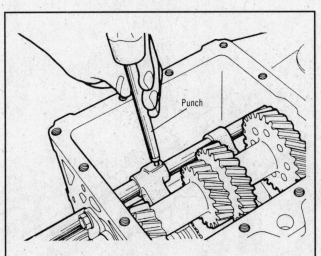

Fig. 4 Using a punch, remove the 3-4 and 1-2 shift fork spring pins

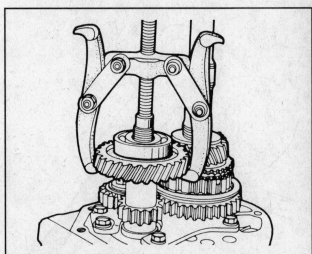

Fig. 7 Using a gear puller, remove the overtop gear and sleeve from the mainshaft

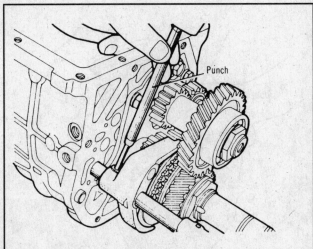

Fig. 5 With the same punch, remove the overtop and reverse shift forks spring pins

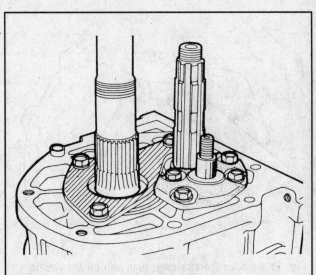

Fig. 8 Remove the rear bearing retainer

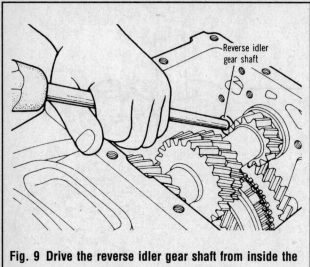

Fig. 9 Drive the reverse idler gear shaft from inside the case

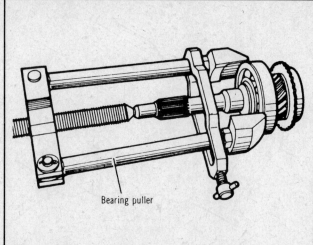

Fig. 12 With a bearing puller, remove the main drive gear bearing

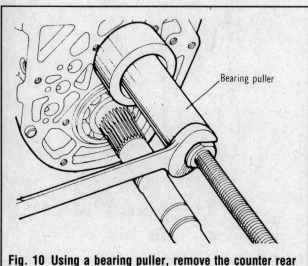

Fig. 10 Using a bearing puller, remove the counter rear bearing

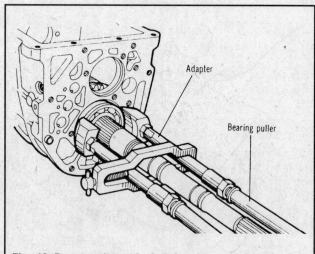

Fig. 13 Remove the mainshaft bearing snapring, then remove the ball bearing

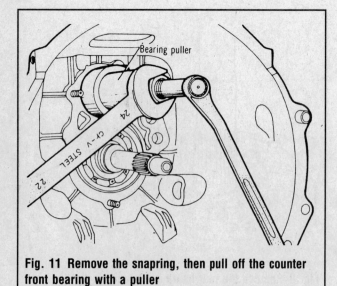

Fig. 11 Remove the snapring, then pull off the counter front bearing with a puller

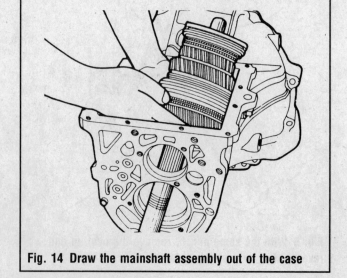

Fig. 14 Draw the mainshaft assembly out of the case

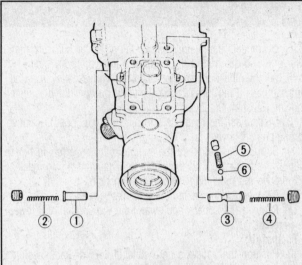

(1) Neutral return plunger (A)
(2) Spring (A)
(3) Neutral return plunger (B)
(4) Spring (B)
(5) Resistance spring
(6) Ball

Fig. 15 Exploded view of the neutral return plunger components

neutral return plunger plug, turn the shift lever down to the left and pull off the extension housing.

4. Remove the snapring and speedometer drive gear.

5. Remove the snapring and the mainshaft rear bearing.

6. Remove the three plugs, and remove the poppet springs and balls.

7. Remove the first-second and third-fourth shift fork pins using a punch. Pull each rail toward the rear of the case and remove the forks and interlock plunger.

8. In the same manner, remove the fifth-reverse forks.

9. Engage the reverse and second gears, remove the mainshaft and countershaft locknuts.

10. Remove the fifth counter gear and bearing using a puller. Remove the spacer and reverse counter gear.

11. Remove the fifth gear and sleeve from the mainshaft. Remove the fifth synchronizer and spacer.

12. Remove the cotter pin, nut and reverse idler gear.

13. Remove the rear bearing retainer.

14. Drive the reverse idler gear shaft from the case.

15. Remove the front bearing retainer.

16. Press the counter gear to the rear and remove the bearing snapring.

17. Use a puller, and remove the counter rear bearing.

18. Remove the snapring and pull the counter front bearing. Remove the counter gear from the case.

19. Remove the main drive pinion from the case.

20. Remove the two snaprings and pull the bearing.

21. Remove the snapring and pull the mainshaft bearing.

22. Remove the mainshaft from the case.

23. Disassemble the mainshaft.

24. Disassemble the extension housing.

To assemble:

25. Inspect all of the transmission components, replace as necessary. Install the bearing on the maindrive pinion and select a snapring which will give a clearance of 0–0.06mm between the snapring and the bearing.

26. Assemble the mainshaft. Use a spacer which will give the third-fourth synchronizer an end-play of 0–0.08mm. Use a snapring that will give the first-second gear end-play of 0.05–0.20mm.

27. Insert the mainshaft into the case and drive in the center bearing.

28. Install the needle bearing and synchronizer ring, then insert the main drive pinion into the case from the front.

29. Insert the countergear into the case.

30. Install the snapring on the countershaft front bearing and drive the bearing into the case carefully.

31. Install the snapring on the countershaft rear bearing and install it in place.

32. Install the front bearing retainer using a spacer that will give a clearance of 0–0.1mm between the retainer and bearing.

33. Install the front retainer oil seal.

34. Install the rear retainer.

35. Install the reverse idler shaft.

36. Install the needle bearing, reverse idler gear, and thrust washer. Tighten the locknut and install the cotter pin. Idler gear end-play should be 0.12–0.28mm. If not replace the thrust washer.

37. Assemble the fifth gear synchronizer.

38. Install the spacer, stop plate and fifth synchronizer assembly, the fifth gear bearing sleeve and needle bearing, the synchronizer ring and fifth gear, in that order, to the mainshaft from the rear. Fifth gear end-play should be 0.10–0.25mm.

39. Install the spacer, counter reverse gear, counter fifth gear and the ball bearing onto the countershaft gear from the rear. Tighten and lock the nut.

40. Insert the third-fourth and the first-second forks into their synchronizer sleeves. Insert each shift rail from the rear of the case. Install the spring pins, with the split of the pins parallel with the rail. Install the interlock plunger.

41. Insert the ball and poppet spring into each shift rail. Tighten the plugs flush with the transmission case.

42. Install the ball bearing on the rear of the mainshaft.

43. Install the speedometer drive gear.

44. Turn the shifter down and to the left and install the extension housing.

45. Install the neutral return plungers, spring, and resistance spring and ball. Tighten the plug flush with the case.

46. Install the speedometer driven gear.

47. Install the backup light switch and ball.

48. Install the bottom cover and torque the bolts to 6–7 ft. lbs.

49. Install the control lever assembly.

MANUAL TRANSAXLE

Understanding the Manual Transaxle

Because of the way an internal combustion engine breathes, it can produce torque, or twisting force, only within a narrow speed range. Most modern, overhead valve pushrod engines must turn at about 2500 rpm to produce their peak torque. By 4500 rpm they are producing so little torque that continued increases in engine speed produce no power increases. The torque peak on overhead camshaft engines is generally much higher, but much narrower.

The manual transaxle and clutch are employed to vary the relationship between engine speed and the speed of the wheels so that adequate engine power can be produced under all circumstances. The clutch allows engine torque to be applied to the transaxle input shaft gradually, due to mechanical slippage. Consequently, the vehicle may be started smoothly from a full stop. The transaxle changes the ratio between the rotating speeds of the engine and the wheels by the use of gears. The gear ratios allow full engine power to be applied to the wheels during acceleration at low speeds and at highway/passing speeds.

In a front wheel drive transaxle, power is usually transmitted from the input shaft to a mainshaft or output shaft located slightly beneath and to the side of the input shaft. The gears of the mainshaft mesh with gears on the input shaft, allowing power to be carried from one to the other. All forward gears are in constant mesh and are free from rotating with the shaft unless the synchronizer and clutch is engaged. Shifting from one gear to the next causes one of the gears to be freed from rotating with the shaft and locks another to it. Gears are locked and unlocked by internal dog clutches which slide between the center of the gear and the shaft. The forward gears employ synchronizers; friction members which smoothly bring gear and shaft to the same speed before the toothed dog clutches are engaged.

Transaxle

REMOVAL & INSTALLATION

Front Wheel Drive, Except 4WD Vista

➡ See Figures 16, 17, 18 and 19

1. Disconnect the negative battery cable and the positive cable. Remove the battery and battery tray.
2. Disconnect from the transaxle; the clutch cable or hydraulic line to slave cylinder, speedometer cable, back-up light harness, starter motor and the four upper bolts connecting the engine to the transaxle. On cars with a turbo-charger, remove the air cleaner case, the actuator mounting bolts, the pin coupling the actuator and shaft and remove the actuator. Discard the collar used with the pin and replace it with a new collar. On cars with a 5-speed transaxle, disconnect the selector control valve.
3. Jack up the car and support on jackstands.
4. Remove the front wheels. Remove the splash shield. Drain the transaxle fluid.
5. Remove the shift rod and extension. It may be necessary to remove any heat shields that can interfere with your progress.

6. On models equipped: Remove the stabilizer bar from the lower arm and disconnect the lower arm from the body side.
7. Remove the right and left halfshafts (driveshafts) from the transaxle case. Plug the transaxle holes to prevent dirt from entering. See Halfshaft Removal.
8. Disconnect the range selector cable (if equipped). Remove the engine rear cover.
9. Support the weight of the engine from above (chain hoist). Support the transaxle with a suitable floor or transmission jack and remove the remaining lower mounting bolts.
10. Remove the transaxle mount insulator bolt.
11. Remove (slide back and away from the engine) and lower the transaxle.
To install:
12. Position the transaxle on a suitable floor or transmission jack and raise it into position under the vehicle.
13. Push the transaxle towards the rear of the engine and align the mainshaft with the clutch disc. Push the transaxle into position against the engine, take care not to knock the transaxle off of the jack.
14. Install and tighten the transaxle to engine lower mounting bolts. Install the transaxle mount through bolt. Disconnect the chain hoist from the engine.
15. Install the halfshafts. Use new retaining ring circlips when installing the halfshafts. Connect the range selector cable. Connect the engine roll control bar, the lower bell housing shield, the lower arms and stabilizer bar.
16. Install the upper transaxle to engine mounting bolts, the starter motor, speedometer cable, ground cable, back-up light harness, select cable, shift cable, clutch linkage or hydraulic connection, and install the splash shield after filling the transaxle with lubricant.
17. Install the battery tray, the battery and connect the cables. Lower the vehicle if not already done.

4-WD Vista

▶ See Figure 20

1. Disconnect the battery cables at the battery. Remove the coolant reserve tank.
2. Disconnect the speedometer cable, shift control cable and back-up light harness at the transaxle.
3. Remove the range select control valves and connectors.
4. Tag and disconnect all other wiring attached to the transaxle.
5. Remove the clutch slave cylinder.
6. Remove the vacuum reservoir tank.
7. Disconnect the starter wiring.
8. Remove the upper 5 engine-to-transaxle bolts.
9. Raise and support the car on jackstands.
10. Remove the front wheels, lower engine cover and skid plate.
11. Drain the transaxle and transfer case.
12. Remove the driveshaft.
13. Remove the transfer case extension housing.
14. Remove the left and right halfshafts.
15. Disconnect the right strut from the lower arm.
16. Remove the right fender liner.
17. Take up the weight of the transaxle with a floor jack.

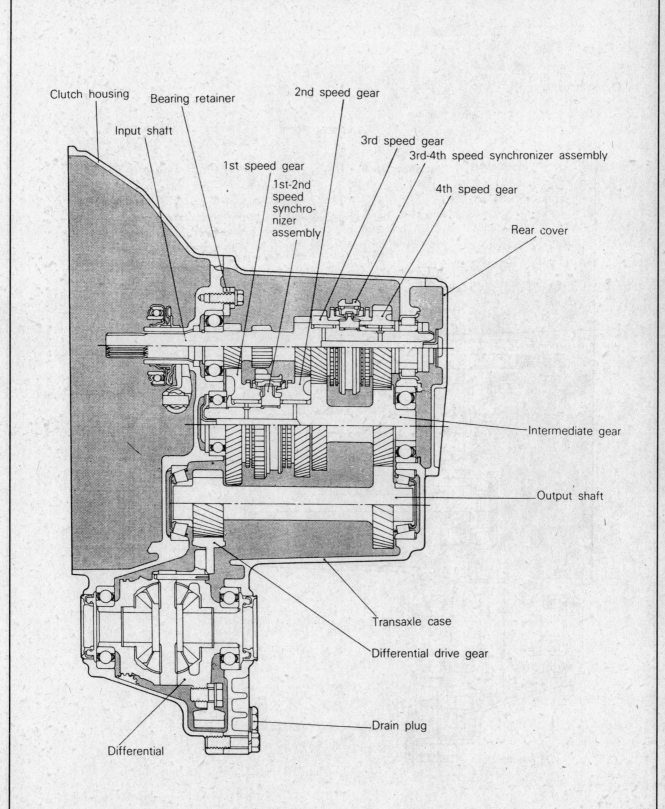

Fig. 16 Cross-section of the 4 speed KM200 transaxle

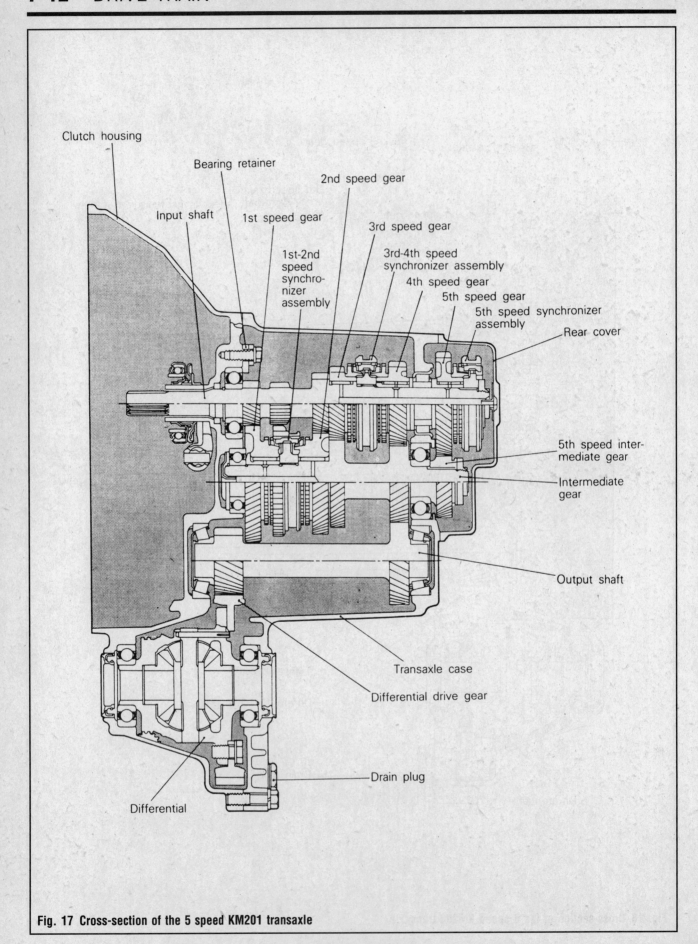

Fig. 17 Cross-section of the 5 speed KM201 transaxle

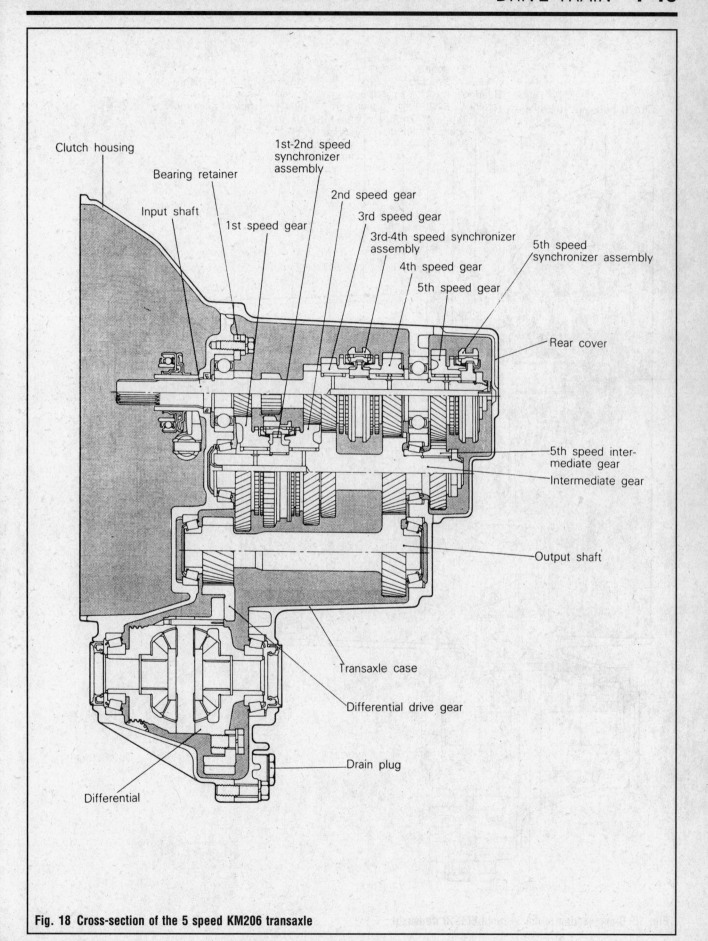

Fig. 18 Cross-section of the 5 speed KM206 transaxle

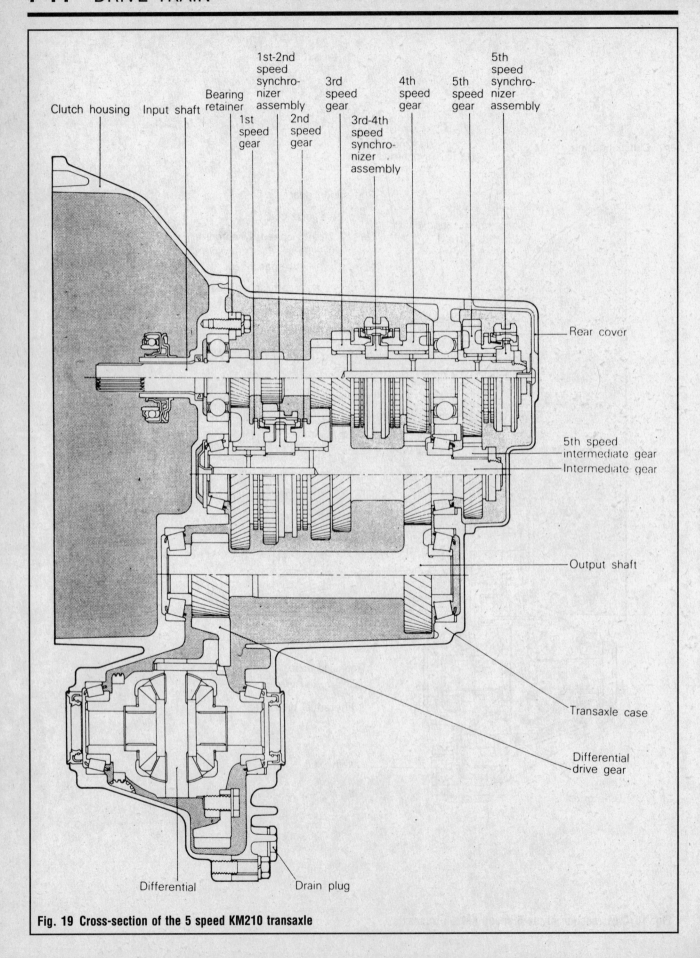

Fig. 19 Cross-section of the 5 speed KM210 transaxle

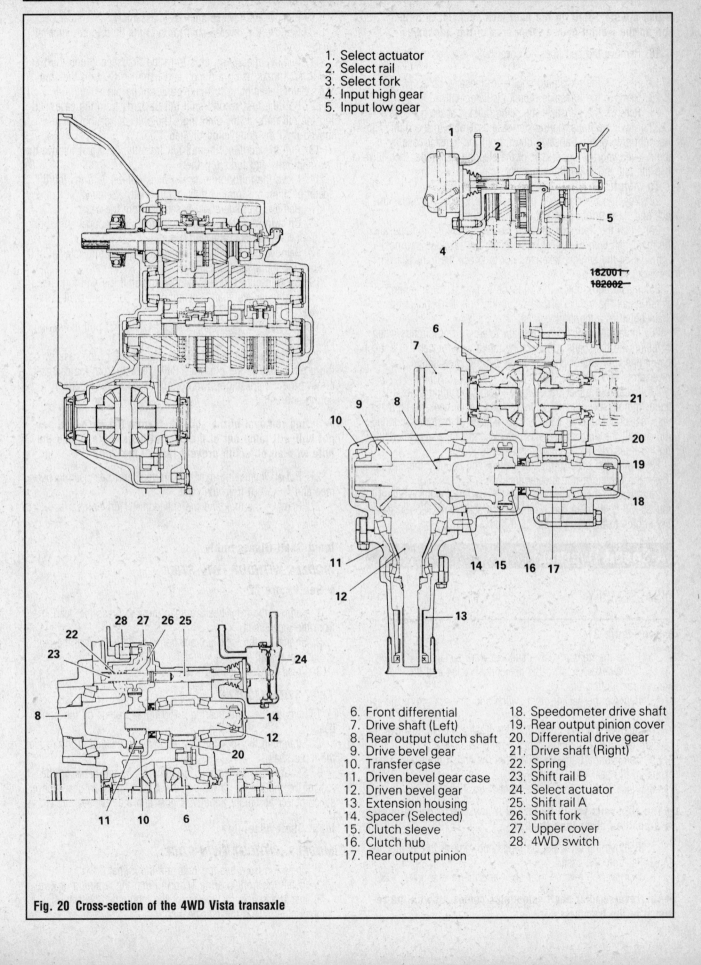

1. Select actuator
2. Select rail
3. Select fork
4. Input high gear
5. Input low gear

6. Front differential
7. Drive shaft (Left)
8. Rear output clutch shaft
9. Drive bevel gear
10. Transfer case
11. Driven bevel gear case
12. Driven bevel gear
13. Extension housing
14. Spacer (Selected)
15. Clutch sleeve
16. Clutch hub
17. Rear output pinion

18. Speedometer drive shaft
19. Rear output pinion cover
20. Differential drive gear
21. Drive shaft (Right)
22. Spring
23. Shift rail B
24. Select actuator
25. Shift rail A
26. Shift fork
27. Upper cover
28. 4WD switch

Fig. 20 Cross-section of the 4WD Vista transaxle

➥**Use a wide board on the floor jack pedestal to help spread the weight over a large area of the transaxle.**

18. Remove the bell housing cover bolts and remove the cover.

19. Remove the remaining engine-to-transaxle bolts.
20. Remove the transaxle mount insulator bolt.
21. Remove the transaxle mounting bracket attaching bolts.
22. Move the transaxle/transfer case assembly to the right. Tilt the right side of the transaxle down, until the transfer case is about level with the upper part of the steering rack tube, then turn it to the left and lower the assembly.

To install:

23. Position the transaxle on a suitable floor or transmission jack and raise it into position under the vehicle.
24. Push the transaxle towards the rear of the engine and align the mainshaft with the clutch disc. Push the transaxle into position against the engine, take care not to knock the transaxle off of the jack.
25. Install and tighten the transaxle to engine lower mounting bolts. Install the transaxle mount through bolt. Disconnect the chain hoist from the engine.
26. Install the halfshafts. Use new retaining ring circlips when installing the halfshafts. Connect the range selector cable. Connect the engine roll control bar, the lower bell housing shield, the lower arms and stabilizer bar.
27. Install the upper transaxle to engine mounting bolts, the starter motor, speedometer cable, ground cable, back-up light harness, select cable, shift cable, clutch linkage or hydraulic connection. Install the driveshaft, splash shield and skid plates after filling the transaxle and transfer case with lubricant.
28. Install the battery tray, the battery and connect the cables. Lower the vehicle if not already done.
29. Observe the following torques: Transaxle mount insulator nut: 55–58 ft. lbs. Transaxle mounting bracket bolts; 25–30 ft. lbs. Engine-to-transaxle bolts: 45 ft. lbs.

4-Speed Overhaul

DISASSEMBLY

◗ **See Figure 21**

1. Place the transaxle on a suitable work surface.
2. Remove the clutch cable operating bracket and the transaxle mounting bracket.
3. Remove the backup light switch and steel ball from the case.
4. Remove the rear cover from the transaxle case. Remove the spacers from the rear of the tapered roller bearings.
5. Remove the transaxle case from the clutch housing, exposing the gear train assembly.
6. Place all shift rails in the Neutral position.

➥**The shift rails would be locked if any one of the rails are in a position other than Neutral.**

7. Remove the three poppet plugs and remove the springs and balls, from the case.
8. Remove the reverse idler shaft and the reverse idler gear.

➥**The reverse idler shaft sometimes comes off with the removal of the transaxle case.**

9. Remove the reverse shift lever assembly.
10. Remove the reverse shift rail and the third/fourth shift rail spacer collar.
11. Remove the spring pins from the first/second and third/fourth shift forks using a punch and hammer. Support the shift forks before attempting to remove the spring pins.
12. Pull the first/second shift rail upwards from the case, sliding the rail through the shift fork. The shift rail cannot be removed until the completion of Step 13.
13. Pull the third/fourth shift rail from the case and remove the two shift rails and forks together.
14. Move the third/fourth speed synchronizer into the fourth speed position and remove the output shaft assembly.
15. Remove the differential assembly from the case.
16. On twin-stick models; Remove the plug, poppet and spring for the two-speed shift rail and fork.
17. Remove the bolts from the input shaft bearing retainer and remove the input shaft assembly.
18. On twin-stick models; remove the shift rail and fork along with the intermediate shaft assembly, when the input shaft is removed.
19. Remove the shift shaft spring retainer and pull the spring pin with pliers.
20. Move the shift shaft towards the outside of the case by using a pin punch in the pin hole. Pull the shaft from the case and remove the control finger, two springs, spacer collar poppet spring and ball.

➥**During removal of the shift shaft from the case, the poppet ball will jump out of the control finger hole. Close the hole with an object to prevent loss of the ball.**

21. Put an identifying mark on the tapered roller bearing outer race and remove it from the case.
22. Remove the lock and the speedometer driven gear assembly.

Input Shaft Disassembly

MODELS WITHOUT TWIN-STICK

◗ **See Figure 22**

1. Remove the front bearing snapring and press the bearing from the input shaft.
2. Straighten the lock tab, and remove the locknut at the rear of the input shaft.
3. Press the rear bearing from the shaft.

TWIN-STICK MODELS

1. Remove the front bearing snapring and press off the front bearing.
2. Straighten the lock tab and remove the locknut at the rear of the input shaft.
3. Support the low gear of the input shaft, and press on the rear of the input shaft to remove the input high gear, gear sleeve, synchronizer assembly, input low gear and the rear bearing.

Input Shaft Assembly

MODELS WITHOUT TWIN-STICK:

1. Press the front bearing onto the input shaft.
2. Install the front bearing snapring into the retaining groove.
3. Install a spacer to the rear of the input shaft, with the stepped side toward the rear bearing.

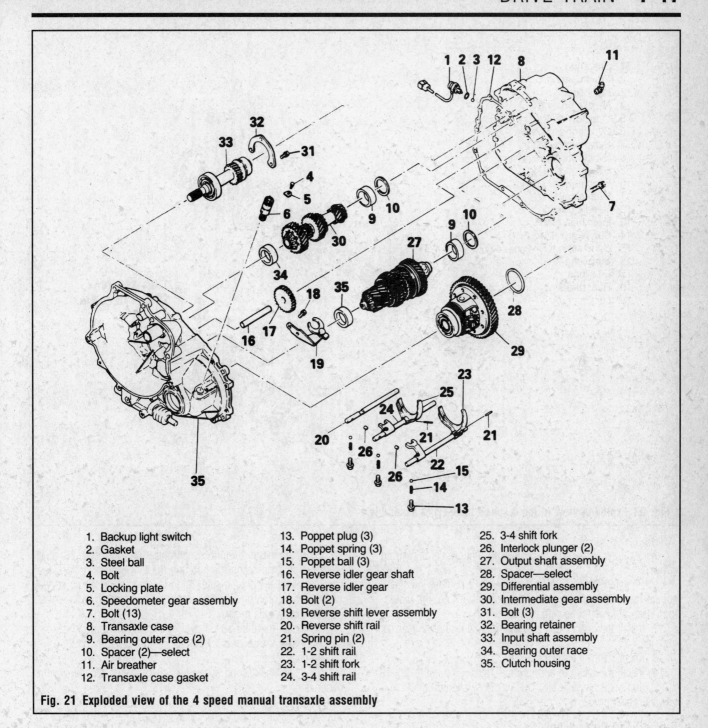

Fig. 21 Exploded view of the 4 speed manual transaxle assembly

1. Backup light switch
2. Gasket
3. Steel ball
4. Bolt
5. Locking plate
6. Speedometer gear assembly
7. Bolt (13)
8. Transaxle case
9. Bearing outer race (2)
10. Spacer (2)—select
11. Air breather
12. Transaxle case gasket
13. Poppet plug (3)
14. Poppet spring (3)
15. Poppet ball (3)
16. Reverse idler gear shaft
17. Reverse idler gear
18. Bolt (2)
19. Reverse shift lever assembly
20. Reverse shift rail
21. Spring pin (2)
22. 1-2 shift rail
23. 1-2 shift fork
24. 3-4 shift rail
25. 3-4 shift fork
26. Interlock plunger (2)
27. Output shaft assembly
28. Spacer—select
29. Differential assembly
30. Intermediate gear assembly
31. Bolt (3)
32. Bearing retainer
33. Input shaft assembly
34. Bearing outer race
35. Clutch housing

4. Press the rear bearing on to the input shaft.

5. Tighten the locknut after install ing the lock tab. Tighten the nut to 66–79 ft. lbs. Bend the locking tab and stake the plate into the notch provided on the shaft.

TWIN-STICK MODELS:

1. Press on the front bearing.
2. Install the front bearing snapring.
3. Install the synchronizer hub with the oil groove slot facing the engine side of the shaft.
4. The synchronizer sleeve must be installed with the thirty degree champfer facing the engine side. The other side of the sleeve is machined at a forty-five degree angle.

5. Install the synchronizer spring with its stepped part positioned on the synchronizer key. Alternate the stepped parts of the front and rear springs to avoid having the stepped parts on the same key.

6. Install the sub-gear to the input high gear and lubricate the entire surface.

7. Install the cone spring and install a new snapring, making sure the inner side of the cone spring is not in the snapring groove.

8. Install the input low gear and the needle bearing on the input shaft.

9. Install the synchronizer ring.

10. Press the synchronizer assembly onto the input shaft with

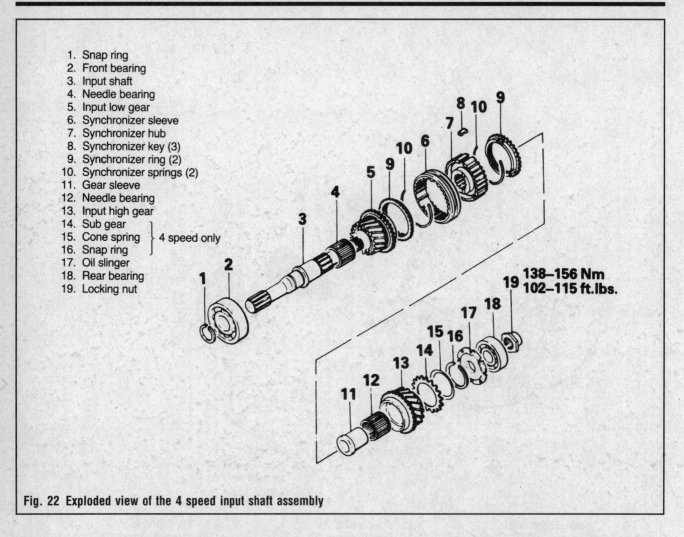

1. Snap ring
2. Front bearing
3. Input shaft
4. Needle bearing
5. Input low gear
6. Synchronizer sleeve
7. Synchronizer hub
8. Synchronizer key (3)
9. Synchronizer ring (2)
10. Synchronizer springs (2)
11. Gear sleeve
12. Needle bearing
13. Input high gear
14. Sub gear
15. Cone spring ⎫ 4 speed only
16. Snap ring ⎭
17. Oil slinger
18. Rear bearing
19. Locking nut

138–156 Nm
102–115 ft.lbs.

Fig. 22 Exploded view of the 4 speed input shaft assembly

the synchronizer key correctly aligned with the synchronizer ring keyway.

11. Press on the input high gear sleeve. The input low gear should rotate smoothly. Install the synchronizer ring, the input high gear and needle bearing.

12. Install the spacer with the stepprd side facing the rear bearing side.

13. Press on the rear bearing.

14. Install the lock tab and locknut. Tighten the nut to 66–79 ft. lbs. and bend the lock tab. The lock plate should be staked into the notch providedon the shaft.

Output Shaft Disassembly

1. Unlock the rear nut lockplate and remove the nut.
2. Remove the front and rear tapered bearings from the output shaft, using a puller or press.
3. Press off the first speed gear, gear sleeve, first/second speed synchronizer and the second speed gear.
4. Press off the second speed gear sleeve, third speed gear and sleeve, third/fourth speed synchronizer assembly and the fourth speed gear.

Output Shaft Assembly

1. Press the fourth speed gear onto the shaft and install the synchronizer ring.
2. Lubricate the contact surfaces.

3. Press the third/fourth synchronizer unit to the output shaft with the oil grooves on the hub and the fork groove in the sleeve facing toward the engine side. Align the synchronizer ring keyway with the synchronizer ring key. After the installation, be sure the fourth gear rotates freely.

4. Install the third speed gear sleeve and third speed gear.
5. Install the second speed gear sleeve, be sure the third speed gear rotates freely.
6. Install the second speed gear and the first/second synchronizer ring.
7. Install the first/second speed synchronizer assembly onto the output shaft. Be sure the second speed gear rotates freely.
8. Install the first/second speed synchronizer ring with the keyways properly aligned.
9. Install the first gear to the gear sleeve and press the unit onto the shaft. Be sure the first speed gear rotates freely.
10. Install the front and rear tapered bearings.
11. Install the lock plate and nut. Tighten the nut to 66–79 ft. lbs. Bend the lock tab and stake the plate into the notch provided.

Intermediate Shaft Disassembly

▶ See Figure 23

1. Press off the front bearing.
2. Remove the sub-gaer and the spring assembly.
3. Press off the rear bearing.

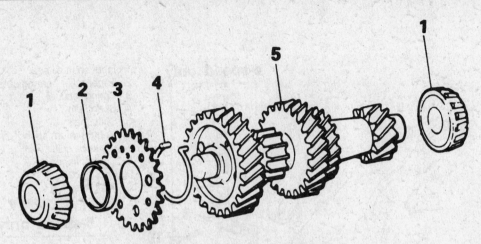

1. Taper roller bearing inner race (2)
2. Spacer
3. Sub gear
4. Spring
5. Intermediate gear

Fig. 23 Exploded view of the 4 speed intermediate gear assembly

Intermediate Shaft Assembly

1. Assemble the sub-gaer spring to the intermediate shaft gear with the longest end of the spring fitted in the hole.

2. Install the sub-gear and insert the remaining end of the spring into the hole in the sub-gear.

3. Press on the front and rear bearings.

TRANSAXLE ASSEMBLY

♦ See Figure 24

1. Lubricate all seals and O-rings during assembly. Prepare the transaxle case for component assembly by replacing all oil seals and case internal small parts that were removed.

2. Install the speedometer driven gear assembly in to the clutch housing. Install the locking plate into the grooves cot into the sleeve.

3. On the Twin-Stick; install an O-ring onto the selector shaft and lubricate the ring and the case bore. Install the shaft into the case and install the selector finger. Install the lock pin so that it is flush on the clutch housing side of the selector finger.

4. Install the poppet spring and steel ball into the control finger. Force the ball into the bore with a special tool and leave the tool in position securing the ball.

5. Install a new O-ring onto the shift shaft and install the shaft into the clutch housing. Engage the reverse restrict spring and the control finger.

6. Press the shift shaft inward until the special tool holding the poppet ball is forced out. Remove the tool. Install the spacer collar and the neutral return spring. Force the shift shaft into its bore on the opposite side of the case.

7. Align the spring pin holes and install the spring pins.

8. Install the spring retainer in place over the control finger assembly.

9. Install the differential gear assembly into the clutch housing.

10. Turn the intermediate shaft sub-gear in the direction of the embossed arrow, until the 8mm hole provided in the intermediate gear aligns with the hole in the sub-gear. Insert a snug fitting pin through the holes to hold the sub-gear in position.

11. Install the input shaft assembly and the intermediate shaft assembly into the clutch housing as a unit. On Twin-Stick models; install the selector shift rail and fork assembly at this time.

12. Install the selector shaft poppet ball. poppet spring and plug. Apply sealer to the plug and seat it flush with the housing surface.

13. Install the input shaft bearing retainer and remove the pin that secured the intermediate shaft sub-gear.

14. Install the output shaft assembly.

15. Install the interlocking plungers into the housing. Assemble the first/second and third/fourth shift rails and forks into position on the housing.

16. Install the spring pins with the split parallel with the center line of the rail.

17. Install the reverse shift rail and install the three poppet balls, springs and plugs. The poppet spring with the white paint ID must be installed in the poppet hole of the reverse shift rail. Install the small diameter ends of the springs toward the balls.

18. Install the reverse shift lever assembly, the reverse idler gear and shaft after lubricating them.

19. Apply sealer to a new gasket and install it on the clutch housing.

20. Install the spacer on the differential bearing and install the transaxle case. Tighten the bolts to 26–30 ft. lbs.

21. Install the intermediate and output shaft tapered bearing races and press them in by hand.

22. Install new halfshaft seals, if not already installed.

23. Apply sealer to the rear cover gasket and install the cover. Tighten the bolts to 14–16 ft. lbs.

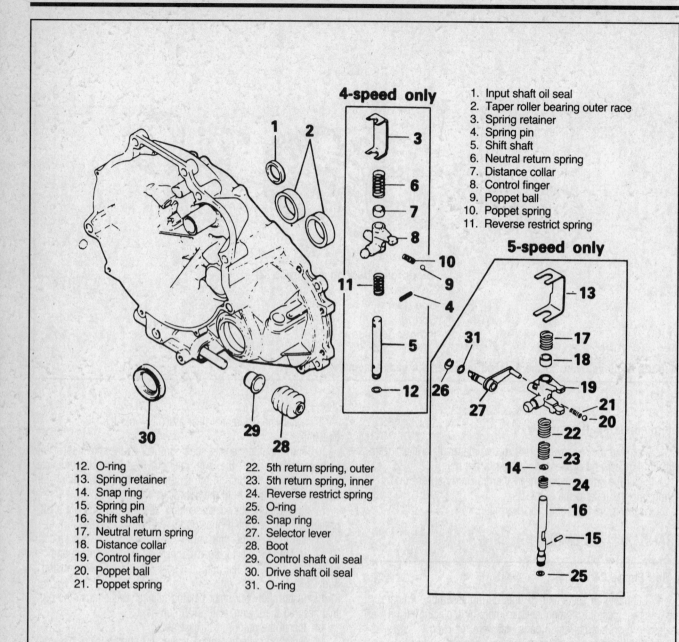

4-speed only

1. Input shaft oil seal
2. Taper roller bearing outer race
3. Spring retainer
4. Spring pin
5. Shift shaft
6. Neutral return spring
7. Distance collar
8. Control finger
9. Poppet ball
10. Poppet spring
11. Reverse restrict spring

5-speed only

12. O-ring
13. Spring retainer
14. Snap ring
15. Spring pin
16. Shift shaft
17. Neutral return spring
18. Distance collar
19. Control finger
20. Poppet ball
21. Poppet spring
22. 5th return spring, outer
23. 5th return spring, inner
24. Reverse restrict spring
25. O-ring
26. Snap ring
27. Selector lever
28. Boot
29. Control shaft oil seal
30. Drive shaft oil seal
31. O-ring

Fig. 24 Exploded view of the clutch housing assembly

5-Speed Overhaul

DISASSEMBLY

▶ **See Figure 25**

1. Place the transaxle assembly on a suitable work service. Remove the transaxle switch and gasket.
2. Remove the rear cover.
3. Remove the backup light switch, gasket and steel ball.
4. Remove the three poppet plugs, springs and balls.
5. Remove the speedometer driven gear assembly.
6. Remove the air breather.
7. Remove the spring pin using a pin punch.
8. Unstake the locknuts on the input and intermediate shafts.

Shift the transaxle into reverse using the control and shift levers. Remove the locknuts.

9. Remove the fifth speed synchronizer assembly and shift fork.
10. Remove the synchronizer ring and fifth speed gear.
11. Remove the needle bearing and the bearing sleeve.
12. Remove the dished washer, roller bearing and the fifth speed intermediate gear.
13. Remove the idler gear shaft bolt.
14. Separate the transmission case from the clutch housing.
15. Remove the oil guide from the transmission case assembly.
16. Remove the bolt, spring washer and stopper bracket. Remove the restrictor ball assembly and gasket.
17. Remove the outer ring and oil seal from the transmission case.

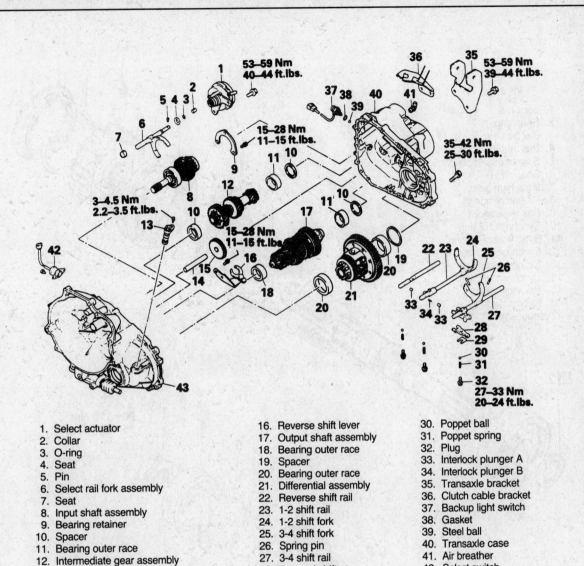

1. Select actuator
2. Collar
3. O-ring
4. Seat
5. Pin
6. Select rail fork assembly
7. Seat
8. Input shaft assembly
9. Bearing retainer
10. Spacer
11. Bearing outer race
12. Intermediate gear assembly
13. Speedometer driven gear assembly
14. Reverse idler gear shaft
15. Reverse idler gear
16. Reverse shift lever
17. Output shaft assembly
18. Bearing outer race
19. Spacer
20. Bearing outer race
21. Differential assembly
22. Reverse shift rail
23. 1-2 shift rail
24. 1-2 shift fork
25. 3-4 shift fork
26. Spring pin
27. 3-4 shift rail
28. 5-speed shift rag
29. Selector spacer
30. Poppet ball
31. Poppet spring
32. Plug
33. Interlock plunger A
34. Interlock plunger B
35. Transaxle bracket
36. Clutch cable bracket
37. Backup light switch
38. Gasket
39. Steel ball
40. Transaxle case
41. Air breather
42. Select switch
43. Clutch housing assembly

Fig. 25 Exploded view of the common 5 speed manual transaxle assembly

18. Remove the three spacers. Remove the shift lever assembly and lever shoe.

19. Remove the reverse idler gear and shaft.

20. Remove the shift lever spring pins. Refer to the four speed transaxle procedures and remove the shift forks and rails. Remove the select spacer.

21. Remove the interlocking plungers from the clutch housing. Remove the fifth speed shift lug and select spacer.

22. Remove the output shaft assembly. Remove the differential assembly.

23. Remove the poppet plug and the poppet spring and ball for the select shift rail.

24. Remove the input shaft front bearing retainer. Lift up the input shaft assembly together with the select shift fork and the intermediate shaft assembly.

25. Refer to the four speed procedures for component servicing and transaxle assembly.

Input Shaft Disassembly

◆ **See Figure 26**

1. Remove the front bearing snapring and press the bearing from the input shaft.

2. Straighten the lock tab, and remove the locknut at the rear of the input shaft.

3. Press the rear bearing from the shaft.

Input Shaft Assembly

1. Press the front bearing onto the input shaft.
2. Install the front bearing snapring into the retaining groove.

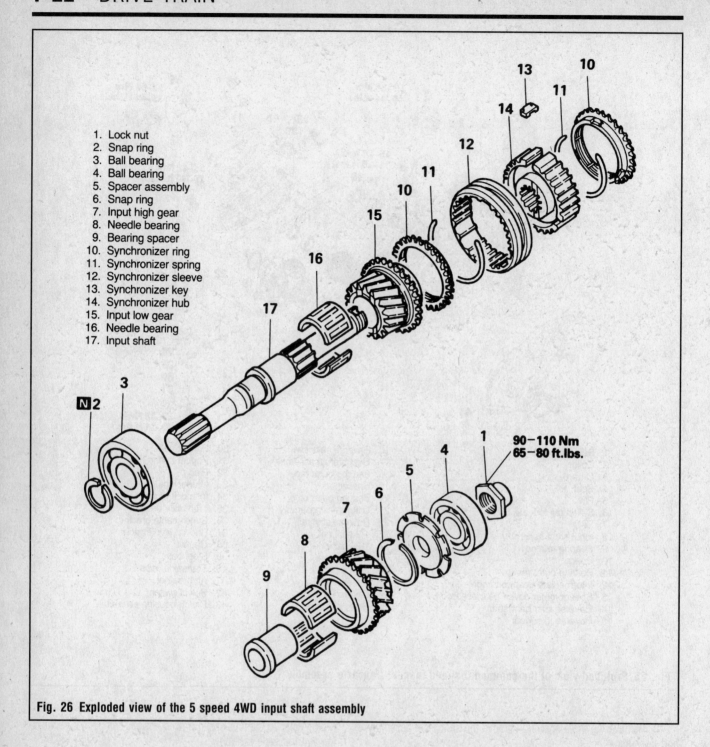

1. Lock nut
2. Snap ring
3. Ball bearing
4. Ball bearing
5. Spacer assembly
6. Snap ring
7. Input high gear
8. Needle bearing
9. Bearing spacer
10. Synchronizer ring
11. Synchronizer spring
12. Synchronizer sleeve
13. Synchronizer key
14. Synchronizer hub
15. Input low gear
16. Needle bearing
17. Input shaft

90–110 Nm
65–80 ft.lbs.

Fig. 26 Exploded view of the 5 speed 4WD input shaft assembly

3. Install a spacer to the rear of the input shaft, with the stepped side toward the rear bearing.

4. Press the rear bearing on to the input shaft.

5. Tighten the locknut after installing the lock tab. Tighten the nut to 66–79 ft. lbs. Bend the locking tab and stake the plate into the notch provided on the shaft.

Output Shaft Disassembly

▶ **See Figure 27**

1. Unlock the rear nut lockplate and remove the nut.

2. Remove the front and rear tapered bearings from the output shaft, using a puller or press.

3. Press off the first speed gear, gear sleeve, first/second speed synchronizer and the second speed gear.

4. Press off the second speed gear sleeve, third speed gear and sleeve, third/fourth speed synchronizer assembly and the fourth speed gear.

Output Shaft Assembly

▶ **See Figure 27A**

1. Press the fourth speed gear onto the shaft and install the synchronizer ring.

2. Lubricate the contact surfaces.

3. Press the third/fourth synchronizer unit to the output shaft

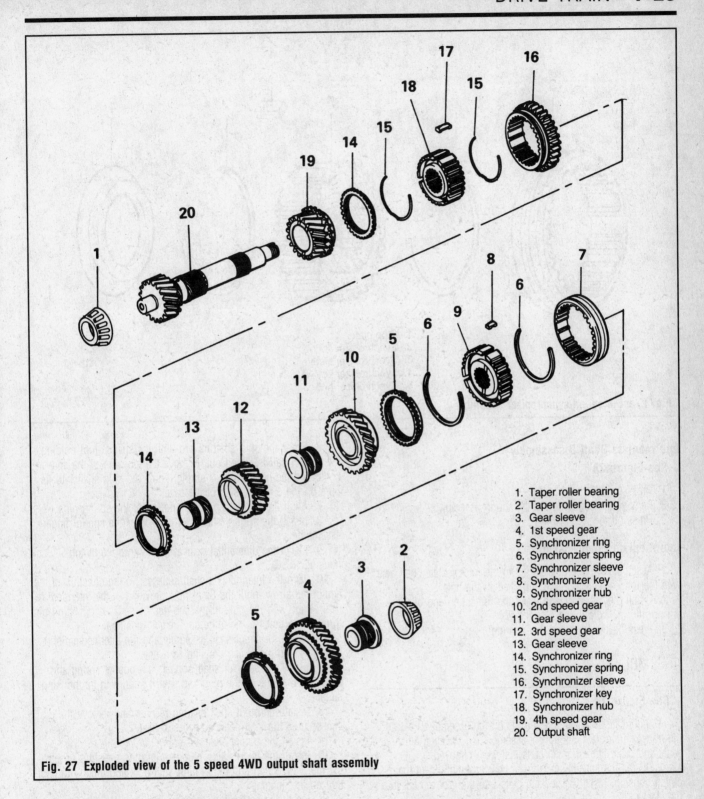

1. Taper roller bearing
2. Taper roller bearing
3. Gear sleeve
4. 1st speed gear
5. Synchronizer ring
6. Synchronzier spring
7. Synchronizer sleeve
8. Synchronizer key
9. Synchronizer hub
10. 2nd speed gear
11. Gear sleeve
12. 3rd speed gear
13. Gear sleeve
14. Synchronizer ring
15. Synchronizer spring
16. Synchronizer sleeve
17. Synchronizer key
18. Synchronizer hub
19. 4th speed gear
20. Output shaft

Fig. 27 Exploded view of the 5 speed 4WD output shaft assembly

with the oil grooves on the hub and the fork groove in the sleeve facing toward the engine side. Align the synchronizer ring keyway with the synchronizer ring key. After the installation, be sure the fourth gear rotates freely.

4. Install the third speed gear sleeve and third speed gear.

5. Install the second speed gear sleeve, be sure the third speed gear rotates freely.

6. Install the second speed gear and the first/second synchronizer ring.

7. Install the first/second speed synchronizer assembly onto the output shaft. Be sure the second speed gear rotates freely.

8. Install the first/second speed synchronizer ring with the keyways properly aligned.

9. Install the first gear to the gear sleeve and press the unit onto the shaft. Be sure the first speed gear rotates freely.

10. Install the front and rear tapered bearings.

11. Install the lock plate and nut. Tighten the nut to 66–79 ft. lbs. Bend the lock tab and stake the plate into the notch provided.

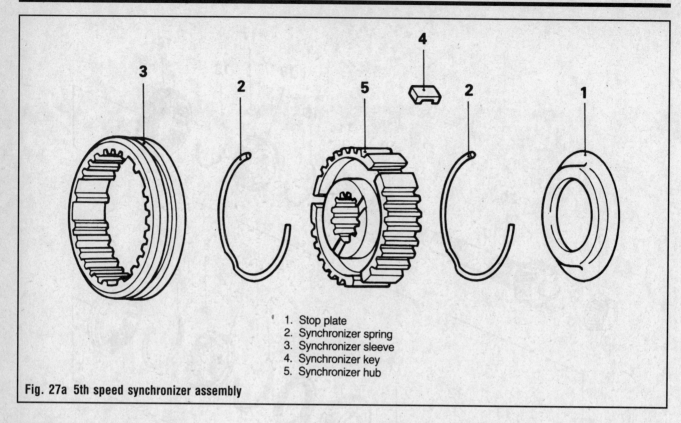

1. Stop plate
2. Synchronizer spring
3. Synchronizer sleeve
4. Synchronizer key
5. Synchronizer hub

Fig. 27a 5th speed synchronizer assembly

Intermediate Shaft Disassembly

▶ **See Figure 28**

1. Press off the front bearing.
2. Remove the sub-gear and the spring assembly.
3. Press off the rear bearing.

Intermediate Shaft Assembly

1. Assemble the sub-gear spring to the intermediate shaft gear with the longest end of the spring fitted in the hole.
2. Install the sub-gear and insert the remaining end of the spring into the hole in the sub-gear.
3. Press on the front and rear bearings.

ASSEMBLY

▶ **See Figure 29**

1. Lubricate all seals and O-rings during assembly. Prepare the transaxle case for component assembly by replacing all oil seals and case internal small parts that were removed.
2. Install the speedometer driven gear assembly in to the clutch housing. Install the locking plate into the grooves cut into the sleeve.
3. Install the shaft into the case and install the selector finger. Install the lock pin so that it is flush on the clutch housing side of the selector finger.
4. Install the poppet spring and steel ball into the control finger. Force the ball into the bore with a special tool and leave the tool in position securing the ball.
5. Install a new O-ring onto the shift shaft and install the shaft into the clutch housing. Engage the the 5th/reverse restrict spring and the control finger.

6. Press the shift shaft inward until the special tool holding the poppet ball is forced out. Remove the tool. Install the spacer collar and the neutral return spring. Force the shift shaft into its bore on the opposite side of the case.
7. Align the spring pin holes and install the spring pins.
8. Install the spring retainer in place over the control finger assembly.
9. Install the differential gear assembly into the clutch housing.
10. Turn the intermediate shaft sub-gear in the direction of the embossed arrow, until the 8mm hole provided in the intermediate gear aligns with the hole in the sub-gear. Insert a snug fitting pin through the holes to hold the sub-gear in position.
11. Install the input shaft assembly and the intermediate shaft assembly into the clutch housing as a unit.
12. Install the selector shaft poppet ball. poppet spring and plug. Apply sealer to the plug and seat it flush with the housing surface.
13. Install the input shaft bearing retainer and remove the pin that secured the intermediate shaft sub-gear.
14. Install the output shaft assembly.
15. Install the interlocking plungers into the housing. Assemble the first/second and third/fourth shift rails and forks into position on the housing.
16. Install the spring pins with the split parallel with the center line of the rail.
17. Install the 5th/reverse shift rail and install the three poppet balls, springs and plugs. The poppet spring with the white paint ID must be installed in the poppet hole of the 5th/reverse shift rail. Install the small diameter ends of the springs toward the balls.
18. Install the 5th/reverse shift lever assembly, the 5th/reverse idler gear and shaft after lubricating them.
19. Apply sealer to a new gasket and install it on the clutch housing.

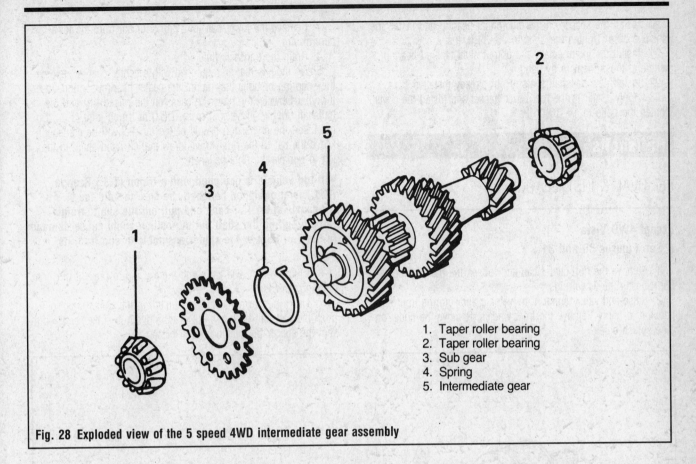

1. Taper roller bearing
2. Taper roller bearing
3. Sub gear
4. Spring
5. Intermediate gear

Fig. 28 Exploded view of the 5 speed 4WD intermediate gear assembly

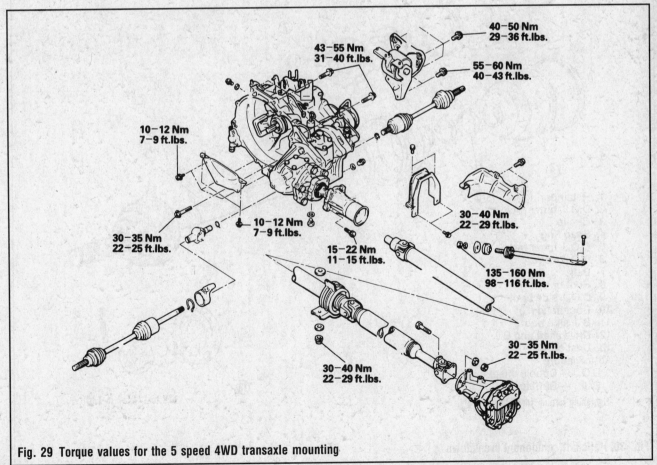

40−50 Nm
29−36 ft.lbs.

43−55 Nm
31−40 ft.lbs.

55−60 Nm
40−43 ft.lbs.

10−12 Nm
7−9 ft.lbs.

30−40 Nm
22−29 ft.lbs.

10−12 Nm
7−9 ft.lbs.

30−35 Nm
22−25 ft.lbs.

15−22 Nm
11−15 ft.lbs.

135−160 Nm
98−116 ft.lbs.

30−40 Nm
22−29 ft.lbs.

30−35 Nm
22−25 ft.lbs.

Fig. 29 Torque values for the 5 speed 4WD transaxle mounting

20. Install the spacer on the differential bearing and install the transaxle case. Tighten the bolts to 26–30 ft. lbs.

21. Install the intermediate and output shaft tapered bearing races and press them in by hand.

22. Install new halfshaft seals, if not already installed.

23. Apply sealer to the rear cover gasket and install the cover. Tighten the bolts to 14–16 ft. lbs.

Halfshafts

REMOVAL & INSTALLATION

Except 4WD Vista

▶ **See Figures 30 and 31**

1. Remove the hub center cap and loosen the halfshaft center nut. Loosen the wheel lugs.

2. Raise and safely support the vehicle allowing the front suspension to hang. Remove the front wheels. Remove the under engine splash shield.

3. Remove the lower ball joint and strut bar from the lower control arm.

4. Drain the transaxle fluid.

5. On models that are equipped with a center bearing; remove the snapring or bolts that mount the center bearing/support. Insert a prybar between the transaxle case (on the raised rib) and the halfshaft double off-set joint case (DOJ) or tripod joint (T.J.). Do not insert the prybar too deeply or the oil seal will be damaged. Move the bar to the right to withdraw the left-hand shaft; to the left to remove the right halfshaft.

➡**If the vehicle is equipped with a tripod (T.J.) Rzeppa (R.J.) joint equipped halfshaft, be sure to hold the (transaxle side) T.J. case and pull out the shaft straight. Simply pulling the shaft out of position could cause damage to the T.J. boot or the spider assembly to slip from its case.**

6. Plug the transaxle case with a clean rag to prevent dirt from entering the case.

7. Use a pusher/puller tool, mounted on the wheel lugs, to push the halfshaft back and out of the drive hub. Take care to prevent the spacer from falling out of place.

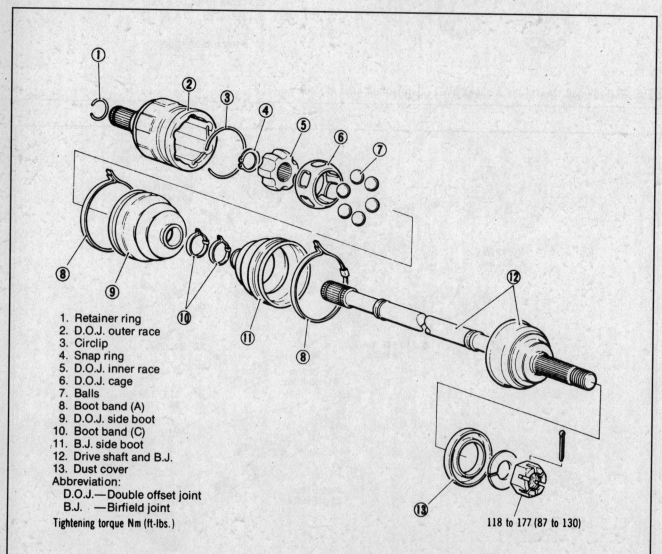

1. Retainer ring
2. D.O.J. outer race
3. Circlip
4. Snap ring
5. D.O.J. inner race
6. D.O.J. cage
7. Balls
8. Boot band (A)
9. D.O.J. side boot
10. Boot band (C)
11. B.J. side boot
12. Drive shaft and B.J.
13. Dust cover
Abbreviation:
   D.O.J.—Double offset joint
   B.J. —Birfield joint
Tightening torque Nm (ft-lbs.)

118 to 177 (87 to 130)

Fig. 30 Halfshaft component breakdown

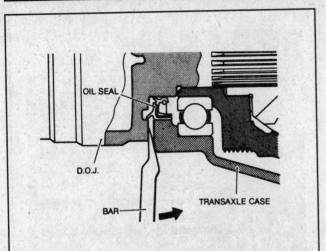

Fig. 31 Insert a prybar between the transaxle case and the double off set joint case

8. Service the halfshaft as required. Install the halfshaft through the drive hub first, then install the transaxle side. Connect the strut bar and lower ball joint. Connect the center bearing on models equipped. ALWAYS install a new retaining circlip ring on the transaxle end when installing the halfshaft. Fill the transaxle with lubricant and install the lower splash shield. Mount the wheels and lower the vehicle. Tighten the wheel lugs, and tighten the halfshaft hub nut to 185 ft. lbs.

4WD Vista

LEFT SIDE

♦ See Figure 32

1. Remove the center wheel hub. Loosen the wheel lugs and the center halfshaft nut.
2. Raise and safely support the front of the vehicle with the suspension hanging.
3. Remove the front wheels.
4. Drain the transaxle fluid.

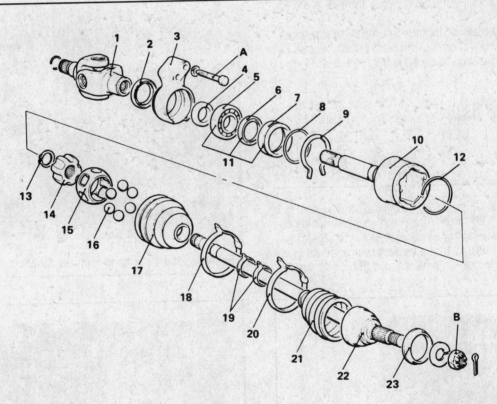

1. Cardan joint assembly	11. Center bearing assembly	21. B.J. boot
2. Dust seal	12. Circlip	22. B.J. Assembly
3. Bearing bracket	13. Snap ring	23. Dust cover
4. Bearing retainer	14. D.O.J. inner race	A = 30–40 ft. lb.
5. Center bearing	15. D.O.J. cage	B = 145–190 ft. lb.
6. Oil seal	16. Ball	B.J.–Birfield joint
7. Oil seal retainer	17. D.O.J. boot	D.O.J.–Double offset joint
8. O-ring	18. D.O.J. boot band	
9. Snap ring	19. Boot band (small)	
10. D.O.J. outer race	20. B.J. boot band	

Fig. 32 Exploded view of the 4WD Vista halfshaft

5. Disconnect the lower ball joint from the steering knuckle.

6. Remove the strut bar and the stabilizer bar from the lower arm.

7. Remove the center bearing mount snapring/bolts from the bracket.

8. Lightly tap the double-offset joint outer race with a wooden mallet and disconnect the cardan joint.

9. Disconnect the halfshaft from the center bearing bracket.

10. Use a pusher/puller tool mounted to the wheel studs and press the halfshaft from the drive hub.

11. Unbolt and remove the bearing bracket.

12. Use a wooden mallet and lightly tap the cardan joint yoke and remove it from the transaxle. DO NOT pry the cardan joint from the transaxle, damage can be caused to the joint and boot.

13. Service the halfshaft as required. Install the cardan joint.

14. Apply grease to the cardan joint contact surfaces.

15. Attach a new O-ring to the oil seal retainer.

16. Install the center bearing bracket. Torque the mounting to 40 ft. lbs.

17. Insert the center bearing into the mounting bracket, make sure it is fully seated. Secure with the snapring bolts.

18. Coat the halfshaft splines with grease and slide it into the cardan joint.

19. Slide the halfshaft into the drive hub. Install the suspension components and wheel. Lower the vehicle and tighten the wheel lugs and the center halfshaft nut. Torque the nut to 188 ft. lbs.

RIGHT SIDE

The right side halfshaft is serviced in the same manner as those on other front wheel drive models. See the except 4WD Vista procedures.

OVERHAUL

Two types of halfshafts are used on front wheel drive models. The 1979 through 1981 models use a shaft equipped with a double offset joint (DOJ) on the transaxle side, and a Birfield joint (BJ) aon the wheel side. In 1981 a halfshaft using a Tripod joint (TJ) on the transaxle side and a Rzeppa joint (RJ) on the wheel

Removing the outer band from the CV-boot

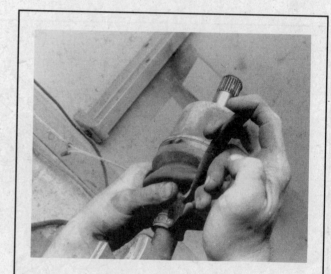
Removing the inner band from the CV-boot

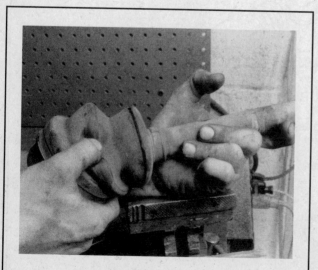
Check the CV-boot for wear

Removing the CV-boot from the joint housing

Clean the CV-joint housing prior to removing boot

Inspecting the CV-joint housing

Removing the CV-joint housing assembly

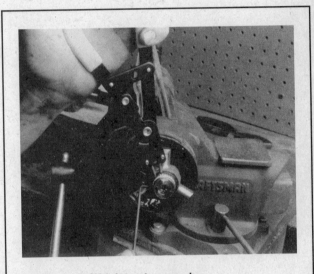

Removing the CV-joint outer snapring

Removing the CV-joint

Checking the CV-joint snapring for wear

CV-joint snapring (typical)

Removing the CV-joint assembly

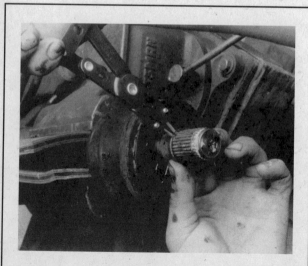

Removing the CV-joint inner snapring

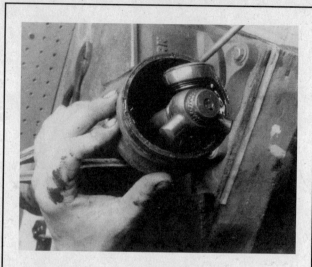

Installing the CV-joint assembly (typical)

side was introduced. 1981 and later models could be equipped with either style halfshaft.

The halfshafts are equipped with different style rubber boots for quick identification. The TJ boot has three folds as opposed to two on the DOJ boot. The RJ boot is equipped with two annular projections on the small end, while the BJ boot is smooth.

➡**Boot kits containing grease, clamps, snapring or circlip and necessary boots are available for all joints. If joint replacement is required, all halfshafts are serviced with a DOJ or BJ kit which replaces the TJ or RJ joint.**

Do not disassemble a BJ or RJ. Service them with a new joint, or clean and pack them using a boot kit. The halfshafts use a special grease! Do not add any grease other then that contained in a repair kit!

Double Offset Joint
▶ See Figures 33 thru 40

1. Remove the boot band from the double offset joint (DOJ) and slide the boot away from the joint.

2. Remove the circlip from the DOJ with a flat bladed tool. Remove the halfshaft from the DOJ and wipe off the grease.

3. Remove the snapring that retains the inner race. Remove the inner race, cage and balls without disassembly.

4. Clean the inner race, cage and balls as an assembly.

5. Remove the Birfield joint boot, clean grease away and inspect the joint for wear; check the splines on both ends of the shaft for wear.

6. Check the DOJ for rust, damage or wear to the outer race, inner race, cage and balls. If any parts show wear, replace with the necessary kit. It is a good idea to at least replace the boots. Kits available are; halfshaft and Birfield joint, Double offset joint, Birfield boot kit and DOJ boot kit.

To assemble:

7. Tape the ends of the splines to prevent damage to the boots when they are installed.

8. Apply gear oil to the shaft and slide the new boots on. If you are not installing a kit apply an equal amount of grease as the amount you wiped away.

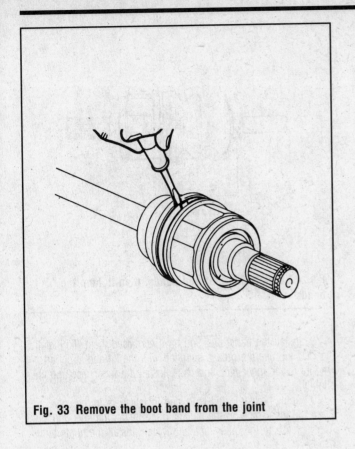

Fig. 33 Remove the boot band from the joint

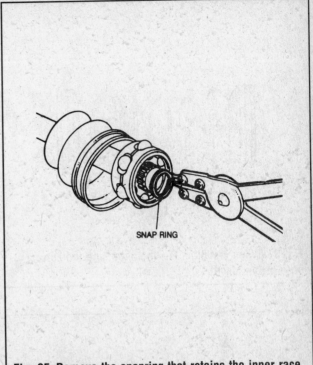

Fig. 35 Remove the snapring that retains the inner race, cage and balls

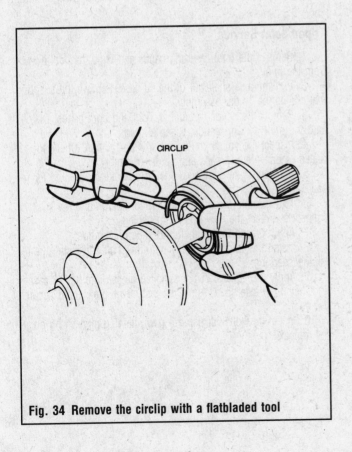

Fig. 34 Remove the circlip with a flatbladed tool

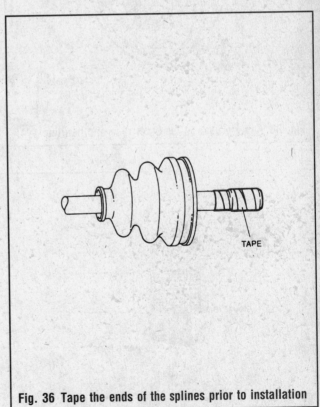

Fig. 36 Tape the ends of the splines prior to installation

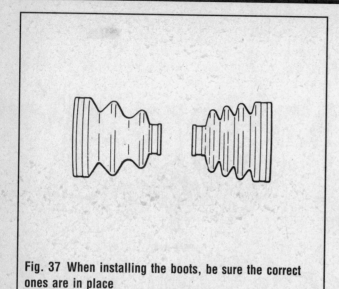

Fig. 37 When installing the boots, be sure the correct ones are in place

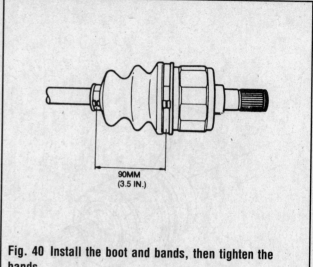

Fig. 40 Install the boot and bands, then tighten the bands

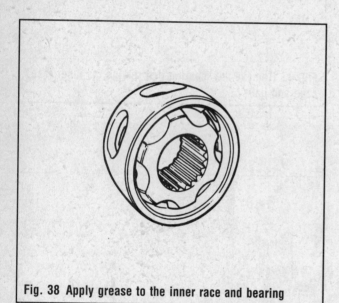

Fig. 38 Apply grease to the inner race and bearing

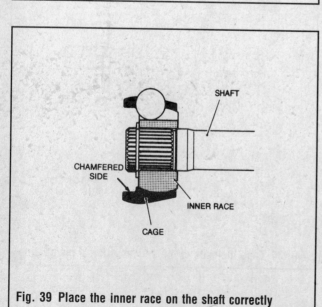

Fig. 39 Place the inner race on the shaft correctly

9. Install the parts after you have regreased them. To install the DOJ kit, use the grease supplied with the kit and apply an amount to the inner race and cage. Install the inner race and cock slightly.

10. Apply grease to the balls and install them in the cage. Place the inner race on the halfshaft and install the snapring. Apply grease to the outer race and install. Install the boots and bands.

11. Install the halfshaft shaft using a new retainer ring on the DOJ side.

Tripod Joint Service

1. Remove the boot retaining bands and slide the boot away from the joint.

2. Pull the axle shaft out of the TJ case. Remove the snapring that retains the spider assembly.

3. Remove the spider assembly, boot and boot bands. Discard the old boot and bands. Clean all parts.

4. Inspect the spider rollers for smooth rotation. Check for rusted or damaged TJ case and spider assembly.

5. If TJ parts are damaged, a DOJ repair kit is required for repair.

6. To assemble the old TJ, first wrap tape around the shaft splines to protect the new boot from getting cut.

7. Apply grease to the shaft and slide on the boot.

8. Install the spider assembly onto the shaft and install the retaining snapring.

9. Apply 2½–3 ozs. of the supplied grease into the TJ case and install the axle shaft. Apply the rest of the grease and secure the boot.

10. Install the halfshaft using a new retaining circlip ring on the transaxle side.

CLUTCH

▶ **See Figure 41**

Understanding the Clutch

The purpose of the clutch is to disconnect and connect engine power at the transmission. A vehicle at rest requires a lot of engine torque to get all that weight moving. An internal combustion engine does not develop a high starting torque (unlike steam engines) so it must be allowed to operate without any load until it builds up enough torque to move the vehicle. To a point, torque increases with engine rpm. The clutch allows the engine to build up torque by physically disconnecting the engine from the transmission, relieving the engine of any load or resistance.

The transfer of engine power to the transmission (the load) must be smooth and gradual; if it weren't, drive line components would wear out or break quickly. This gradual power transfer is made possible by gradually releasing the clutch pedal. The clutch disc and pressure plate are the connecting link between the engine and transmission. When the clutch pedal is released, the disc and plate contact each other (the clutch is engaged) physically joining the engine and transmission. When the pedal is pushed in, the disc and plate separate (the clutch is disengaged) disconnecting the engine from the transmission.

Most clutch assemblies consists of the flywheel, the clutch disc, the clutch pressure plate, the throw out bearing and fork, the actuating linkage and the pedal. The flywheel and clutch pressure plate (driving members) are connected to the engine crankshaft and rotate with it. The clutch disc is located between the flywheel and pressure plate, and is splined to the transmission shaft. A driving member is one that is attached to the engine and transfers engine power to a driven member (clutch disc) on the transmission shaft. A driving member (pressure plate) rotates (drives) a driven member (clutch disc) on contact and, in so doing, turns the transmission shaft.

There is a circular diaphragm spring within the pressure plate cover (transmission side). In a relaxed state (when the clutch pedal is fully released) this spring is convex; that is, it is dished outward toward the transmission. Pushing in the clutch pedal actuates the attached linkage. Connected to the other end of this is the throw-out fork, which hold the throw out bearing. When the clutch pedal is depressed, the clutch linkage pushes the fork and bearing forward to contact the diaphragm spring of the pressure plate. The outer edges of the spring are secured to the pressure plate and are pivoted on rings so that when the center of the spring is compressed by the throw-out bearing, the outer edges bow outward and, by so doing, pull the pressure plate in the same direction — away from the clutch disc. This action separates the disc from the plate, disengaging the clutch and allowing the transmission to be shifted into another gear. A coil type clutch return spring attached to the clutch pedal arm permits

full release of the pedal. Releasing the pedal pulls the throw out bearing away from the diaphragm spring resulting in a reversal of spring position. As bearing pressure is gradually released from the spring center, the outer edges of the spring bow outward, pushing the pressure plate into closer contact with the clutch disc. As the disc and plate move closer together, friction between the two increases and slippage is reduced until, when full spring pressure is applied (by fully releasing the pedal) the speed of the disc and plate are the same. This stops all slipping, creating a direct connection between the plate and disc which results in the transfer of power from the engine to the transmission. The clutch disc is now rotating with the pressure plate at engine speed and, because it is splined to the transmission shaft, the shaft now turns at the same engine speed.

The clutch is operating properly if:

1. It will stall the engine when released with the vehicle held stationary.

2. The shift lever can be moved freely between 1st and reverse gears when the vehicle is stationary and the clutch disengaged.

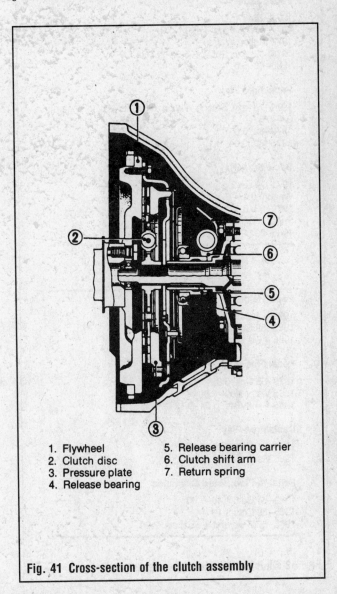

1. Flywheel
2. Clutch disc
3. Pressure plate
4. Release bearing
5. Release bearing carrier
6. Clutch shift arm
7. Return spring

Fig. 41 Cross-section of the clutch assembly

Adjustments

PEDAL HEIGHT

♦ See Figures 42 and 43

1. Measure the distance between the floor and the top of the clutch pedal.
2. Refer to the height chart in this chapter for proper distance.

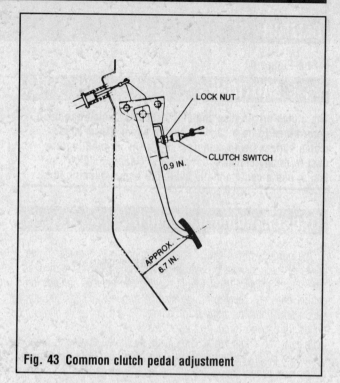

Fig. 43 Common clutch pedal adjustment

Loosen the clutch switch locknut and move the switch in or out as necessary.

3. Tighten the locknut.

CABLE AND FREE-PLAY

Except Conquest and 4-WD Vista

♦ See Figure 44

1. Slightly pull the cable out from the firewall.
2. Turn the adjusting wheel on the cable until the play between the wheel and the cable retainer is set to the distance shown in the chart.

Clutch Adjustments (in.)
Rear Wheel Drive Cars

Pedal Height
1971–77: 6.5–6.7
1978–80: exc. 2555cc: 6.8; 2555cc: 7.2
1981–83: 7.1
1985–89: 7.4–7.6

Pedal Stroke
1971–76: 5.1
1977, exc. Station Wagon: 5.9
1977 Station Wagon: 5.1
1978–79: exc. 2555cc: 5.5; 2555cc: 5.9
1980–83: 6.0

Pedal Free-Play
1971–78: exc. Station Wagon: 0.8–1.4; Station Wagon: 0.4–0.6
1979–83: 0.6–0.8
1985–89: 0.04–0.10

Cable Free-Play
1971–78: exc. Station Wagon: 0.20–0.24; Station Wagon: 0.14–0.18
1979–83: 0.12–0.16
Pedal pad surface-to-floor
1985–89: 1.4

Front Wheel Drive Cars

Pedal Height
1979–84 Colt: 7.10–7.30
1985–89 Colt and Vista: 6.20–6.40
1985 4-wd Vista: 7.10–7.30

Pedal Free-Play
1979–85 Colt: 0.80–1.20
1985 Vista: 0.60–0.80
1985 4-wd Vista: 0.04–0.12

Cable Free-Play
1979–85 Colt: 0.20–0.24
1985 Vista: 0–0.04

Pedal-to-Floorboard Clearance
1979–84 Colt: 1.40–1.60
1985–89 Colt: 3.10 +
1985–89 2-wd and 4-wd Vista: 2.20 +

Fig. 42 Clutch adjustment specifications

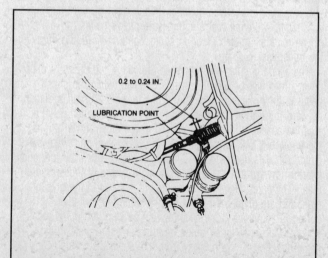

Fig. 44 The clutch free-play adjustment and lubrication point

3. Check the clutch free-play: Jack up the front of the car and support it on stands. Slide under and remove the rubber cover from the clutch housing. Using a 0.8mm feeler gauge, check the clearance between the pressure plate diaphragm spring and the throwout bearing.

4. If the free travel is not correct, make further adjustments at the cable adjusting wheel.

➡**Each turn of the adjusting wheel equals 1.5mm of adjustment to the wheel and retainer clearance.**

5. Lower the car and check the clutch operation.

Conquest and 4-WD Vista

If pedal free-play and pedal surface-to-floor clearance are not within the value specified in the chart, there is air in the hydraulic system. Bleed the system.

Driven Disc and Pressure Plate

REMOVAL & INSTALLATION

▶ **See Figures 45 and 46**

1. Remove the transmission or transaxle as outlined.
2. Insert a pilot shaft or an old input shaft into the center of the clutch disc, pressure plate, and the pilot bearing in the crankshaft.
3. With the pilot tool supporting the clutch disc, loosen the pressure plate bolts gradually and in a criss-cross pattern.
4. Remove the pressure plate and clutch disc.

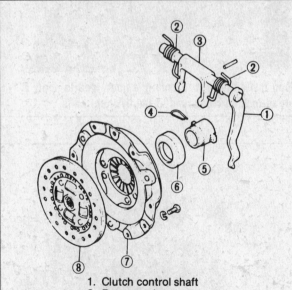

1. Clutch control shaft
2. Return spring
3. Clutch shift arm
4. Return clip
5. Release bearing carrier
6. Release bearing
7. Pressure plate assembly
8. Clutch disc

Fig. 45 Exploded view of the clutch and throwout bearing components

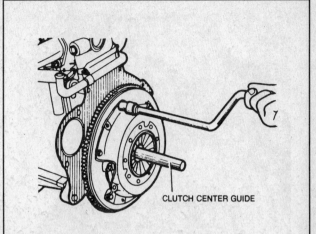

CLUTCH CENTER GUIDE

Fig. 46 A pilot tool must be used during clutch installation

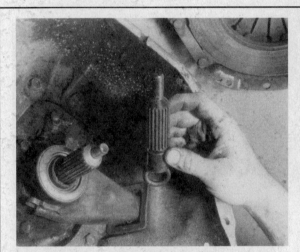

Typical clutch alignment tool, note how the splines match the transmission's input shaft

Loosen and remove the clutch and pressure plate bolts evenly, a little at a time . . .

. . . then carefully remove the clutch and pressure plate assembly from the flywheel

. . . then remove the flywheel from the crankshaft in order replace it or have it machined

Check across the flywheel surface, it should be flat

Upon installation, it is usually a good idea to apply a thread-locking compound to the flywheel bolts

If necessary, lock the flywheel in place and remove the retaining bolts . . .

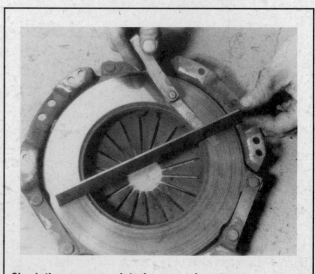

Check the pressure plate for excessive wear

Be sure that the flywheel surface is clean, before installing the clutch

Clutch plate and pressure plate installed with the alignment arbor in place

Install a clutch alignment arbor, to align the clutch assembly during installation

Pressure plate-to-flywheel bolt holes should align

Clutch plate installed with the arbor in place

You may want to use a thread locking compound on the clutch assembly bolts

Install the clutch assembly bolts and tighten in steps, using an X pattern

Be sure to use a torque wrench to tighten all bolts

View of the clutch and pressure plate assembly

5. Clean the transmission and clutch housing. Clean the flywheel surface with a non-oil based solvent. Wash your hands before installing or handling the clutch assembly parts. Hold the clutch disc by the center hub only.

➡ **Before assembly, slide the clutch disc up and down on the transmission input shaft to check for any binding. Remove any rough spots with crocus cloth and then lightly coat the shaft with Lubriplate.**

6. To remove the throwout bearing assembly: Remove the return clip and take out the throwout bearing carrier and the bearing.

7. To replace the throwout arm use a ³⁄₁₆ in. punch, knock out the throwout shaft spring pin and remove the shaft, springs, and the center lever.

8. Do not immerse the throwout bearing in solvent; it is permanently lubricated. Blow and wipe it clean. Check the bearing for wear, deterioration, or burning. Replace the bearing if there is any question about its condition.

9. Check the shafts, lever, and springs for wear and defects. Replace them if necessary.

10. If you hadn't planned on replacing the clutch disc, examine it for the following before reusing it. Loose rivets. Burned facing. Oil or grease on the facing. Less than 0.3mm left between the rivet head and the top of the facing.

➡ **On early 1600cc models, when replacing a clutch disc, use the later model which is identified by a number and letter on one of the rivet heads. This disc is effective in dampening rumbling or growling sounds from the transmission when decelerating or coasting between 25 and 65 mph.**

11. Check the pressure plate and replace it if any of the following conditions exist: Scored or excessively worn. Bent or distorted diaphragm spring. Loose rivets.

12. Insert the control lever into the clutch housing. Install the two return springs and the throwout shaft.

13. Lock the shift lever to the shaft with the spring pin.

14. Fill the shaft oil seal with multipurpose grease.

15. Install the throwout bearing carrier and the bearing. Install the return clip.

16. Grease the carrier groove and inner surface.

17. Lightly grease the clutch disc splines.

➡ **The clutch is installed with the larger boss facing the transmission.**

18. Support the clutch disc and pressure plate with the pilot tool.

19. Turn the pressure plate so that its balance mark aligns with the notch in the flywheel.

20. Install the pressure plate-to-flywheel bolts head-tight. Using a torque wrench and, working in a criss-cross pattern, tighten the bolts to 11–15 ft. lbs.

21. Install the transmission or transaxle as outlined.

22. Adjust the clutch as described in the following section.

Clutch Cable

REMOVAL & INSTALLATION

1. Loosen the cable adjusting wheel inside the engine compartment.

2. Loosen the clutch pedal adjusting bolt locknut and loosen the adjusting bolt.

3. Remove the cable end from the clutch throwout lever.

4. Remove the cable end from the clutch pedal.

5. Install the cable end to the clutch pedal and throwout lever. Adjust the clutch.

➡ **Lubricate the cable with engine oil and after installation, install pads isolating the cable from the intake manifold and from the rear side of the engine mount insulator on coupe, sedan, and hatchbacks only.**

Clutch Master Cylinder

REMOVAL & INSTALLATION

1. Loosen the bleeder screw on the slave cylinder and drain the system.

2. Disconnect the pushrod from the clutch pedal.

3. Disconnect the clutch pedal from the pedal bracket.

4. Disconnect the fluid line from the master cylinder.

5. Unbolt and remove the master cylinder.

➡ **On the 4-WD Vista, the lower master cylinder mounting nut is accessed from inside the car.**

6. Install the master cylinder and bleed the system.

Slave Cylinder

REMOVAL & INSTALLATION

1. Disconnect the clutch hose from the slave cylinder.

2. Unbolt and remove the cylinder from the clutch housing.

3. Install the slave cylinder and bleed the system.

SYSTEM BLEEDING

➡ **You'll need an assistant for this job.**

1. Raise and support the car on jackstands.

2. Loosen the bleeder screw at the slave cylinder.

3. Make sure that the master cylinder is full.

4. Attach a length of rubber hose to the bleeder screw nipple and place the other end in a glass jar half full of clean brake fluid.

5. Have your assistant push the clutch pedal down slowly to the floor. If air is in the system, bubbles will appear in the jar as the pedal is being depressed.

6. When the pedal is at the floor, have the assistant hold it there while you tighten the bleeder screw.

7. Repeat Steps 5 & 6 until no bubbles are found. Check the master cylinder level frequently to make sure that you don't run low on fluid.

Troubleshooting Basic Clutch Problems

Problem	Cause
Excessive clutch noise	Throwout bearing noises are more audible at the lower end of pedal travel. The usual causes are: · Riding the clutch · Too little pedal free-play · Lack of bearing lubrication A bad clutch shaft pilot bearing will make a high pitched squeal, when the clutch is disengaged and the transmission is in gear or within the first 2″ of pedal travel. The bearing must be replaced. Noise from the clutch linkage is a clicking or snapping that can be heard or felt as the pedal is moved completely up or down. This usually requires lubrication. Transmitted engine noises are amplified by the clutch housing and heard in the passenger compartment. They are usually the result of insufficient pedal free-play and can be changed by manipulating the clutch pedal.
Clutch slips (the car does not move as it should when the clutch is engaged)	This is usually most noticeable when pulling away from a standing start. A severe test is to start the engine, apply the brakes, shift into high gear and SLOWLY release the clutch pedal. A healthy clutch will stall the engine. If it slips it may be due to: · A worn pressure plate or clutch plate · Oil soaked clutch plate · Insufficient pedal free-play
Clutch drags or fails to release	The clutch disc and some transmission gears spin briefly after clutch disengagement. Under normal conditions in average temperatures, 3 seconds is maximum spin-time. Failure to release properly can be caused by: · Too light transmission lubricant or low lubricant level · Improperly adjusted clutch linkage
Low clutch life	Low clutch life is usually a result of poor driving habits or heavy duty use. Riding the clutch, pulling heavy loads, holding the car on a grade with the clutch instead of the brakes and rapid clutch engagement all contribute to low clutch life.

AUTOMATIC TRANSMISSION

Understanding Automatic Transmissions

The automatic transmission allows engine torque and power to be transmitted to the rear wheels within a narrow range of engine operating speeds. It will allow the engine to turn fast enough to produce plenty of power and torque at very low speeds, while keeping it at a sensible rpm at high vehicle speeds (and it does this job without driver assistance). The transmission uses a light fluid as the medium for the transmission of power. This fluid also works in the operation of various hydraulic control circuits and as a lubricant. Because the transmission fluid performs all of these functions, trouble within the unit can easily travel from one part to another. For this reason, and because of the complexity and unusual operating principles of the transmission, a very sound understanding of the basic principles of operation will simplify troubleshooting.

TORQUE CONVERTER

The torque converter replaces the conventional clutch. It has three functions:

1. It allows the engine to idle with the vehicle at a standstill, even with the transmission in gear.

2. It allows the transmission to shift from range-to-range smoothly, without requiring that the driver close the throttle during the shift.

3. It multiplies engine torque to an increasing extent as vehicle speed drops and throttle opening is increased. This has the effect of making the transmission more responsive and reduces the amount of shifting required.

The torque converter is a metal case which is shaped like a sphere that has been flattened on opposite sides. It is bolted to the rear end of the engine's crankshaft. Generally, the entire metal case rotates at engine speed and serves as the engine's flywheel.

The case contains three sets of blades. One set is attached directly to the case. This set forms the torus or pump. Another set is directly connected to the output shaft, and forms the turbine. The third set is mounted on a hub which, in turn, is mounted on a stationary shaft through a one-way clutch. This third set is known as the stator.

A pump, which is driven by the converter hub at engine speed, keeps the torque converter full of transmission fluid at all times. Fluid flows continuously through the unit to provide cooling.

Under low speed acceleration, the torque converter functions as follows:

The torus is turning faster than the turbine. It picks up fluid at the center of the converter and, through centrifugal force, slings it outward. Since the outer edge of the converter moves faster than the portions at the center, the fluid picks up speed.

The fluid then enters the outer edge of the turbine blades. It then travels back toward the center of the converter case along the turbine blades. In impinging upon the turbine blades, the fluid loses the energy picked up in the torus.

If the fluid was now returned directly into the torus, both halves of the converter would have to turn at approximately the same speed at all times, and torque input and output would both be the same.

In flowing through the torus and turbine, the fluid picks up two types of flow, or flow in two separate directions. It flows through the turbine blades, and it spins with the engine. The stator, whose blades are stationary when the vehicle is being accelerated at low speeds, converts one type of flow into another. Instead of allowing the fluid to flow straight back into the torus, the stator's curved blades turn the fluid almost 90° toward the direction of rotation of the engine. Thus the fluid does not flow as fast toward the torus, but is already spinning when the torus picks it up. This has the effect of allowing the torus to turn much faster than the turbine. This difference in speed may be compared to the difference in speed between the smaller and larger gears in any gear train. The result is that engine power output is higher, and engine torque is multiplied.

As the speed of the turbine increases, the fluid spins faster and faster in the direction of engine rotation. As a result, the ability of the stator to redirect the fluid flow is reduced. Under cruising conditions, the stator is eventually forced to rotate on its one-way clutch in the direction of engine rotation. Under these conditions, the torque converter begins to behave almost like a solid shaft, with the torus and turbine speeds being almost equal.

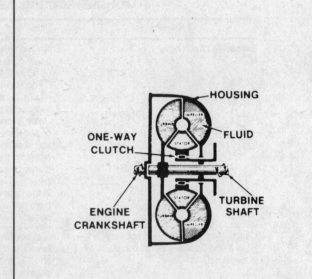

The torque converter housing is rotated by the engine's crankshaft, and turns the impeller—The impeller then spins the turbine, which gives motion to the turbine shaft, driving the gears

PLANETARY GEARBOX

The ability of the torque converter to multiply engine torque is limited. Also, the unit tends to be more efficient when the turbine is rotating at relatively high speeds. Therefore, a planetary gearbox is used to carry the power output of the turbine to the driveshaft.

Planetary gears function very similarly to conventional transmission gears. However, their construction is different in that three elements make up one gear system, and, in that all three elements are different from one another. The three elements are: an outer gear that is shaped like a hoop, with teeth cut into the inner surface; a sun gear, mounted on a shaft and located at the very center of the outer gear; and a set of three planet gears, held by pins in a ring-like planet carrier, meshing with both the sun gear and the outer gear. Either the outer gear or the sun gear may be held stationary, providing more than one possible torque multiplication factor for each set of gears. Also, if all three gears are forced to rotate at the same speed, the gearset forms, in effect, a solid shaft.

Most automatics use the planetary gears to provide various reductions ratios. Bands and clutches are used to hold various portions of the gearsets to the transmission case or to the shaft on which they are mounted. Shifting is accomplished, then, by changing the portion of each planetary gearset which is held to the transmission case or to the shaft.

SERVOS AND ACCUMULATORS

The servos are hydraulic pistons and cylinders. They resemble the hydraulic actuators used on many other machines, such as bulldozers. Hydraulic fluid enters the cylinder, under pressure, and forces the piston to move to engage the band or clutches.

The accumulators are used to cushion the engagement of the servos. The transmission fluid must pass through the accumulator on the way to the servo. The accumulator housing contains a thin piston which is sprung away from the discharge passage of the accumulator. When fluid passes through the accumulator on the way

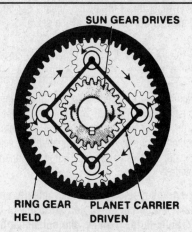

Planetary gears in the minimum reduction (drive) range. The ring gear is allowed to revolve, providing a higher gear ratio

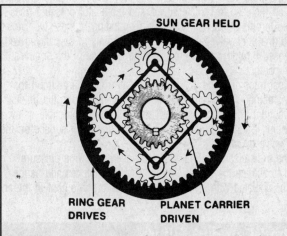

Planetary gears in the minimum reduction (drive) range. The ring gear is allowed to revolve, providing a higher gear ratio

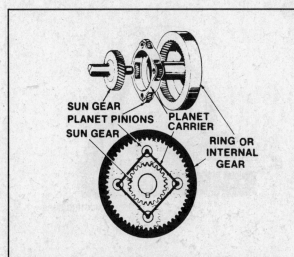

Planetary gears work in a similar fashion to manual transmission gears, but are composed of three parts

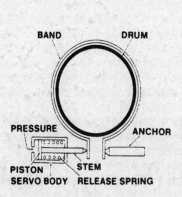

Servos, operated by pressure, are used to apply or release the bands, to either hold the ring gear or allow it to rotate

to the servo, it must move the piston against spring pressure, and this action smooths out the action of the servo.

HYDRAULIC CONTROL SYSTEM

The hydraulic pressure used to operate the servos comes from the main transmission oil pump. This fluid is channeled to the various servos through the shift valves. There is generally a manual shift valve which is operated by the transmission selector lever and an automatic shift valve for each automatic upshift the transmission provides.

➡**Many new transmissions are electronically controlled. On these models, electrical solenoids are used to better control the hydraulic fluid. Usually, the solenoids are regulated by an electronic control module.**

There are two pressures which affect the operation of these valves. One is the governor pressure which is effected by vehicle speed. The other is the modulator pressure which is effected by intake manifold vacuum or throttle position. Governor pressure rises with an increase in vehicle speed, and modulator pressure rises as the throttle is opened wider. By responding to these two pressures, the shift valves cause the upshift points to be delayed with increased throttle opening to make the best use of the engine's power output.

Most transmissions also make use of an auxiliary circuit for downshifting. This circuit may be actuated by the throttle linkage the vacuum line which actuates the modulator, by a cable or by a solenoid. It applies pressure to a special downshift surface on the shift valve or valves.

The transmission modulator also governs the line pressure, used to actuate the servos. In this way, the clutches and bands will be actuated with a force matching the torque output of the engine.

Fluid Pan and Filter

REMOVAL & INSTALLATION

Borg-Warner and JM600

1. Jack up the front of the car and support it safely on stands.
2. Slide a drain pan under the transmission. Some late model JM600 transmissions are equipped with an oil drain plug. On these models, loosen and remove the plug to drain the fluid. On models not equipped with a drain plug: Loosen the rear oil pan bolts first, to allow most of the fluid to drain off without making a mess on your garage floor.
3. Remove the remaining bolts and drop the pan.
4. Discard the old gasket, clean the pan, and re-install the pan with a new gasket.
5. Tighten the pan bolts to 8–13 ft. lbs. on the Borg-Warner and 4–6 ft. lbs. on the JM 600 in a criss-cross pattern.

➡**The transmission case is aluminum, so don't exert too much force on the bolts.**

6. Install the drain plug, on models equipped. Fill the transmission through the dipstick tube. Check the fluid level as described in Section 1.

TorqueFlite

1. Jack up the front of the car and support it safely on jackstands. Place a drain container with a large opening, under transmission and pan.
2. Loosen pan bolts and tap the pan at one corner to break it loose allowing fluid to drain, then remove the oil pan.
3. If necessary, adjust the reverse band.
4. Install a new filter on bottom of the valve body, and tighten retaining screws to 35 in. lbs.
5. Clean the oil pan, and reinstall using a new gasket. Tighten oil pan bolts to 150 in. lbs. in a criss-cross pattern. Lower the car.
6. Pour four quarts of DEXRON®II type automatic transmission fluid through the filler tube.
7. Start the engine and allow to idle for at least two minutes. Then, with parking brake on, move selector lever momentarily to each position, ending in the neutral position.
8. Add sufficient fluid to bring level to the ADD 1 PINT mark. Check fluid level after transmission is at normal operating temperature. The level should be between the FULL and ADD 1 PINT mark.

Adjustments

FRONT BAND

Borg-Warner

▶ **See Figure 47**

1. Remove the transmission pan as previously outlined.
2. Loosen the locknut.
3. While pulling the servo lever toward the outside, insert a 6mm feeler gauge between the adjusting screw and the servo piston pin.

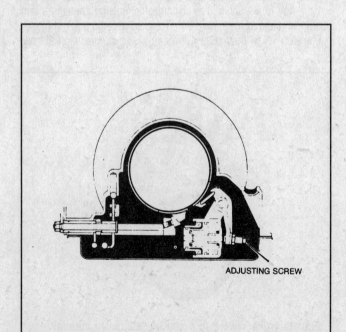

ADJUSTING SCREW

Fig. 47 Borg-Warner front band adjusting screw location

4. Under the conditions of Step 3, tighten the servo adjusting screw to 10 inch lbs.

➡**That's inch lbs., not ft. lbs.! Use an inch lbs. torque wrench, or don't attempt this adjustment.**

5. Install the locknut and remove the feeler gauge.
6. Install the transmission pan.

KICKDOWN BAND

TorqueFlite
▶ **See Figure 48**

The kickdown band adjusting screw is located on the left-side of the transmission case.

1. Loosen the locknut and back off approximately 5 turns. Test the adjustment screw for free turning in the transmission case.
2. On models through 1980: Use an inch pound torque wrench and tighten the adjusting screw to 72 inch pounds. On 1981 and later; tighten the adjusting screw to 69 inch pounds. (The torque specifications shown are true torque with no adapter on the wrench).
3. On models through 1980; back off the adjusting screw 3 full turns. On 1981 and later models; back off the adjusting screw 3½ turns.
4. Hold the adjusting screw to prevent turning and secure the locknut to 30–41 foot pounds.

LOW AND REVERSE BAND

TorqueFlite
▶ **See Figure 49**

1. Raise and safely support the front of the car. Drain the transmission fluid and remove the oil pan.
2. The allen socket headed adjusting screw is located at the servo end of the strut. On models through 1980; loosen and remove the locknut from the adjusting screw. Tighten the adjusting screw to 41 inch pounds of true torque (no adapter on wrench). Back off adjusting screw 7½ turns. On 1981 and later models; Loosen and remove the locknut from the adjusting screw. Tighten the adjusting screw to 43 inch pounds of true torque. Back off the adjusting screw 7 turns.
3. Install the locknut on the adjusting screw. Hold the adjusting screw in position and tighten the locknut to 25–35 ft. lbs.
4. Install the oil pan using a new gasket. Fill the transmission with the proper amount of transmission fluid.

REAR BAND

Borg-Warner
▶ **See Figure 50**

This adjustment is performed externally at the adjustment screw on the right-side of the transmission.

1. Loosen the locknut.

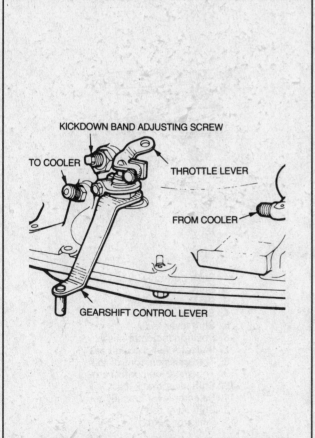

Fig. 48 TorqueFlite kick down band adjustment points

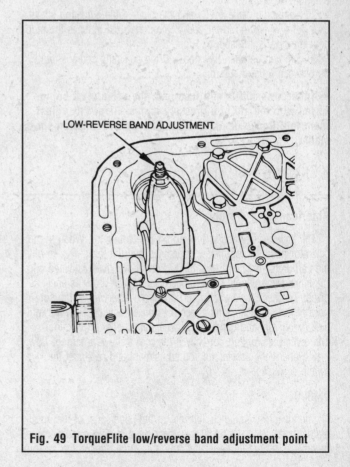

Fig. 49 TorqueFlite low/reverse band adjustment point

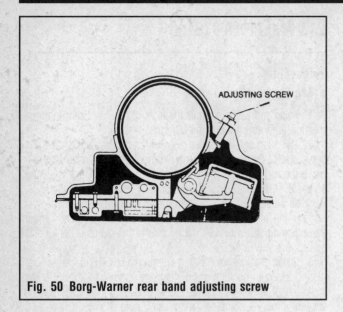

Fig. 50 Borg-Warner rear band adjusting screw

2. Tighten the adjusting screw to 10 ft. lbs. (ft. lbs. not in. lbs.).

3. Back the screw of ¾ of a turn and tighten the locknut.

DOWNSHIFT CABLE

British Borg-Warner

1. Run the engine at an idle until it reaches the normal operating temperature.

2. Adjust the cable by turning the outer cable adjusting screw to a point where the lower end of the screw just touches the stop near the downshift cable end fork.

3. The gap between the stop and the adjusting screw should be between 0.05–0.10mm.

➡ **If the downshift is still incorrect, the cable must be adjusted with the aid of a pressure gauge. Refer this adjustment to a Dodge dealer or an automatic transmission specialist.**

KICKDOWN SWITCH

American Borg-Warner

The kickdown switch is located on the carburetor. When the accelerator pedal is completely depressed and the throttle valve of the carburetor is wide open, the kickdown switch is activated and the kickdown solenoid at the transmission valve body is energized. To check the switch, disconnect the lead wire to the solenoid at the connector and attach it to an ohmmeter. Turn the ignition switch ON and depress the accelerator pedal on the floor. The switch is working correctly if the meter shows a current flow. If not, check the accelerator rod adjustment and re-adjust the switch or replace it.

JM600

The kickdown switch is located on the upper post of the accelerator pedal. With the pedal fully depressed, a click should be heard just before the pedal bottoms out. If not, loosen the locknut

and extend the switch until the pedal lever contacts the switch and a click is heard at the proper time.

SHIFT LINKAGE

Borg-Warner
➡ **See Figure 51**

The shifter end of the linkage rod is slotted. With the lever and transmission both in Neutral, loosen the locknut and adjust the

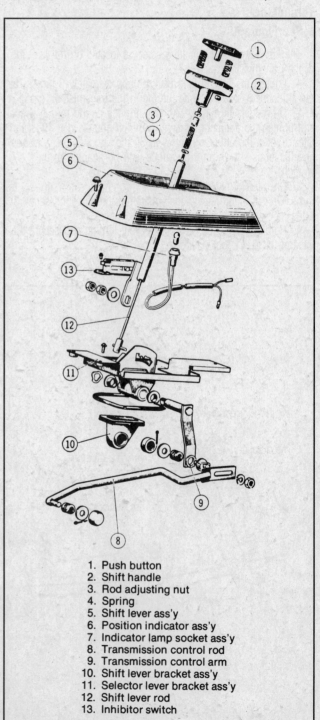

1. Push button
2. Shift handle
3. Rod adjusting nut
4. Spring
5. Shift lever ass'y
6. Position indicator ass'y
7. Indicator lamp socket ass'y
8. Transmission control rod
9. Transmission control arm
10. Shift lever bracket ass'y
11. Selector lever bracket ass'y
12. Shift lever rod
13. Inhibitor switch

Fig. 51 Exploded view of the Borg-Warner shift linkage

linkage for smooth operation. Grease the sliding parts of the linkage and tighten the nut to 10 ft. lbs.

JM600
▶ **See Figure 52**

1. Apply chassis lube to all sliding parts.
2. Place the selector in the NEUTRAL position.
3. Turn the adjusting cam until the distance between the adjusting cam and the selector lever end is 15–16mm.

NEUTRAL SWITCH

Borg-Warner
▶ **See Figure 53**

1. Install the switch with the slit mark aligned with the (N) position.
2. If the switch is not properly connected, loosen the attaching screws and adjust its position by moving it forward or backward.
3. The gap between the switch and the lever should be adjusted at 1.5mm so that the switch is free from the lever and turns smoothly.
4. Adjust the connection range of the switch so that in any position, the lever can be moved an equal distance in either direction.

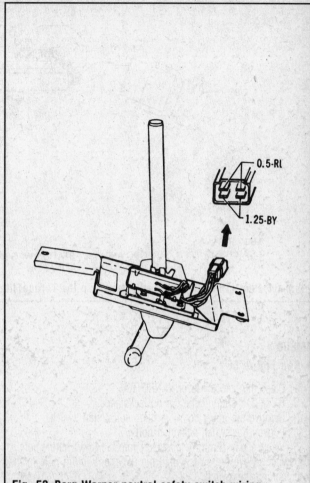

Fig. 53 Borg-Warner neutral safety switch wiring connector descriptions

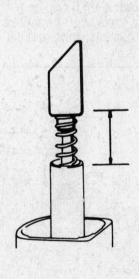

Fig. 52 The LM600 throttle rod adjustment point is located in between the arrowed section

TorqueFlite
▶ **See Figure 54**

1. The inhibitor (Neutral) switch is located at the base of the shift control under the console cover.
2. Loosen the set screw that retains the shift lever handle to the shift lever. Remove the handle.
3. Remove the screws at the top and rear of the console, place the shift lever in L and remove the console. Put lever in P position.
4. Remove the top and side shift indicator panel mounting screws and pull the panel up. The inhibitor switch can now be disconnected and removed if necessary.
5. Adjust the switch by moving the selector lever to the N position. Loosen the mounting screws and adjust the inhibitor switch so that the pin on the forward end of the rod assembly will be in the position near the lobe of the detent plate and that this position will be at the front end of the range of the N connection of the switch. Temporarily tighten the switch mounting screws. After adjusting the selector lever clearance to 1.5mm tighten the mounting screws.
6. To test the switch: Disconnect the wiring connector and set the selector lever in each of its positions. With a continuity tester connected current should be available in the P, N and R positions only. Replace switch if necessary. Install console and shift handle.

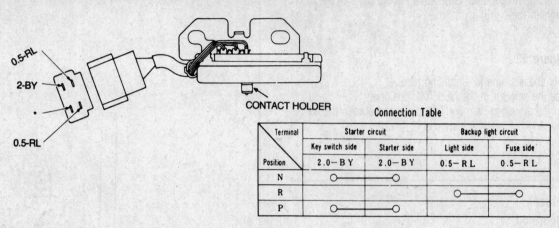

CONTACT HOLDER

Terminal	Starter circuit		Backup light circuit	
	Key switch side	Starter side	Light side	Fuse side
Position	2.0—B Y	2.0—B Y	0.5—R L	0.5—R L
N	○——————○			
R			○——————○	
P	○——————○			

Connection Table

0.5-RL
2-BY
0.5-RL

2-BG (ARROW)
2-BY (CHALLENGER, SAPPORO AND COLT STATION WAGON)

Fig. 54 Neutral safety switch adjustment on the TorqueFlite transmission

JM600

♦ **See Figure 55**

1. Place the selector lever in NEUTRAL.
2. Raise and support the car on jackstands.
3. Remove the lower screw on the neutral start switch.
4. Loosen the switch attaching bolts.
5. Insert a pin, (2mm in diameter) into the lower screw hole in the switch. Move the switch until the pin drops into a hole in the rotor behind the switch.
6. Hold the switch in that position and tighten the attaching bolts to 5 ft. lbs.
7. Using an ohmmeter, check the switch across the leads for continuity.

DOWNSHIFT SOLENOID INSPECTION

JM600

♦ **See Figure 56**

1. Raise and support the car on jackstands.
2. Uncouple the connectors on the wiring at the solenoid.

➡**Transmission fluid will drain from the hole after the solenoid is removed. Have a drain pan ready to catch it.**

3. Remove the solenoid and O-ring.
4. Connect a 12V source across the solenoid wires to verify that the plunger is operational. If not, replace it.

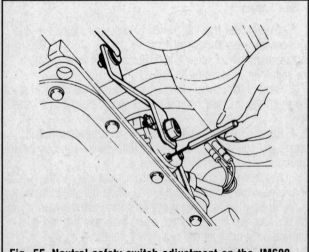

Fig. 55 Neutral safety switch adjustment on the JM600 transmission

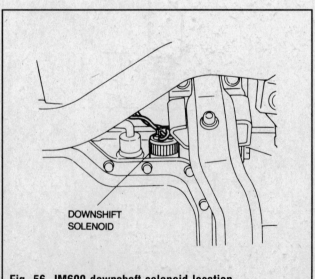

DOWNSHIFT SOLENOID

Fig. 56 JM600 downshaft solenoid location

5. Apply a coating of clean transmission fluid to the O-ring and install the solenoid. Fill the transmission.

THROTTLE ROD

TorqueFlite

♦ **See Figure 57**

Warm the engine until it reaches the normal operating temperature. With the carburetor automatic choke off the fast idle cam, adjust the engine idle speed by using a tachometer. Then make the throttle rod adjustment.

1. Install each linkage. Loosen its bolts so that the rods **B** and **C** can slide properly.

2. Lightly push the rod **A** or the transmission throttle lever and the rod **C** toward the idle stopper and set the rods to idle position. In this case the carburetor automatic choke must be fully released. Tighten the bolt securely to connect the rods **B** and **C.**

3. Make sure that when the carburetor throttle valve is wide-open, the transmission throttle lever smoothly moves from idle to wide-open position (operating angle: 45–54°) and that there exists some room in the lever stroke.

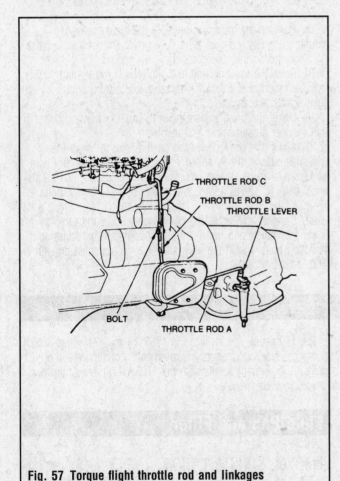

Fig. 57 Torque flight throttle rod and linkages

Automatic Transmission

REMOVAL & INSTALLATION

Borg-Warner

1. Remove the air cleaner, battery with cables (disconnect the negative cable first), starter, and the upper bolts which attach the engine to the transmission.

2. Place the car on jackstands. Drain the transmission. Disconnect the gear shift linkage, and wire harness (if equipped). Remove the speedometer cable and disconnect the driveshaft.

3. Remove the exhaust system from the connecting pipe rearward to the muffler.

4. Remove the transmission oil cooler lines.

5. Remove the control rod from its attachment to the arm.

6. Remove the starter motor. Loosen and remove the lower bellhousing cover plate. Rotate the engine in the normal direction of rotation and remove the torque converter mounting bolts.

7. Place a jack under the transmission and support it.

➡**Do not support the transmission on the oil pan.**

8. Remove the transmission mounting insulator attaching bolts, ground cabls, and spacer. Remove the insulator and crossmember.

9. Pry the torque converter back from the engine flexplate. Pull the transmission away from the engine. Lower the jack and remove the transmission.

10. Position the transmission, with the torque converter mounted properly, on a suitable floor or transmission jack. Raise the transmission into position behind the engine.

11. Raise the transmission and align the converter and engine flexplate mountings. Push the transmission forward until it is flush against the engine.

12. Install the lower transmission to engine mounting bolts. Install the rear crossmember and insulator.

13. Attach the converter to the engine flexplate. Install the driveshaft, starter motor, speedometer, shift linkage, control wire harnesses, exhaust system, and fluid cooler lines.

14. Connect any remaining components under the vehicle. Lower the vehicle and install the upper engine to transmission mounting bolts. Fill the transmission with fluid.

TorqueFlite

1. The transmission and converter must be removed as an assembly; otherwise, converter drive plate, pump bushing, or oil the seal may be damaged. The drive plate will not support a load; therefore, none of the weight of the transmission should be allowed to rest on the plate during removal.

2. Disconnect the negative cable.

3. Remove the cooler lines at transmission.

4. Remove the starter motor, lower cover, cooler line bracket and any exhaust system component that will interfere with the removal of the transmission.

5. Loosen the oil pan and drain the transmission fluid.

6. Rotate the engine clockwise to position the bolts attaching the torque converter to the engine drive plate, and remove them.

7. Mark parts for reassembly then disconnect the driveshaft at rear universal joint. Carefully pull the shaft assembly out of the extension housing.

8. Disconnect the gearshift rod and torque shaft assembly from the transmission.

9. Disconnect the throttle rod from the lever at the left-side of transmission. Remove the linkage bell-crank from transmission if so equipped.

10. Remove the oil filler tube and speedometer cable.

11. Support the rear of the engine with a jack.

12. Position a suitable floor or transmission jack under the transmission. Raise the transmission slightly with a service jack to relieve the load on the supports.

13. Remove the bolts securing the transmission mount to the crossmember and the crossmember to the frame. Remove the crossmember.

14. Remove all bellhousing bolts.

15. Carefully work the transmission converter assembly rearward off of the engine block dowels and disengage the converter hub from end of crankshaft. Attach a small C-clamp to edge of bellhousing to hold converter in place during transmission removal.

16. Lower the transmission and remove the assembly from under the vehicle.

17. To remove converter assembly, remove C-clamp from edge of bellhousing, then carefully slide assembly out of transmission.

18. Position the transmission, with the torque converter mounted properly, on a suitable floor or transmission jack. Raise the transmission into position behind the engine.

19. Raise the transmission and align the converter and engine flexplate mountings. Push the transmission forward until it is flush against the engine.

20. Install the lower transmission to engine mounting bolts. Install the rear crossmember and insulator.

21. Attach the converter to the engine flexplate. Install the driveshaft, starter motor, speedometer, shift linkage, control wire harnesses, exhaust system, and fluid cooler lines. Tighten the flywheel bolts to 42–46 ft. lbs.; the transmission-to-engine bolts to 32–40 ft. lbs.

22. Connect any remaining components under the vehicle. Lower the vehicle and install the upper engine to transmission mounting bolts. Install the filler tube. Fill the transmission with fluid. Adjust linkages.

JM600

1. Drain the fluid.

2. Disconnect the battery ground cable.

3. Remove the transmission dipstick and unbolt the filler tube.

4. Raise the front and rear of the car and support it on jackstands.

5. Remove the two topmost transmission-to-engine bolts.

6. Remove the starter.

7. Disconnect the oil cooler lines and cap them to avoid spillage.

8. Remove the bell housing cover.

9. Turn the crankshaft so that the torque converter bolts appear and remove them, turning the crankshaft for each bolt in turn.

10. Disconnect the speedometer cable at the transmission.

11. Disconnect the linkage and cross shaft.

12. Disconnect the ground strap.

13. Matchmark the flanges and remove the driveshaft.

14. Support the transmission with a transmission jack, and the engine with a floor jack.

15. Remove the rear engine support bracket.

16. Remove the remaining engine-to-transmission bolts.

17. Slowly lower the transmission while pulling it rearward to disengage it from the engine. Be careful to avoid dropping the torque converter.

18. Position the transmission, with the torque converter mounted properly, on a suitable floor or transmission jack. Raise the transmission into position behind the engine.

19. Raise the transmission and align the converter and engine flexplate mountings. Push the transmission forward until it is flush against the engine.

20. Install the lower transmission to engine mounting bolts. Install the rear crossmember and insulator.

21. Attach the converter to the engine flexplate. Install the driveshaft, starter motor, speedometer, shift linkage, control wire harnesses, exhaust system, and fluid cooler lines. Tighten the flywheel bolts to 42–46 ft. lbs.; the transmission-to-engine bolts to 32–40 ft. lbs.

22. Connect any remaining components under the vehicle. Lower the vehicle and install the upper engine to transmission mounting bolts. Install the filler tube. Fill the transmission with fluid. Adjust linkages.

AUTOMATIC TRANSAXLE

General Information

The KM170 automatic transaxle appeared in 1980 models. It uses a torque converter in a fully automatic 3-speed transaxle, including transfer gearing and differential into a compact front wheel drive unit. There are four centers of rotation in the KM170. They are: main center line plus valve body, idler gear center line, transfer shaft center line and differential center line. An aluminum die-cast converter housing and transaxle case are used and the transaxle and differential oil sump is common to both. The torque converter is attached to the crankshaft through a flexible driving plate. Converter cooling is through an oil-to-water cooler, located in the radiator lower tank. The torque converter is a sealed unit and cannot be disassembled.

The 170 series was replaced in 1985, by the 171 series, which incorporates several internal improvements. For service and adjustments, it is vertually identical to the 170. A 172 series transaxle is used in Vista models.

Fluid Pan and Filter

REMOVAL & INSTALLATION

KM 170, 171, 172

1. Jack up the front of the car and support it safely on jackstands. Remove splash shield.

The automatic transaxle dipstick is located near the pan on some models

. . . and clean the pan gasket edge and magnet

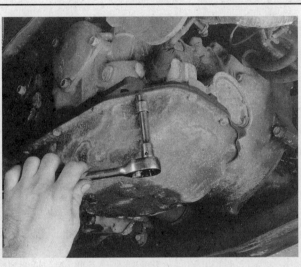

Loosen the pan retaining bolts in a crisscross sequence

The filter is bolted to the valve body as shown here

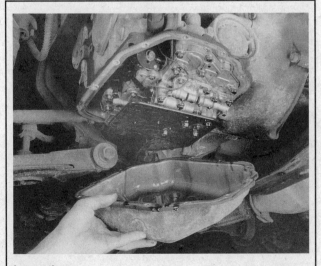

Lower the pan . . .

Remove the filter mounting bolts . . .

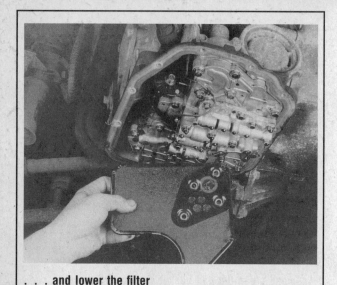

. . . and lower the filter

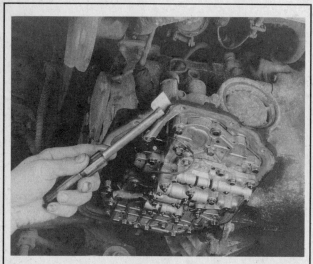

Don't forget to clean the transaxle mating surface

2. Slide a drain pan under the differential drain plug. Loosen and remove the plug and drain the fluid. Move the drain pan under the transaxle oil pan, remove the drain plug (models equipped) or the oil pan and drain the fluid. The transaxle fluid cannot all be drained by just draining the oil pan.

3. Remove the pan retaining evenly and allow the fluid to drain. Remove the pan.

4. The filter may be serviced at this time.

5. Use a new oil pan gasket and install the pan. Install and tighten the bolts evenly in a criss-cross pattern.

6. Replace both drain plugs (if equipped). Lower the vehicle. Fill the transaxle with 4.2 pts of DEXRON®II fluid. Start the engine and allow it to idle for at least two minutes. With the parking brake applied, move the selector to each position ending neutral.

7. Add sufficient fluid to bring the level to the lower mark. Check the fluid level after the transaxle is up to normal operating temperature.

Adjustments

KICKDOWN BAND

KM170

➡**No adjustment is possible on KM171, 172 models.**

1. Wipe all dirt and other contamination from the kickdown servo cover and the surrounding area. The cover is located to the right of the dipstick hole.

2. Remove the snapring and then the cover.

3. Loosen the locknut.

4. Holding the kickdown servo piston from turning, tighten the adjusting screw to 7 ft. lbs. (84 in. lbs.) and then back it off. Repeat the tightening and backing off two times in order to ensure seating of the bank on the drum.

5. Tighten the adjusting screw to 3.5 ft. lbs. (42 inch lbs.) and back off 3.5 turns (counterclockwise).

6. While holding the adjusting screw against rotation, tighten the locknut nut to 11–15 ft. lbs.

7. Install a new seal ring (D-shaped) in the groove in the outside surface of the cover. Use care not to distort the seal ring.

8. Install the cover and then the snapring.

SHIFT LINKAGE

KM 170, 171, 172

1. Apply grease to all sliding parts.

2. Place the selector lever in Neutral position.

3. Depress the selector lever knob and turn it to adjust clearance between detent plate and at the end of the selector lever. Detent plate to selector lever end pin clearance should be 0.20–0.90mm.

4. Turn the adjusting nut to remove slack from the manual control cable.

5. Confirm that the selector lever operates smoothly and is set properly in every selector position. Be sure that the respective position indicator turns red.

THROTTLE CONTROL CABLE

KM 170, 171, 172

♦ **See Figures 58 and 59**

1980–81

1. Place the carburetor throttle lever in wide open position.

2. Loosen the lower cable bracket mounting bolt.

3. Move the lower cable bracket until there is 0.5–1.5mm between the nipple at the bracket and the center of the nipple at the other end. Fasten the lower bracket in position.

4. Check the cable for freedom of movement. If it is binding it may need replacement.

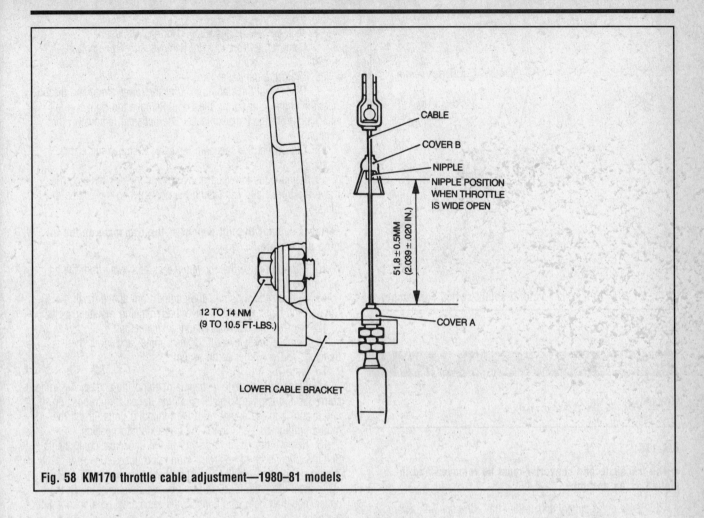

Fig. 58 KM170 throttle cable adjustment—1980–81 models

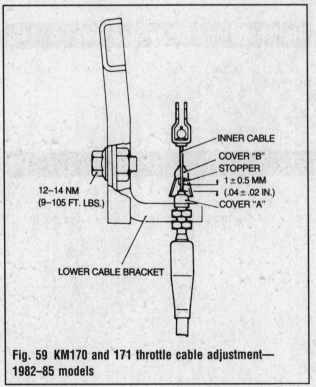

Fig. 59 KM170 and 171 throttle cable adjustment— 1982–85 models

1982–88

1. Run the engine to normal operating temperature. Shut it off and make sure the throttle plate is closed (curb idle position).

2. Raise the small cone-shaped cover on the throttle cable to expose the nipple.

3. Loosen the lower cable bracket bolt.

4. Move the lower cable bracket until the distance between the nipple and the lower cover directly underneath it is 0.5–1.5mm.

5. Tighten the bracket bolt to 9–11 ft. lbs.

NEUTRAL SWITCH

KM 170, 171, 172

◆ **See Figure 60**

1. Place manual control lever in the Neutral position.

2. Loosen the two switch attaching bolts. Switch is located on side of transmission.

3. Turn the switch body until the flat end of the manual lever is centered over the square end of the swwitch body flange.

4. While keeping the switch body flange and manual lever aligned tighten the two attaching bolts to 7–8 ft. lbs.

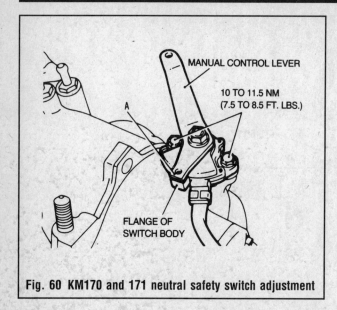

MANUAL CONTROL LEVER

10 TO 11.5 NM
(7.5 TO 8.5 FT. LBS.)

A

FLANGE OF
SWITCH BODY

Fig. 60 KM170 and 171 neutral safety switch adjustment

Transaxle

REMOVAL & INSTALLATION

KM 170, 171, 172

➡**The transaxle and converter must be removed and installed as an assembly.**

1. Remove the battery and battery tray. On cars with a turbocharger, or fuel injection; remove the air cleaner case.
2. Disconnect the throttle control cable at the carburetor and the manual control cable at the transaxle. On fuel injected models; disconnect the oil cooler hose connection, control cable, throttle control cable and wiring harness connecters to the transaxle.
3. Disconnect from the transaxle; the inhibitor switch (neutral safety) connector, fluid cooler hoses and the four upper bolts connecting the engine to the transaxle.

4. Jack up the car and support on jackstands.
5. Remove the front wheels. Remove the engine splash shield.
6. Drain the transaxle fluid.
7. Disconnect the stabilizer bar at the lower arms, and disconnect the control arms from the body. Remove the right and left halfshafts from the transaxle case. See halfshaft removal in this section.
8. Disconnect the speedometer cable. Remove the starter motor.
9. Remove the lower cover from the converter housing. Remove the three bolts connecting the converter to the engine drive plate.

➡**Never support the full weight of the transaxle on the engine drive plate.**

10. Turn and force the converter back and away from the engine drive plate.
11. Support the weight of the engine from above (chain hoist). Support the transaxle and remove the remaining mounting bolts.
12. Remove the transaxle mount insulator bolt.
13. Remove (slide away from the engine) and lower the transaxle and converter as an assembly.
   To install:
14. Raise the transaxle in position behind the engine. Align the converter and engine flexplate, push the transaxle into position and secure it to the engine with the mounting bolts. Install the mount through bolt and lower the transaxle into position.
15. Remove the chain hoist. Install the under car components. Be sure to connect all controls, wiring and hoses. Use new retaining rings when installing the halfshafts. Torque all 7T bolts to 39 ft. lbs.; 10T bolts to 25 ft. lbs. Lower the vehicle. Install the upper mounting bolts and connect the remaining components. Fill the transaxle.

Halfshafts and CV Joints

Refer to the proceeding Manual Transaxle section for service procedures.

TRANSFER CASE

Transfer Case

REMOVAL & INSTALLATION

4-WD Vista
◆ **See Figures 61 and 62**

1. Remove the transaxle as described previously.
2. Unbolt the transfer case from the transaxle and, using a small prybar, separate the two.

3. Install the transfer case to the transaxle. Install the transaxle. The transfer case to transaxle mounting bolts are tightened to: 40–43 ft. lbs.

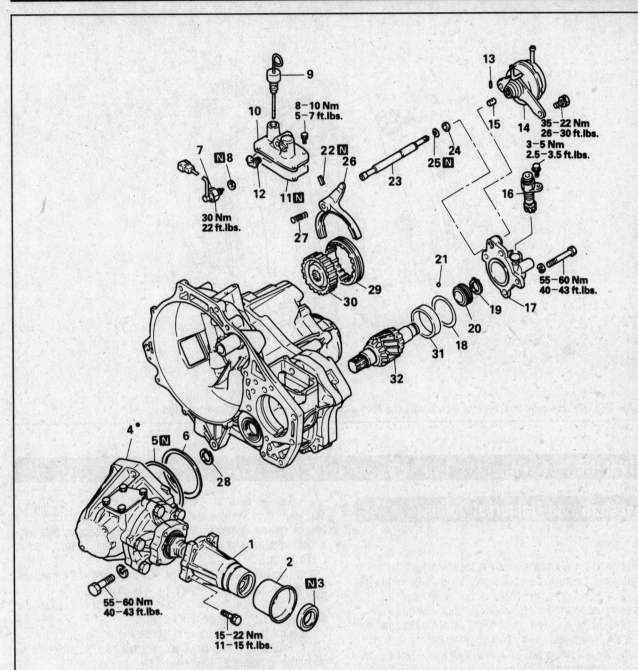

8—10 Nm
5—7 ft.lbs.

30 Nm
22 ft.lbs.

35—22 Nm
26—30 ft.lbs.

3—5 Nm
2.5—3.5 ft.lbs.

55—60 Nm
40—43 ft.lbs.

55—60 Nm
40—43 ft.lbs.

15—22 Nm
11—15 ft.lbs.

1. Extension housing
2. Dust seal guard
3. Rear oil seal
4. Transfer assembly*
5. O-ring
6. Spacer
7. Indicator lamp switch
8. Gasket
9. Level gauge
10. Upper cover
11. Upper cover gasket
12. Air breather
13. Pin
14. Actuator
15. Cover
16. Speedometer driven gear assembly

17. Rear output pinion cover
18. Spacer
19. Spacer ring
20. Speedometer drive gear
21. Steel ball
22. Spring pin
23. 2-4 shift rail
24. Seat
25. O-ring
26. 2-4 shift fork
27. Spring
28. Snap ring
29. Clutch sleeve
30. Clutch hub
31. Bearing outer race
32. Rear output pinion assembly

Fig. 61 Exploded view of the transfer case and mounting components

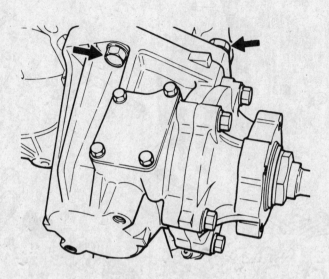

Fig. 62 The transfer case has several mounting bolts that attach it to the transaxle/transmission

DRIVELINE

Driveshaft and Universal Joints

▶ **See Figure 63**

The driveshaft is the means by which the power from the engine and transmission (in the front of the car) is transferred to the differential and rear axles, and finally to the rear wheels.

The driveshaft assembly incorporates (through 1980) two universal joints-one at each end- and a slip yoke at the front end of the assembly, which fits into the back of the transmission. Beginning with 1981 models, a two piece driveshaft with a center bearing support and universal joint is installed.

All driveshafts are balanced when installed in a car. It is, therefore, imperative that before applying undercoating to the chassis, the driveshaft and universal joint assembly be completely covered to prevent the accidental application of undercoating to their surfaces, and the subsequent loss of balance.

REMOVAL & INSTALLATION

Except 4-WD Vista

1. Mark the relationship of the rear driveshaft yoke and the drive pinion flange of the axle. The purpose of this marking is to facilitate installation of the assembly in its exact original position, thereby maintaining proper balance of the driveshaft assembly.

2. Remove the four bolts which hold the rear universal joint to the pinion flange. Remove center support bolts if equipped.

3. Pull the driveshaft toward the rear of the vehicle until the slip yoke clears the transmission housing and the seal. Plug the hole at the rear of the transmission housing or place a container under the opening to catch any fluid which might leak out.

To install:

4. Carefully inspect the rubber seal in the end of the transmission extension housing. Replace it if it is damaged.

5. Examine the lugs on the axle pinion flange and replace the flange if the lugs are shaved or distorted.

6. Coat the yoke spline with lubricant.

7. Remove the plug which you inserted into the rear of the transmission housing.

8. Insert the yoke into the transmission housing and onto the transmission output shaft. Make sure that the yoke assembly does not bottom on the output shaft with excessive force.

9. Locate the marks which you made on the rear driveshaft yoke and the pinion flange prior to removal of the driveshaft assembly. Install the driveshaft assembly with the marks properly aligned. Secure center support.

10. Install the bolts that attach the universal joint to the pinion flange. Torque the bolts to 25–30 ft. lbs. Center support bolts are tightened to 22–29 ft. lbs.

4-WD Vista

▶ **See Figure 64**

1. Raise and support the car on jackstands.
2. Drain the transfer case.
3. Matchmark the differential companion flange and the driveshaft flange yoke.

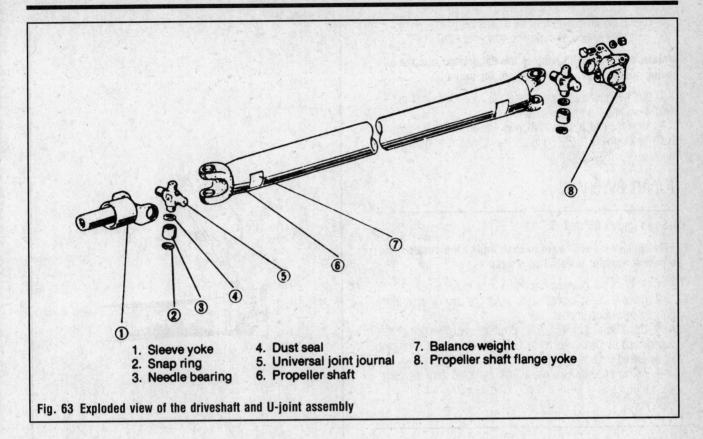

1. Sleeve yoke
2. Snap ring
3. Needle bearing
4. Dust seal
5. Universal joint journal
6. Propeller shaft
7. Balance weight
8. Propeller shaft flange yoke

Fig. 63 Exploded view of the driveshaft and U-joint assembly

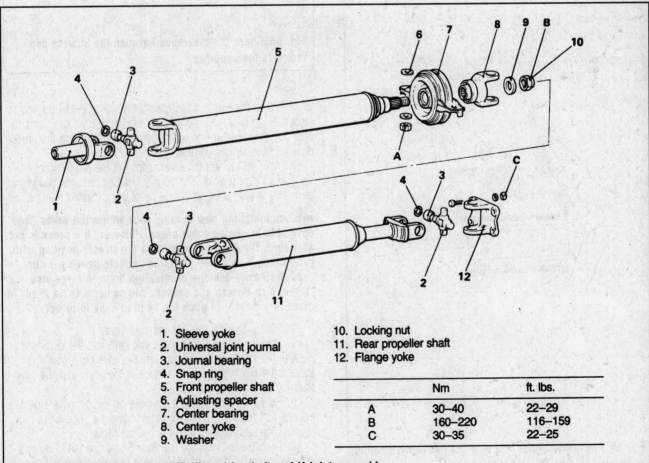

1. Sleeve yoke
2. Universal joint journal
3. Journal bearing
4. Snap ring
5. Front propeller shaft
6. Adjusting spacer
7. Center bearing
8. Center yoke
9. Washer
10. Locking nut
11. Rear propeller shaft
12. Flange yoke

	Nm	ft. lbs.
A	30–40	22–29
B	160–220	116–159
C	30–35	22–25

Fig. 64 Exploded view of the 4WD Vista driveshaft and U-joint assembly

4. Unbolt the driveshaft from the differential flange.

5. Remove the two center bearing attaching nuts.

➡**Make sure you don't confuse the flat washer and the adjusting spacer. Keep them separate for assembly.**

6. Pull the driveshaft from the transfer case. Be careful to avoid damaging the transfer case oil seal.

7. Align the matchmarks and install the driveshaft. Torque the center bearing nuts to 25–30 ft. lb.; the driveshaft-to-differential flange nuts to 20–25 ft. lbs.

U-JOINT OVERHAUL

◆ **See Figures 65 and 66**

➡**Matchmark the rear yoke to shaft and/or the center yoke to yoke for proper installation reference.**

1. Position the driveshaft assembly in a sturdy vise.

2. Remove the snaprings which retain the bearing caps in the slip yoke and the driveshaft.

3. Use a large punch or an arbor press and drive one of the bearing caps in toward the center of the universal joint. The joint will be forced through the opposite side of the yoke.

4. As the opposite side bearing cap is forced from the yoke, grip it with a pair of pliers and pull it, in a twisting motion, out of the yoke.

Fig. 66 Check the clearance between the bearing cap face and the snapring

5. Press the spider cross toward the side you just pushed to force the cap back into the yoke. When the bearing cap starts to clear the yoke, pull it free with a pair of pliers. Repeat the procedure with the other side bearing caps.

6. After removing the bearing caps, lift the bearing (spider)cross from the yoke. Thoroughly clean all dirt and foreign matter from the yoke area on both ends of the driveshaft.

➡**When installing new bearing caps within the yokes, it is advisable to use an arbor press. However, if a press is not available, the bearings should be driven into position with extreme care. A heavy jolt on the needle bearing, in the cap, can easily damage or misalign them. A large vise and correct size drivers and spacers can sometimes be used, in place of a punch, to push the bearing caps in or out.**

7. Start a bearing cap into the yoke bore.

8. Position the spider into the yoke and into the bearing cap. Push the cap the rest of the way into the yoke bore until it is about 6mm below the outside surface of the yoke. Install a new snapring.

9. Start a bearing cap into the yoke on the opposite side of the one just installed. Carefully press it into the yoke while aligning the spider cross with the bearing center.

10. Continue to press the cap in until the opposite side bearing cap contacts the snapring. Install a new snapring on the side just installed. Check the clearance between the bearing cap face

Fig. 65 Place the U-joint in a vise to remove the bearing end caps

and the snapring. If it exceeds 0.025mm, install a thicker snapring. Check the joint for free movement. Complete the installation of the yoke and bearing caps.

11. Position the driveshaft and work on the other end if service is required.

12. After service is completed, check the assembled joints and yokes for freedom of movement. If misalignment of any part causes it to bind, a sharp rap on the side of the yoke with a brass hammer should seat the needle bearings, and provide the desired freedom of movement. Care should be exercised to firmly support the shaft end during this operation, as well as to prevent blows to the bearing caps themselves. Under no circumstances should a driveshaft be installed in a vehicle if there is any bind in the U-joints. If the binding remains, disassemble the yoke and joint a check the needle bearings for correct vertical alignment.

Center Bearing and Support

REMOVAL & INSTALLATION

Except 4WD Vista

1. After removing the driveshaft, put mating marks on the front shaft flange, center yoke and rear shaft flange for installation alignment.

2. Disconnect the front and rear shaft sections by disassembling the universal joint.

3. Remove the center yoke from the front shaft by removing the center retaining nut. Remove the center support bracket. The support will slide off of the bearing by applying alternate side pressure.

4. Remove the center bearing, if necessary, use a two legged puller.

5. Inspect the center support; the bracket for damage, the rubber for deterioration and the bearing for noise, looseness or rough rotation. Replace as necessary.

6. Fill the groove on the inside center of the bearing with multi-purpose grease (NIGI Grade 2). Partially install the bearing onto the driveshaft and install the center bearing bracket over the bearing. Make sure the bearing is securely fitted in the rubber mount. Slide the assembly into place on the driveshaft. Install the yoke and rear driveshaft.

➡ **Always use a new self-locking nut to secure the center yoke.**

4WD Vista

1. Remove the driveshaft and center bearing as in the previous procedure.

2. Matchmark the two driveshafts with the center bearing.

3. Disassemble the universal joint connecting the center bearing with the rear driveshaft.

4. Remove and discard the self-locking nut holding the yoke half to the center bearing.

5. Pull the yoke from the center bearing.

6. Pull off the center bearing bracket.

➡ **The mounting rubber is not removable from the center bearing bracket.**

7. Using a two-jawed puller, remove the center bearing from the forward driveshaft.

8. Apply a coating of chassis lube to the grease holder on the center bearing and to the outer circumference of the dust boot at the point at which the shaft is inserted.

9. Install the bearing in the groove of the center bearing bracket mounting rubber. Make sure it is securely installed.

10. Install the center bearing assembly to the forward driveshaft.

11. Align the matchmarks and slide the yoke half into the center bearing. Using a new self-locking nut, seat the yoke in the center bearing. Torque the nut to 160 ft. lbs.

12. Align the matchmarks and assemble the yoke. Make sure the snaprings securing the bearings caps are installed with a clearance of 0–0.03mm between the snapring and groove in the yoke.

BASIC DRIVESHAFT PROBLEMS

Problem	Cause	Solution
Shudder as car accelerates from stop or low speed	• Loose U-joint • Defective center bearing	• Replace U-joint • Replace center bearing
Loud clunk in driveshaft when shifting gears	• Worn U-joints	• Replace U-joints
Roughness or vibration at any speed	• Out-of-balance, bent or dented driveshaft • Worn U-joints • U-joint clamp bolts loose	• Balance or replace driveshaft • Replace U-joints • Tighten U-joint clamp bolts
Squeaking noise at low speeds	• Lack of U-joint lubrication	• Lubricate U-joint; if problem persists, replace U-joint
Knock or clicking noise	• U-joint or driveshaft hitting frame tunnel • Worn CV joint	• Correct overloaded condition • Replace CV joint

BASIC REAR AXLE PROBLEMS

First, determine when the noise is most noticeable.

Drive Noise: Produced under vehicle acceleration.

Coast Noise: Produced while the car coasts with a closed throttle.

Float Noise: Occurs while maintaining constant car speed (just enough to keep speed constant) on a level road.

Road Noise

Brick or rough surfaced concrete roads produce noises that seem to come from the rear axle. Road noise is usually identical in Drive or Coast and driving on a different type of road will tell whether the road is the problem.

Tire Noise

Tire noises are often mistaken for rear axle problems. Snow treads or unevenly worn tires produce vibrations seeming to originate elsewhere. **Temporarily** inflating the tires to 40 lbs will significantly alter tire noise, but will have no effect on rear axle noises (which normally cease below about 30 mph).

Engine/Transmission Noise

Determine at what speed the noise is most pronounced, then stop the car in a quiet place. With the transmission in Neutral, run the engine through speeds corresponding to road speeds where the noise was noticed. Noises produced with the car standing still are coming from the engine or transmission.

Front Wheel Bearings

While holding the car speed steady, lightly apply the footbrake; this will often decease bearing noise, as some of the load is taken from the bearing.

Rear Axle Noises

Eliminating other possible sources can narrow the cause to the rear axle, which normally produces noise from worn gears or bearings. Gear noises tend to peak in a narrow speed range, while bearing noises will usually vary in pitch with engine speeds.

NOISE DIAGNOSIS

The Noise Is	Most Probably Produced By
• Identical under Drive or Coast	• Road surface, tires or front wheel bearings
• Different depending on road surface	• Road surface or tires
• Lower as the car speed is lowered	• Tires
• Similar with car standing or moving	• Engine or transmission
• A vibration	• Unbalanced tires, rear wheel bearing, unbalanced driveshaft or worn U-joint
• A knock or click about every 2 tire revolutions	• Rear wheel bearing
• Most pronounced on turns	• Damaged differential gears
• A steady low-pitched whirring or scraping, starting at low speeds	• Damaged or worn pinion bearing
• A chattering vibration on turns	• Wrong differential lubricant or worn clutch plates (limited slip rear axle)
• Noticed only in Drive, Coast or Float conditions	• Worn ring gear and/or pinion gear

REAR DRIVE AXLES

Understanding Rear Axles

▶ See Figure 67

The rear axle is a special type of transmission that reduces the speed of the drive from the engine and transmission and divides the power to the rear wheels.

Power enters the rear axle from the driveshaft via the companion flange. The flange is mounted on the drive pinion shaft. The drive pinion shaft and gear which carry the power into the differential turn at engine speed. The gear on the end of the pinion shaft drives a large ring gear the axis of rotation of which is ninety degrees away from that of the pinion. The pinion and gear reduce the speed and multiply the power by the gear ratio of the axle, and change the direction of rotation to turn the axleshafts which

drive both wheels. The rear axle gear ratio is found by dividing the number of pinion gear teeth into the number of ring gear teeth.

The ring gear drives the differential case. The case provides the two mounting points for the ends of a pinion shaft on which are mounted two pinion gears. The pinion gears drive the two side pinion gears, one of which is located on the inner end of each axleshaft.

By driving the axleshafts through this arrangement, the differential allows the outer drive wheel to turn faster than the inner drive wheel in a turn.

The main drive pinion and the side bearings, which bear the weight of the differential case, are shimmed to provide proper bearing preload, and to position the pinion and ring gears properly.

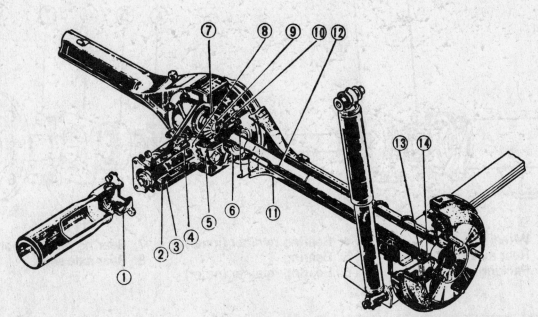

1. Propeller shaft flange yoke
2. Drive pinion oil seal
3. Drive pinion front bearing
4. Drive pinion rear bearing
5. Final drive gear
6. Differential carrier side bearing
7. Differential case
8. Drive pinion
9. Differential pinion
10. Differential side pinion
11. Rear axle housing
12. Rear axle shaft
13. Rear axle shaft oil seal
14. Rear axle shaft bearing

Fig. 67 Exploded view of the common rear axle and differential assembly

➡The proper adjustment of a relationship of the ring and pinion gears is critical. It should only be attempted by those with extensive equipment and or experience.

The rear wheels are connected to the differential assembly by axleshafts. The axleshafts are supported in the rear axle housing by bearings and are retained in the housing by bearing retainer plates which bolt to the rear brake mounting plates.

The differential assembly is mounted on two tapered bearings. These bearings are retained in the axle housing with removable bearing caps.

The drive pinion is mounted in the axle on two roller bearings.

An identification tag is attached to one of the inspection plate bolts. The information on this tag must be used when ordering replacement parts.

Axleshaft/Bearing

REMOVAL & INSTALLATION

Except Conquest and 4WD Vista
▶ See Figure 68

➡A press is necessary for bearing removal and installation. After the axle has been removed, an automotive machine shop can press off and install the axle bearing.

1. Remove the wheel, tire and brake drum.
2. Remove the nuts holding the axle retainer plate to the backing plate.

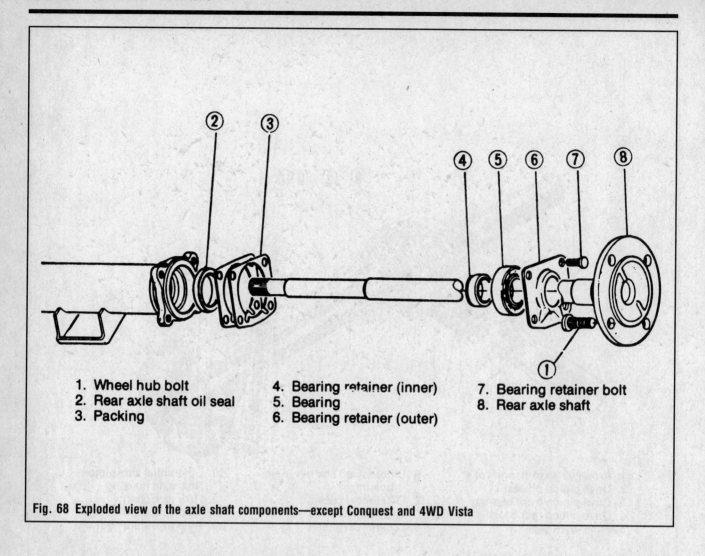

1. **Wheel hub bolt**
2. **Rear axle shaft oil seal**
3. **Packing**

4. **Bearing retainer (inner)**
5. **Bearing**
6. **Bearing retainer (outer)**

7. **Bearing retainer bolt**
8. **Rear axle shaft**

Fig. 68 Exploded view of the axle shaft components—except Conquest and 4WD Vista

3. Remove the retainer. Install the nuts finger-tight, to prevent the backing plate from being dislodged.

4. Pull the axleshaft and bearing from the axle housing. A slide hammer puller will make the job easier. Remove the oil seal from the axle housing.

5. Using a chisel, nick the bearing retainer ring in three or four places. The retainer does not have to be cut, merely collapsed sufficiently to allow the retainer ring to slide from the shaft and not resist when the bearing is pressed off.

6. Press off the old bearing, and install the new one.

7. Press on the new retaining ring.

➡**Do not attempt to press the bearing and retainer on at the same time.**

8. Install a new oil seal in the axle housing, after cleaning the mounting surface of the housing.

9. Install the axle. Secure the retaining plate. Install the brake drum and wheel.

Conquest

◆ **See Figure 69**

➡**The term axleshaft refers to the shaft enclosed in the flange and housing at the rear wheel. The shaft between the differential and axleshaft is termed the intermediate shaft. A press is required for bearing replacement.**

1. Raise and safely support the vehicle on jackstands.

2. Disconnect the parking brake cable from the rear calipers.

3. Remove the caliper, caliper support and rotor. Don't disconnect the brake line from the caliper, just suspend the caliper out of the way with wire.

4. Remove the intermediate shaft and companion shaft.

5. Remove the axleshaft housing from the lower control arm.

6. Remove the strut assembly from the axleshaft housing.

7. Loosen the companion flange nut and tap the axleshaft out of the housing with a plastic mallet. Take care not to damage the oil seal.

8. Remove the spacer and dust covers from inside the housing.

➡**Don't remove the bearings unless you intend to replace them, since they will be damaged during removal.**

9. Remove the outer bearing with a puller.

10. Using a brass drift, drive the inner bearing and seal from the housing.

11. Press the new outer bearing onto the shaft with the seal side facing the companion flange side of the shaft.

12. Pack the housing with lithium based wheel bearing grease.

13. Press the inner bearing onto the shaft with the seal side facing the companion side of the shaft.

14. Grease the seal bore in the housing and drive the new seal into position.

15. Install the dust covers.

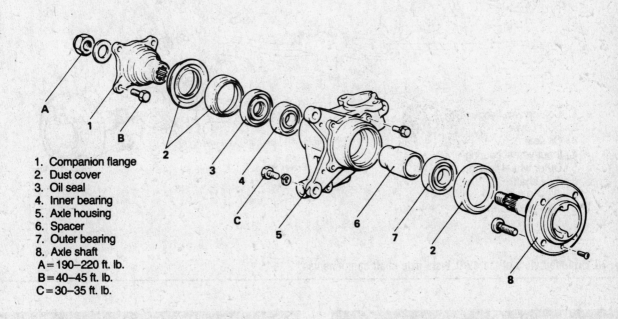

1. Companion flange
2. Dust cover
3. Oil seal
4. Inner bearing
5. Axle housing
6. Spacer
7. Outer bearing
8. Axle shaft
  A = 190—220 ft. lb.
  B = 40—45 ft. lb.
  C = 30—35 ft. lb.

Fig. 69 Exploded view of the Conquest axle shaft components

16. Insert the axleshaft and spacer into the housing and attach the companion flange.

17. Place the housing in a vise, then install and tighten the companion flange nut to 200—220 ft. lbs.

18. Install all the other parts. Check the axleshaft end-play with a dial indicator. End-play should be 0.8mm on vehicles with four lug wheel, and 0.13—0.20mm on vehicles with five lug wheels. If the end-play exceeds the limits, the bearing needs replacing or it has been assembled incorrectly.

4WD Vista

▶ **See Figure 70**

1. Raise and safely support the rear of the vehicle, with the suspension hanging free.

2. Remove the rear wheels.

3. Remove the brake drums.

4. Remove the bolts securing the axle flange to the intermediate shaft flange.

5. Remove the axle flange nut.

6. Use a slide hammer puller, and remove the axleshaft from the housing.

7. Remove the lower control arm.

8. Remove the dust cover and outer wheel bearing and seal from the axleshaft with an appropriate puller.

9. Press the inner bearing and seal from the housing. Pack the new bearing with grease and press into place.

10. Install the new inner bearing seal.

11. Install the dust cover into place evenly in the housing.

12. Coat the lip of a new seal and pack the outer bearing with grease.

13. Press in the bearing and seal.

14. Press the axleshaft into the inner arm.

15. Install the inner arm assembly.

16. Install the companion flange and nut. Torque the nut to 160 ft. lbs.

17. Connect the intermediate shaft and axleshaft. Torque the bolts to 43 ft. lbs.

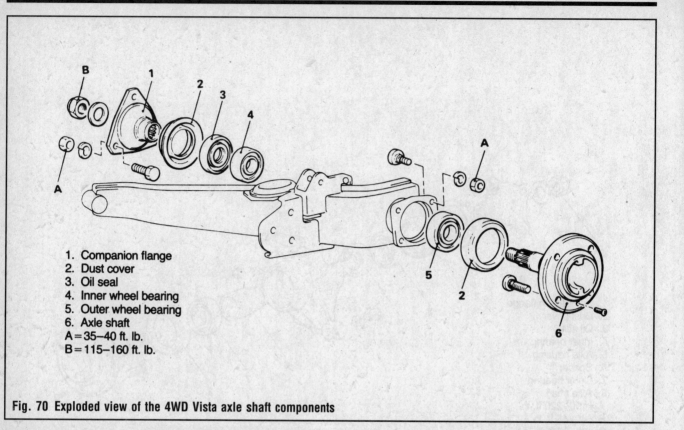

1. Companion flange
2. Dust cover
3. Oil seal
4. Inner wheel bearing
5. Outer wheel bearing
6. Axle shaft
A = 35–40 ft. lb.
B = 115–160 ft. lb.

Fig. 70 Exploded view of the 4WD Vista axle shaft components

Intermediate Shaft

REMOVAL & INSTALLATION

Conquest

♦ See Figure 71

1. Remove the bolts and separate the intermediate shaft from the companion flange.
2. Use a slide hammer puller and remove the intermediate shaft from the differential. Be careful to avoid damaging the oil seal. It is always a good idea to install a new oil seal at shaft installation time.
3. Pry the oil seal carefully from the housing. Install a new seal after cleaning the housing mounting surface.
4. Service the intermediate shaft as require. Install the shaft after coating the seal surface of the shaft and the oil seal lip with grease. Tap the shaft into position carefully, with the slide hammer if necessary. Take care that the shaft assembly does not fall from the differential during removal or installation operations.

4WD Vista

1. Raise and support the rear of the vehicle with jackstands placed under the frame.
2. Disconnect the intermediate shaft and axleshaft flanges.
3. Use a small prybar and carefully remove the intermediate shaft from the differential.
4. Service the intermediate shaft as required. Install a new seal into the differential. Install the intermediate shaft. Connect the intermediate shaft to the axleshaft. Tighten the bolts to 43 ft. lbs.

Intermediate Shaft
Constant Velocity Joints

OVERHAUL

➡Two types of CV joints are used on each shaft. On the inner end of the shaft is a Birfield joint; on the outer end, a double offset joint. The DOJ can be disassembled; the Birfield joint cannot. CV joint repair kits are the only way to rebuild the joint. These kits come with a special grease. Use it.

1. Remove the boot bands.
2. Remove the circlip from the DOJ outer race.
3. Separate the intermediate shaft from the DOJ outer race.
4. Remove the balls from the DOJ cage.
5. Remove the cage from the inner race, in the direction of the Birfield joint.
6. Remove the snapring from the shaft and pull the DOJ inner race and cage from the shaft. Remove the circlip.
7. Wrap plastic tape around the splines on the shaft and slide the boots off. Pay attention to the boots, they are different from each other. Be sure to use the correct boot for each end when installing them.
8. Clean all parts in a non-flammable solvent. Check all parts for wear or damage. Replace any suspect parts. If the Birfield joint is defective, the shaft and joint must be replaced as an assembly.
9. Apply the special grease to the intermediate shaft and install the boots and bands. Be sure to install the different boots to their correct shaft end.

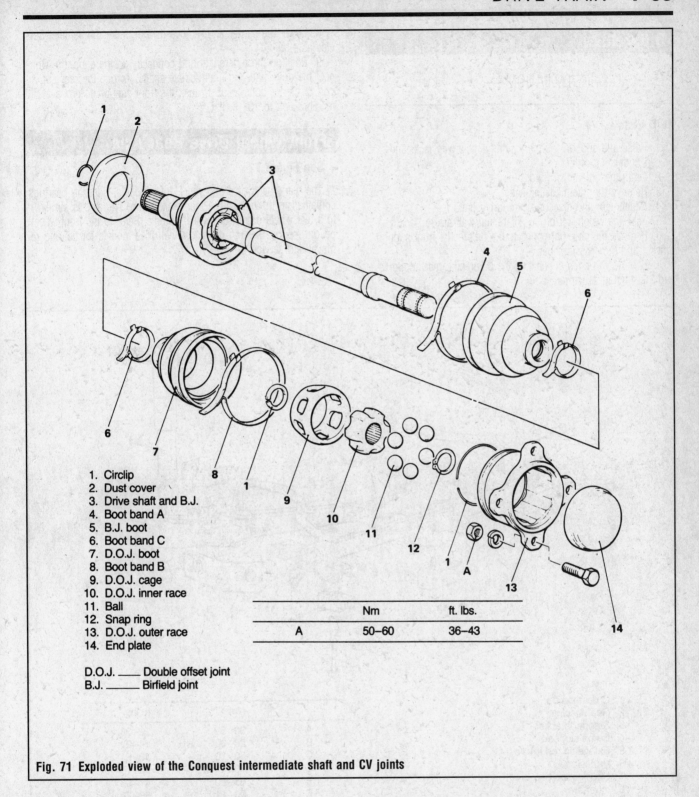

1. Circlip
2. Dust cover
3. Drive shaft and B.J.
4. Boot band A
5. B.J. boot
6. Boot band C
7. D.O.J. boot
8. Boot band B
9. D.O.J. cage
10. D.O.J. inner race
11. Ball
12. Snap ring
13. D.O.J. outer race
14. End plate

D.O.J. —— Double offset joint
B.J. —— Birfield joint

	Nm	ft. lbs.
A	50–60	36–43

Fig. 71 Exploded view of the Conquest intermediate shaft and CV joints

10. Install the cage onto the shaft, smaller end first.
11. Install the circlip.
12. Install the inner race and snapring.
13. Coat the inner race and cage with the special grease and fit them together.
14. Apply the special grease to the balls and insert them into the cage and race.
15. Apply about 2.5 ounces of the special grease to the outer race.

16. Insert the shaft into the outer race and apply another 2.5 ounces of grease on the race.
17. Install the circlip on the outer race.
18. Position the boot over the DOJ and secure it with the band.
19. Install the smaller band and position it so that 76mm exists between the two bands. Tighten the band.
20. Pack the Birfield joint with 4–5 ounces of the special grease.

Differential

REMOVAL & INSTALLATION

4WD Vista

1. Raise and support the rear of the vehicle with jackstand placed under the frame.
2. Drain the differential fluid.
3. Remove the intermediate shafts.
4. Matchmark and disconnect the driveshaft.
5. Take the weight off of the differential with a floor jack.
6. Remove the bolt that connects the differential front support bracket and the crossmember.
7. Remove the bolts connecting the differential rear support and the differential carrier.

8. Lower the carrier and remove it from under the vehicle. Service as required.
9. Position the differential and connect it to the supports. Connect the driveshaft and intermediate shafts. Torque the rear support to carrier bolts to 95 ft. lbs.; the front support to crossmember bolt to 101 ft. lbs.

Front Wheel Drive Rear Axle

♦ See Figure 72

The rear wheel, on front wheel drive models, rides on bearings contained in the hub of the rear brake drum. The axle is similar to a rear wheel drive front wheel spindle. Refer to the front wheel bearing service section on rear wheel drive models for bearing removal and service.

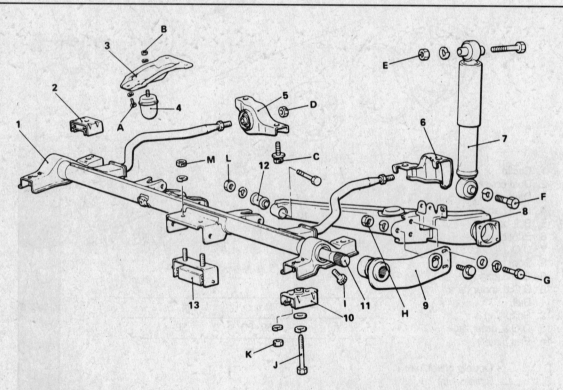

1. Crossmember
2. Rear insulator
3. Stopper bracket
4. Bump stopper
5. Extension rod fixture
6. Protector
7. Shock absorber
8. Inner arm
9. Outer arm
10. Front insulator
11. Torsion bar
12. Inner arm bushing
13. Dynamic damper

	Nm	ft. lbs.
A	30–50	22–36
B	20–30	14–22
C	50–70	36–51
D	100–140	72–101
E	65–80	47–58
F	80–110	58–79
G	80–100	58–72
H	120–140	87–101
I	22–30	16–22
J	80–120	58–87
K	10–15	7–10
L	70–90	51–65
M	19–28	14–20

Fig. 72 Exploded view of the 4WD Vista rear suspension

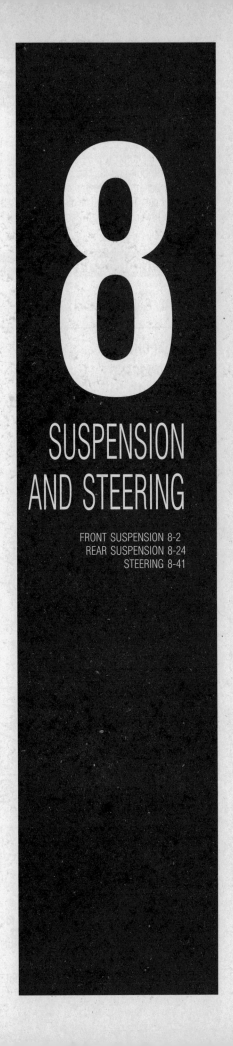

8

SUSPENSION AND STEERING

FRONT SUSPENSION 8-2
REAR SUSPENSION 8-24
STEERING 8-41

FRONT SUSPENSION

The front suspension consists of MacPherson struts, lower control arms and a stabilizer bar. The strut assembly performs several suspension functions: It provides the steering knuckle mounting, the concentric coil acts as the springing medium, the integral shock absorber provides dampening and the strut assembly locates the wheel. The stabilizer bar minimizes body roll when cornering. The lower control arm acts to longitudinally locate the suspension/wheel.

MacPherson Struts

REMOVAL & INSTALLATION

Rear Wheel Drive

EXCEPT CONQUEST

▶ **See Figure 1**

1. Loosen the lug nuts, jack up the front of the vehicle (after blocking the rear wheels) and support safely on jackstands.

2. Remove the wheel assembly, brake caliper, hub and brake disc rotor. Disconnect the stabilizer link from the lower arm, remove the steering knuckle-to-strut assembly bolts. Carefully force the lower arm down and separate the strut assembly and the steering knuckle. Unscrew the retaining nuts at the top of the strut and remove the strut assembly.

➡ **On some models the lower splash shield may interfere with the strut removal and installation. If so, remove the splash shield.**

To install:

3. Position the strut assembly in the fender. Install the upper retainer nuts hand-tight.

4. Apply sealer on the mounting flange and fasten the strut assembly to the steering knuckle. Connect the brake line if it was removed.

5. Tighten the upper retaining nuts to 7–11 ft. lbs. Torque the knuckle bolts to 30–36 ft. lbs.

6. Assemble the stabilizer link and fasten it to the lower control arm if removed.

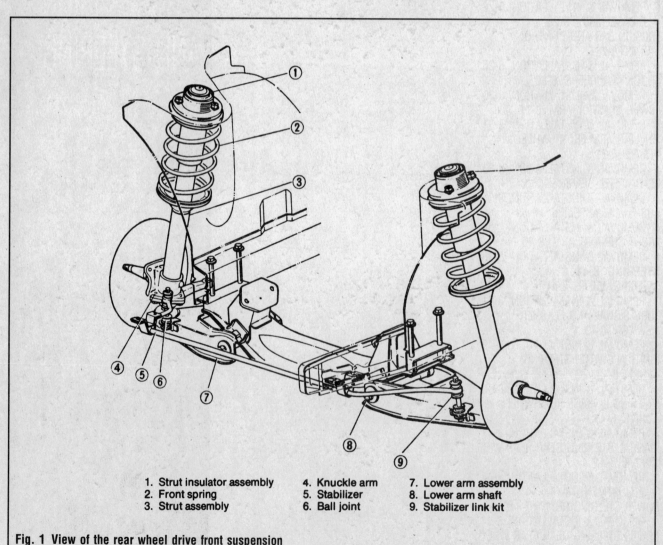

1. Strut insulator assembly
2. Front spring
3. Strut assembly
4. Knuckle arm
5. Stabilizer
6. Ball joint
7. Lower arm assembly
8. Lower arm shaft
9. Stabilizer link kit

Fig. 1 View of the rear wheel drive front suspension

7. Assemble the remaining parts. Bleed the brakes if any brake lines were disconnected during strut removal.

CONQUEST

♦ **See Figures 2 and 3**

1. Raise and support the front end of the vehicle on jackstands. Remove the wheels. Allow the front suspension to hang.

2. Remove the brake caliper and suspend it out of the way with wire. Do not allow any strain to be put on the brake hose.

3. Remove the wheel hub and disc rotor.

4. Remove the brake dust cover.

5. Unbolt the strut from the steering knuckle.

6. Remove the strut to upper fender mount securing nuts and remove the strut assembly.

7. Service the strut as required. Secure the strut to the upper mounting. Secure the strut to the steering knuckle. Install the dust shield, hub, rotor and caliper. Torque the upper mounting nuts to 18–25 ft. lbs.; the strut to knuckle bolts to 58–72 ft. lbs.

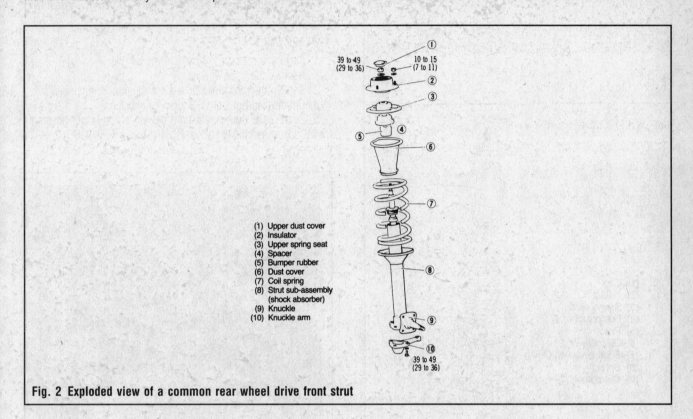

(1) Upper dust cover
(2) Insulator
(3) Upper spring seat
(4) Spacer
(5) Bumper rubber
(6) Dust cover
(7) Coil spring
(8) Strut sub-assembly (shock absorber)
(9) Knuckle
(10) Knuckle arm

39 to 49 (29 to 36)
10 to 15 (7 to 11)
39 to 49 (29 to 36)

Fig. 2 Exploded view of a common rear wheel drive front strut

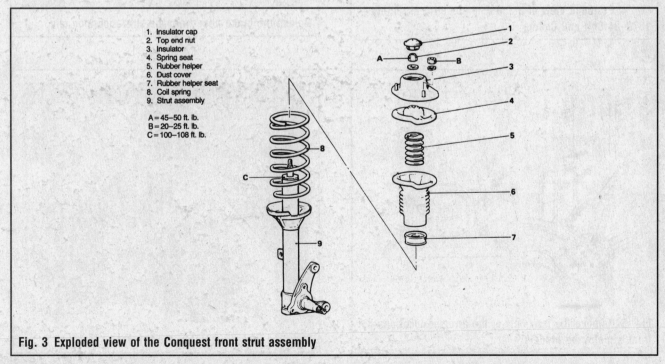

1. Insulator cap
2. Top end nut
3. Insulator
4. Spring seat
5. Rubber helper
6. Dust cover
7. Rubber helper seat
8. Coil spring
9. Strut assembly

A = 45–50 ft. lb.
B = 20–25 ft. lb.
C = 100–108 ft. lb.

Fig. 3 Exploded view of the Conquest front strut assembly

Front Wheel Drive

1979–84 COLT AND 1985–89 VISTA

▶ **See Figures 4 and 5**

1. Raise and safely support the front of the vehicle.
2. Remove the front wheels.
3. Detach the brake hose from the clip on the strut.

4. Remove the mounting nuts that secure the upper end of the strut to the fender housing.
5. Unbolt the strut from the steering knuckle.
6. Remove the strut from the vehicle.

To install:

7. Service as required. Bolt the strut to the steering knuckle, and the upper fender mounting. Secure the brake hose to the strut mounting clip.
8. Torque the strut to knuckle bolts to 55–65 ft. lbs.; Torque the strut to fender housing bolts to; Colt, 7–11 ft. lbs. Vista, 18–25 ft. lbs.

1985–89 COLT

1. Raise and support the front of the vehicle.
2. Remove the front wheels.
3. Detach the front brake hose from the strut mounting clip.
4. Unbolt the strut from the steering knuckle.
5. Remove the dust shield from the top of the fender housing mount. Insert a suitable socket (special tool MB991036, or the equivalent) into the top of the strut to loosen the mounting nut.

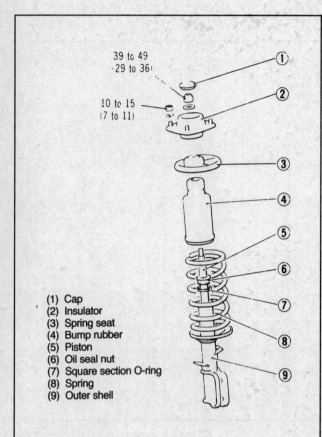

(1) Cap
(2) Insulator
(3) Spring seat
(4) Bump rubber
(5) Piston
(6) Oil seal nut
(7) Square section O-ring
(8) Spring
(9) Outer shell

Fig. 4 Exploded view of the McPherson strut assembly—1979–84 Colt and Champ

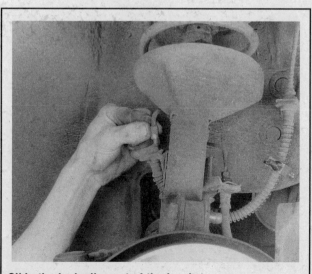

Detach the brake hose from the strut mounting clip

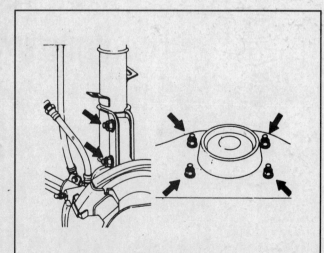

Fig. 5 Remove the nuts only at the arrowed locations on front wheel drive models

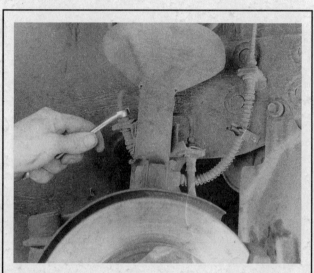

Slide the brake line out of the bracket

Pull the clip off and move aside

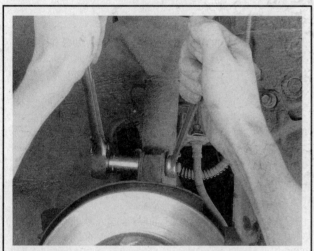

Using a ratchet and a wrench, loosen strut lower mounting bolt and nut

Remove the mounting bolt, nut and washer and set aside

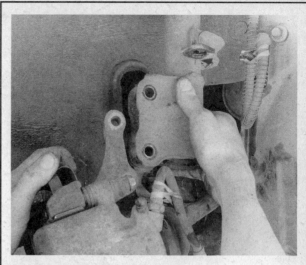

Separate the knuckle from the strut

6. Insert an allen wrench through the socket, into the top of the strut shaft. Remove the mounting nut, while holding the shaft with the allen wrench.

7. Remove the strut. Service as required.

To install:

8. Mount the strut into position and secure the upper mount. Attach the lower strut bracket to the steering knuckle.

9. Torque the strut to knuckle bolts to 55–65 ft. lbs.; the upper retaining nut to 25–36 ft. lbs. Check the wheel alignment.

Coil Spring

REMOVAL & INSTALLATION

Except 1985–89 Colt

◆ See Figures 6, 7 and 8

1. Remove the strut assembly as previously outlined. Clamp the strut assembly in a soft-jawed vise or wrap heavy rags around the strut before tightening the vise.

2. Install a spring compressor on the spring and tighten to compress the spring slightly. The compressor will keep the spring compressed while the strut cover and spring seat are removed.

✳✳ CAUTION

A compressed coil spring can release tremendous energy. Be very careful when compressing or releasing the spring. Be sure the jaws of the compressor grip the coils of the spring firmly.

3. Remove the upper dust cover.

4. Remove the nuts that retain the insulator to the strut. Remove the insulator.

5. Remove the spring. Service the strut as required.

To install:

6. If a new spring is to be installed, compress the spring.

7. Install the spring on the strut.

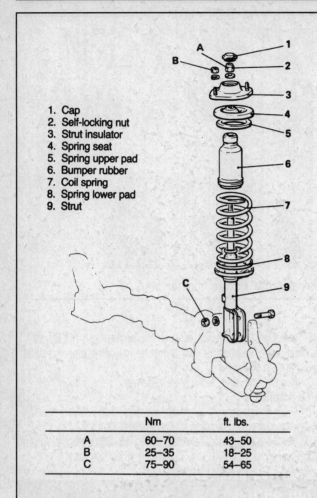

1. Cap
2. Self-locking nut
3. Strut insulator
4. Spring seat
5. Spring upper pad
6. Bumper rubber
7. Coil spring
8. Spring lower pad
9. Strut

	Nm	ft. lbs.
A	60–70	43–50
B	25–35	18–25
C	75–90	54–65

Fig. 6 Vista front strut torque specifications

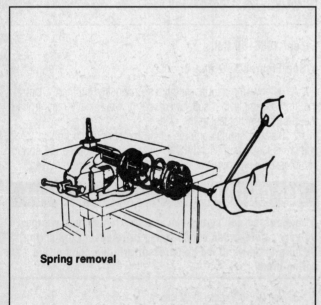

Spring removal

Fig. 7 When removing the spring, be sure to keep it secured in a vise

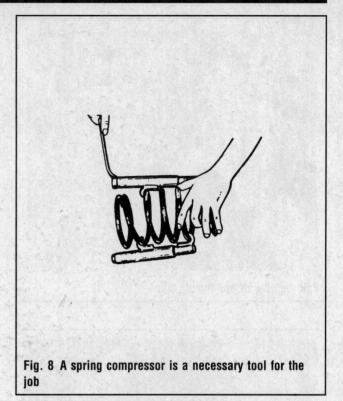

Fig. 8 A spring compressor is a necessary tool for the job

8. Fully extend the shock absorber piston rod.
9. Align the spring seat upper assembly with the indent on the piston rod and the D-shaped hole.
10. Install the insulator assembly. Temporarily tighten the self-locking nut.

➡**Always install a new self-locking nut. DO NOT use the old nut.**

11. After correctly seating the upper and lower ends of the coil spring on the grooves of the upper and lower seats, release the spring compressor.
   Hold the upper spring seat stationary and tighten the self-locking retaining nut. Torque the nut to 30–36 ft. lbs. on all models except the Conquest. Tighten to 43–51 ft. lbs. on the Conquest.

1985–89 Colt

▶ **See Figure 9**

1. Remove the strut assembly from the vehicle.
2. Using a spring compressor, fully compress the spring.

✳✳ CAUTION

A compressed coil spring can release tremendous energy. Be very careful when compressing or releasing the spring. Be sure the jaws of the compressor grip the coils of the spring firmly.

3. Using special tool MB9910036, or the equivalent, and an allen wrench, remove the retaining nut.
4. Remove the rubber insulator, support, spring seat rubber bumper and spring.
5. Use a brass drift and carefully remove the bearing from the support.
6. Check all parts for wear. Service as require.

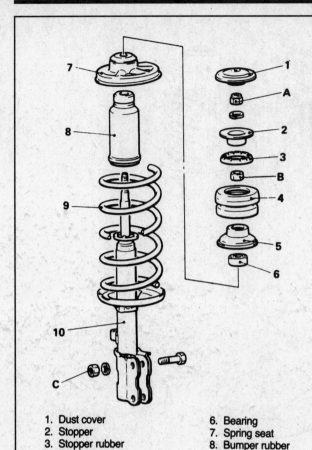

1. Dust cover	6. Bearing
2. Stopper	7. Spring seat
3. Stopper rubber	8. Bumper rubber
4. Rubber insulator	9. Coil spring
5. Support	10. Strut

	Nm	ft. lbs.
A	45–60	33–43
B	35–50	25–36
C	75–90	54–65

Fig. 9 Torque specifications for the 1985–86 Colt front strut

To install:

7. Install the bearing, spring, seat rubber bumper, support, rubber insulator and secure them with a new self-locking nut.

8. Make sure that both spring seat grooves align with the coil spring ends.

➡**Always install a new self-locking nut. DO NOT use the old nut.**

9. Tighten the retaining nut to 25–36 ft. lbs.

OVERHAUL

1. Remove the strut from the vehicle. Remove the coil spring from the strut.

➡**Matchmark the upper end of the coil spring and bearing plate to avoid confusion during assembly.**

2. Keep the upper mounting parts in the order of their removal, again to avoid confusion during assembly.

3. Clean the outside of the strut body, especially around the top. Use the proper size wrench to loosen the top strut body nut.

4. Remove the body nut. If a new nut came with the strut overhaul kit, discard the old nut.

5. Use a suitable tool and remove the O-ring from the top of the strut housing bore.

6. Grasp the piston rod and slowly pull the cartridge out of the housing. Remove the cartridge slowly to prevent the oil between the housing and the cartridge from splashing.

7. Pour all of the strut oil into a suitable container. Clean the inside of the housing and inspect the cylinder for dents and to insure that all loose parts have been removed from the inside of the strut body.

8. Keep the strut upright and replenish the strut cylinder with one ounce (or whatever amount is suggested by the overhaul kit instructions) of the original or fresh oil. The oil helps dissipate internal heat during operation and results in cooler strut operation. Do not put too much oil in, or the oil may leak at the body nut when the shock heats up and causes expansion.

9. Insert the replacement cartridge into the strut body. Push the piston rod all of the way down to avoid damage if the wrench slips when installing the top nut. Carefully install the top body nut, take care not to cross-thread. Tighten the top body nut to 100 ft. lbs. (or whatever the instruction sheet calls for).

10. Install the coil spring and top parts. Pay attention to the alignment reference marks made when taking apart the strut.

11. Install the strut on the vehicle.

Lower Control Arm

REMOVAL & INSTALLATION

Rear Wheel Drive

EXCEPT CONQUEST

◆ **See Figure 10**

1. Loosen the wheel lug nuts, raise and support the front of the vehicle allowing the suspension to hang.

2. Remove the wheels, caliper, hub and disc rotor.

3. Disconnect the stabilizer link and strut bar from the lower control arm. Depending on the year, remove the idler support from the chassis and move the steering linkage to gain working clearance.

4. Remove the steering knuckle to strut mounting bolts.

5. Carefully force the lower control arm down and separate the strut assembly from the steering knuckle.

6. Remove the strut assembly, if necessary, to gain working room.

7. Use a puller and disconnect the steering knuckle arm from the tie rod end assembly.

8. Use a puller and disconnect the knuckle arm and lower control arm ball joint.

9. Remove the control arm to inner crossmember mounting bolt and remove the control arm.

To install:

10. Service as necessary. Install the control arm to the inner crossmember. Tighten the bolts to 51–57 ft. lbs. (through 1980) and 58–69 ft. lbs. (from 1981). The chamfered end of the nut should be facing the round surface of the bracket.

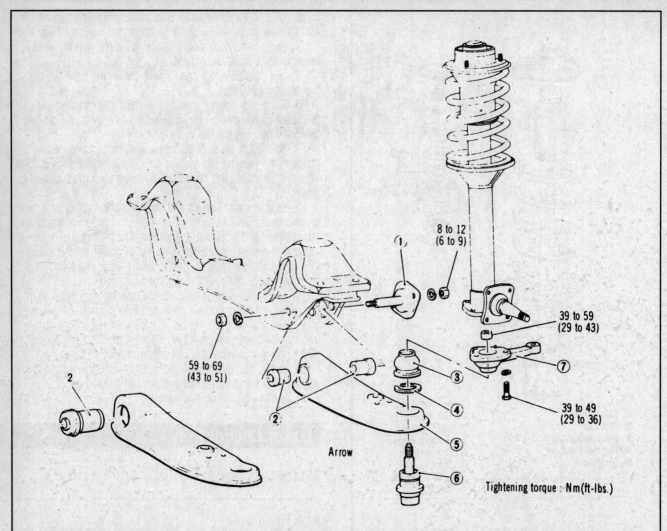

Fig. 10 Exploded view of the lower control arm and ball joint assembly used on all rear wheel drive cars except Conquest

11. Tighten the steering knuckle to control arm ball joint nut to 30–40 ft. lbs. (through 1980) and 52–69 ft. lbs. (from 1981).

12. Install the strut assembly into the fender mount. Tighten the upper mounting bolts to 7–10 ft. lbs. (through 1980) and 18–25 ft. lbs. (from 1981).

13. Apply sealer to the lower end of the strut. Install and tighten the strut to steering knuckle arm bolts to 30–36 ft. lbs. (through 1980) and 58–72 ft. lbs. (from 1981).

14. Assemble the stabilizer link and fasten it and the strut bar to the lower control arm.

15. Install the brake disc rotor, hub and caliper. Tighten the strut bar to 18–25 ft. lbs.

16. Install the wheels and lower the vehicle. Jounce the vehicle up and down several times, then tighten the stabilizer bolt to 7–10 ft. lbs.

CONQUEST

♦ See Figures 11 and 12

➡This procedure requires the use of a special tool MB990635, or equivalent.

1. Loosen the wheel lugs. Raise and support the front of the vehicle allowing the suspension to hang.

2. Remove the wheels.

3. Remove the brake caliper and suspend it out of the way. Take care not to put strain on the brake hose.

4. Remove the hub and disc rotor.

5. Disconnect the stabilizer bar and strut bar from the lower arm.

6. Use a separator and disconnect the tie rod assembly from the steering knuckle, after removing the locknut.

7. Unbolt the strut from the lower control arm.

8. Unbolt the control arm and strut assembly from the inner crossmember.

➡The inner control arm mounting bolt is an eccentric and used to adjust alignment. Mark the tab and crossmember for installation reference.

9. Use the special tool MB990635, or equivalent and separate the steering knuckle from the lower control arm.

10. Service as required. Install the lower control arm and strut. Connect the tie rod, strut bar and stabilizer. Install the disc rotor, hub and caliper. Install the front wheels and lower the vehicle. Torque the lower control arm inner mounting bolt to 60–70 ft. lbs.; the ball joint to knuckle arm nut to 45–55 ft. lbs.

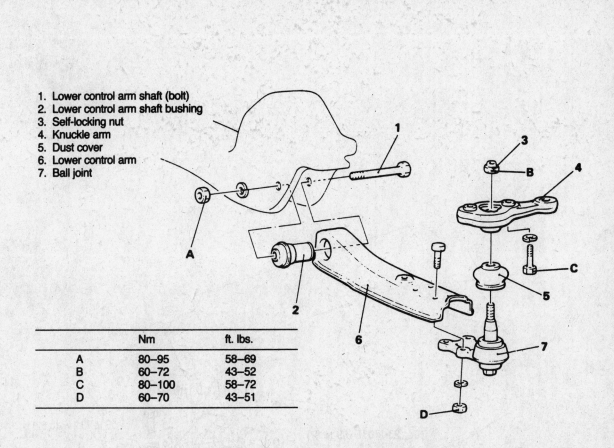

1. Lower control arm shaft (bolt)
2. Lower control arm shaft bushing
3. Self-locking nut
4. Knuckle arm
5. Dust cover
6. Lower control arm
7. Ball joint

	Nm	ft. lbs.
A	80–95	58–69
B	60–72	43–52
C	80–100	58–72
D	60–70	43–51

Fig. 11 The Conquest lower control arm and ball joint are slightly different than other models

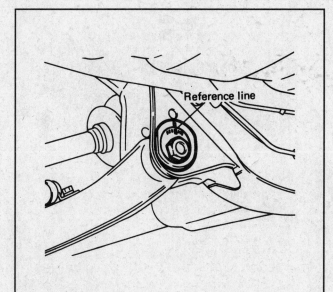

Fig. 12 Alignment marks on the Conquest lower control arm

Front Wheel Drive

1979–84 MODELS

▶ See Figures 13 and 14

1. Loosen the front wheel lugs. Block the rear wheels. Jack up the front of the vehicle, allowing the front suspension to hang, and safely support the vehicle on jackstands.

2. Remove the front wheels. Remove the lower engine splash shield.

3. Disconnect the lower ball joint by unfastening the nuts and bolts mounting it to the control arm. It is not necessary to remove the ball joint from the knuckle.

4. Remove the strut bar and the control arm inner mounting nut and bolt. Remove the control arm.

To install:

5. Service as required. Position the control arm to the cross-member, install and tighten the mounting bolt and nut. Install the strut bar. Fasten the ball joint to the control arm. Install the front wheels and lower the vehicle.

6. Torque the mounting bolts to the following: inner mount bolt; 69–87 ft. lbs.; ball joint; 69–87 ft. lbs.; ball joint nut; 40–51 ft. lbs.

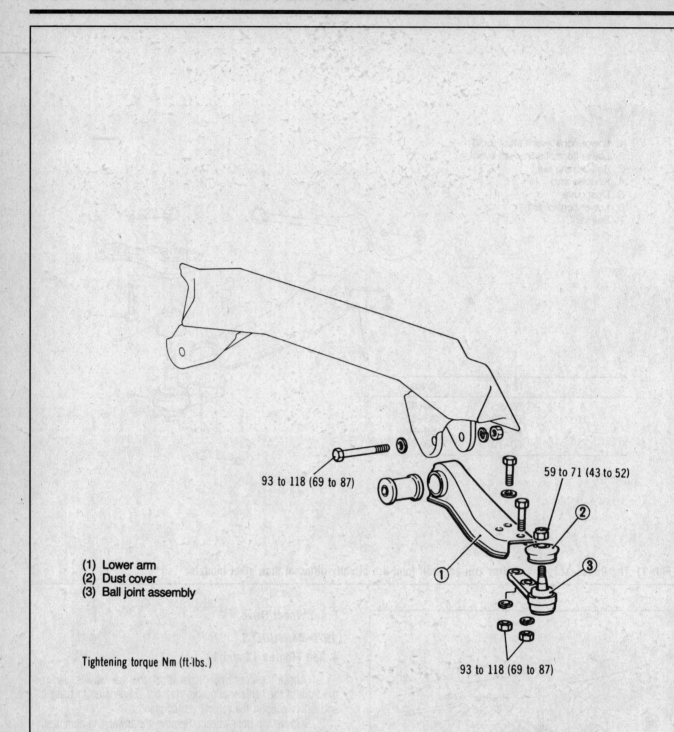

93 to 118 (69 to 87)

59 to 71 (43 to 52)

(1) Lower arm
(2) Dust cover
(3) Ball joint assembly

Tightening torque Nm (ft-lbs.)

93 to 118 (69 to 87)

Fig 13 Tightening specification on the 1979–84 front wheel drive Colt control arm and ball joint

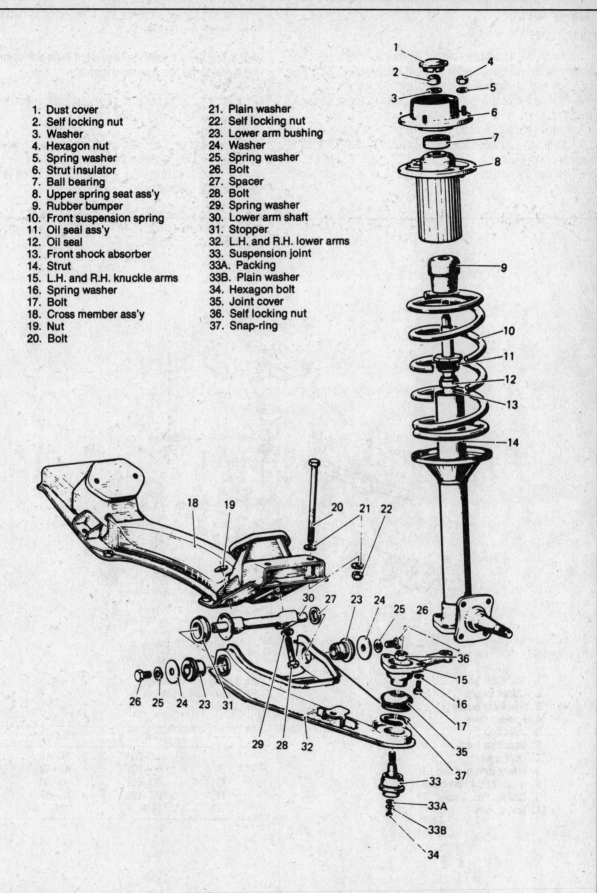

1. Dust cover
2. Self locking nut
3. Washer
4. Hexagon nut
5. Spring washer
6. Strut insulator
7. Ball bearing
8. Upper spring seat ass'y
9. Rubber bumper
10. Front suspension spring
11. Oil seal ass'y
12. Oil seal
13. Front shock absorber
14. Strut
15. L.H. and R.H. knuckle arms
16. Spring washer
17. Bolt
18. Cross member ass'y
19. Nut
20. Bolt

21. Plain washer
22. Self locking nut
23. Lower arm bushing
24. Washer
25. Spring washer
26. Bolt
27. Spacer
28. Bolt
29. Spring washer
30. Lower arm shaft
31. Stopper
32. L.H. and R.H. lower arms
33. Suspension joint
33A. Packing
33B. Plain washer
34. Hexagon bolt
35. Joint cover
36. Self locking nut
37. Snap-ring

Fig. 14 Exploded view of a common lower control arm and strut on a front wheel drive vehicle

1985–88 COLT

◗ **See Figure 15**

1. Loosen the front wheel lugs. Block the rear wheels. Jack up the front of the vehicle, allowing the front suspension to hang, and safely support the vehicle on jackstands.

2. Remove the front wheels. Remove the lower engine splash shield.

3. Remove the nut securing the ball joint to the control arm.

4. Use a ball joint separator and disconnect the ball joint from the steering knuckle.

5. Remove the retainers securing the stabilizer bar to the control arm.

6. Unbolt the lower control arm from the crossmember and remove it from the vehicle.

➡**The ball joint cannot be separated from the control arm, but must be replaced as an assembly.**

7. If the stabilizer bar is to be removed, disconnect the tie rod from the knuckle, unbolt it and remove.

To install:

8. Check all parts for wear and damage. Service as required.

9. Use an inch pound torque wrench and check the ball joint torque. Nominal starting effort should be 22–87 inch lbs. Replace the assembly if otherwise.

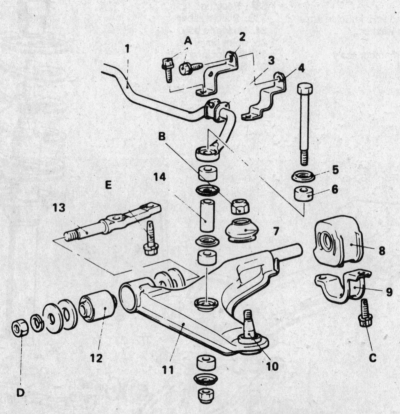

1. Stabilizer bar
2. Upper fixture
3. Stabilizer bushing
4. Lower fixture
5. Joint cup
6. Stabilizer rubber
7. Dust cover
8. Lower arm bushing (B)
9. Bushing support bracket
10. Ball joint assembly
11. Lower arm
12. Lower arm bushing
13. Lower arm shaft
14. Collar

	Nm	ft. lbs.
A	17–26	12–19
B	60–72	43–52
C	60–80	43–58
D	95–120	69–87
E	160–190	116–137

Fig. 15 The 1985 Colt lower control arm ball joint can not be separated from the arm

Loosen the mounting nut between the knuckle and the control arm

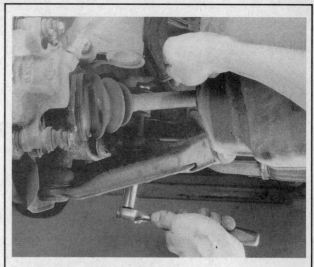

Separate the stabilizer-to-control arm mounting bushings

Using a separating tool and a hammer, carefully tap the two components apart

Inspect the bushings for wear, replace if necessary

Separate the ball joint from the steering knuckle

Loosen and remove the mounting nut and washer attached to the control arm shaft

Inspect the nut for any crossthreading

. . . then remove the U-bracket

Behind the nut and washer are two more washers, set them aside

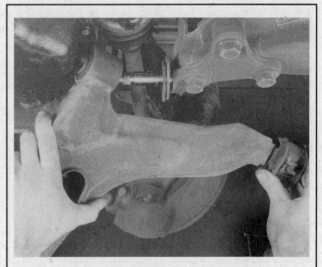

Slide the control arm out from under the vehicle

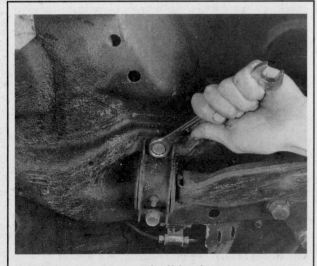

Unbolt the control arm at the U-bracket . . .

If necessary to remove the stabilizer bar, remove the cotter pin from the tie rod

. . . then remove the nut attaching the tie rod to the knuckle

Use a ball joint separator tool to detach the two components

10. Install the stabilizer, if removed. Connect the tie rod. Position and attach the lower control arm to the crossmember. Connect the ball joint. Install the splash shield and front wheels. Lower the vehicle.

11. Torque the mounting bolts as follows: knuckle–to–strut; 54–65 ft. lbs.; lower arm–to–body; 118–125 ft. lbs.; stabilizer bar–to–body; 12–20 ft. lbs.; ball joint–to–knuckle; 44–53 ft. lbs.; lower arm–to–shaft; 70–88 ft. lbs.

1985–88 VISTA

▶ See Figure 16

1. Raise and support the front end.
2. Remove the wheels.
3. Disconnect the stabilizer bar and strut bar from the lower arm.
4. Remove the nut and disconnect the ball joint from the knuckle with a separator.
5. Unbolt the lower arm from the crossmember.
6. Check all parts for wear or damage and replace any suspect part.

7. Using an inch lb. torque wrench, check the ball joint starting torque. Starting torque should be 20–86 inch lbs. If it is not within that range, replace the ball joint.

8. Install the lower arm to the crossmember. Install the strut bar and stabilizer. Attach the front wheels and lower the vehicle. Tighten all fasteners with the wheels hanging freely. Observe the following torques:
- Ball joint-to-knuckle: 44–53 ft. lbs.
- Arm-to-crossmember: 90–111 ft. lbs.
- 2-wd: 90–111 ft. lbs.
- 4-wd: 58–68 ft. lbs.
- Stabilizer bar hanger brackets: 7–9 ft. lbs.

➡ **When installing the stabilizer bar, the nut on the bar-to-crossmember bolts and the bar-to-lower arm bolts, are not torqued, but turned on until a certain length of thread is exposed above the nut: 2-wd stabilizer bar–to–crossmember: 8–10mm; stabilizer bar to lower control arm: 8–10mm; 4-wd stabilizer bar–to–crossmember: 8–10mm; stabilizer bar–to–lower arm: 13–15mm.**

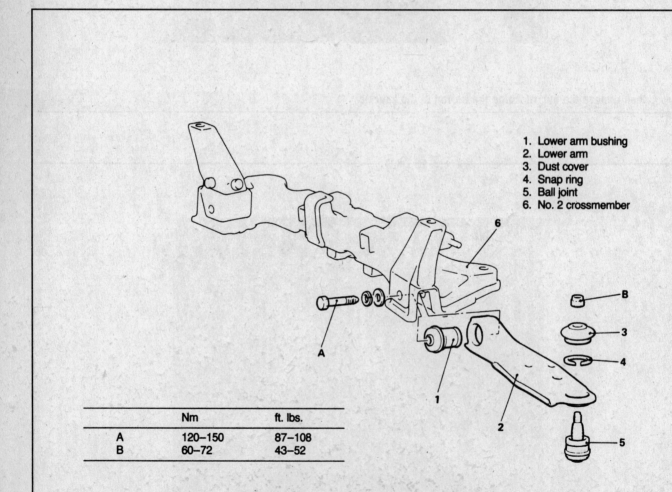

1. Lower arm bushing
2. Lower arm
3. Dust cover
4. Snap ring
5. Ball joint
6. No. 2 crossmember

	Nm	ft. lbs.
A	120–150	87–108
B	60–72	43–52

Fig. 16 The Vista ball joint is a replaceable component, tighten to specifications during replacement

Ball Joints

INSPECTION

1. Jack up the front and support the car on jackstands. There must be no weight on the front wheels.

2. Apply downward and upward pressure to the wheel avoiding any compression to the spring. If excessive play is encountered between the control arm and the steering knuckle, the ball joint probably needs replacing.

REMOVAL & INSTALLATION

1971–80 Rear Wheel Drive

Remove the lower control arm as previously outlined. Remove the snapring retaining the ball joint to the control arm. Press out the ball joint using a ball joint remover or have your local automotive machine shop do the job for you. Press a new ball joint into the control arm. Make sure the ball joint does not cock when installing in control arm seat. Installation is in reverse order. Refer to control arm section for torque specifications.

Rear Wheel Drive from 1981

1. Remove the tire and wheel assembly.
2. Remove the brake caliper and support from the mounting adapter.
3. Anchor assembly out of the way with wire to the strut spring.
4. Remove the tie rod end nut and separate the tie rod end from the steering knuckle using a removing tool. Remove the bolts securing the strut assembly to the steering knuckle. Tap the connection with a plastic hammer to separate.
5. Remove the ball joint to control arm mounting bolts and remove the ball joint with the knuckle arm attached. Remove the ball joint stud nut and separate the ball joint and knuckle arm.
6. Installation is the reverse of removal. Torque specifications are: ball joint stud nut 43–52 ft. lbs., strut–to–knuckle bolts 58–78 ft. lbs., ball joint–to–control arm bolts 43–51 ft. lbs.

➡When self-locking nuts are removed, always replace with new self-locking nuts.

1979–84 Front Wheel Drive

Unbolt the ball joint from the control arm. Use a ball joint removing tool and separate the ball joint from the steering knuckle after removing the stud retaining nut. Install in the reverse order. Torque specifications are: Ball joint to control arm 69–87 ft. lbs., ball joint stud nut 40–51 ft. lbs.

1985–89 Colt

The ball joint is not replaceable. The ball joint and lower control arm must be replaced as an assembly.

1985–89 Vista

➡This procedure requires a hydraulic press.

1. See the Lower Control Arm procedure and disconnect the lower arm.

2. Remove the ball joint dust cover.
3. Using snapring pliers, remove the snapring from the ball joint.
4. Using an adapter plate and driver, such as tool MB990800, press the ball joint from the arm.
5. Install the ball joint, inverting the tool in the press for installation. Coat the lip and interior of the dust cover with lithium based chassis lub.

Front Wheel Drive Hub, Knuckle and Wheel Bearings

REMOVAL & INSTALLATION

1979–83 and 1984 Non-Turbocharged

▶ See Figures 17 thru 23

➡A press and several special tools are needed for this procedure.

1. Remove the halfshaft.

➡Keep the bearing spacers separate for installation.

2. Remove the caliper, and suspend it out of the way, without disconnecting the brake line.
3. Disconnect the tie rod end from the knuckle.
4. Disconnect the strut from the knuckle and remove the hub and knuckle assembly.
5. Pry the hub and knuckle assembly apart. If separation is difficult, mount the knuckle in a vise and drive out the hub with a plastic mallet. Drive out the oil seals, bearings and races with a brass drift.
6. Inspect all parts for wear and damage; replace any suspect parts.

To install:
7. Install the outer races of the inner and outer bearings, using a brass drift or press. If a press is used, 4,400 lb. installation pressure is necessary.
8. Apply lithium based wheel bearing grease to the inside of

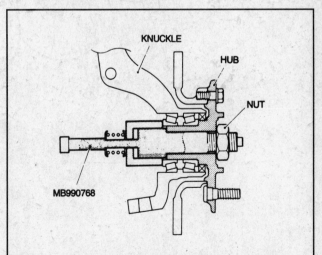

Fig 17 Install a spacer selection gauge on the hub and tighten the nut to specification

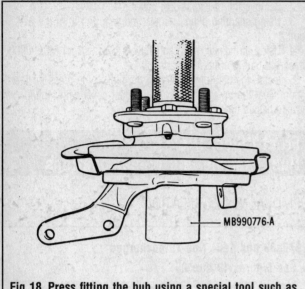

Fig 18 Press fitting the hub using a special tool such as MB990776-A

Averaged TIR (in.)	Spacer Part Number	Thickness (in.)	Identifying Color
.020–.023	MB109291	.223	Pink
.023–.025	MB109292	.226	Green
.025–.028	MB109293	.228	Red
.028–.030	MB109294	.230	White
.030–.032	MB109295	.233	None
.032–.035	MB109296	.235	Yellow
.035–.037	MB109297	.237	Blue
.037–.039	MB109298	.240	Orange
.039–.042	MB109299	.242	Light Green
.042–.044	MB109300	.244	Brown
.044–.046	MB109301	.247	Grey
.046–.049	MB109302	.249	Navy Blue
.049–.051	MB109303	.252	Vermilion
.051–.054	MB109304	.254	Purple
.137–.141	MB109126	.139	Red
.141–.146	MB109127	.144	White
.146–.151	MB109128	.149	Black
.151–.156	MB109129	.154	Yellow
.156–.160	MB109165	.159	Blue

Fig 19 Spacer chart

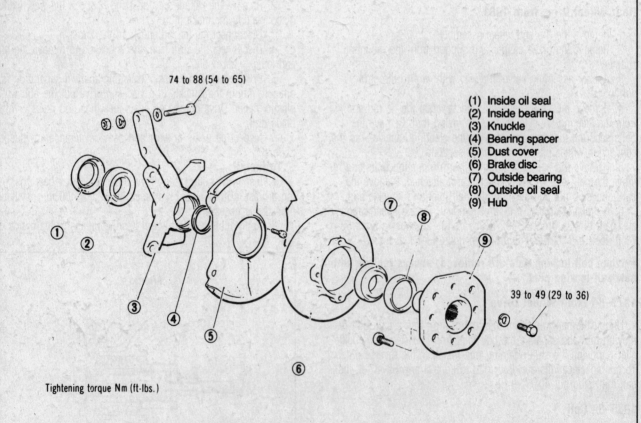

74 to 88 (54 to 65)

(1) Inside oil seal
(2) Inside bearing
(3) Knuckle
(4) Bearing spacer
(5) Dust cover
(6) Brake disc
(7) Outside bearing
(8) Outside oil seal
(9) Hub

39 to 49 (29 to 36)

Tightening torque Nm (ft-lbs.)

Fig 20 Exploded view of the front hub and knuckle assembly on the 1979–83 and non-Turbo 1984 front wheel drive vehicles

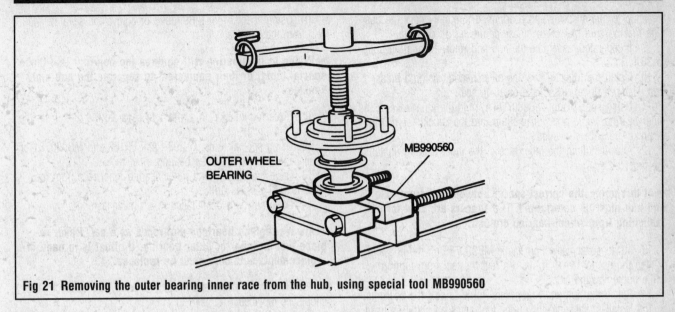

Fig 21 Removing the outer bearing inner race from the hub, using special tool MB990560

OUTER WHEEL BEARING

MB990560

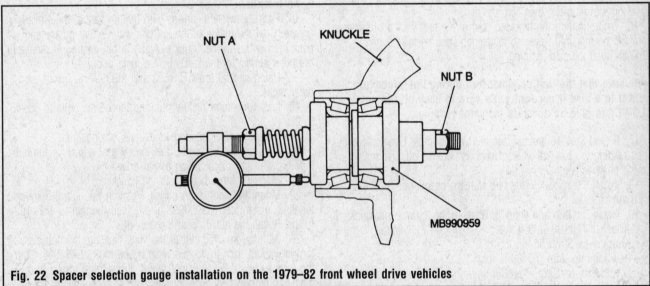

NUT A

KNUCKLE

NUT B

MB990959

Fig. 22 Spacer selection gauge installation on the 1979–82 front wheel drive vehicles

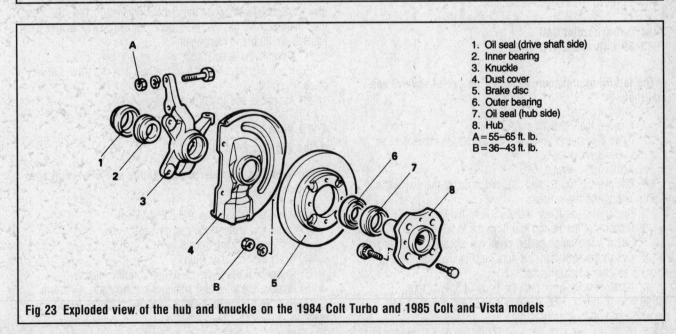

1. Oil seal (drive shaft side)
2. Inner bearing
3. Knuckle
4. Dust cover
5. Brake disc
6. Outer bearing
7. Oil seal (hub side)
8. Hub
A = 55–65 ft. lb.
B = 36–43 ft. lb.

Fig 23 Exploded view of the hub and knuckle on the 1984 Colt Turbo and 1985 Colt and Vista models

the knuckle, the oil seals and bearings. Thoroughly pack the bearings making sure that clean grease permeates all cavities.

9. If separated, assemble the hub and rotor. Torque the bolts to 36 ft. lbs.

10. Install the inner race of the outer bearing using a brass drift. Using a driver, install the outer oil seal.

11. Using special tool MB990776-A, hold the inner race of the outer bearing, while pressing the hub into the knuckle. 1,100 lb. of press pressure is needed.

12. After installing the inner race of the inner bearing, install the inner oil seal.

➡**At this point, the correct spacer between the front axle and hub must be determined. The spacers are vital for establishing front wheel bearing preload.**

13. Install spacer selection gauge MB990768 on the hub and tighten the nut to 14–15 ft. lbs. Prevent the tool from turning while tightening the nut.

14. Rotate the hub and tool several turns to seat the bearings.

15. Install a dial indicator on the tool and load about 5mm of travel on the indicator, then zero the dial.

16. While holding the threaded stud of the tool with a wrench, back off the nut until travel no longer registers on the gauge. Note the total indicator reading.

➡**Be sure that the tool does not turn during this procedure. Hold it in a vise if necessary. Be sure to back off the nut SLOWLY to give an accurate indicator reading.**

17. Repeat Step 16 and average the two readings. Use the averaged reading to calculate what spacers will be needed. Use the following chart as a guide:

18. Install the spacer in the hub with the chamferred side toward the knuckle.

19. Install the hub and knuckle. Observe the following torques:
- Axleshaft Nut: 88–130 ft. lbs.
- Knuckle–to–Strut: 55–65 ft. lbs.
- Ball Joint–to–Arm: 70–88 ft. lbs.
- Lower Arm–to–Strut: 70–88 ft. lbs.
- Knuckle–to–Tie Rod: 11–25 ft. lbs.

1984 Turbocharged Colt
1985–89 Colt and 2-WD Vista

➡**The following procedure requires the use of several special tools**

1. Remove the axleshaft nut.

2. Raise and support the car with jackstands positioned so that the wheels hang freely.

3. Remove the wheels.

4. Remove the caliper and suspend it out of the way without disconnecting the brake hose.

5. Disconnect the lower ball joint from the knuckle.

6. Disconnect the tie rod end from the knuckle.

7. Using a two-jawed puller, press the axleshaft from the hub.

8. Unbolt the strut from the knuckle. Remove the hub and knuckle assembly from the car.

9. Install first the arm, then the body of special tool MB991056 (Colt), or MB991001 (Vista) or equivalent on the knuckle and tighten the nut.

10. Using special tool MB990998 or equivalent, separate the hub from the knuckle.

➡**Prying or hammering will damage the bearing. Use these special tools, or their equivalent to separate the hub and knuckle.**

11. Place the knuckle in a vise and separate the rotor from the hub.

12. Using special tools, C-293-PA, SP3183 and MB990781 or equivalent, remove the outer bearing inner race.

13. Drive the oil seal and inner bearing inner race from the knuckle with a brass drift.

14. Drive out both outer races in a similar fashion.

➡**Always replace bearings and races as a set. Never replace just an inner or outer bearing. If either is in need of replacement, both sets must be replaced.**

15. Thoroughly clean and inspect all parts. Any suspect part should be replaced.

To install:

16. Pack the wheel bearings with lithium based wheel bearing grease. Coat the inside of the knuckle with similar grease and pack the cavities in the knuckle. Apply a thin coating of grease to the outer surface of the races before installation.

17. Using special tools C-3893 and MB990776, install the outer races.

18. Install the rotor on the hub and torque the bolts to 36–43 ft. lbs.

19. Drive the outer bearing inner race into position.

20. Coat the out rim and lip of the oil seal and drive the hub side oil seal into place, using a seal driver.

21. Place the inner bearing in the knuckle.

22. Mount the knuckle in a vise. Position the hub and knuckle together. Install tool MB990998 and tighten the tool to 147–192 ft. lbs. Rotate the hub to seat the bearing.

23. With the knuckle still in the vise, measure the hub starting torque with an inch lb. torque wrench and tool MB990998. Starting torque should be 11.5 inch lbs. If the starting torque is 0, measure the hub bearing axial play with a dial indicator. If axial play exceeds 0.2mm, while the nut is tightened to 145–192 ft. lbs., the assembly has not been done correctly. Disassemble the knuckle and hub and start again.

24. Remove the special tool.

25. Place the outer bearing in the hub and drive the seal into place.

26. Assemble and install the knuckle.

4-WD Vista
◆ **See Figures 24 and 25**

➡**The following procedure requires the use of several special tools.**

1. Remove the hub cap and halfshaft nut.

2. Raise and support the car on jackstands.

3. Remove the front wheels.

4. Drain the transaxle fluid.

5. Disconnect the lower ball joint from the knuckle.

6. Remove the strut and stabilizer bar from the lower arm.

7. Remove the center bearing snapring from the bearing bracket.

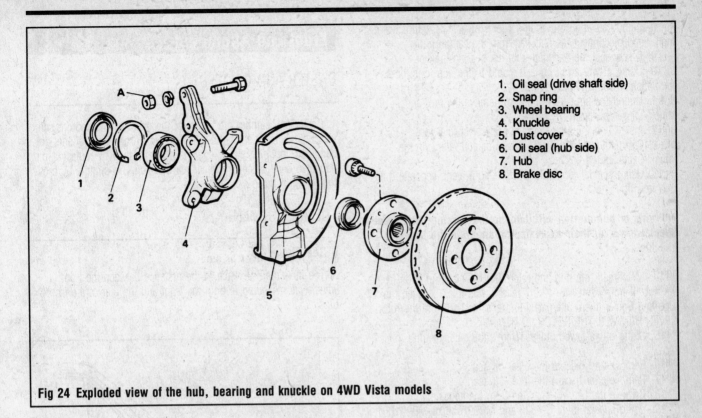

1. Oil seal (drive shaft side)
2. Snap ring
3. Wheel bearing
4. Knuckle
5. Dust cover
6. Oil seal (hub side)
7. Hub
8. Brake disc

Fig 24 Exploded view of the hub, bearing and knuckle on 4WD Vista models

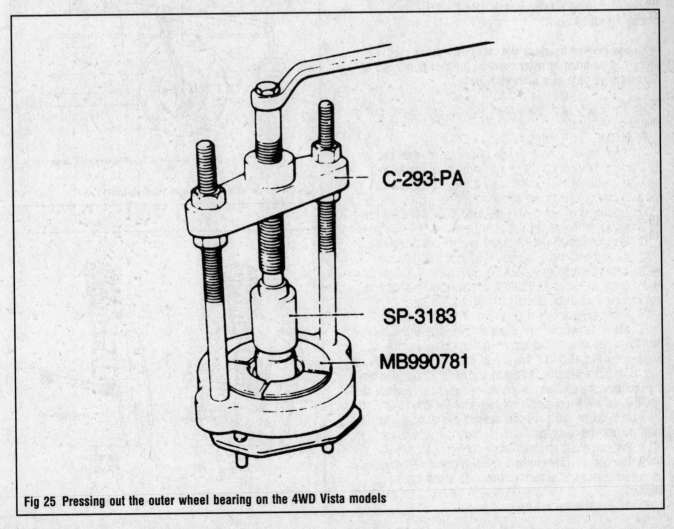

C-293-PA

SP-3183

MB990781

Fig 25 Pressing out the outer wheel bearing on the 4WD Vista models

8. Lightly tap the double off-set joint outer race with a wood mallet and disconnect the halfshaft from the cardan joint.

9. Disconnect the halfshaft from the bearing bracket.

10. Using a two-jawed puller secured to the hub lugs, press the halfshaft from the hub.

11. Unbolt the strut from the hub. Remove the hub and knuckle assembly from the car.

12. Install first the arm, then the body of special tool MB991056 (Colt) or MB991001 (Vista) or equivalent on the knuckle and tighten the nut.

13. Using special tool MB990998 or equivalent, separate the hub from the knuckle.

➡**Prying or hammering will damage the bearing. Use these special tools, or their equivalent to separate the hub and knuckle.**

14. Matchmark the hub and rotor. The rotor should slide from the hub. If not, insert M8 × 1.25 bolts in the holes between the lugs and tighten them alternately to press the hub from the rotor. NEVER HAMMER THE ROTOR TO REMOVE IT!

15. Using a two-jawed puller, remove the outer bearing inner race.

16. Remove and discard the outer oil seal.

17. Remove and discard the inner oil seal.

18. Remove the bearing snapring from the knuckle.

19. Using special tools C-4628 and MB991056 or MB991001, remove the bearing from the knuckle. Using a driver, drive the bearing from the knuckle.

➡**Always replace bearings and races as a set. Never replace just an inner or outer bearing. If either is in need of replacement, both sets must be replaced.**

20. Thoroughly clean and inspect all parts. Any suspect part should be replaced.

To install:

21. Pack the wheel bearings with lithium based wheel bearing grease. Coat the inside of the knuckle with similar grease and pack the cavities in the knuckle. Apply a thin coating of grease to the outer surface of the races before installation.

22. Using special tool C-4171 and MB990985, press the bearing into place in the knuckle. Install the snapring.

23. Coat the lips of a new hub-side seal with lithium grease. Using a seal driver, install the seal. Make sure it is flush.

24. Install the rotor on the hub.

25. Using special tool MB990998 or equivalent, join the hub and knuckle. Torque the special tool nut to 188 ft. lbs.

26. Rotate the hub several times to seat the bearing.

27. Mount the knuckle in a vise. Using MB990998 and an inch lb. torque wrench, measure the turning torque. Turning torque should be 15.6 inch lbs. or less. Next, measure the axial play using a dial indicator. Axial play should be 0.2mm. If either the axial play or the turning torque are not within the specified values, the hub and knuckle have not been properly assembled. You will have to do the procedure over again. If everything checks out okay, go onto the next step.

28. Remove all the special tools.

29. Using a seal driver, drive a new seal coated with lithium grease, into place on the halfshaft side, until it contacts the snapring.

30. Assemble and install the knuckle.

Front End Alignment

CASTER AND CAMBER

Caster and camber are preset at the factory. They require service only if the suspension and steering linkage components are damaged, in which case, repair is accomplished by replacing the damaged part. Caster, however, can be adjusted slightly by moving the strut bar nut.

TOE ADJUSTMENT

◆ **See Figure 26**

Toe-in is the difference in the distance between the front wheels, as measured at both the front and the rear of the front tires.

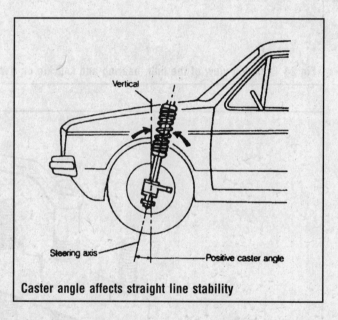

Caster angle affects straight line stability

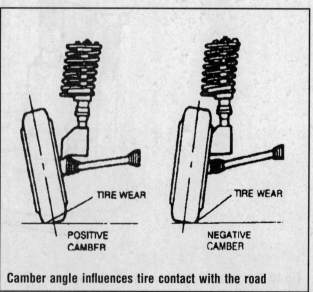

Camber angle influences tire contact with the road

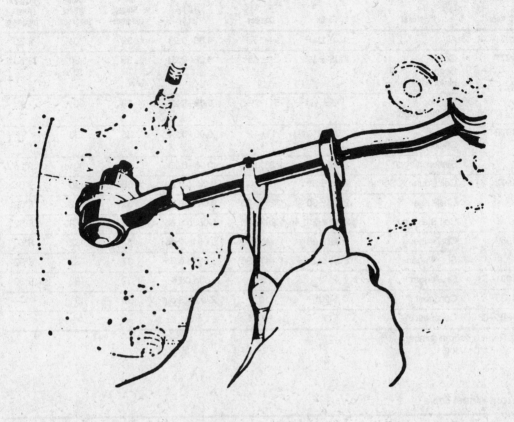

Fig 26 Adjust the toe through the tie rod ends

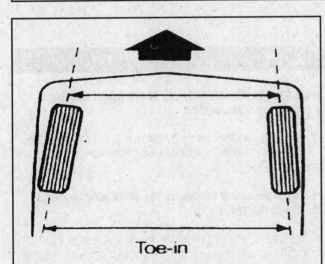

Toe-in

Toe-in means the distance between the wheels is closer at the front than at the rear of the wheels

1. Raise the front of the car so that its front wheels are just clear of the ground.

2. Use a scribing block to hold a piece of chalk at the center of each tire tread while rotating the wheels by hand.

3. Measure the distance between the marked lines at both the front and rear.

➡**Take both measurements at equal distances from the ground.**

4. Toe-in is equal to the difference between the front and rear measurements. This difference should be 2–6mm.

5. Toe-in is adjusted by screwing the tie rod turnbuckle in or out as necessary. Left side toe-in may be reduced by turning the tie rod turn-buckle toward the rear of the car. The turn-buckles should always be tightened or loosened the same amount for both tie rods; the difference in length between the two tie rods should not exceed 5mm. Tighten the locknuts to 36–40 ft. lbs.

Wheel Alignment Specifications

Rear Wheel Drive

| Year | Model | Caster | Camber | Toe-in (in.) | Steering Angle | | King Pin Angle (degrees) |
					Inner Wheel (degrees)	Outer Wheel (degrees)	
1971–76	All	1¼–1½P	½–1½P	0.08–0.23	39	30½	8°50′
1977	Coupe Sedan Hatchback	2°05′±½°	1°±45′	0.08–0.23	35	30	8°53′
	Hardtop Station Wagon	1°9′±½°	51′±½°	0.08–0.23	39	30½	9°
1978	All exc. Station Wagon	2°05′±½°	1°±½′	0.08–0.24	35	36	9°
	Station Wagon	2°38′±½°	1°28′±½°	0.08–0.35	39	30½	8°25′
1979	Colt Coupe & Sedan	2°05′±30′	1°±30′	0.08 to 0.24	35	30	9°01′
	Challenger	2°38′±30′	1°28′±30′	0.08 to 0.35	37	32	8°52′
	Colt Sta. Wagon	2°38′±30′	1°28′±30′	0.08 to 0.35	39	30°30′	8°52′
1980	Challenger	2°38′±30′	1°14′±30′	0.08 to 0.35	37	32	8°52′
	Sta. Wagon	2°38′±30′	1°14′±30′	0.08 to 0.35	37	32	8°52′
1981–83	Challenger	2°40′	1°10′	0 to 0.28	37	32	9°30′
1985	Conquest	5°20′	0	.2 in to .2 out	39	31	—
1986–88	Conquest ①	5¹³⁄₁₆	–½N	0	—	—	—

① Rear: 0 degree camber
　　0 in. toe

Front Wheel Drive

| Year | Model | Caster | Camber | Toe-in (in.) | Steering Angle | |
					Inner	Outer
1979–84	All	50′ P20′	30′P 30′	.16 in–.08 out	35.68	29.31
1985–88	Colt	³⁄₁₆–1³⁄₁₆	½N–½P	0	35.68	29.31
	Vista	⁵⁄₁₆–1⁵⁄₁₆	¹⁄₁₆N–¹⁵⁄₁₆P	⅛	37.45	30.40
	4-wd Vista	48′P 30′	50′P 30′	0	37.45	30.40

REAR SUSPENSION

Leaf Springs

REMOVAL & INSTALLATION

Rear Wheel Drive
Except Station Wagon and Conquest

◆ **See Figures 27, 28 and 29**

1. Remove the hub cap or wheel cover. Loosen the lug nuts.
2. Block the front wheels. Raise the rear of the car and support it on jackstands. The dimples on the sill flange locate the support point to place the jackstands.

➡**Damage to the unit body can result from installing a stand at any other location.**

3. Disconnect the lower mounting nut of the shock absorber.
4. Remove the four U-bolt fastening nuts from the spring seat.

➡**It's not necessary to remove the shock absorber; leave the top connected.**

5. Place a floor jack under the rear axle and raise it just enough to remove the load from the springs. Remove the spring pad and seat.
6. Remove the two rear shackle attaching nuts and the rear shackle.

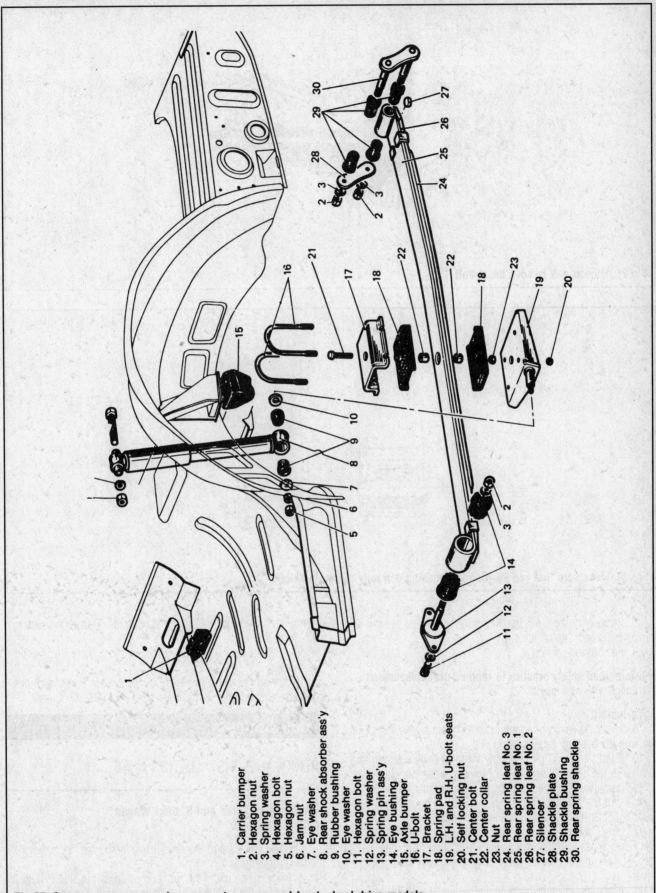

1. Carrier bumper
2. Hexagon nut
3. Spring washer
4. Hexagon bolt
5. Hexagon nut
6. Jam nut
7. Eye washer
8. Rear shock absorber ass'y
9. Rubber bushing
10. Eye washer
11. Hexagon bolt
12. Spring washer
13. Spring pin ass'y
14. Eye bushing
15. Axle bumper
16. U-bolt
17. Bracket
18. Spring pad
19. L.H. and R.H. U-bolt seats
20. Self locking nut
21. Center bolt
22. Center collar
23. Nut
24. Rear spring leaf No. 3
25. Rear spring leaf No. 1
26. Rear spring leaf No. 2
27. Silencer
28. Shackle plate
29. Shackle bushing
30. Rear spring shackle

Fig 27 Common rear suspension—except wagons and front wheel drive models

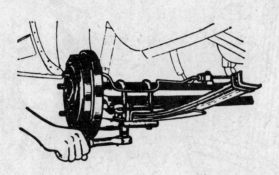

Fig 28 Loosen and remove the U-bolt

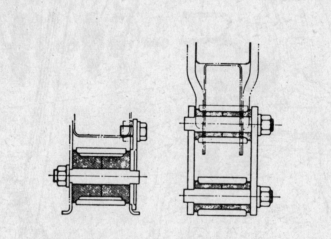

Fig 29 Make sure that you position the bushing correctly during installation

7. Remove the front pin retaining nut. Remove the two pin retaining bolts and take off the pin.

8. Remove the spring.

➡**It is a good safety practice to replace used suspension fasteners with new parts.**

To install:

9. Install the front spring eye bushings from both sides of the eye with the bushing flanges facing out.

10. Insert the spring pin assembly from the body side and fasten it with the bolts. Temporarily tighten the spring pin nut.

11. Install the rear eye bushings in the same manner as the front, insert the shackle pins from the outside of the car, and temporarily tighten the nut after installing the shackle plate.

12. Install the pads on both sides of the spring, aligning the pad center holes with the spring center bolt collar, and then install the spring seat with its center hole through the spring center collar.

13. Attach the assembled spring and spring seat to the axle housing with the axle housing spring center hole meeting the spring center bolt and install the U-bolt nuts. Tighten the nuts to 33–36 ft. lbs.

14. Tighten the lower shock absorber nut to 12–15 ft. lbs. on all models.

15. Lower the car to the floor, jounce it a few times, and then tighten the spring pin and shackle pin nuts to 36–43 ft. lbs.

Coil Springs

REMOVAL & INSTALLATION

Front Wheel Drive and Station Wagon
◆ **See Figure 30**

1. Raise and support the car safely allowing the rear axle to hang unsupported.

2. Place a jack under the rear axle or under the side trailing arm. Remove the bottom bolts or nuts mounting the shock absorbers.

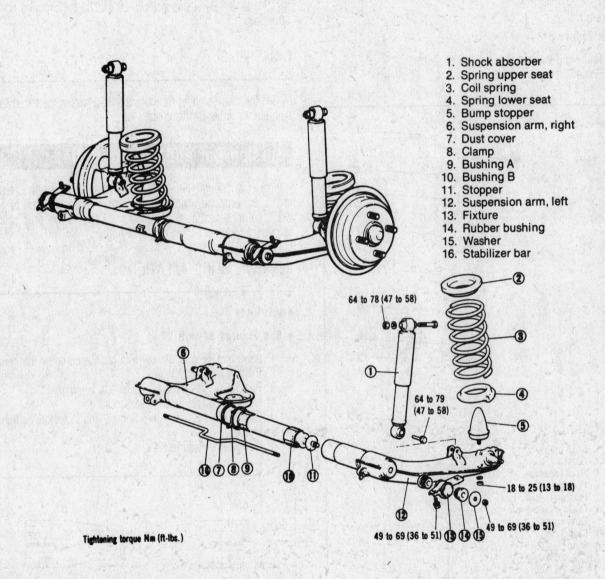

1. Shock absorber
2. Spring upper seat
3. Coil spring
4. Spring lower seat
5. Bump stopper
6. Suspension arm, right
7. Dust cover
8. Clamp
9. Bushing A
10. Bushing B
11. Stopper
12. Suspension arm, left
13. Fixture
14. Rubber bushing
15. Washer
16. Stabilizer bar

64 to 78 (47 to 58)

64 to 79
(47 to 58)

18 to 25 (13 to 18)

49 to 69 (36 to 51)

49 to 69 (36 to 51)

Tightening torque Nm (ft-lbs.)

Fig. 30 Exploded view of the rear suspension on front wheel drive models

3. Lower the rear axle or trailing arm and remove the coil spring.

4. To install, position the spring and raise the axle or trailing arm. Connect the shock absorber. Lower the vehicle.

Struts

REMOVAL & INSTALLATION

Conquest

◆ **See Figure 31**

1. Raise and support the rear end on jackstands.
2. Remove the rear wheels.

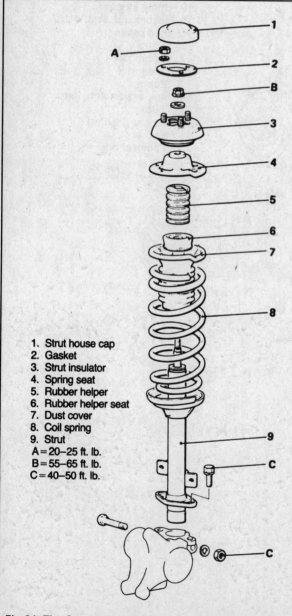

1. Strut house cap
2. Gasket
3. Strut insulator
4. Spring seat
5. Rubber helper
6. Rubber helper seat
7. Dust cover
8. Coil spring
9. Strut
A = 20–25 ft. lb.
B = 55–65 ft. lb.
C = 40–50 ft. lb.

Fig 31 The Conquest models are equipped with rear struts

3. Unclip the brake hose at the strut.
4. Unbolt the intermediate shaft from the companion flange.
5. Unbolt the strut assembly from the axleshaft housing. Remove the housing coupling bolt. Separate the strut from the housing by pushing the housing downward while prying open the coupling on the housing.
6. Remove the strut upper end attaching nuts, found under the side trim in the cargo area.
7. Lift out the strut.
8. Install the strut. Torque the upper end nuts to 20–25 ft. lbs.; the strut–to–housing bolts to 50 ft. lbs.; the coupling bolt to 50 ft. lbs.

DISASSEMBLY

See the disassembly procedure for MacPherson front suspension struts, earlier in this chapter.

Torsion Bar and Control Arms

Instead of springs, the 4-wd Vista uses transversely mounted torsion bars housed inside the rear crossmember, attached to which are inner and outer control arms. Conventional style shock absorbers are mounted on the inner arms.

REMOVAL & INSTALLATION

4-WD Vista

◆ **See Figures 32 thru 37**

1. Raise and support the car with jackstands under the frame.
2. Remove the differential.
3. Remove the intermediate shafts and axleshafts.
4. Remove the rear brake assemblies.
5. Disconnect the brake lines and parking brake cables from the inner arms.
6. Remove the main muffler.

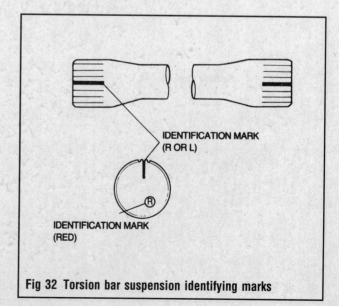

IDENTIFICATION MARK
(R OR L)

IDENTIFICATION MARK
(RED)

Fig 32 Torsion bar suspension identifying marks

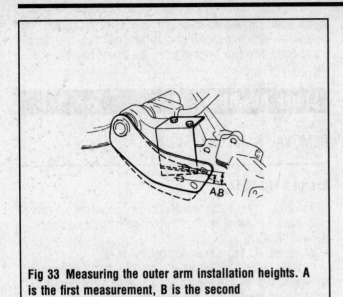

Fig 33 Measuring the outer arm installation heights. A is the first measurement, B is the second

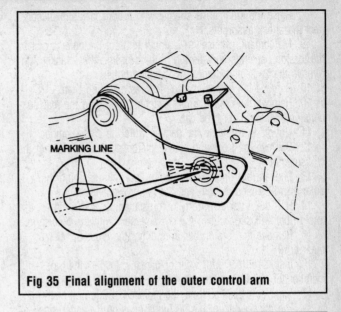

MARKING LINE

Fig 35 Final alignment of the outer control arm

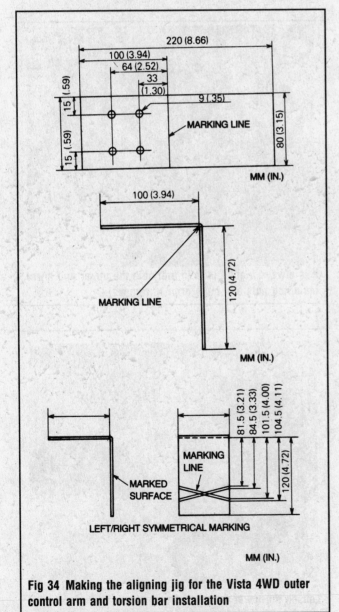

220 (8.66)

100 (3.94)

64 (2.52)

33 (1.30)

9 (.35)

(.59)

15

(.59)

15

MARKING LINE

80 (3.15)

MM (IN.)

100 (3.94)

MARKING LINE

120 (4.72)

MM (IN.)

81.5 (3.21)
84.5 (3.33)
101.5 (4.00)
104.5 (4.11)

MARKING LINE

120 (4.72)

MARKED SURFACE

LEFT/RIGHT SYMMETRICAL MARKING

MM (IN.)

Fig 34 Making the aligning jig for the Vista 4WD outer control arm and torsion bar installation

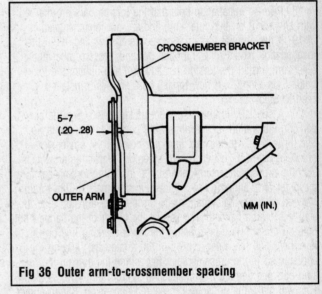

CROSSMEMBER BRACKET

5–7 (.20–.28)

OUTER ARM

MM (IN.)

Fig 36 Outer arm-to-crossmember spacing

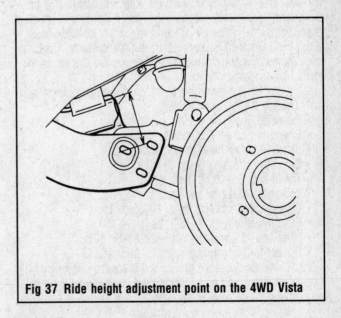

Fig 37 Ride height adjustment point on the 4WD Vista

7. Raise the inner arms slightly with a floor jack and disconnect the shock absorbers.

8. Matchmark, precisely, the upper ends of the outer arms, the torsion bar ends and the top of the crossmember bracket and remove the inner and outer arm attaching bolts.

9. Remove the extension rods fixtures attaching bolts.

10. Remove the crossmember attaching bolts and the rear suspension assembly from the car.

11. Unbolt and remove the damper from the crossmember.

12. Remove the front and rear insulators from both ends of the crossmember.

13. Loosen, but do not remove, the lockbolts securing the outer arm bushings at both ends of the crossmember.

14. Pull the outer arm from the crossmember. Many times, the torsion bar will slide out of the crossmember with the outer arm.

15. Remove the torsion bar from either the crossmember or outer arm.

16. Inspect all parts for wear or damage. Inspect the crossmember for bending or deformation.

17. Inner arm bushings may be replaced at this time using a press. The thicker end of the bushings goes on the inner side.

18. Prior to installation note that the torsion bars are marked with an L or R on the outer end, and are not interchangeable.

19. If the original torsion bars are being installed, align the identification marks on the torsion bar end, crossmember and outer arm, install the torsion bar and arm and tighten the lockbolts. Skip Step 20. If new torsion bars are being installed, proceed to Step 20.

20. A special alignment jig must be fabricated. See the accompanying illustration for the dimension needed to make this jig. The jig is bolted to the rear insulator hole on the crossmember bracket as shown. Install the crossmember bracket as shown. Install the crossmember and inner arms. Insert the torsion bar into the outer arm, aligning the red identification mark on the torsion bar end with the matchmark made on the outer arm top side. Install the torsion bar and arm so that the center of the flanged bolt hole on the arm is 32mm below the lower marking line on the jig. Then, pull the outer arm off of the torsion bar, leaving the bar undisturbed in the crossmember. Reposition the arm on the torsion bar, one serration counterclockwise from its former position. This will make the previously measured dimension, 33mm above the lower line. In any event, when the outer arm and torsion bar are properly positioned, the marking lines on the jig will run diagonally across the center of the toe-in adjustment hole as shown. When the adjustment is complete, tighten the lockbolts. The clearance between the outer arm and the crossmember bracket, at the torsion bar, should be 5mm.

21. Complete the remainder of the component parts installation. Observe the following torques:
- Extension Rod Fixture bolts: 45–50 ft. lbs.
- Extension Rod-to-Fixture nut: 95–100 ft. lbs.
- Shock Absorber lower bolt: 75–80 ft. lbs.
- Outer Arm attaching bolts: 65–70 ft. lbs.
- Toe-In bolt: 95–100 ft. lbs.
- Lockbolts: 20–22 ft. lbs.
- Crossmember attaching bolts: 80–85 ft. lbs.
- Front Insulator nuts: 7–10 ft. lbs.
- Inner Arm-to-Crossmember bolts: 60–65 ft. lbs.
- Damper-to-Crossmember nuts: 15–20 ft. lbs.

22. Lower the car to the ground and check the ride height. The ride height is checked on both sides and is determined by measuring the distance between the center line of the toe-in bolt hole on the outer arm, and the lower edge of the rebound bumper. The distance on each side should be 102–104mm. If not, or if there is a significant difference between sides, the torsion bar(s) positioning is wrong.

Shock Absorbers

REMOVAL & INSTALLATION

Except 4-WD Vista

1. Remove the hub cap or wheel cover. Loosen the lug nuts.

2. Raise the rear of the car. Support the car with jackstands. Remove the wheel.

3. Remove the upper mounting bolt/nut or nut.

4. While holding the bottom stud mount nut with one wrench, remove the locknut with another wrench, or on some models remove the nut and bolt from the mounting bracket.

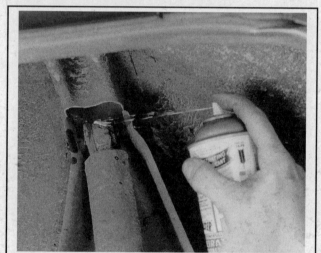

It is always a good idea to lubricate the upper and lower mounting nuts and bolts prior to removal

Loosen the lower nut . . . .

. . . and separate the assembly from the frame

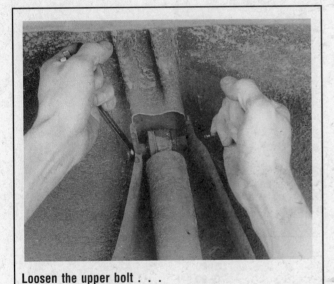

Loosen the upper bolt . . .

. . . then remove the mounting bolt and nut

5. Remove the shock absorber.
6. Check the shock for:
   a. Excessive oil leakage, some minor weeping is permissible.
   b. Bent center rod, damaged outer case, or other defects.
   c. Pump the shock absorber several times, if it offers even resistance on full strokes it may be considered serviceable.
7. Install the upper shock mounting nut and bolt. Hand-tighten the nut.
8. Install the bottom eye of the shock over the spring stud or into the mounting bracket and insert the bolt and nut. Tighten the nut to 12–15 ft. lbs. on rear wheel drive car; 47–58 ft. lbs. on front wheel drive cars.
9. Finally, tighten the upper nut to 47–58 ft. lbs. on all models except station wagons, which are tightened to 12–15 ft. lbs.

4-WD Vista

1. Raise and support the rear end on jackstands under the frame.
2. Remove the rear wheels.
3. Using a floor jack, raise the inner control arm slightly.
4. Unbolt the top, then the bottom of the shock absorber. Remove it from the car.
5. Install and attach the shock absorber. Torque the top nut to 55–58 ft. lbs.; the bottom bolt to 75–80 ft. lbs.

Lower Control Arm

REMOVAL & INSTALLATION

Rear Wheel Drive, Except Conquest
▶ **See Figure 38**

1. Support the vehicle body on safety stands. Use a jack under the rear axle to raise the rear axle assembly slightly.
2. Remove the wheel and the upper control arm rod.
3. Detach the parking brake rear cable from the lower arm.
4. Remove the lower arm from the rear axle housing and from the bracket attached to the body.
5. Temporarily install the lower arm (check for marking on left side arm) and torque the bolts to 94–108 ft. lbs. Torque the assist link bushing bolt to 47–58 ft. lbs.
6. With the special nut assembly placed securely against the rear axle housing bracket, install the upper control arm rod to the bracket. Torque the bolt to 94 ft. lbs.

➡ **Always use new bolts.**

Conquest
▶ **See Figure 39**

1. Raise and support the rear end on jackstands. Allow the wheels to hang freely.
2. Remove the rear wheels.
3. Disconnect the parking brake cable from the lower arm.
4. Disconnect the stabilizer bar.
5. Unbolt the lower control arm from the axleshaft housing.
6. Unbolt the lower control arm from the front support.
7. Unbolt the lower control arm from the crossmember and remove it.

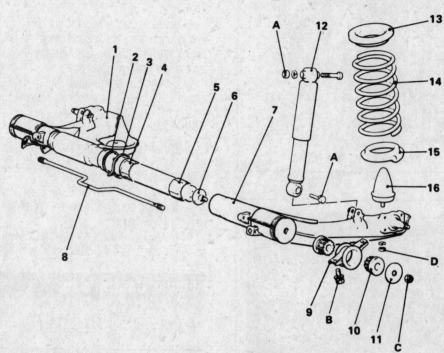

1. Suspension arm (R.H.)
2. Dust cover
3. Clamp
4. Bushing A
5. Bushing B
6. Rubber stopper
7. Suspension arm (L.H.)
8. Stabilizer bar
9. Fixture
10. Rubber bushing
11. Washer
12. Shock absorber

13. Spring upper seat
14. Coil spring
15. Spring lower seat
16. Bump stopper

	Nm	ft. lbs.
A	65–80	47–58
B	70–90	51–65
C	130–150	94–108
D	18–25	13–18

Fig 38 Rear suspension on the 1979–84 Colt and 1985 Vista

8. Install the control arm to the crossmember, front support and housing.

9. Connect the stabilizer bar. Insert the brake cable into the retaining clip.

10. Attach the wheels and lower the vehicle.

11. Apply a thin coating of chassis lube to the cutout portion of the lower control arm-to-axleshaft housing shaft. Do not allow the grease to touch the bushings.

12. Insert the shaft with the mark on its head facing downward. When positioning the lower control arm on the crossmember, align the mark on the crossmember with the line on the plate. Torque the lower control arm-to-front support bolts to 108 ft. lbs.; the arm-to-crossmember bolts to 108 ft. lbs.; the arm-to-axleshaft housing bolts to 60 ft. lbs.; the arm locking pin to 15 ft. lbs.

13. Have the rear wheel alignment checked.

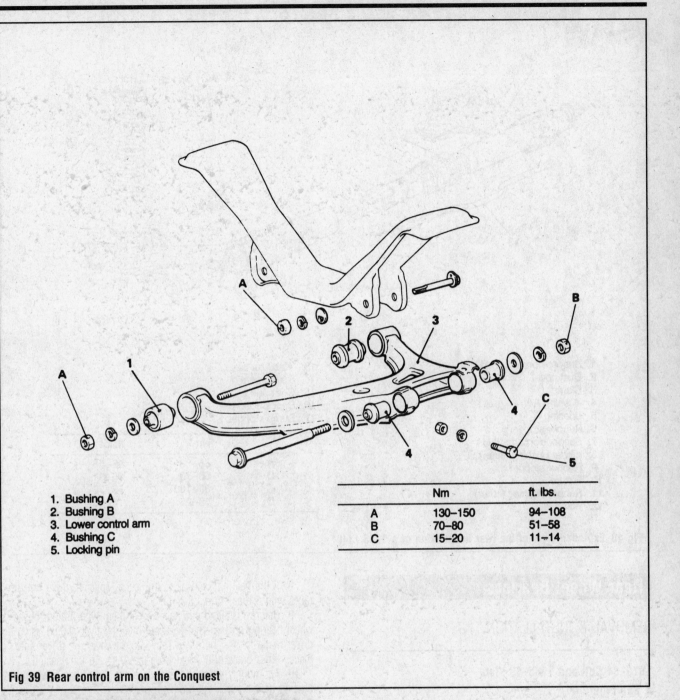

1. Bushing A
2. Bushing B
3. Lower control arm
4. Bushing C
5. Locking pin

	Nm	ft. lbs.
A	130–150	94–108
B	70–80	51–58
C	15–20	11–14

Fig 39 Rear control arm on the Conquest

Trailing Arm
Front Wheel Drive

REMOVAL & INSTALLATION

◗ **See Figure 40**

1. Support the side frame on jack stands and remove the rear wheels. Remove the rear brake assembly.

2. Remove the muffler and jack the control arm just enough to raise it slightly. Disconnect the parking brake cable from the arm.

3. Remove the shock absorber and lower the jack. Remove the coil spring.

4. Disconnect the brake hoses at the rear suspension arms, and remove the rear suspension from the body as an assembly.

To install:

5. Install the fixture–to–body bolts and tighten to 36–51 ft. lbs. on Colt models; 51–65 ft. lbs. on Vista models.

6. Install the coil springs and loosely install the shock absorbers. Tighten the shock absorber bolts to specification after the vehicle is lowered to the floor.

7. Install the rear brake assembly.

8. Lower the vehicle and tighten the suspension arm end nuts to 36–51 ft. lbs. on 1979–84 models; 56–70 ft. lbs. on 1985 Colt; 94–108 ft. lbs. on Vista; the shock bolts to 47–58 ft. lbs.

9. Install the brake drums and wheels.

10. Bleed the brake system and adjust the rear brake shoe clearance.

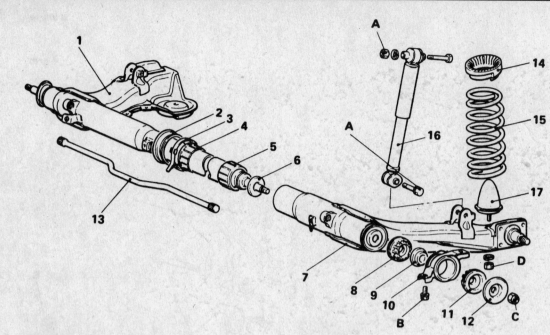

1. Suspension arm (R.H.)
2. Dust cover
3. Clamp
4. Bushing A
5. Bushing B
6. Rubber stopper
7. Suspension arm (L.H.)
8. rubber bushing (inner)
9. Rubber stopper
10. Fixture
11. Rubber bushing (outer)
12. Washer

13. Stabilizer bar
14. Spring seat
15. Coil spring
16. Shock absorber
17. Bump stopper

	Nm	ft. lbs.
A	65–80	46–56
B	50–70	36–51
C	80–100	56–70
D	18–25	13–18

Fig 40 Exploded view of the rear suspension of a 1985 Colt

Rear Wheel Bearings

REMOVAL & INSTALLATION

1979–84 Colt and 1985–89 Vista

♦ **See Figure 41**

1. Loosen the lug nuts, raise the rear of the car and support it on jackstands. Remove the wheel.
2. Remove the grease cap, cotter pin, nut and washer.
3. Remove the brake drum. While pulling the drum, the outer bearing will fall out. Position your hand to catch it.
4. Pry out the grease seal and discard it.
5. Remove the inner bearing.
To install:
6. Check the bearing races. If any scoring, heat checking or damage is noted, they should be replaced.

➡**When bearings or races need replacement, replace them as a set.**

7. Inspect the bearings. If wear or looseness or heat checking is found, replace them.

8. If the bearings and races are to be replaced, drive out the races with a brass drift.
9. Before installing new races, coat them with lithium based wheel bearing grease. The races are most easily installed using a driver made for that purpose. They can, however, be driven into place with a brass drift. Make sure that they are fully seated.
10. Thoroughly pack the bearings with lithium based wheel bearing grease. Pack the hub with grease.
11. Install the inner bearing and coat the lip and rim of the grease seal with grease. Drive the seal into place with a seal driver.
12. Mount the drum onto the hub, slide the outer bearing into place, install the washer and thread the nut into place, finger-tight.
13. Install a torque wrench on the nut. While turning the drum by hand, tighten the nut to 15 ft. lbs. Back off the nut until it is loose, then tighten it to 4 ft. lbs. If your torque wrench is not all that accurate below 10 ft. lbs. (most aren't), use an inch lb. torque wrench and tighten the nut to 48 inch lbs.
14. Install the lock cap and insert a new cotter pin. If the lock cap and hole don't align, and repositioning the cap can't accomplish alignment, back off the nut no more than 15 degrees. If that won't align the holes either, try the adjustment procedure over again.

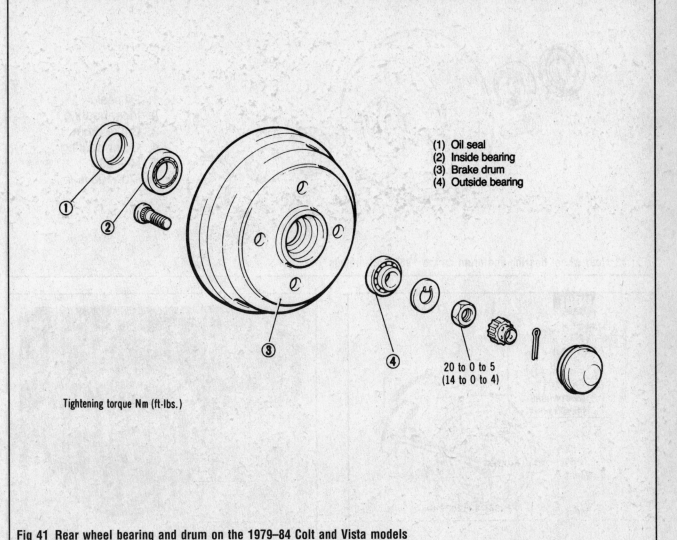

(1) Oil seal
(2) Inside bearing
(3) Brake drum
(4) Outside bearing

20 to 0 to 5
(14 to 0 to 4)

Tightening torque Nm (ft-lbs.)

Fig 41 Rear wheel bearing and drum on the 1979–84 Colt and Vista models

1985–89 Colt

▶ **See Figures 42 and 43**

➡**Special tools are needed for this procedure.**

1. Loosen the lug nuts. Raise the rear of the car and support it on jackstands.
2. Remove the wheel.
3. Remove the grease cap.
4. Remove the nut.
5. Pull the drum off. The outer bearing will fall out while the drum is coming off, so position your hand to catch it.
6. Pry out the oil seal. Discard it.
7. Remove the inner bearing.

To install:

8. Check the bearing races. If any scoring, heat checking or damage is noted, they should be replaced.

➡**When bearings or races need replacement, replace them as a set.**

9. Inspect the bearings. If wear or looseness or heat checking is found, replace them.

10. If the bearings and races are to be replaced, drive out the races with a brass drift.
11. Before installing new races, coat them with lithium based wheel bearing grease. The races are most easily installed using a driver made for that purpose. They can, however, be driven into place with a brass drift. Make sure that they are fully seated.
12. Thoroughly pack the bearings with lithium based wheel bearing grease. Pack the hub with grease.
13. Install the inner bearing and coat the lip and rim of the grease seal with grease. Drive the seal into place with a seal driver.
14. Mount the drum on the axleshaft. Install the outer bearing. Don't install the nut at this point.
15. Using a pull scale attached to one of the lugs, measure the starting force necessary to get the drum to turn. Starting force should be 5 lbs. If the starting torque is greater than specified, replace the bearings.
16. Install the nut on the axleshaft. Thread the nut on, by hand, to a point at which the back face of the nut is 2–3mm from the shoulder of the shaft (where the threads end).
17. Using an inch lb. torque wrench, turn the nut counterclockwise 2 to 3 turns, noting the average force needed during the turn-

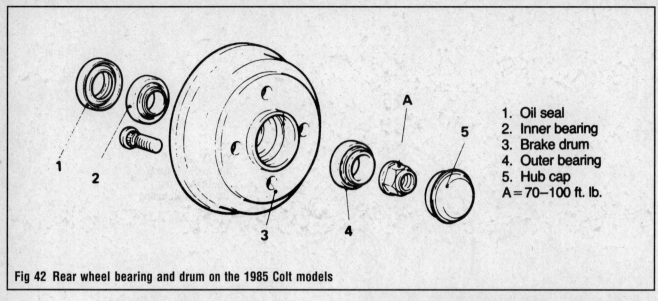

1. Oil seal
2. Inner bearing
3. Brake drum
4. Outer bearing
5. Hub cap
A = 70–100 ft. lb.

Fig 42 Rear wheel bearing and drum on the 1985 Colt models

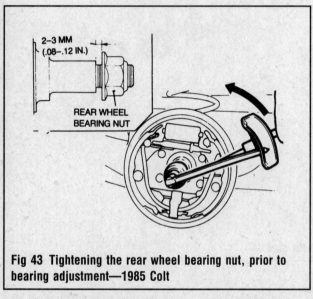

Fig 43 Tightening the rear wheel bearing nut, prior to bearing adjustment—1985 Colt

Carefully pry off the dust cover . . .

The rear wheel bearing can be accessed after removing the dust cover

. . . and set aside on a clean surface

Loosen the axle nut . . .

. . . and the drum

. . . and remove

With the drum removed, take the opportunity to inspect the brakes for wear

Remove the outer wheel bearing . . .

Pry the old seal out of the drum . . .

. . . and discard. Never reuse an old seal

Place the inner bearing into the drum

Pull the bearing out from inside the drum

Install a new seal . . .

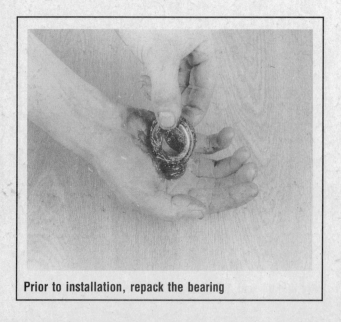

Prior to installation, repack the bearing

. . . using a seal driver

ing procedure. Turning torque for the nut should be above 48 in. lbs. If turning torque is not within 5 inch lbs., either way, replace the nut.

18. Tighten the nut to 75–110 ft. lbs.

19. Using a stand-mounted gauge, check the axial play of the wheel bearings. Play should be less than 0.2mm. If play cannot be brought within that figure, you probably have assembled the unit incorrectly.

20. Pack the grease cap with wheel bearing grease and install it.

Sub-Frame Assembly

REMOVAL & INSTALLATION

Conquest

▶ **See Figure 44**

➡**An assistant will make this job easier and safer.**

1. Support the rear end on jackstands placed under the body frame rails, forward of the rear wheels. The jackstands must extend at least 24 inches.

2. Using wire or rope, tie the struts to the crossmember to keep them from flopping to the side when the top nuts are removed.

3. Support the sub-frame with a floor jack, bearing on a 4 × 4 wood beam placed across the sub-frame.

4. Disconnect the driveshaft.

5. Remove the exhaust pipe and muffler.

6. Disconnect the parking brake cables at the calipers and the clips on the lower arms.

7. Disconnect the brake hose at the floor.

8. Remove the strut upper end attaching nuts from under the trim panels in the cargo area.

9. Remove the crossmember attaching nuts.

10. Remove the front support attaching nuts.

11. Have your assistant steady the sub-frame assembly while you lower the jack slowly.

12. Position the sub-frame and attach it to the crossmember. Attach the struts and removed components. Torque the front support nut-to-pin to 60 ft. lbs.; the front support lower stopper bolt-to-body to 36 ft. lbs.; the crossmember bolts to 60 ft. lbs.; the upper strut nuts to 25 ft. lbs.

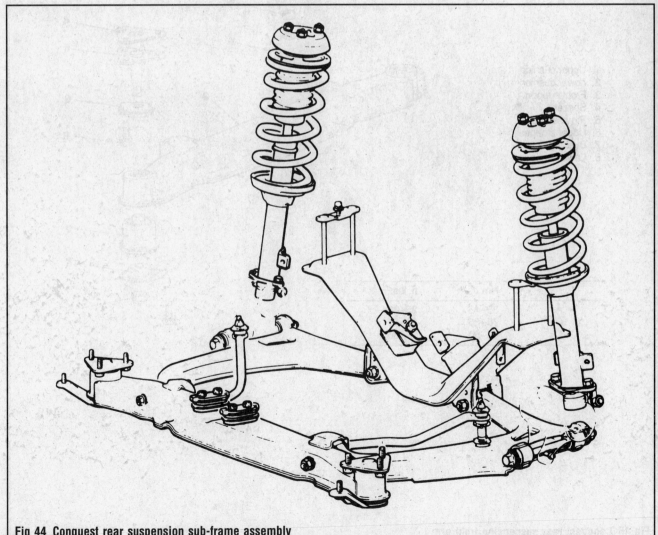

Fig 44 Conquest rear suspension sub-frame assembly

Front Support Arm

REMOVAL & INSTALLATION

Conquest

▶ See Figure 45

1. Remove the exhaust pipe.
2. Remove the stabilizer bar brackets from the front support.

3. Unbolt the lower control arms from the front support.
4. Unbolt the torque tube from the front support.
5. Support the torque tube with a floor jack.
6. Remove the nut, bolt and lower stopper from each end of the front support and remove the support.
7. Install the support and attach the components. Torque the lower stopper nuts to 60 ft. lbs.; the lower stopper bolts to 36 ft. lbs.; the torque tube mounting bolts to 33 ft. lbs.

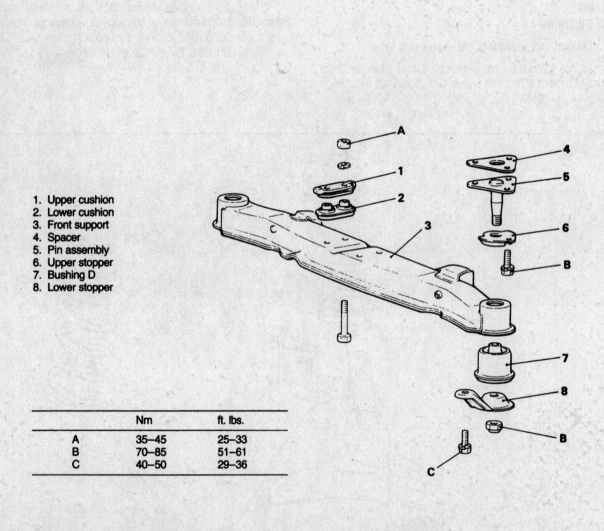

1. Upper cushion
2. Lower cushion
3. Front support
4. Spacer
5. Pin assembly
6. Upper stopper
7. Bushing D
8. Lower stopper

	Nm	ft. lbs.
A	35–45	25–33
B	70–85	51–61
C	40–50	29–36

Fig 45 Conquest rear suspension front arm

STEERING

Steering Wheel

REMOVAL & INSTALLATION

1. Disconnect the battery ground cable. Remove the center pad retaining screws located on the back of the wheel on some models, or pull off the horn pad using steady pressure.

2. Paint or chalk matchmarks on the steering shaft and the steering wheel so that they can be correctly reinstalled.

3. Unscrew the hub nut and, using a puller, remove the steering wheel.

➡**Don't hammer or otherwise pound on the steering column, as it is collapsible.**

4. Align the matchmarks and install the steering wheel. Torque the nut to 30 ft. lbs. Install the horn pad and connect the battery cable.

Remove the horn pad from the steering wheel . . .

Matchmark the wheel with the steering shaft

. . . and separate the horn connection

Remove the mounting nut

Using a puller, separate the steering wheel from the shaft . . .

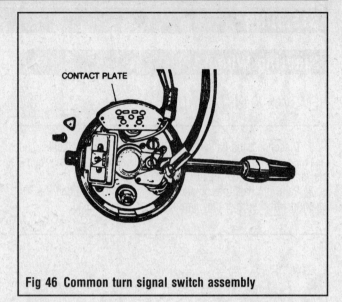

Fig 46 Common turn signal switch assembly

. . . then remove the assembly from the shaft

Turn Signal and Flasher Switch

REMOVAL & INSTALLATION

Rear Wheel Drive Cars

▶ **See Figure 46**

1. Remove the steering wheel as previously outlines.
2. Remove the instrument cluster using the procedure in Chapter 5.
3. Undo the retaining screws and remove the top and bottom steering column covers.
4. Disconnect each column switch harness, then remove the column switch from the column tube.
5. Remove the switch assembly retaining screws from the back of the column switch.
6. Remove the turn signal and flasher switch contact points.

To install:

7. Examine the switch contact points for corrosion. Clean or replace them as necessary.
8. Install the switch. Be sure that the switch is centered in the column or the self-cancelling will be affected. The switch wiring harness should be securely retained with clips.

Front Wheel Drive Cars

1. Remove the steering wheel.
2. Remove the lap heater duct.
3. Remove the column covers.
4. Remove the switch retaining screws, disconnect the wiring and remove the switch.
5. Install the switch. Connect the wiring. Install the column covers, heater duct and steering wheel.

Ignition Switch/Steering Lock

REMOVAL & INSTALLATION

▶ **See Figure 47**

1. Remove the turn signal switch as described above.
2. Disconnect the electrical wiring to the switch.
3. Drill out the shear bolts or cut a slot in the mounting screw heads and bracket with a hack saw and remove with a flat blade screwdriver.

➡ **Use new screws and bracket when installing the switch.**

4. Remove the switch.

To install:

5. Align the column tube hole with the wheel lock guide dowel for initial assembly.
6. Insert the ignition key to make sure that the lock functions correctly.
7. Install the shear bolts. Tighten them evenly until the heads break off.
8. Complete the installation of the removed components.

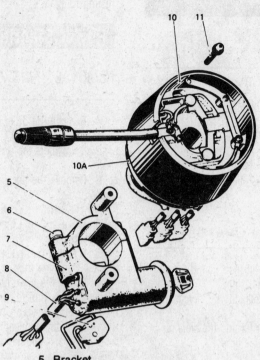

5. Bracket
6. Bolt
7. Body and cylinder
8. Ignition and starter switch
9. Door warning switch
10. Column switch
10A. Column switch rubber ring
11. Washer assembled machine screw

Fig 47 Exploded view of the ignition switch and steering lock turn signal

Steering Linkage Rear Wheel Drive

REMOVAL & INSTALLATION

Tie Rods

1. Using a puller, disconnect the tie rod ends from the steering knuckle.
2. Loosen the jam nut and remove the tie rod ends from the tie rod. The outer end is left-hand threaded and the inner is right-hand threaded.
   To install:
3. Grease the tie rod threads and install the ends. Turn each end in an equal amount.
4. Install the tie rod assembly on the steering knuckle and relay rod. Tighten the castellated nuts to 29–36 ft. lbs. Use new cotter pins.
5. Adjust the toe-in as described under Wheel Alignment.

Relay Rod

1. Disconnect the tie rod ends from the steering knuckles with a puller.
2. Again using the puller, disconnect the relay rod from the idler arm and the pitman arm.
3. Remove the relay rod.
   To install:
4. Install the rod. Tighten the tie rod end nuts to 29–36 ft. lbs. Tighten the relay rod-to-pitman arm nut and relay rod-to-idler arm nut to 29–43 ft. lbs. Always use new cotter pins.

Idler Arm

1. Disconnect the idler arm from the relay rod using a puller.
2. Remove the retaining bolts and the idler arm.
   To install:
3. Mount the idler arm on the frame and tighten the bolts to 25–29 ft. lbs.
4. Attach the relay rod to the idler arm and tighten the stud nut to 29–43 ft. lbs. Use a new cotter pin.

Manual Steering Gear Rear Wheel Drive

REMOVAL & INSTALLATION

▶ **See Figure 48**

1. Remove the clamp bolt connecting the steering shaft with the steering gear.
2. Disconnect the tie rod and pitman arm from the relay rod using a linkage puller.
3. Remove the gear box from the frame by loosening the side mounting bolts. To install, fasten the box to the frame and connect the linkage.

ADJUSTMENT

1. Measure the mainshaft preload with an inch pound torque wrench. The allowable torque is 3 to 4.8 inch lbs.
2. The preload torque is corrected by reducing or increasing the number of shims under the end plate.
3. Seat the cross-shaft and bearings by turning the steering mainshaft and the adjusting bolt two or three times.

4. Tighten the adjusting bolt to obtain zero free-play with the cross-shaft in the center position. Tighten the locknut on the adjusting bolt.

Power Steering Pump

REMOVAL & INSTALLATION

1. Remove the drive belt. If the pulley is to be removed do so now.
2. Disconnect the pressure and return lines. Catch any leaking fluid.
3. Remove the pump attaching bolts and lift the pump from the brackets.

To install:

4. Make sure the bracket bolts are tight and install the pump to the brackets.
5. If pulley had been removed install it and tighten the nut securely. Bend the lock tab over the nut.
6. Install the drive belt and adjust to a tension of 22 lbs. at a deflection of 7mm to the housing mainshaft.
7. Fill the reservoir with Dexron®II fluid and air bleed the system. (Refer to the bleeding procedure).
8. Start the engine and inspect for leakage.

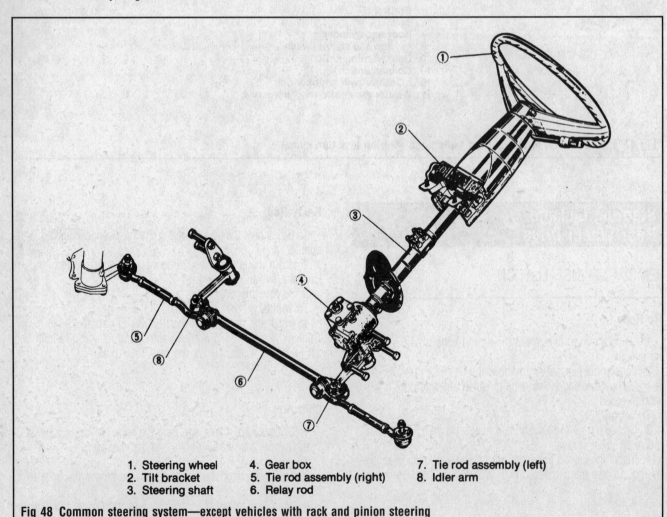

1. Steering wheel	4. Gear box	7. Tie rod assembly (left)
2. Tilt bracket	5. Tie rod assembly (right)	8. Idler arm
3. Steering shaft	6. Relay rod	

Fig 48 Common steering system—except vehicles with rack and pinion steering

✳✳ WARNING

When installing the pressure and return hoses, be careful not to twist or strip the fittings and pipes. Route the lines so as not to interfere with adjacent parts.

Power Steering Gear Rear Wheel Drive

REMOVAL & INSTALLATION

◆ **See Figure 49**

1. Matchmark and disconnect the steering shaft from the gearbox main shaft.
2. Matchmark and disconnect the tie rod end and pitman arm from the relay rod.
3. Remove the air cleaner and disconnect the pressure and return lines from the steering gear assembly.
4. Remove any interfering splash pans from underneath the vehicle.
5. If necessary, remove the kickdown linkage splash pan shield and bolts. Move the fuel line aside to avoid damage during removal.
6. Remove the frame bolts from the gearbox and lower the unit from the vehicle.

To install:

7. Install the box to the frame and connect the linkage and fluid lines. Make sure that all matchmarks align. After tightening the pitman arm nut make sure that the distance between the centerline of the lowest steering gear mounting bolt and the top of the pitman arm is 19.5mm. Observe the following torques: pitman arm nut: 94–109 ft. lbs. steering gear mounting bolts: 40–47 ft. lbs. tie rod socket and relay rod: 25–33 ft. lbs. high pressure hose: 22–29 ft. lbs. return hose: 29–36 ft. lbs.

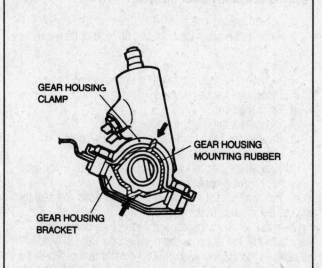

Fig 49 Matchmark and disconnect the steering shaft from the gearbox main shaft

ADJUSTMENT

➡**The steering gear must be disconnected from the steering shaft.**

1. Measure the mainshaft preload with an inch pound torque wrench. The preload should be 3.5–6.9 inch lbs., with the cross-haft adjusting bolt backed off.
2. Adjust the valve housing top cover to obtain the proper preload. When correct, lock the top cover with the locking nut.
3. Tighten the cross-shaft adjusting bolt until zero lash is present. Check the total starting torque to rotate the main shaft. The torque should be 5.2–8.7 inch lbs.
4. Adjust the cross-shaft until the required starting torque is obtained and lock the adjusting bolt nut securely.

BLEEDING THE SYSTEM

1. The reservoir should be full of Dexron®II fluid.
2. Jack up the front wheels and support the vehicle safely.
3. Turn the steering wheel fully to the right and left until no air bubbles appear in the fluid. Maintain the reservoir level.
4. Lower the vehicle and with the engine idling, turn the wheels fully to the right and left. Stop the engine.
5. Install a tube from the bleeder screw on the steering gear box to the reservoir.
6. Start the engine, turn the steering wheel fully to the left and loosen the bleeder screw.
7. Repeat the procedure until no air bubbles pass through the tube.
8. Tighten the bleeder screw and remove the tube. Refill the reservoir as needed, and check that no further bubbles are present in the fluid.

➡**An abrupt rise in the fluid level after stopping the engine is a sign of incomplete bleeding. This will cause noise from the pump or control valve.**

Rack and Pinion Steering Gear Front Wheel Drive

REMOVAL & INSTALLATION

1979–84 Colt Manual and Power Steering
1985–89 Colt Manual Steering

◆ **See Figure 50**

1. Loosen the lug nuts.
2. Raise and support the front end on jackstands under the frame.
3. Remove the wheels.
4. Remove the steering shaft-to-pinion coupling bolt.
5. Disconnect the tie rod ends with a separator. On cars with power steering, drain the fluid and disconnect the hoses at the gear unit.
6. Removing the clamps securing the rack to the crossmember and remove the unit from the car.

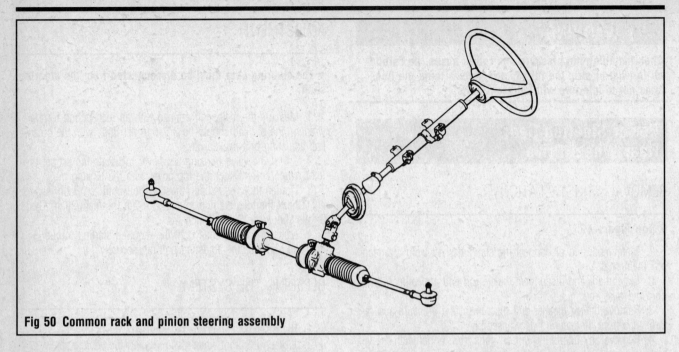

Fig 50 Common rack and pinion steering assembly

To install:

7. Install the rubber mount for the gear box with the slit on the downside. Connect the steering gear to the crossmember. Connect the power steering lines, the tie rod ends and the steering shaft to column connector. Torque the rack-to-crossmember bolts to 22–29 ft. lbs. (1979–84); 45–60 ft. lbs. (1985–89); the coupling bolt to 11–14 ft. lbs. (1979–84): 22–25 ft. lbs. (1985–89) and the tie-rod nuts to 11–25 ft. lbs. Fill the system and road test the car.

2-WD Vista

1. Loosen the lug nuts.
2. Raise and support the front end on jackstands under the frame.
3. Remove the wheels.
4. Remove the steering shaft-to-pinion coupling bolt.
5. Disconnect the tie rod ends with a separator. On cars with power steering, disconnect the hoses at the gear unit.
6. Remove the crossmember support bracket from the crossmember on the right side of the car.
7. Unbolt the gearbox from the crossmember.

➡**The gearbox is most easily removed using a ratchet and long extension, working from the engine compartment side.**

8. Pull the gearbox out the right side of the car. Pull it slowly to avoid damage.
9. Install the gear to the crossmember and install the components. Torque the rack clamp bolts to 43–58 ft. lbs., the tie rod nuts to 17–25 ft. lbs., and the coupling bolt to 22–25 ft. lbs. Fill the system and road test the car.

4-WD Vista

1. Remove the steering column.
2. Raise and support the car on jackstands under the frame.
3. Remove the front wheels.
4. Using a separator, disconnect the tie rod from the knuckle.
5. Disconnect the steering shaft joint at the gear box.
6. Disconnect the fluid lines at the gear box.
7. Remove the air cleaner.

8. Remove the gear box attaching bolts from the rear of the No. 2 crossmember. The bolts are most easily accessed using a long extension and working from the top of the engine compartment.
9. From under the car, remove the gear box mounting bolts from the front of the No. 2 crossmember, and pull out and to the left on the gear box.
10. Lower the gear box until the left edge of the left feed tube contacts the lower part of the left fender shield. At this point, remove the left and right feed tubes.
11. Remove the gear box from the car.
12. Install the gear to the crossmember and connect the components. When installing the clamps, make sure that the rubber projections are aligned with the holes in the clamps. Install the tie rods so that 191–193mm shows between the tie rod end locknut and the beginning of the boot. Torque the gear box mounting bolts to 55–60 ft. lbs.; the tie rod-to-knuckle nut to 20–25 ft. lbs.

1985–89 Colt with Power Steering

1. Loosen the lug nuts.
2. Raise and support the front end on jackstands under the frame.
3. Remove the wheels.
4. Remove the steering shaft-to-pinion coupling bolt.
5. Disconnect the tie rod ends with a separator.
6. Drain the fluid.
7. Disconnect the hoses from the gearbox.
8. Remove the band from the steering joint cover.
9. Unbolt and remove the stabilizer bar.
10. Remove the rear roll stopper-to-center member bolt and move the rear roll stopper forward.
11. Remove the rack unit mounting clamp bolts and take the unit out the left side of the car.
12. Install the steering gear and connect the components. Make sure that the rubber isolators have their nubs aligned with the holes in the clamps. Apply rubber cement to the slits in the gear mounting grommet. Tighten the clamp bolt to 43–58 ft. lbs., the tie-rod nuts to 11–25 ft. lbs., and the coupling bolt to 22–25 ft. lbs.
13. Fill the system and road test the car.

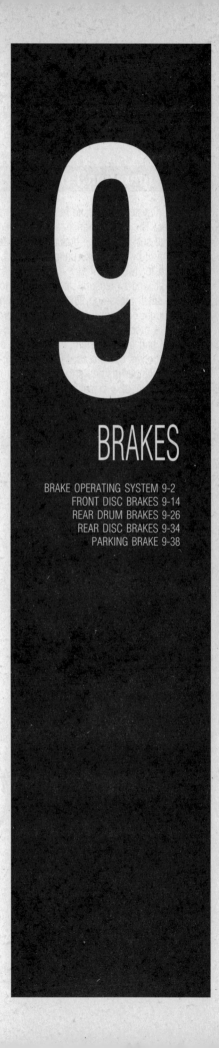

9

BRAKES

BRAKE OPERATING SYSTEM

▶ **See Figure 1**

Basic Operating Principles

Hydraulic systems are used to actuate the brakes of all modern automobiles. The system transports the power required to force the frictional surfaces of the braking system together from the pedal to the individual brake units at each wheel. A hydraulic system is used for two reasons.

First, fluid under pressure can be carried to all parts of an automobile by small pipes and flexible hoses without taking up a significant amount of room or posing routing problems.

Second, a great mechanical advantage can be given to the brake pedal end of the system, and the foot pressure required to actuate the brakes can be reduced by making the surface area of the master cylinder pistons smaller than that of any of the pistons in the wheel cylinders or calipers.

The master cylinder consists of a fluid reservoir along with a double cylinder and piston assembly. Double type master cylinders are designed to separate the front and rear braking systems hydraulically in case of a leak. The master cylinder coverts me-

chanical motion from the pedal into hydraulic pressure within the lines. This pressure is translated back into mechanical motion at the wheels by either the wheel cylinder (drum brakes) or the caliper (disc brakes).

Steel lines carry the brake fluid to a point on the vehicle's frame near each of the vehicle's wheels. The fluid is then carried to the calipers and wheel cylinders by flexible tubes in order to allow for suspension and steering movements.

In drum brake systems, each wheel cylinder contains two pistons, one at either end, which push outward in opposite directions and force the brake shoe into contact with the drum.

In disc brake systems, the cylinders are part of the calipers. At least one cylinder in each caliper is used to force the brake pads against the disc.

All pistons employ some type of seal, usually made of rubber, to minimize fluid leakage. A rubber dust boot seals the outer end of the cylinder against dust and dirt. The boot fits around the outer end of the piston on disc brake calipers, and around the brake actuating rod on wheel cylinders.

The hydraulic system operates as follows: When at rest, the entire system, from the piston(s) in the master cylinder to those in the wheel cylinders or calipers, is full of brake fluid. Upon applica-

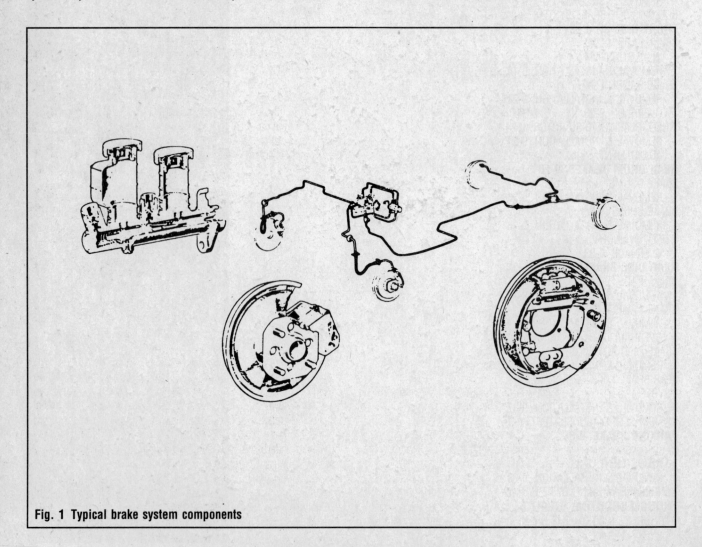

Fig. 1 Typical brake system components

tion of the brake pedal, fluid trapped in front of the master cylinder piston(s) is forced through the lines to the wheel cylinders. Here, it forces the pistons outward, in the case of drum brakes, and inward toward the disc, in the case of disc brakes. The motion of the pistons is opposed by return springs mounted outside the cylinders in drum brakes, and by spring seals, in disc brakes.

Upon release of the brake pedal, a spring located inside the master cylinder immediately returns the master cylinder pistons to the normal position. The pistons contain check valves and the master cylinder has compensating ports drilled in it. These are uncovered as the pistons reach their normal position. The piston check valves allow fluid to flow toward the wheel cylinders or calipers as the pistons withdraw. Then, as the return springs force the brake pads or shoes into the released position, the excess fluid reservoir through the compensating ports. It is during the time the pedal is in the released position that any fluid that has leaked out of the system will be replaced through the compensating ports.

Dual circuit master cylinders employ two pistons, located one behind the other, in the same cylinder. The primary piston is actuated directly by mechanical linkage from the brake pedal through the power booster. The secondary piston is actuated by fluid trapped between the two pistons. If a leak develops in front of the secondary piston, it moves forward until it bottoms against the front of the master cylinder, and the fluid trapped between the pistons will operate the rear brakes. If the rear brakes develop a leak, the primary piston will move forward until direct contact with the secondary piston takes place, and it will force the secondary piston to actuate the front brakes. In either case, the brake pedal moves farther when the brakes are applied, and less braking power is available.

All dual circuit systems use a switch to warn the driver when only half of the brake system is operational. This switch is usually located in a valve body which is mounted on the firewall or the frame below the master cylinder. A hydraulic piston receives pressure from both circuits, each circuit's pressure being applied to one end of the piston. When the pressures are in balance, the piston remains stationary. When one circuit has a leak, however, the greater pressure in that circuit during application of the brakes will push the piston to one side, closing the switch and activating the brake warning light.

In disc brake systems, this valve body also contains a metering valve and, in some cases, a proportioning valve. The metering valve keeps pressure from traveling to the disc brakes on the front wheels until the brake shoes on the rear wheels have contacted the drums, ensuring that the front brakes will never be used alone. The proportioning valve controls the pressure to the rear brakes to lessen the chance of rear wheel lock-up during very hard braking.

Warning lights may be tested by depressing the brake pedal and holding it while opening one of the wheel cylinder bleeder screws. If this does not cause the light to go on, substitute a new lamp, make continuity checks, and, finally, replace the switch as necessary.

The hydraulic system may be checked for leaks by applying pressure to the pedal gradually and steadily. If the pedal sinks very slowly to the floor, the system has a leak. This is not to be confused with a springy or spongy feel due to the compression of air within the lines. If the system leaks, there will be a gradual change in the position of the pedal with a constant pressure.

Check for leaks along all lines and at wheel cylinders. If no external leaks are apparent, the problem is inside the master cylinder.

DISC BRAKES

Instead of the traditional expanding brakes that press outward against a circular drum, disc brake systems utilize a disc (rotor) with brake pads positioned on either side of it. An easily-seen analogy is the hand brake arrangement on a bicycle. The pads squeeze onto the rim of the bike wheel, slowing its motion. Automobile disc brakes use the identical principle but apply the braking effort to a separate disc instead of the wheel.

The disc (rotor) is a casting, usually equipped with cooling fins between the two braking surfaces. This enables air to circulate between the braking surfaces making them less sensitive to heat buildup and more resistant to fade. Dirt and water do not drastically affect braking action since contaminants are thrown off by the centrifugal action of the rotor or scraped off the by the pads. Also, the equal clamping action of the two brake pads tends to ensure uniform, straight line stops. Disc brakes are inherently self-adjusting. There are three general types of disc brake:

1. A fixed caliper.
2. A floating caliper.
3. A sliding caliper.

The fixed caliper design uses two pistons mounted on either side of the rotor (in each side of the caliper). The caliper is mounted rigidly and does not move.

The sliding and floating designs are quite similar. In fact, these two types are often lumped together. In both designs, the pad on the inside of the rotor is moved into contact with the rotor by hydraulic force. The caliper, which is not held in a fixed position, moves slightly, bringing the outside pad into contact with the rotor. There are various methods of attaching floating calipers. Some pivot at the bottom or top, and some slide on mounting bolts. In any event, the end result is the same.

DRUM BRAKES

Drum brakes employ two brake shoes mounted on a stationary backing plate. These shoes are positioned inside a circular drum which rotates with the wheel assembly. The shoes are held in place by springs. This allows them to slide toward the drums (when they are applied) while keeping the linings and drums in alignment. The shoes are actuated by a wheel cylinder which is mounted at the top of the backing plate. When the brakes are applied, hydraulic pressure forces the wheel cylinder's actuating links outward. Since these links bear directly against the top of the brake shoes, the tops of the shoes are then forced against the inner side of the drum. This action forces the bottoms of the two shoes to contact the brake drum by rotating the entire assembly slightly (known as servo action). When pressure within the wheel cylinder is relaxed, return springs pull the shoes back away from the drum.

Most modern drum brakes are designed to self-adjust themselves during application when the vehicle is moving in reverse. This motion causes both shoes to rotate very slightly with the drum, rocking an adjusting lever, thereby causing rotation of the adjusting screw. Some drum brake systems are designed to self-adjust during application whenever the brakes are applied. This on-board adjustment system reduces the need for maintenance adjustments and keeps both the brake function and pedal feel satisfactory.

POWER BOOSTERS

Virtually all modern vehicles use a vacuum assisted power brake system to multiply the braking force and reduce pedal effort. Since vacuum is always available when the engine is operating, the system is simple and efficient. A vacuum diaphragm is located on the front of the master cylinder and assists the driver in applying the brakes, reducing both the effort and travel he must put into moving the brake pedal.

The vacuum diaphragm housing is normally connected to the intake manifold by a vacuum hose. A check valve is placed at the point where the hose enters the diaphragm housing, so that during periods of low manifold vacuum brakes assist will not be lost.

Depressing the brake pedal closes off the vacuum source and allows atmospheric pressure to enter on one side of the diaphragm. This causes the master cylinder pistons to move and apply the brakes. When the brake pedal is released, vacuum is applied to both sides of the diaphragm and springs return the diaphragm and master cylinder pistons to the released position.

If the vacuum supply fails, the brake pedal rod will contact the end of the master cylinder actuator rod and the system will apply the brakes without any power assistance. The driver will notice that much higher pedal effort is needed to stop the car and that the pedal feels harder than usual.

Vacuum Leak Test

1. Operate the engine at idle without touching the brake pedal for at least one minute.
2. Turn off the engine and wait one minute.
3. Test for the presence of assist vacuum by depressing the brake pedal and releasing it several times. If vacuum is present in the system, light application will produce less and less pedal travel. If there is no vacuum, air is leaking into the system.

System Operation Test

1. With the engine **OFF**, pump the brake pedal until the supply vacuum is entirely gone.
2. Put light, steady pressure on the brake pedal.
3. Start the engine and let it idle. If the system is operating correctly, the brake pedal should fall toward the floor if the constant pressure is maintained.

Power brake systems may be tested for hydraulic leaks just as ordinary systems are tested.

Adjustments

➡ **All brakes used on these cars, beginning mid-year 1973, are self-adjusting.**

DRUM BRAKES

1971–Mid 1973 Models

➡ **If you are experiencing low brake pedal (soft pedal), first perform the rear brake adjustment, as outlined below, before blaming the hydraulic system.**

1. Make sure that the hand brake lever is completely lowered.
2. Jack up the rear of the car and support it on stands. Block the front wheels.
3. The square-lugged adjuster is located on the rear of the backing plate. Using an adjustable wrench, turn the adjuster as far as it will go clockwise.
4. Back the adjuster off slightly until, while turning the wheel, you feel no drag. Maximum brake shoe-to-drum clearance should be less than 0.3mm. Each 90 degrees turn of the adjuster decreases clearance by 0.15mm.

Master Cylinder

➡ **Be careful not to spill brake fluid on the painted surfaces of your car. The brake fluid will cause damage to the paint.**

REMOVAL & INSTALLATION

Rear Wheel Drive

1. Disconnect all hydraulic lines from the master cylinder. On models with remote reservoir, remove and plug the hoses from the master cylinder caps. If the master cylinder has a fluid level warning device, disconnect the wiring harness.
2. On non-power brake cars, remove the clevis pin that connects the master cylinder pushrod to the brake pedal.
3. Loosen and remove the master cylinder mounting nuts, either from the firewall (manual brakes) or from the power brake booster. Remove the master cylinder.

To install:
4. Mount the master cylinder to the firewall (manual brakes) or to the power brake booster. Torque the nuts to 10 ft. lbs.
5. Connect the pushrod to the brake pedal (manual brakes).
6. Connect all brake lines and wiring harnesses and fill the master cylinder reservoirs with clean fluid.

✳✳ WARNING

Clean, high quality brake fluid is essential to the safe and proper operation of the brake system. You should always buy the highest quality brake fluid that is available. If the brake fluid becomes contaminated, drain and flush the system, then refill the master cylinder with new fluid. Never reuse any brake fluid. Any brake fluid that is removed from the system should be discarded.

7. Bleed the brake system as outlined in this chapter.

Front Wheel Drive

1. Disconnect the fluid level sensor.
2. Disconnect the brake tubes from the master cylinder and cap them immediately.
3. On cars with a turbocharger, remove the reservoir from the reservoir holder.
4. Unbolt and remove the master cylinder from the booster.
5. Install the master cylinder to the booster. Install the reservoir. Connect the brake lines and the fluid level sensor. Torque the mounting bolts to 6–9 ft. lbs. (72–108 inch lbs.).

Using a flare nut wrench, disconnect the brake lines leading to the brake master cylinder

If equipped, separate the wiring for the level sensor

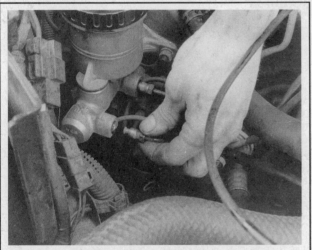

Push the brake lines back *slightly,* be careful not to bend the lines

Remove the master cylinder, with the cap tightened so not to spill any fluid

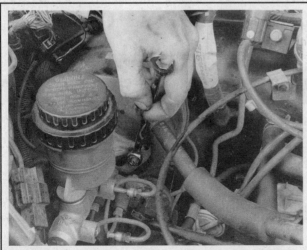

Remove the mounting nuts retaining the master cylinder to the brake booster

OVERHAUL

▶ See Figure 2

This is a tedious, time-consuming job. You can save yourself a lot of trouble by buying a rebuilt master cylinder from your dealer or a parts supply house. The small difference in cost between a re-building kit and a rebuilt part usually makes it more economical, in terms of time and work, to buy the rebuilt part.

1. Remove the master cylinder from the car.

2. Remove the reservoir caps and filters and drain the brake fluid. Discard this fluid.

3. Remove the piston stopper snapring from the open end of the master cylinder with a pair of snapring pliers, or other suitable tool.

4. Remove the stopper screw and washer (if equipped) from the bottom of the master cylinder and then remove the primary and secondary piston assemblies from the master cylinder bore.

5. Remove the caps on the underside of the master cylinder to gain access to the check valves for cleaning.

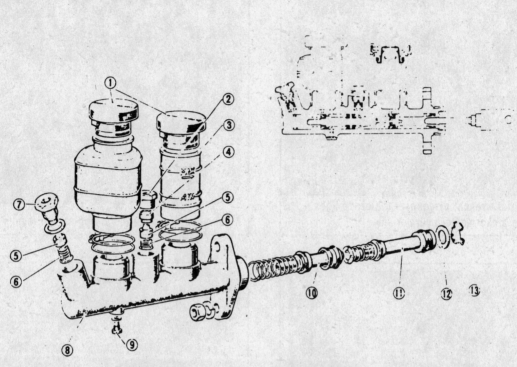

1. Reservoir cap
2. Check valve cap
3. Fluid reservoir
4. Outer pipe seat
5. Check valve
6. Check valve spring
7. Valve case
8. Master cylinder
9. Piston stopper
10. Secondary piston assembly
11. Primary piston assembly
12. Piston stopper
13. Stopper ring

Fig 2 Exploded view of the common dual master cylinder and internal components

➡ **Do not disassemble the brake fluid level gauge, if equipped.**

6. Discard all used rubber parts and gaskets. These parts should be replaced with the new components included in the rebuilding kit.

➡ **Do not remove the master cylinder reservoir tanks unless they are leaking.**

7. Clean all the parts in clean brake fluid. Do not use mineral oil or alcohol for cleaning.

8. Check the cylinder bore and piston for wear, scoring, corrosion, or any other damage. The piston and cylinder bore can be dressed with crocus cloth, or a brake cylinder hone, soaked in brake fluid. Move the crocus cloth around the cylinder bore, not in and out. Do the same to the piston, if necessary. Wash both the cylinder bore and the piston with clean brake fluid.

9. Check the piston-to-cylinder bore clearance; it should measure 0.15mm. If greater clearance exists, replace the piston, the cylinder, or both.

10. Assemble the master cylinder. Soak all of the components in clean brake fluid before assembling them.

⁕⁕ WARNING

Clean, high quality brake fluid is essential to the safe and proper operation of the brake system. You should always buy the highest quality brake fluid that is available. If the brake fluid becomes contaminated, drain and flush the system, then refill the master cylinder with new fluid. Never reuse any brake fluid. Any brake fluid that is removed from the system should be discarded.

11. Clamp the master cylinder in a vise by one of its flanges. Fill the reservoirs with fresh fluid, and pump the piston with a screwdriver until fluid squirts from the outlet ports. Install the master cylinder and bleed the system.

Power Brake Boosters

OPERATION

Power brakes operate just as standard brake systems except in the actuation of the master cylinder pistons. A vacuum diaphragm is located on the front of the master cylinder and assists the driver in applying the brakes, reducing both the effort and travel he must put into moving the brake pedal.

The vacuum diaphragm housing is connected to the intake manifold by a vacuum hose. A check valve is placed at the point where the hose enters the diaphragm housing, so that during periods of low manifold vacuum brake assist vacuum will not be lost.

Depressing the brake pedal closes off the vacuum source and allows atmospheric pressure to enter on one side of the diaphragm. This causes the master cylinder pistons to move and apply the brakes. When the brake pedal is released, vacuum is applied to both sides of the diaphragm, and return springs return the diaphragm and master cylinder pistons to the released position. If the vacuum fails, the brake pedal rod will butt against the end of the master cylinder actuating rod, and direct mechanical application will occur as the pedal is depressed. The hydraulic and mechanical problems that apply to conventional brake systems also apply to power brakes, and should be checked for if the tests below do not reveal the problem. Test for a system vacuum leak as described below:

1. Operate the engine at idle with the transmission in Neutral without touching the brake pedal for at least one minute.
2. Turn **off** the engine, and wait one minute.

3. Test for the presence of assist vacuum by depressing the brake pedal and releasing it several times. Light application will produce less and less pedal travel, if vacuum was present. If there is no vacuum, air is leaking into the system somewhere.
4. Test for system operation as follows:
5. Pump the brake pedal (with engine off) until the supply vacuum is entirely gone.
6. Put a light, steady pressure on the pedal.
7. Start the engine, and operate it at idle with the transmission in Neutral. If the system is operating, the brake pedal should fall toward the floor if constant pressure is maintained on the pedal.

➡ **Power brake systems may be tested for hydraulic leaks just as ordinary systems are tested, except that the engine should be idling with the transmission in Neutral (manual) or Park (automatic) with the wheels blocked throughout the test.**

REMOVAL & INSTALLATION

▶ See Figure 3

1. Remove the master cylinder.
2. Disconnect the vacuum line from the booster.
3. Remove the pin connecting the power brake operating rod and the brake lever.
4. Unbolt and remove the booster.
5. Replace the packing on both sides of the booster-to-firewall spacer with new packing.
6. If the check valve was removed, make sure the direction of installation marking on the valve is followed.

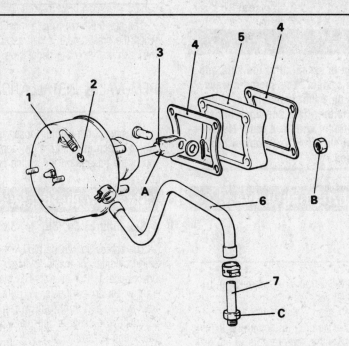

1. Brake booster
2. Check valve
3. Operating rod
4. Sealer
5. Spacer
6. Vacuum hose
7. Fitting

	Nm	ft. lbs.
A	19–25	14–18
B	8–12	6–9
C	15–18	11–13

Fig 3 Exploded view of a common brake booster mounting

7. Install the booster and master cylinder. Torque the booster-to-firewall nuts to 6–9 ft. lbs. (72–108 inch lbs.) Torque the master cylinder-to-booster nuts to 6–9 ft. lbs.

Combination Valve or Proportioning Valve

OPERATION

The valve performs one or more of the following functions:
1. Controls the amount of hydraulic pressure to the rear brakes.
2. Warns of failure in the brake system (warning light on dash).
3. Inactivates rear pressure control in case of failure in the front service brake system.

REMOVAL & INSTALLATION

1. Disconnect the brake lines at the valve.

➡**Use a flare nut wrench, if possible, to avoid damage to the lines and fittings.**

2. Remove the mounting bolts and remove the valve.

➡**Do not disassemble the valve, replace with a new one if necessary.**

3. Install the valve and connect the lines. Make sure the brake lines are tight. Fill the system with fluid and bleed the brakes.

✳✳ WARNING

Clean, high quality brake fluid is essential to the safe and proper operation of the brake system. You should always buy the highest quality brake fluid that is available. If the brake fluid becomes contaminated, drain and flush the system, then refill the master cylinder with new fluid. Never reuse any brake fluid. Any brake fluid that is removed from the system should be discarded.

Load Sensing Proportioning Valve

OPERATION

A load sensing proportioning valve (LSPV) is installed in the rear brake line on some late model vehicles.

Brake fluid pressure, from the master cylinder, to the rear wheels is controlled by the LSPV according to the vehicle loading conditions, i.e., weight carried. Adjusting the pressure to the rear wheels, depending on the load, improves straight line stopping and helps prevent rear wheel lock up.

The LSPV is connected to a rear lateral rod by a link, lever, cable, and spring. The space between the vehicle floor and lateral rod determines the amount of pressure adjustment to the rear wheels. When the space is greater (light load), the spring pressure to the LSPV is light and less brake pressure is applied. As the vehicle load is increased, so is the LSPV spring pressure and more braking pressure to the rear wheels is provided.

ADJUSTMENT

1. Park the unloaded vehicle on a level surface. Do NOT support the vehicle on a jack or other support.
2. Measure the length, of the spring, between the attaching holes in the fixed end of the LSPV and the operating lever. The length should be 89–91mm.
3. If the length of the spring is not correct, adjust it to the correct length by turning the adjusting nut at the end of the cable located on the opposite side of the operating lever.

Brake Warning Light Switch

The warning light switch is unrepairable, and must be replaced as a unit if problems occur. The switch may be located in the combination valve, in the master cylinder reservoir or mounted in line between the master cylinder and combination/proportioning valve. Replacement is made by disconnecting the brake lines or unscrewing the switch. If the switch is located in line, the brake system will have to be bled after replacement.

Stoplight Switch

OPERATION

The stoplight switch is a mechanical plunger type, activated when the brake pedal is depressed. The switch is located under the dash on the brake pedal stop.

REMOVAL & INSTALLATION

Disconnect the wiring, loosen the locknut and unscrew the switch. When installing, allow about 0.5mm clearance between the top of the threads on the switch and the brake pedal arm.

Bleeding the Brake System

◆ **See Figures 3a, 3b, 3c, 3d and 3e**

The brakes should be bled whenever a brake line, caliper, wheel cylinder, or master cylinder has been removed or when the brake pedal is low or soft. The bleeding sequence (except for front wheel drive models) is, right rear wheel, left rear wheel, left front wheel, and right front wheel. The bleeding sequence for front wheel drive models is, left rear wheel, right front wheel, right rear wheel and left front wheel.

➡**Some 1976 and later rear wheel drive models don't have a bleeder fitting on the left rear brake. Both rear brakes must be bled from the right rear.**

1. Check the master cylinder fluid level. If necessary, add fluid to bring the level up.
2. Remove the bleeder cap at the wheel cylinder or caliper.

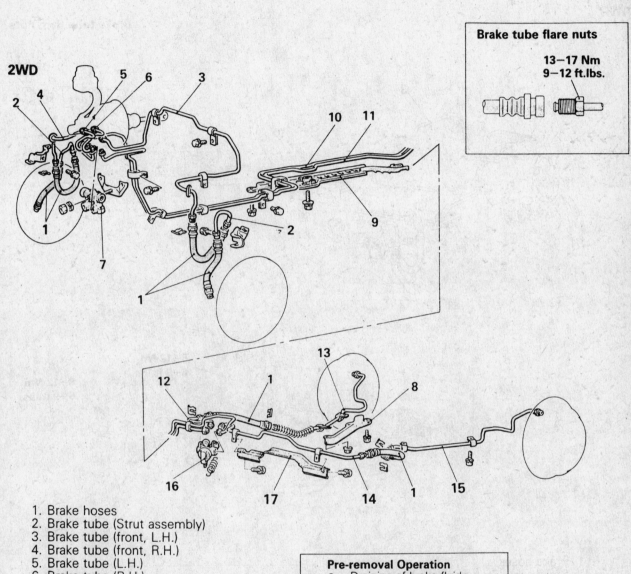

2WD

Brake tube flare nuts

13–17 Nm
9–12 ft.lbs.

1. Brake hoses
2. Brake tube (Strut assembly)
3. Brake tube (front, L.H.)
4. Brake tube (front, R.H.)
5. Brake tube (L.H.)
6. Brake tube (R.H.)
7. 6-way connector
9. Stone guard
10. Brake tube (main, L.H.)
11. Brake tube (main, R.H.)
12. Brake tube (center, R.H.)
13. Brake tube (rear, R.H.)
14. Brake tube (center, L.H.)
15. Brake tube (rear, L.H.)
16. Load sensing proportioning valve
17. Heat protector

Pre-removal Operation
- Draining of brake fluid

Post-installation Operation
- Filling of brake fluid
- Air bleeding of brake line

Fig 3a Brake line routing—2WD Colt and Vista

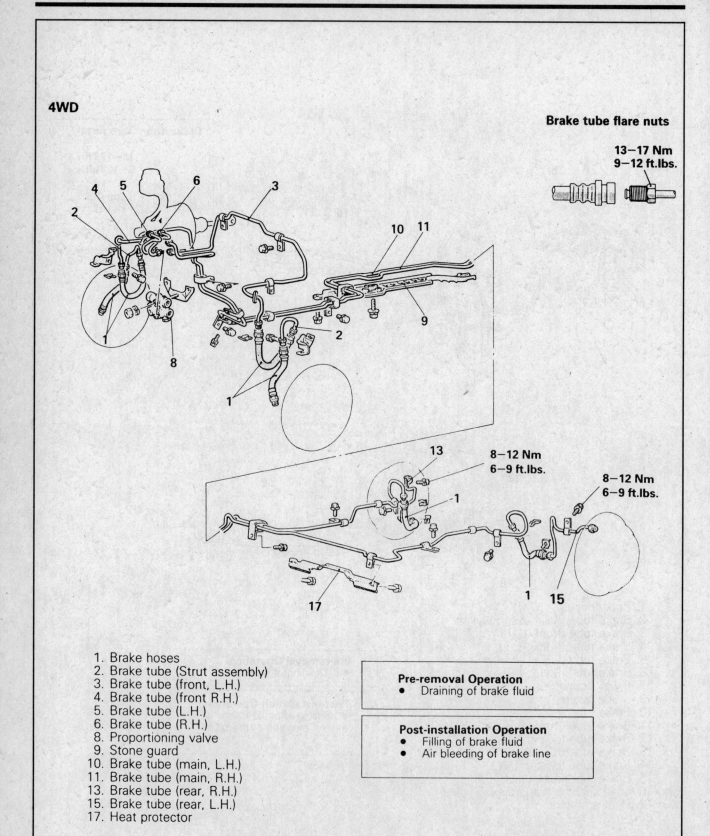

4WD

Brake tube flare nuts

13–17 Nm
9–12 ft.lbs.

8–12 Nm
6–9 ft.lbs.

8–12 Nm
6–9 ft.lbs.

1. Brake hoses
2. Brake tube (Strut assembly)
3. Brake tube (front, L.H.)
4. Brake tube (front R.H.)
5. Brake tube (L.H.)
6. Brake tube (R.H.)
8. Proportioning valve
9. Stone guard
10. Brake tube (main, L.H.)
11. Brake tube (main, R.H.)
13. Brake tube (rear, R.H.)
15. Brake tube (rear, L.H.)
17. Heat protector

Pre-removal Operation
- Draining of brake fluid

Post-installation Operation
- Filling of brake fluid
- Air bleeding of brake line

Fig 3b Brake line routing—4WD Colt and Vista

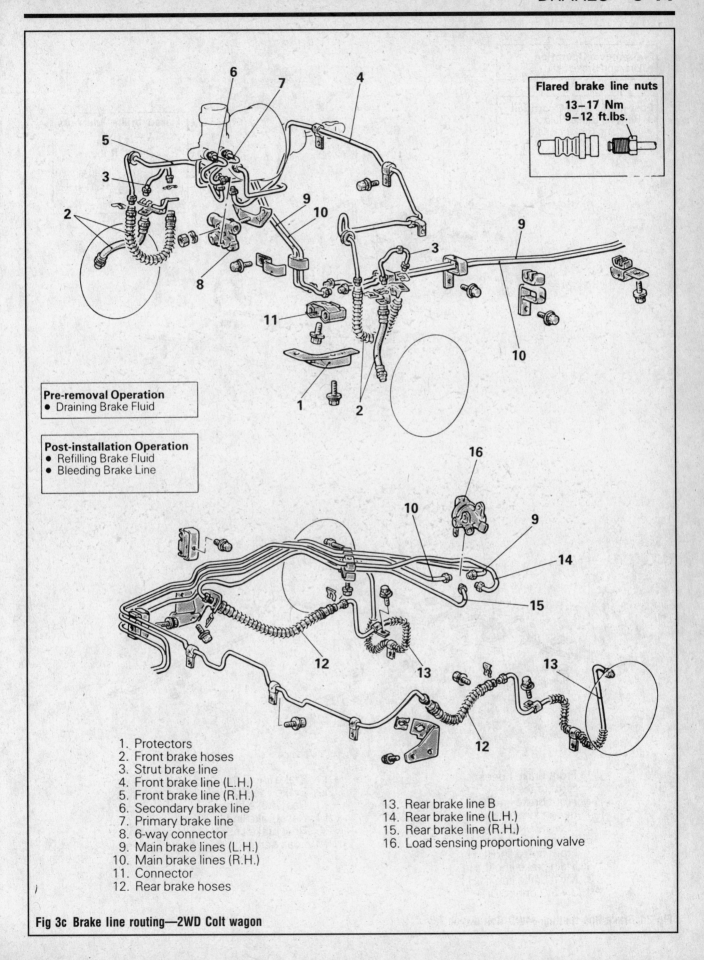

Flared brake line nuts
13–17 Nm
9–12 ft.lbs.

Pre-removal Operation
● Draining Brake Fluid

Post-installation Operation
● Refilling Brake Fluid
● Bleeding Brake Line

1. Protectors
2. Front brake hoses
3. Strut brake line
4. Front brake line (L.H.)
5. Front brake line (R.H.)
6. Secondary brake line
7. Primary brake line
8. 6-way connector
9. Main brake lines (L.H.)
10. Main brake lines (R.H.)
11. Connector
12. Rear brake hoses

13. Rear brake line B
14. Rear brake line (L.H.)
15. Rear brake line (R.H.)
16. Load sensing proportioning valve

Fig 3c Brake line routing—2WD Colt wagon

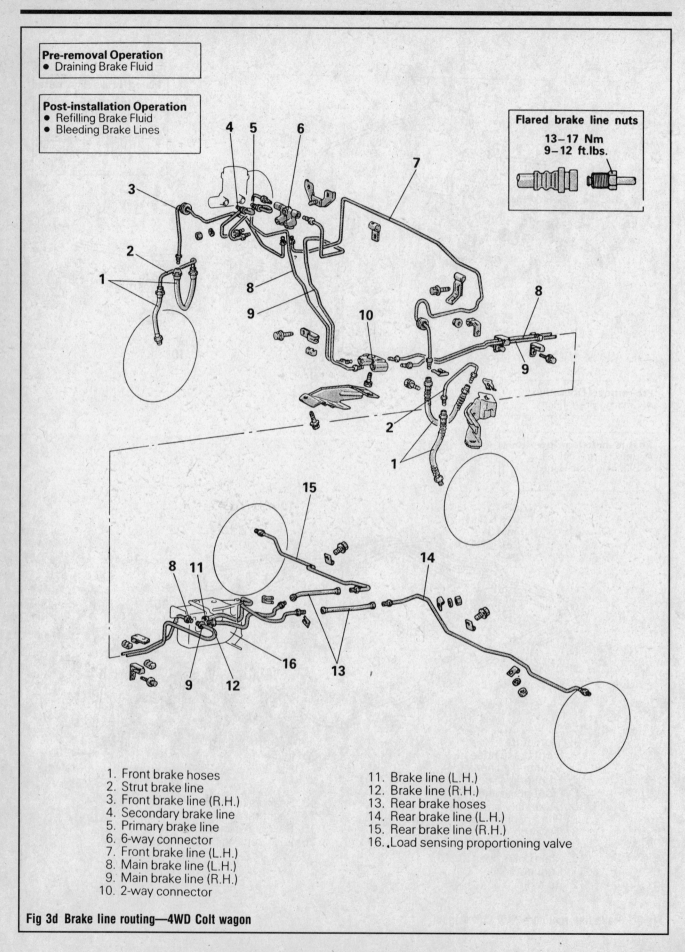

Pre-removal Operation
- Draining Brake Fluid

Post-installation Operation
- Refilling Brake Fluid
- Bleeding Brake Lines

Flared brake line nuts
13—17 Nm
9—12 ft.lbs.

1. Front brake hoses
2. Strut brake line
3. Front brake line (R.H.)
4. Secondary brake line
5. Primary brake line
6. 6-way connector
7. Front brake line (L.H.)
8. Main brake line (L.H.)
9. Main brake line (R.H.)
10. 2-way connector

11. Brake line (L.H.)
12. Brake line (R.H.)
13. Rear brake hoses
14. Rear brake line (L.H.)
15. Rear brake line (R.H.)
16. Load sensing proportioning valve

Fig 3d Brake line routing—4WD Colt wagon

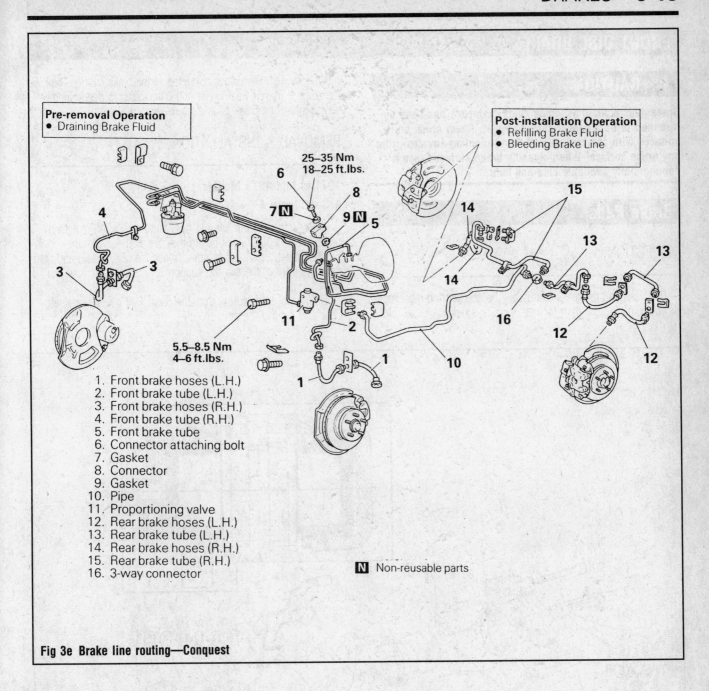

25–35 Nm
18–25 ft.lbs.

5.5–8.5 Nm
4–6 ft.lbs.

1. Front brake hoses (L.H.)
2. Front brake tube (L.H.)
3. Front brake hoses (R.H.)
4. Front brake tube (R.H.)
5. Front brake tube
6. Connector attaching bolt
7. Gasket
8. Connector
9. Gasket
10. Pipe
11. Proportioning valve
12. Rear brake hoses (L.H.)
13. Rear brake tube (L.H.)
14. Rear brake hoses (R.H.)
15. Rear brake tube (R.H.)
16. 3-way connector

N Non-reusable parts

Fig 3e Brake line routing—Conquest

Connect a rubber hose to the bleeder and immerse the other end in a glass container half filled with brake fluid.

3. Have an assistant depress the brake pedal to the floor, and then pause until the fluid flow stops and the bleeder nipple is closed.

4. Allow the pedal to return and repeat the procedure until a steady, bubble-free flow is seen.

5. Tighten the bleeder valve and replace the cap. Move on to the next wheel in sequence.

➡**Frequently check the master cylinder level during this procedure. If the reservoir goes dry, air will enter the system and it will have to be rebled.**

FRONT DISC BRAKES

✳✳ CAUTION

Brake pads contain asbestos fibers. Asbestos has been determined to be a cancer-causing agent. Never clean brake surfaces with compressed air! Avoid inhaling any dust from any brake surface! When cleaning brake surfaces, use a commercially available cleaning fluid.

Brake Pads

INSPECTION

The brake pad thickness can usually be checked (on most models) by removing the front (or rear, models equipped) wheel, and looking through the cutout at the top of the brake caliper. Replace the pads if uneven wear (inner and outer pads) is determined. Always replace the brake pads as a set (both wheels).

REMOVAL & INSTALLATION

1971 to Mid-1973 Models
◗ See Figure 4

Always replace both left and right-hand sets when replacing brake pads. Replace pads before they are worn past 2mm.

1. Loosen the wheel lug nuts, block the rear wheels and then raise the front of the car and support it on stands. Remove the wheels.
2. Pry the cross-spring from the pads. Pull out the retaining clips and remove the pins.

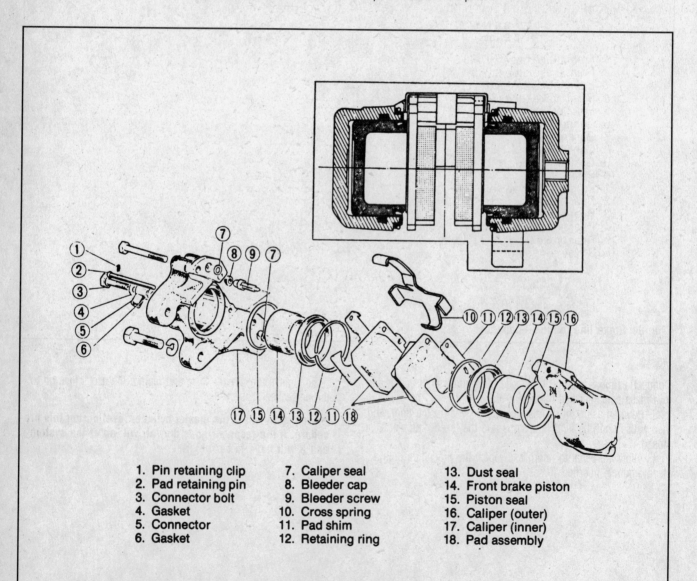

1. Pin retaining clip	7. Caliper seal	13. Dust seal
2. Pad retaining pin	8. Bleeder cap	14. Front brake piston
3. Connector bolt	9. Bleeder screw	15. Piston seal
4. Gasket	10. Cross spring	16. Caliper (outer)
5. Connector	11. Pad shim	17. Caliper (inner)
6. Gasket	12. Retaining ring	18. Pad assembly

Fig 4 Exploded view of the front disc brake pads and caliper—1971–73 models

3. Using a pair of locking pliers, pull the one pad out of the caliper.

4. Siphon off about ½ of the brake fluid in the reservoir. This prevents air overflow when the pistons are pushed back for the new pad.

To install:

5. Push the caliper piston back with a flat piece of metal or smooth hardwood and a large C-clamp. Place the piece of metal or wood against the piston. Position the C-clamp, centered on the wood and over the caliper and push the piston into its bore by tightening the clamp.

6. Insert the new pad along with its shim (arrow on shim pointing forward).

➡**If you have a 1971 or early 1972 Colt and have been experiencing brake squeaking, replace the shims with the newer square type.**

7. Remove the opposite pad and repeat Steps 5 and 6.

8. Install the retaining pins and clips. Install the cross-spring as shown in the illustration.

9. Repeat the above operation on the other wheel.

10. Fill the master cylinder (bleed the system if necessary) and lower the car. Pump the brakes several times. Do not move the car until a firm brake pedal is present.

Mid 1973–83, Rear Wheel Drive
Except Station Wagon and Challenger

1. Follow the preceeding procedure through Step 1.

2. Pry the dust shield off the top of the caliper by lifting the clip in the center of the shield with a screwdriver.

3. Using needlenose pliers, unsnap the M-clip from the brake pad and the two retaining pins.

4. Remove the K-clip from the holes in the retaining pins.

5. Use a small punch or screwdriver to tap the retaining pins out of the caliper.

6. Grip the ears of each brake pad with a pliers and pull it from the caliper. Minimum serviceable thickness for the brake lining on the pad is 2mm. Always replace both sets at the same time.

To install:

7. Using a flat piece of hardwood and C-clamp, push the piston back into the cylinder.

8. Install the pads in the caliper.

9. Insert the retaining pins and install the K and M-clips. Be sure that they are installed properly in the positions from which they were removed. Fill the master cylinder (bleed the system if necessary) and lower the car. Pump the brakes several times. Do not move the car until a firm brake pedal is present.

1973 and Later
▶ See Figure 5

A sliding caliper disc brake is used on station wagons and Challengers.

1. Loosen the wheel lugs, block the rear wheels, raise the front of the car and support on jackstands. Remove the wheels.

2. Remove approximately half of the brake fluid from the master cylinder.

3. Remove the spring pin(s) and pull the stopper plug(s) from the upper end of the caliper.

4. Move the caliper back and forth to loosen, then remove the caliper from the support.

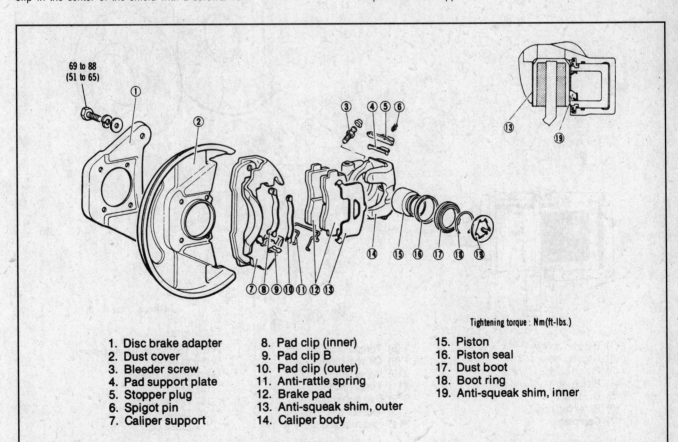

Tightening torque : Nm(ft-lbs.)

1. Disc brake adapter
2. Dust cover
3. Bleeder screw
4. Pad support plate
5. Stopper plug
6. Spigot pin
7. Caliper support
8. Pad clip (inner)
9. Pad clip B
10. Pad clip (outer)
11. Anti-rattle spring
12. Brake pad
13. Anti-squeak shim, outer
14. Caliper body
15. Piston
16. Piston seal
17. Dust boot
18. Boot ring
19. Anti-squeak shim, inner

Fig 5 Exploded view of the front disc brake sliding type caliper

➡**The hydraulic brake hose need not be removed from the caliper, but do not allow the caliper weight to hang from the hose. Secure the caliper with a piece of wire.**

5. Take the time to examine the pad holder with its related clips and springs. All parts must be returned to the same place when reinstalling the old pads or replacing with new pads.

6. Remove the anti-squeak clips then remove the brake pads from the mounting bracket. Do not remove the caliper support springs (two large wire hair pins).

To install:

7. Under each brake pad there is a pad support plate. These are not interchangeable and must be installed correctly.

8. Insert the new pads in the mounting bracket over the pad support plates and install the anti-squeak clips.

9. Seat the caliper piston fully into the caliper bore. Do this by opening the bleeder screw and push the piston in with a hammer handle, or C-clamp. If you meet too much resistance, the piston might be hanging up on a scored bore or have a gaulded piston wall, if so rebuild or replace the caliper.

10. Seat the caliper over the mounting bracket. Clean and apply No. 2 brake grease to the sliding surfaces, plug plates and stopper plug. Install the caliper stopper plug and the spring pin.

11. Fill the master cylinder and bleed the brake system.

12. Install the tire and wheel, lower the car to the ground and road test. Pump the brakes several times. Do not move the car until a firm brake pedal is present.

1979–84 Front Wheel Drive Without Turbo

◆ **See Figure 6**

1. Raise and support the front end on jackstands.
2. Remove the front wheels.
3. Pry off the dust shield from the caliper.
4. Depress the center of the outboard spring clip and remove the clip by slipping the ends from the pins.
5. Remove the inboard spring clip with pliers.
6. Using pliers, pull the retaining pins from the caliper.
7. Lift the pads and anti-squeal shims from the caliper.

To install:

8. Clean all caliper parts, especially the torque plate shafts, with a solvent made for brake parts.

➡**Replace all brake pads at the same time. Never replace the pads on one wheel only!**

9. If the dust protector or spring clips are weak, damaged or deformed, replace them.

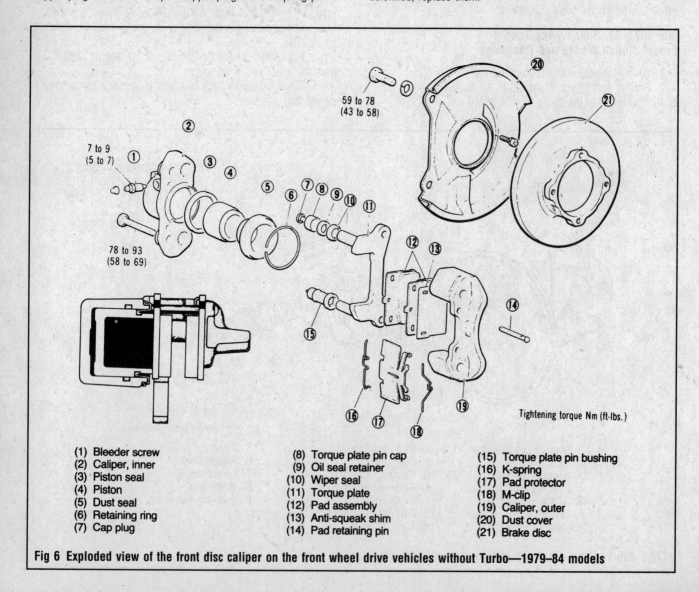

(1) Bleeder screw	(8) Torque plate pin cap	(15) Torque plate pin bushing
(2) Caliper, inner	(9) Oil seal retainer	(16) K-spring
(3) Piston seal	(10) Wiper seal	(17) Pad protector
(4) Piston	(11) Torque plate	(18) M-clip
(5) Dust seal	(12) Pad assembly	(19) Caliper, outer
(6) Retaining ring	(13) Anti-squeak shim	(20) Dust cover
(7) Cap plug	(14) Pad retaining pin	(21) Brake disc

Fig 6 Exploded view of the front disc caliper on the front wheel drive vehicles without Turbo—1979–84 models

10. Remove the cap from the master cylinder reservoir and, using a clean suction gun, remove about ¼ inch of fluid.

11. Using a C-clamp, force the caliper piston back into the caliper as far as it will go.

12. Install the inboard pad and anti-squeal shim.

13. Install the outboard pad and anti-squeal shim.

14. Install the pins.

15. Install the two spring clips.

16. Install the dust shield.

17. Install the wheels and lower the car. Get in the car and depress the brake pedal a few times. The first couple of strokes on the pedal will feel overly long. However, the pads will set themselves and the stroke will return to normal. Pump the brakes several more times. Do not move the car until a firm brake pedal is present.

1985–89 Colt Without Turbo

♦ See Figure 7

1. Raise and support the front end on jackstands. Remove the wheels.

➡ On late models equipped with the PFS15 type front disc brakes; the caliper and pads are retained to the adapter by two sleeve pin bolts. Remove the pin bolts and service the assembly as required. Sleeve pin torque is 16–23 ft. lbs.

2. Remove the lower sleeve bolt from the caliper and rotate the caliper upward.

➡ There is a grease coating on the bolt. Make sure that it is not removed or contaminated.

3. Support the caliper by suspending it with wire or string from a nearby suspension member.

4. Remove the inner, then outer shims from the caliper.

5. Lift out the brake pads.

6. Remove the pad liners.

7. Clean all parts in solvent made for brake parts.

To install:

8. Inspect the dust boot on the caliper piston. If it is torn or brittle, replace it, and consider rebuilding the caliper.

9. Inspect the shims and liners and replace them if damaged.

✳✳ WARNING

Clean, high quality brake fluid is essential to the safe and proper operation of the brake system. You should always buy the highest quality brake fluid that is available. If the brake fluid becomes contaminated, drain and flush the system, then refill the master cylinder with new fluid. Never reuse any brake fluid. Any brake fluid that is removed from the system should be discarded.

10. Remove the cap from the master cylinder reservoir and siphon off about ¼ inch of fluid.

11. Using a C-clamp, force the piston back into the caliper as far as it will go. Remove the clamp.

12. Install the liners, pads and inner, then outer shims.

➡ Never replace just one set of pads, pads should be replaced on both front wheels at the same time.

13. Lower the caliper and install the lower sleeve bolt. Torque the bolt to 16–23 ft. lbs.

14. Start the engine and depress the brake pedal several times. Hold it depressed for about 5 seconds. Turn the engine off.

15. Rotate the brake rotor a few times. Using a spring scale hooked to one of the lugs, measure the brake drag. Remove the pads and perform the spring scale test again. The difference between the drag test with and without the pads should not exceed

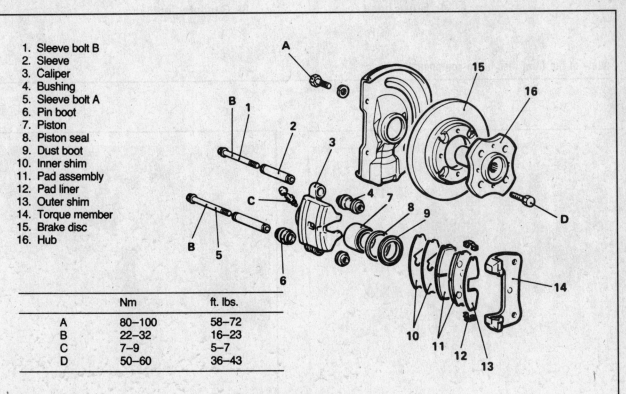

1. Sleeve bolt B
2. Sleeve
3. Caliper
4. Bushing
5. Sleeve bolt A
6. Pin boot
7. Piston
8. Piston seal
9. Dust boot
10. Inner shim
11. Pad assembly
12. Pad liner
13. Outer shim
14. Torque member
15. Brake disc
16. Hub

	Nm	ft. lbs.
A	80–100	58–72
B	22–32	16–23
C	7–9	5–7
D	50–60	36–43

Fig 7 Exploded view of the front disc caliper on 1985 Colts without Turbo

1. Brake rotor
2. Caliper
3. Brake pad
4. Brake hose
5. Backing plate
6. Stud
7. Cotter pin
8. Castlated nut

View of the front disc brake components

Loosen the lower sleeve bolt from the caliper . . .

. . . and remove

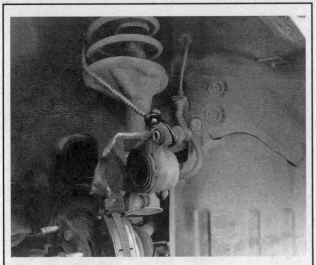

Rotate the caliper upwards and suspend

Use a C-clamp to force the piston back into the caliper

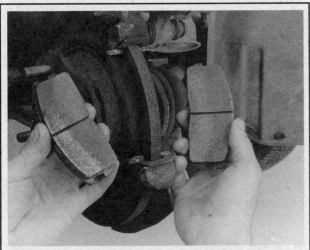

Remove the pad clips and slide the pads off the mounting bracket

Remove and inspect all retainer clips

15 lbs. If the difference does exceed 15 lbs., the caliper will have to be rebuilt or replaced. Service if required. When servicing is complete, pump the brakes several times. Do not move the car until a firm brake pedal is present.

1984–89 Colt Turbo 1985–89 Vista
◆ **See Figure 8**

1. Raise and support the front end on jackstands. Remove the front wheels.

➡ **On late models equipped with the PFS15 type front disc brakes; the caliper and pads are retained to the adapter by two sleeve pin bolts. Remove the pin bolts and service the assembly as required. Sleeve bolt torque is 16–23 ft. lbs.**

2. Remove the lower pin bolt and rotate the caliper upwards. Support the caliper with wire or string from a nearby suspension member.
3. Remove the inner shim, the anti-squeal shim and the pads from the caliper support assembly.
4. Remove the clips from the pads.
5. Clean all parts in solvent made for brake parts.
   To install:
6. Inspect the dust boot on the caliper piston. If it is torn or brittle, replace it, and consider rebuilding the caliper.
7. Inspect the shims and liners and replace them if damaged.
8. Remove the cap from the master cylinder reservoir and siphon off about ¼ inch of fluid.
9. Using tool MB990520, force the piston back into the caliper as far as it will go. Remove the clamp.
10. Install the pads with clips attached and the proper shims, in position, on the support.

➡ **Never replace just one set of pads. Pads should be replaced on both front wheels at the same time.**

11. Lower the caliper and install the lower pin bolt. Torque the bolt to 16–23 ft. lbs.
12. Start the engine and depress the brake pedal. Hold it depressed for about 5 seconds. Turn the engine off.

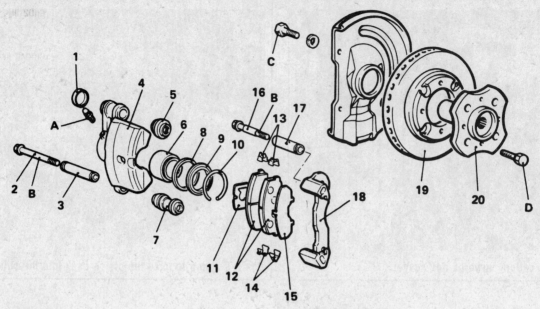

1. Lid
2. Lock pin
3. Sleeve
4. Caliper body
5. Guide pin boot
6. Piston
7. Lock pin boot
8. Piston seal
9. Piston boot
10. Boot ring
11. Inner shim
12. Pad assembly
13. Pad clip B
14. Pad clip C

15. Anti-squeak shim
16. Guide pin
17. Sleeve
18. Support mounting
19. Brake disc
20. Hub

	Nm	ft. lbs.
A	7–9	5–7
B	22–32	16–23
C	80–100	58–72
D	50–60	36–43

Fig 8 Exploded view of the front disc brake pads and caliper—Colt Turbo and Vista models

13. Rotate the brake rotor a few times. Using a spring scale hooked to one of the lugs, measure the brake drag. Remove the pads and perform the spring scale test again. The difference between the drag test with and without the pads should not exceed 15 lbs. If the difference does exceed 15 lbs., the caliper will have to be rebuilt or replaced.

14. When servicing is complete, pump the brakes several times, do not operate the vehicle until a firm brake pedal is present. Bleed the brakes if necessary.

Conquest

⟐ **See Figures 9 and 9A**

1. Raise and support the front end on jackstands.
2. Remove the front wheels.
3. Remove the caliper lower slide pin.

➡**There is a grease coating on the bolt. Make sure that it is not removed or contaminated.**

4. Rotate the caliper upward and suspend it with string from a nearby suspension member.
5. Remove the brake pads and shims.
6. Remove the clips from the pads.
7. Clean all parts in solvent made for brake parts.

To install:

8. Inspect the dust boot on the caliper piston. If it is torn or brittle, replace it, and consider rebuilding the caliper.

9. Inspect the shims and liners and replace them if damaged.

10. Remove the cap from the master cylinder reservoir and siphon off about ¼ inch of fluid.

11. Using tool MB990520, force the piston back into the caliper as far as it will go. Remove the clamp.

12. Install the pads with clips attached and the proper shims, in position, on the support.

➡**Never replace just one set of pads, pads should be replaced on both front wheels at the same time.**

13. Rotate the caliper back into position and install the lower slider pin. Torque the pin to 70 ft. lbs.

14. Start the engine and depress the brake pedal. Hold it depressed for about 5 seconds. Turn the engine **OFF**.

15. Rotate the brake rotor a few times. Using a spring scale hooked to one of the studs, measure the brake drag. Remove the pads and perform the spring scale test again. The difference between the drag test with and without the pads should not exceed 15 lbs. If the difference does exceed 15 lbs., the caliper will have to be rebuilt or replaced.

16. When servicing is complete, pump the brakes several

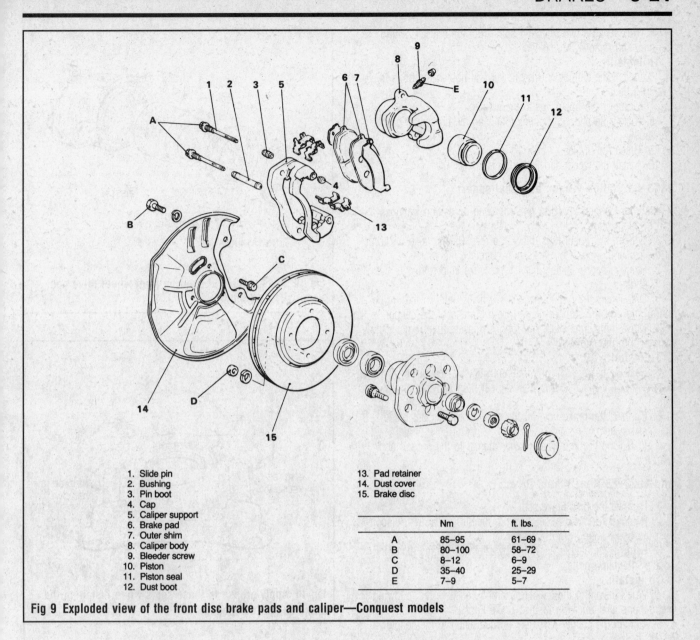

1. Slide pin
2. Bushing
3. Pin boot
4. Cap
5. Caliper support
6. Brake pad
7. Outer shim
8. Caliper body
9. Bleeder screw
10. Piston
11. Piston seal
12. Dust boot

13. Pad retainer
14. Dust cover
15. Brake disc

	Nm	ft. lbs.
A	85–95	61–69
B	80–100	58–72
C	8–12	6–9
D	35–40	25–29
E	7–9	5–7

Fig 9 Exploded view of the front disc brake pads and caliper—Conquest models

Fig 9a With a spring scale attached to a stud, measure the brake drag

times, do not operate the vehicle until a firm brake pedal is present. Bleed the brakes if necessary.

Brake Caliper

REMOVAL & INSTALLATION

1971 to Mid-1973 Models

1. Block the rear wheel, loosen the wheel lugs and raise front of the car. Support safely on jackstands and remove the wheel.

2. Disconnect the brake line from the brake hose. Remove the union bolt of the flexible hose which is connected to caliper.

3. Remove the cross-spring. Remove the clips and the retaining pins.

4. Using a pair of locking pliers, remove both brake pads and shims. Mark them left and right, if they are being reused.

5. Unscrew the two retaining bolts from the bracket behind the disc and remove the caliper.

To install:

6. Install the caliper on the bracket and tighten the bolts to 29–36 ft. lbs.

7. Connect the brake line to the caliper.

8. Install the pads and shims following the procedure given previously.

9. Bleed the brakes.

10. Install the wheel and lower the car.

1973–83 Station Wagon and Challenger

A sliding caliper type disc brake is used on station wagons and Challengers.

1. Loosen the wheel lugs, block the rear wheels, raise the front of the car and support on jackstands. Remove the wheels.

2. Remove approximately half of the brake fluid from the master cylinder.

3. Disconnect the brake line at the caliper. Remove the spring pin(s) and pull the stopper plug(s) from the end of the caliper.

4. Move the caliper back and forth to loosen, then remove the caliper from the support.

To install:

5. Seat the caliper over the mounting bracket (caliper piston seated in bore). Install the caliper stopper plug and the spring pin.

6. Connect the brake line, fill the master cylinder and bleed the brake system.

7. Install the tire and wheel, lower the car to the ground and road test.

Mid-1973–83 Rear Wheel Drive

1. Remove the disc brake pad.

2. Remove the brake hose clip from the strut area, then disconnect the brake hose from the caliper.

3. Remove the caliper assembly by removing torque plate and adapter mounting bolts.

To install:

4. When installing the caliper assembly, observe the following instructions after referring to Disc Brake Pads.

5. Tighten the caliper assembly (torque plate) to the adapter to 51–66 ft. lbs.

6. After tightening the brake hose to 9–12 ft. lbs., bleed the brake hydraulic system.

➡**Since the wheel cylinder uses a large piston, even the presence of a small amount of air, will have a great effect on the brake pedal stroke. Bleeding, therefore, should be performed carefully and thoroughly.**

1979–84 Front Wheel Drive Without Turbo

▶ **See Figures 10, 11 and 12**

1. Remove the brake pads.

2. Remove the brake hose from the clip on the strut.

3. Disconnect the hose from the caliper.

4. Remove the torque plate and adapter housing bolts and lift off the caliper.

To install:

5. Install the caliper and install the torque plate/adapter mounting bolts. Torque the bolts to 43–58 ft. lbs. Connect the brake hose and install the brake pads. Bleed the system and road test the car.

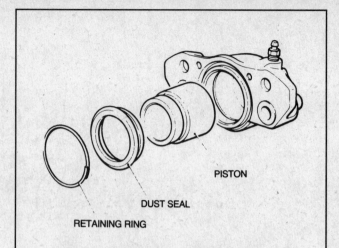

Fig 10 Piston and seal used on front wheel drive non Turbo 1979–84 models

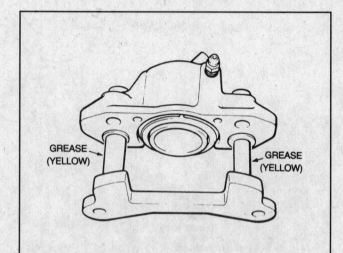

Fig 11 Apply grease to these spots when installing the brake caliper components

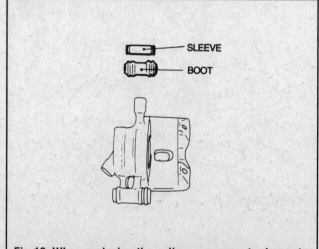

Fig 12 When replacing the caliper components, inspect any seals and bushings/boots for deterioration

1984–89 Colt Turbo, 1985–89 Colt Without Turbo and Vista

1. Disconnect the brake hose from the clip at the strut.
2. Remove the pads.

➡ **On late models equipped with the PFS15 type front disc brakes; the caliper and pads are retained to the adapter by two sleeve pin bolts. Remove the pin bolts and service the assembly as required. Sleeve bolt torque is 16–23 ft. lbs.**

3. Remove the upper pin bolt.
4. Lift off the caliper.
5. Clean all parts thoroughly.
6. Place the caliper into position and install the pin bolt. Torque the pin bolts to 16–23 ft. lbs. Bleed the system. Road test the car.

Conquest

1. Remove the front pads, as described above.
2. Remove the slider pin(s).
3. Loosen the brake hose at the caliper.
4. Lift off the caliper and unscrew the hose.
5. Install the caliper and brake pads. Connect the brake hose. Torque the pins to 70 ft. lbs. Check the brake dragging force as described under Pad Removal and Installation.

OVERHAUL

1971-Mid-1973 Models

◆ **See Figures 13 and 14**

1. Remove the caliper as previously outlined. Remove the retaining ring and seal from the outer piston.
2. While holding the piston with a piece of hardwood, apply air pressure through the brake line fitting and force the outer piston from the caliper.

✳✳ CAUTION

If the piston on the other side isn't held, both pistons could pop out simultaneously, causing possible injury.

3. Remove the inner piston by inserting a drift through the union bolt opening and tapping it out.
4. Remove the piston seals, being careful not to damage the cylinder seal grooves.
5. Clean all the removed parts in brake fluid.
6. Replace worn, damaged, or corroded cylinders and pistons.
7. Replace rubber parts as a matter of course during caliper disassembly.
8. Apply silicone grease to the surfaces of the piston seal and the inner side of the dust seal.
9. Lubricate the cylinder walls and the outer side of the piston, insert the piston into the cylinder without twisting it. Install the dust seal and the retaining ring.
10. Repeat the assembly operation for the second piston. Install the caliper as previously outlined.

Mid 1973–83 Rear Wheel Drive Except Wagon and Challenger

1. Loosen and remove the caliper half retaining bolt.

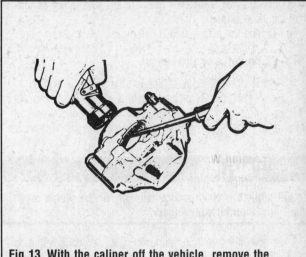

Fig 13 With the caliper off the vehicle, remove the retaining ring and seal

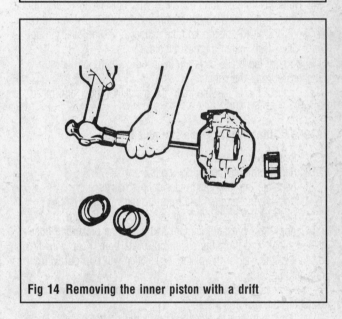

Fig 14 Removing the inner piston with a drift

2. Separate the two caliper halves.
3. Remove the dust seal, and then remove the piston by applying compressed air to the hose fitting.

✳✳ CAUTION

Be careful that the piston doesn't fly out and cause injury.

4. Carefully remove the piston seal, so as not to damage the cylinder.
5. Clean all parts in denatured alcohol.
6. Inspect the piston and cylinder for scoring or corrosion. Replace any defective parts.
7. Assemble the caliper using the new parts supplied in the rebuilding kit.
8. Apply brake fluid to the piston before assembly. Insert the piston seal into the piston carefully so that the seal isn't twisted.
9. Whenever the torque plate has been removed from the inner caliper half, it is necessary to clean the torque plate shaft and the shaft bore of the caliper and apply brake assembly grease to

the rubber bushing, wiper seal inner surface, and torque plate shaft before assembly.

10. Tighten the caliper bridge bolts to 58–59 ft. lbs.

1973–83 Wagon and Challenger

1. Remove the caliper as outlined in the following section.
2. Remove the caliper piston dust boot. Cover the piston with a rag and piece of hardwood. While holding the wood, inject air pressure into the brake hose fitting and force the piston from the caliper.

※※ CAUTION

Do not apply the air pressure suddenly or the piston may shoot out, injuring your fingers.

3. Remove the seal from the piston. Clean all parts with alcohol or brake fluid. Inspect the piston for scoring, replace if necessary.
4. Hone the caliper bore and clean with brake fluid or alcohol.
5. Install a new seal on the piston, lubricate the piston and caliper bore. Install the piston into the caliper bore and seat the bottom of its travel. Install the dust shield.
6. Be sure the brake pads are installed correctly on the support and reinstall the caliper.
7. Connect the brake line, refill the master cylinder and bleed the brake system.

1979–84 Front Wheel Drive Without Turbo

1. Remove the caliper.
2. Remove the caliper bridge bolts.
3. Separate the inner and outer caliper halves.
4. Remove the torque plate from the inner caliper half.
5. Remove the dust seal from the piston and discard it.
6. Apply low pressure compressed air to the brake line hose in the caliper, and force the piston out of its bore. Keep your fingers out of the way of the piston, as it often will pop out with considerable force.
7. Remove the seal from the piston, being careful to avoid scratching the piston surface.
8. Clean all parts in alcohol. Discard all rubber parts.
9. Replace the piston if it appears worn, damaged or pitted.
10. Using a rebuilding kit, replace all worn and rubber parts. Most kits for these brakes contain two types of grease. One type is colored red; the other, yellow. The yellow grease is applied to the torque plate shafts. The red grease goes on the piston seal. If this type of kit is not available, use rubber grease on the seal and silicone grease on the shafts.
11. Assemble the caliper. Don't forget to grease the seal and shafts. Torque the bridge bolts to 58–69 ft. lbs.

1985–89 Models and 1984–89 Colt Turbo

1. Remove the caliper assembly from the car.
2. Remove the pads.
3. Remove and discard the piston dust boot.
4. Apply low pressure compressed air to the brake line hose in the caliper, and force the piston out of its bore. Keep your fingers out of the way of the piston, as it often will pop out with considerable force.
5. Remove the seal from the piston, being careful to avoid scratching the piston surface.

6. Clean all parts in alcohol. Discard all rubber parts.
7. Replace the piston if it appears worn, damaged or pitted. Replace all rubber parts.
8. Coat the piston and bore with clean brake fluid.
9. Coat the piston seal with rubber grease. Install it on the piston.
10. Insert the piston into the bore, being careful to avoid twisting the seal.
11. Apply silicone grease to the new dust boot and install it.
12. Install the caliper and brake pads. Coat the pin bolt threads with clean brake fluid on Colt without a turbocharger; RTV silicone sealant on Colt Turbo and Vista.

Wheel Bearings/Disc Rotor

REMOVAL & INSTALLATION

Rear Wheel Drive

▶ **See Figures 15 and 16**

1. Remove the caliper (pin type) or the caliper and support (sliding type).

➡ **On the sliding type calipers, remove the caliper and support as a unit by unfastening the bolts holding it to the adapter (backing plate). Support the caliper with wire, do not allow the weight to be supported by the brake hose.**

2. Pry off the dust cap. Tap out and discard the cotter pin. Remove the locknut.
3. Being careful not to drop the outer bearing, pull off the brake disc and wheel hub.
4. Remove the grease inside the wheel hub.
5. Using a brass drift, carefully drive the outer bearing race out of the hub.
6. Remove the inner bearing seal and bearing.
7. Check the bearings for wear or damage and replace them if necessary.
8. Coat the inner surface of the hub with grease.
9. Grease the outer surface of the bearing race and drift it into place in the hub.
10. Pack the inner and outer wheel bearings with grease (see Repacking).

➡ **If the brake disc has been removed and/or replaced, tighten the retaining bolts to 25–29 ft. lbs.**

11. Install the inner bearing in the hub. Being careful not to distort it, install the oil seal with its lip facing the bearing. Drive the seal on until its outer edge is even with the edge of the hub.
12. Install the hub/disc assembly on the spindle, being careful not to damage the oil seal.
13. Install the outer bearing, washer, and spindle nut. Adjust the bearing as follows.

ADJUSTMENT

1. Tighten the spindle nut to 15 ft. lbs. and then loosen it.
2. Tighten the nut to 4 ft. lbs.
3. Install the cap on the nut. Insert and bend the cotter pin. Do

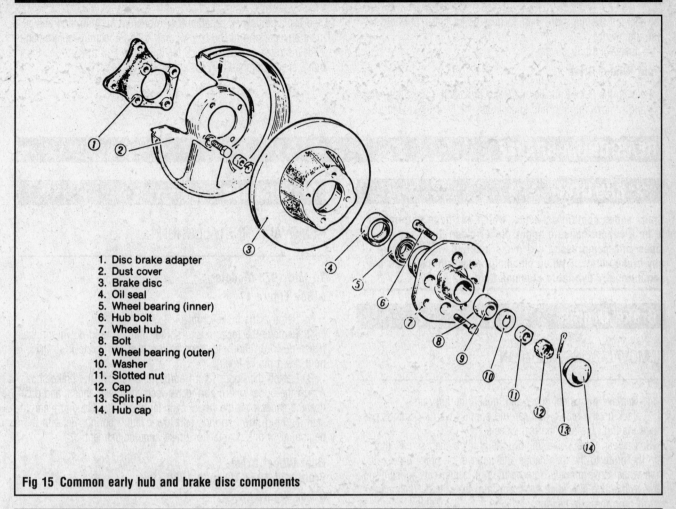

1. Disc brake adapter
2. Dust cover
3. Brake disc
4. Oil seal
5. Wheel bearing (inner)
6. Hub bolt
7. Wheel hub
8. Bolt
9. Wheel bearing (outer)
10. Washer
11. Slotted nut
12. Cap
13. Split pin
14. Hub cap

Fig 15 Common early hub and brake disc components

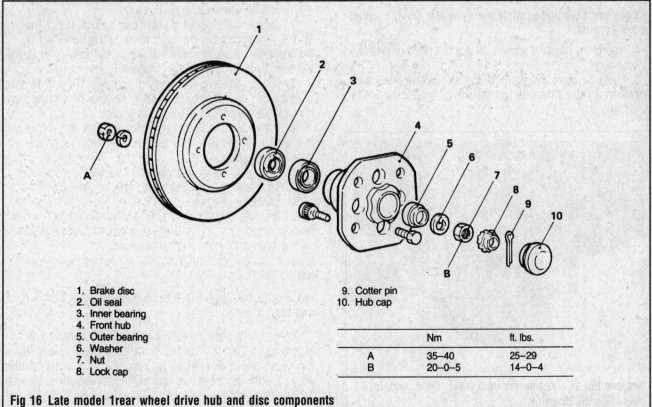

1. Brake disc
2. Oil seal
3. Inner bearing
4. Front hub
5. Outer bearing
6. Washer
7. Nut
8. Lock cap

9. Cotter pin
10. Hub cap

	Nm	ft. lbs.
A	35–40	25–29
B	20–0–5	14–0–4

Fig 16 Late model 1rear wheel drive hub and disc components

not back off the nut more than 15 degrees for cotter pin hold-to-slot alignment.

4. Install the hub cover.

Front Wheel Drive

Refer to the Hub, Knuckle and Rotor procedure (preceding chapter) and remove the hub and knuckle assembly. This procedure also explains how to separate the rotor from the hub, and adjustment and packing of the bearings as well as bearing replacement. With the rotor removed, check for thickness and runout. See the brake specifications chart for appropriate values.

REAR DRUM BRAKES

✳✳ CAUTION

Brake shoes contain asbestos, which has been determined to be a cancer causing agent. Never clean the brake surfaces with compressed air! Avoid inhaling any dust from any brake surface! When cleaning brake surfaces, use a commercially available cleaning fluid.

Brake Drums

REMOVAL & INSTALLATION

1. Remove the wheel cover and loosen the lug nuts.
2. Jack up the rear of the car and support with jackstands. Remove the lug nuts and the rear wheels.
3. On rear wheel drive, remove the phillips head screws that retain the drum to the axle flange and remove the brake drum. On front wheel drive models, remove the hub center cap, loosen and remove the axle nut, slide the drum from the spindle (take care not to drop the axle bearing).

➡**If you meet resistance while removing the drum, back off on the adjuster.**

4. Inspect the drum for grooves, have it machined or replaced as necessary.
5. Install the drum and adjust the brakes. On front wheel drive models repack the wheel bearings (refer to the bearing section in this chapter).

Remove the axle nut on the front wheel drive models, then slide the drum off

Brake Shoes

REMOVAL & INSTALLATION

To Mid-1973 Models

➧ **See Figure 17**

1. Remove the brake drum.
2. Remove the lower return spring and the hold-down springs. (Push down on the hold-down spring seat and rotate it so the hold-down pin is freed).
3. Detach the upper return spring and remove the brake shoes. Attach the upper return spring between the brake shoes, and position the shoes over the wheel cylinder and to the backing plate. Install the hold-down springs and lower return spring. Refer to the beginning of this chapter for brake shoe adjustment.

Rear Wheel Drive
From Mid-1973 Through 1980

➧ **See Figure 18**

1. Remove wheel and brake drum.
2. Remove the brake shoe hold-down springs. Detach the strut-to-shoe spring and the upper return spring from the rear (trailing) brake shoe. Remove the brake shoes (both) as an assembly, with the lower return spring attached.
3. Pull the adjusting lever toward the center of the brake shoe while holding the adjusting latch down. Remove the adjuster from the shoe. Remove the strut and return springs.
4. The wheel cylinder can be removed at this time for service or replacement. The parking brake lever and strut may be removed, if necessary.
5. Clean the backing plate with a wire brush to remove dirt. Reinstall the parking brake lever and strut, if removed. Install the wheel cylinder, if removed.
6. Lubricate the contact surfaces on the backing plate, wheel cylinder piston ends, anchor plate shoe contact surfaces and the parking brake strut joints and contact surfaces.
7. Install the adjusting lever and latch spring assembly on the leading (front) shoe.

➡**The adjusting lever and latch spring are different for right and left.**

8. Install the brake shoes in position on the backing plate with the hold-down springs. Install the top shoe-to-shoe spring. Make sure the top web (metal) is in the slot of the wheel cylinder piston and the bottom web is against the anchor block of the backing plate with the lower return spring installed.
9. Set the amount of engagement of the adjusting lever with

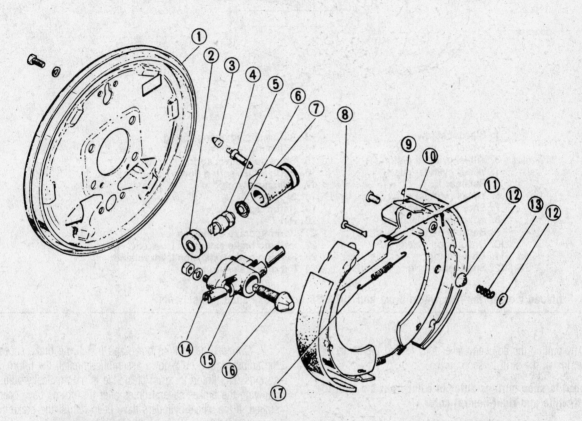

1. Backing plate
2. Wheel cylinder boot
3. Bleeder screw cap
4. Bleeder screw
5. Wheel cylinder piston
6. Piston cup
7. Wheel cylinder body
8. Shoe hold-down spring pin
9. Brake shoe ass'y
10. Brake lining
11. Parking brake extension lever
12. Shoe hold-down spring seat
13. Shoe hold-down spring
14. Slack adjuster anchor
15. Slack adjuster body
16. Slack adjuster
17. Shoe return spring

Fig 17 Exploded view of the 1971—mid 73 rear brake shoe components

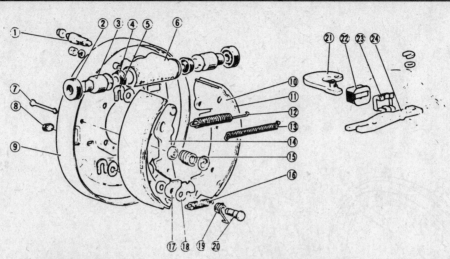

1. Bleeder screw
2. Wheel cylinder boot
3. Wheel cylinder piston
4. Wheel cylinder cup
5. Retainer
6. Wheel cylinder body
7. Shoe hold-down pin
8. Adjusting wheel cover
9. Backing plate
10. Brake shoe assembly
11. Brake lining
12. Shoe return spring (upper)
13. Automatic adjusting spring
14. Adjusting lever
15. Shoe hold-down spring
16. Shoe return spring (lower)
17. Adjusting latch
18. Stopper
19. Return spring
20. Pin
21. Parking brake extension lever
22. Parking brake extension lever cup
23. Parking brake extension lever retainer
24. Parking brake strut

Fig 18 Exploded view of the rear wheel drive mid 1973–80 rear brake shoe components

the strut by pulling the adjusting lever fully toward the center of the brake. Install the strut to shoe spring.

➡**The strut to shoe springs differ in color from the side-to-side; left-white and right-neutral color.**

10. Return the adjusting lever until it touches the shoe rim.
11. Install the brake drums. The lining to drum clearance is automatically adjusted by applying the brakes several times; however, if the wheel cylinders have been serviced the brake system will have to be bled before proper adjustment is possible.
12. Adjust the parking brake stroke. Road test the car.

1981 and Later Rear Wheel Drive

1. Raise the back of the car and support on jackstands.
2. Remove the wheel. Make sure the front wheels are blocked securely, release the parking brake and remove the brake drum.

➡**The brake drum is retained by two small bolts.**

3. Disconnect the shoe-to-shoe spring and the strut-to-shoe spring. Disconnect the shoe return spring and remove the brake hold-down assemblies.
4. Disconnect the parking brake cable from the parking brake lever and remove the rear brake shoe.
5. Remove the front brake shoe. Transfer the levers and adjusters to the new brake shoes using new U-shaped locks.
6. Prior to assembly, apply No. 2 brake grease to the contact area of the strut and parking brake lever and strut and adjusting lever. After cleaning the backing plate apply grease to the brake shoe contact points.

7. Connect the parking brake and install the brake shoes with the adjusters and hold-down assemblies. Install the return springs. The lining to drum clearance is automatically adjusted by applying the brakes several times after the drums have been installed. If the wheel cylinders have been rebuilt the brake system must be bled before correct adjustment is possible.

1979–89 Front Wheel Drive Colt

◗ **See Figure 19**

1. Remove rear wheel and brake drum.
2. Remove the lower pressed metal spring clip, the shoe return spring (the large one piece spring between the two shoes), and the two shoe hold-down springs.
3. Remove the shoes and adjuster as an assembly. Disconnect the parking brake cable from the lever, remove the spring between the shoes and the lever from the rear (trailing) shoe. Disconnect the adjuster retaining spring and remove the adjuster, turn the star wheel in to the adjuster body after cleaning and lubricating the threads.
4. The wheel cylinder may be removed for service or replacement, if necessary.
5. Clean the backing plate. Install the wheel cylinder if it was removed. Lubricate all contact points on the backing plate, anchor plate, wheel cylinder to shoe contact and parking brake strut joints and contacts. Install the brake shoes after attaching the parking brake, lever and adjuster assemblies. Install the hold-down and return springs.
6. Pre-adjustment of the brake shoe can be made by turning the adjuster star wheel out until the drum will just slide on over

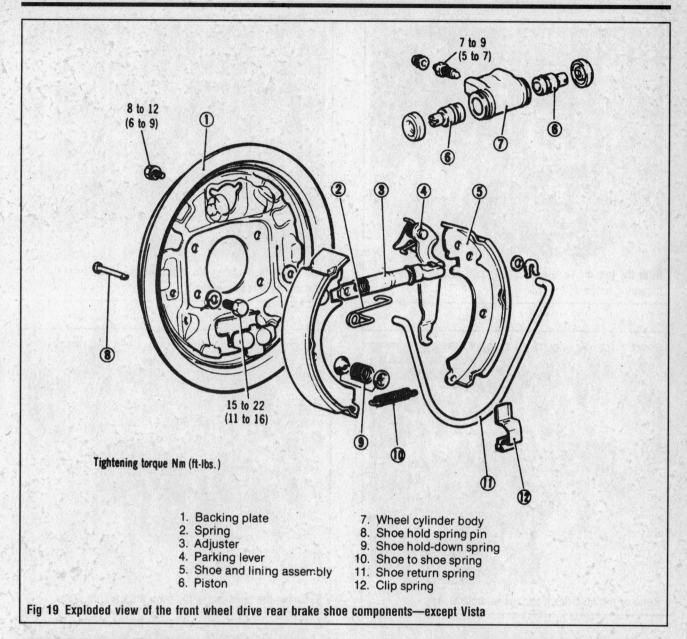

8 to 12
(6 to 9)

7 to 9
(5 to 7)

15 to 22
(11 to 16)

Tightening torque Nm (ft-lbs.)

1. Backing plate
2. Spring
3. Adjuster
4. Parking lever
5. Shoe and lining assembly
6. Piston
7. Wheel cylinder body
8. Shoe hold spring pin
9. Shoe hold-down spring
10. Shoe to shoe spring
11. Shoe return spring
12. Clip spring

Fig 19 Exploded view of the front wheel drive rear brake shoe components—except Vista

Remove the lower pressed metal spring . . .

. . . and the large shoe return spring

After the tension is released, it should pull out of the mounting holes with ease

The hold-down spring pin should be removed from the rear of the backing plate

Release the hold-down springs on both sides . . .

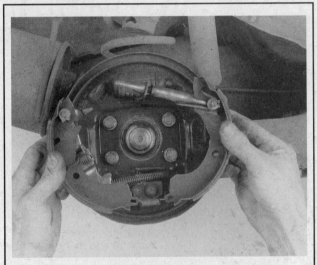

Separate the shoe assembly from the backing plate

. . . then remove the springs and washers

Unhook the two shoes . . .

. . . then disconnect the parking brake cable

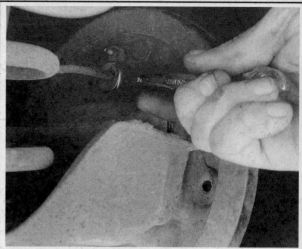

If the wheel cylinder needs replacement, disconnect the brake line behind the cylinder

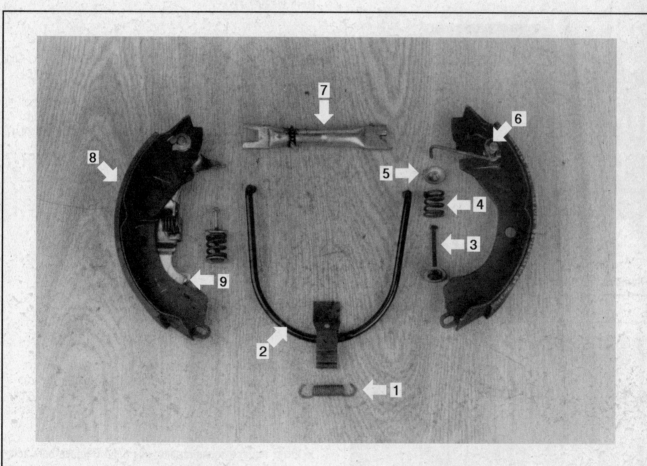

1. Shoe-to-shoe spring
2. Shoe return spring
3. Hold-down pin
4. Hold-down spring
5. Hold-down washer
6. C-clip
7. Adjuster
8. Brake shoe
9. Parking lever

View of the rear drum brake components

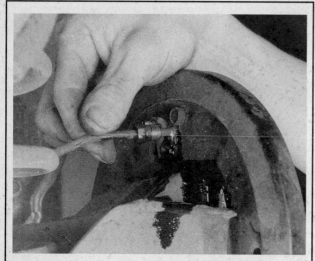
Some fluid will leak out of the line once separated

Remove the two mounting nuts or bolts . . .

. . . then from the front, remove the wheel cylinder

Attach a hose and clear bottle filled with brake fluid to the bleeder port

the brake shoes. Before installing the drum make sure the parking brake is not adjusted too tightly, if it is—loosen, or the adjustment of the rear brakes will not be correct.

7. If the wheel cylinders were serviced, bleed the brake system. The brake shoes are then adjusted by pumping the brake pedal and applying and releasing the parking brake. Adjust the parking brake stroke. Road test the car.

1985–89 Vista

♦ **See Figure 20**

1. Raise and support the rear on jackstands.
2. Remove the wheels.
3. Remove the brake drums.
4. Remove the shoe-to-strut spring.
5. Remove the shoe-to-shoe spring.
6. Remove the shoe hold-down spring.
7. Remove the shoe retainer clip.
8. Remove the leading shoe.
9. Remove the brake cable from the lever.
10. Remove the trailing shoe.
11. Remove the brake cable snapring and remove the cable.
12. Inspect all parts for wear or damage. Heat damage is a problem common to brake systems. Sign of heat damage are bluing and cracking. It's a good idea, when replacing brake shoes, to replace all the brake hardware, i.e., springs and clips.

➡**Never replace shoes on one side only! Replace both sets of shoes at the same time.**

13. Assemble the parking brake and adjuster assemblies on the brake shoes. Install the brake shoes and hold-downs. Connect the return springs. Apply a small amount of lithium based grease to the contact pads of the backing plate before installing the shoes. When installing the shoe-to-shoe spring and shoe-to-strut spring, set the adjuster lever all the way back against the shoe. When everything is assembled, pump the pedal several times and adjust the brakes.

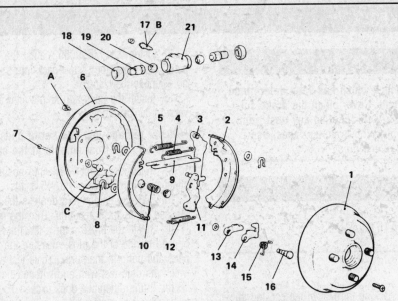

1. Brake drum
2. Shoe lining assembly
3. Parking brake lever
4. Shoe-to-strut spring
5. Shoe-to-shoe spring
6. Backing plate
7. Shoe hold-down pin
8. Retainer
9. Strut
10. Shoe hold-down spring
11. Adjuster lever
12. Shoe retainer spring
13. Latch
14. Stopper

15. Auto adjuster latch spring
16. Pin
17. Bleeder screw
18. Wheel cylinder boot
19. Wheel cylinder piston
20. Piston cup
21. Wheel cylinder body

	Nm	ft. lbs.
A	8–12	6–9
B	7–9	5–7
C	50–60	36–43

Fig 20 Exploded view of the front wheel drive rear brake shoe components—Vista

Wheel Cylinders

OVERHAUL

Since the piston travel in the wheel cylinder changes when new brake shoes are installed, it is possible for previously good wheel cylinders to start leaking after new brakes are installed. Therefore, to save yourself the expense of having to replace new brakes that become saturated with brake fluid and the aggravation of having to take everything apart again, it is strongly recommended that wheel cylinders be rebuilt every time new brake shoes are installed. This is especially true for cars with high mileage.

➡**Most wheel cylinders can be rebuilt while mounted in position on the brake backing plate. However, if the cylinder must be removed, disconnect the brake line and unbolt the cylinder after the brake shoes have been removed.**

1. Remove the brake shoes.
2. Place a bucket or some old newspapers under the brake backing plate to catch the brake fluid that will run out of the wheel cylinder. Disconnect the brake line and remove the cylinder mounting bolts. Remove the cylinder from the backing plate.
3. Remove the boots from the ends of the wheel cylinder.
4. Push one piston toward the center of the cylinder to force the opposite piston and cup out the other end of the cylinder.

Reach in the open end of the cylinder and push the spring, cup, and piston out of the cylinder.
5. Remove the bleeder screw from the rear of the cylinder.
6. Inspect the inside of the wheel cylinder. If it is scored in any way, the cylinder must be honed with a wheel cylinder hone or fine emery paper, and finished with crocus cloth if emery paper is used. If the inside of the cylinder is excessively worn, the cylinder will have to be replaced, as only 0.08mm of material can be removed from the cylinder walls. Whenever honing or cleaning wheel cylinders, keep a small amount of brake fluid in the cylinder to serve as a lubricant.
7. Clean any foreign matter from the pistons. The sides of the pistons must be smooth for the wheel cylinders to operate properly.
8. Clean the cylinder bore with alcohol and a lint-free rag. Pull the rag through the bore several times to remove all foreign matter and dry the cylinder.
9. Install the bleeder screw and the return spring in the cylinder.
10. Coat new cylinder cups with new brake fluid and install them in the cylinder. Make sure they are square in the bore or they will leak.
11. Install the pistons in the cylinder after coating them with new brake fluid.
12. Coat the insides of the boots with new brake fluid and install them on the cylinder. Reinstall the wheel cylinder. Install and bleed the brakes.

REAR DISC BRAKES

✳✳ CAUTION

Brake shoes contain asbestos, which has been determined to be a cancer causing agent. Never clean the brake surfaces with compressed air! Avoid inhaling any dust from any brake surface! When cleaning brake surfaces, use a commercially available cleaning fluid.

Brake Pads

REMOVAL & INSTALLATION

Challenger

1. Block the front wheels, jack up the rear of the car and support on jackstands. Remove the rear wheel and the caliper dust cover.
2. Disconnect the parking brake cable.
3. Remove the spring pin and stopper plug.
4. Move the caliper back and forth to loosen, then remove the caliper from the support.

➡**The brake hose need not be disconnected; however, do not suspend the weight of the caliper from the hose.**

5. Take time to examine the location of the various clips and springs. Remove the pads from the support. Do not mix up the inner and outer clips, they must be installed in the same location.
6. Seat the caliper piston by pushing in while turning clockwise (use a special tool). When fully seated, one of the grooves on the piston must be located vertically at 12 o'clock to accommodate a projection of the brake pad. Install new pads into the support and install the caliper.

Conquest
▶ **See Figure 21**

1. Raise and support the rear end on jackstands.
2. Remove the wheels.
3. Disconnect the parking brake cable.
4. Remove the lower caliper lockpin, and (depending on year), the upper guide pin.

➡**There is a grease coating on the bolt. Make sure that it is not removed or contaminated.**

5. Rotate the caliper upward (if upper guide pin removal is not required) and suspend it with string from a nearby suspension member.
6. Remove the brake pads and shims.
7. Remove the clips from the pads.
8. Clean all parts in solvent made for brake parts.
9. Inspect the dust boot on the caliper piston. If it is torn or brittle, replace it, and consider rebuilding the caliper.
10. Inspect the shims and liners and replace them if damaged.
11. Remove the cap from the master cylinder reservoir and siphon off about ¼ in. of fluid.

12. Using tool MB990652, align the grooves in the caliper and piston and force the piston back into the caliper as far as it will go. Remove the clamp.
13. Install the pads and shims after attaching the clips in reverse order of removal.

➡**Never replace just one set of pads, pads should be replaced on both front wheels at the same time.**

14. Rotate the caliper back into position and install the lower slider pin. Torque the pin to 45 ft. lbs.
15. Start the engine and depress the brake pedal. Hold it depressed for about 5 seconds. Turn the engine **OFF**.
16. Rotate the brake rotor a few times. Using a spring scale hooked to one of the lugs, measure the brake drag. Remove the pads and perform the spring scale test again. The difference between the drag test with and without the pads should not exceed 15 lbs. If the difference does exceed 15 lbs., the caliper will have to be rebuilt or replaced.

Brake Caliper

REMOVAL & INSTALLATION

For Challenger, follow the pad replacement procedure and disconnect the brake lines. For Conquest, follow the pad replacement procedure, then remove the upper pin and disconnect the brake line.

OVERHAUL

Challenger
▶ **See Figures 22 thru 27**

1. Remove caliper from support after disconnecting the brake hose.
2. Remove the clevis pin connecting the parking brake lever.
3. Remove the ring that retains the lever cap and the cap. Remove the lever assembly.
4. Remove the automatic adjuster spindle by unscrewing it.
5. Remove the piston boot and the piston. The piston may be pushed from the caliper by inserting a soft round drift through the adjuster spindle hole. Remove the seal from the piston and clean all parts.
6. Hone the caliper bore.
7. Install a new piston and adjuster seal on the piston, lubricate and install into caliper. Seat the piston and install the dust shield (boot). Lubricate and install the adjuster spindle.

➡**When installing the adjuster spindle the spring washers must be in the proper direction, i.e. The first, nearest the piston, must curve toward the piston. The second, away from the piston, the third, toward and so on. It may be necessary to apply pressure while installing the lever cap and retaining ring. Install the parking brake lever assembly by reversing the removal procedure.**

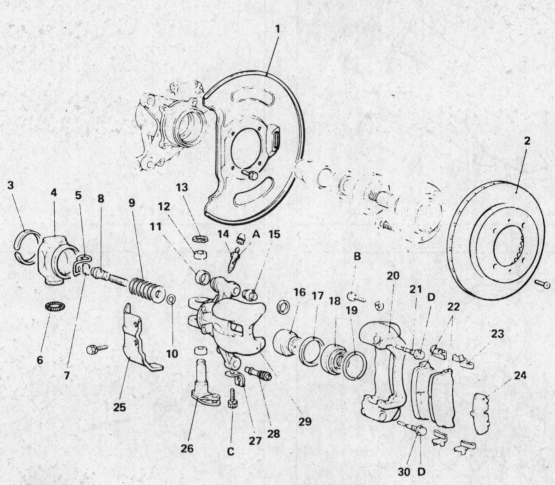

1. Dust cover
2. Brake disc
3. Cap ring
4. Lever cap
5. Return spring
6. Garter spring
7. Connecting link
8. Spindle
9. Spring washer
10. Spindle seal
11. Lid
12. Bearing
13. Retaining ring
14. Bleeder screw
15. Guide pin boot
16. Piston assembly
17. Piston seal
18. Piston boot
19. Boot ring

20. Caliper support
21. Guide pin
22. Brake pad
23. Pad clip
24. Outer shim
25. Dust cover
26. Parking lever assembly
27. Parking cable bracket
28. Lock pin boot
29. Caliper body
30. Lock pin

	Nm	ft. lbs.
A	7–9	5–7
B	40–50	29–36
C	40–55	29–40
D	50–60	36–43

Fig 21 Exploded view of the Conquest rear disc brake system

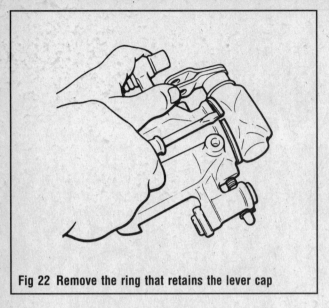

Fig 22 Remove the ring that retains the lever cap

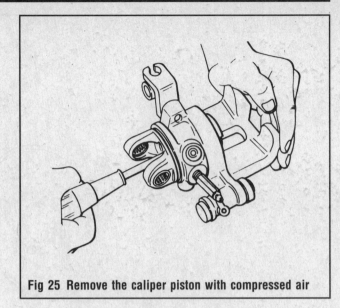

Fig 25 Remove the caliper piston with compressed air

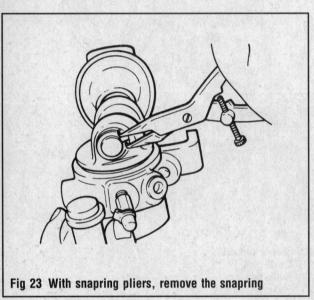

Fig 23 With snapring pliers, remove the snapring

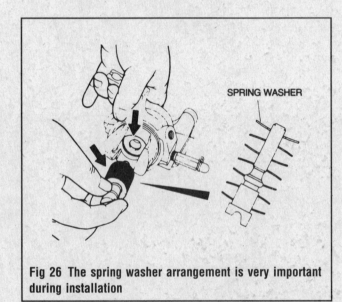

Fig 26 The spring washer arrangement is very important during installation

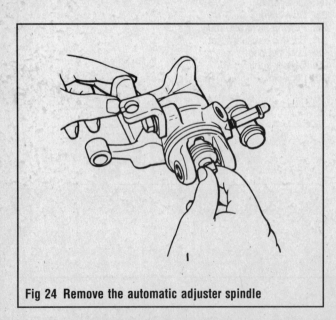

Fig 24 Remove the automatic adjuster spindle

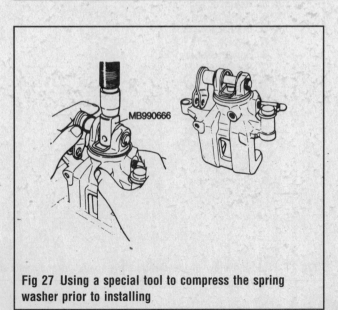

Fig 27 Using a special tool to compress the spring washer prior to installing

✷✷ WARNING

Clean, high quality brake fluid is essential to the safe and proper operation of the brake system. You should always buy the highest quality brake fluid that is available. If the brake fluid becomes contaminated, drain and flush the system, then refill the master cylinder with new fluid. Never reuse any brake fluid. Any brake fluid that is removed from the system should be discarded.

8. Install the caliper, connect the brake hose and bleed the brakes.

Conquest

1. Follow Steps 1–5 of the Challenger procedure.
2. Press the bushing from the caliper with special tool MB990665.
3. Clean all parts with alcohol. Check all parts for wear or damage. Replace any suspect part. Replace all rubber parts.
4. Assemble all parts in reverse order (refer to the Challenger procedure). Coat all rubber parts sparingly with rubber lubricant. Coat the piston and bore with clean brake fluid. Coat the pins sparingly with silicone grease. When installing the adjuster spindle, screw it in until it turns freely. The spring washer on the spindle must be installed with the first one curving toward the piston then rest curving toward or away alternately.

Brake Disc Rotor

REMOVAL & INSTALLATION

1. Remove the caliper, brake pads, and support.
2. Remove the retaining bolts.
3. Remove the rotor. Service as required. Install the rotor and secure the bolts. Install the support, pads and caliper.

Rear Brake Lock-Up Control System

The late model Conquest is equipped with a rear wheel lock-up control system that is designed to achieve maximum braking efficiency for quick stops on wet or icy roads, and to reduce the possibility of vehicle skidding causes by rear wheel lock-up.

The rear wheel lock-up system is composed of five units, which are: A pulse generator. A G-sensor. A control unit. A modulator. And a fail indication light. The pulse generator generates a rotation pulse in accordance with the speed of the rear wheels. The G-sensor generates a voltage in accordance with the reduction of the vehicle speed. The control unit controls each of the signals received from the pulse generator and G-sensor. The modulator controls the brake fluid pressure. The fail indication light warns of a malfunction in the control unit.

REMOVAL & INSTALLATION

Modulator

1. The modulator is located on the passenger's side fender well. Remove the heat protector.

2. Remove the vacuum lines, the brake fluid lines and the solenoid wiring harness.
3. Disconnect the mounting brackets and remove the modulator.
4. Service as required. Mount the modulator in position and connect the lines and wiring harness. Bleed the brake system.

➡**Bleed the modulator before bleeding the front wheels.**

5. If the modulator solenoid is suspected improper operation check the resistance value between the electrical terminals with an ohmmeter. On the solenoid release side: Terminals 1 and 3, resistance should measure 3.8–4.8 ohms. On the build up side: Terminals 2 and 4, the resistance should measure 4.5–5.5 ohms. Service as required.

G-Sensor

1. The G-Sensor is located in the luggage compartment.
2. Disconnect the wiring harness and remove the mounting bolts and the sensor.
3. Install the G-Sensor and connect the wiring harness.

➡**When handling the G-Sensor, be careful not to subject it to any impact or violent shaking.**

4. While the G-Sensor is mounted, check the voltage across the R wire and ground. Voltage should be 7.0–7.5 volts. If voltage is not within specs, the control unit should be suspect.

Control Unit

1. The control unit is located under the side panel on the right side of the luggage compartment.
2. Remove the mounting screws, lower the unit and disconnect the wiring harness.
3. Connect the wiring harness and mount the control unit in position with the mounting screws.

Pulse Generator

1. The pulse generator is mounted on the transmission side of the speedometer cable.
2. Disconnect the speedometer cable and wiring. Look for mating marks between the generator housing and the transmission. If none are seen, scribe a pair (on generator and transmission). Remove the clamp bolt and remove the pulse generator.
3. Align the mating marks and mount the pulse generator with the clamp. Be sure the clamp is positioned in the grooves provided in the generator body. Connect the speedometer cable and wiring.
4. The resistance between the terminals of the pulse generator should be 600–800 ohms.

Control Relay

1. The control relay is located on the left front cowl side of the vehicle.
2. Disconnect the wiring harness and unbolt the relay.
3. Mount and secure the relay in position and connect the wiring harness.

System Self-Diagnosis Test

Operate the engine for five seconds or longer, but don't move the vehicle. Turn the key to the Lock position and depress the brake pedal. Turn the key to the **On** position. A sound dull clicking should be heard from the modulator solenoid. If the operating sound can be heard the solenoid is operating correctly.

PARKING BRAKE

Cable

ADJUSTMENT

Through 1984 Models

▶ See Figures 28, 29, 30, 31 and 32

Release the parking brake lever. Loosen the lock (rear) nuts on each side of the lever or on the frame bracket. Tighten the adjusting (front) nuts to increase tension, or loosen to reduce. Any adjustment must be made evenly on both sides. Be sure, after adjustment, that when the parking brake is released the rear wheels will turn freely with no brake shoe drag. Handbrake travel should be; through 1976—10 notches. From 1977—6 to 8 notches.

➡**Lever stroke of less than 5 notches, will cause the adjuster to malfunction i.e., not adjust.**

1985–89 Except Conquest

1. Pull the parking brake lever up with a force of about 45 lbs. If that value cannot be determined, just pull it up as far as you can. The total number of clicks heard should be 5–7.
2. If the number of clicks was not within that range, release the lever and back off the cable adjuster locknut at the base of the lever and tighten the adjusting nut until there is no more slack in the cable.
3. Operate the lever and brake pedal several times, until no more clicks are heard from the automatic adjuster.
4. Turn the adjusting nut to give the proper number of clicks when the lever is raised full travel.
5. Raise and support the rear of the car on jackstands.
6. Release the brake lever and make sure that the rear

wheels turn freely. If not, back off on the adjusting nut until they do.

Conquest

1. Pull up on the lever, counting the number of clicks. Total travel should yield 4–5 clicks.
2. If not, remove the center console and turn the adjusting nut on the lever rod to obtain the required travel.
3. Raise and support the rear of the car on jackstands.
4. With the parking brake released, make sure that the rear wheels turn freely.

REMOVAL & INSTALLATION

Rear Wheel Drive

1. Block the front wheels, jack up the rear of the car and support with jackstands.
2. Release the parking brake. Pull off the clevis pins from both sides of the rear brake. Disconnect the cable from the extension lever.
3. On drum brake models (through 1980): loosen the parking brake lever mounting bolts and disconnect the front end of the rear cable from the equalizer. On 1981 and later models; remove brake drums, disconnect cable from lever, remove retaining clip and remove cable through brake backing plate. Remove the front cable after disconnecting the parking brake lever. On rear disc brake models: Remove the rubber hanger from the center of the axle housing. Remove the parking brake lever and clevis pin linking the lever and cable. Remove the clips under the floor and remove the cable.
4. Install the cable. When installing, make sure that the cable clips do not interfere with a rotating part. Adjust the extension

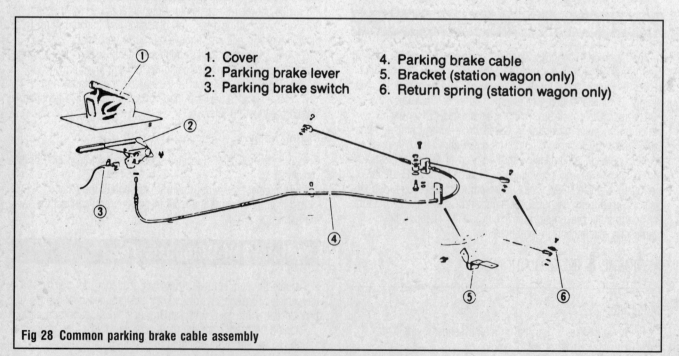

1. Cover
2. Parking brake lever
3. Parking brake switch
4. Parking brake cable
5. Bracket (station wagon only)
6. Return spring (station wagon only)

Fig 28 Common parking brake cable assembly

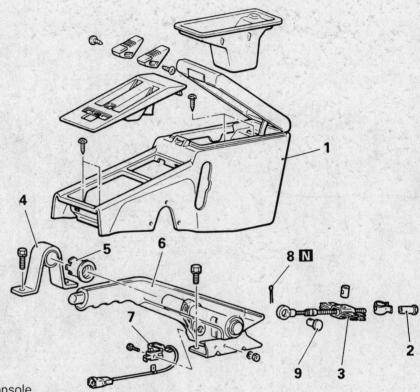

Removal steps

1. Rear floor console
   Adjustment of parking brake lever stroke
2. Adjuster
3. Equalizer
4. Stay
5. Bushing
6. Parking brake lever
7. Parking brake switch
8. Cotter pin
9. Clevis pin

N: Non-reusable parts

Fig 29 Parking brake lever mounting

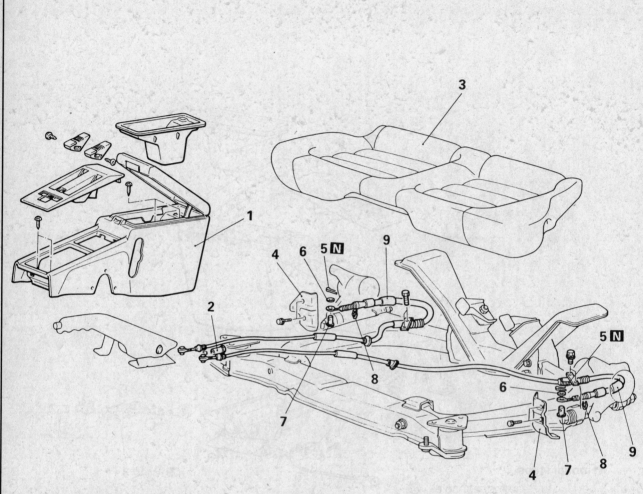

Removal steps

1. Rear floor console
   Adjustment of parking brake lever stroke
2. Adjuster
3. Rear seat cushion
4. Dust cover
5. Cotter pin
6. Washer
7. Clevis pin
8. Clip
9. Parking brake cable

N: Non-reusable parts

Fig 30 Exploded view of the parking brake cable system—1989 Conquest

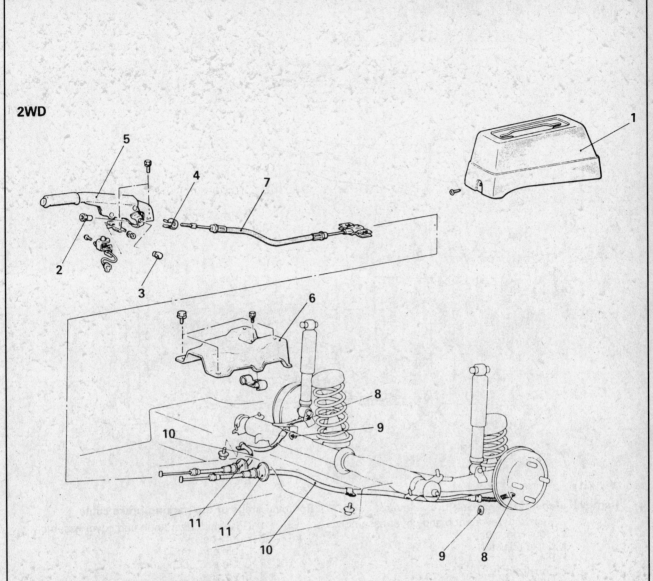

2WD

Removal steps of the parking brake lever

1. Parking brake cover
2. Cable adjuster
3. Pin
4. Nut holder
5. Parking brake lever

Removal steps of the parking brake cable

1. Parking brake cover
2. Cable adjuster
6. Equalizer cover
7. Front parking brake cable
8. Cable end connection
9. Snap ring

10. Rear parking brake cable
11. Grommet

Post-installation Operation
- Adjustment of parking brake lever stroke

Fig 31 Exploded view of the parking brake cable system—2WD 1989 Colt and Vista

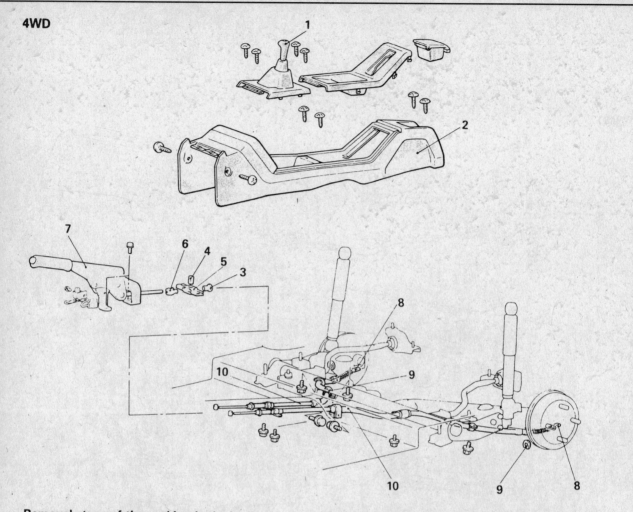

4WD

Removal steps of the parking brake lever

1. Gear shift lever knob and cover assembly
2. Floor console
3. Cable adjuster
4. Pin
5. Equalizer
6. Nut holder
7. Parking brake lever

Removal steps of the parking brake cable

1. Gear shift lever knob and cover assembly
2. Floor console
3. Cable adjuster
8. Cable end connection
9. Snap ring
10. Parking brake cable

Post-installation Operation
● Adjustment of parking brake lever stroke

Fig 32 Exploded view of the parking brake cable system—2WD 1989 Colt and Vista

lever to stop first. Then adjust the left cable, then the right on the Challenger and Wagons.

Front Wheel Drive

1. Block front wheels, raise rear of car and support on jackstands.

2. Disconnect the brake cable at the parking brake lever (brakes released). Remove the cable clamps inside the driver's compartment (two bolts). On 1985 Colt, remove the rear seat. Disconnect the clamps on the rear suspension arm.

3. Remove the rear brake drums and the brake shoes assem-blies. Disconnect the parking brake cable from the lever on the trailing (rear) brake shoe. Remove the brake cables.

4. Install the cable and adjust.

Handbrake Warning Switch

On most models, a dash mounted warning light indicates when the hand brake is applied. The light should go on when the parking brake lever is pulled one or more notches, and go out when the lever is fully released. Adjustment is made by loosening the mounting bolt and changing the mounted positions of the switch.

Troubleshooting the Brake System

Problem	Cause	Solution
Low brake pedal (excessive pedal travel required for braking action.)	• Excessive clearance between rear linings and drums caused by inoperative automatic adjusters	• Make 10 to 15 alternate forward and reverse brake stops to adjust brakes. If brake pedal does not come up, repair or replace adjuster parts as necessary.
	• Worn rear brakelining	• Inspect and replace lining if worn beyond minimum thickness specification
	• Bent, distorted brakeshoes, front or rear	• Replace brakeshoes in axle sets
	• Air in hydraulic system	• Remove air from system. Refer to Brake Bleeding.
Low brake pedal (pedal may go to floor with steady pressure applied.)	• Fluid leak in hydraulic system	• Fill master cylinder to fill line; have helper apply brakes and check calipers, wheel cylinders, differential valve tubes, hoses and fittings for leaks. Repair or replace as necessary.
	• Air in hydraulic system	• Remove air from system. Refer to Brake Bleeding.
	• Incorrect or non-recommended brake fluid (fluid evaporates at below normal temp).	• Flush hydraulic system with clean brake fluid. Refill with correct-type fluid.
	• Master cylinder piston seals worn, or master cylinder bore is scored, worn or corroded	• Repair or replace master cylinder
Low brake pedal (pedal goes to floor on first application—o.k. on subsequent applications.)	• Disc brake pads sticking on abutment surfaces of anchor plate. Caused by a build-up of dirt, rust, or corrosion on abutment surfaces	• Clean abutment surfaces
Fading brake pedal (pedal height decreases with steady pressure applied.)	• Fluid leak in hydraulic system	• Fill master cylinder reservoirs to fill mark, have helper apply brakes, check calipers, wheel cylinders, differential valve, tubes, hoses, and fittings for fluid leaks. Repair or replace parts as necessary.
	• Master cylinder piston seals worn, or master cylinder bore is scored, worn or corroded	• Repair or replace master cylinder
Decreasing brake pedal travel (pedal travel required for braking action decreases and may be accompanied by a hard pedal.)	• Caliper or wheel cylinder pistons sticking or seized	• Repair or replace the calipers, or wheel cylinders
	• Master cylinder compensator ports blocked (preventing fluid return to reservoirs) or pistons sticking or seized in master cylinder bore	• Repair or replace the master cylinder
	• Power brake unit binding internally	• Test unit according to the following procedure: (a) Shift transmission into neutral and start engine (b) Increase engine speed to 1500 rpm, close throttle and fully depress brake pedal (c) Slow release brake pedal and stop engine (d) Have helper remove vacuum check valve and hose from power unit. Observe for backward movement of brake pedal. (e) If the pedal moves backward, the power unit has an internal bind—replace power unit

Troubleshooting the Brake System (cont.)

Problem	Cause	Solution
Spongy brake pedal (pedal has abnormally soft, springy, spongy feel when depressed.)	• Air in hydraulic system • Brakeshoes bent or distorted • Brakelining not yet seated with drums and rotors • Rear drum brakes not properly adjusted	• Remove air from system. Refer to Brake Bleeding. • Replace brakeshoes • Burnish brakes • Adjust brakes
Hard brake pedal (excessive pedal pressure required to stop vehicle. May be accompanied by brake fade.)	• Loose or leaking power brake unit vacuum hose • Incorrect or poor quality brakelining • Bent, broken, distorted brakeshoes • Calipers binding or dragging on mounting pins. Rear brakeshoes dragging on support plate. • Caliper, wheel cylinder, or master cylinder pistons sticking or seized • Power brake unit vacuum check valve malfunction • Power brake unit has internal bind • Master cylinder compensator ports (at bottom of reservoirs) blocked by dirt, scale, rust, or have small burrs (blocked ports prevent fluid return to reservoirs). • Brake hoses, tubes, fittings clogged or restricted • Brake fluid contaminated with improper fluids (motor oil, transmission fluid, causing rubber components to swell and stick in bores • Low engine vacuum	• Tighten connections or replace leaking hose • Replace with lining in axle sets • Replace brakeshoes • Replace mounting pins and bushings. Clean rust or burrs from rear brake support plate ledges and lubricate ledges with molydisulfide grease. **NOTE:** If ledges are deeply grooved or scored, do not attempt to sand or grind them smooth—replace support plate. • Repair or replace parts as necessary • Test valve according to the following procedure: (a) Start engine, increase engine speed to 1500 rpm, close throttle and immediately stop engine (b) Wait at least 90 seconds then depress brake pedal (c) If brakes are not vacuum assisted for 2 or more applications, check valve is faulty • Test unit according to the following procedure: (a) With engine stopped, apply brakes several times to exhaust all vacuum in system (b) Shift transmission into neutral, depress brake pedal and start engine (c) If pedal height decreases with foot pressure and less pressure is required to hold pedal in applied position, power unit vacuum system is operating normally. Test power unit. If power unit exhibits a bind condition, replace the power unit. • Repair or replace master cylinder **CAUTION:** Do not attempt to clean blocked ports with wire, pencils, or similar implements. Use compressed air only. • Use compressed air to check or unclog parts. Replace any damaged parts. • Replace all rubber components, combination valve and hoses. Flush entire brake system with DOT 3 brake fluid or equivalent. • Adjust or repair engine

Troubleshooting the Brake System (cont.)

Problem	Cause	Solution
Grabbing brakes (severe reaction to brake pedal pressure.)	• Brakelining(s) contaminated by grease or brake fluid	• Determine and correct cause of contamination and replace brakeshoes in axle sets
	• Parking brake cables incorrectly adjusted or seized	• Adjust cables. Replace seized cables.
	• Incorrect brakelining or lining loose on brakeshoes	• Replace brakeshoes in axle sets
	• Caliper anchor plate bolts loose	• Tighten bolts
	• Rear brakeshoes binding on support plate ledges	• Clean and lubricate ledges. Replace support plate(s) if ledges are deeply grooved. Do not attempt to smooth ledges by grinding.
	• Incorrect or missing power brake reaction disc	• Install correct disc
	• Rear brake support plates loose	• Tighten mounting bolts
Dragging brakes (slow or incomplete release of brakes)	• Brake pedal binding at pivot	• Loosen and lubricate
	• Power brake unit has internal bind	• Inspect for internal bind. Replace unit if internal bind exists.
	• Parking brake cables incorrrectly adjusted or seized	• Adjust cables. Replace seized cables.
	• Rear brakeshoe return springs weak or broken	• Replace return springs. Replace brakeshoe if necessary in axle sets.
	• Automatic adjusters malfunctioning	• Repair or replace adjuster parts as required
	• Caliper, wheel cylinder or master cylinder pistons sticking or seized	• Repair or replace parts as necessary
	• Master cylinder compensating ports blocked (fluid does not return to reservoirs).	• Use compressed air to clear ports. Do not use wire, pencils, or similar objects to open blocked ports.
Vehicle moves to one side when brakes are applied	• Incorrect front tire pressure	• Inflate to recommended cold (reduced load) inflation pressure
	• Worn or damaged wheel bearings	• Replace worn or damaged bearings
	• Brakelining on one side contaminated	• Determine and correct cause of contamination and replace brakelining in axle sets
	• Brakeshoes on one side bent, distorted, or lining loose on shoe	• Replace brakeshoes in axle sets
	• Support plate bent or loose on one side	• Tighten or replace support plate
	• Brakelining not yet seated with drums or rotors	• Burnish brakelining
	• Caliper anchor plate loose on one side	• Tighten anchor plate bolts
	• Caliper piston sticking or seized	• Repair or replace caliper
	• Brakelinings water soaked	• Drive vehicle with brakes lightly applied to dry linings
	• Loose suspension component attaching or mounting bolts	• Tighten suspension bolts. Replace worn suspension components.
	• Brake combination valve failure	• Replace combination valve
Chatter or shudder when brakes are applied (pedal pulsation and roughness may also occur.)	• Brakeshoes distorted, bent, contaminated, or worn	• Replace brakeshoes in axle sets
	• Caliper anchor plate or support plate loose	• Tighten mounting bolts
	• Excessive thickness variation of rotor(s)	• Refinish or replace rotors in axle sets
Noisy brakes (squealing, clicking, scraping sound when brakes are applied.)	• Bent, broken, distorted brakeshoes	• Replace brakeshoes in axle sets
	• Excessive rust on outer edge of rotor braking surface	• Remove rust

Troubleshooting the Brake System (cont.)

Problem	Cause	Solution
Noisy brakes (squealing, clicking, scraping sound when brakes are applied.) (cont.)	• Brakelining worn out—shoes contacting drum of rotor	• Replace brakeshoes and lining in axle sets. Refinish or replace drums or rotors.
	• Broken or loose holdown or return springs	• Replace parts as necessary
	• Rough or dry drum brake support plate ledges	• Lubricate support plate ledges
	• Cracked, grooved, or scored rotor(s) or drum(s)	• Replace rotor(s) or drum(s). Replace brakeshoes and lining in axle sets if necessary.
	• Incorrect brakelining and/or shoes (front or rear).	• Install specified shoe and lining assemblies
Pulsating brake pedal	• Out of round drums or excessive lateral runout in disc brake rotor(s)	• Refinish or replace drums, re-index rotors or replace

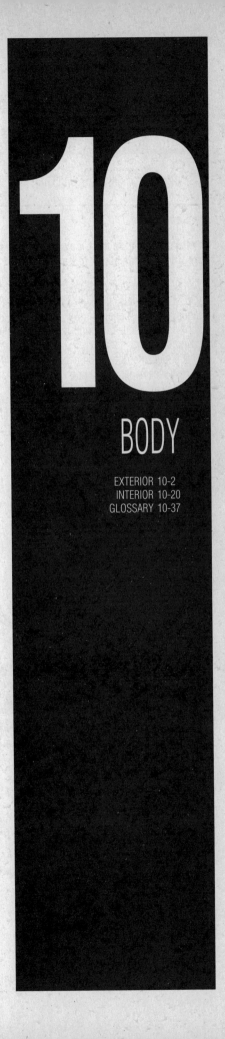

10

BODY

EXTERIOR

Doors

REMOVAL & INSTALLATION

▶ **See Figure 1**

➡**On some models, it may be necessary to remove the front fender for hinge to body side bolt removal.**

1. Open the door and remove the inner door panel covering (On some models, the light harness can be disconnected without requiring inner panel removal.) Disconnect the interior light wiring harness and feed it through the access hole. Disconnect the door swing stop.

2. Open the door wide enough to gain access to the hinge bolts. Place a padded support under the door edge that will hold the door in a level position when the hinges have been unbolted from the frame.

3. Scribe around the door hinge on the door frame. Remove the hinge mounting bolts, lower hinge first than the upper from the door frame.

4. Remove the door.

5. Place the door on the padded support and install the hinge mounting bolts until they are snug enough to support the door, but not tight enough to prevent door adjustment. Adjust the door position until correctly aligned and tighten the hinge bolts. Adjust the striker as necessary. Connect the door stop and interior light harness. Install the inner trim panel.

ALIGNMENT

The doors should be adjusted so that there is an even clearance all around the door edge and body. Adjust the door to position and raise or lower it so that the stamped edge line matches the body panel line. Secure the door in proper position after necessary adjustments. Loosen the door striker mounting screws to

Front

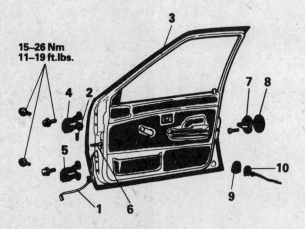

Rear

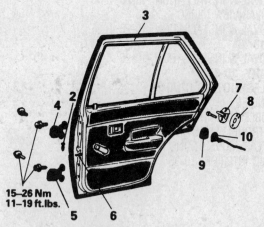

1. Door harness connection
2. Spring pin
3. Door
4. Door upper hinge
5. Door lower hinge
6. Door check
7. Striker
8. Striker shim
9. Door switch cap
10. Door switch

Fig 1 Front and rear door mounting components on the FWD Colt

adjust the alignment of the door panel. Increase or decrease the number of shims behind the striker as required.

Hood

REMOVAL & INSTALLATION

▶ **See Figures 2, 3 and 3a**

1. Raise the hood. Scribe mark the hinge to hood panel location.

2. Place padding between the windshield/cowl and hood edge to prevent damage should the hood slip during removal.

3. Have a helper hold the front of the hood to prevent it from falling or sliding when the mounting bolts are removed.

4. Remove the hood panel to hinge mounting bolts and remove the hood.

5. Position the hood panel over the hinges and align the panel with the scribed lines. Install and tighten the mounting bolts.

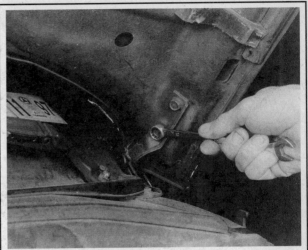

After scribing the hood hinges, loosen and remove the hood with the help of an assistant

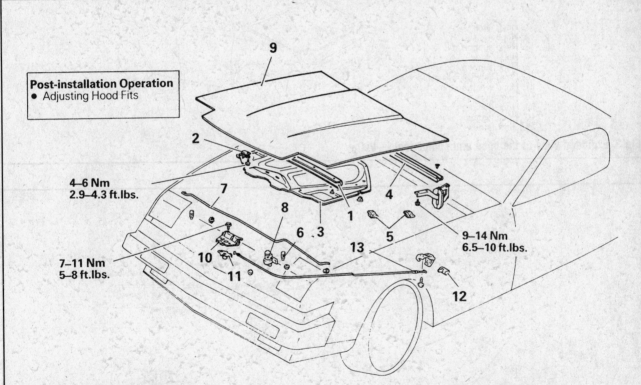

Post-installation Operation
● Adjusting Hood Fits

4–6 Nm
2.9–4.3 ft.lbs.

7–11 Nm
5–8 ft.lbs.

9–14 Nm
6.5–10 ft.lbs.

Hood panel removal steps

1. Hood weatherstrip, front
2. Hood hook
3. Heat protector
4. Hood weatherstrip, rear
5. Hood damper
6. Hood bumper
7. Hood support rod
8. Hood switch
9. Hood panel

Release cable removal steps

10. Hood lock plate
11. Hood lock
12. Hood release handle
13. Release cable

NOTE
Reverse the removal procedures to reinstall.

Fig 2 Exploded view of the hood and components—Conquest

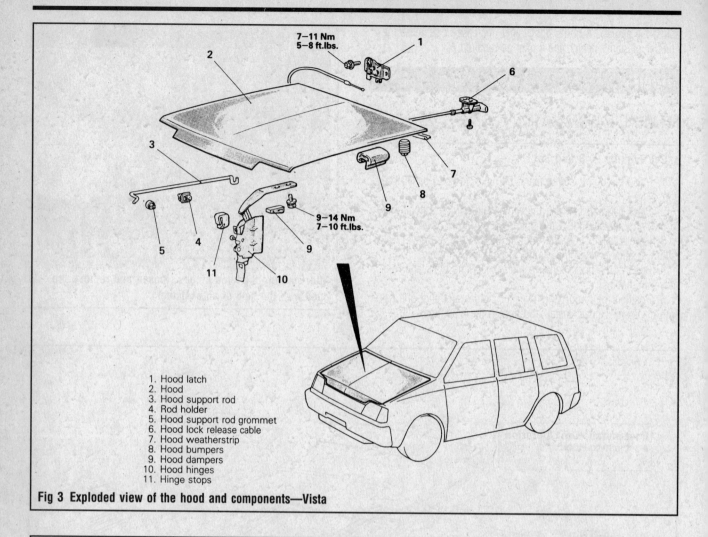

7–11 Nm
5–8 ft.lbs.

9–14 Nm
7–10 ft.lbs.

1. Hood latch
2. Hood
3. Hood support rod
4. Rod holder
5. Hood support rod grommet
6. Hood lock release cable
7. Hood weatherstrip
8. Hood bumpers
9. Hood dampers
10. Hood hinges
11. Hinge stops

Fig 3 Exploded view of the hood and components—Vista

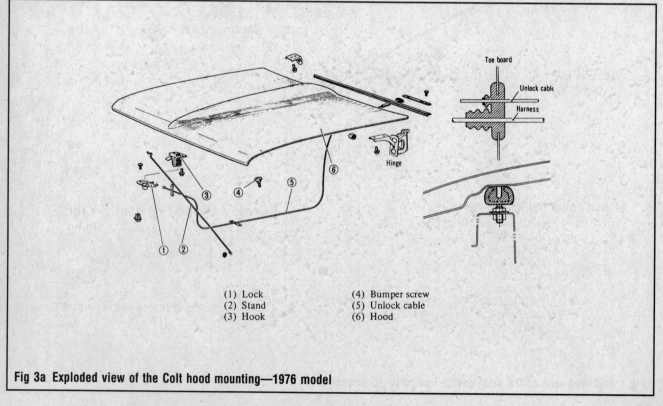

Toe board
Unlock cable
Harness
Hinge

(1) Lock   (4) Bumper screw
(2) Stand   (5) Unlock cable
(3) Hook   (6) Hood

Fig 3a Exploded view of the Colt hood mounting—1976 model

ALIGNMENT

1. One, or both sets of hood hinge mounting holes or the hood panel attaching captive mounting nut locations are elongated to permit panel to fender and cowl adjustment.

2. Locate the mounting bolts that are in the elongated holes. Loosen them slightly until the hood panel position can be shifted.

3. Move the panel as required for even spacing around the hood outer edges. Tighten the bolts.

4. Adjustable (up or down) bumpers are provided, in most cases, to permit the front of the hood to be raised or lower to match the fender edges. Raise or lower the bumpers, by screwing them in or out, to adjust.

Liftgate

REMOVAL & INSTALLATION

▶ **See Figure 4, 5, 6, 7 and 8**

1. Support the liftgate in the full opened position. Depending on the model, remove the one piece plastic headliner if it covers the hinge mounting.

2. Scribe a mark on the liftgate to mark the hinge positions.

3. Place masking tape on the roof edge and liftgate edge to protect the paint surfaces during removal and installation.

4. Remove the liftgate prop fasteners and remove the props.

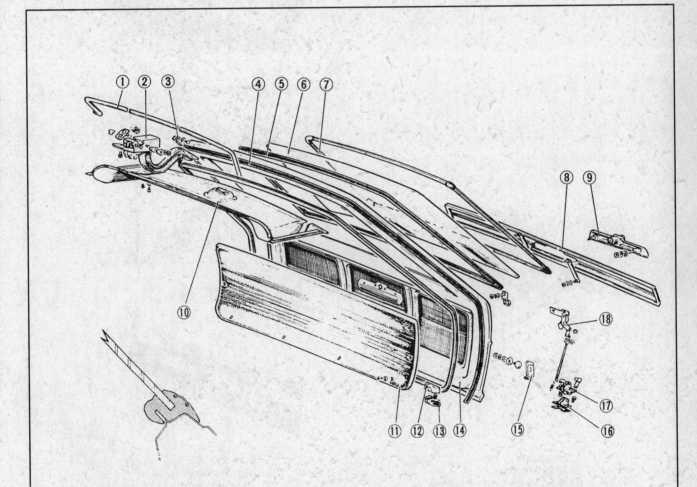

(1) Torsion bar	(7) Rear window moulding	(13) Bumper rubber
(2) Tail gate hinge	(8) Rear grille	(14) Tail gate body
(3) Guide rubber	(9) Tail gate handle	(15) Bumper plate
(4) Tail gate weatherstrip	(10) Hinge cover	(16) Stopper
(5) Tail gate window weatherstrip	(11) Tail gate trim	(17) Lock
(6) Tail gate window glass	(12) Bumper female	(18) Lever

Fig 4 Tailgate components on the 1976 Colt wagon

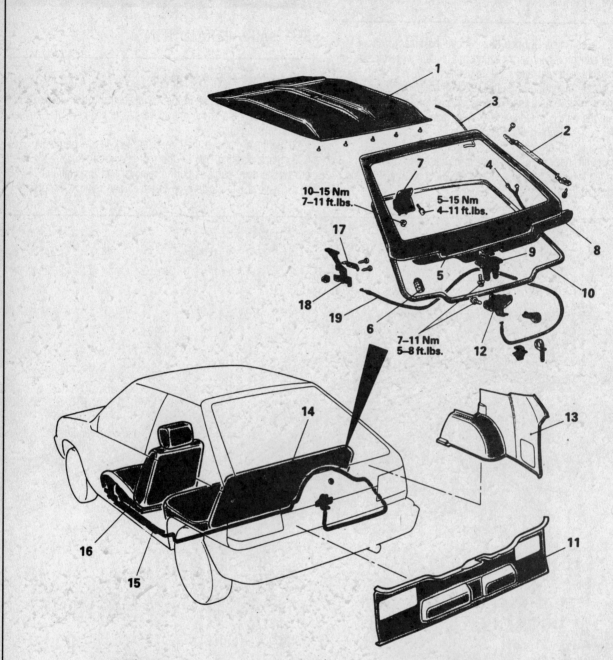

1. Headlining
2. Liftgate stopper
3. Rear washer tube connection
4. Tailgate wiring harness connector connection
5. Liftgate
6. Liftgate bumper
7. Liftgate hinge
8. Liftgate trim
9. Liftgate latch
10. Liftgate opening weatherstrip
11. Rear end trim
12. Liftgate striker
13. Trunk side trim
14. Rear seat
15. Scuff plate
16. Front seat
17. Release handle cover
18. Release handle
19. Liftgate lock release cable

Fig 5 Liftgate components on the FWD Colt

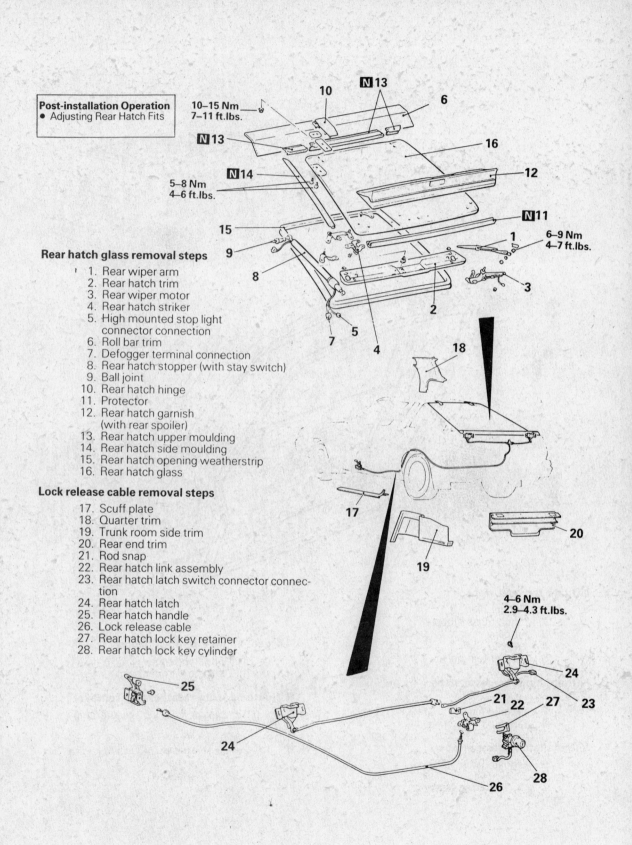

Post-installation Operation
● Adjusting Rear Hatch Fits

10–15 Nm
7–11 ft.lbs.

5–8 Nm
4–6 ft.lbs.

6–9 Nm
4–7 ft.lbs.

4–6 Nm
2.9–4.3 ft.lbs.

Rear hatch glass removal steps

1. Rear wiper arm
2. Rear hatch trim
3. Rear wiper motor
4. Rear hatch striker
5. High mounted stop light connector connection
6. Roll bar trim
7. Defogger terminal connection
8. Rear hatch stopper (with stay switch)
9. Ball joint
10. Rear hatch hinge
11. Protector
12. Rear hatch garnish (with rear spoiler)
13. Rear hatch upper moulding
14. Rear hatch side moulding
15. Rear hatch opening weatherstrip
16. Rear hatch glass

Lock release cable removal steps

17. Scuff plate
18. Quarter trim
19. Trunk room side trim
20. Rear end trim
21. Rod snap
22. Rear hatch link assembly
23. Rear hatch latch switch connector connection
24. Rear hatch latch
25. Rear hatch handle
26. Lock release cable
27. Rear hatch lock key retainer
28. Rear hatch lock key cylinder

Fig 6 Rear hatch components on the 1989 Conquest

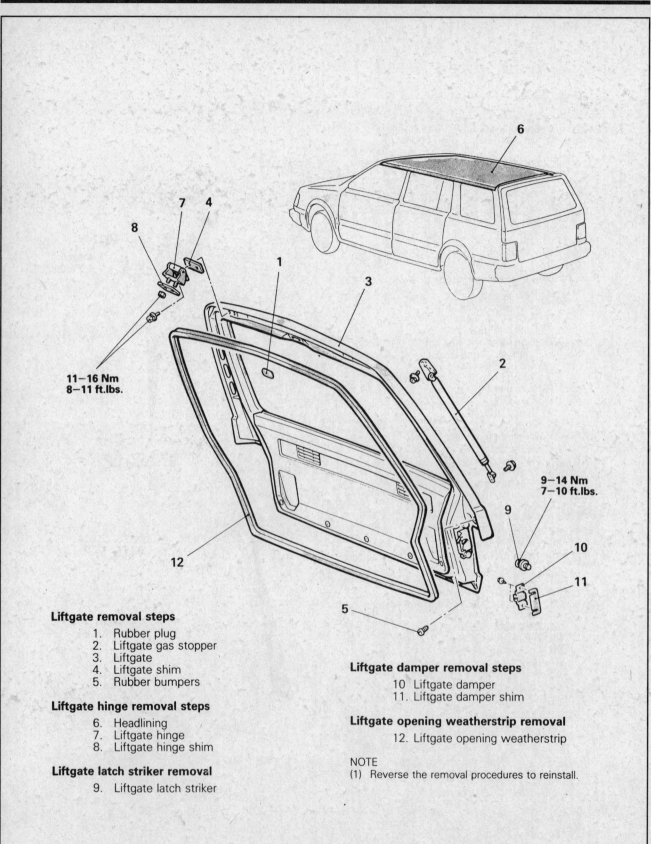

11–16 Nm
8–11 ft.lbs.

9–14 Nm
7–10 ft.lbs.

Liftgate removal steps

1. Rubber plug
2. Liftgate gas stopper
3. Liftgate
4. Liftgate shim
5. Rubber bumpers

Liftgate hinge removal steps

6. Headlining
7. Liftgate hinge
8. Liftgate hinge shim

Liftgate latch striker removal

9. Liftgate latch striker

Liftgate damper removal steps

10 Liftgate damper
11. Liftgate damper shim

Liftgate opening weatherstrip removal

12. Liftgate opening weatherstrip

NOTE
(1) Reverse the removal procedures to reinstall.

Fig 7 Liftgate components on the 1989 Colt Vista

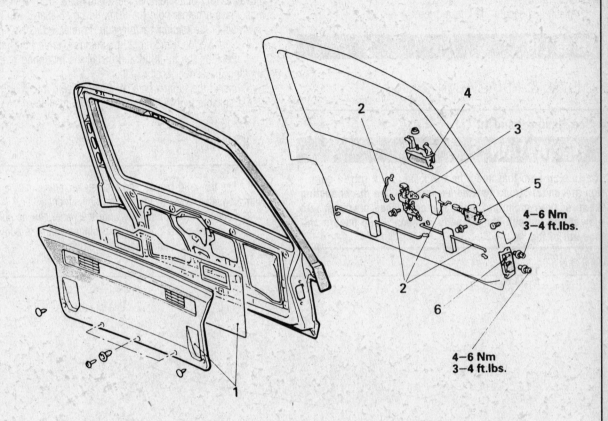

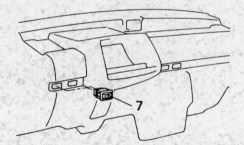

4–6 Nm
3–4 ft.lbs.

4–6 Nm
3–4 ft.lbs.

Liftgate removal steps

1. Liftgate trim and waterproof film
2. Handle rod
   Liftgate link assembly adjustment
3. Liftgate link assembly
4. Release handle
5. Liftgate lock actuator
6. Liftgate latch

Liftgate lock release switch removal

7. Liftgate lock release switch

NOTE
(1) Reverse the removal procedures to reinstall.

Fig 8 Liftgate handle and hatch components on the 1989 Colt Vista

5. Have a helper on hand to support the liftgate. Remove the hinge mounting bolts and remove the liftgate.

6. Raise the liftgate into position and install the hinge mounting bolts. Tighten the bolts until they are snug, but not tight enough to prevent liftgate adjustment.

7. Shift the liftgate until the hinge scribe marks are in position and tighten the hinge mounting bolts.

8. Attach and secure the liftgate props.

Trunk Lid

REMOVAL & INSTALLATION

▶ See Figures 9 and 10

✳✳ CAUTION

The torsion bars that keep the trunk lid in the raised position are under strong twisted pressure. When disconnecting them for their mounting holes and/or notched brackets, they may spring out and cause bodily damage. Keep fingers and face out of the way.

1. Scribe the hinge outline to the mounting panel. On some models it will be necessary to remove the rear package tray from in front of the rear window to gain access to the hinge mount.

2. On models with a remote release, disconnect the cable if it runs on the inside of the trunk panel. If necessary for hinge removal, CAREFULLY remove the torsion bars from their mountings. Have a helper hold the trunk lid up so that it will not slam down when the torsion bar pressure is released.

3. Remove the trunk hinge mounting bolts and the lid.

4. Position the trunk lid and install the mounting bolts after aligning the scribe locator marks.

5. Install the torsion bars, if disconnected, into their notches. Use a suitable tool to tension them while installing.

ALIGNMENT

1. The trunk lid hinges and lock striker are usually equipped with elongated holes to provide for adjustment.

2. Loosen the bolts slightly until the panel can be shifted.

3. Move the panel until even spacing around the edges is present. Tighten the mounting bolts and striker.

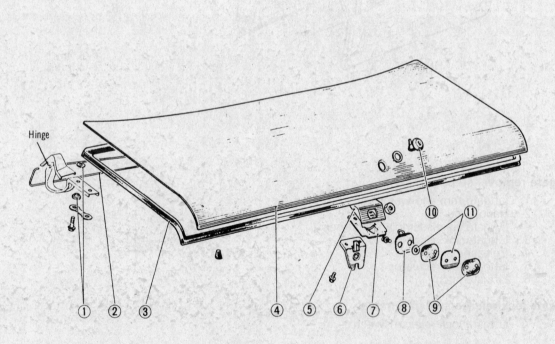

(1) Insulator
(2) Torsion bar
(3) Weatherstrip
(4) Deck lid
(5) Plate
(6) Lid latch
(7) Cylinder lock cover
(8) Striker
(9) Striker shim
(10) Cylinder lock
(11) Insulator

Fig 9 Exploded view of the trunk lid components—1976 Colt

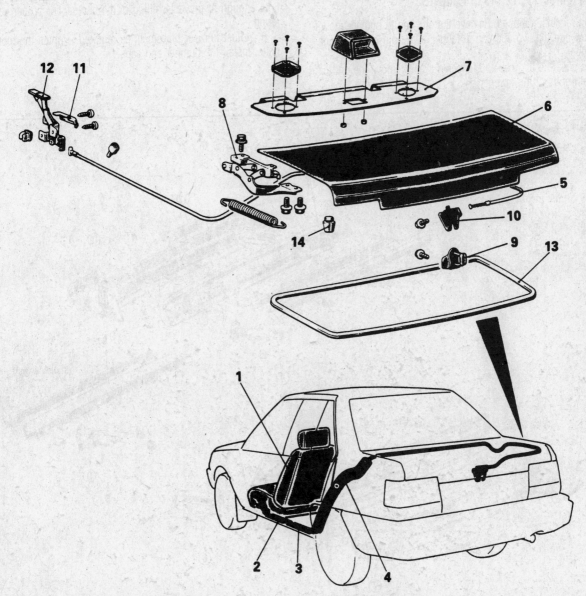

1. Front seat
2. Front scuff plate
3. Rear scuff plate
4. Rear wheel arch trim
5. Trunk lid lock release cable
6. Trunk lid
7. Rear shelf trim
8. Trunk lid hinge
9. Trunk lid striker
10. Trunk lid latch
11. Release handle cover
12. Trunk lid lock release handle
13. Trunk lid weatherstrip
14. Damper

Fig 10 Exploded view of the trunk lid components—FWD Colt

Bumpers

REMOVAL & INSTALLATION

♦ **See Figures 11, 12, 13, 14 and 15**

1. On models equipped: Remove the end cap to bumper mounting screw and the two end cap to fender nuts from both ends of the bumper.

2. Remove the end cap to bumper nut and remove the end cap from both ends of the bumper.

3. Support the lower edge of the bumper on a padded jack.

4. Remove the bolts that mount the bumper to the body brackets/impact absorber mount and remove the bumper.

5. Place the bumper into the proper position, use a padded jack to support the bumper, and install the bracket to bumper mounting bolts. Tighten the bolts until they are snug, but not tight enough to prevent shifting of the bumper for proper centering.

6. Adjust bumper placement as required. Tighten the mounting bolts. Install the bumper end caps.

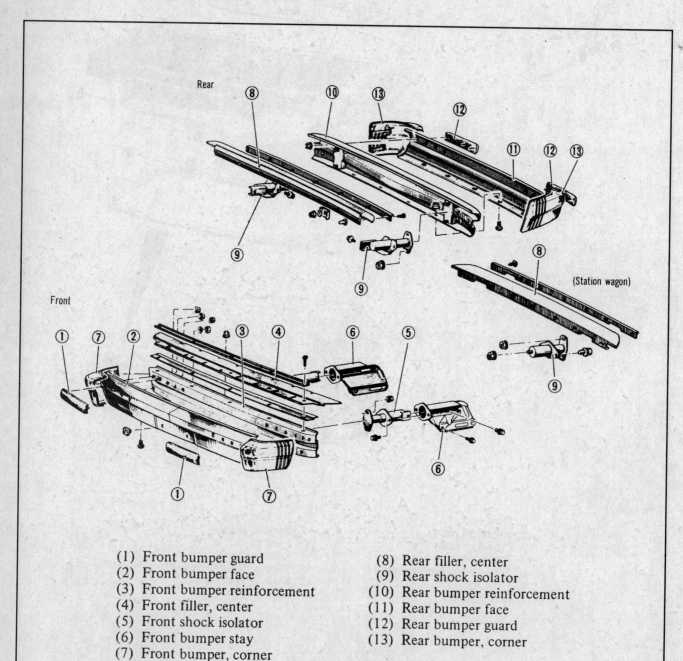

(1) Front bumper guard
(2) Front bumper face
(3) Front bumper reinforcement
(4) Front filler, center
(5) Front shock isolator
(6) Front bumper stay
(7) Front bumper, corner

(8) Rear filler, center
(9) Rear shock isolator
(10) Rear bumper reinforcement
(11) Rear bumper face
(12) Rear bumper guard
(13) Rear bumper, corner

Fig 11 Exploded view of the front and rear bumper mountings on the 1976 Colt sedan, coupe and wagon

Front

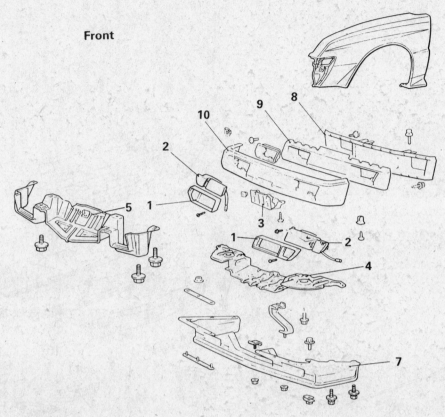

Rear

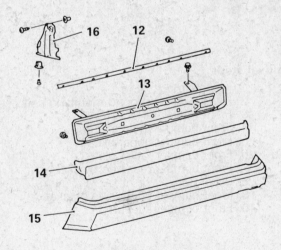

Front bumper removal steps

1. Front combination light bezel
2. Front combination light
3. Licence plate bracket
4. Air guide panel (Vehicles with a manual transmission)
5. Air guide panel (Vehicles with an automatic transmission)
6. Front bumper assembly with front skirt panel (Parts 7 through 10)
7. Front skirt panel
8. Bumper reinforcement
9. Bumper core
10. Bumper face

Rear bumper removal steps

11. Rear bumper assembly (Parts 12 through 15)
12. Bumper plate
13. Bumper reinforcement
14. Bumper core
15. Bumper face
16. Bumper guide plate

NOTE
(1) Reverse the removal procedures to reinstall.

Fig 12 Exploded view of the front and rear bumper mounting on the 1989 Conquest

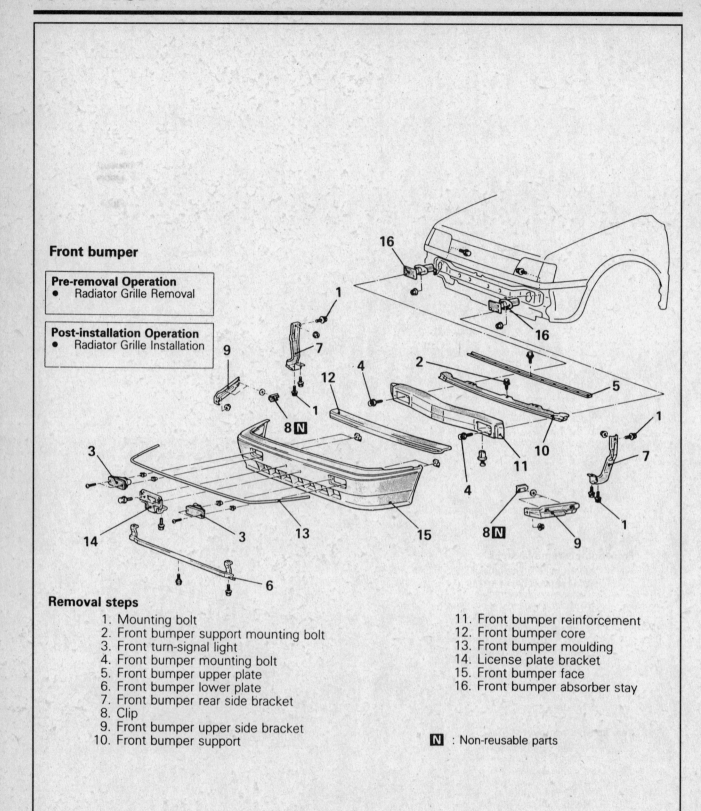

Front bumper

Pre-removal Operation
● Radiator Grille Removal

Post-installation Operation
● Radiator Grille Installation

Removal steps

1. Mounting bolt
2. Front bumper support mounting bolt
3. Front turn-signal light
4. Front bumper mounting bolt
5. Front bumper upper plate
6. Front bumper lower plate
7. Front bumper rear side bracket
8. Clip
9. Front bumper upper side bracket
10. Front bumper support
11. Front bumper reinforcement
12. Front bumper core
13. Front bumper moulding
14. License plate bracket
15. Front bumper face
16. Front bumper absorber stay

N : Non-reusable parts

Fig 13 Exploded view of the front bumper mounting on the 1989 Colt Vista

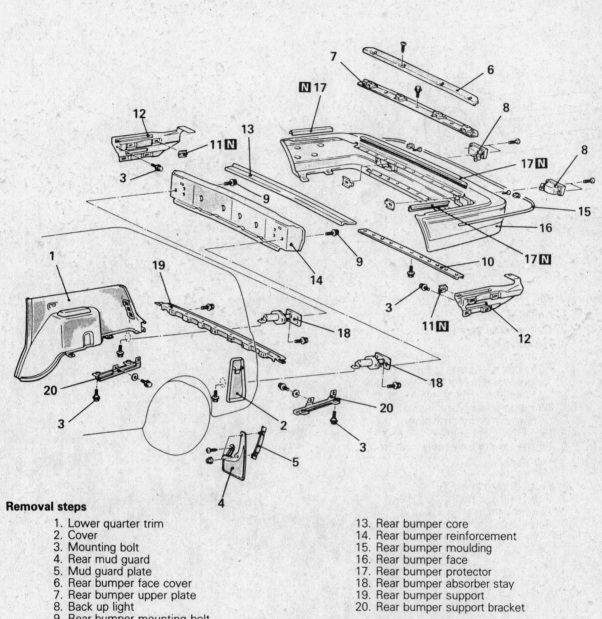

Removal steps

1. Lower quarter trim
2. Cover
3. Mounting bolt
4. Rear mud guard
5. Mud guard plate
6. Rear bumper face cover
7. Rear bumper upper plate
8. Back up light
9. Rear bumper mounting bolt
10. Rear bumper lower plate
11. Clip
12. Rear bumper side reinforcement

13. Rear bumper core
14. Rear bumper reinforcement
15. Rear bumper moulding
16. Rear bumper face
17. Rear bumper protector
18. Rear bumper absorber stay
19. Rear bumper support
20. Rear bumper support bracket

N : Non-reusable parts

Fig 14 Exploded view of the rear bumper mounting on the 1989 Colt Vista

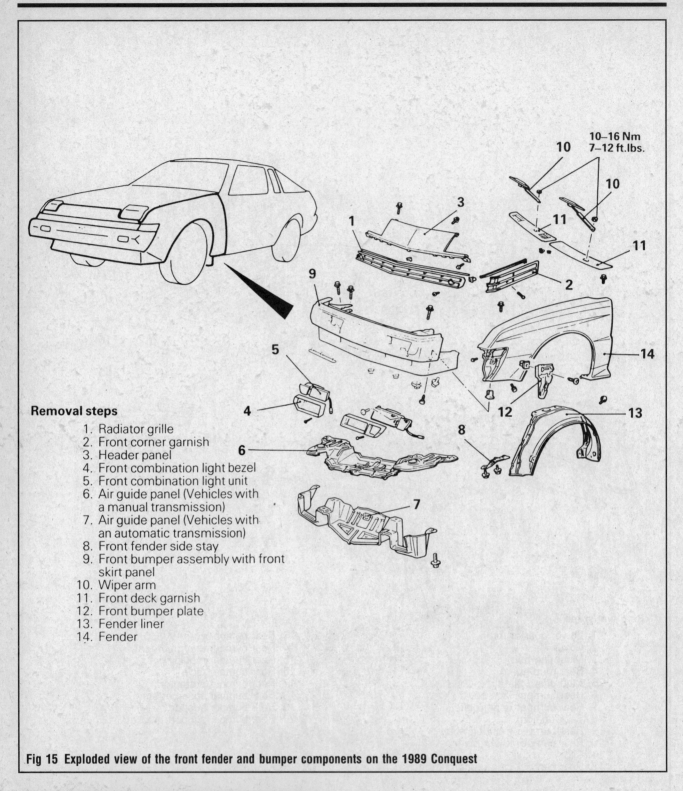

10–16 Nm
7–12 ft.lbs.

Removal steps

1. Radiator grille
2. Front corner garnish
3. Header panel
4. Front combination light bezel
5. Front combination light unit
6. Air guide panel (Vehicles with a manual transmission)
7. Air guide panel (Vehicles with an automatic transmission)
8. Front fender side stay
9. Front bumper assembly with front skirt panel
10. Wiper arm
11. Front deck garnish
12. Front bumper plate
13. Fender liner
14. Fender

Fig 15 Exploded view of the front fender and bumper components on the 1989 Conquest

Grille

REMOVAL & INSTALLATION

▶ **See Figures 16 and 17**

1. Remove the screws from the headlamp bezels. Remove the screws from the sides of the grille.

2. Remove the screws from the grille to center support bracket.
3. Remove the grille.
4. Place the grille into position. Install the center support screws and the outer mounting screws. Center the grille and tighten the mounting screws.
5. Install the headlamp bezel screws.

Remove all mounting screws securing the grille . . .

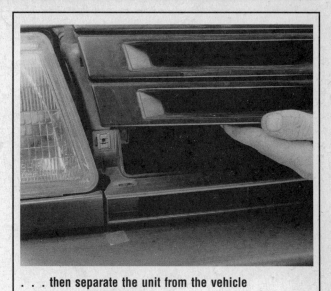

. . . then separate the unit from the vehicle

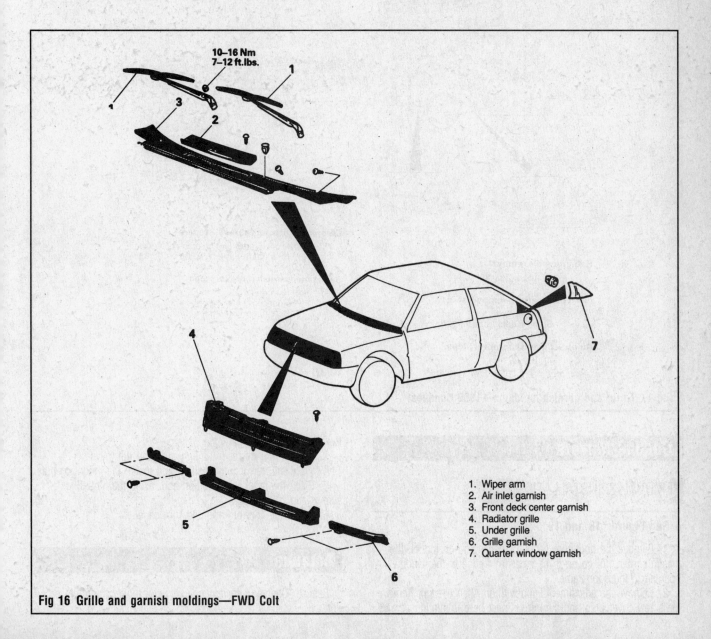

1. Wiper arm
2. Air inlet garnish
3. Front deck center garnish
4. Radiator grille
5. Under grille
6. Grille garnish
7. Quarter window garnish

10–16 Nm
7–12 ft.lbs.

Fig 16 Grille and garnish moldings—FWD Colt

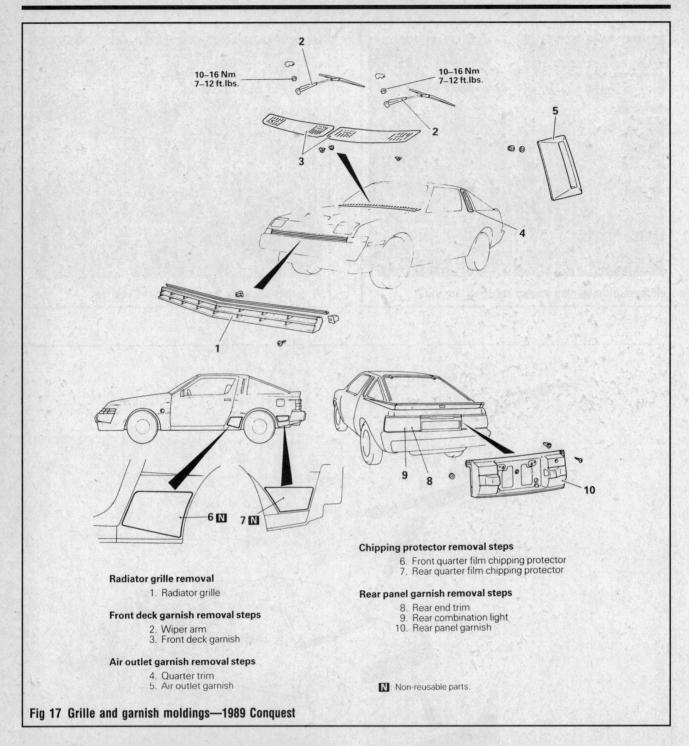

Radiator grille removal
1. Radiator grille

Front deck garnish removal steps
2. Wiper arm
3. Front deck garnish

Air outlet garnish removal steps
4. Quarter trim
5. Air outlet garnish

Chipping protector removal steps
6. Front quarter film chipping protector
7. Rear quarter film chipping protector

Rear panel garnish removal steps
8. Rear end trim
9. Rear combination light
10. Rear panel garnish

N: Non-reusable parts.

Fig 17 Grille and garnish moldings—1989 Conquest

Outside Mirrors

REMOVAL & INSTALLATION

▶ **See Figures 18 and 19**

1. Remove the door trim panel, or depending on model, the plastic corner trim cover at the inner front edge of the window opening in the door frame.

2. Remove the adjustment knob with an Allen wrench. Remove the screw cover plug and the mirror inner bezel mounting screws.

Remove the bezel.

3. Remove the mirror mounting nuts and the mirror.

4. Place the mirror into position and install the mounting nuts.

5. Place the bezel into position and install the mounting screws and cover plug.

6. Install the control knob and trim panel.

Antenna

Refer to Chapter 6 for antenna servicing under the Radio section.

Remove the screws securing the cover . . .

Remove the inner trim panel which hides the mirror mounting nuts

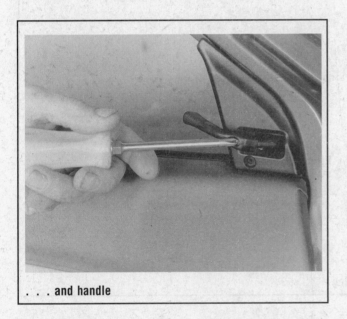

. . . and handle

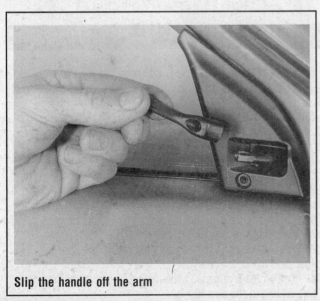

Slip the handle off the arm

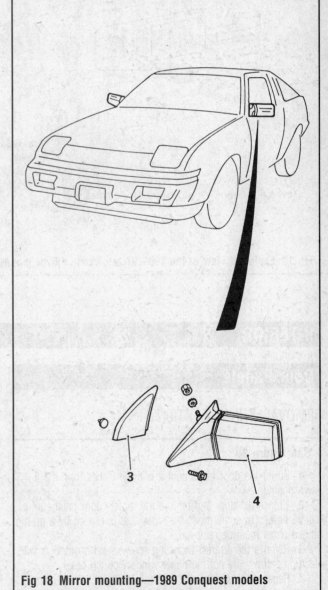

Fig 18 Mirror mounting—1989 Conquest models

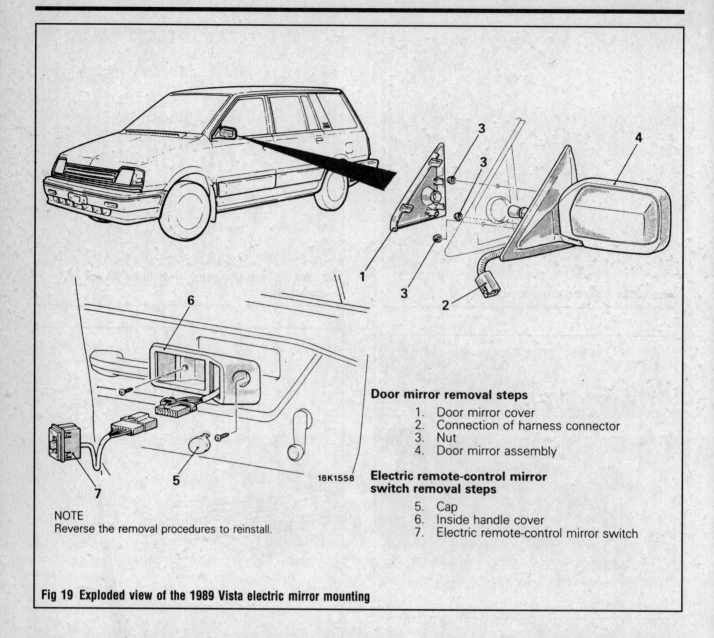

Door mirror removal steps

1. Door mirror cover
2. Connection of harness connector
3. Nut
4. Door mirror assembly

Electric remote-control mirror switch removal steps

5. Cap
6. Inside handle cover
7. Electric remote-control mirror switch

NOTE
Reverse the removal procedures to reinstall.

18K1558

Fig 19 Exploded view of the 1989 Vista electric mirror mounting

INTERIOR

Door Panels

REMOVAL & INSTALLATION

♦ **See Figure 20**

1. Lower the door glass until it is three inches from the full down position.

2. Unlock the door and remove the remote door latch control handle bezel. On some models a screw that is hidden by a plastic hinged panel must be removed.

3. Remove the armrest mounting screws, and on models with electric controls, pry out the power window switch bezel.

4. Remove the window crank handle on models with manual window regulators.

5. Remove the two edge inserts that cover the mounting screws for the door pull strap, and remove the mounting screws and strap.

6. Insert a wide flat tool between the panel and door frame and carefully twist the tool to unfasten the retainer clips from the door.

7. If the vehicle is equipped with power locks, slide the switch bezel through the trim panel.

8. Disconnect the courtesy lamp connector. Remove the door trim panel.

9. Remove the inner plastic cover and service the components as required.

10. Place sealer along the edges of the plastic liner and put the liner onto the door frame.

11. Position the trim panel, slide the power lock bezel through the panel, connect the courtesy lamp.

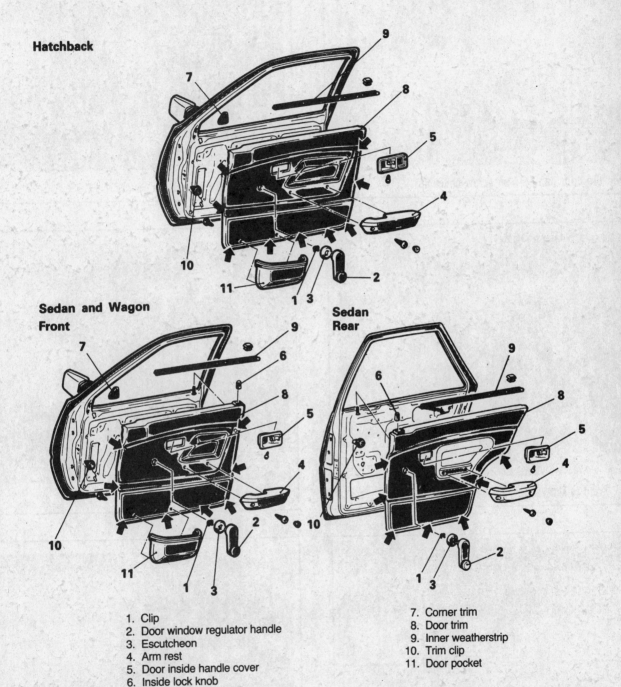

Hatchback

Sedan and Wagon Front

Sedan Rear

1. Clip
2. Door window regulator handle
3. Escutcheon
4. Arm rest
5. Door inside handle cover
6. Inside lock knob
7. Corner trim
8. Door trim
9. Inner weatherstrip
10. Trim clip
11. Door pocket

Fig 20 Interior door trim panels—FWD Colt

Pop the door handle trim screw cover up . . .

Unsnap the armrest screw covers . . .

. . . and unscrew the door handle trim

. . . and remove the screws

While pulling the handle up, slide the trim out and around the handle as shown

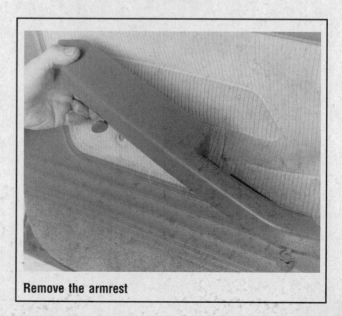

Remove the armrest

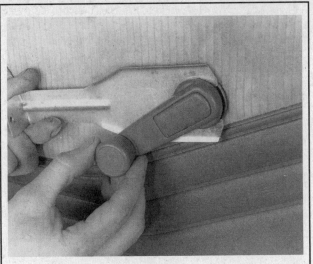

A special tool is available to . . .

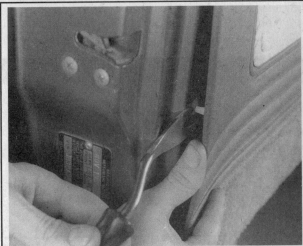

Using a suitable prytool, carefully pry the trim panel off the door shell . . .

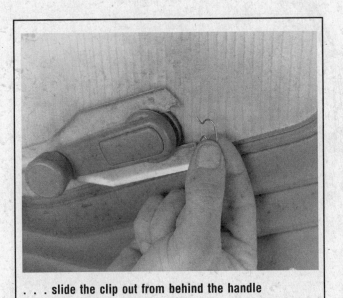

. . . slide the clip out from behind the handle

. . . then remove the door trim panel

12. Position the panel clips over their mounting holes and push the panel against the door frame to lock the clips.

13. Install the pull strap, the armrest, window handle/power switch, remote latch control/bezel.

Door Locks/Latch

REMOVAL & INSTALLATION

1. Remove the door trim panel and inner cover.
2. Raise the window to the full up position.
3. Disconnect all the locking clips from the remote linkage at the latch.
4. Remove the retaining screws at the door edge and remove the latch assembly.
5. Position the latch to the door frame and secure it with the retaining screws.

Separate the handle and trim washer from the door panel

6. Connect all of the remote linkage to the latch levers.

7. Check latch operation. Install the inner cover and door trim panel.

Door Glass Regulator

REMOVAL & INSTALLATION

▶ **See Figure 21**

1. Remove the door trim panel and inner liner.
2. Remove the window glass from the regulator and the door.
3. If equipped with power windows, disconnect the wiring harness and remove the retainer clip.

4. Unbolt, or if riveted, drill out the regulator mounting rivets.

5. Remove the regulator through the larger access hole. Rotate the regulator through the hole as required for removal.

6. Install the regulator to the mounting holes. If riveted use ¼-20 × ½ in. screws and nuts. Tighten the screws to 90 inch lbs.

7. Install the window glass, connect the motor wiring harness, and install the inner liner and door trim panel.

➡**The window glass is mounted to the regulator by two mounting studs and nuts, or a pin and clip. Raise the glass until the mounting nuts, or pi and clip align with the large access hole. Remove the nuts, or clip. Raise the glass up through the door frame. Rotate the glass so that the mounting studs pass through the notch at the rear of the door and remove the glass from the door.**

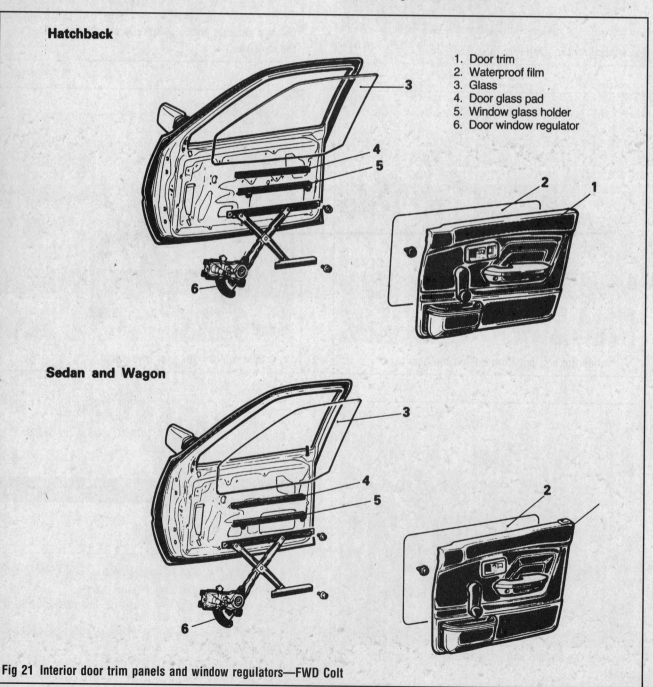

Hatchback

1. Door trim
2. Waterproof film
3. Glass
4. Door glass pad
5. Window glass holder
6. Door window regulator

Sedan and Wagon

Fig 21 Interior door trim panels and window regulators—FWD Colt

Electric Window Motor

REMOVAL & INSTALLATION

1. Remove the window regulator. See procedure.
2. Remove the electric motor mounting screws and the motor.
3. Place the window motor into position and secure the mounting screws.
4. Install the window regulator.

Windshield Glass

REMOVAL & INSTALLATION

✳✳ CAUTION

Do not operate the vehicle for at least 24 hours after the windshield installation. The windshield may not perform properly in the event of a collision if the urethane adhesive is not sufficiently cured.

It is difficult to salvage (to keep it from breaking or to reuse it) a windshield during the removal operation. The windshield is part of the structural support for the roof. The urethane bonding used to secure the windshield to the fence is difficult to cut or clean from any surface. If the moldings are set in urethane, it would also be unlikely they can be salvaged. Before starting this procedure, check on the availability of the windshield and moldings from a parts supplier.

➡**Protect the skin from coming in contact with the urethane, and wear eye and hand protection when working with glass.**

1. Remove the inside rear view mirror—refer to the necessary service procedures later in this section. Remove the windshield wiper arms and cowl cover.
2. Remove the windshield moldings using a trim stick.
3. Cut the urethane bonding from around windshield using a sharp, cold knife.
4. Remove the windshield from the vehicle.

To install:
Open the left front door window before installing the windshield to avoid pressurizing the passenger compartment; if a door or the trunk lid is slammed shut before the urethane bonding has had the chance to cure completely, leaks around the windshield may result.

➡**Allow the urethane sealer at least 24 hours to cure before returning the vehicle to use. The windshield fence should be cleaned of old bonding material. Support spacers should also be cleaned and properly installed on the weld studs or repair screws at the bottom of the windshield opening.**

5. Place the replacement windshield into the windshield opening with the glass in the center of the opening against the support spacers.
6. Mark the glass at the support spacers with a grease pencil, or pieces of masking tape and a pen, to use as a reference for installation. Remove the replacement windshield from the windshield opening.
7. Position the windshield inside on a suitable work surface with two padded 4×4×20 in. (10×10×50cm) blocks of wood. The blocks of wood should be positioned approximately 2.5 ft. (76cm) apart.
8. Clean the inside of the windshield with Mopar® Glass Cleaner, or equivalent, and a lint-free cloth.
9. Apply clear glass primer in a 1 in. (25mm) wide strip around the perimeter of the windshield and wipe clean.
10. Install the moldings onto the windshield. Apply black-out primer 0.75 in. (19mm) wide on the top and sides of the windshield and 1 in. (25mm) on bottom of the windshield. Allow at least 3 minutes drying time.
11. Position windshield bonding compression spacers on lower fence above the support spacers at the edge of the windshield opening.
12. Apply a 0.04 in. (1mm) bead of urethane around perimeter of windshield along the inside of the moldings.
13. With the aid of an assistant, position the windshield over the windshield opening. Align the reference marks at the bottom of the windshield to the support spacers.
14. Slowly lower the windshield glass to the windshield opening fence. Guide the top molding into proper position as necessary.
15. Push windshield inward to fence spacers at bottom and until the top molding is flush to the roof line.
16. Clean excess urethane from the exterior. Install cowl cover and wipers.
17. Install inside rear view mirror.
18. After repair has cured, water test windshield.

Rear Window Stationary Glass

REMOVAL & INSTALLATION

1. Remove any trim panels as necessary to gain access to the glass pane.
2. If removing the quarter glass, remove the nuts holding the glass module to the quarter glass opening.
3. Cut the urethane sealer around the perimeter of the glass opening fence.
4. Lift the glass module out of the glass opening. Separate the glass module from the vehicle.

To install:
5. Clean all surfaces of the opening, fence and glass module.
6. Prepare the fence and glass module using the same method as described in the windshield removal and installation service procedures earlier in this section.
7. Install the window into the opening.
8. If applicable, install the nuts to hold the quarter glass module in the opening.
9. Wipe excess urethane from around the window, then install the quarter window molding and trim panel.
10. Allow adequate time for the urethane to cure before driving the vehicle. For more details, refer to the windshield removal and installation procedure earlier in this section.

Inside Rear View Mirror

REMOVAL & INSTALLATION

1. Loosen the mounting set screw on the mounting arm.
2. Slide the mirror off of the windshield mounting button.
3. Slide the mirror mounting arm over the mounting button and secure the set screw.

Seats

REMOVAL & INSTALLATION

◆ **See Figures 22, 23, 24 and 25**

1. Depending on year and model, the front seat(s) are mounted by bolts accessible from underneath the vehicle, or a combination of nuts and bolts. The nuts usually are used to mount the front of

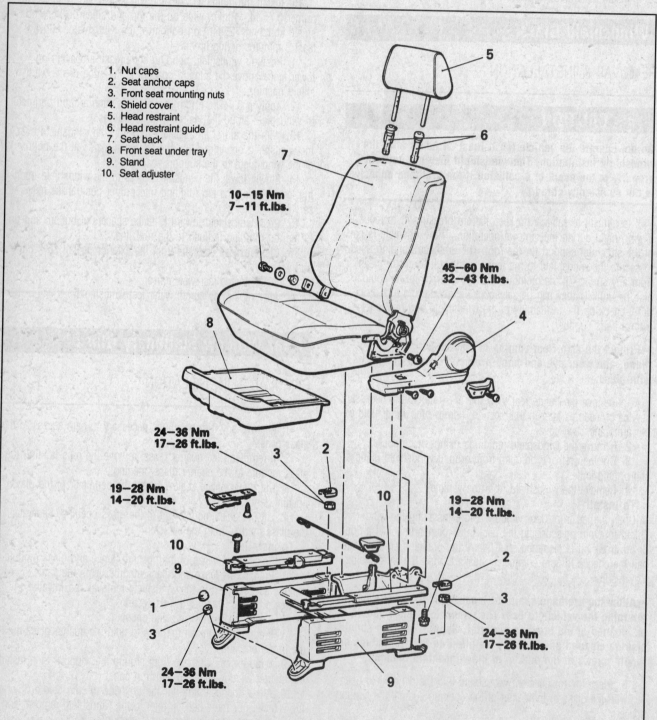

1. Nut caps
2. Seat anchor caps
3. Front seat mounting nuts
4. Shield cover
5. Head restraint
6. Head restraint guide
7. Seat back
8. Front seat under tray
9. Stand
10. Seat adjuster

10—15 Nm
7—11 ft.lbs.

45—60 Nm
32—43 ft.lbs.

24—36 Nm
17—26 ft.lbs.

19—28 Nm
14—20 ft.lbs.

19—28 Nm
14—20 ft.lbs.

24—36 Nm
17—26 ft.lbs.

24—36 Nm
17—26 ft.lbs.

Fig 22 Exploded view of the Vista front seat mounting

the seat brackets, and are loosened from the passenger's compartment. The nuts are usually covered by a trim plug which must be removed first. The rear of the seat bracket mounting bolts are accessed from underneath the vehicle mounting are loosen.

2. The second seat (Vista models) is mounted by nuts and bolts that can be removed from the passengers compartment.

3. Rear seats are removed by pushing the front of the seat cushion back towards the rear of the vehicle and lifting it up to free it from the mounting clips. Or, removing the bolts from the front of the seat cushion brackets. The seat back is usually retained by bolts through the floor pan that are visible after the cushion has been removed.

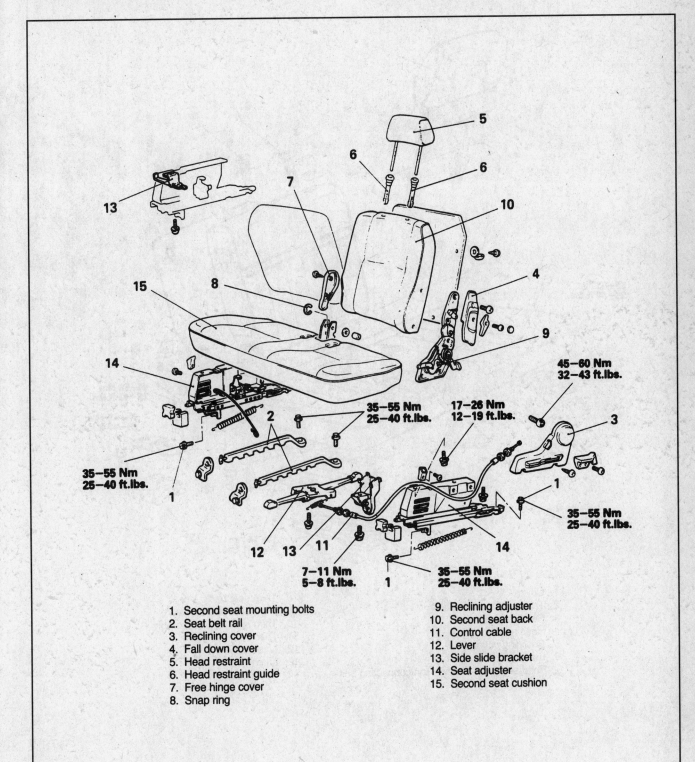

1. Second seat mounting bolts
2. Seat belt rail
3. Reclining cover
4. Fall down cover
5. Head restraint
6. Head restraint guide
7. Free hinge cover
8. Snap ring
9. Reclining adjuster
10. Second seat back
11. Control cable
12. Lever
13. Side slide bracket
14. Seat adjuster
15. Second seat cushion

Fig 23 Exploded view of the Vista second seat mounting

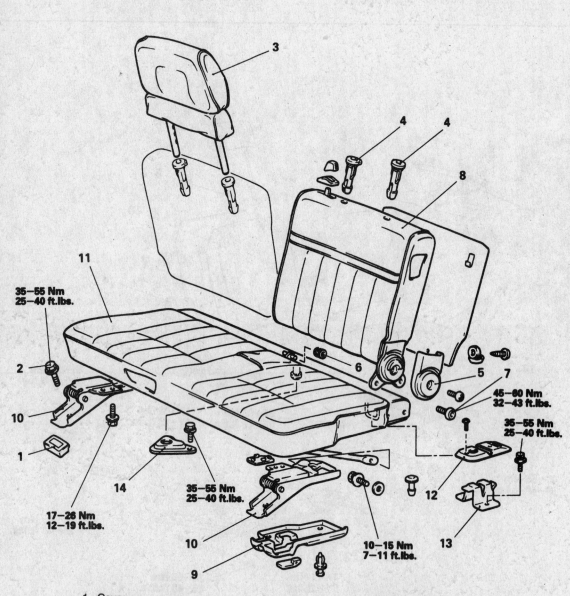

35—55 Nm
25—40 ft.lbs.

45—60 Nm
32—43 ft.lbs.

35—55 Nm
25—40 ft.lbs.

35—55 Nm
25—40 ft.lbs.

17—26 Nm
12—19 ft.lbs.

10—15 Nm
7—11 ft.lbs.

1. Cover
2. Third seat mounting bolt
3. Head restraint
4. Head restraint guide
5. Reclining cover
6. Bushing
7. Third seat back and cushion connecting bolt

8. Third seat back
9. Third seat hinge cover
10. Third seat hinge assembly
11. Third seat cushion
12. Latch cover
13. Latch
14. Anchor plate

Fig 24 Exploded view of the Vista third seat mounting

Front seat

Rear seat

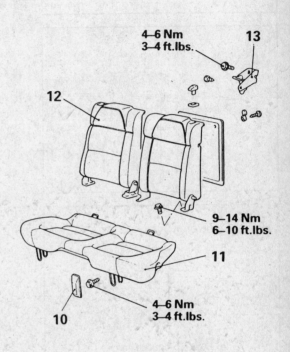

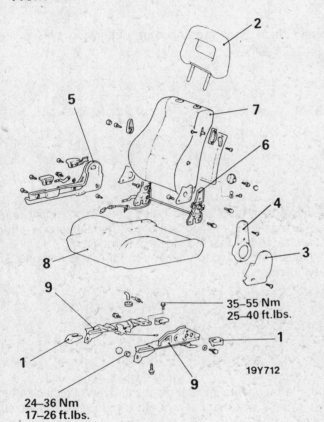

4–6 Nm
3–4 ft.lbs.

9–14 Nm
6–10 ft.lbs.

4–6 Nm
3–4 ft.lbs.

35–55 Nm
25–40 ft.lbs.

24–36 Nm
17–26 ft.lbs.

19Y712

Front seat removal steps

1. Cover
2. Head restraint
3. Upper reclining cover
4. Lower reclining cover
5. Cushion shield
6. Reclining adjuster
7. Seatback
8. Seat cushion
9. Seat side adjuster

Rear seat removal steps

10. Cover
11. Rear seat cushion
12. Rear seatback
13. Striker

Fig 25 Exploded view of the Conquest front and rear seat mounting

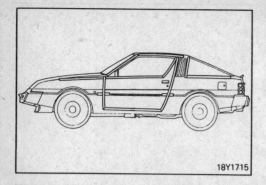

18Y1715

TROUBLESHOOTING OF WIND NOISE

(1) Apply cloth tape to all potential sources of wind noise such as panel joints, protrusions, moulding joints, glass to body joints in the direction from which noises are heard.

(2) Drive under this condition to make sure that wind noises are eliminated.

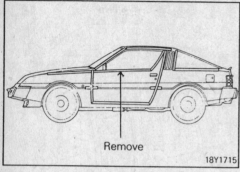

Remove

18Y1715

(3) Remove tape one after another until wind noises are produced again.

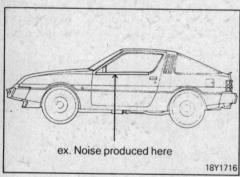

ex. Noise produced here

18Y1716

(4) If removal of a tape causes noise generation, apply tape again to that location and remove other tapes one after another to check that no noise is produced.

(5) The location with tape left applied to the last is responsible for wind noise.

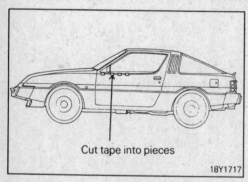

Cut tape into pieces

18Y1717

(6) Cut the left tape into smaller pieces and remove piece after piece in the same manner as before to localize suspected source.

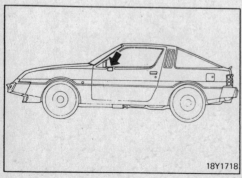

18Y1718

(7) Remove the last piece left and check that its removal causes wind noise and its application stops wind noise.

(8) Apply butyl tape or body sealer to the thus located area to minimize gap.

TROUBLE SHOOTING

Trouble and possible cause	Remedy

1. Rain water leaks from windshield and toe board to foot area.

   (1) Defectively bonded or loose windshield weatherstrip.
     Apply adhesive and sealer.

   (2) Deformed or broken windshield weatherstrip.
     Replace weatherstrip.

   (3) Sealer defectively applied to grommets in toe board
     (for wiring harness, hood unlock cable, heater water hose
     and speedometer cable through holes).
     Apply sealer to all surfaces of each grommet.

2. Rain water leaks into luggage compartment.

   (1) Defectively bonded or loose rear window weatherstrip.
     Apply adhesive.

   (2) Sealer in rear deck quarter panel joint cracked.
     Apply sealer from inside luggage compartment.

   (3) Loose bonded rear part of deck lid, or loose clip.
     Apply adhesive and, after correction of flange, securely clip the lid.

   (4) Defectively sealed floor panel joints (wheel house, quarter
     panel and rear panel to floor panel joints)
     Apply sealer.

   (5) Weak contact of deck lid weatherstrip.
     Adjust at deck lid hinges and striker.

   (6) Defectively sealed quarter panel and filler neck bracket
     attaching area.
     Apply sealer.

   (7) Unevenly contacting or cracked rear combination lamp
     packing.
     Retighten or replace packing.

3. Rain water leaks into rear room (station wagon).

   (1) Loose or defectively bonded tail gate window weatherstrip.
     Apply adhesive.

   (2) Loose tail gate weatherstrip.
     Apply adhesive.

   (3) Weak contact of tail gate.
     Adjust guide rubber and bumper plate.

   (4) Loose quarter window weatherstrip.
     Apply sealer.

   (5) Defectively sealed floor panel joints.
     Apply sealer.

4. Rain water leaks at around doors.

   (1) Loose door weatherstrip, or improperly fitted clip.
     Apply adhesive, or securely clip weatherstrip.

   (2) Weak front door contact at front corner above sash
     (sedan and station wagon).
     Bend sash to obtain firm door contact.

   (3) Weak front door contact at front corner above door glass
     (hardtop and coupe).
     Adjust tilt of main roller guide.

   (4) Front door glass clearance at top (hardtop and coupe).
     Adjust upper stopper and tilt.

   (5) Defective contact of quarter window vertical weatherstrip
     with door weatherstrip (hardtop).
     Adjust longitudinal and lateral positions of quarter window and door window.

   (6) Weak contact of quarter window (hardtop).
     Adjust tilt of main roller guide and quarter glass guide.

   (7) Loose or broken door inner panel weather film.
     Apply adhesive or replace weather film.

   (8) Loose rear door quarter glass weatherstrip
     (sedan and station wagon).
     Apply adhesive.

5. Entry of dust into room. (For other than the following items, refer to para. 1 to 4.)

   (1) Cracked sealer or improperly filled sealer at floor joints.
     Apply sealer.

   (2) Side ventilator valve defectively shut.
     Adjust control linkage to correct its contact.

   (3) Rear ventilator screen broken.
     Replace screen.

Trouble and possible cause	Remedy
6. Wind noise from front of car.	
(1) Door window glass defectively contacting (hardtop and coupe).	Adjust tilt of main roller guide.
(2) Loose or missing front door seal rubber (MA154216). (sedan and station wagon).	Reline seal rubber by applying adhesive.
(3) Loose or missing rear door corner weatherstrip (MA 154526)	Reline weatherstrip by applying adhesive.
7. Heavy locking and unlocking of front hood.	
(1) Short hood hook lock bolt.	Adjust length of lock bolt.
(2) Incorrectly centered hood hook and lock.	Adjust hook and lock.
8. Uneven or floating front hood.	
(1) Incorrect height of bumper screws.	Adjust height of bumper screws.
(2) Hook lock bolts too long.	Adjust length of lock bolts.
9. Uneven clearance between front hood and car body.	
(1) Defectively installed hood.	Adjust clearance at hinges.
10. Defectively opening and closing deck lid.	
(1) Latch and striker out of adjustment.	Adjust latch and striker.
11. Uneven height of deck lid.	
(1) Defectively installed lid.	Adjust height of lid at hinges. Adjust height of lid at striker.
12. Uneven clearance between deck lid and car body.	
(1) Defectively installed lid.	Adjust longitudinal and lateral positions of lid at hinges.
13. Defective door operation.	
(1) Door striker out of adjustment.	Adjust vertical, horizontal and longitudinal positions of striker.
14. Uneven clearance between door and car body, and uneven height between door and car body.	
(1) Defectively installed door.	Adjust at door hinges.
15. Defective tail gate opening and closing.	
(1) Weak torsion bar spring.	Insert adjusting plate.
(2) Bumper female and rubber maladjusted.	Adjust.

Symptom	Probable cause	Remedy
Improper door position	Worn bushing and hinge of door	Replace
	Loose tightening bolt to door hinge	Retighten
	Deformed door hinge	Repair by sheet metal working or replace
Noise from door interior	Worn door check	Replace
	Worn bushing and hinge of door	Replace
	Bent interior rod from inside door handle	Repair by hand
	Detached interior rod from inside door lock	Attach
	Loose tightening screw to door latch-striker	Retighten
	Loose tightening screw to door latch	Retighten
	Damaged portion-caulked of rod in door locking system	Repair by sheet metal working or replace at door latch assembly
	Bent interior rod of outside door handle	Repair by hand or replace
	Detached interior rod of outside door handle	Attach
Broken door	Cracked mount portion to door hinge	Repair by welding
Malfunctionated door checker	Worn door check	Replace
	Damaged door check	Replace
Door fails opening	Malfunction in door latch	Repair or replace
	Detached interior rod from outside door handle	Attach
	Broken interior rod from outside door handle	Replace
	Detached interior rod from inside door handle	Attach
	Broken interior rod from inside door handle	Replace
	Detached interior rod from door inside lock	Attach
	Broken interior rod from door inside lock	Replace
	Broken caulking pin to door locking system	Replace
Door fails closing	Bent interior rod from outside door handle	Repair by hand
	Bent interior rod from inside door handle	Repair by hand
	Loose tightening screw to door latch striker	Retighten
	Broken door latch striker	Replace
	Loose tightening screw to door latch	Retighten
	Malfunction in door latch	Repair or replace
	Broken door latch	Replace
Hard movement of door	Improper door position	Adjust door position
	Seized door hinge with corrosion	Clean up or replace
	Excessive play of outside door handle	Adjust the play
	Excessive play of inside door handle	Adjust the play
	Deformed door check	Reform or replace
Ajar door	Deformed door hinge	Repair by sheet metal working or replace
	Improper door position	Adjust position
	Excessive play of outside door handle	Adjust the play
	Excessive play of inside door handle	Adjust the play
Inoperative center door lock	Broken interior rod from inside door lock	Replace
	Detached interior rod from inside door lock	Attach
	Bent interior rod from inside door lock	Repair by hand

Symptom	Probable cause	Remedy
Inoperative center door lock	Broken caulking pin to door latch	Replace
	Broken door latch	Replace
	Malfunction in child lock operation	Repair or replace
	Broken door lock cylinder	Replace
Malfunction in center door lock	Insufficient holding effort of actuator	Replace
	Insufficient stroke of actuator	Replace
	Misassembled locking rod	Reassemble
	Dismounted actuator	Remount
	Improper adjustment of regulating pin	Adjust position
	Broken electrical circuit	Repair
Door glass falis up and down	Detached sash	Attach
	Broken sash	Replace
	Collapsed sash	Repair by sheet metal working or replace
	Dismount window glass regulator	Remount
	Collapsed window glass regulator arm	Repair by sheet metal working or replace
	Broken window glass regulator	Replace
Door glass operates up and down hardly	Collapsed sash	Repair by sheet metal working or replace
	Collapsed window regulator arm	Repair by sheet metal working or replace
	Broken window regulator handle	Replace
	Improper window glass position	Adjust position
Inoperative hood support	Detached link from hood support	Attach
	Collapsed hood support	Repair by sheet metal working or replace
	Broken hood support	Replace
Noise from hood	Improper hood position	Adjust position
	Loose tightening screw to hood latch	Retighten
	Loose tightening screw to hood support	Retighten
Hood fails lock or unlock	Improper adjustment of hood lock-cable length	Adjust installation
	Broken hood lock-cable	Replace
	Detached hood lock-cable	Attach
	Detached bracket to hood lock-cable	Attach
	Broken bracket to hood lock-cable	Replace
	Broken hood latch	Replace
	Improper hood latch position	Adjust position
Ajar hood	Improper hood position	Adjust position
	Improper hood latch position	Adjust position
	Improper adjustment of hood lock-cable length	Adjust installation
	Loose tightening screw in bracket to hood lock-cable	Retighten
Improper door glass position	Improper adjustment of door window regulator	Adjust position

Symptom	Probable cause	Remedy
Improper bumper position	Improper bumper stay	Adjust position
	Collapsed bumper stay	Replace
	Improper bumper corner bracket	Adjust position
	Deformed mount portion to bumper stay	Replace
Damaged bumper	Cracked bumper	Replace
	Discolored bumper	Repair by painting or replace
	Heated deformation of bumper	Replace
Noise from bumper	Loose tightening bolt to bumper	Retighten
	Cracked bumper	Replace
Detached bumper	Detached tightening bolt to bumper	Attach
	Broken bumper stay	Replace
Damaged body panel	Corrosived body panel	Clean-up and repair by painting
	Discolored body panel	Repair by painting
Detached liftgate	Detached tightening bolt to liftgate hinge	Attach
	Broken pin to liftgate hinge	Replace
	Broken liftgate hinge	Replace
Improper liftgate position	Improper liftgate hinge position	Adjust position
	Improper liftgate latch position	Adjust position
	Improper liftgate striker position	Adjust position
Noise from liftgate	Loose tightening bolt to liftgate hinge	Retighten
	Loose tightening bolt to liftgate striker	Retighten
	Loose tightening bolt to liftgate gas stopper	Retighten
	Loose tightening bolt to liftgate latch	Retighten
Water leakage from liftgate	Damaged weatherstrip to liftgate	Replace
	Damaged weatherstrip to glass of liftgate	Replace
Improper liftgate movement feeling	Collapsed liftgate hinge	Repair by sheet metal working or replace
	Improper liftgate latch position	Adjust position
	Improper liftgate striker position	Adjust position
	Damaged liftgate gas stopper	Replace
	Deformed mount portion to liftgate gas stopper	Repair by sheet metal working or replace
Hard movement of liftgate	Collapsed liftgate hinge	Repair by sheet metal working or replace
	Improper liftgate latch position	Adjust position
	Improper liftgate striker position	Adjust position
	Damaged liftgate gas stopper	Replace
	Deformed mount portion to liftgate gas stopper	Repair by sheet metal working or replace
Liftgate falis lock or unlock	Liftgate hinge fails to turn	Replace
	Deformed pin of liftgate hinge	Replace
	Damaged liftgate hinge	Replace
	Damaged liftgate latch	Replace
	Damaged liftgate striker	Replace
	Damaged lifigate gas stopper	Replace

How to Remove Stains from Fabric Interior

For rest results, spots and stains should be removed as soon as possible. Never use gasoline, lacquer thinner, acetone, nail polish remover or bleach. Use a 3' x 3" piece of cheesecloth. Squeeze most of the liquid from the fabric and wipe the stained fabric from the outside of the stain toward the center with a lifting motion. Turn the cheesecloth as soon as one side becomes soiled. When using water to remove a stain, be sure to wash the entire section after the spot has been removed to avoid water stains. Encrusted spots can be broken up with a dull knife and vacuumed before removing the stain.

Type of Stain	How to Remove It
Surface spots	Brush the spots out with a small hand brush or use a commercial preparation such as K2R to lift the stain.
Mildew	Clean around the mildew with warm suds. Rinse in cold water and soak the mildew area in a solution of 1 part table salt and 2 parts water. Wash with upholstery cleaner.
Water stains	Water stains in fabric materials can be removed with a solution made from 1 cup of table salt dissolved in 1 quart of water. Vigorously scrub the solution into the stain and rinse with clear water. Water stains in nylon or other synthetic fabrics should be removed with a commercial type spot remover.
Chewing gum, tar, crayons, shoe polish (greasy stains)	Do not use a cleaner that will soften gum or tar. Harden the deposit with an ice cube and scrape away as much as possible with a dull knife. Moisten the remainder with cleaning fluid and scrub clean.
Ice cream, candy	Most candy has a sugar base and can be removed with a cloth wrung out in warm water. Oily candy, after cleaning with warm water, should be cleaned with upholstery cleaner. Rinse with warm water and clean the remainder with cleaning fluid.
Wine, alcohol, egg, milk, soft drink (non-greasy stains)	Do not use soap. Scrub the stain with a cloth wrung out in warm water. Remove the remainder with cleaning fluid.
Grease, oil, lipstick, butter and related stains	Use a spot remover to avoid leaving a ring. Work from the outisde of the stain to the center and dry with a clean cloth when the spot is gone.
Headliners (cloth)	Mix a solution of warm water and foam upholstery cleaner to give thick suds. Use only foam—liquid may streak or spot. Clean the entire headliner in one operation using a circular motion with a natural sponge.
Headliner (vinyl)	Use a vinyl cleaner with a sponge and wipe clean with a dry cloth.
Seats and door panels	Mix 1 pint upholstery cleaner in 1 gallon of water. Do not soak the fabric around the buttons.
Leather or vinyl fabric	Use a multi-purpose cleaner full strength and a stiff brush. Let stand 2 minutes and scrub thoroughly. Wipe with a clean, soft rag.
Nylon or synthetic fabrics	For normal stains, use the same procedures you would for washing cloth upholstery. If the fabric is extremely dirty, use a multi-purpose cleaner full strength with a stiff scrub brush. Scrub thoroughly in all directions and wipe with a cotton towel or soft rag.

GLOSSARY

AIR/FUEL RATIO: The ratio of air-to-gasoline by weight in the fuel mixture drawn into the engine.

AIR INJECTION: One method of reducing harmful exhaust emissions by injecting air into each of the exhaust ports of an engine. The fresh air entering the hot exhaust manifold causes any remaining fuel to be burned before it can exit the tailpipe.

ALTERNATOR: A device used for converting mechanical energy into electrical energy.

AMMETER: An instrument, calibrated in amperes, used to measure the flow of an electrical current in a circuit. Ammeters are always connected in series with the circuit being tested.

AMPERE: The rate of flow of electrical current present when one volt of electrical pressure is applied against one ohm of electrical resistance.

ANALOG COMPUTER: Any microprocessor that uses similar (analogous) electrical signals to make its calculations.

ARMATURE: A laminated, soft iron core wrapped by a wire that converts electrical energy to mechanical energy as in a motor or relay. When rotated in a magnetic field, it changes mechanical energy into electrical energy as in a generator.

ATMOSPHERIC PRESSURE: The pressure on the Earth's surface caused by the weight of the air in the atmosphere. At sea level, this pressure is 14.7 psi at 32°F (101 kPa at 0°C).

ATOMIZATION: The breaking down of a liquid into a fine mist that can be suspended in air.

AXIAL PLAY: Movement parallel to a shaft or bearing bore.

BACKFIRE: The sudden combustion of gases in the intake or exhaust system that results in a loud explosion.

BACKLASH: The clearance or play between two parts, such as meshed gears.

BACKPRESSURE: Restrictions in the exhaust system that slow the exit of exhaust gases from the combustion chamber.

BAKELITE: A heat resistant, plastic insulator material commonly used in printed circuit boards and transistorized components.

BALL BEARING: A bearing made up of hardened inner and outer races between which hardened steel balls roll.

BALLAST RESISTOR: A resistor in the primary ignition circuit that lowers voltage after the engine is started to reduce wear on ignition components.

BEARING: A friction reducing, supportive device usually located between a stationary part and a moving part.

BIMETAL TEMPERATURE SENSOR: Any sensor or switch made of two dissimilar types of metal that bend when heated or cooled due to the different expansion rates of the alloys. These types of sensors usually function as an on/off switch.

BLOWBY: Combustion gases, composed of water vapor and unburned fuel, that leak past the piston rings into the crankcase during normal engine operation. These gases are removed by the PCV system to prevent the buildup of harmful acids in the crankcase.

BRAKE PAD: A brake shoe and lining assembly used with disc brakes.

BRAKE SHOE: The backing for the brake lining. The term is, however, usually applied to the assembly of the brake backing and lining.

BUSHING: A liner, usually removable, for a bearing; an anti-friction liner used in place of a bearing.

CALIPER: A hydraulically activated device in a disc brake system, which is mounted straddling the brake rotor (disc). The caliper contains at least one piston and two brake pads. Hydraulic pressure on the piston(s) forces the pads against the rotor.

CAMSHAFT: A shaft in the engine on which are the lobes (cams) which operate the valves. The camshaft is driven by the crankshaft, via a belt, chain or gears, at one half the crankshaft speed.

CAPACITOR: A device which stores an electrical charge.

CARBON MONOXIDE (CO): A colorless, odorless gas given off as a normal byproduct of combustion. It is poisonous and extremely dangerous in confined areas, building up slowly to toxic levels without warning if adequate ventilation is not available.

CARBURETOR: A device, usually mounted on the intake manifold of an engine, which mixes the air and fuel in the proper proportion to allow even combustion.

CATALYTIC CONVERTER: A device installed in the exhaust system, like a muffler, that converts harmful byproducts of combustion into carbon dioxide and water vapor by means of a heat-producing chemical reaction.

CENTRIFUGAL ADVANCE: A mechanical method of advancing the spark timing by using flyweights in the distributor that react to centrifugal force generated by the distributor shaft rotation.

CHECK VALVE: Any one-way valve installed to permit the flow of air, fuel or vacuum in one direction only.

CHOKE: A device, usually a moveable valve, placed in the intake path of a carburetor to restrict the flow of air.

CIRCUIT: Any unbroken path through which an electrical current can flow. Also used to describe fuel flow in some instances.

CIRCUIT BREAKER: A switch which protects an electrical circuit from overload by opening the circuit when the current flow exceeds a predetermined level. Some circuit breakers must be reset manually, while most reset automatically.

COIL (IGNITION): A transformer in the ignition circuit which steps up the voltage provided to the spark plugs.

COMBINATION MANIFOLD: An assembly which includes both the intake and exhaust manifolds in one casting.

COMBINATION VALVE: A device used in some fuel systems that routes fuel vapors to a charcoal storage canister instead of venting them into the atmosphere. The valve relieves fuel tank pressure and allows fresh air into the tank as the fuel level drops to prevent a vapor lock situation.

COMPRESSION RATIO: The comparison of the total volume of the cylinder and combustion chamber with the piston at BDC and the piston at TDC.

CONDENSER: 1. An electrical device which acts to store an electrical charge, preventing voltage surges. 2. A radiator-like device in the air conditioning system in which refrigerant gas condenses into a liquid, giving off heat.

CONDUCTOR: Any material through which an electrical current can be transmitted easily.

CONTINUITY: Continuous or complete circuit. Can be checked with an ohmmeter.

COUNTERSHAFT: An intermediate shaft which is rotated by a mainshaft and transmits, in turn, that rotation to a working part.

CRANKCASE: The lower part of an engine in which the crankshaft and related parts operate.

CRANKSHAFT: The main driving shaft of an engine which receives reciprocating motion from the pistons and converts it to rotary motion.

CYLINDER: In an engine, the round hole in the engine block in which the piston(s) ride.

CYLINDER BLOCK: The main structural member of an engine in which is found the cylinders, crankshaft and other principal parts.

CYLINDER HEAD: The detachable portion of the engine, usually fastened to the top of the cylinder block and containing all or most of the combustion chambers. On overhead valve engines, it contains the valves and their operating parts. On overhead cam engines, it contains the camshaft as well.

DEAD CENTER: The extreme top or bottom of the piston stroke.

DETONATION: An unwanted explosion of the air/fuel mixture in the combustion chamber caused by excess heat and compression, advanced timing, or an overly lean mixture. Also referred to as "ping".

DIAPHRAGM: A thin, flexible wall separating two cavities, such as in a vacuum advance unit.

DIESELING: A condition in which hot spots in the combustion chamber cause the engine to run on after the key is turned off.

DIFFERENTIAL: A geared assembly which allows the transmission of motion between drive axles, giving one axle the ability to turn faster than the other.

DIODE: An electrical device that will allow current to flow in one direction only.

DISC BRAKE: A hydraulic braking assembly consisting of a brake disc, or rotor, mounted on an axle, and a caliper assembly containing, usually two brake pads which are activated by hydraulic pressure. The pads are forced against the sides of the disc, creating friction which slows the vehicle.

DISTRIBUTOR: A mechanically driven device on an engine which is responsible for electrically firing the spark plug at a predetermined point of the piston stroke.

DOWEL PIN: A pin, inserted in mating holes in two different parts allowing those parts to maintain a fixed relationship.

DRUM BRAKE: A braking system which consists of two brake shoes and one or two wheel cylinders, mounted on a fixed backing plate, and a brake drum, mounted on an axle, which revolves around the assembly.

DWELL: The rate, measured in degrees of shaft rotation, at which an electrical circuit cycles on and off.

ELECTRONIC CONTROL UNIT (ECU): Ignition module, module, amplifier or igniter. See Module for definition.

ELECTRONIC IGNITION: A system in which the timing and firing of the spark plugs is controlled by an electronic control unit, usually called a module. These systems have no points or condenser.

END-PLAY: The measured amount of axial movement in a shaft.

ENGINE: A device that converts heat into mechanical energy.

EXHAUST MANIFOLD: A set of cast passages or pipes which conduct exhaust gases from the engine.

FEELER GAUGE: A blade, usually metal, of precisely predetermined thickness, used to measure the clearance between two parts.

FIRING ORDER: The order in which combustion occurs in the cylinders of an engine. Also the order in which spark is distributed to the plugs by the distributor.

FLOODING: The presence of too much fuel in the intake manifold and combustion chamber which prevents the air/fuel mixture from firing, thereby causing a no-start situation.

FLYWHEEL: A disc shaped part bolted to the rear end of the crankshaft. Around the outer perimeter is affixed the ring gear. The starter drive engages the ring gear, turning the flywheel, which rotates the crankshaft, imparting the initial starting motion to the engine.

FOOT POUND (ft. lbs. or sometimes, ft.lb.): The amount of energy or work needed to raise an item weighing one pound, a distance of one foot.

FUSE: A protective device in a circuit which prevents circuit overload by breaking the circuit when a specific amperage is present. The device is constructed around a strip or wire of a lower amperage rating than the circuit it is designed to protect. When an amperage higher than that stamped on the fuse is present in the circuit, the strip or wire melts, opening the circuit.

GEAR RATIO: The ratio between the number of teeth on meshing gears.

GENERATOR: A device which converts mechanical energy into electrical energy.

HEAT RANGE: The measure of a spark plug's ability to dissipate heat from its firing end. The higher the heat range, the hotter the plug fires.

HUB: The center part of a wheel or gear.

HYDROCARBON (HC): Any chemical compound made up of hydrogen and carbon. A major pollutant formed by the engine as a byproduct of combustion.

HYDROMETER: An instrument used to measure the specific gravity of a solution.

INCH POUND (inch lbs.; sometimes in.lb. or in. lbs.): One twelfth of a foot pound.

INDUCTION: A means of transferring electrical energy in the form of a magnetic field. Principle used in the ignition coil to increase voltage.

INJECTOR: A device which receives metered fuel under relatively low pressure and is activated to inject the fuel into the engine under relatively high pressure at a predetermined time.

INPUT SHAFT: The shaft to which torque is applied, usually carrying the driving gear or gears.

INTAKE MANIFOLD: A casting of passages or pipes used to conduct air or a fuel/air mixture to the cylinders.

JOURNAL: The bearing surface within which a shaft operates.

KEY: A small block usually fitted in a notch between a shaft and a hub to prevent slippage of the two parts.

MANIFOLD: A casting of passages or set of pipes which connect the cylinders to an inlet or outlet source.

MANIFOLD VACUUM: Low pressure in an engine intake manifold formed just below the throttle plates. Manifold vacuum is highest at idle and drops under acceleration.

MASTER CYLINDER: The primary fluid pressurizing device in a hydraulic system. In automotive use, it is found in brake and hydraulic clutch systems and is pedal activated, either directly or, in a power brake system, through the power booster.

MODULE: Electronic control unit, amplifier or igniter of solid state or integrated design which controls the current flow in the ignition primary circuit based on input from the pick-up coil. When the module opens the primary circuit, high secondary voltage is induced in the coil.

NEEDLE BEARING: A bearing which consists of a number (usually a large number) of long, thin rollers.

OHM: (Ω) The unit used to measure the resistance of conductor-to-electrical flow. One ohm is the amount of resistance that limits current flow to one ampere in a circuit with one volt of pressure.

OHMMETER: An instrument used for measuring the resistance, in ohms, in an electrical circuit.

OUTPUT SHAFT: The shaft which transmits torque from a device, such as a transmission.

OVERDRIVE: A gear assembly which produces more shaft revolutions than that transmitted to it.

OVERHEAD CAMSHAFT (OHC): An engine configuration in which the camshaft is mounted on top of the cylinder head and operates the valve either directly or by means of rocker arms.

OVERHEAD VALVE (OHV): An engine configuration in which all of the valves are located in the cylinder head and the camshaft is located in the cylinder block. The camshaft operates the valves via lifters and push-rods.

OXIDES OF NITROGEN (NOx): Chemical compounds of nitrogen produced as a byproduct of combustion. They combine with hydrocarbons to produce smog.

OXYGEN SENSOR: Used with the feedback system to sense the presence of oxygen in the exhaust gas and signal the computer which can reference the voltage signal to an air/fuel ratio.

PINION: The smaller of two meshing gears.

PISTON RING: An open-ended ring which fits into a groove on the outer diameter of the piston. Its chief function is to form a seal between the piston and cylinder wall. Most automotive pistons have three rings: two for compression sealing; one for oil sealing.

PRELOAD: A predetermined load placed on a bearing during assembly or by adjustment.

PRIMARY CIRCUIT: The low voltage side of the ignition system which consists of the ignition switch, ballast resistor or resistance wire, bypass, coil, electronic control unit and pick-up coil as well as the connecting wires and harnesses.

PRESS FIT: The mating of two parts under pressure, due to the inner diameter of one being smaller than the outer diameter of the other, or vice versa; an interference fit.

RACE: The surface on the inner or outer ring of a bearing on which the balls, needles or rollers move.

REGULATOR: A device which maintains the amperage and/or voltage levels of a circuit at predetermined values.

RELAY: A switch which automatically opens and/or closes a circuit.

RESISTANCE: The opposition to the flow of current through a circuit or electrical device, and is measured in ohms. Resistance is equal to the voltage divided by the amperage.

RESISTOR: A device, usually made of wire, which offers a preset amount of resistance in an electrical circuit.

RING GEAR: The name given to a ring-shaped gear attached to a differential case, or affixed to a flywheel or as part of a planetary gear set.

ROLLER BEARING: A bearing made up of hardened inner and outer races between which hardened steel rollers move.

ROTOR: 1. The disc-shaped part of a disc brake assembly, upon which the brake pads bear; also called, brake disc. 2. The device mounted atop the distributor shaft, which passes current to the distributor cap tower contacts.

SECONDARY CIRCUIT: The high voltage side of the ignition system, usually above 20,000 volts. The secondary includes the ignition coil, coil wire, distributor cap and rotor, spark plug wires and spark plugs.

SENDING UNIT: A mechanical, electrical, hydraulic or electromagnetic device which transmits information to a gauge.

SENSOR: Any device designed to measure engine operating conditions or ambient pressures and temperatures. Usually electronic in nature and designed to send a voltage signal to an on-board computer, some sensors may operate as a simple on/off switch or they may provide a variable voltage signal (like a potentiometer) as conditions or measured parameters change.

SHIM: Spacers of precise, predetermined thickness used between parts to establish a proper working relationship.

SLAVE CYLINDER: In automotive use, a device in the hydraulic clutch system which is activated by hydraulic force, disengaging the clutch.

SOLENOID: A coil used to produce a magnetic field, the effect of which is to produce work.

SPARK PLUG: A device screwed into the combustion chamber of a spark ignition engine. The basic construction is a conductive core inside of a ceramic insulator, mounted in an outer conductive base. An electrical charge from the spark plug wire travels along the conductive core and jumps a preset air gap to a grounding point or points at the end of the conductive base. The resultant spark ignites the fuel/air mixture in the combustion chamber.

SPLINES: Ridges machined or cast onto the outer diameter of a shaft or inner diameter of a bore to enable parts to mate without rotation.

TACHOMETER: A device used to measure the rotary speed of an engine, shaft, gear, etc., usually in rotations per minute.

THERMOSTAT: A valve, located in the cooling system of an engine, which is closed when cold and opens gradually in response to engine heating, controlling the temperature of the coolant and rate of coolant flow.

TOP DEAD CENTER (TDC): The point at which the piston reaches the top of its travel on the compression stroke.

TORQUE: The twisting force applied to an object.

TORQUE CONVERTER: A turbine used to transmit power from a driving member to a driven member via hydraulic action, providing changes in drive ratio and torque. In automotive use, it links the driveplate at the rear of the engine to the automatic transmission.

TRANSDUCER: A device used to change a force into an electrical signal.

TRANSISTOR: A semi-conductor component which can be actuated by a small voltage to perform an electrical switching function.

TUNE-UP: A regular maintenance function, usually associated with the replacement and adjustment of parts and components in the electrical and fuel systems of a vehicle for the purpose of attaining optimum performance.

TURBOCHARGER: An exhaust driven pump which compresses intake air and forces it into the combustion chambers at higher than atmospheric pressures. The increased air pressure allows more fuel to be burned and results in increased horsepower being produced.

VACUUM ADVANCE: A device which advances the ignition timing in response to increased engine vacuum.

VACUUM GAUGE: An instrument used to measure the presence of vacuum in a chamber.

VALVE: A device which control the pressure, direction of flow or rate of flow of a liquid or gas.

VALVE CLEARANCE: The measured gap between the end of the valve stem and the rocker arm, cam lobe or follower that activates the valve.

VISCOSITY: The rating of a liquid's internal resistance to flow.

VOLTMETER: An instrument used for measuring electrical force in units called volts. Voltmeters are always connected parallel with the circuit being tested.

WHEEL CYLINDER: Found in the automotive drum brake assembly, it is a device, actuated by hydraulic pressure, which, through internal pistons, pushes the brake shoes outward against the drums.

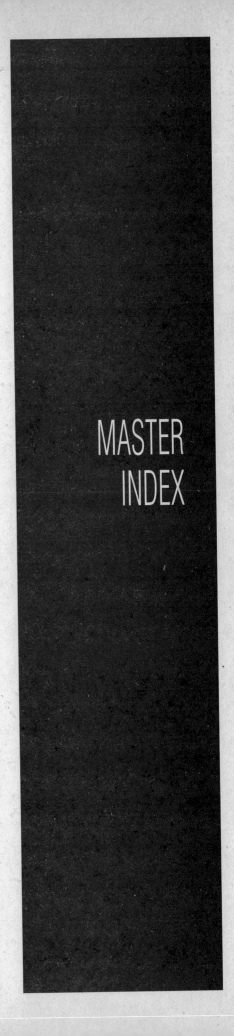

MASTER

INDEX